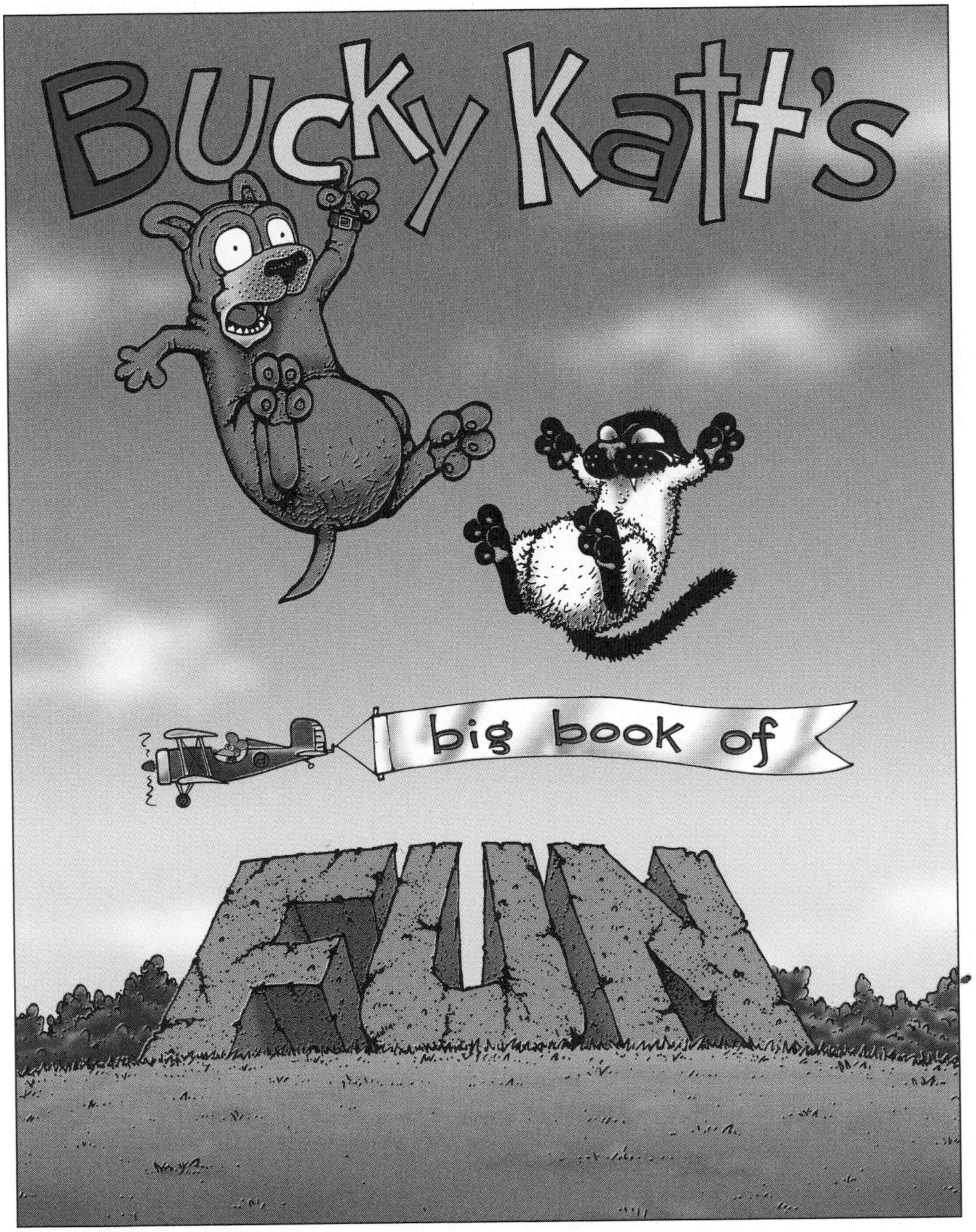
Bucky Katt's
big book of
FUN

Other books by Darby Conley

The Dog Is Not a Toy (House Rule #4)
Fuzzy Logic: Get Fuzzy 2
Groovitude: A Get Fuzzy Treasury
The Get Fuzzy Experience: Are You Bucksperienced
I Would Have Bought You a Cat, But . . .
Blueprint for Disaster

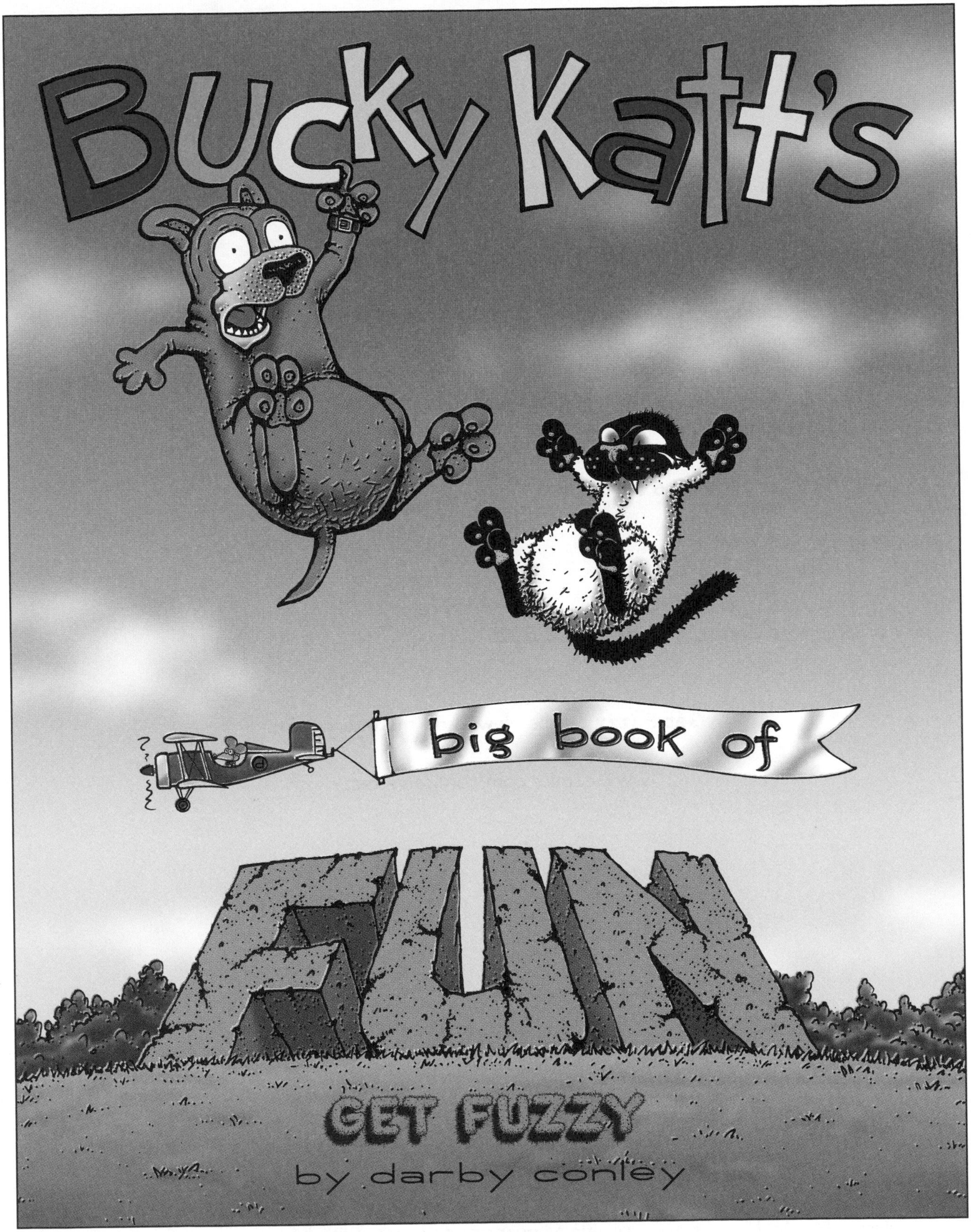
Bucky Katt's
big book of
FUN
GET FUZZY
by darby conley

Andrews McMeel
Publishing

Kansas City

Get Fuzzy is distributed internationally by United Feature Syndicate.

Bucky Katt's Big Book of Fun copyright © 2004 by Darby Conley. All rights reserved. Printed in the United States of America. No part of this book may be used or reproduced in any manner whatsoever without written permission except in the case of reprints in the context of reviews. For information, write Andrews McMeel Publishing, an Andrews McMeel Universal company, 4520 Main Street, Kansas City, Missouri 64111.

04 05 06 07 08 BAM 10 9 8 7 6 5 4 3 2 1

ISBN: 0-7407-4136-5

Library of Congress Control Number: 2003113251

Get Fuzzy can be viewed on the Internet at:

www.comics.com/comics/getfuzzy

—— **ATTENTION: SCHOOLS AND BUSINESSES** ——

Andrews McMeel books are available at quantity discounts with bulk purchase for educational, business, or sales promotional use. For information, please write to: Special Sales Department, Andrews McMeel Publishing, 4520 Main Street, Kansas City, Missouri 64111.

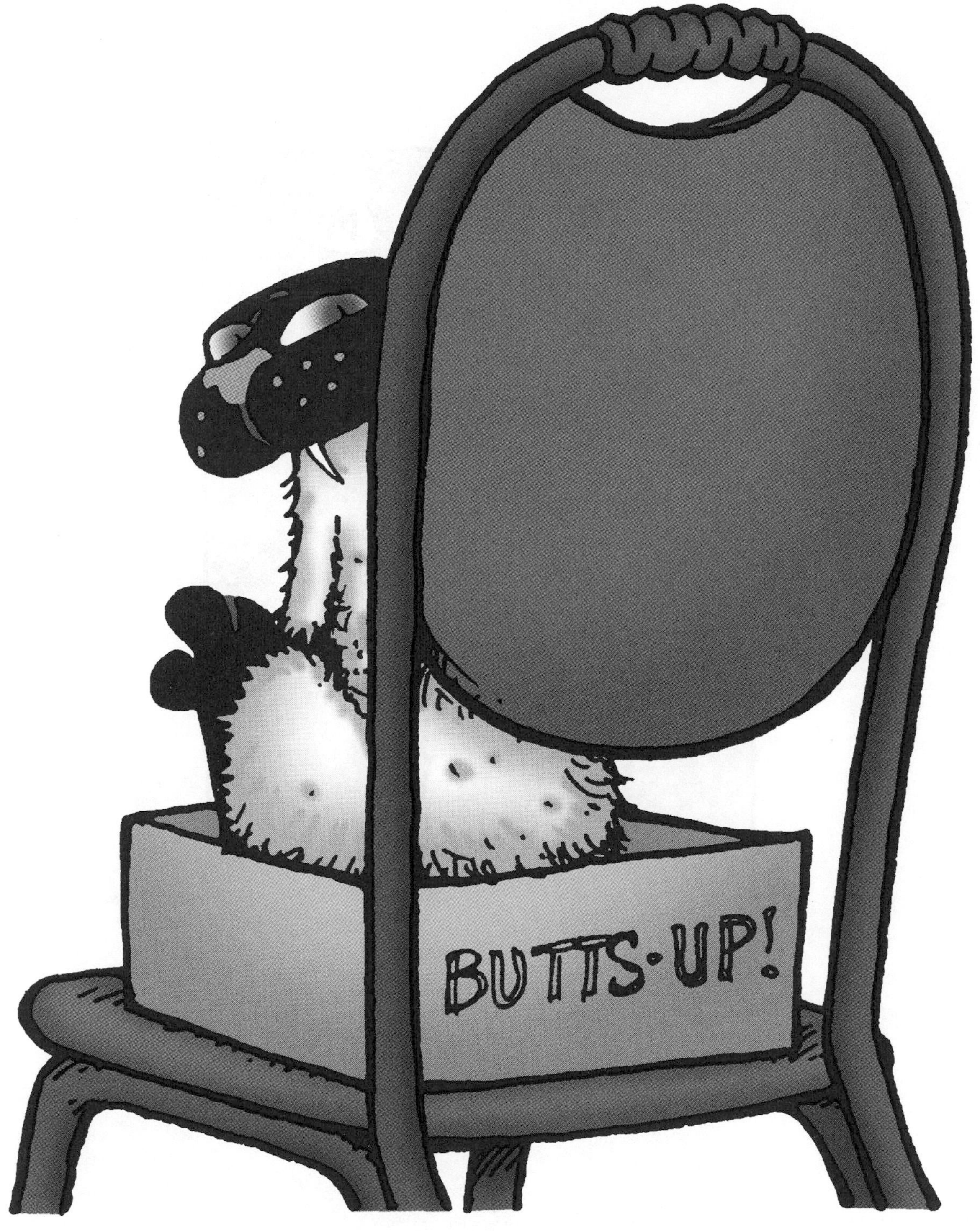
BUTTS-UP!

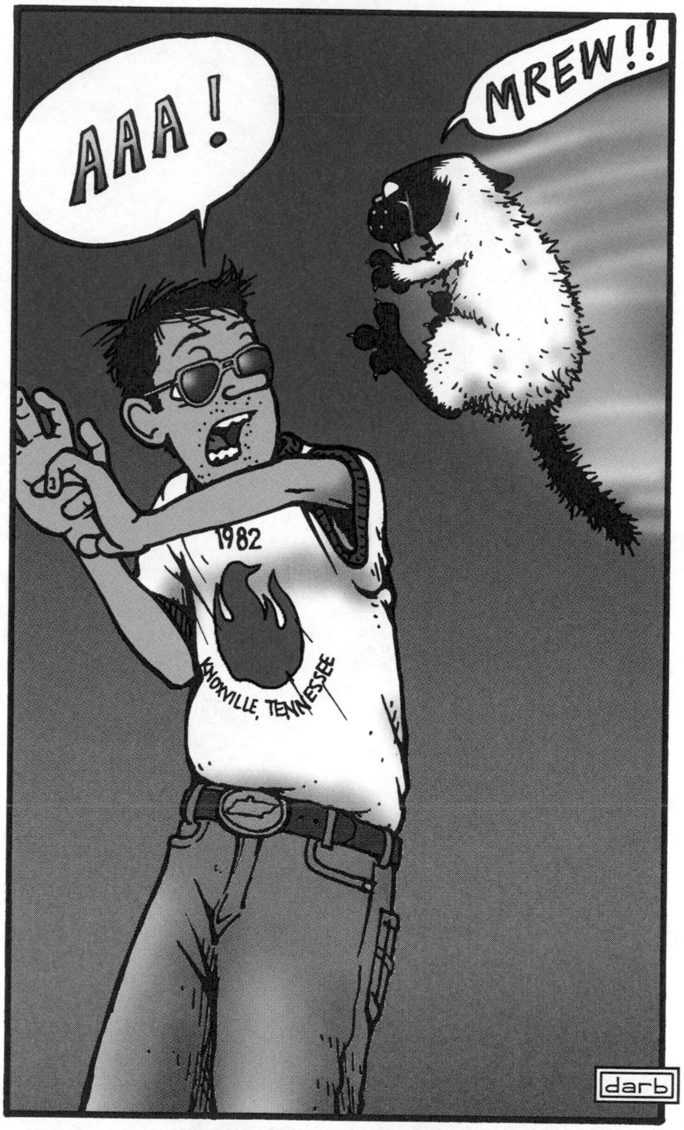
AAA!
MREW!!
1982
KNOXVILLE, TENNESSEE
darb

get fuzzy
an apology

I must confess that when I invented the characters for what was to become the comic strip "get fuzzy," I had never owned a cat.

I never really spent too much time with them, either, as I grew up in Tennessee, smack-dab in the middle of America's hound belt. The cats in Knoxville in the '70s and '80s were few, far between, and deep in hiding.

I thought the idea of psychotic cats, scratched-up furniture, and gooey hairballs was funny.

But now I have a cat.
And I have furniture that's been destroyed.
And I have a cabinet full of enzyme-based cleaning products.
And I have some of those flesh wounds which seemed so comical on other people.

And I've come to the conclusion that, well . . . cats aren't funny. I understand that now. So as you read this book, please remember that it was written out of ignorance, and I am sorry.

Sorry and ignorant.

But mostly just sorry, 'cause, you know . . . I got the cat now.

Sorry.

Respectfully,
darby conley

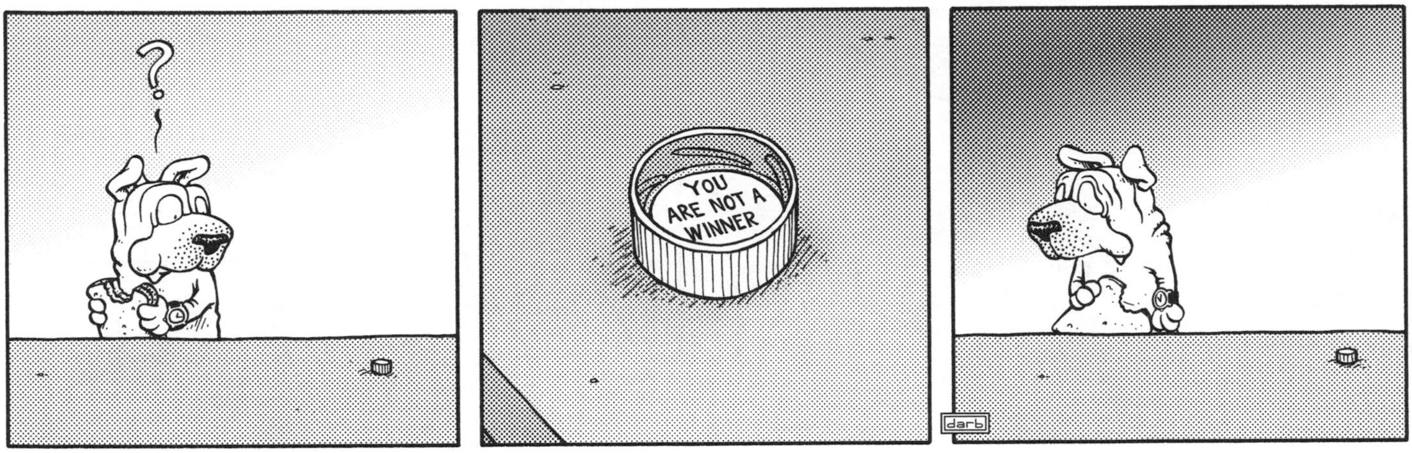
?
YOU ARE NOT A WINNER
darb

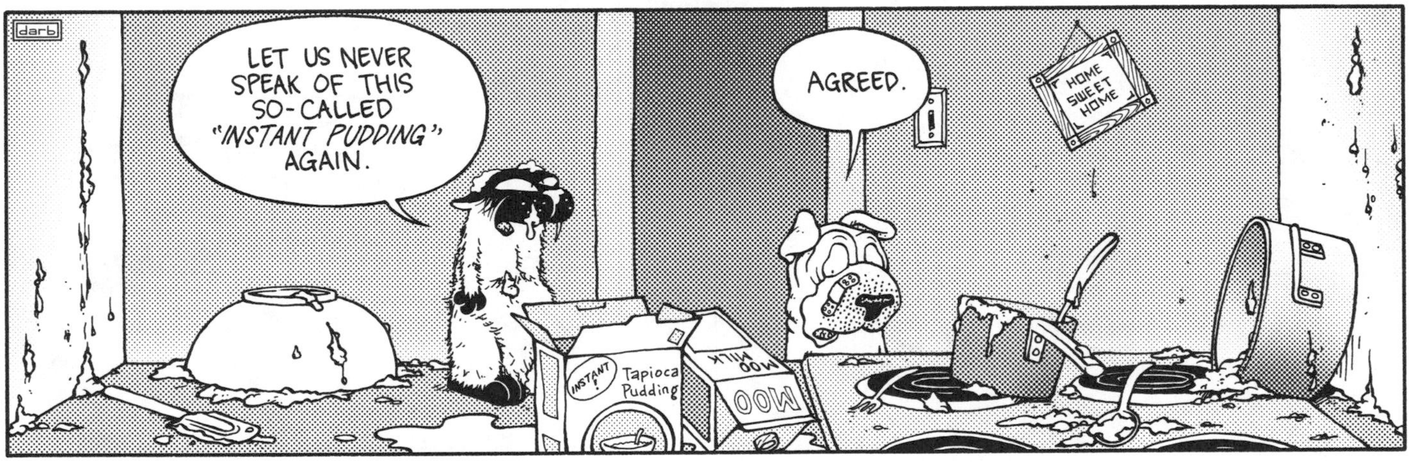
darb
LET US NEVER SPEAK OF THIS SO-CALLED "INSTANT PUDDING" AGAIN.
AGREED.
HOME SWEET HOME
INSTANT
Tapioca Pudding
MOO MILK
MOO

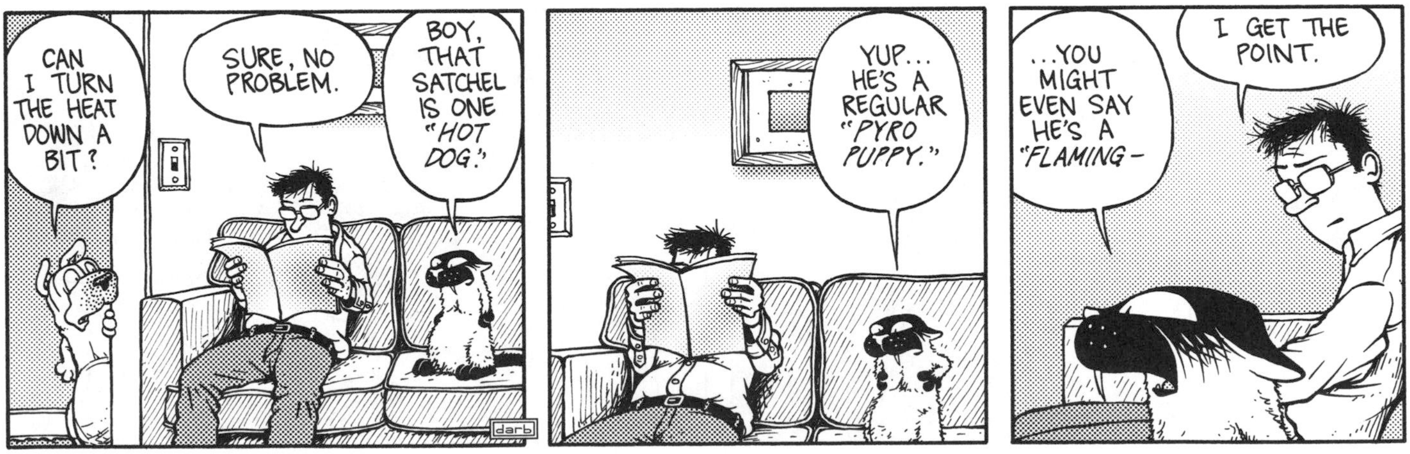
CAN I TURN THE HEAT DOWN A BIT?
SURE, NO PROBLEM.
BOY, THAT SATCHEL IS ONE "HOT DOG."
darb
YUP... HE'S A REGULAR "PYRO PUPPY."
...YOU MIGHT EVEN SAY HE'S A "FLAMING–
I GET THE POINT.

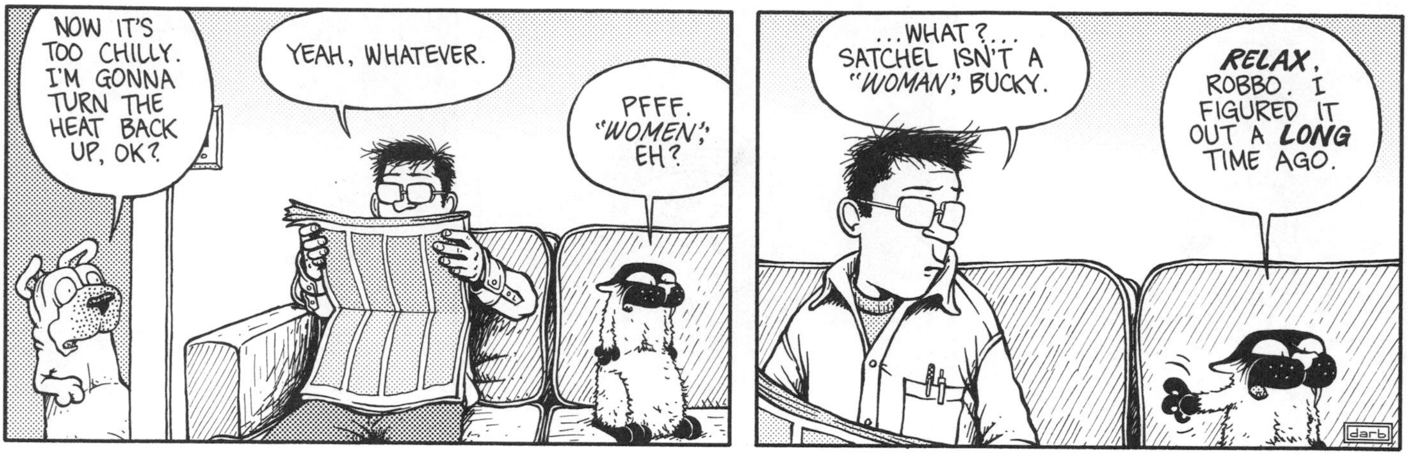
NOW IT'S TOO CHILLY. I'M GONNA TURN THE HEAT BACK UP, OK?
YEAH, WHATEVER.
PFFF. "*WOMEN*," EH?
...WHAT?... SATCHEL ISN'T A "*WOMAN*," BUCKY.
RELAX, ROBBO. I FIGURED IT OUT A ***LONG*** TIME AGO.
darb

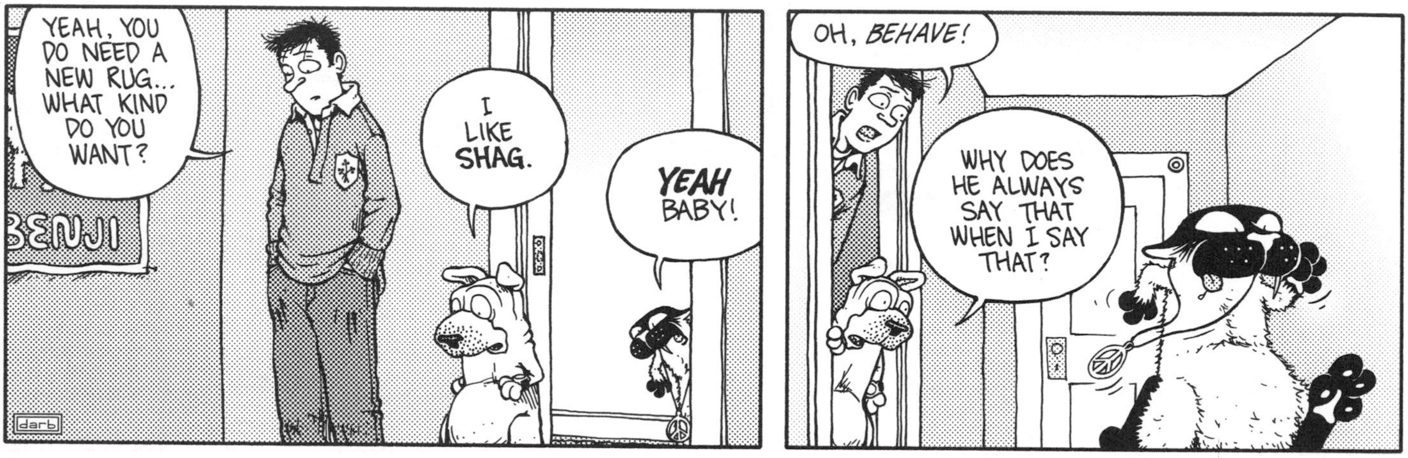
YEAH, YOU DO NEED A NEW RUG... WHAT KIND DO YOU WANT?
BENJI
I LIKE **SHAG**.
YEAH BABY!
darb
OH, *BEHAVE!*
WHY DOES HE ALWAYS SAY THAT WHEN I SAY THAT?

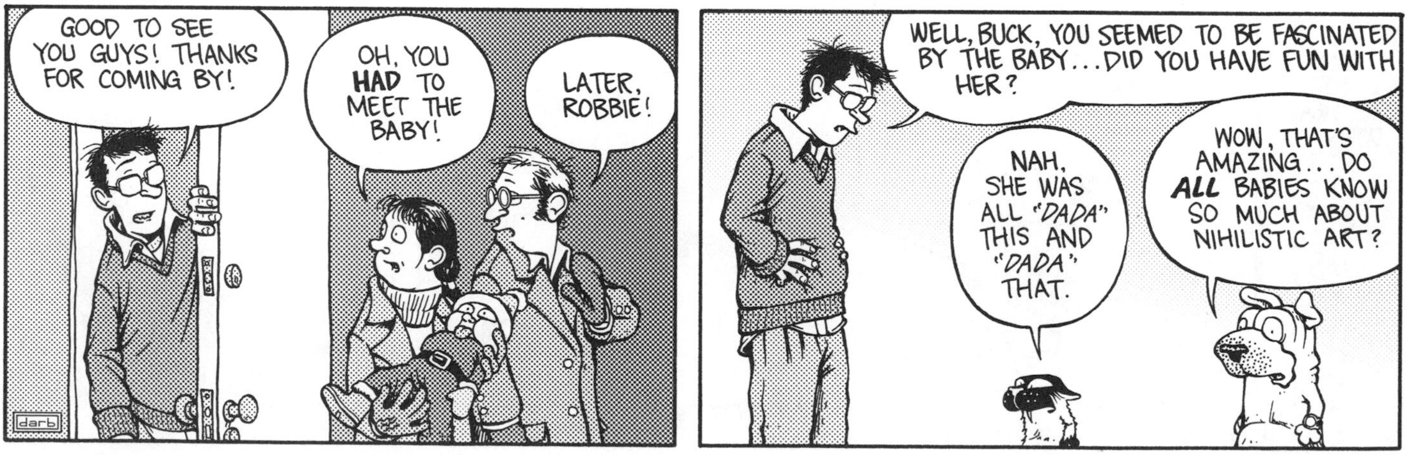
GOOD TO SEE YOU GUYS! THANKS FOR COMING BY!
OH, YOU **HAD** TO MEET THE BABY!
LATER, ROBBIE!
darb
WELL, BUCK, YOU SEEMED TO BE FASCINATED BY THE BABY... DID YOU HAVE FUN WITH HER?
NAH, SHE WAS ALL "*DADA*" THIS AND "*DADA*" THAT.
WOW, THAT'S AMAZING... DO ***ALL*** BABIES KNOW SO MUCH ABOUT NIHILISTIC ART?

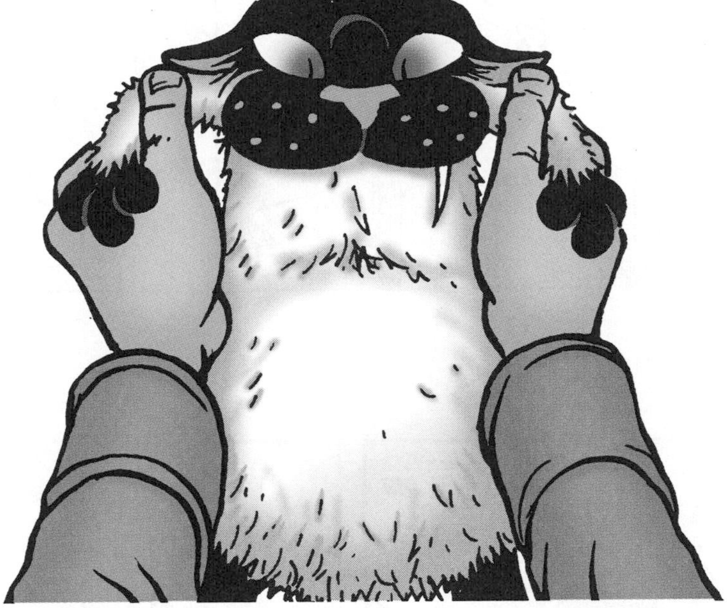

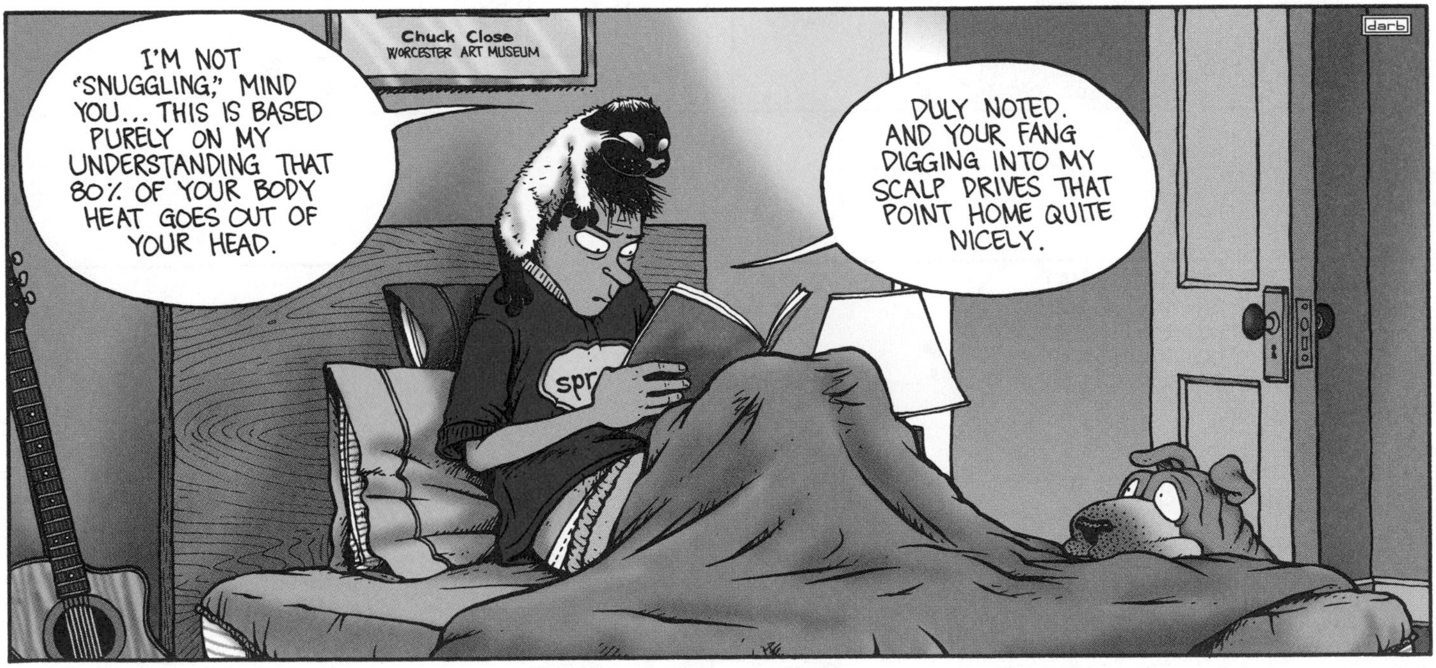
Chuck Close
WORCESTER ART MUSEUM
darb
I'M NOT "SNUGGLING," MIND YOU... THIS IS BASED PURELY ON MY UNDERSTANDING THAT 80% OF YOUR BODY HEAT GOES OUT OF YOUR HEAD.
DULY NOTED. AND YOUR FANG DIGGING INTO MY SCALP DRIVES THAT POINT HOME QUITE NICELY.

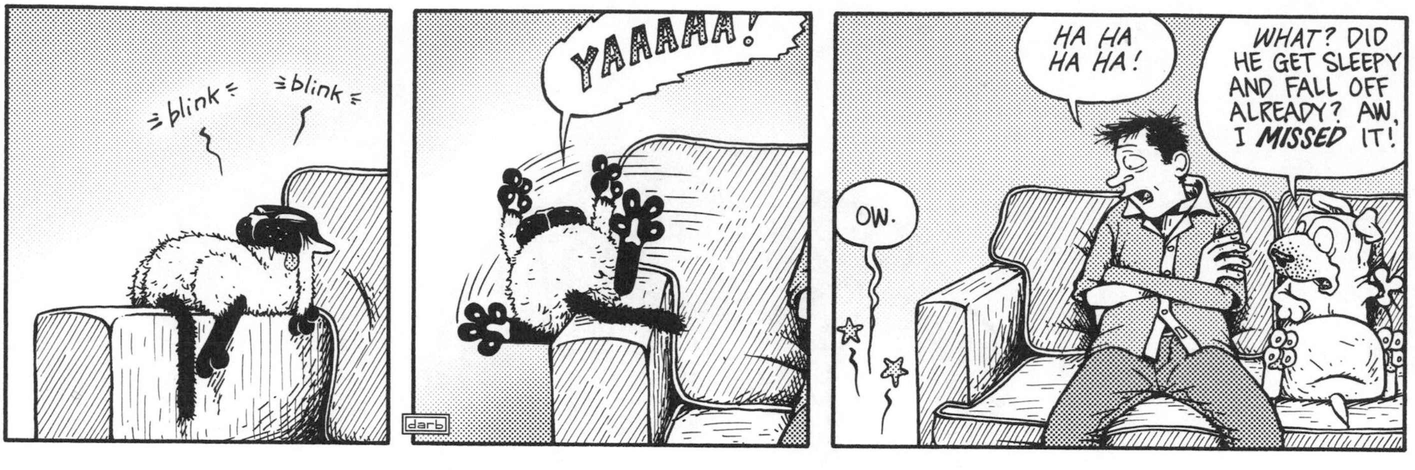
blink
blink
YAAAAA!
HA HA
HA HA!
WHAT? DID HE GET SLEEPY AND FALL OFF ALREADY? AW, I ***MISSED*** IT!
OW.
darb

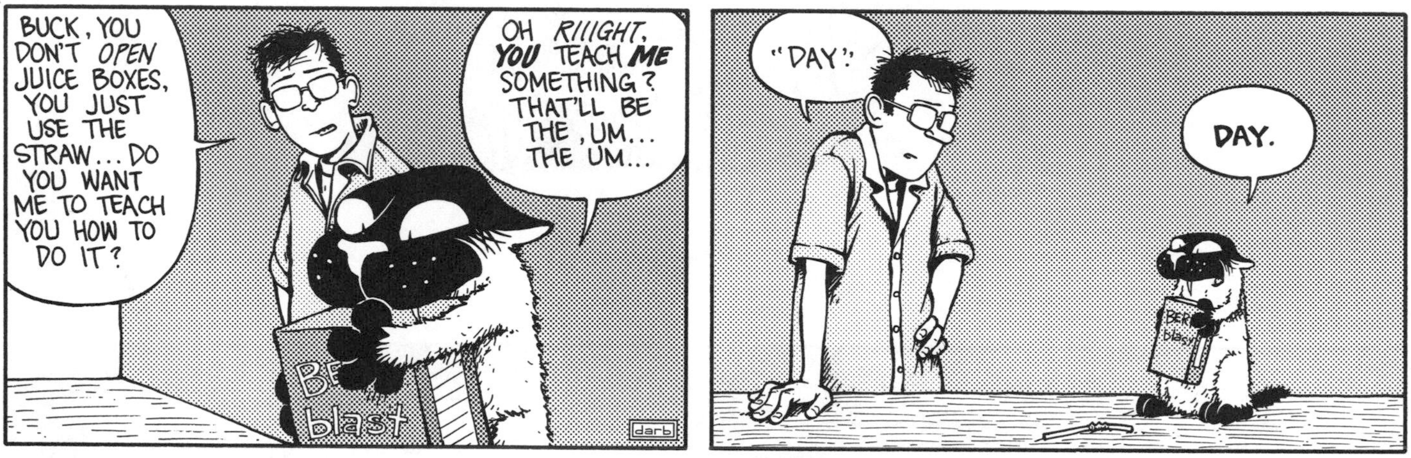
BUCK, YOU DON'T *OPEN* JUICE BOXES, YOU JUST USE THE STRAW... DO YOU WANT ME TO TEACH YOU HOW TO DO IT?
OH *RIIIGHT,* ***YOU*** TEACH ***ME*** SOMETHING? THAT'LL BE THE, UM... THE UM...
"DAY."
DAY.
darb

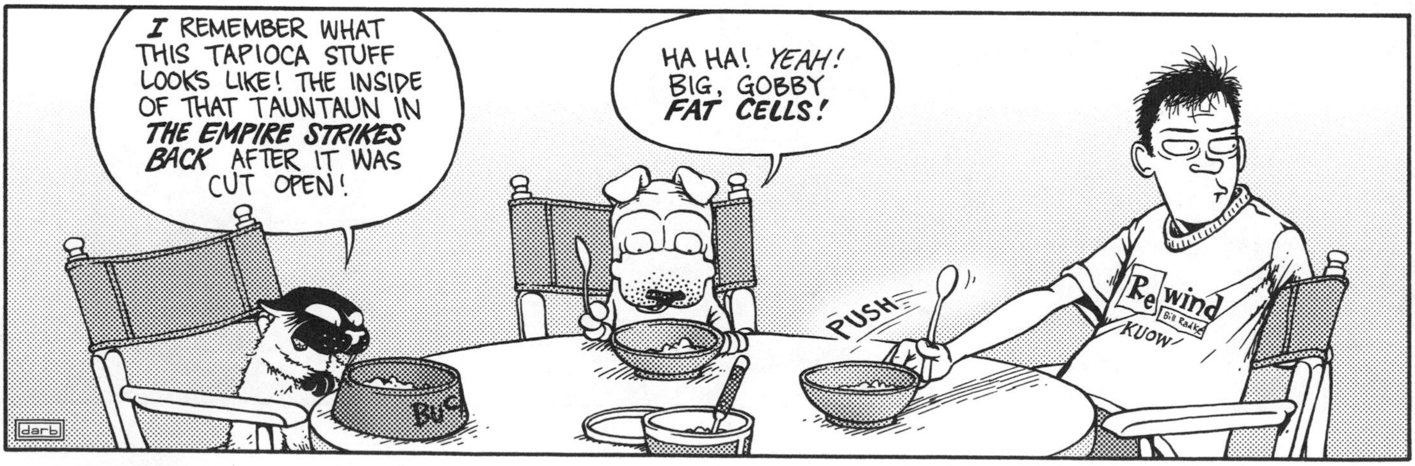
I REMEMBER WHAT THIS TAPIOCA STUFF LOOKS LIKE! THE INSIDE OF THAT TAUNTAUN IN ***THE EMPIRE STRIKES BACK*** AFTER IT WAS CUT OPEN!
HA HA! *YEAH!* BIG, GOBBY ***FAT CELLS!***
PUSH
Rewind
Bill Radke
KUOW
darb

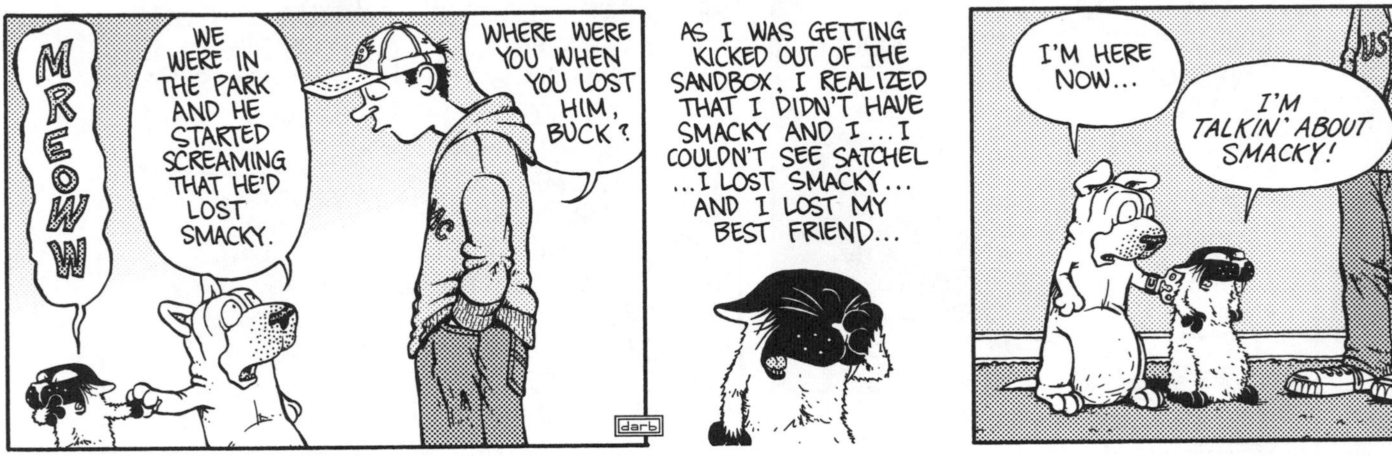
MREOWW
WE WERE IN THE PARK AND HE STARTED SCREAMING THAT HE'D LOST SMACKY.
WHERE WERE YOU WHEN YOU LOST HIM, BUCK?
darb
AS I WAS GETTING KICKED OUT OF THE SANDBOX, I REALIZED THAT I DIDN'T HAVE SMACKY AND I... I COULDN'T SEE SATCHEL ...I LOST SMACKY... AND I LOST MY BEST FRIEND...
I'M HERE NOW...
I'M TALKIN' ABOUT SMACKY!

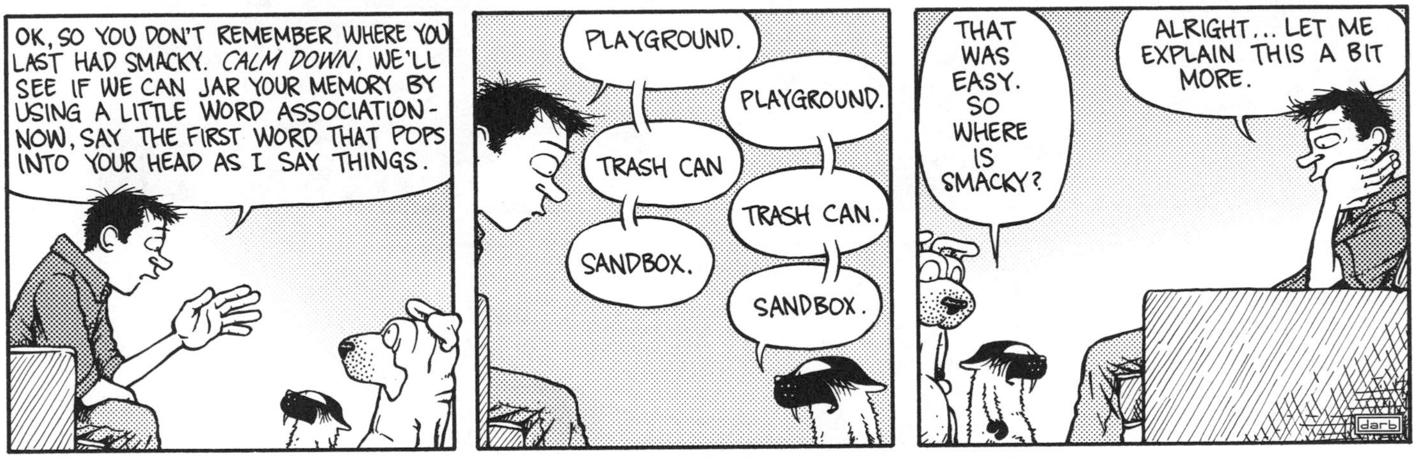
OK, SO YOU DON'T REMEMBER WHERE YOU LAST HAD SMACKY. CALM DOWN, WE'LL SEE IF WE CAN JAR YOUR MEMORY BY USING A LITTLE WORD ASSOCIATION- NOW, SAY THE FIRST WORD THAT POPS INTO YOUR HEAD AS I SAY THINGS.
PLAYGROUND.
PLAYGROUND.
TRASH CAN
TRASH CAN.
SANDBOX.
SANDBOX.
THAT WAS EASY. SO WHERE IS SMACKY?
ALRIGHT... LET ME EXPLAIN THIS A BIT MORE.
darb

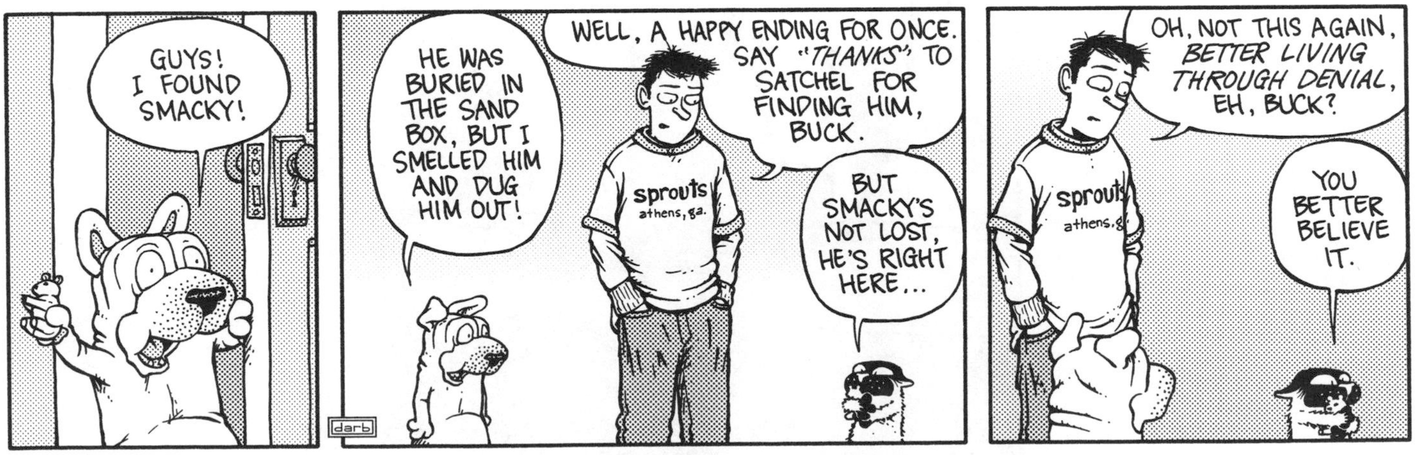
GUYS! I FOUND SMACKY!
darb
HE WAS BURIED IN THE SAND BOX, BUT I SMELLED HIM AND DUG HIM OUT!
WELL, A HAPPY ENDING FOR ONCE. SAY "THANKS" TO SATCHEL FOR FINDING HIM, BUCK.
sprouts athens, ga.
BUT SMACKY'S NOT LOST, HE'S RIGHT HERE...
OH, NOT THIS AGAIN, BETTER LIVING THROUGH DENIAL, EH, BUCK?
YOU BETTER BELIEVE IT.

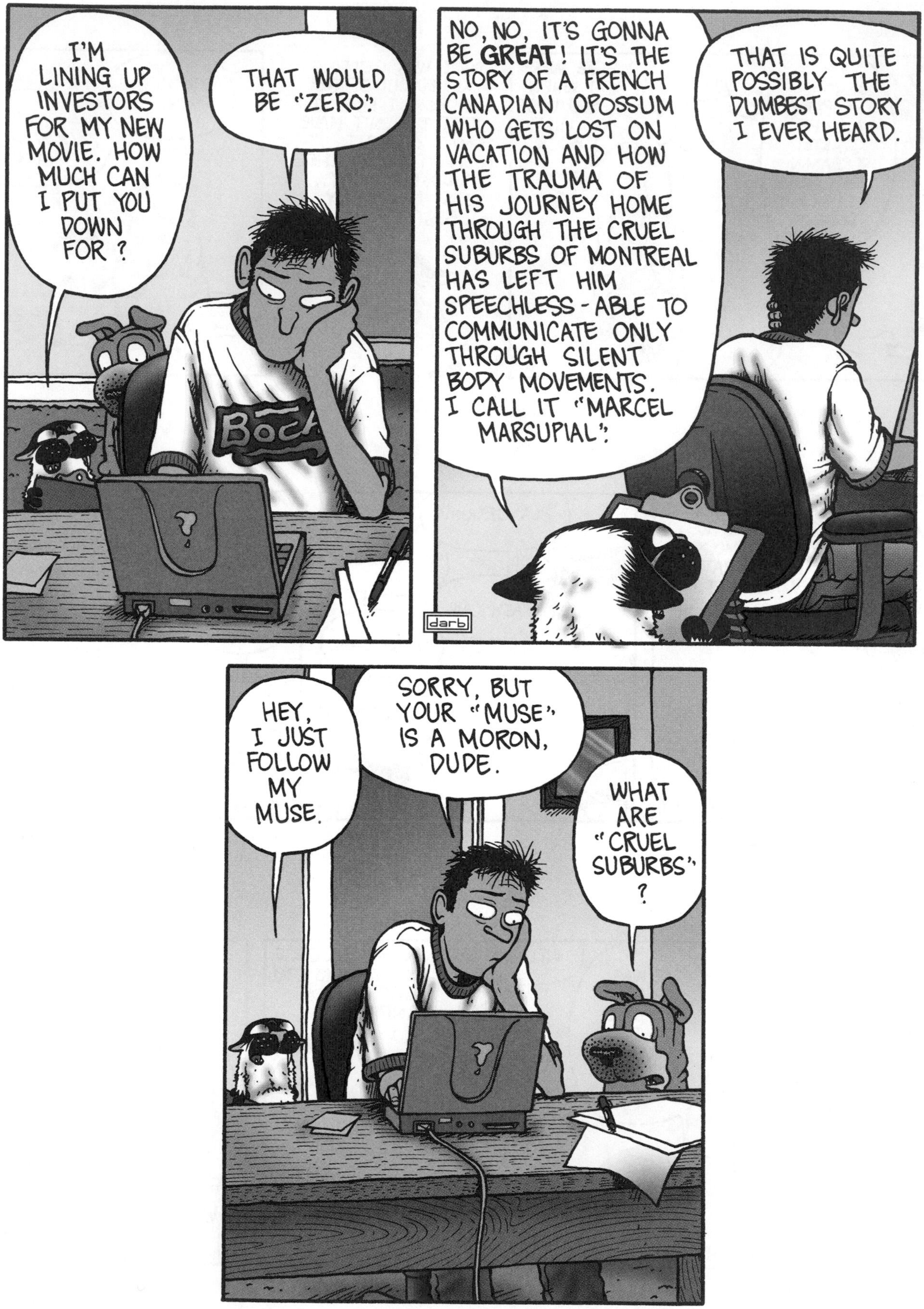
I'M LINING UP INVESTORS FOR MY NEW MOVIE. HOW MUCH CAN I PUT YOU DOWN FOR ?
THAT WOULD BE "ZERO".
NO, NO, IT'S GONNA BE **GREAT**! IT'S THE STORY OF A FRENCH CANADIAN OPOSSUM WHO GETS LOST ON VACATION AND HOW THE TRAUMA OF HIS JOURNEY HOME THROUGH THE CRUEL SUBURBS OF MONTREAL HAS LEFT HIM SPEECHLESS - ABLE TO COMMUNICATE ONLY THROUGH SILENT BODY MOVEMENTS. I CALL IT "MARCEL MARSUPIAL".
THAT IS QUITE POSSIBLY THE DUMBEST STORY I EVER HEARD.
darb
HEY, I JUST FOLLOW MY MUSE.
SORRY, BUT YOUR "MUSE" IS A MORON, DUDE.
WHAT ARE "CRUEL SUBURBS" ?

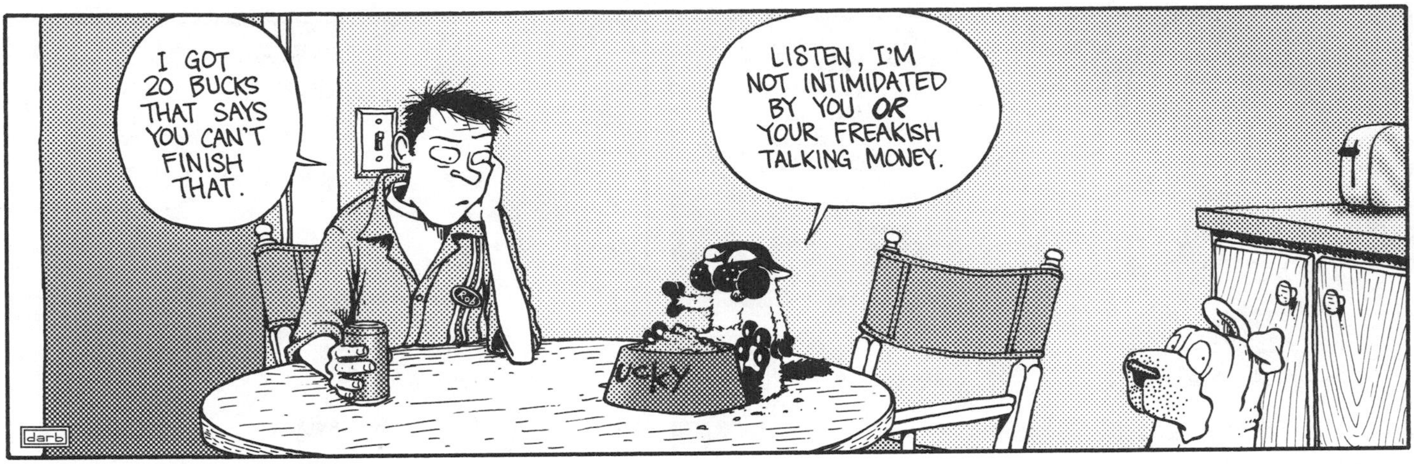

I GOT 20 BUCKS THAT SAYS YOU CAN'T FINISH THAT.
LISTEN, I'M NOT INTIMIDATED BY YOU **OR** YOUR FREAKISH TALKING MONEY.

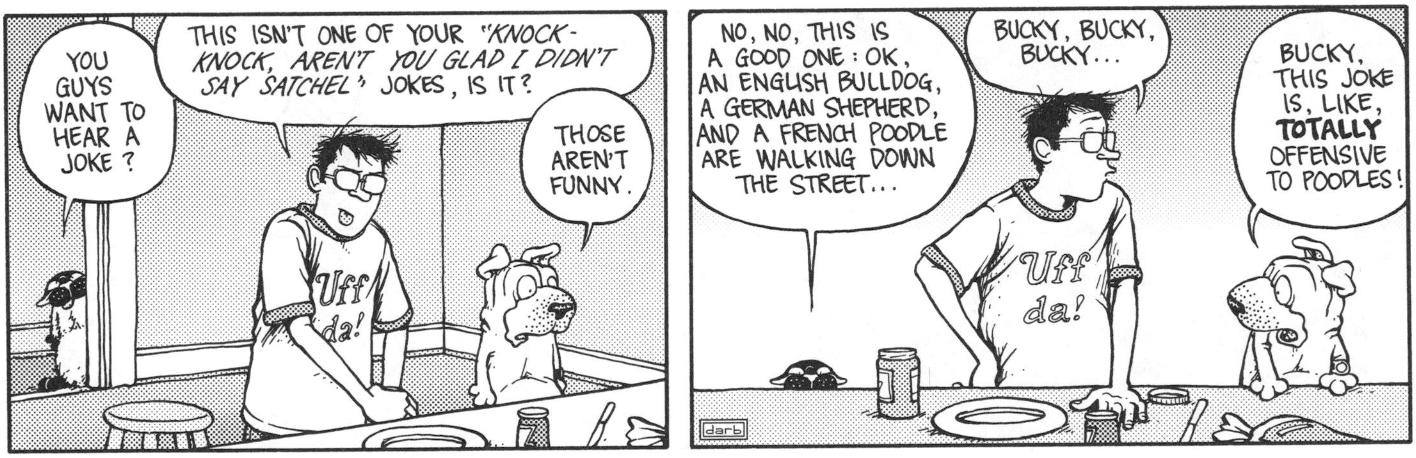

YOU GUYS WANT TO HEAR A JOKE?
THIS ISN'T ONE OF YOUR *"KNOCK-KNOCK, AREN'T YOU GLAD I DIDN'T SAY SATCHEL"* JOKES, IS IT?
THOSE AREN'T FUNNY.
NO, NO, THIS IS A GOOD ONE: OK, AN ENGLISH BULLDOG, A GERMAN SHEPHERD, AND A FRENCH POODLE ARE WALKING DOWN THE STREET...
BUCKY, BUCKY, BUCKY...
BUCKY, THIS JOKE IS, LIKE, **TOTALLY** OFFENSIVE TO POODLES!

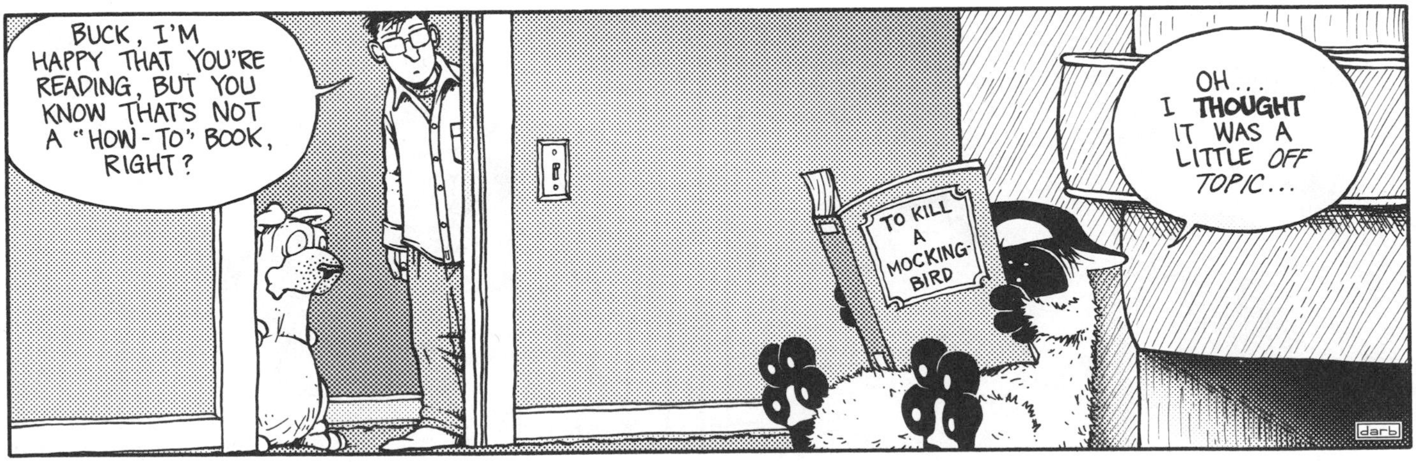

BUCK, I'M HAPPY THAT YOU'RE READING, BUT YOU KNOW THAT'S NOT A "HOW-TO" BOOK, RIGHT?
TO KILL A MOCKINGBIRD
OH... I **THOUGHT** IT WAS A LITTLE *OFF TOPIC*...

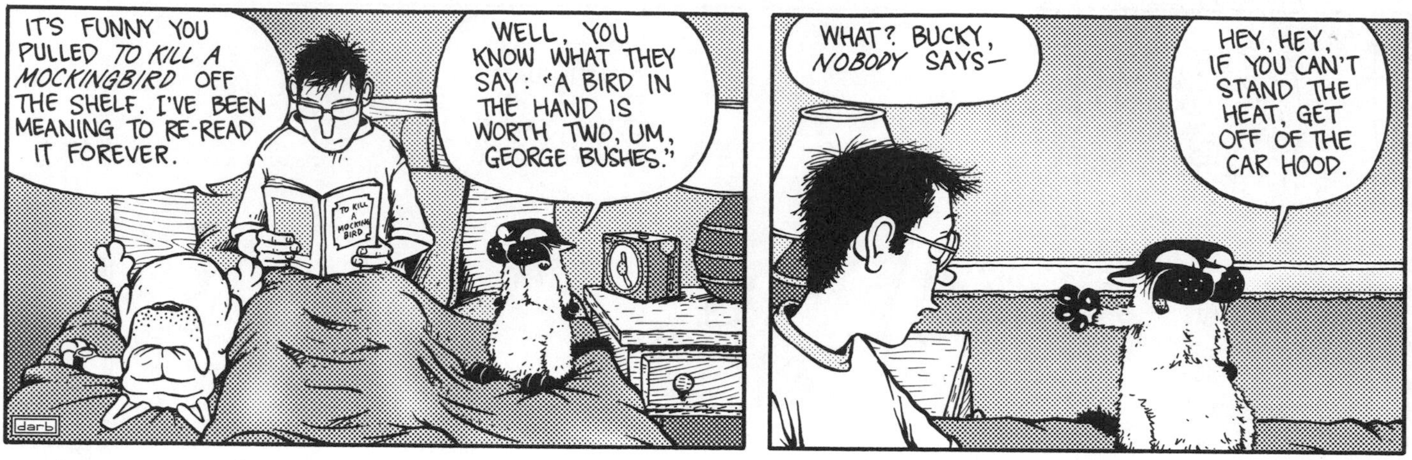

IT'S FUNNY YOU PULLED *TO KILL A MOCKINGBIRD* OFF THE SHELF. I'VE BEEN MEANING TO RE-READ IT FOREVER.
WELL, YOU KNOW WHAT THEY SAY: "A BIRD IN THE HAND IS WORTH TWO, UM, GEORGE BUSHES."
WHAT? BUCKY, *NOBODY* SAYS—
HEY, HEY, IF YOU CAN'T STAND THE HEAT, GET OFF OF THE CAR HOOD.

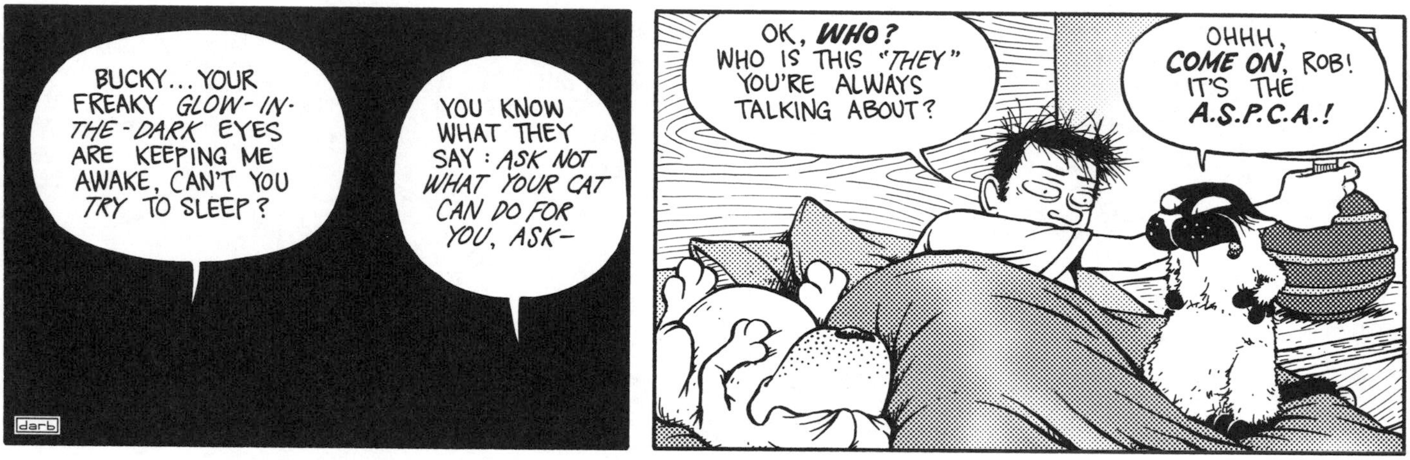

BUCKY... YOUR FREAKY *GLOW-IN-THE-DARK* EYES ARE KEEPING ME AWAKE, CAN'T YOU *TRY* TO SLEEP?
YOU KNOW WHAT THEY SAY: *ASK NOT WHAT YOUR CAT CAN DO FOR YOU, ASK*—
OK, ***WHO?*** WHO IS THIS *"THEY"* YOU'RE ALWAYS TALKING ABOUT?
OHHH, ***COME ON***, ROB! IT'S THE ***A.S.P.C.A.!***

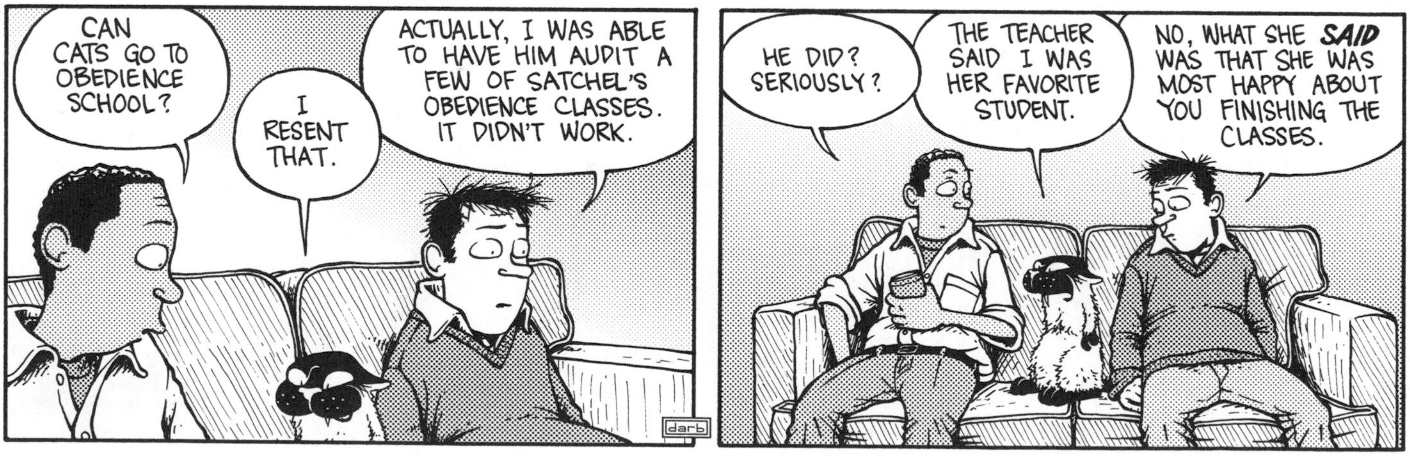

CAN CATS GO TO OBEDIENCE SCHOOL?
I RESENT THAT.
ACTUALLY, I WAS ABLE TO HAVE HIM AUDIT A FEW OF SATCHEL'S OBEDIENCE CLASSES. IT DIDN'T WORK.
HE DID? SERIOUSLY?
THE TEACHER SAID I WAS HER FAVORITE STUDENT.
NO, WHAT SHE ***SAID*** WAS THAT SHE WAS MOST HAPPY ABOUT YOU FINISHING THE CLASSES.

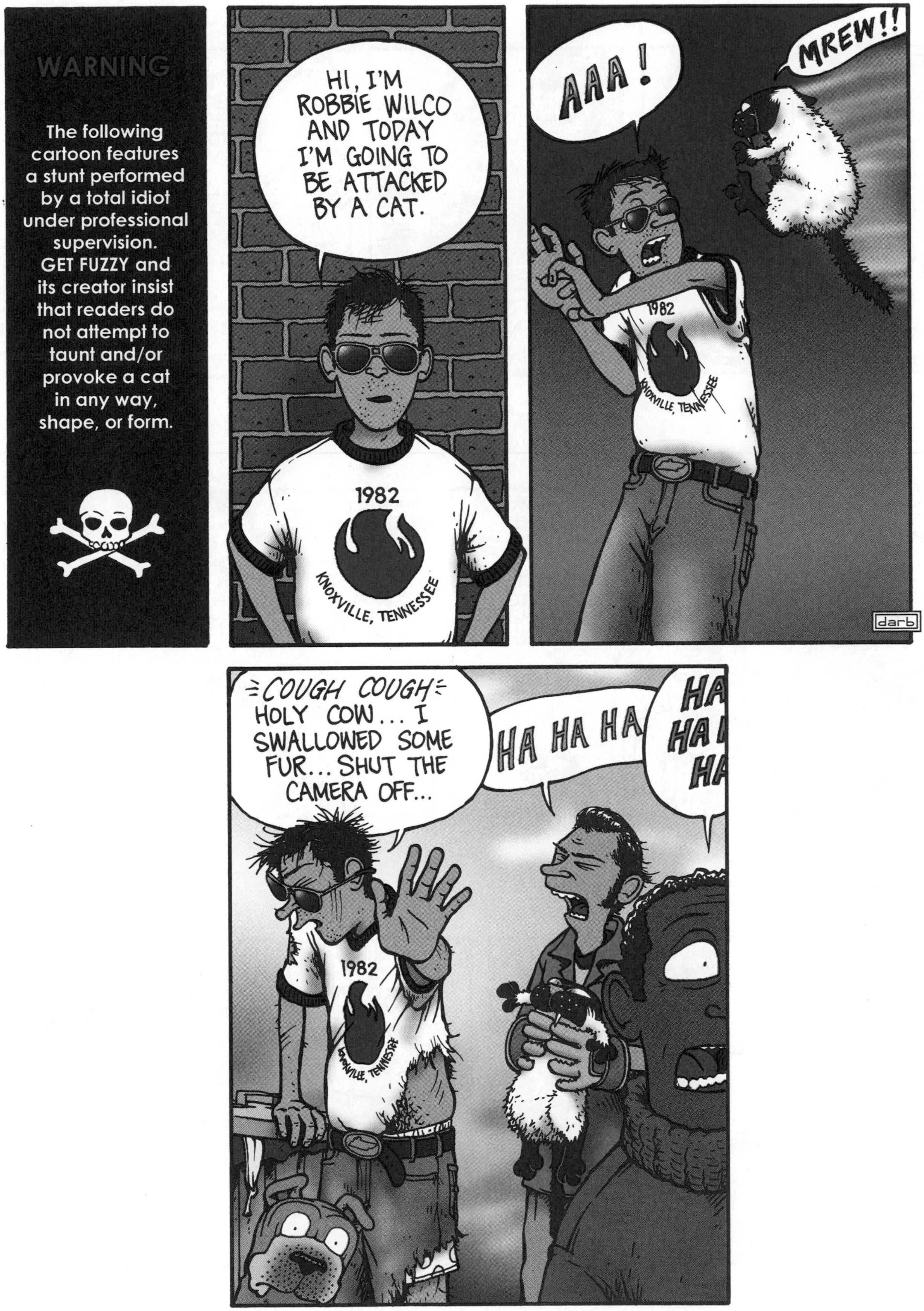
WARNING
The following cartoon features a stunt performed by a total idiot under professional supervision. GET FUZZY and its creator insist that readers do not attempt to taunt and/or provoke a cat in any way, shape, or form.
HI, I'M ROBBIE WILCO AND TODAY I'M GOING TO BE ATTACKED BY A CAT.
1982
KNOXVILLE, TENNESSEE
AAA!
MREW!!
darb
COUGH COUGH HOLY COW... I SWALLOWED SOME FUR... SHUT THE CAMERA OFF...
HA HA HA

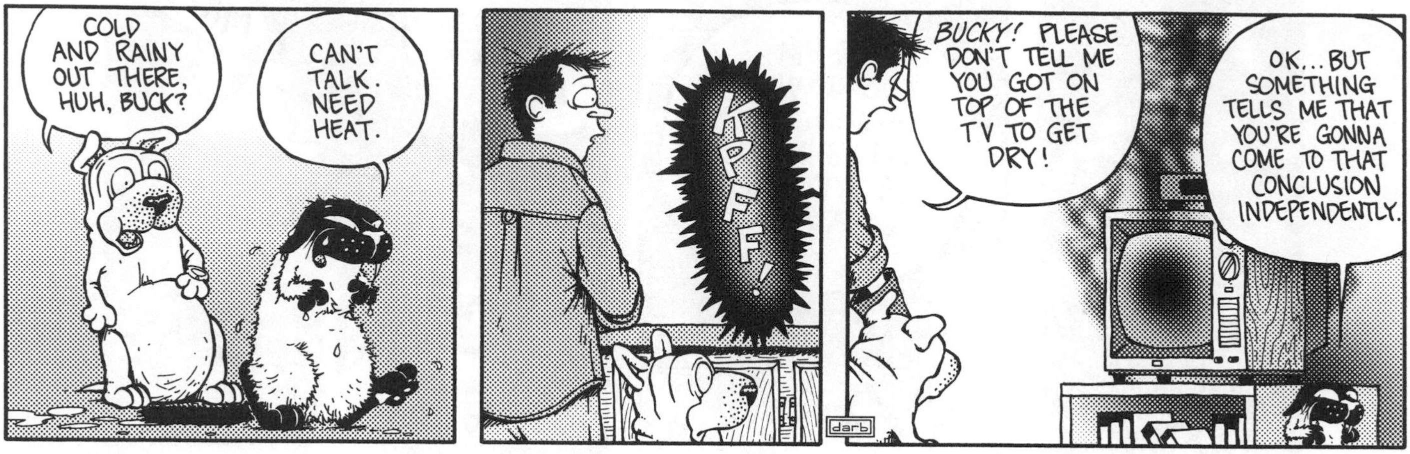
COLD AND RAINY OUT THERE, HUH, BUCK?
CAN'T TALK. NEED HEAT.
KPFF!
BUCKY! PLEASE DON'T TELL ME YOU GOT ON TOP OF THE TV TO GET DRY!
OK... BUT SOMETHING TELLS ME THAT YOU'RE GONNA COME TO THAT CONCLUSION INDEPENDENTLY.

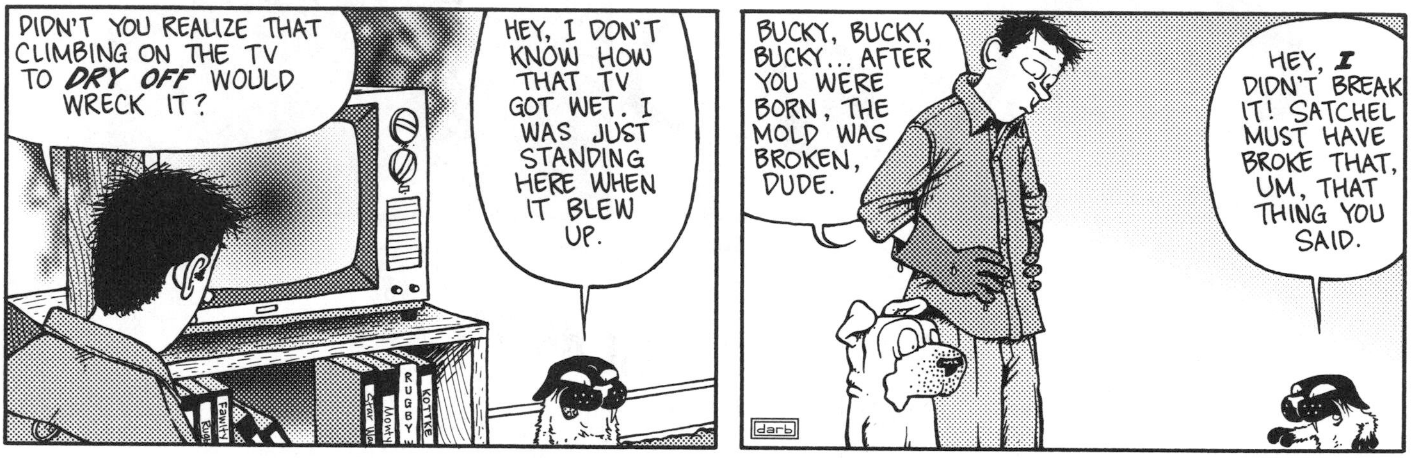
DIDN'T YOU REALIZE THAT CLIMBING ON THE TV TO DRY OFF WOULD WRECK IT?
HEY, I DON'T KNOW HOW THAT TV GOT WET. I WAS JUST STANDING HERE WHEN IT BLEW UP.
BUCKY, BUCKY, BUCKY... AFTER YOU WERE BORN, THE MOLD WAS BROKEN, DUDE.
HEY, I DIDN'T BREAK IT! SATCHEL MUST HAVE BROKE THAT, UM, THAT THING YOU SAID.

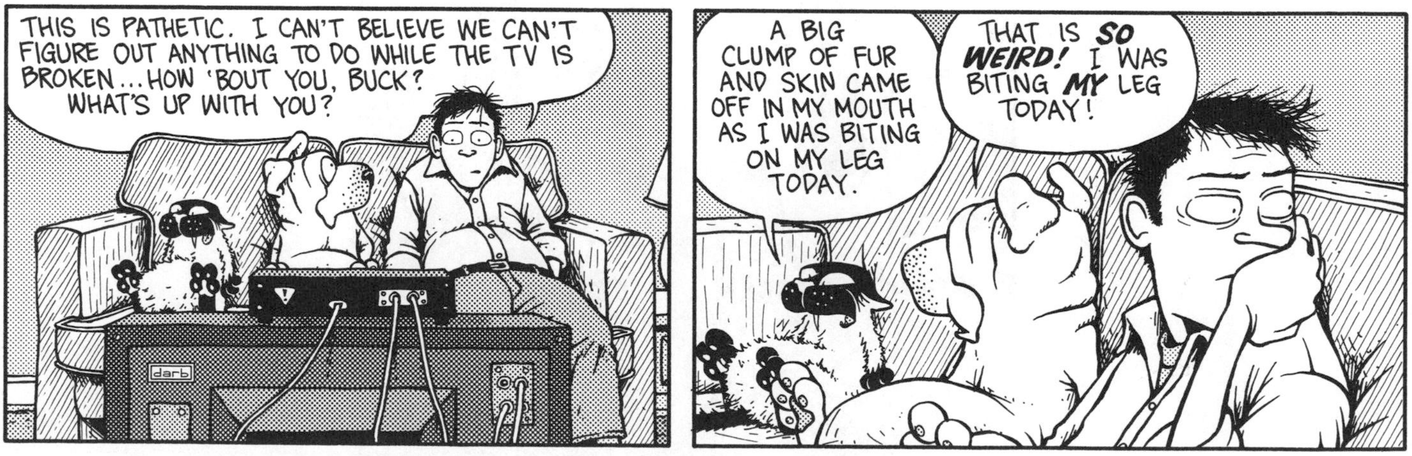
THIS IS PATHETIC. I CAN'T BELIEVE WE CAN'T FIGURE OUT ANYTHING TO DO WHILE THE TV IS BROKEN... HOW 'BOUT YOU, BUCK? WHAT'S UP WITH YOU?
A BIG CLUMP OF FUR AND SKIN CAME OFF IN MY MOUTH AS I WAS BITING ON MY LEG TODAY.
THAT IS SO WEIRD! I WAS BITING MY LEG TODAY!

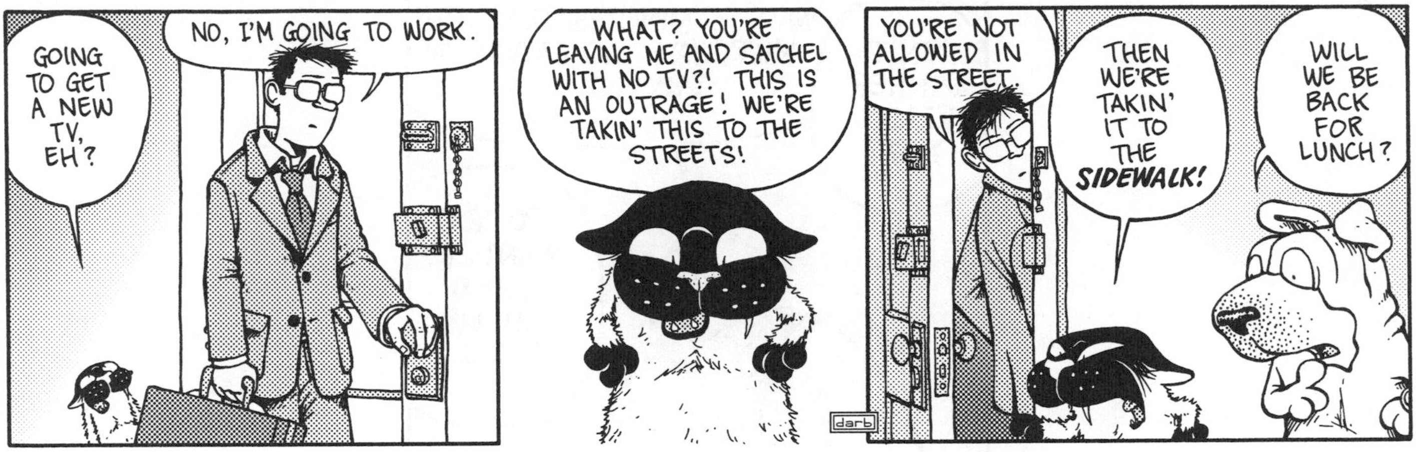
GOING TO GET A NEW TV, EH?
NO, I'M GOING TO WORK.
WHAT? YOU'RE LEAVING ME AND SATCHEL WITH NO TV?! THIS IS AN OUTRAGE! WE'RE TAKIN' THIS TO THE STREETS!
darb
YOU'RE NOT ALLOWED IN THE STREET.
THEN WE'RE TAKIN' IT TO THE SIDEWALK!
WILL WE BE BACK FOR LUNCH?

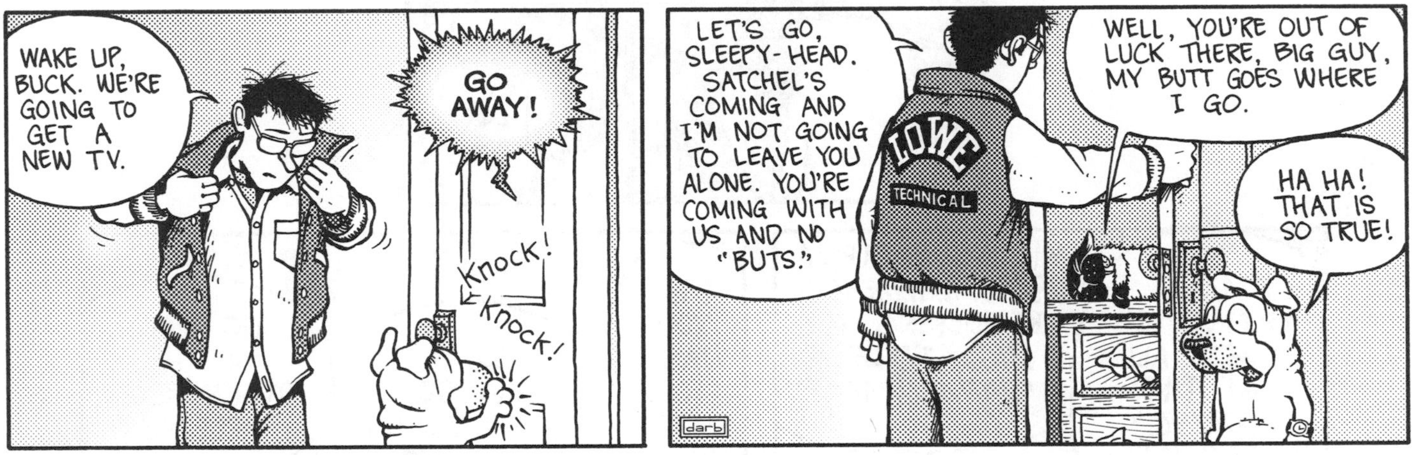
WAKE UP, BUCK. WE'RE GOING TO GET A NEW TV.
GO AWAY!
Knock!
Knock!
darb
LET'S GO, SLEEPY-HEAD. SATCHEL'S COMING AND I'M NOT GOING TO LEAVE YOU ALONE. YOU'RE COMING WITH US AND NO "BUTS."
LOWE
TECHNICAL
WELL, YOU'RE OUT OF LUCK THERE, BIG GUY, MY BUTT GOES WHERE I GO.
HA HA! THAT IS SO TRUE!

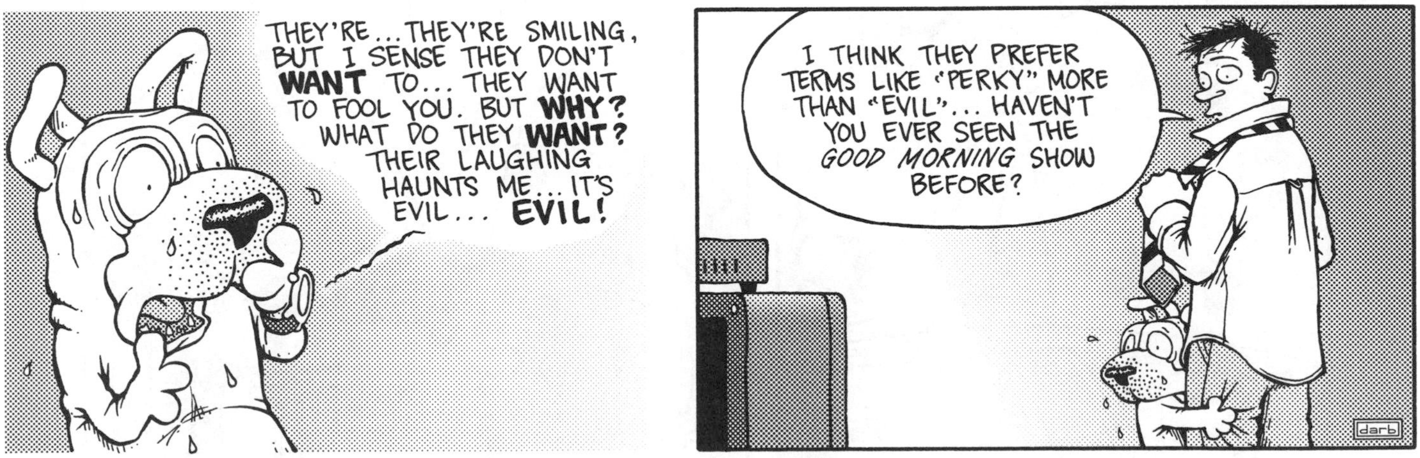
THEY'RE... THEY'RE SMILING, BUT I SENSE THEY DON'T WANT TO... THEY WANT TO FOOL YOU. BUT WHY? WHAT DO THEY WANT? THEIR LAUGHING HAUNTS ME... IT'S EVIL... EVIL!
I THINK THEY PREFER TERMS LIKE "PERKY" MORE THAN "EVIL"... HAVEN'T YOU EVER SEEN THE GOOD MORNING SHOW BEFORE?
darb

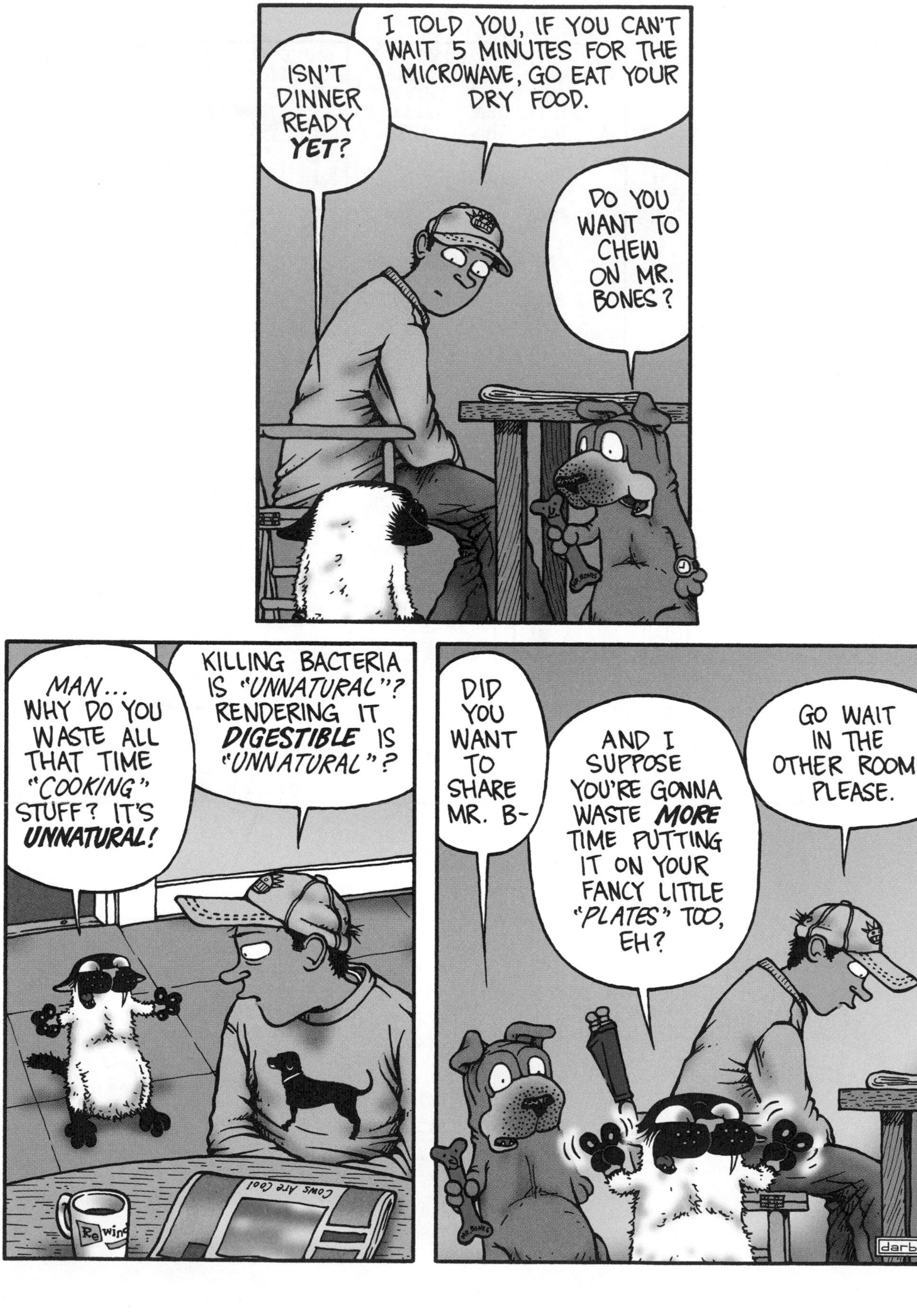
ISN'T DINNER READY YET?
I TOLD YOU, IF YOU CAN'T WAIT 5 MINUTES FOR THE MICROWAVE, GO EAT YOUR DRY FOOD.
DO YOU WANT TO CHEW ON MR. BONES?
MR. BONES
MAN... WHY DO YOU WASTE ALL THAT TIME "COOKING" STUFF? IT'S UNNATURAL!
KILLING BACTERIA IS "UNNATURAL"? RENDERING IT DIGESTIBLE IS "UNNATURAL"?
Cows Are Cool
Rewind
DID YOU WANT TO SHARE MR. B-
AND I SUPPOSE YOU'RE GONNA WASTE MORE TIME PUTTING IT ON YOUR FANCY LITTLE "PLATES" TOO, EH?
GO WAIT IN THE OTHER ROOM, PLEASE.
MR. BONES
darb

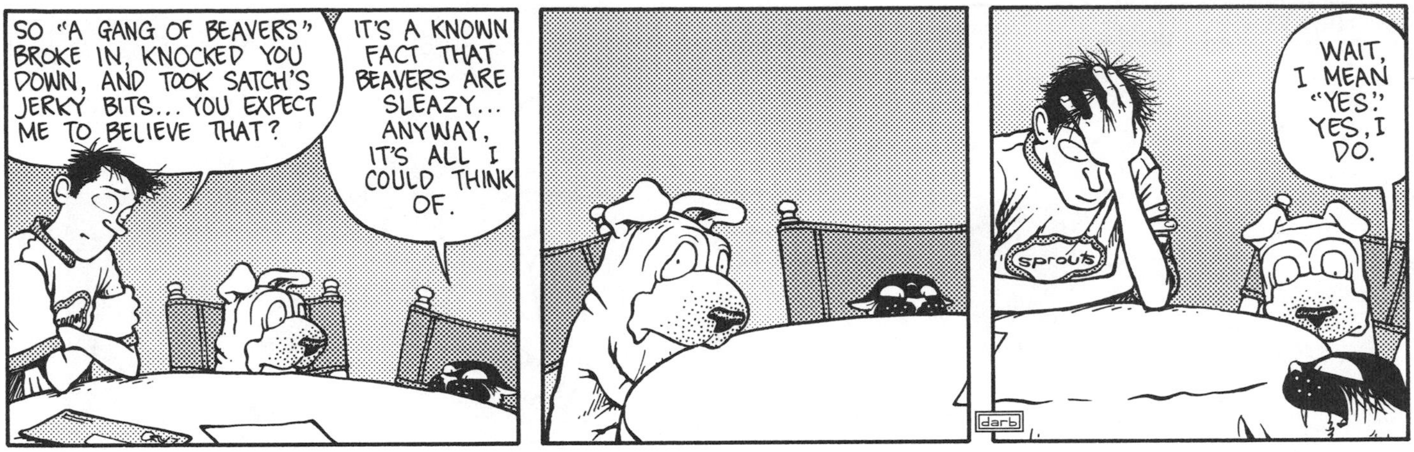
SO "A GANG OF BEAVERS" BROKE IN, KNOCKED YOU DOWN, AND TOOK SATCH'S JERKY BITS... YOU EXPECT ME TO BELIEVE THAT?
IT'S A KNOWN FACT THAT BEAVERS ARE SLEAZY... ANYWAY, IT'S ALL I COULD THINK OF.
sprouts
WAIT, I MEAN "YES." YES, I DO.
darb

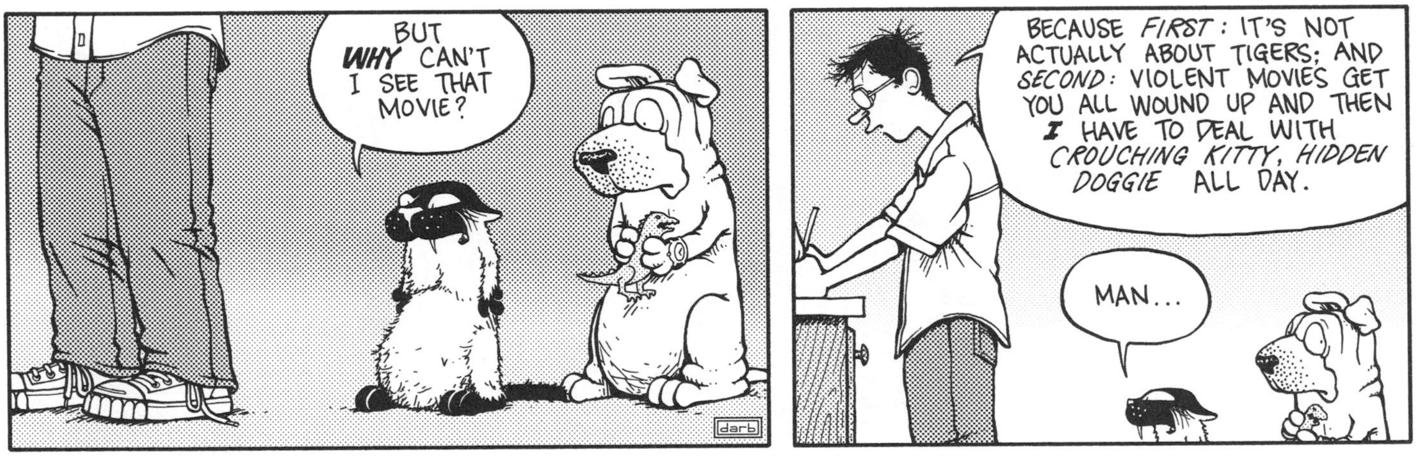
BUT *WHY* CAN'T I SEE THAT MOVIE?
darb
BECAUSE *FIRST*: IT'S NOT ACTUALLY ABOUT TIGERS; AND *SECOND*: VIOLENT MOVIES GET YOU ALL WOUND UP AND THEN *I* HAVE TO DEAL WITH *CROUCHING KITTY, HIDDEN DOGGIE* ALL DAY.
MAN...

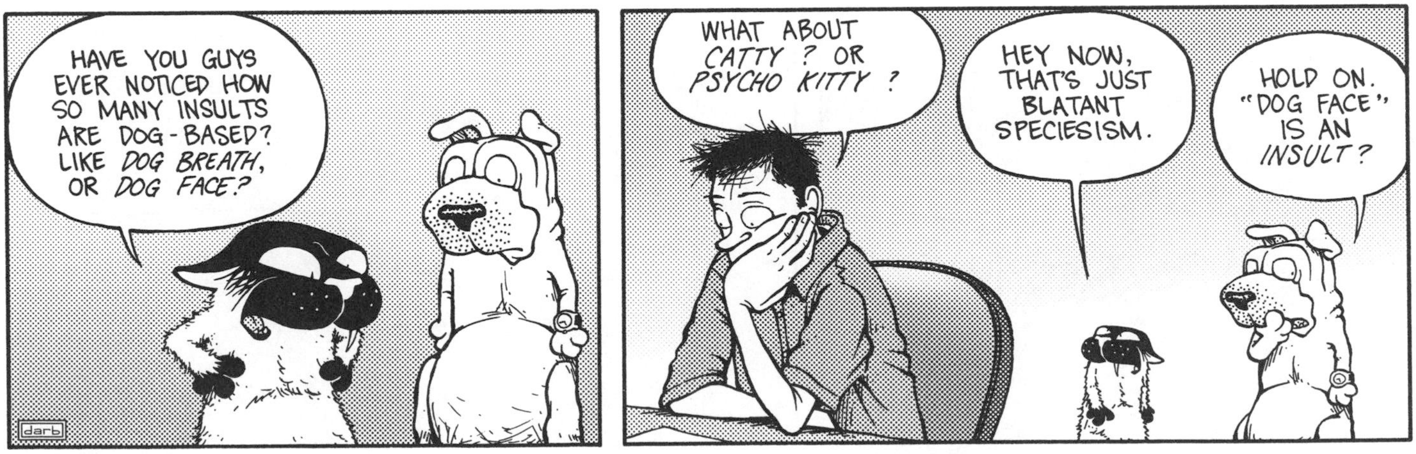
HAVE YOU GUYS EVER NOTICED HOW SO MANY INSULTS ARE DOG-BASED? LIKE *DOG BREATH*, OR *DOG FACE*?
darb
WHAT ABOUT *CATTY*? OR *PSYCHO KITTY*?
HEY NOW, THAT'S JUST BLATANT SPECIESISM.
HOLD ON. "DOG FACE" IS AN *INSULT*?

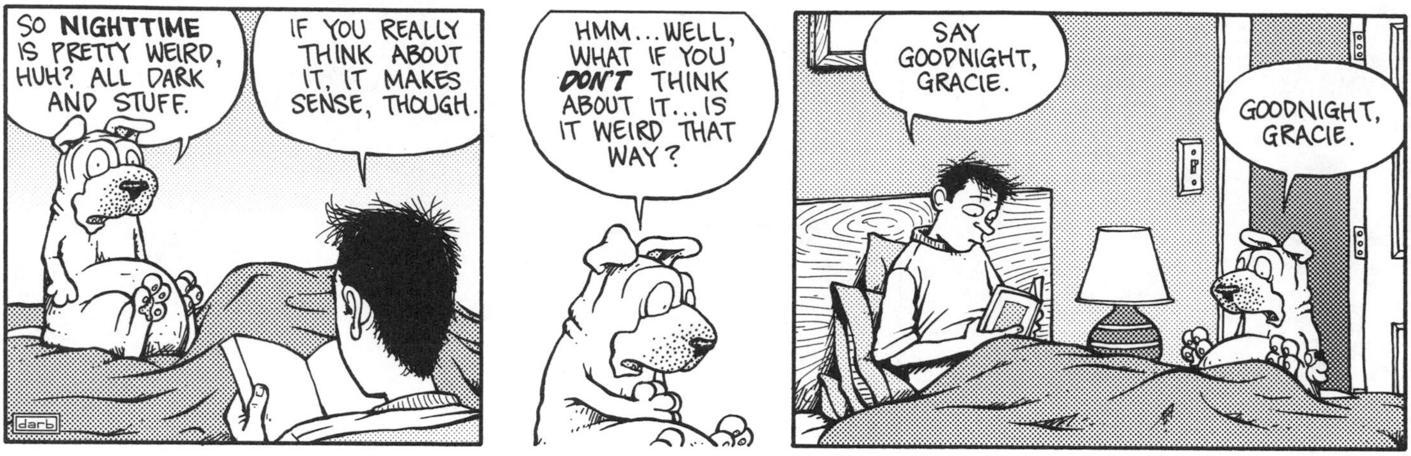
SO **NIGHTTIME** IS PRETTY WEIRD, HUH? ALL DARK AND STUFF.
IF YOU REALLY THINK ABOUT IT, IT MAKES SENSE, THOUGH.
darb
HMM... WELL, WHAT IF YOU ***DON'T*** THINK ABOUT IT... IS IT WEIRD THAT WAY?
SAY GOODNIGHT, GRACIE.
GOODNIGHT, GRACIE.

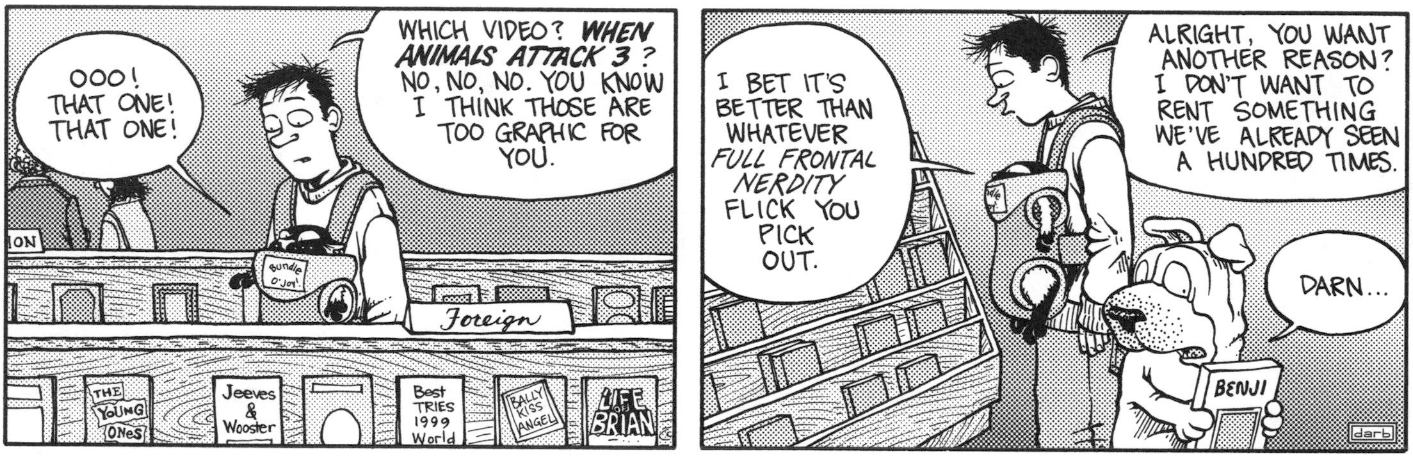
OOO! THAT ONE! THAT ONE!
WHICH VIDEO? ***WHEN ANIMALS ATTACK 3***? NO, NO, NO. YOU KNOW I THINK THOSE ARE TOO GRAPHIC FOR YOU.
Bundle O'Joy
Foreign
THE YOUNG ONES
Jeeves & Wooster
Best TRIES 1999 World
BALLY KISS ANGEL
LIFE OF BRIAN
I BET IT'S BETTER THAN WHATEVER *FULL FRONTAL NERDITY* FLICK YOU PICK OUT.
ALRIGHT, YOU WANT ANOTHER REASON? I DON'T WANT TO RENT SOMETHING WE'VE ALREADY SEEN A HUNDRED TIMES.
DARN...
BENJI
darb

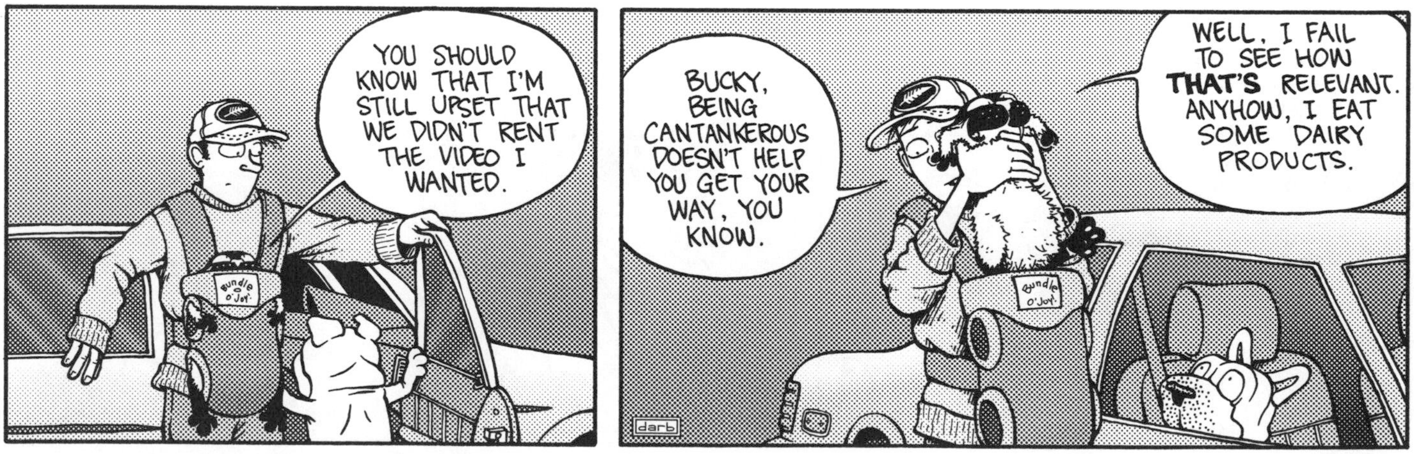
YOU SHOULD KNOW THAT I'M STILL UPSET THAT WE DIDN'T RENT THE VIDEO I WANTED.
Bundle O'Joy
darb
BUCKY, BEING CANTANKEROUS DOESN'T HELP YOU GET YOUR WAY, YOU KNOW.
WELL, I FAIL TO SEE HOW **THAT'S** RELEVANT. ANYHOW, I EAT SOME DAIRY PRODUCTS.
Bundle O'Joy

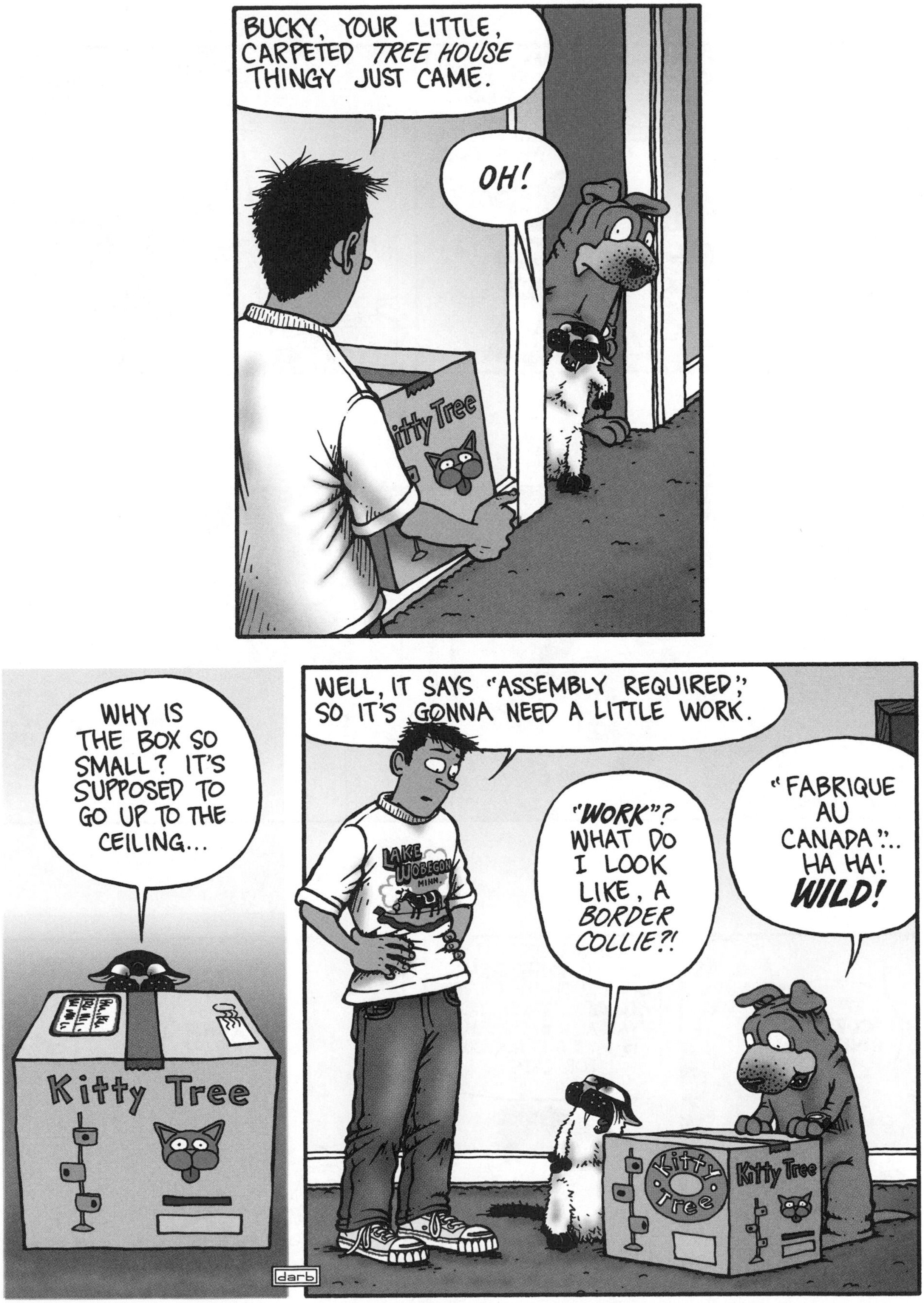
BUCKY, YOUR LITTLE, CARPETED *TREE HOUSE* THINGY JUST CAME.
OH!
Kitty Tree
WHY IS THE BOX SO SMALL? IT'S SUPPOSED TO GO UP TO THE CEILING...
Kitty Tree
darb
WELL, IT SAYS "ASSEMBLY REQUIRED," SO IT'S GONNA NEED A LITTLE WORK.
LAKE WOBEGON MINN.
"*WORK*"? WHAT DO I LOOK LIKE, A *BORDER COLLIE*?!
"FABRIQUE AU CANADA"... HA HA! ***WILD!***
Kitty Tree
Kitty Tree

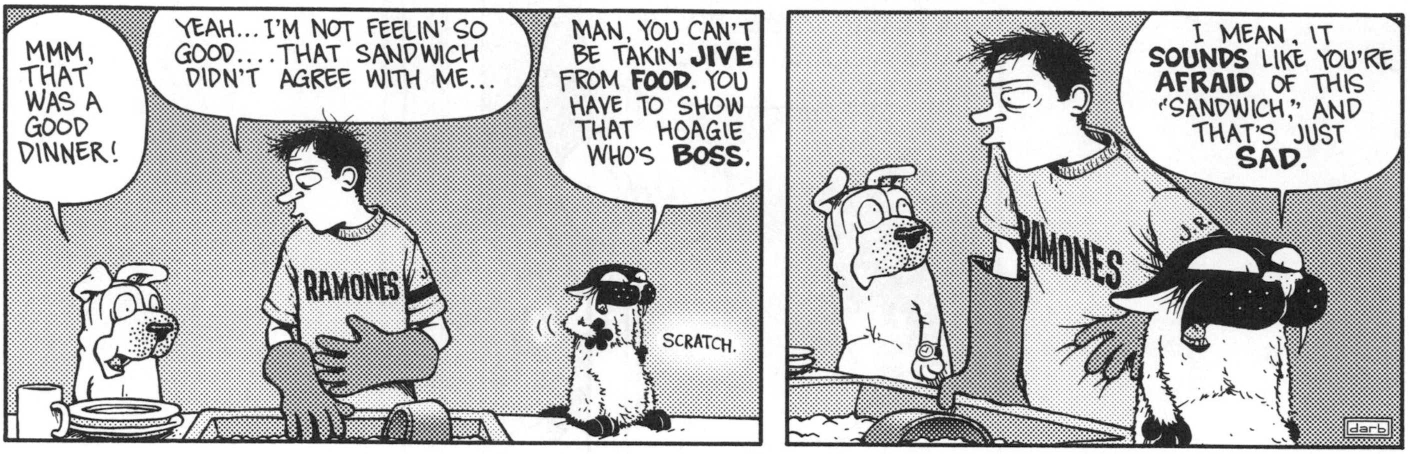
MMM, THAT WAS A GOOD DINNER!
YEAH... I'M NOT FEELIN' SO GOOD.... THAT SANDWICH DIDN'T AGREE WITH ME...
RAMONES
MAN, YOU CAN'T BE TAKIN' **JIVE** FROM **FOOD**. YOU HAVE TO SHOW THAT HOAGIE WHO'S **BOSS**.
SCRATCH.
I MEAN, IT **SOUNDS** LIKE YOU'RE **AFRAID** OF THIS "SANDWICH," AND THAT'S JUST **SAD**.
RAMONES
darb

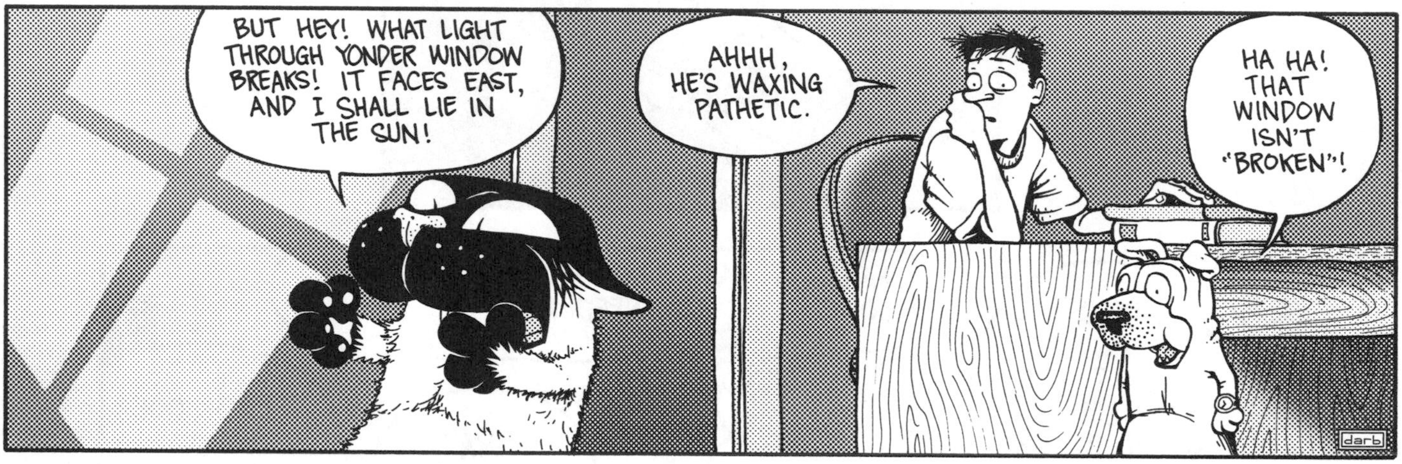
BUT HEY! WHAT LIGHT THROUGH YONDER WINDOW BREAKS! IT FACES EAST, AND I SHALL LIE IN THE SUN!
AHHH, HE'S WAXING PATHETIC.
HA HA! THAT WINDOW ISN'T "BROKEN"!
darb

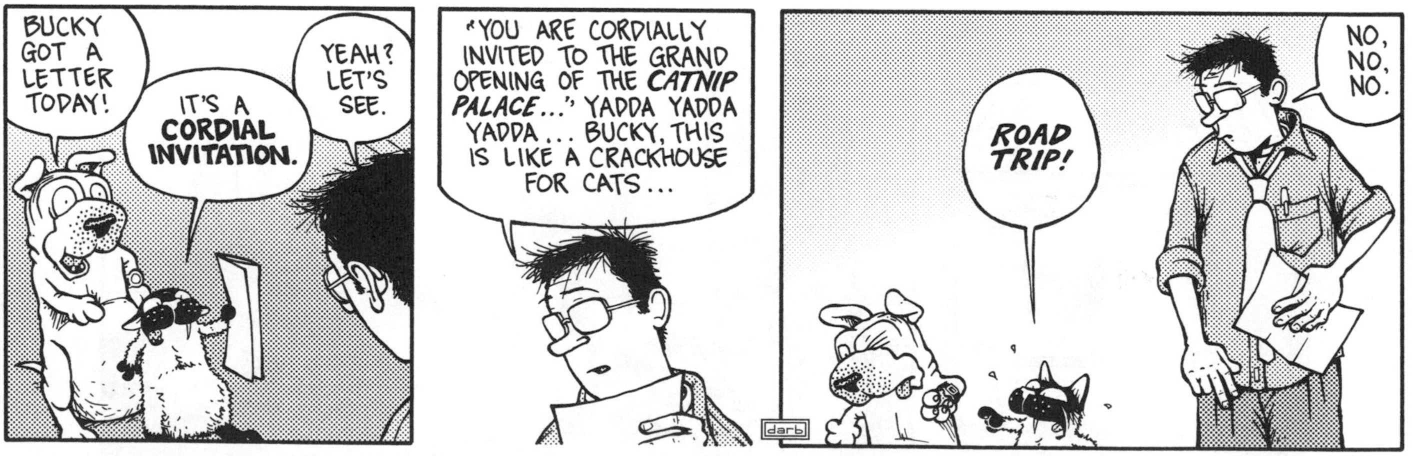
BUCKY GOT A LETTER TODAY!
IT'S A **CORDIAL INVITATION.**
YEAH? LET'S SEE.
"YOU ARE CORDIALLY INVITED TO THE GRAND OPENING OF THE ***CATNIP PALACE...***" YADDA YADDA YADDA... BUCKY, THIS IS LIKE A CRACKHOUSE FOR CATS...
darb
ROAD TRIP!
NO, NO, NO.

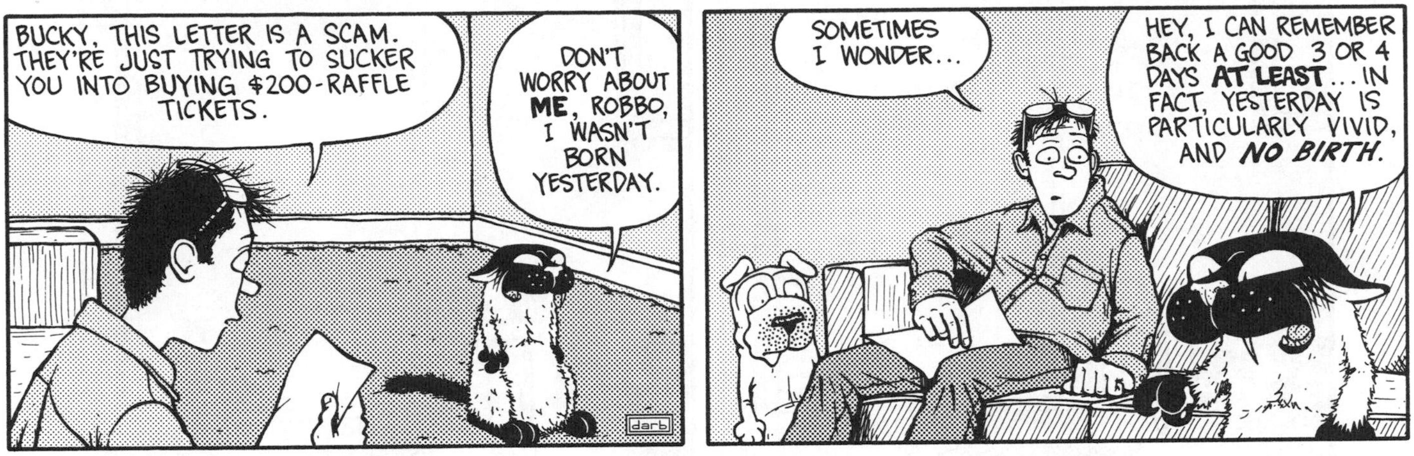
BUCKY, THIS LETTER IS A SCAM. THEY'RE JUST TRYING TO SUCKER YOU INTO BUYING $200-RAFFLE TICKETS.
DON'T WORRY ABOUT **ME**, ROBBO, I WASN'T BORN YESTERDAY.
SOMETIMES I WONDER...
HEY, I CAN REMEMBER BACK A GOOD 3 OR 4 DAYS **AT LEAST**... IN FACT, YESTERDAY IS PARTICULARLY VIVID, AND ***NO BIRTH.***
darb

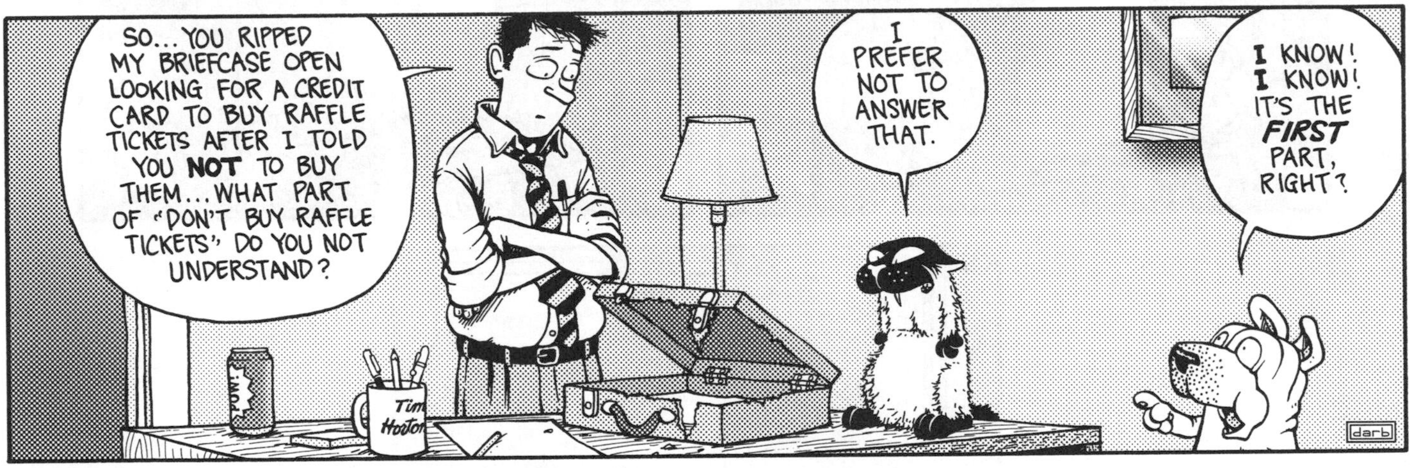
SO... YOU RIPPED MY BRIEFCASE OPEN LOOKING FOR A CREDIT CARD TO BUY RAFFLE TICKETS AFTER I TOLD YOU **NOT** TO BUY THEM... WHAT PART OF "DON'T BUY RAFFLE TICKETS" DO YOU NOT UNDERSTAND?
I PREFER NOT TO ANSWER THAT.
I KNOW! **I** KNOW! IT'S THE ***FIRST*** PART, RIGHT?
Tim Horton
darb

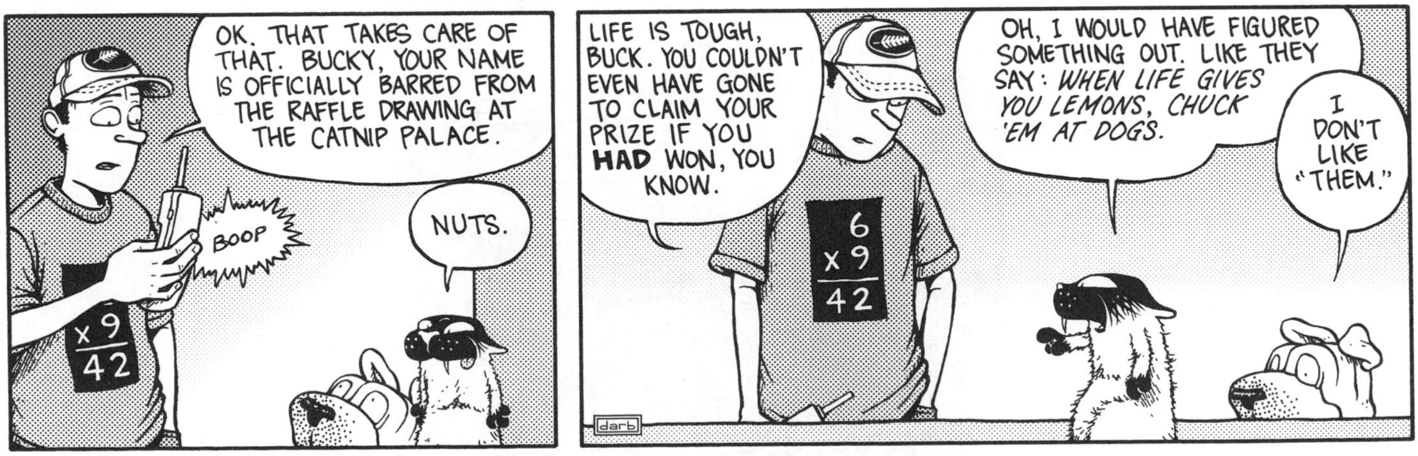
OK. THAT TAKES CARE OF THAT. BUCKY, YOUR NAME IS OFFICIALLY BARRED FROM THE RAFFLE DRAWING AT THE CATNIP PALACE.
BOOP
NUTS.
LIFE IS TOUGH, BUCK. YOU COULDN'T EVEN HAVE GONE TO CLAIM YOUR PRIZE IF YOU **HAD** WON, YOU KNOW.
OH, I WOULD HAVE FIGURED SOMETHING OUT. LIKE THEY SAY: *WHEN LIFE GIVES YOU LEMONS, CHUCK 'EM AT DOGS.*
I DON'T LIKE "THEM."
6 x 9 42
darb

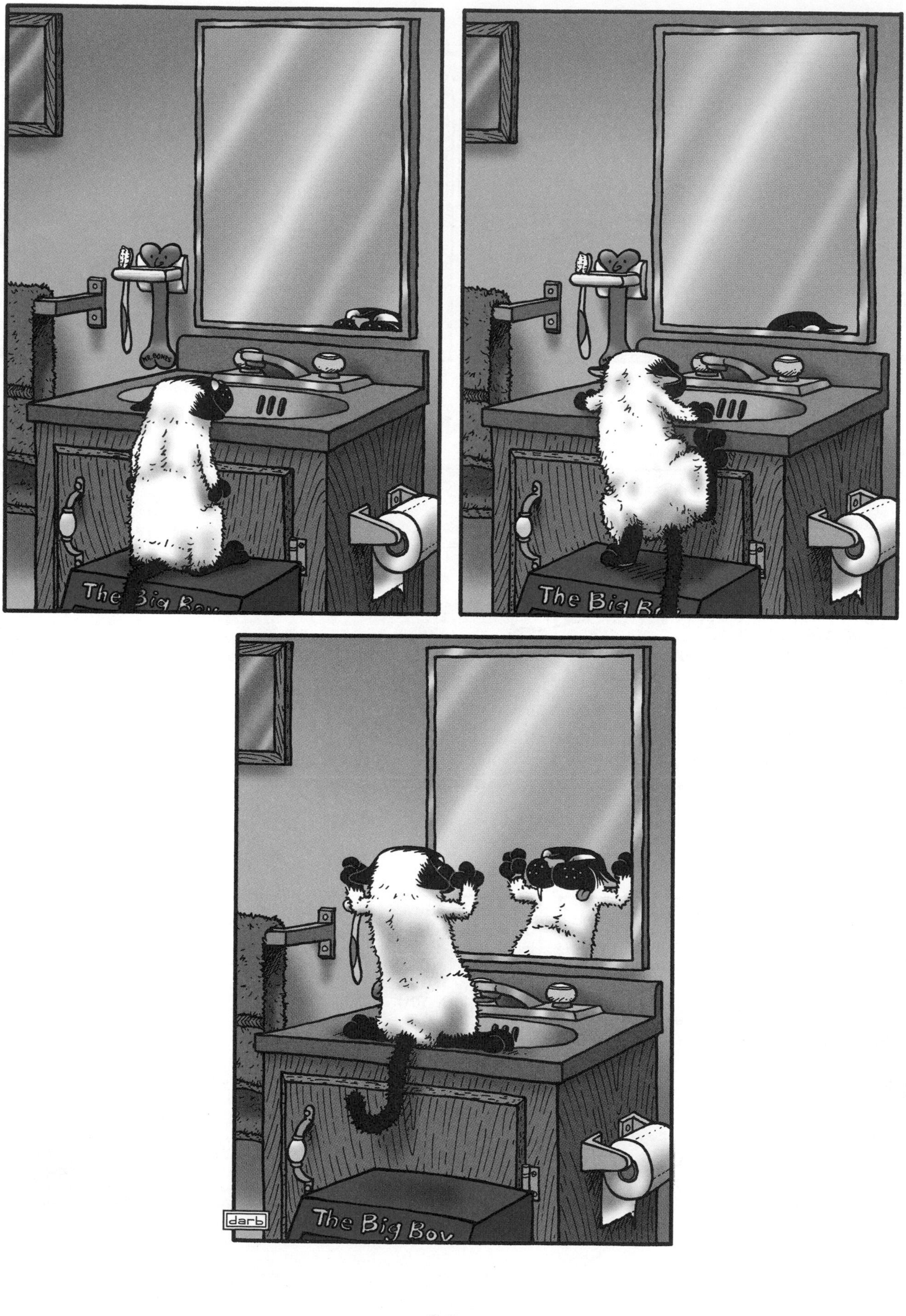
The Big
darb

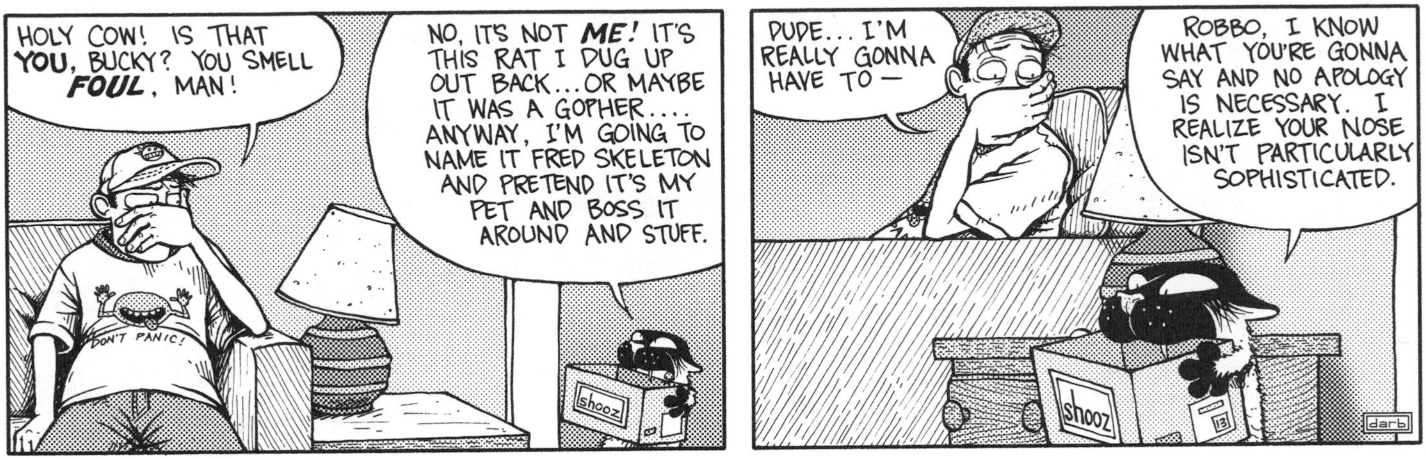
HOLY COW! IS THAT **YOU**, BUCKY? YOU SMELL ***FOUL***, MAN!
NO, IT'S NOT ***ME!*** IT'S THIS RAT I DUG UP OUT BACK...OR MAYBE IT WAS A GOPHER.... ANYWAY, I'M GOING TO NAME IT FRED SKELETON AND PRETEND IT'S MY PET AND BOSS IT AROUND AND STUFF.
DON'T PANIC!
shooz
DUDE... I'M REALLY GONNA HAVE TO—
ROBBO, I KNOW WHAT YOU'RE GONNA SAY AND NO APOLOGY IS NECESSARY. I REALIZE YOUR NOSE ISN'T PARTICULARLY SOPHISTICATED.
shooz
darb

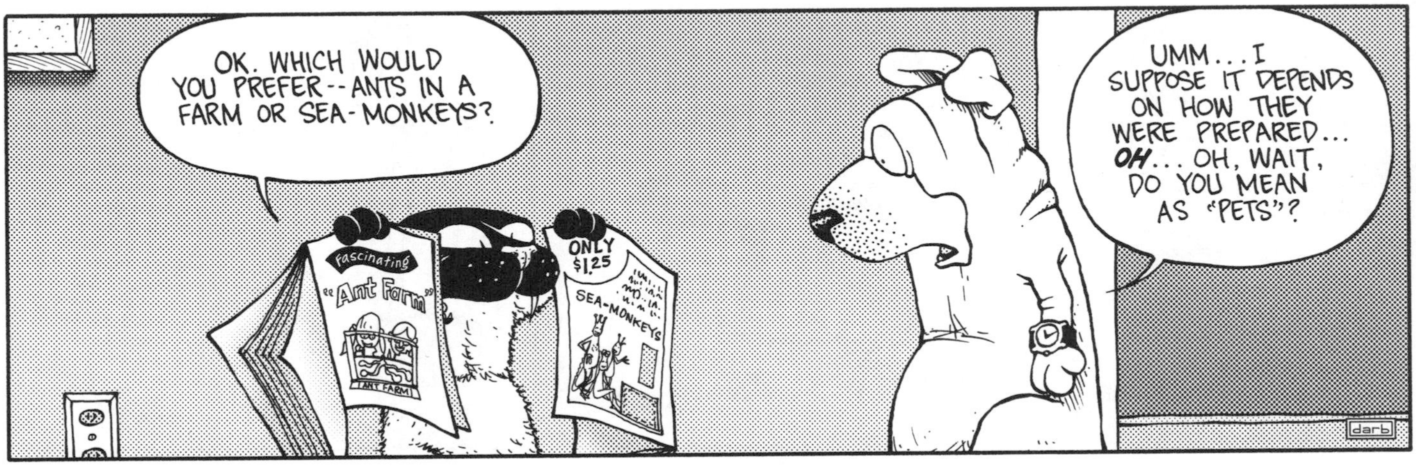
OK. WHICH WOULD YOU PREFER--ANTS IN A FARM OR SEA-MONKEYS?
UMM... I SUPPOSE IT DEPENDS ON HOW THEY WERE PREPARED... ***OH***... OH, WAIT, DO YOU MEAN AS "PETS"?
Fascinating "Ant Farm"
ANT FARM
ONLY $1.25
SEA-MONKEYS
darb

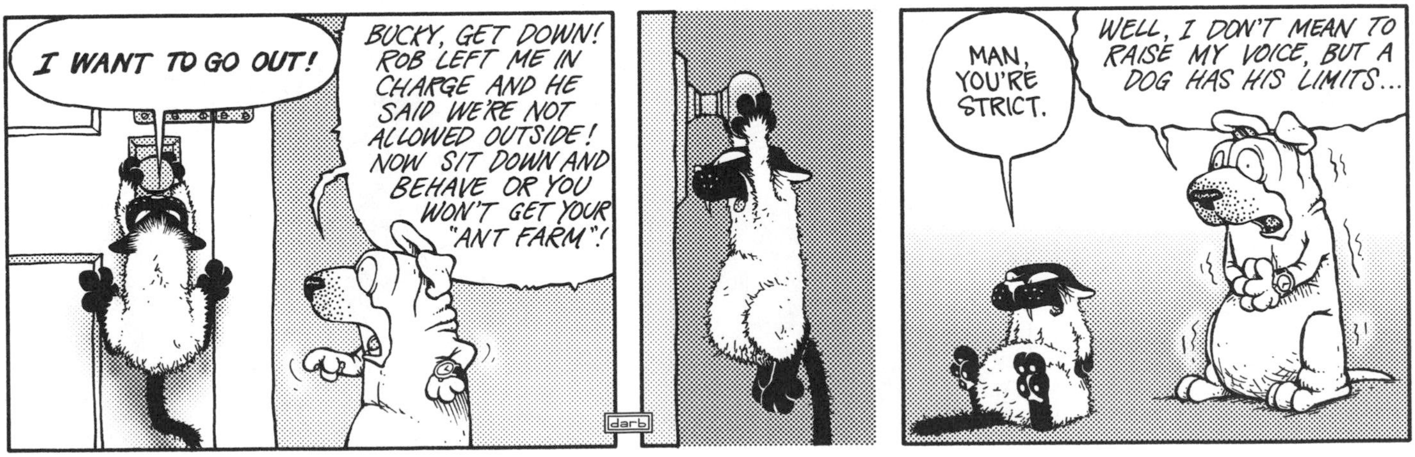
I WANT TO GO OUT!
BUCKY, GET DOWN! ROB LEFT ME IN CHARGE AND HE SAID WE'RE NOT ALLOWED OUTSIDE! NOW SIT DOWN AND BEHAVE OR YOU WON'T GET YOUR "ANT FARM"!
darb
MAN, YOU'RE STRICT.
WELL, I DON'T MEAN TO RAISE MY VOICE, BUT A DOG HAS HIS LIMITS...

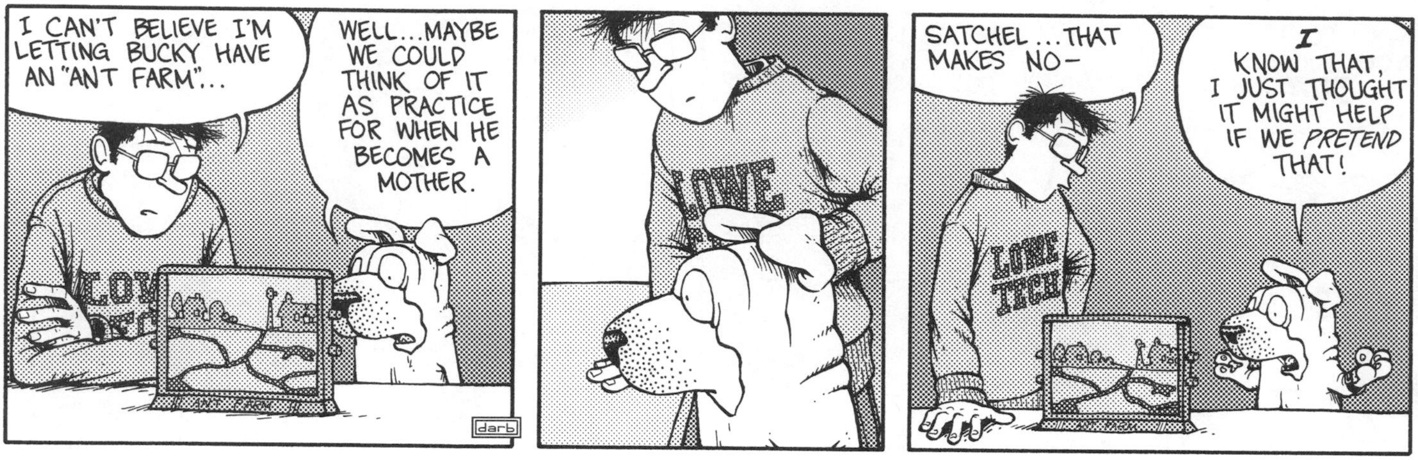
I CAN'T BELIEVE I'M LETTING BUCKY HAVE AN "ANT FARM"...
WELL...MAYBE WE COULD THINK OF IT AS PRACTICE FOR WHEN HE BECOMES A MOTHER.
darb
SATCHEL...THAT MAKES NO–
I KNOW THAT, I JUST THOUGHT IT MIGHT HELP IF WE *PRETEND* THAT!

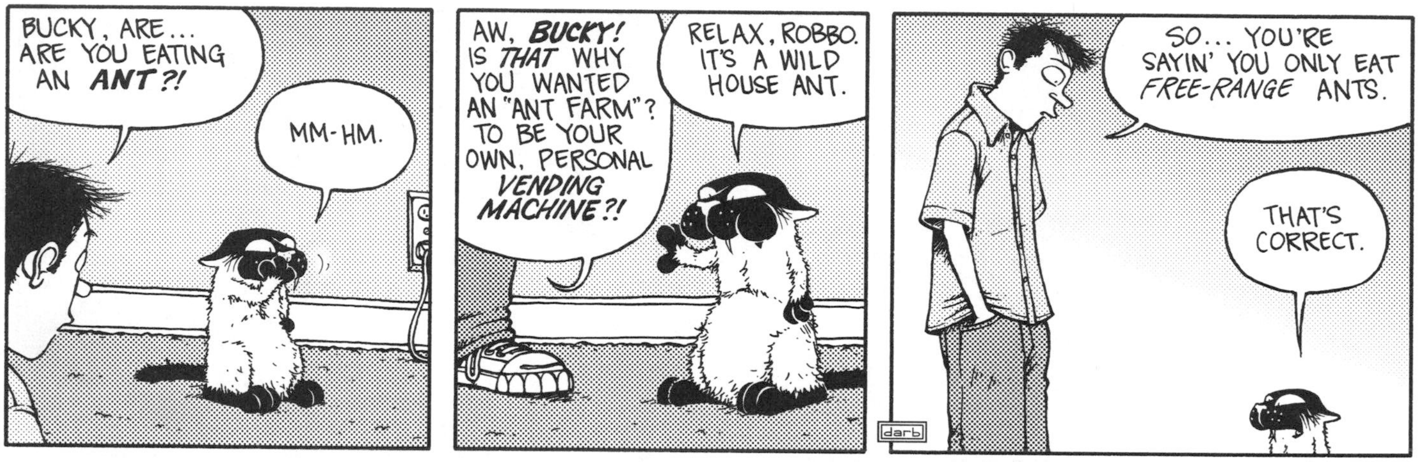
BUCKY, ARE... ARE YOU EATING AN ***ANT***?!
MM-HM.
AW, ***BUCKY!*** IS ***THAT*** WHY YOU WANTED AN "ANT FARM"? TO BE YOUR OWN, PERSONAL ***VENDING MACHINE***?!
RELAX, ROBBO. IT'S A WILD HOUSE ANT.
darb
SO... YOU'RE SAYIN' YOU ONLY EAT *FREE-RANGE* ANTS.
THAT'S CORRECT.

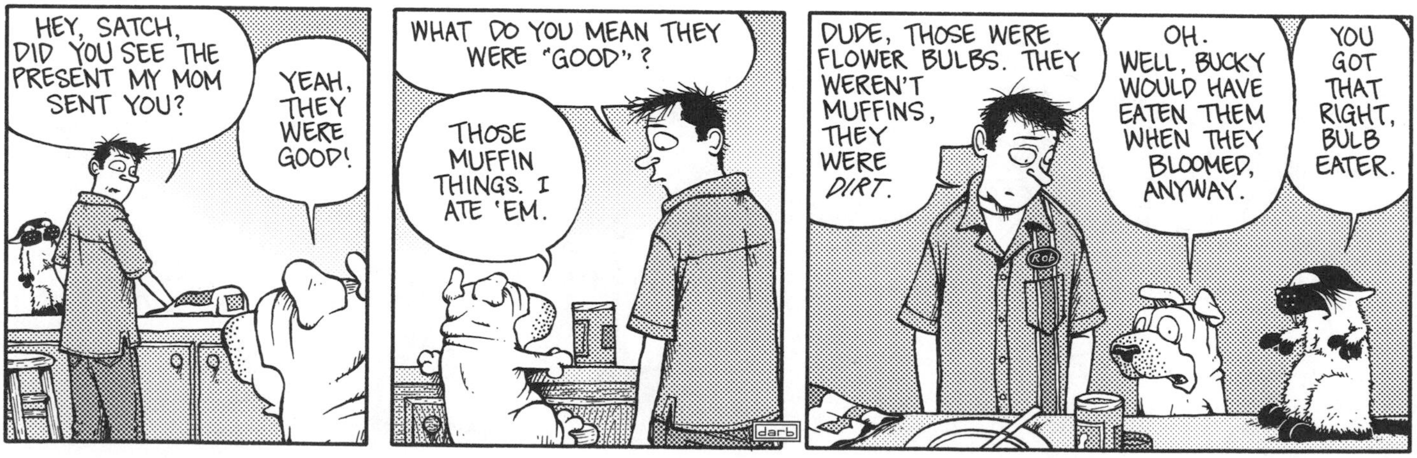
HEY, SATCH, DID YOU SEE THE PRESENT MY MOM SENT YOU?
YEAH, THEY WERE GOOD!
WHAT DO YOU MEAN THEY WERE "GOOD"?
THOSE MUFFIN THINGS. I ATE 'EM.
darb
DUDE, THOSE WERE FLOWER BULBS. THEY WEREN'T MUFFINS, THEY WERE *DIRT*.
OH. WELL, BUCKY WOULD HAVE EATEN THEM WHEN THEY BLOOMED, ANYWAY.
YOU GOT THAT RIGHT, BULB EATER.

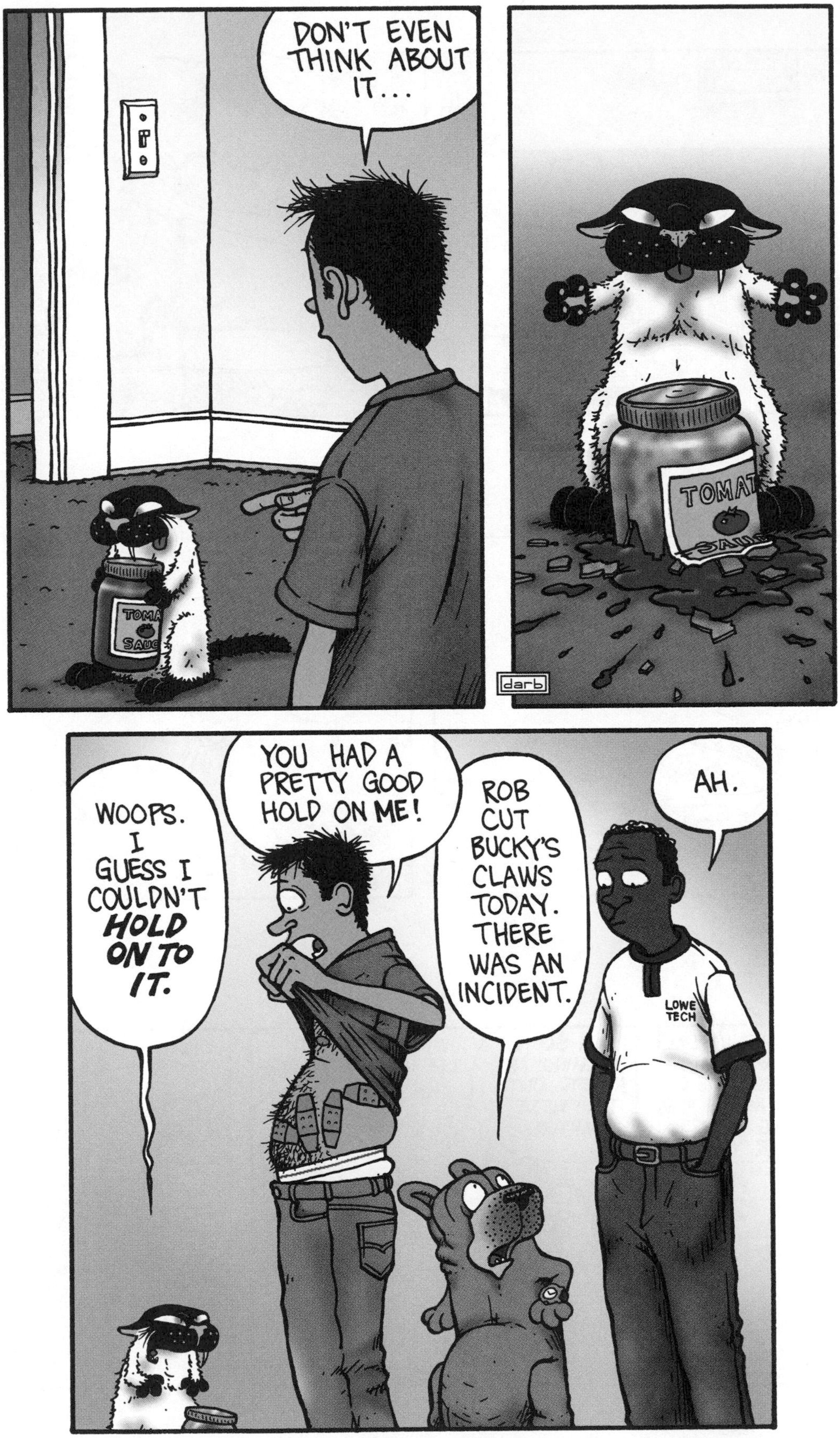
DON'T EVEN THINK ABOUT IT...
TOMA SAUC
TOMAT SAUC
darb
WOOPS. I GUESS I COULDN'T HOLD ON TO IT.
YOU HAD A PRETTY GOOD HOLD ON ME!
ROB CUT BUCKY'S CLAWS TODAY. THERE WAS AN INCIDENT.
AH.
LOWE TECH

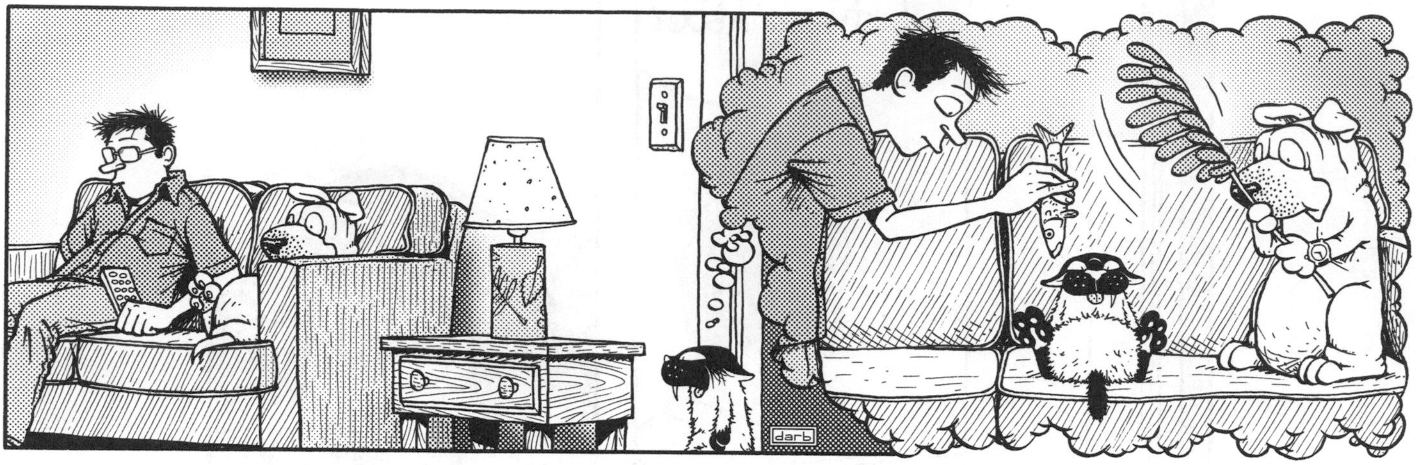
darb

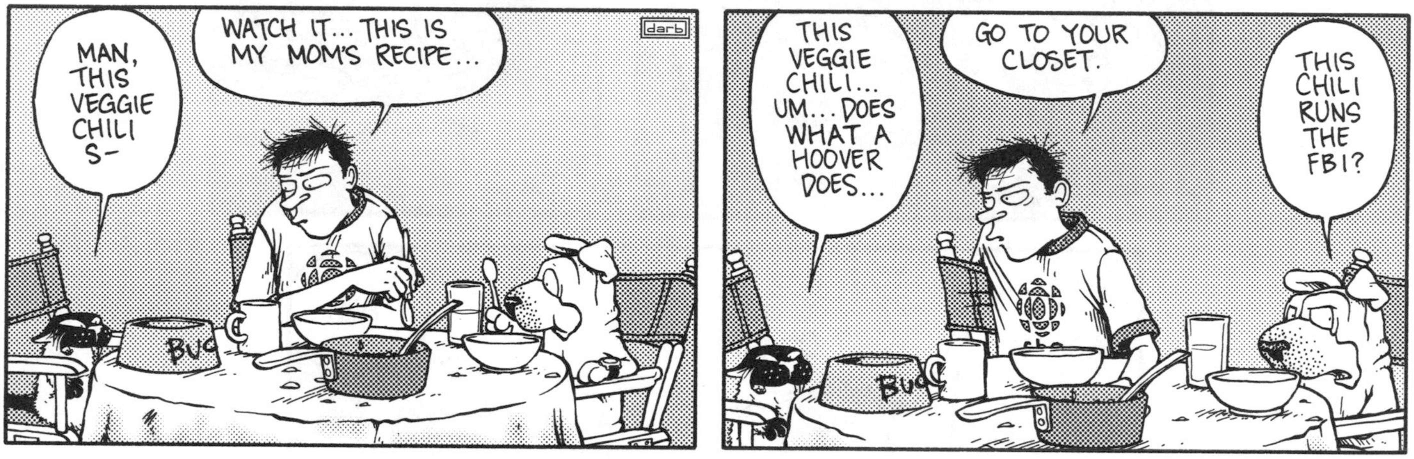
darb
MAN, THIS VEGGIE CHILI S-
WATCH IT... THIS IS MY MOM'S RECIPE...
BUC
THIS VEGGIE CHILI... UM... DOES WHAT A HOOVER DOES...
GO TO YOUR CLOSET.
THIS CHILI RUNS THE FBI?
BUC

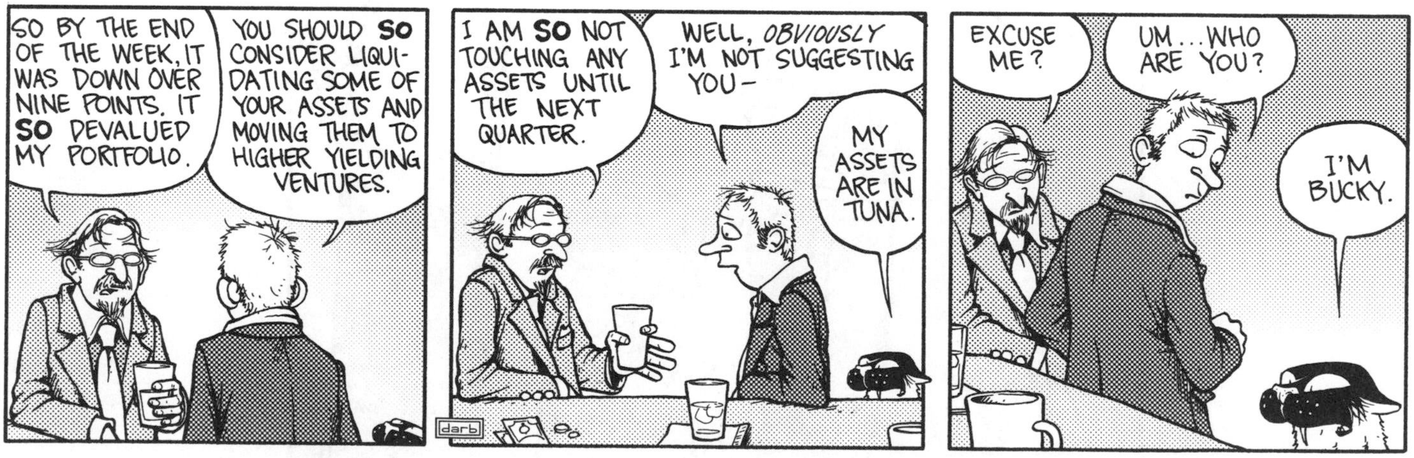
SO BY THE END OF THE WEEK, IT WAS DOWN OVER NINE POINTS. IT **SO** DEVALUED MY PORTFOLIO.
YOU SHOULD **SO** CONSIDER LIQUI-DATING SOME OF YOUR ASSETS AND MOVING THEM TO HIGHER YIELDING VENTURES.
I AM **SO** NOT TOUCHING ANY ASSETS UNTIL THE NEXT QUARTER.
WELL, *OBVIOUSLY* I'M NOT SUGGESTING YOU-
MY ASSETS ARE IN TUNA.
darb
EXCUSE ME?
UM...WHO ARE YOU?
I'M BUCKY.

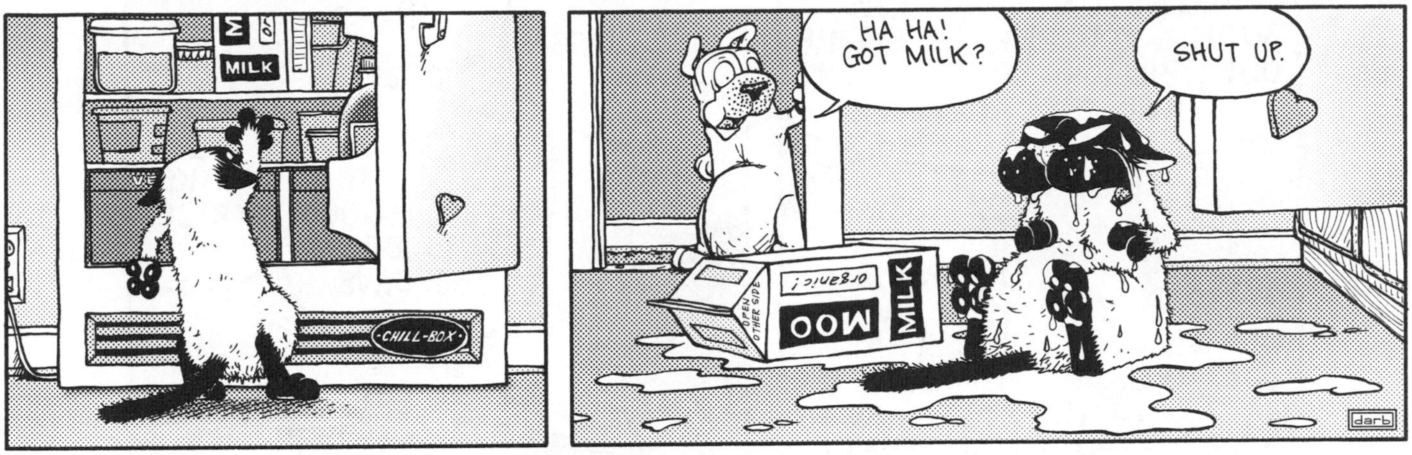
MILK
CHILL-BOX
HA HA! GOT MILK?
SHUT UP.
MOO
MILK
organic!
OPEN OTHER SIDE
darb

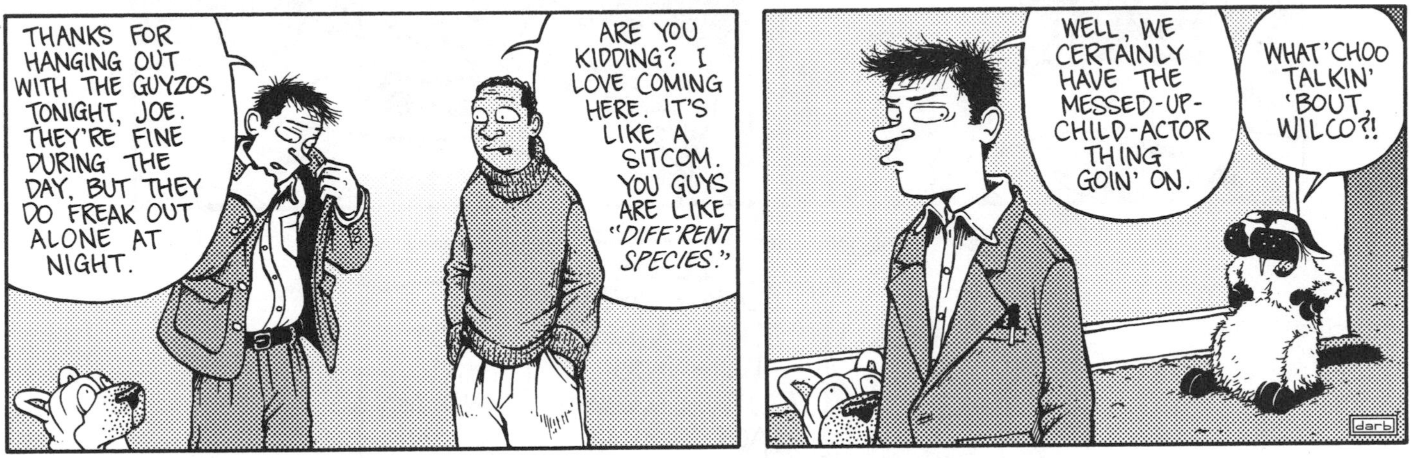
THANKS FOR HANGING OUT WITH THE GUYZOS TONIGHT, JOE. THEY'RE FINE DURING THE DAY, BUT THEY DO FREAK OUT ALONE AT NIGHT.
ARE YOU KIDDING? I LOVE COMING HERE. IT'S LIKE A SITCOM. YOU GUYS ARE LIKE *"DIFF'RENT SPECIES."*
WELL, WE CERTAINLY HAVE THE MESSED-UP-CHILD-ACTOR THING GOIN' ON.
WHAT'CHOO TALKIN' 'BOUT, WILCO?!
darb

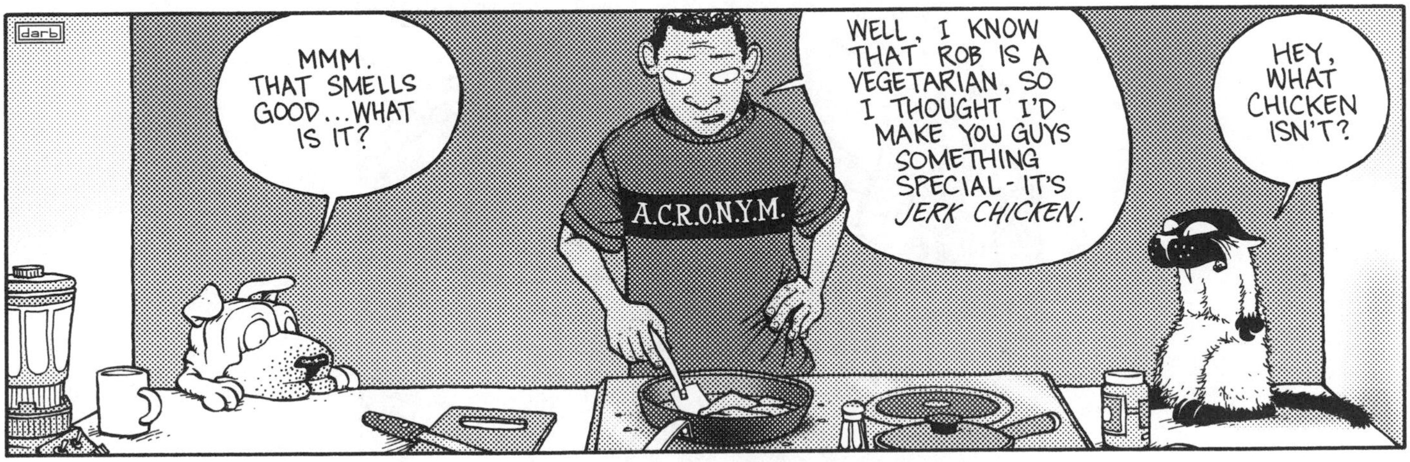
darb
MMM. THAT SMELLS GOOD... WHAT IS IT?
A.C.R.O.N.Y.M.
WELL, I KNOW THAT ROB IS A VEGETARIAN, SO I THOUGHT I'D MAKE YOU GUYS SOMETHING SPECIAL - IT'S *JERK CHICKEN.*
HEY, WHAT CHICKEN ISN'T?

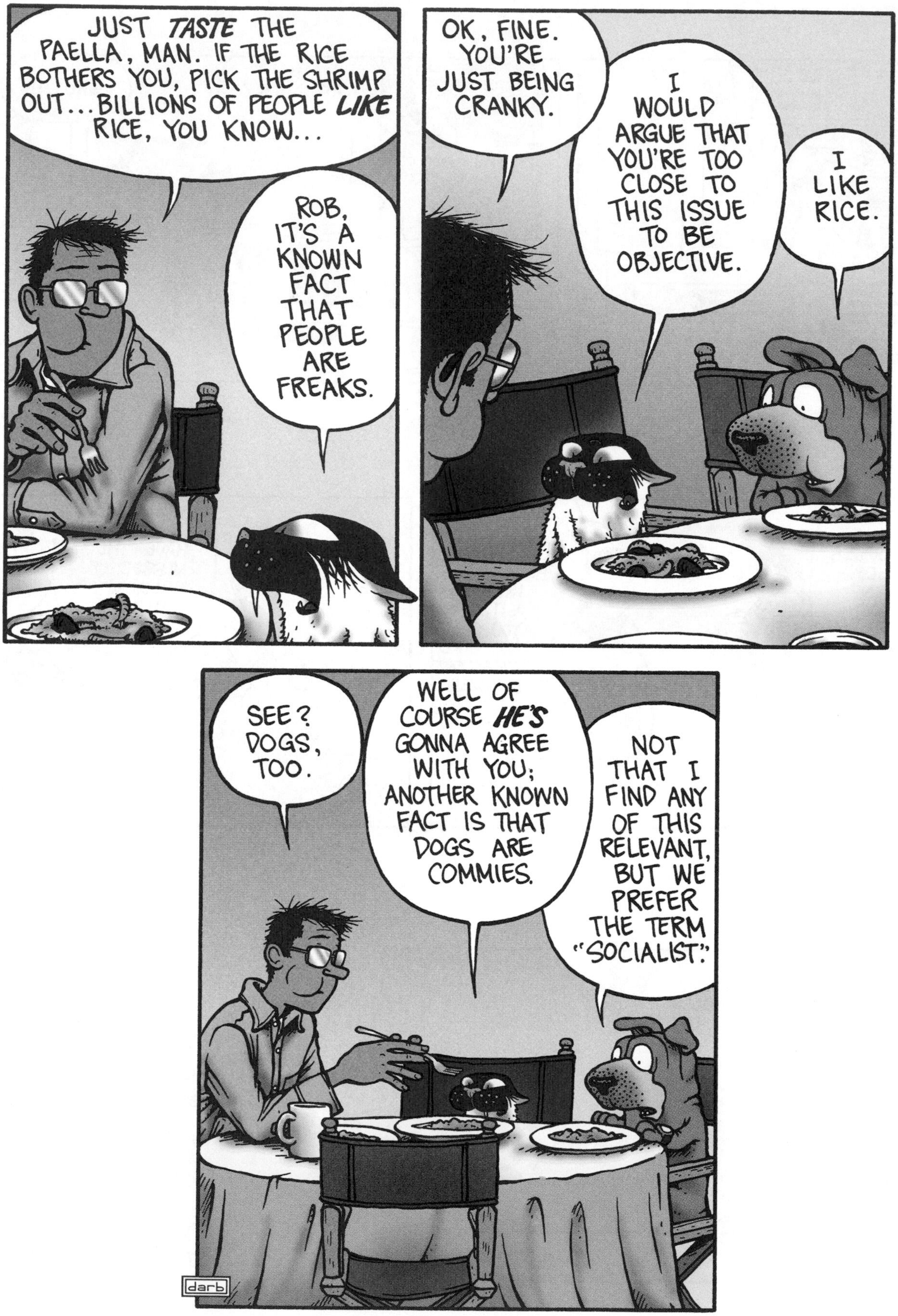

JUST *TASTE* THE PAELLA, MAN. IF THE RICE BOTHERS YOU, PICK THE SHRIMP OUT...BILLIONS OF PEOPLE *LIKE* RICE, YOU KNOW...
ROB, IT'S A KNOWN FACT THAT PEOPLE ARE FREAKS.
OK, FINE. YOU'RE JUST BEING CRANKY.
I WOULD ARGUE THAT YOU'RE TOO CLOSE TO THIS ISSUE TO BE OBJECTIVE.
I LIKE RICE.
SEE? DOGS, TOO.
WELL OF COURSE *HE'S* GONNA AGREE WITH YOU; ANOTHER KNOWN FACT IS THAT DOGS ARE COMMIES.
NOT THAT I FIND ANY OF THIS RELEVANT, BUT WE PREFER THE TERM "SOCIALIST."
darb

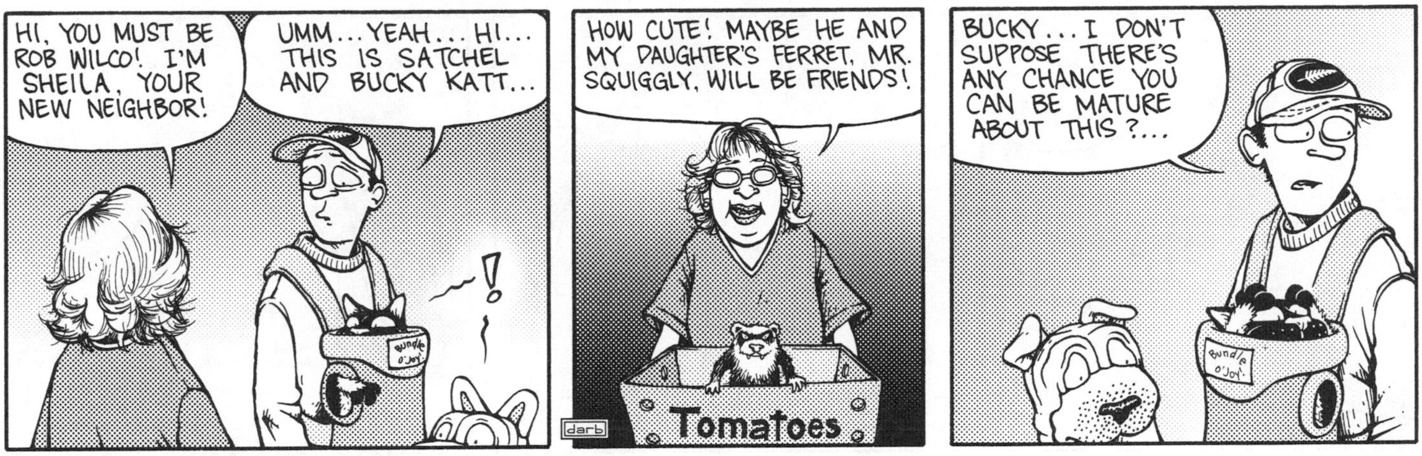
HI, YOU MUST BE ROB WILCO! I'M SHEILA, YOUR NEW NEIGHBOR!
UMM... YEAH... HI... THIS IS SATCHEL AND BUCKY KATT...
!
Bundle o'Joy!
darb
HOW CUTE! MAYBE HE AND MY DAUGHTER'S FERRET, MR. SQUIGGLY, WILL BE FRIENDS!
Tomatoes
BUCKY... I DON'T SUPPOSE THERE'S ANY CHANCE YOU CAN BE MATURE ABOUT THIS?...
Bundle o'Joy!

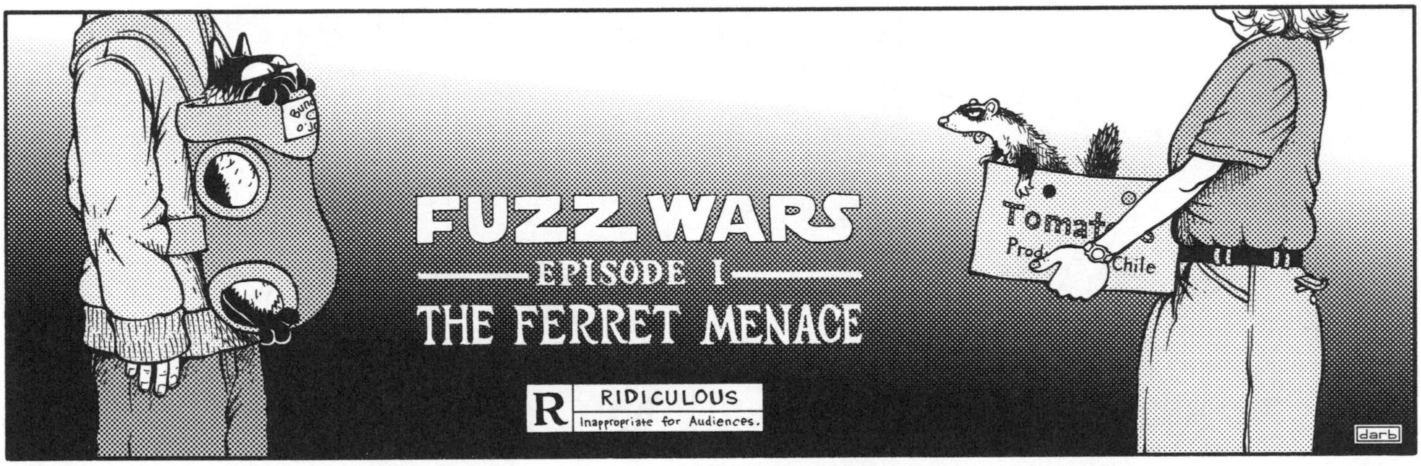
FUZZ WARS
EPISODE I
THE FERRET MENACE
R RIDICULOUS
Inappropriate for Audiences.
Chile
darb

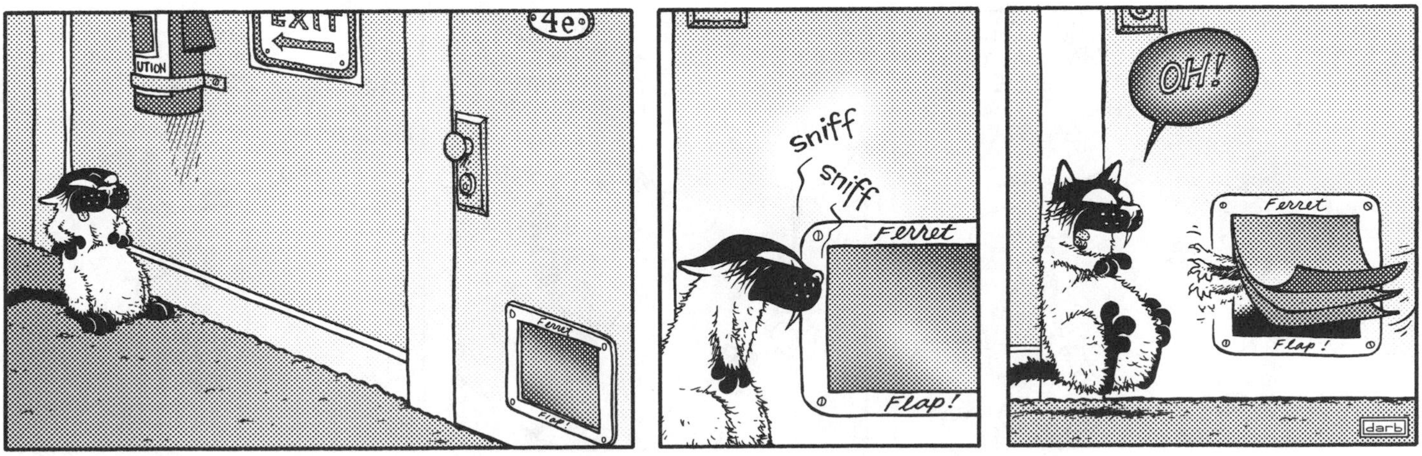
EXIT
4e
Ferret
Flap!
sniff
sniff
Ferret
Flap!
OH!
Ferret
Flap!
darb

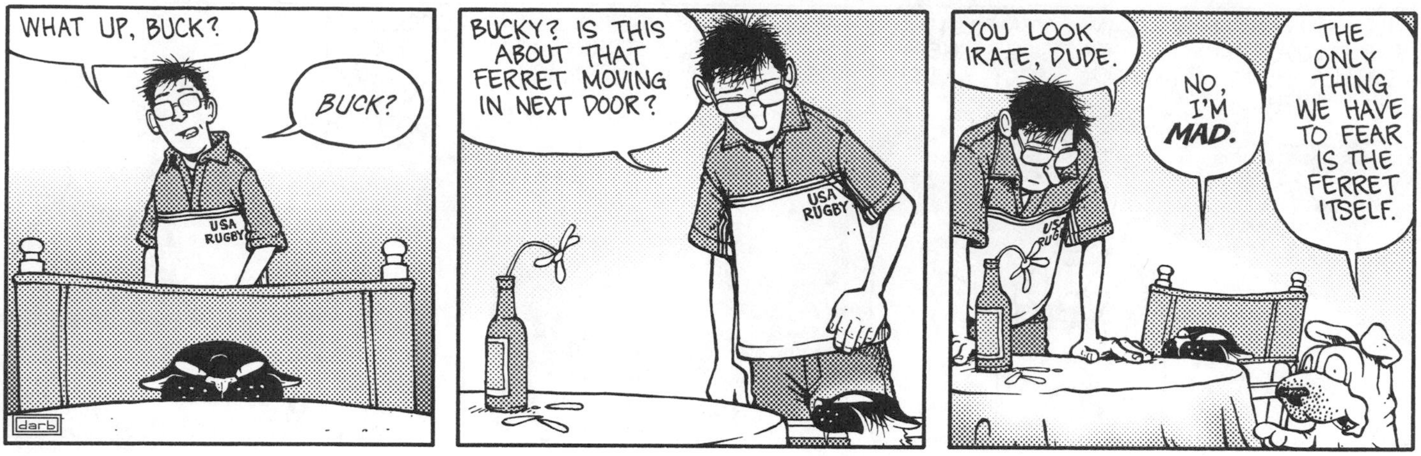
WHAT UP, BUCK?
BUCK?
USA RUGBY
BUCKY? IS THIS ABOUT THAT FERRET MOVING IN NEXT DOOR?
YOU LOOK IRATE, DUDE.
NO, I'M **MAD.**
THE ONLY THING WE HAVE TO FEAR IS THE FERRET ITSELF.
darb

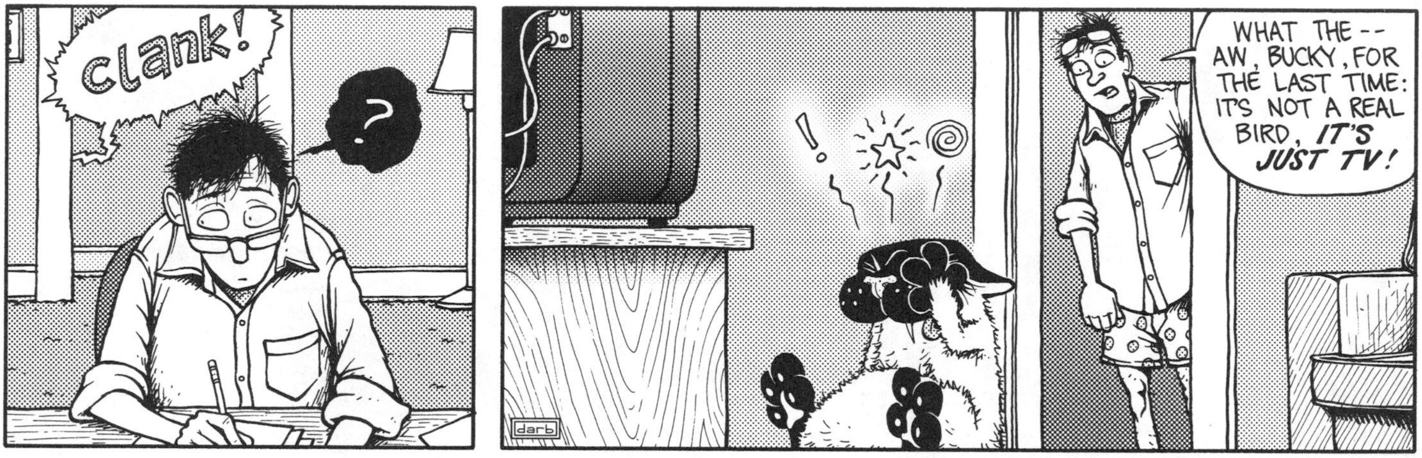
clank!
?
WHAT THE -- AW, BUCKY, FOR THE LAST TIME: IT'S NOT A REAL BIRD, ***IT'S JUST TV!***
darb

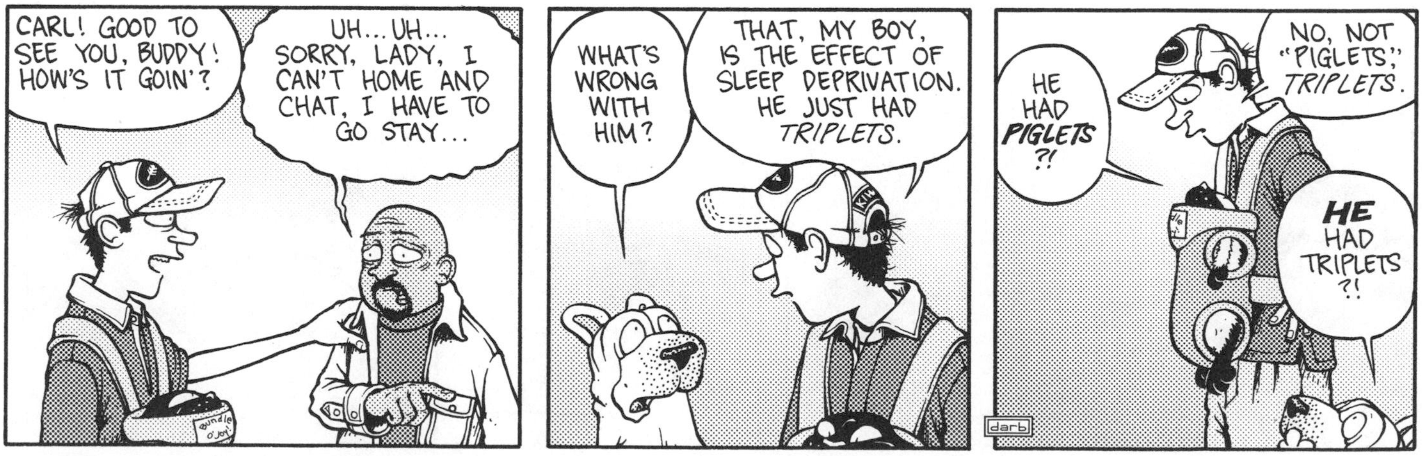
CARL! GOOD TO SEE YOU, BUDDY! HOW'S IT GOIN'?
UH... UH... SORRY, LADY, I CAN'T HOME AND CHAT, I HAVE TO GO STAY...
WHAT'S WRONG WITH HIM?
THAT, MY BOY, IS THE EFFECT OF SLEEP DEPRIVATION. HE JUST HAD *TRIPLETS.*
HE HAD ***PIGLETS*** ?!
NO, NOT "PIGLETS," *TRIPLETS.*
HE HAD TRIPLETS ?!
darb

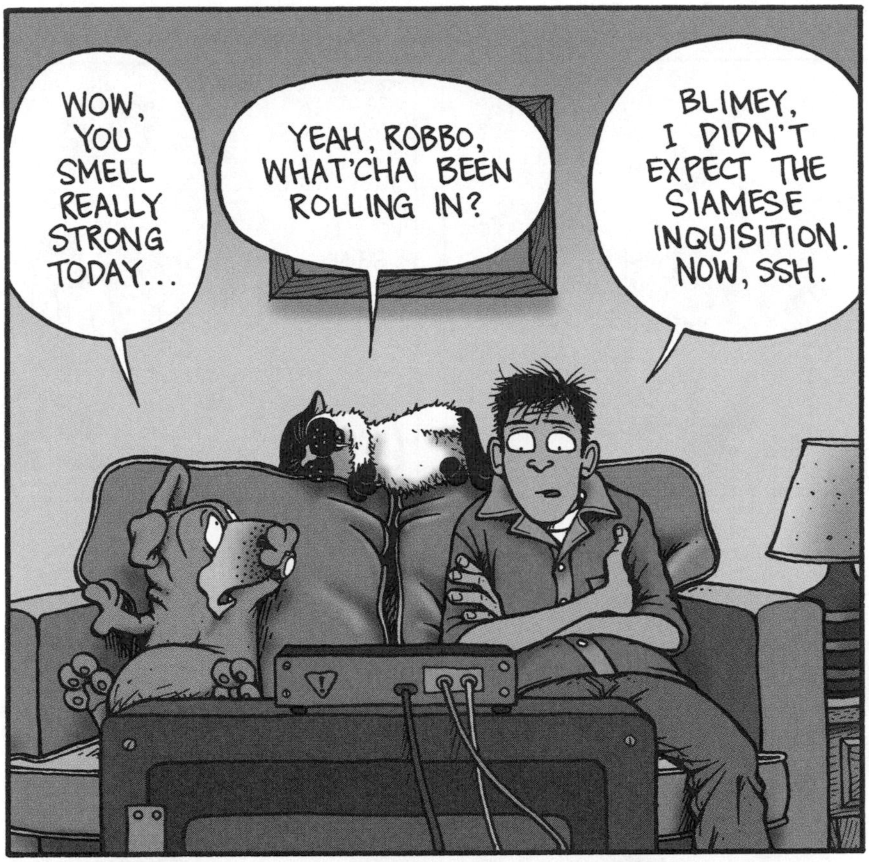
WOW, YOU SMELL REALLY STRONG TODAY...
YEAH, ROBBO, WHAT'CHA BEEN ROLLING IN?
BLIMEY, I DIDN'T EXPECT THE SIAMESE INQUISITION. NOW, SSH.

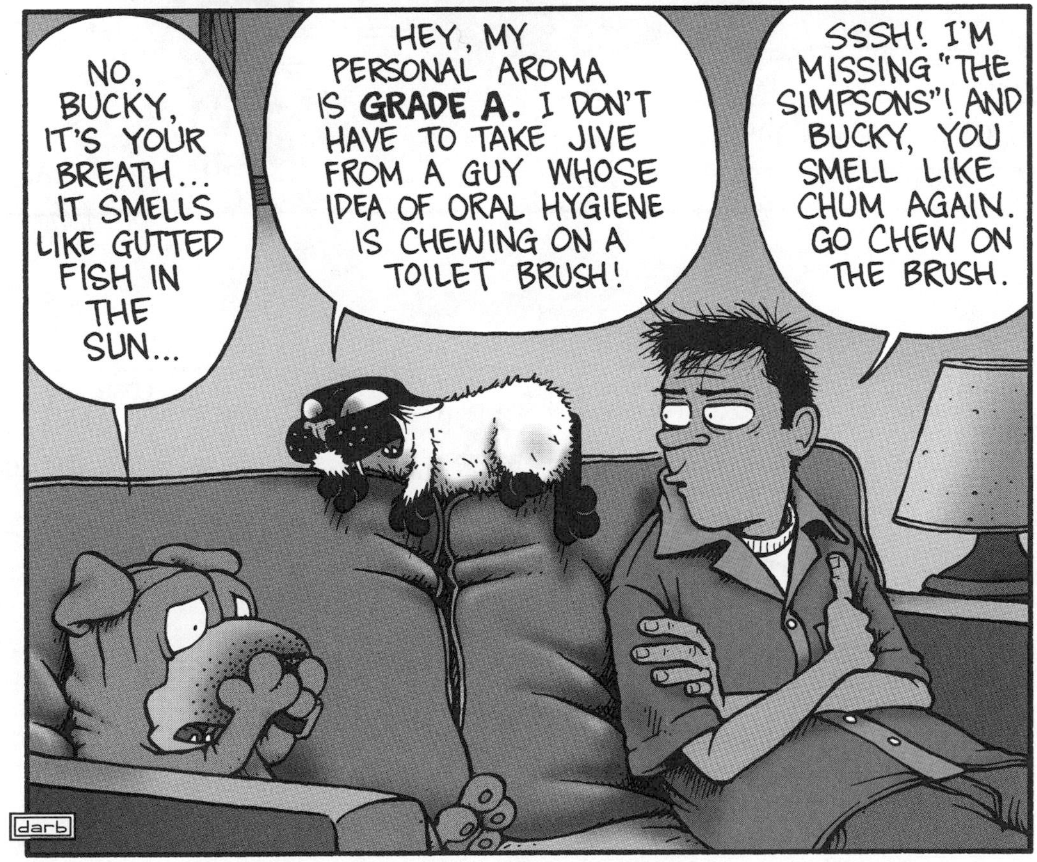
NO, BUCKY, IT'S YOUR BREATH... IT SMELLS LIKE GUTTED FISH IN THE SUN...
HEY, MY PERSONAL AROMA IS GRADE A. I DON'T HAVE TO TAKE JIVE FROM A GUY WHOSE IDEA OF ORAL HYGIENE IS CHEWING ON A TOILET BRUSH!
SSSH! I'M MISSING "THE SIMPSONS"! AND BUCKY, YOU SMELL LIKE CHUM AGAIN. GO CHEW ON THE BRUSH.
darb

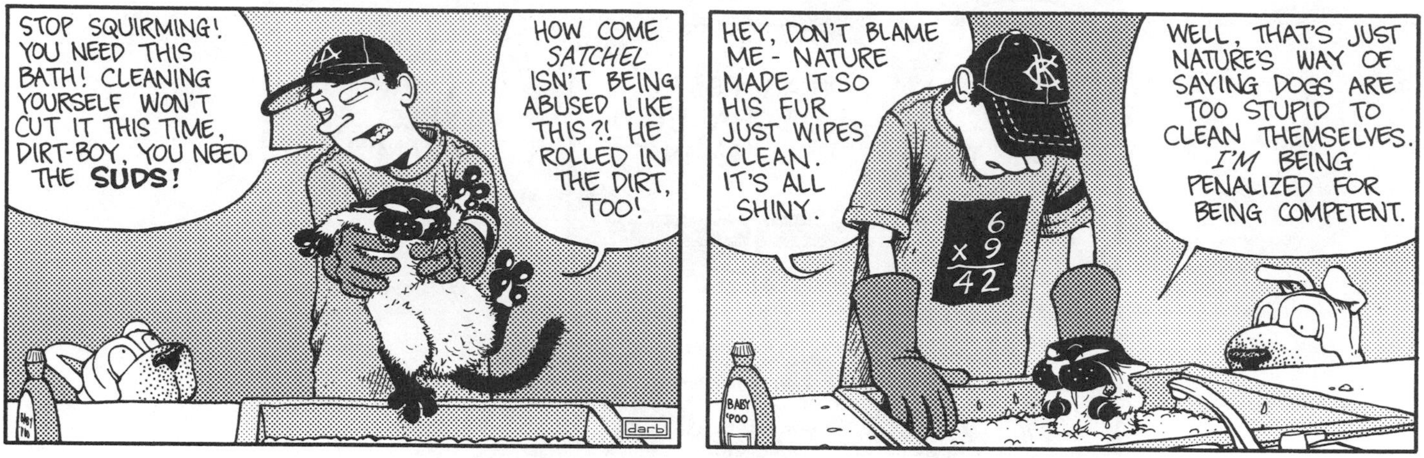
STOP SQUIRMING! YOU NEED THIS BATH! CLEANING YOURSELF WON'T CUT IT THIS TIME, DIRT-BOY, YOU NEED THE **SUDS**!
HOW COME *SATCHEL* ISN'T BEING ABUSED LIKE THIS?! HE ROLLED IN THE DIRT, TOO!
darb
HEY, DON'T BLAME ME - NATURE MADE IT SO HIS FUR JUST WIPES CLEAN. IT'S ALL SHINY.
6
x 9
42
WELL, THAT'S JUST NATURE'S WAY OF SAYING DOGS ARE TOO STUPID TO CLEAN THEMSELVES. *I'M* BEING PENALIZED FOR BEING COMPETENT.
BABY 'POO

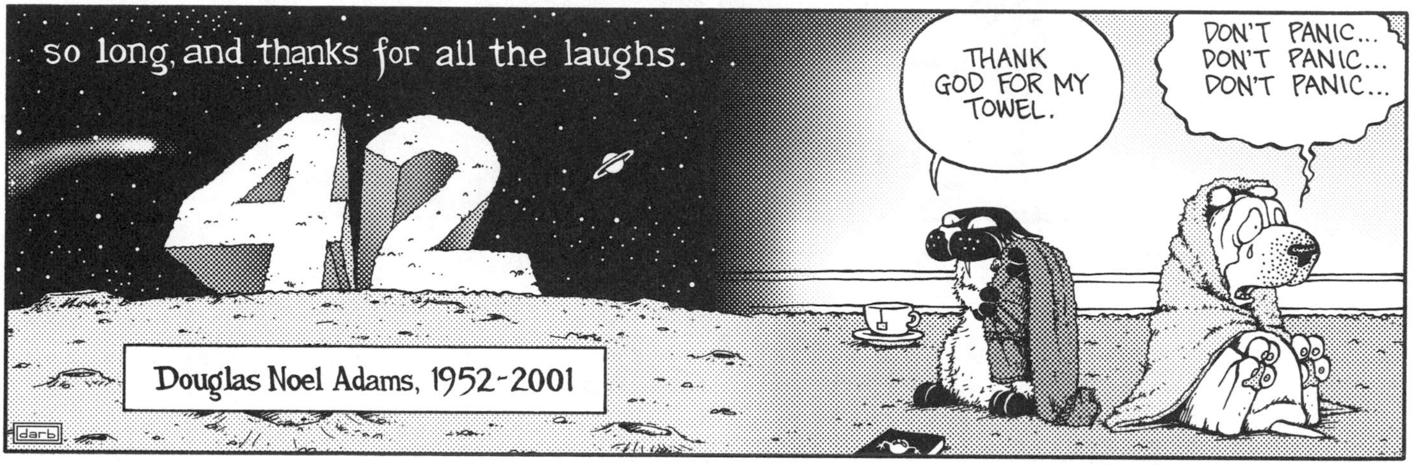
so long, and thanks for all the laughs.
42
Douglas Noel Adams, 1952-2001
darb
THANK GOD FOR MY TOWEL.
DON'T PANIC... DON'T PANIC... DON'T PANIC...

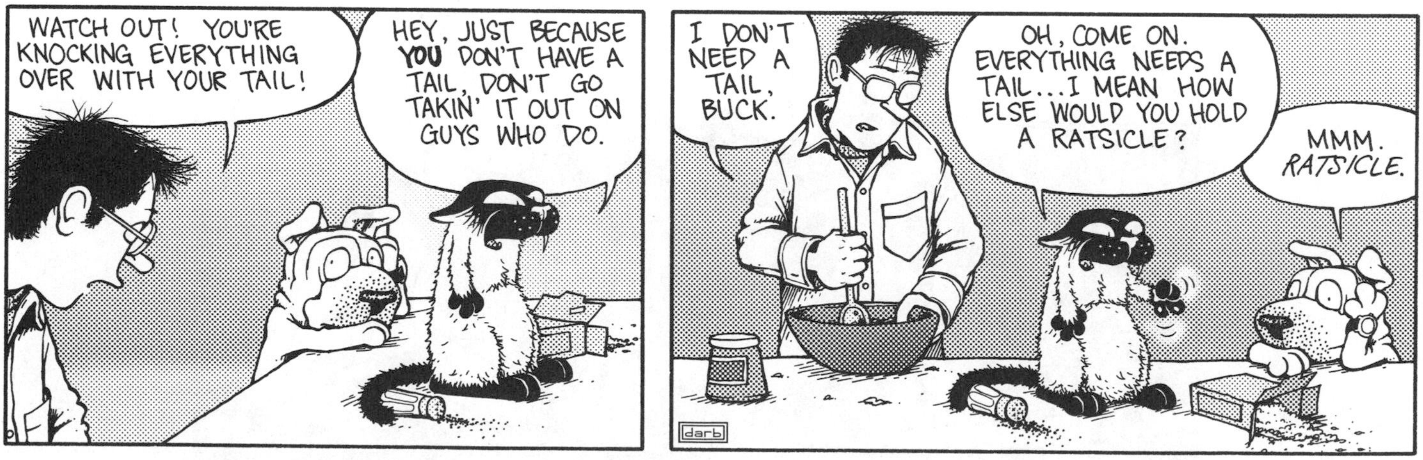
WATCH OUT! YOU'RE KNOCKING EVERYTHING OVER WITH YOUR TAIL!
HEY, JUST BECAUSE **YOU** DON'T HAVE A TAIL, DON'T GO TAKIN' IT OUT ON GUYS WHO DO.
I DON'T NEED A TAIL, BUCK.
OH, COME ON. EVERYTHING NEEDS A TAIL... I MEAN HOW ELSE WOULD YOU HOLD A RATSICLE?
MMM. *RATSICLE.*
darb

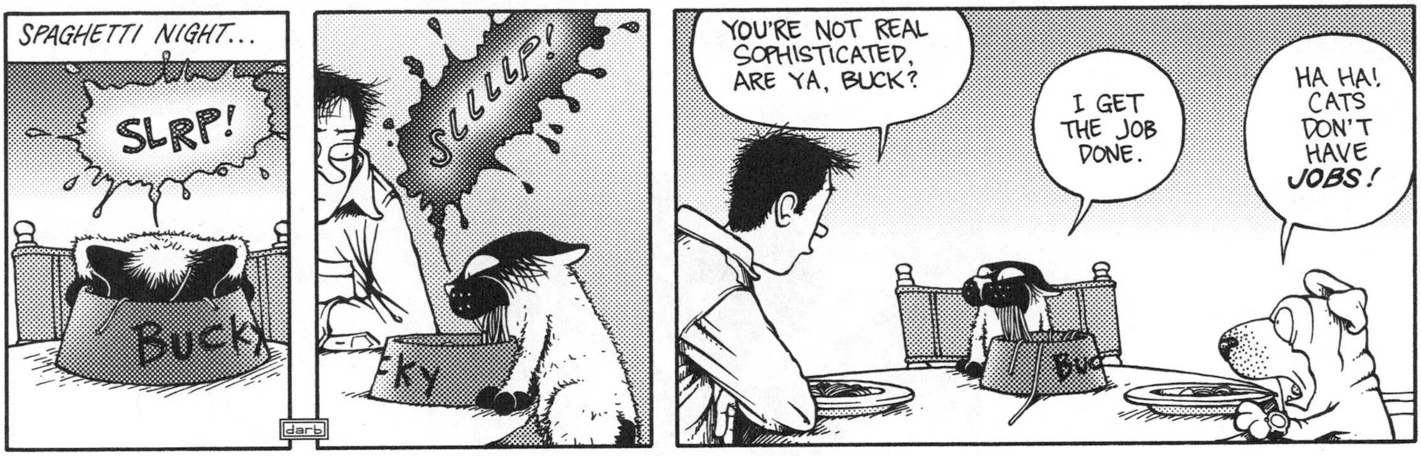
SPAGHETTI NIGHT...
SLRP!
BUCKY
SLLLLP!
KY
YOU'RE NOT REAL SOPHISTICATED, ARE YA, BUCK?
I GET THE JOB DONE.
HA HA! CATS DON'T HAVE JOBS!
darb

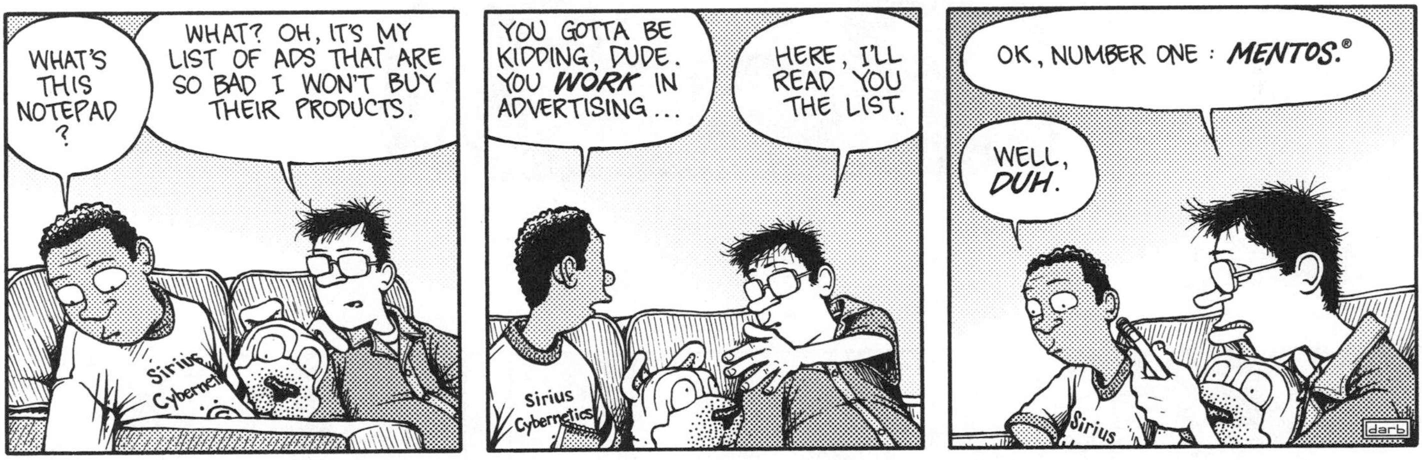
WHAT'S THIS NOTEPAD ?
WHAT? OH, IT'S MY LIST OF ADS THAT ARE SO BAD I WON'T BUY THEIR PRODUCTS.
YOU GOTTA BE KIDDING, DUDE. YOU WORK IN ADVERTISING...
HERE, I'LL READ YOU THE LIST.
OK, NUMBER ONE : MENTOS.®
WELL, DUH.
Sirius Cybernetics
darb

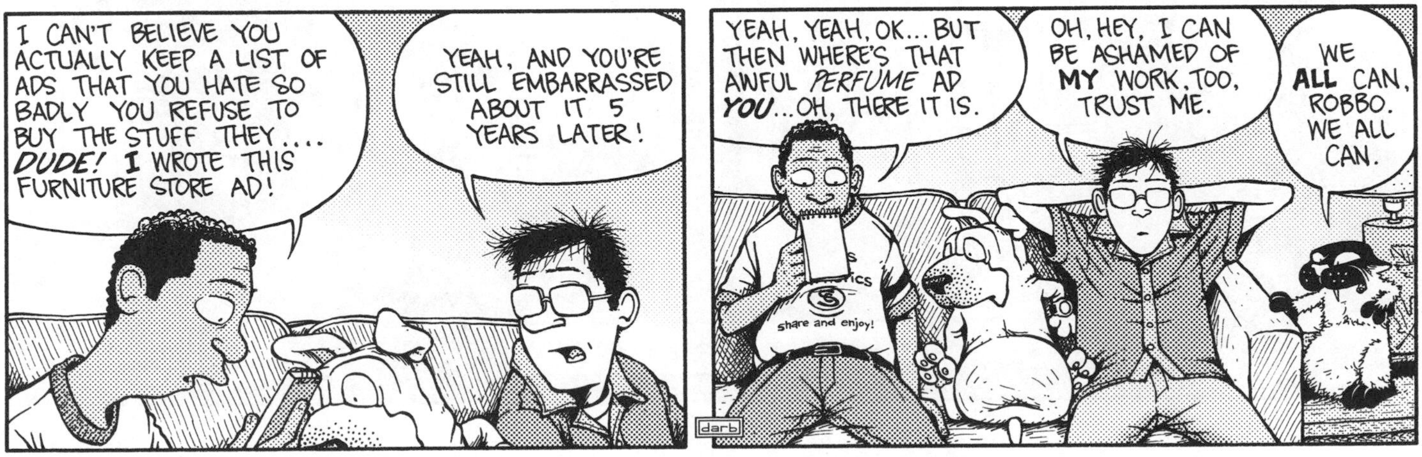
I CAN'T BELIEVE YOU ACTUALLY KEEP A LIST OF ADS THAT YOU HATE SO BADLY YOU REFUSE TO BUY THE STUFF THEY.... DUDE! I WROTE THIS FURNITURE STORE AD!
YEAH, AND YOU'RE STILL EMBARRASSED ABOUT IT 5 YEARS LATER!
YEAH, YEAH, OK... BUT THEN WHERE'S THAT AWFUL PERFUME AD YOU...OH, THERE IT IS.
OH, HEY, I CAN BE ASHAMED OF MY WORK, TOO, TRUST ME.
WE ALL CAN, ROBBO. WE ALL CAN.
share and enjoy!
darb

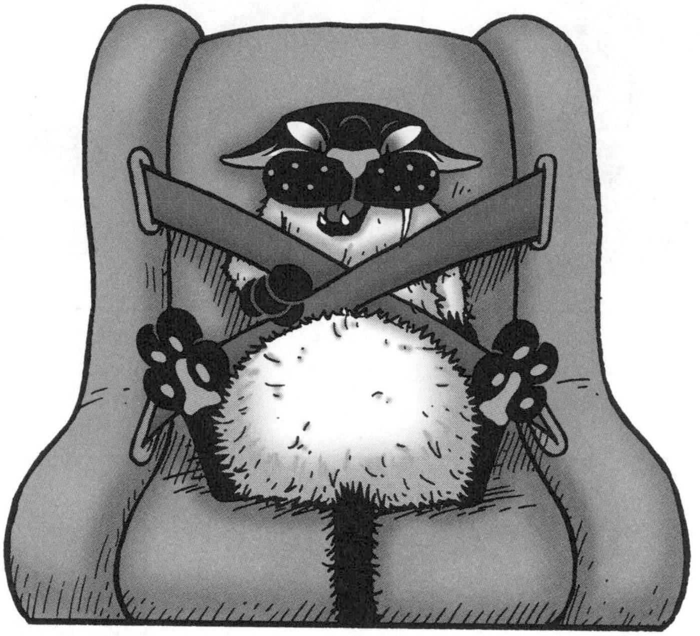

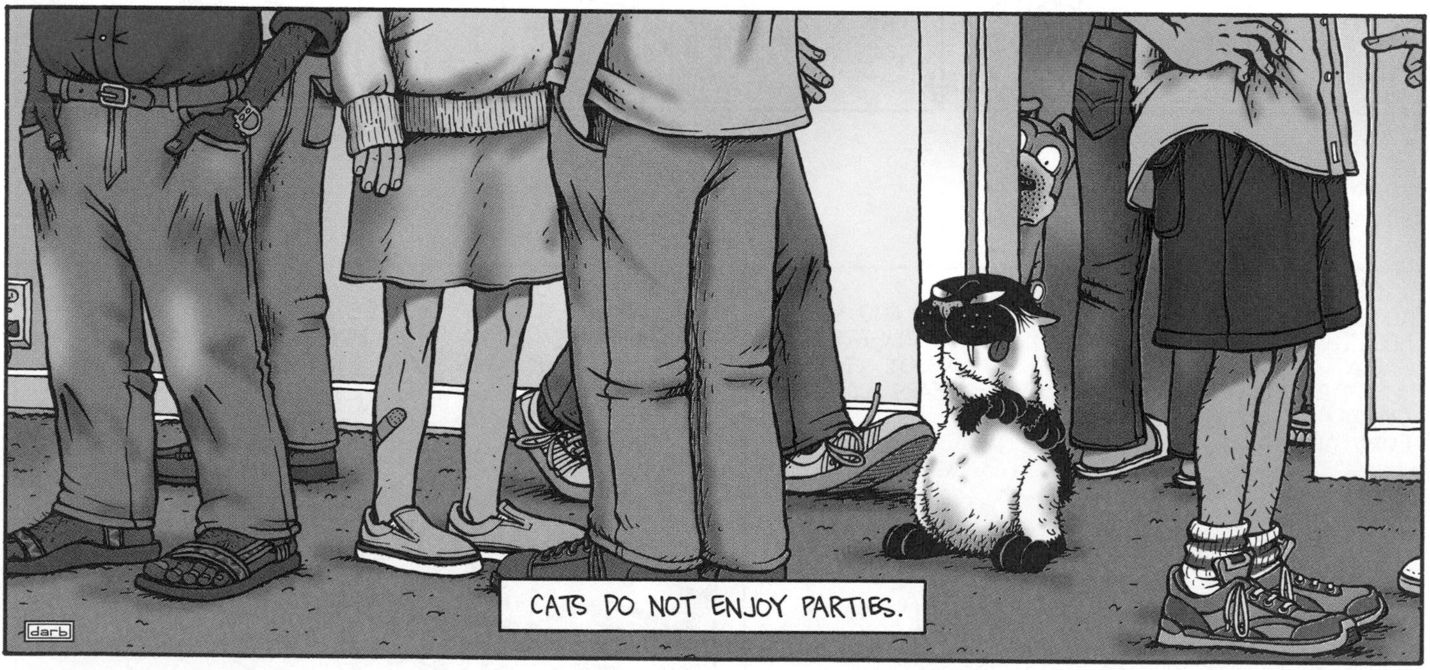
CATS DO NOT ENJOY PARTIES.
darb

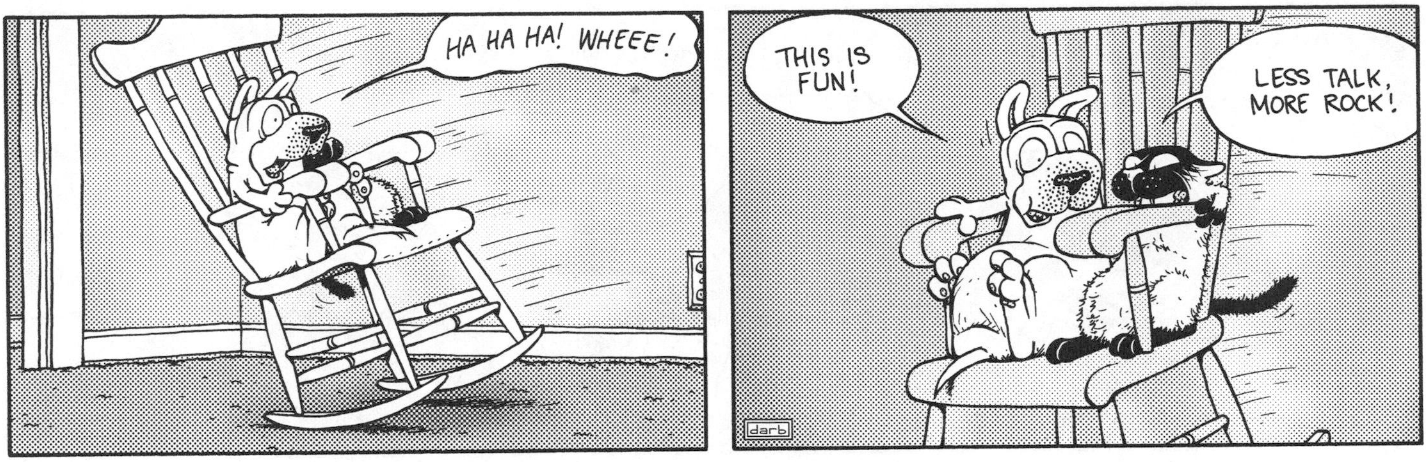
HA HA HA! WHEEE!
THIS IS FUN!
LESS TALK, MORE ROCK!
darb

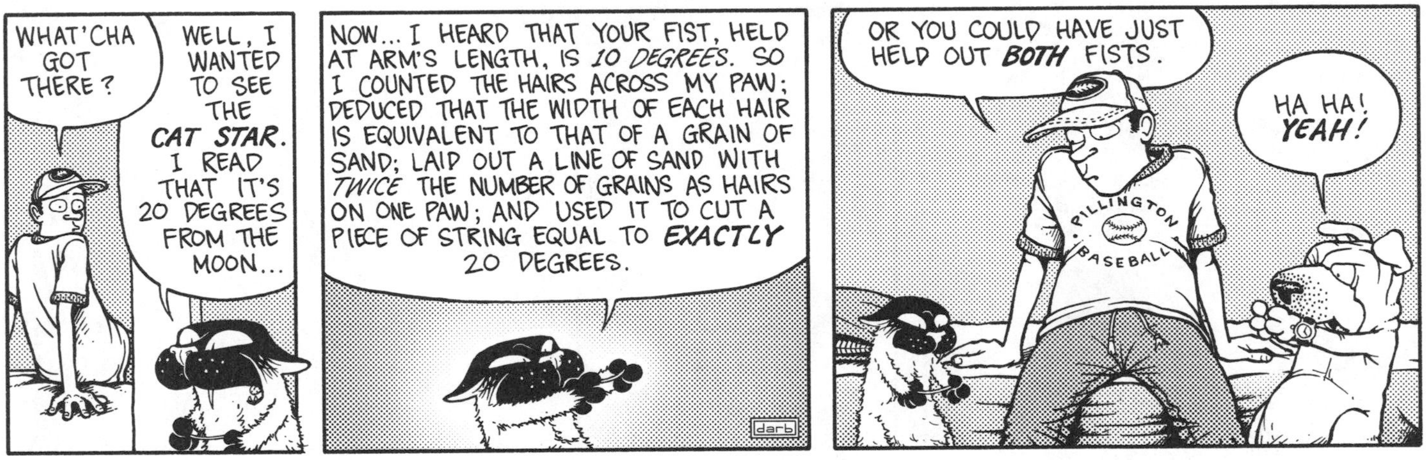
WHAT'CHA GOT THERE?
WELL, I WANTED TO SEE THE CAT STAR. I READ THAT IT'S 20 DEGREES FROM THE MOON...
NOW... I HEARD THAT YOUR FIST, HELD AT ARM'S LENGTH, IS 10 DEGREES. SO I COUNTED THE HAIRS ACROSS MY PAW; DEDUCED THAT THE WIDTH OF EACH HAIR IS EQUIVALENT TO THAT OF A GRAIN OF SAND; LAID OUT A LINE OF SAND WITH TWICE THE NUMBER OF GRAINS AS HAIRS ON ONE PAW; AND USED IT TO CUT A PIECE OF STRING EQUAL TO EXACTLY 20 DEGREES.
darb
OR YOU COULD HAVE JUST HELD OUT BOTH FISTS.
HA HA! YEAH!
PILLINGTON BASEBALL

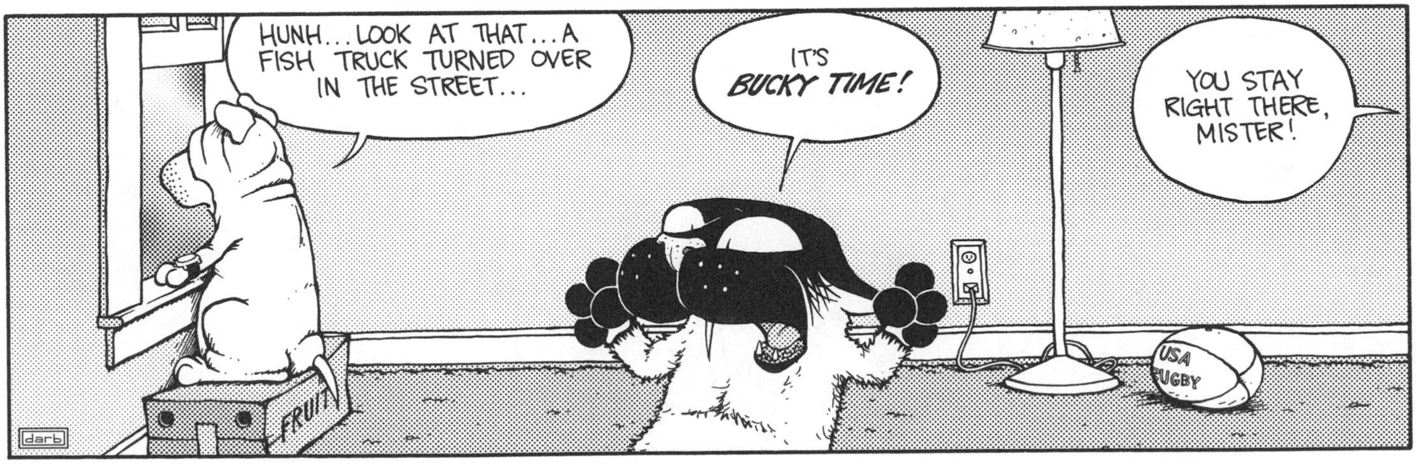
HUNH... LOOK AT THAT... A FISH TRUCK TURNED OVER IN THE STREET...
IT'S BUCKY TIME!
YOU STAY RIGHT THERE, MISTER!
FRUIT
USA RUGBY
darb

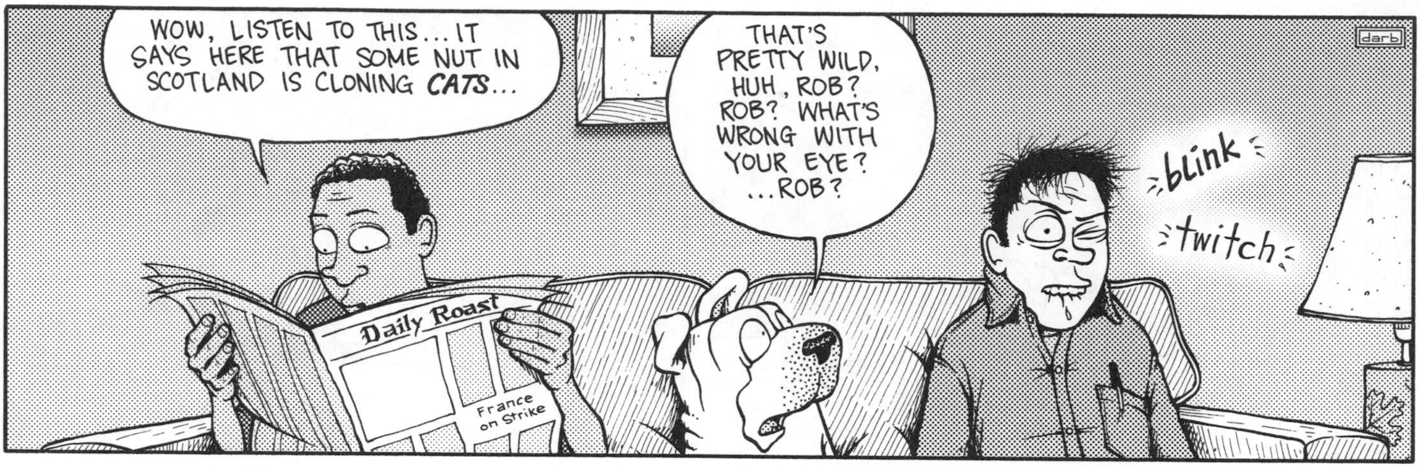
darb
WOW, LISTEN TO THIS... IT SAYS HERE THAT SOME NUT IN SCOTLAND IS CLONING CATS...
THAT'S PRETTY WILD, HUH, ROB? ROB? WHAT'S WRONG WITH YOUR EYE? ...ROB?
blink
twitch
Daily Roast
France on Strike

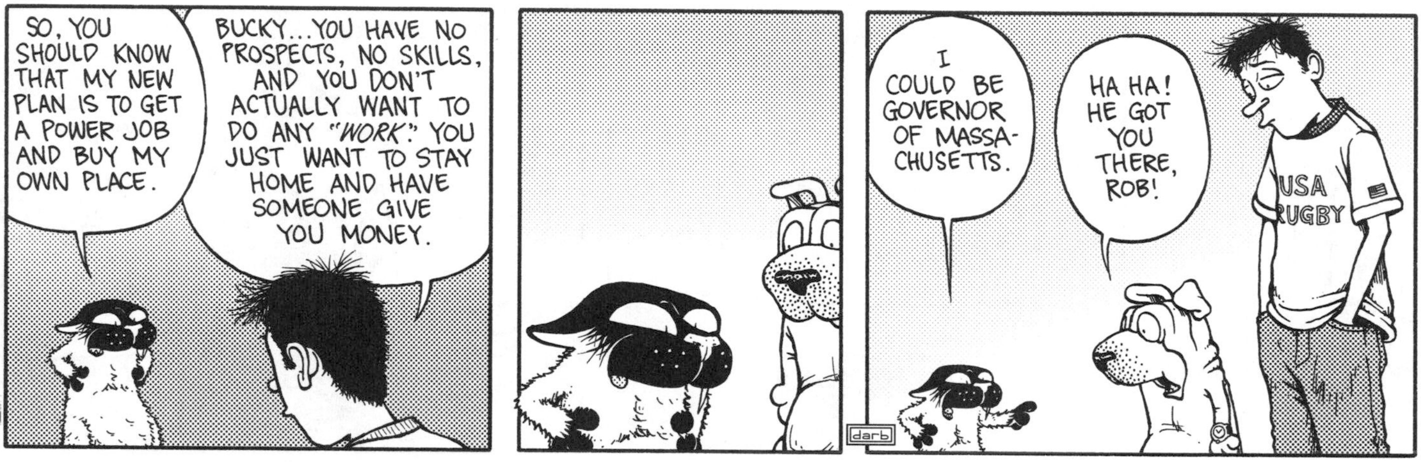
SO, YOU SHOULD KNOW THAT MY NEW PLAN IS TO GET A POWER JOB AND BUY MY OWN PLACE.
BUCKY... YOU HAVE NO PROSPECTS, NO SKILLS, AND YOU DON'T ACTUALLY WANT TO DO ANY "WORK." YOU JUST WANT TO STAY HOME AND HAVE SOMEONE GIVE YOU MONEY.
darb
I COULD BE GOVERNOR OF MASSA-CHUSETTS.
HA HA! HE GOT YOU THERE, ROB!
USA RUGBY

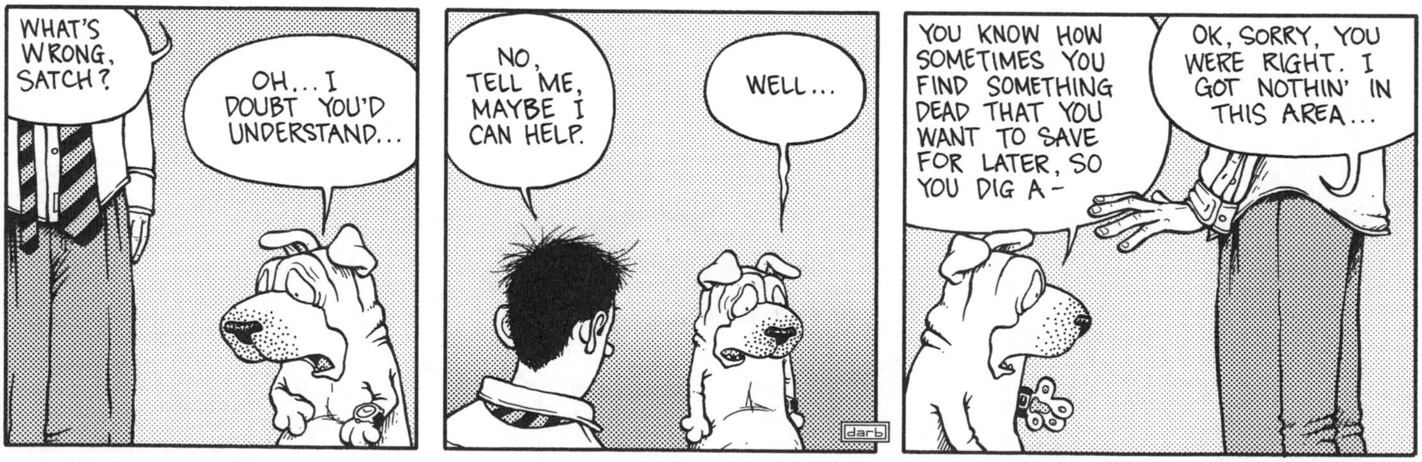
WHAT'S WRONG, SATCH?
OH... I DOUBT YOU'D UNDERSTAND...
NO, TELL ME, MAYBE I CAN HELP.
WELL...
darb
YOU KNOW HOW SOMETIMES YOU FIND SOMETHING DEAD THAT YOU WANT TO SAVE FOR LATER, SO YOU DIG A-
OK, SORRY, YOU WERE RIGHT. I GOT NOTHIN' IN THIS AREA...

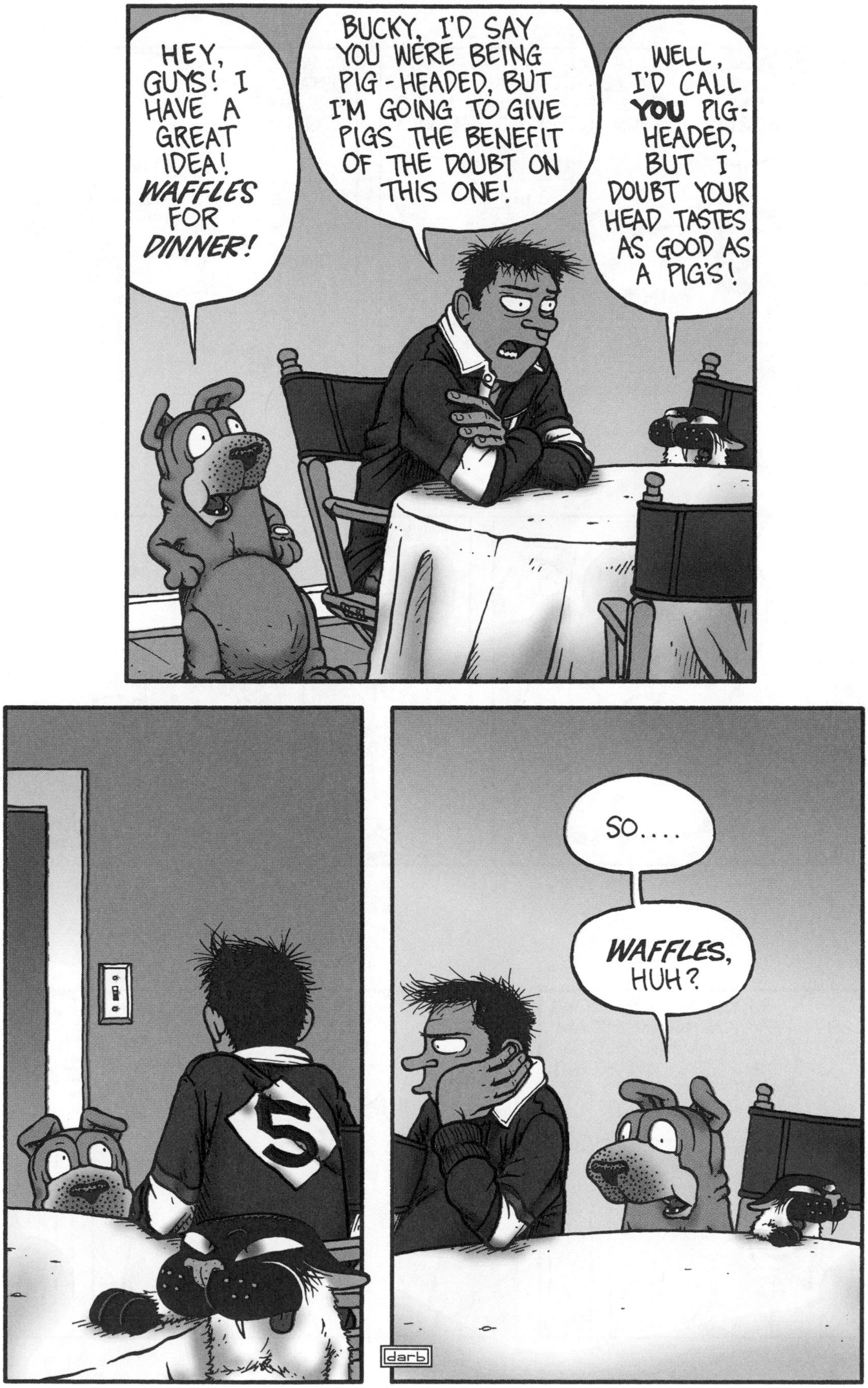
HEY, GUYS! I HAVE A GREAT IDEA! *WAFFLES* FOR *DINNER!*
BUCKY, I'D SAY YOU WERE BEING PIG-HEADED, BUT I'M GOING TO GIVE PIGS THE BENEFIT OF THE DOUBT ON THIS ONE!
WELL, I'D CALL **YOU** PIG-HEADED, BUT I DOUBT YOUR HEAD TASTES AS GOOD AS A PIG'S!
SO....
WAFFLES, HUH?
darb

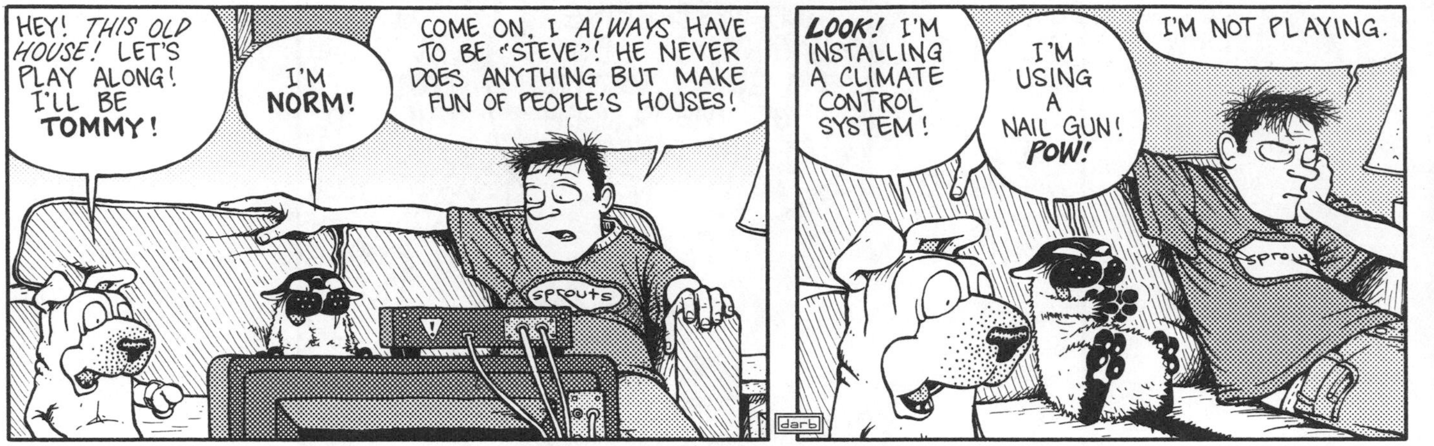
HEY! *THIS OLD HOUSE!* LET'S PLAY ALONG! I'LL BE **TOMMY**!
I'M **NORM!**
COME ON. I *ALWAYS* HAVE TO BE "STEVE"! HE NEVER DOES ANYTHING BUT MAKE FUN OF PEOPLE'S HOUSES!
LOOK! I'M INSTALLING A CLIMATE CONTROL SYSTEM!
I'M USING A NAIL GUN! **POW!**
I'M NOT PLAYING.
darb

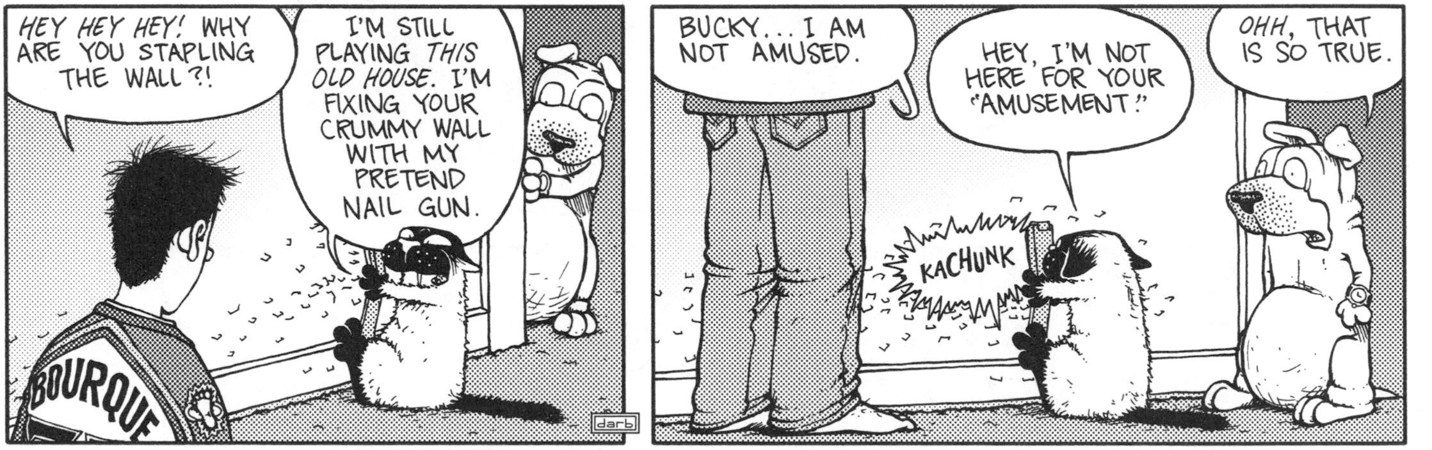
HEY HEY HEY! WHY ARE YOU STAPLING THE WALL?!
I'M STILL PLAYING *THIS OLD HOUSE.* I'M FIXING YOUR CRUMMY WALL WITH MY PRETEND NAIL GUN.
BOURQUE
darb
BUCKY... I AM NOT AMUSED.
HEY, I'M NOT HERE FOR YOUR "AMUSEMENT."
OHH, THAT IS SO TRUE.
KACHUNK

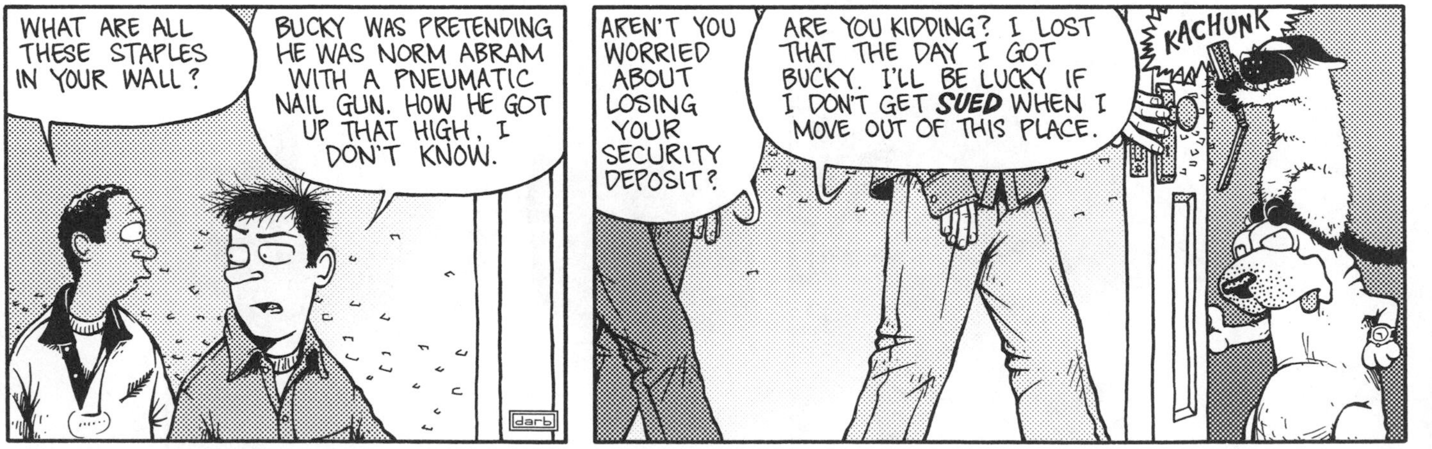
WHAT ARE ALL THESE STAPLES IN YOUR WALL?
BUCKY WAS PRETENDING HE WAS NORM ABRAM WITH A PNEUMATIC NAIL GUN. HOW HE GOT UP THAT HIGH, I DON'T KNOW.
darb
AREN'T YOU WORRIED ABOUT LOSING YOUR SECURITY DEPOSIT?
ARE YOU KIDDING? I LOST THAT THE DAY I GOT BUCKY. I'LL BE LUCKY IF I DON'T GET **SUED** WHEN I MOVE OUT OF THIS PLACE.
KACHUNK

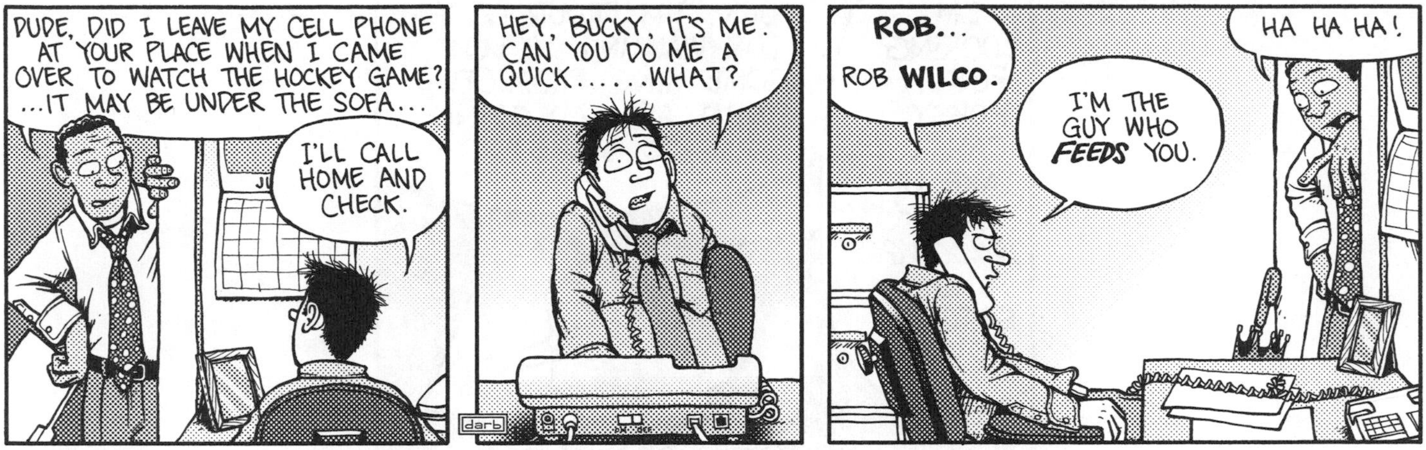

DUDE, DID I LEAVE MY CELL PHONE AT YOUR PLACE WHEN I CAME OVER TO WATCH THE HOCKEY GAME? ...IT MAY BE UNDER THE SOFA...
I'LL CALL HOME AND CHECK.
HEY, BUCKY, IT'S ME. CAN YOU DO ME A QUICK......WHAT?
ROB... ROB WILCO.
I'M THE GUY WHO FEEDS YOU.
HA HA HA!
darb

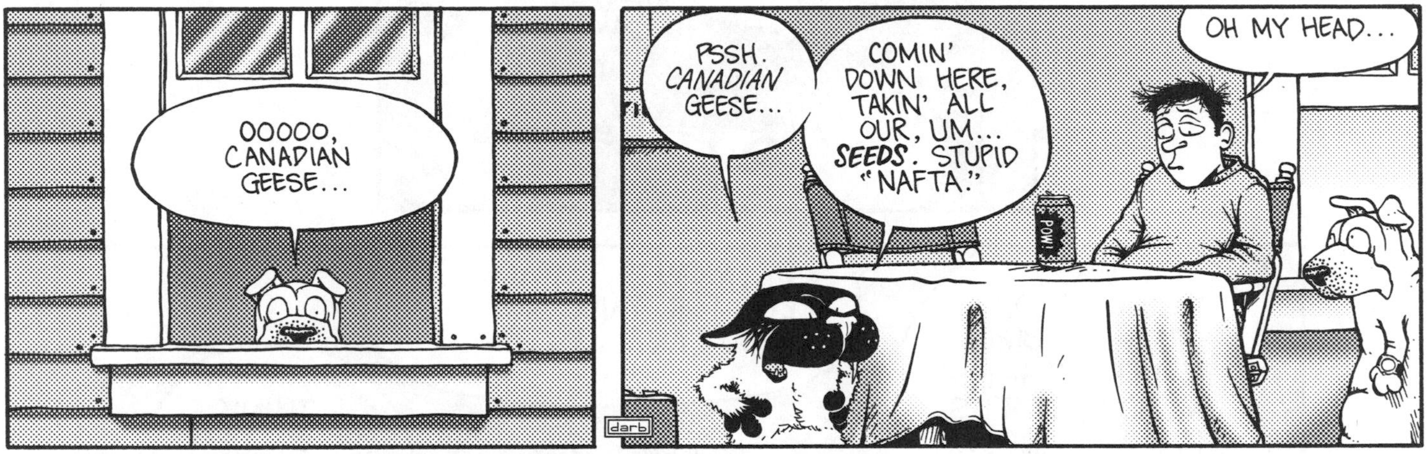

OOOOO, CANADIAN GEESE...
darb
PSSH. CANADIAN GEESE...
COMIN' DOWN HERE, TAKIN' ALL OUR, UM... SEEDS. STUPID "NAFTA."
OH MY HEAD...
POW!

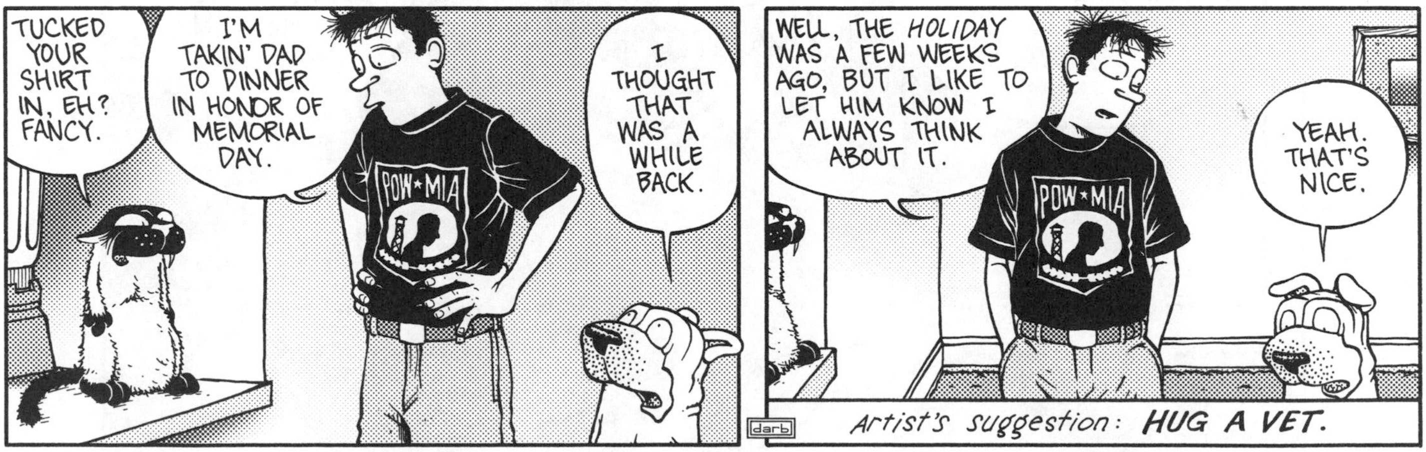

TUCKED YOUR SHIRT IN, EH? FANCY.
I'M TAKIN' DAD TO DINNER IN HONOR OF MEMORIAL DAY.
I THOUGHT THAT WAS A WHILE BACK.
POW ★ MIA
WELL, THE HOLIDAY WAS A FEW WEEKS AGO, BUT I LIKE TO LET HIM KNOW I ALWAYS THINK ABOUT IT.
YEAH. THAT'S NICE.
POW ★ MIA
darb
Artist's suggestion: HUG A VET.

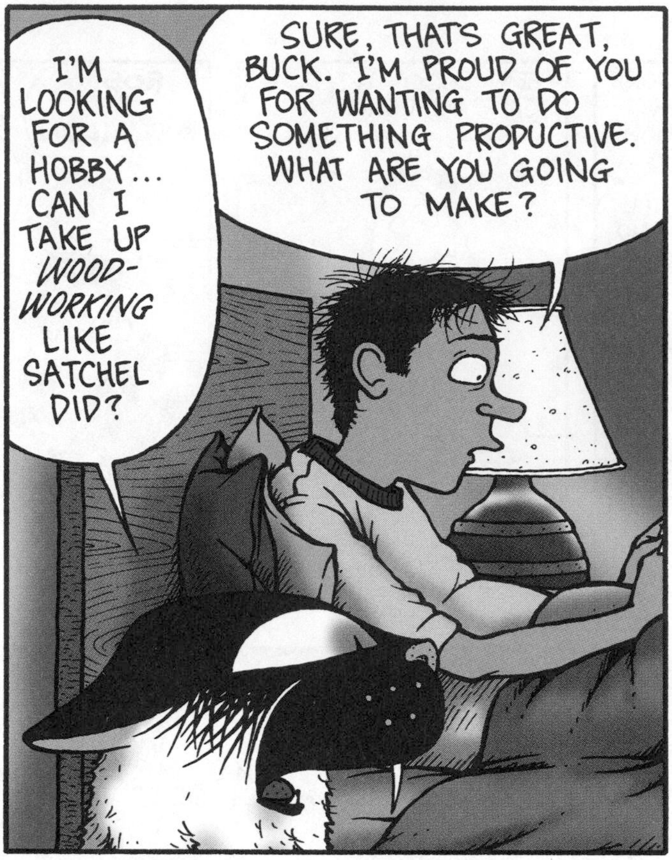
I'M LOOKING FOR A HOBBY... CAN I TAKE UP *WOOD-WORKING* LIKE SATCHEL DID?
SURE, THAT'S GREAT, BUCK. I'M PROUD OF YOU FOR WANTING TO DO SOMETHING PRODUCTIVE. WHAT ARE YOU GOING TO MAKE?

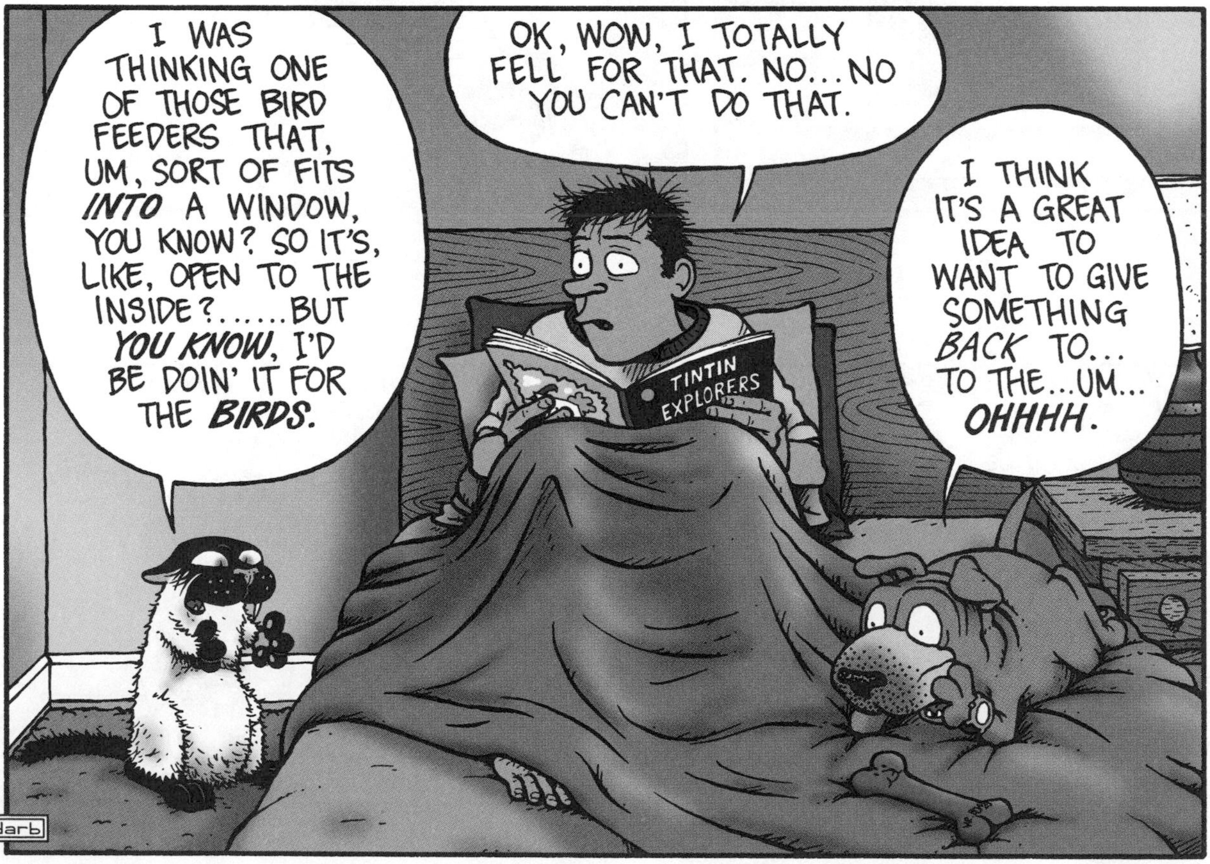
I WAS THINKING ONE OF THOSE BIRD FEEDERS THAT, UM, SORT OF FITS *INTO* A WINDOW, YOU KNOW? SO IT'S, LIKE, OPEN TO THE INSIDE?......BUT ***YOU KNOW***, I'D BE DOIN' IT FOR THE ***BIRDS***.
OK, WOW, I TOTALLY FELL FOR THAT. NO...NO YOU CAN'T DO THAT.
I THINK IT'S A GREAT IDEA TO WANT TO GIVE SOMETHING *BACK* TO... TO THE...UM... **OHHHH**.
TINTIN EXPLORERS
darb

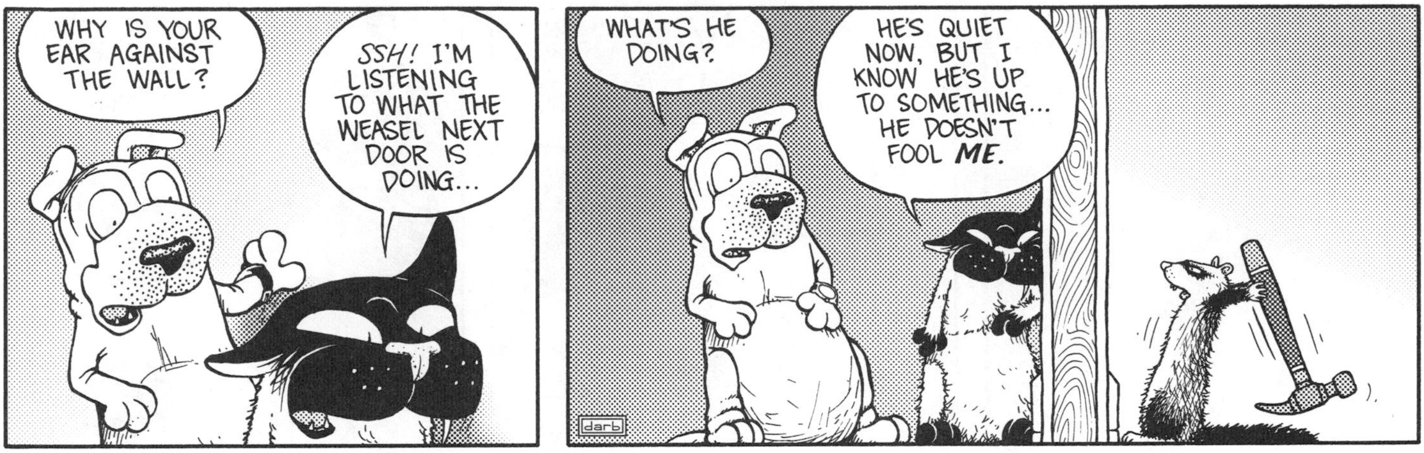
WHY IS YOUR EAR AGAINST THE WALL?
SSH! I'M LISTENING TO WHAT THE WEASEL NEXT DOOR IS DOING...
WHAT'S HE DOING?
HE'S QUIET NOW, BUT I KNOW HE'S UP TO SOMETHING... HE DOESN'T FOOL ME.
darb

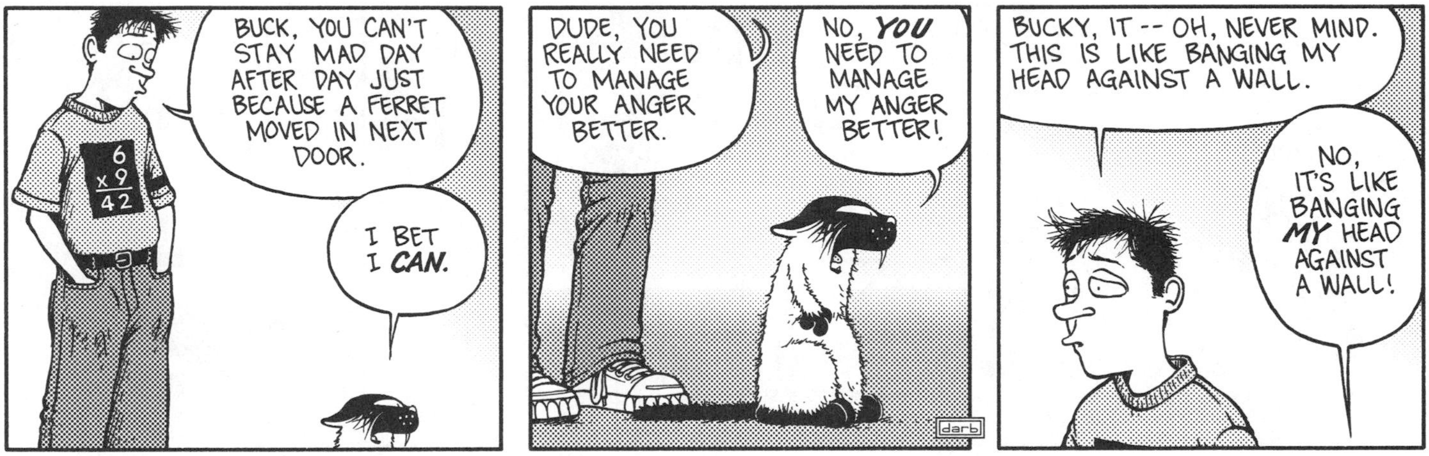
BUCK, YOU CAN'T STAY MAD DAY AFTER DAY JUST BECAUSE A FERRET MOVED IN NEXT DOOR.
6 x 9 42
I BET I CAN.
DUDE, YOU REALLY NEED TO MANAGE YOUR ANGER BETTER.
NO, YOU NEED TO MANAGE MY ANGER BETTER!
darb
BUCKY, IT -- OH, NEVER MIND. THIS IS LIKE BANGING MY HEAD AGAINST A WALL.
NO, IT'S LIKE BANGING MY HEAD AGAINST A WALL!

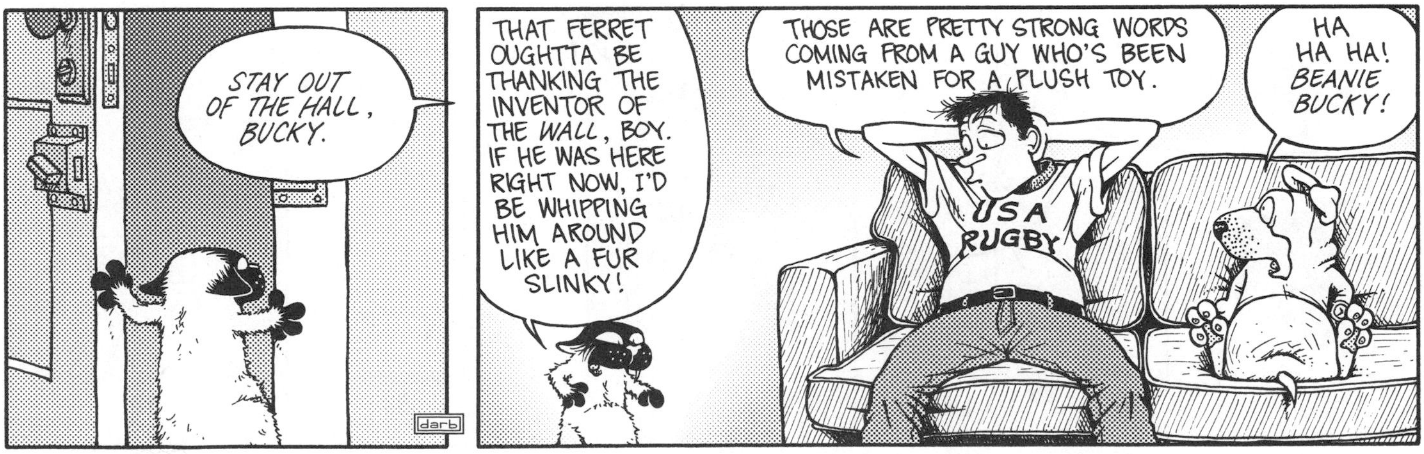
STAY OUT OF THE HALL, BUCKY.
darb
THAT FERRET OUGHTTA BE THANKING THE INVENTOR OF THE WALL, BOY. IF HE WAS HERE RIGHT NOW, I'D BE WHIPPING HIM AROUND LIKE A FUR SLINKY!
THOSE ARE PRETTY STRONG WORDS COMING FROM A GUY WHO'S BEEN MISTAKEN FOR A PLUSH TOY.
HA HA HA! BEANIE BUCKY!
USA RUGBY

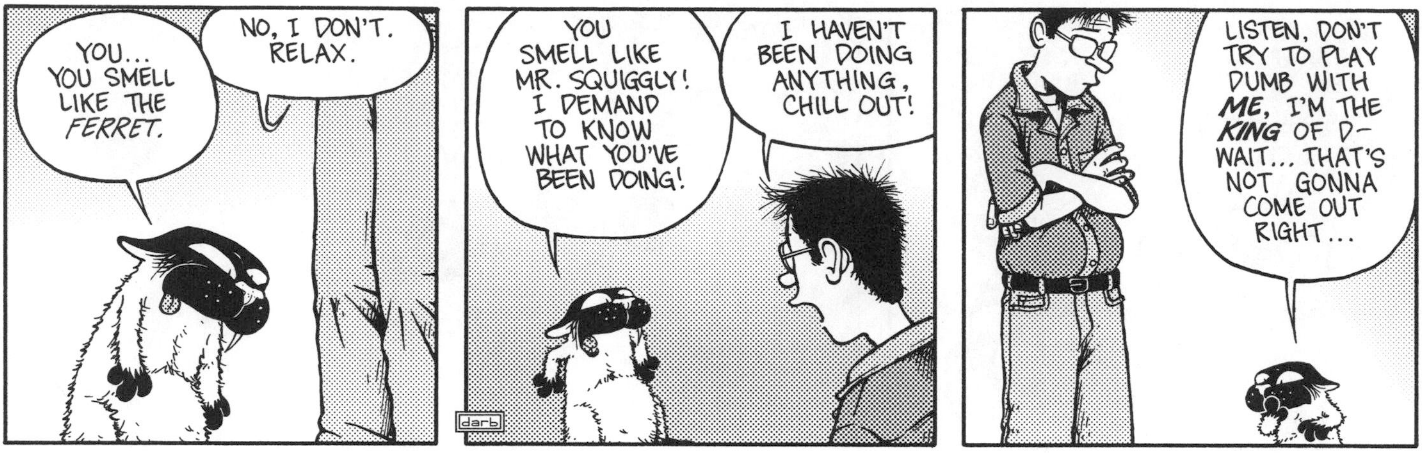
YOU... YOU SMELL LIKE THE *FERRET.*
NO, I DON'T. RELAX.
YOU SMELL LIKE MR. SQUIGGLY! I DEMAND TO KNOW WHAT YOU'VE BEEN DOING!
I HAVEN'T BEEN DOING ANYTHING, CHILL OUT!
LISTEN, DON'T TRY TO PLAY DUMB WITH ***ME,*** I'M THE ***KING*** OF D- WAIT... THAT'S NOT GONNA COME OUT RIGHT...

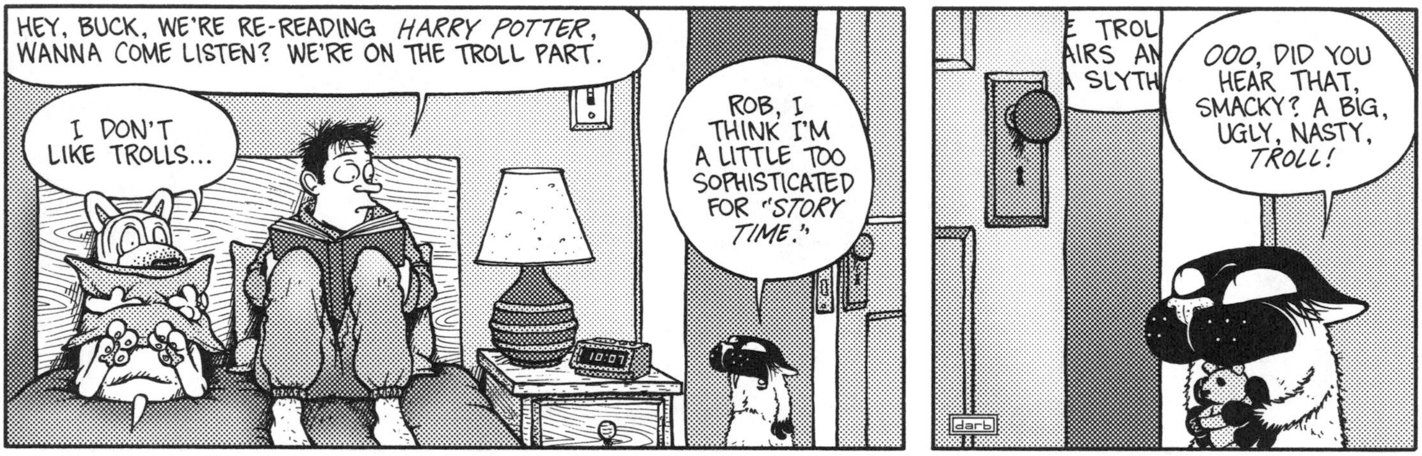
HEY, BUCK, WE'RE RE-READING *HARRY POTTER,* WANNA COME LISTEN? WE'RE ON THE TROLL PART.
I DON'T LIKE TROLLS...
ROB, I THINK I'M A LITTLE TOO SOPHISTICATED FOR *"STORY TIME."*
OOO, DID YOU HEAR THAT, SMACKY? A BIG, UGLY, NASTY, *TROLL!*

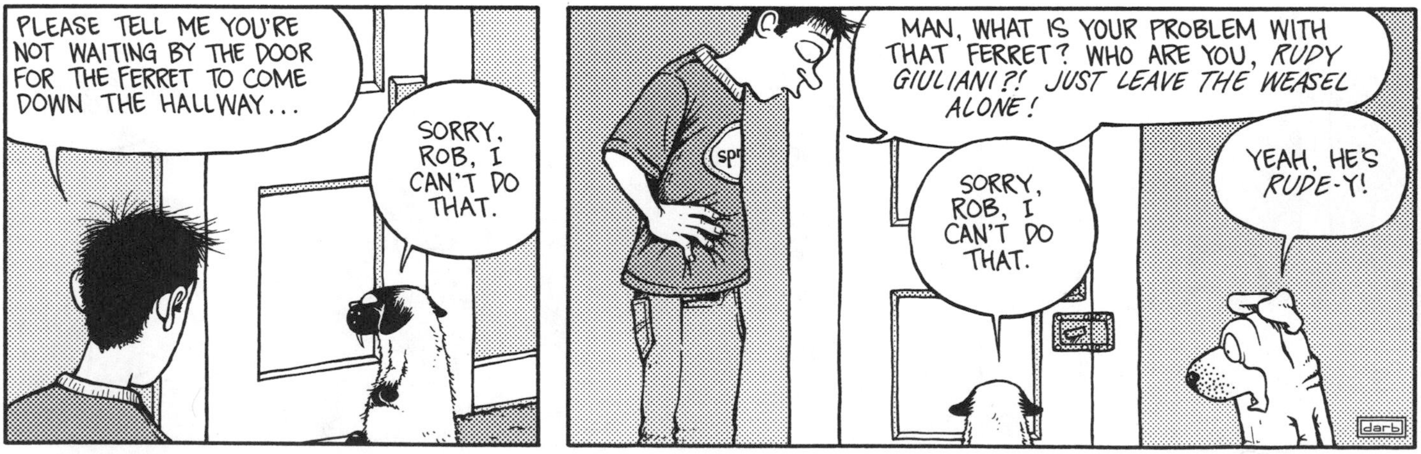
PLEASE TELL ME YOU'RE NOT WAITING BY THE DOOR FOR THE FERRET TO COME DOWN THE HALLWAY...
SORRY, ROB, I CAN'T DO THAT.
MAN, WHAT IS YOUR PROBLEM WITH THAT FERRET? WHO ARE YOU, *RUDY GIULIANI?! JUST LEAVE THE WEASEL ALONE!*
SORRY, ROB, I CAN'T DO THAT.
YEAH, HE'S *RUDE*-Y!

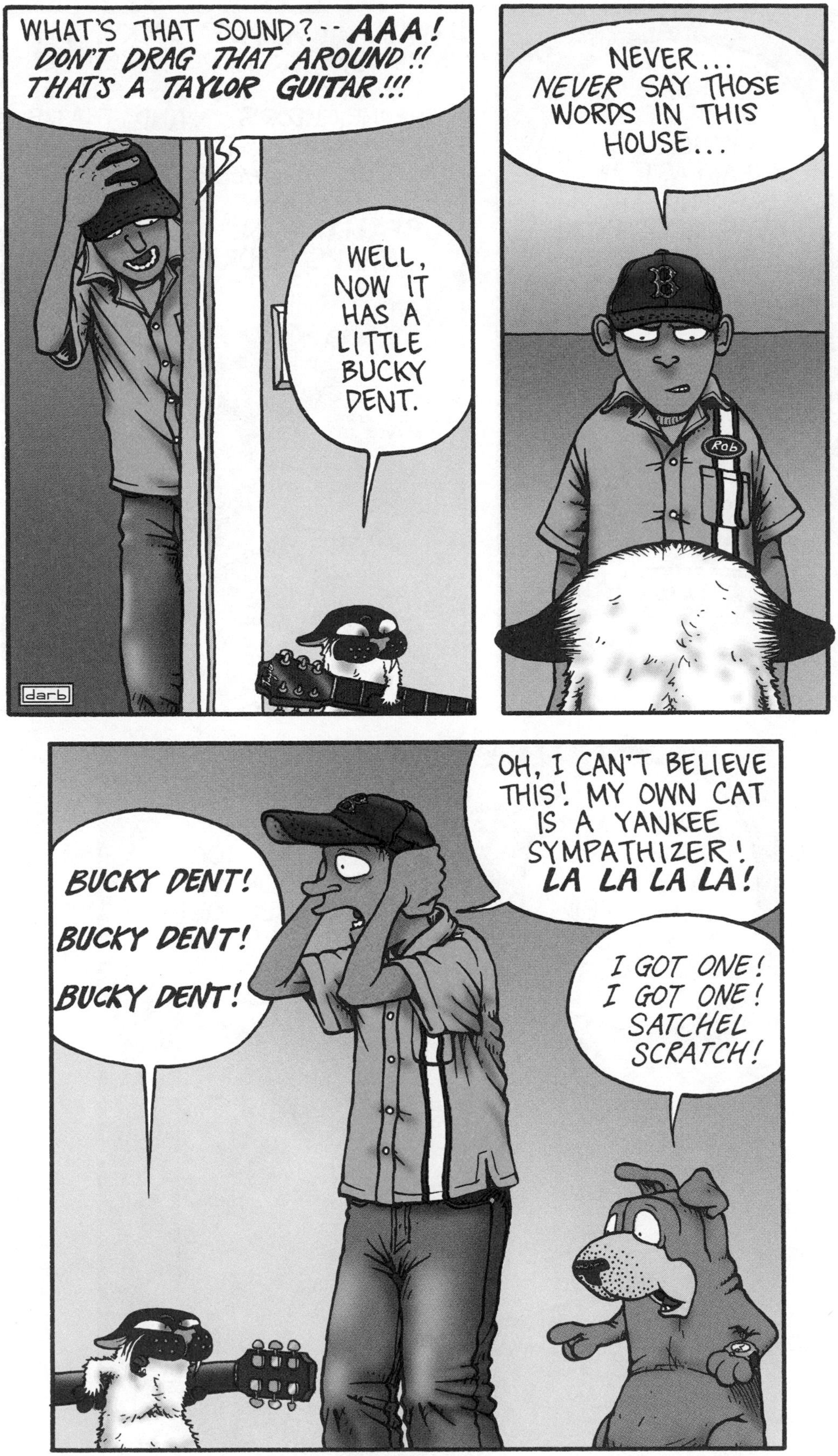
WHAT'S THAT SOUND?-- AAA! DON'T DRAG THAT AROUND!! THAT'S A TAYLOR GUITAR!!!
WELL, NOW IT HAS A LITTLE BUCKY DENT.
darb
NEVER... NEVER SAY THOSE WORDS IN THIS HOUSE...
Rob
BUCKY DENT!
BUCKY DENT!
BUCKY DENT!
OH, I CAN'T BELIEVE THIS! MY OWN CAT IS A YANKEE SYMPATHIZER! LA LA LA LA!
I GOT ONE! I GOT ONE! SATCHEL SCRATCH!

ROB... WAKE UP... I BROUGHT YOU BREAKFAST IN BED AND THE NEWSPAPER FROM THE HALLWAY. WAKE UP.
WHA---? WHAT? BUCKY, MY NEWSPAPER IS DELIVERED TO THE OFFICE, YOU JUST STOLE THE NEIGHBOR'S....AND THAT'S NOT BREAKFAST CEREAL, IT'S A BOWL OF CHEEZ-ITS® WITH MILK ON THEM..... WHAT'S REALLY GOING ON HERE? WHAT'S YOUR AGENDA?
Roast
"AGENDA"? ROB, I'M A BOY... I ASSUMED YOU KNEW THAT.
OK, IT'S TOO EARLY FOR YOU. SERIOUSLY, GET OUT OF HERE.
Daily Roast
darb

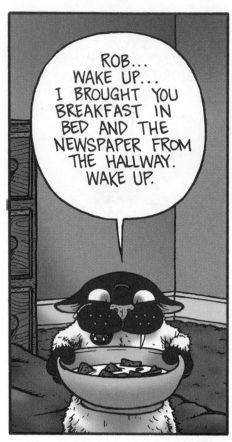

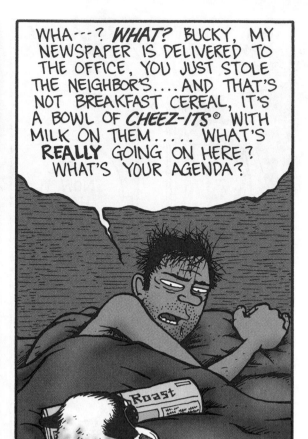

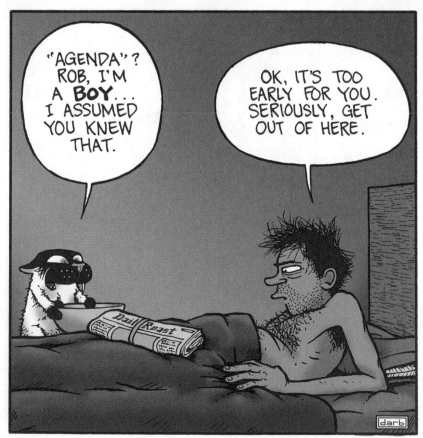

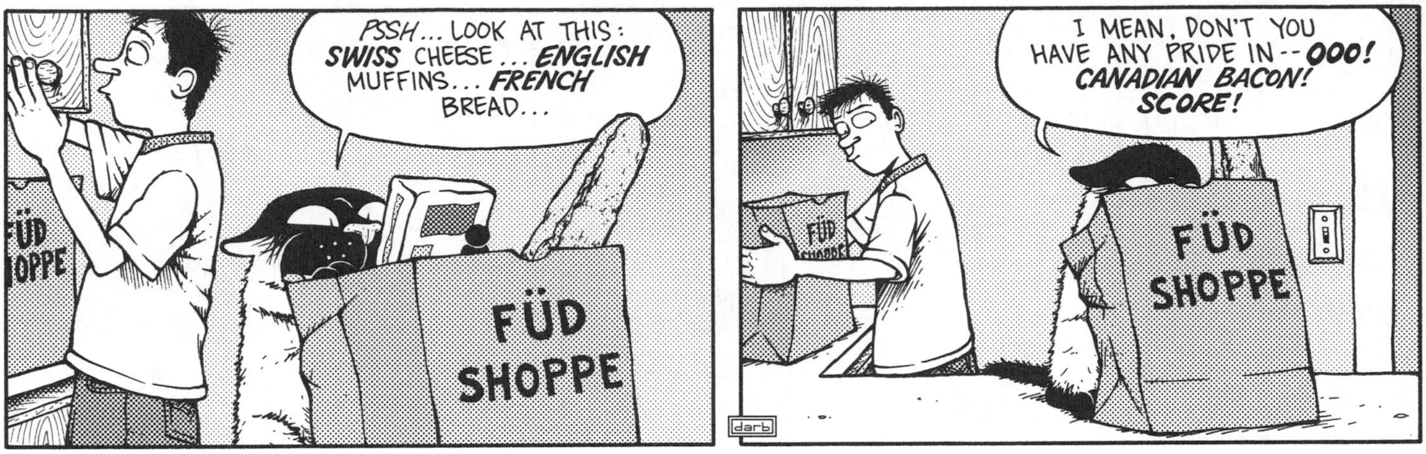
PSSH... LOOK AT THIS: SWISS CHEESE... ENGLISH MUFFINS... FRENCH BREAD...
FÜD SHOPPE
I MEAN, DON'T YOU HAVE ANY PRIDE IN--OOO! CANADIAN BACON! SCORE!
FÜD SHOPPE
darb

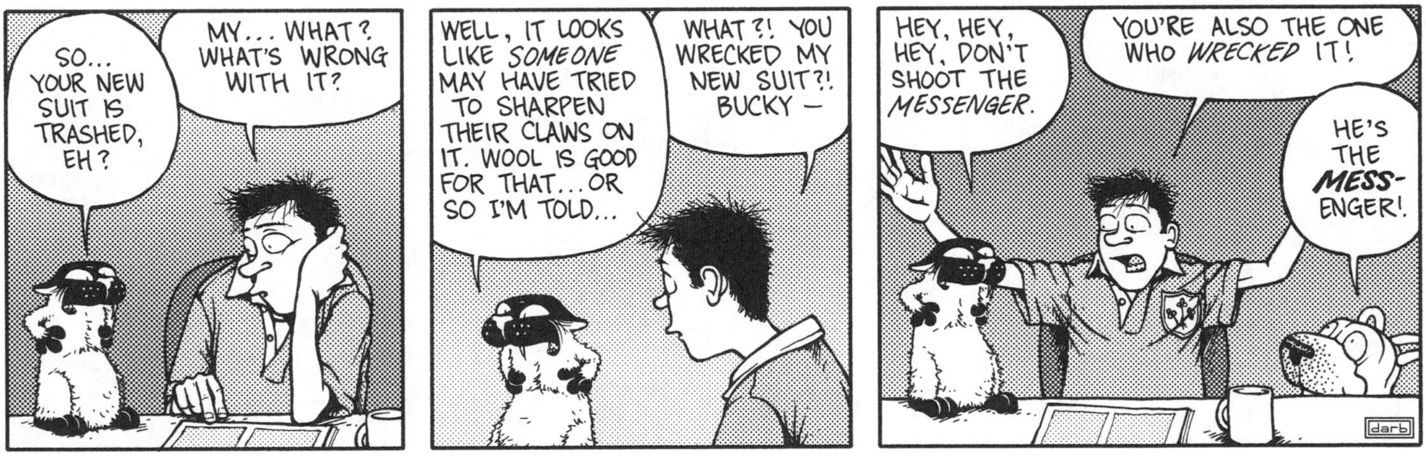
SO... YOUR NEW SUIT IS TRASHED, EH?
MY... WHAT? WHAT'S WRONG WITH IT?
WELL, IT LOOKS LIKE SOMEONE MAY HAVE TRIED TO SHARPEN THEIR CLAWS ON IT. WOOL IS GOOD FOR THAT... OR SO I'M TOLD...
WHAT?! YOU WRECKED MY NEW SUIT?! BUCKY —
HEY, HEY, HEY, DON'T SHOOT THE MESSENGER.
YOU'RE ALSO THE ONE WHO WRECKED IT!
HE'S THE MESS-ENGER!
darb

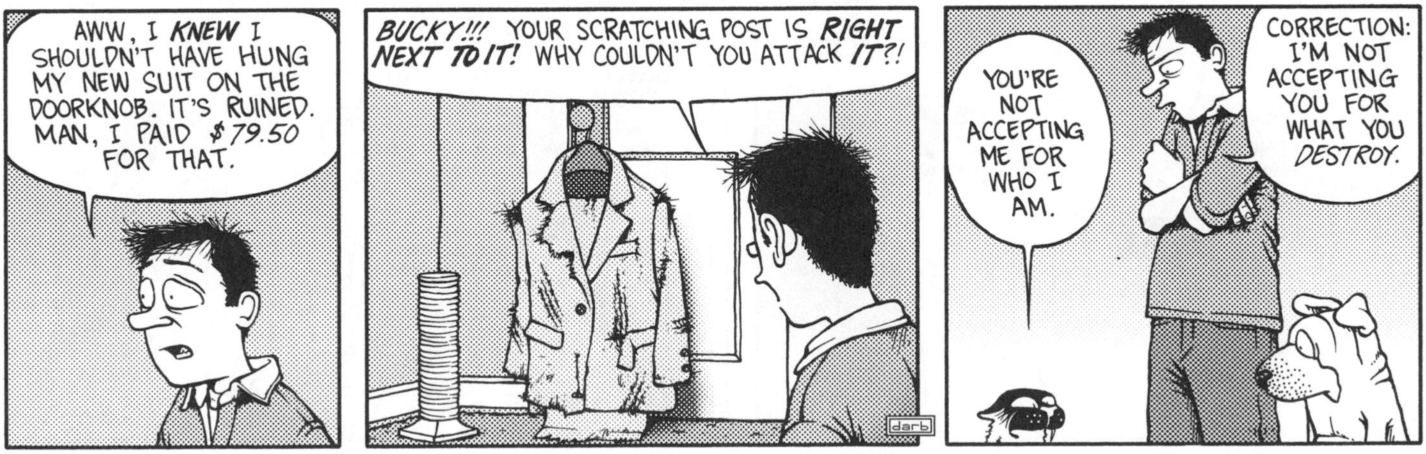
AWW, I KNEW I SHOULDN'T HAVE HUNG MY NEW SUIT ON THE DOORKNOB. IT'S RUINED. MAN, I PAID $79.50 FOR THAT.
BUCKY!!! YOUR SCRATCHING POST IS RIGHT NEXT TO IT! WHY COULDN'T YOU ATTACK IT?!
darb
YOU'RE NOT ACCEPTING ME FOR WHO I AM.
CORRECTION: I'M NOT ACCEPTING YOU FOR WHAT YOU DESTROY.

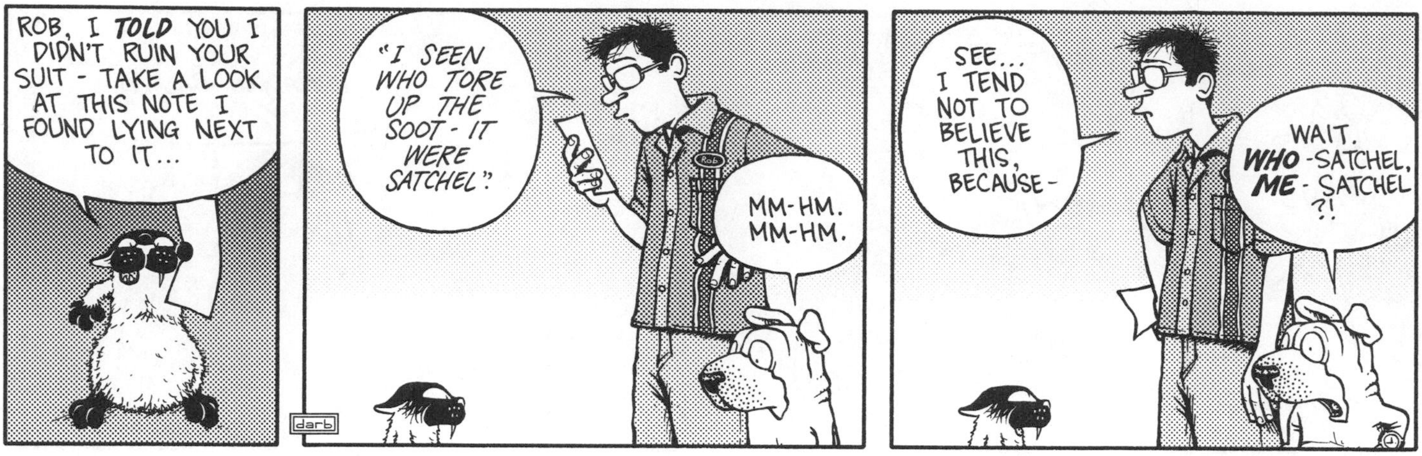
ROB, I **TOLD** YOU I DIDN'T RUIN YOUR SUIT - TAKE A LOOK AT THIS NOTE I FOUND LYING NEXT TO IT...
"I SEEN WHO TORE UP THE SOOT - IT WERE SATCHEL."
MM-HM. MM-HM.
SEE... I TEND NOT TO BELIEVE THIS, BECAUSE-
WAIT. **WHO**-SATCHEL, **ME**-SATCHEL ?!

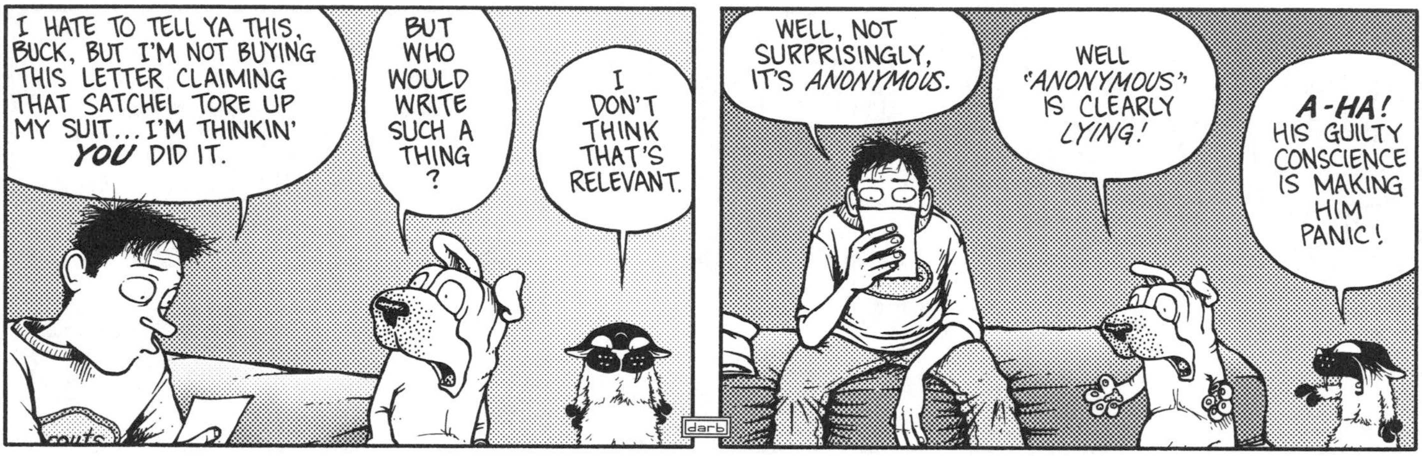
I HATE TO TELL YA THIS, BUCK, BUT I'M NOT BUYING THIS LETTER CLAIMING THAT SATCHEL TORE UP MY SUIT... I'M THINKIN' **YOU** DID IT.
BUT WHO WOULD WRITE SUCH A THING ?
I DON'T THINK THAT'S RELEVANT.
WELL, NOT SURPRISINGLY, IT'S *ANONYMOUS.*
WELL *"ANONYMOUS"* IS CLEARLY *LYING!*
A-HA! HIS GUILTY CONSCIENCE IS MAKING HIM PANIC!

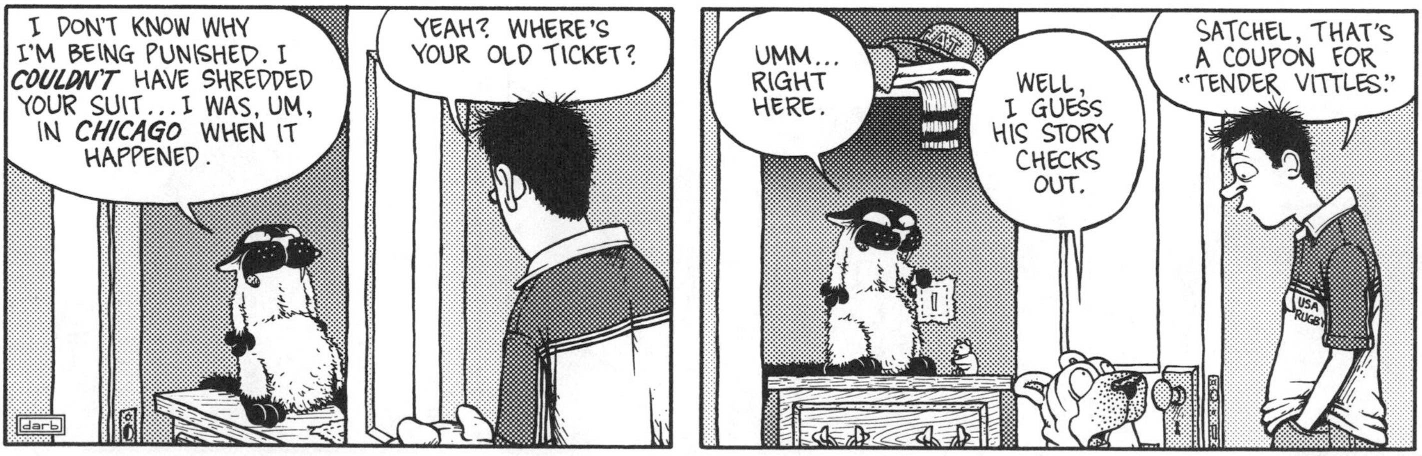
I DON'T KNOW WHY I'M BEING PUNISHED. I ***COULDN'T*** HAVE SHREDDED YOUR SUIT... I WAS, UM, IN **CHICAGO** WHEN IT HAPPENED.
YEAH? WHERE'S YOUR OLD TICKET?
UMM... RIGHT HERE.
WELL, I GUESS HIS STORY CHECKS OUT.
SATCHEL, THAT'S A COUPON FOR "TENDER VITTLES."

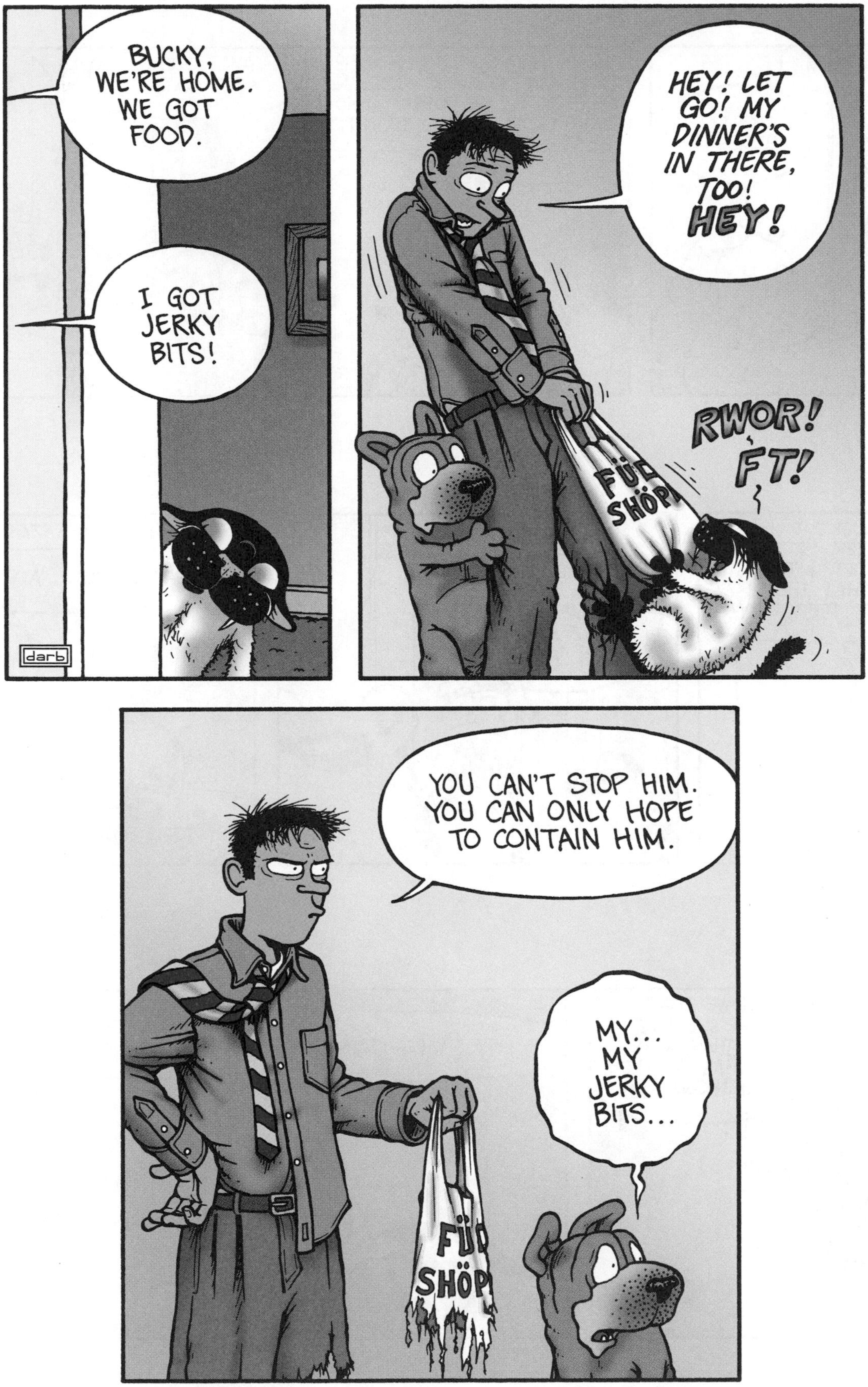
BUCKY, WE'RE HOME. WE GOT FOOD.
I GOT JERKY BITS!
darb
HEY! LET GO! MY DINNER'S IN THERE, TOO! HEY!
FÜD SHÖP
RWOR! FT!
YOU CAN'T STOP HIM. YOU CAN ONLY HOPE TO CONTAIN HIM.
MY... MY JERKY BITS...
FÜD SHÖP

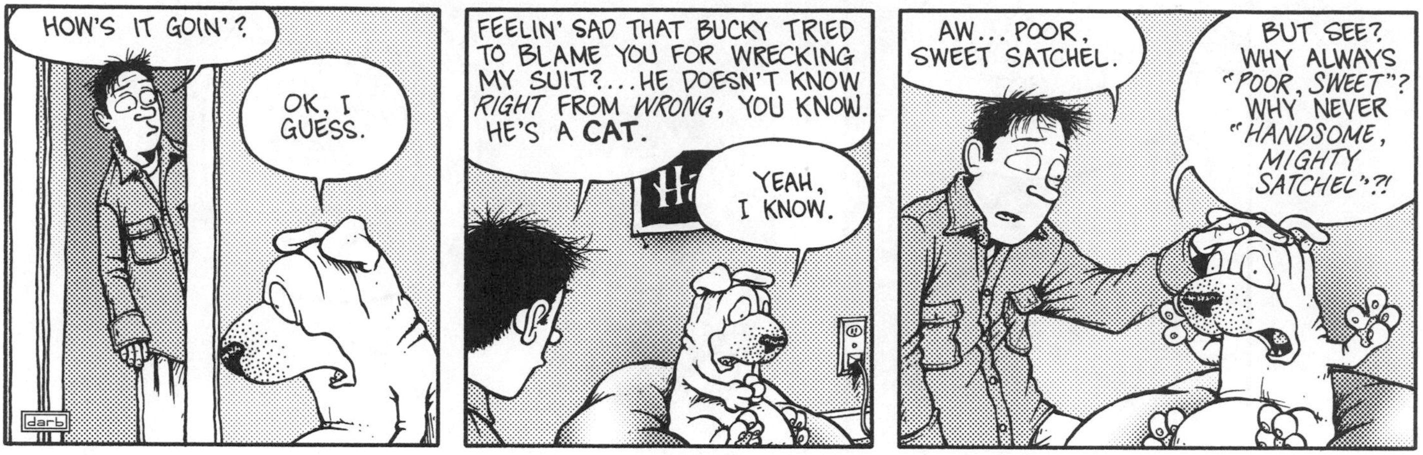
HOW'S IT GOIN'?
OK, I GUESS.
darb
FEELIN' SAD THAT BUCKY TRIED TO BLAME YOU FOR WRECKING MY SUIT?... HE DOESN'T KNOW *RIGHT* FROM *WRONG*, YOU KNOW. HE'S A **CAT**.
YEAH, I KNOW.
AW... POOR, SWEET SATCHEL.
BUT SEE? WHY ALWAYS *"POOR, SWEET"*? WHY NEVER *"HANDSOME, MIGHTY SATCHEL"*?!

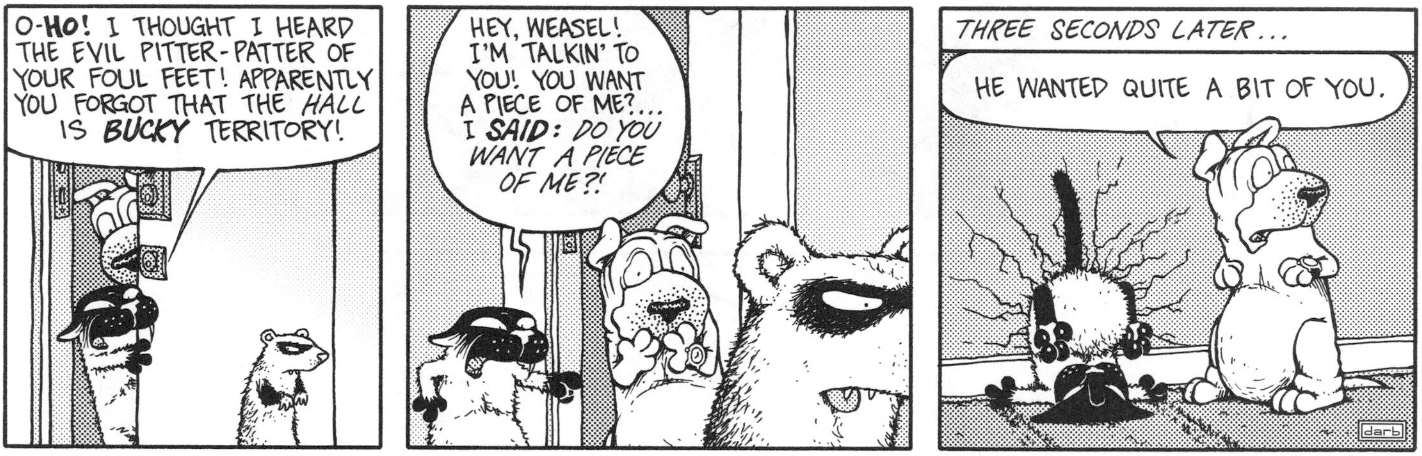
O-**HO!** I THOUGHT I HEARD THE EVIL PITTER-PATTER OF YOUR FOUL FEET! APPARENTLY YOU FORGOT THAT THE *HALL* IS ***BUCKY*** TERRITORY!
HEY, WEASEL! I'M TALKIN' TO YOU! YOU WANT A PIECE OF ME?... I **SAID:** *DO YOU WANT A PIECE OF ME?!*
THREE SECONDS LATER...
HE WANTED QUITE A BIT OF YOU.
darb

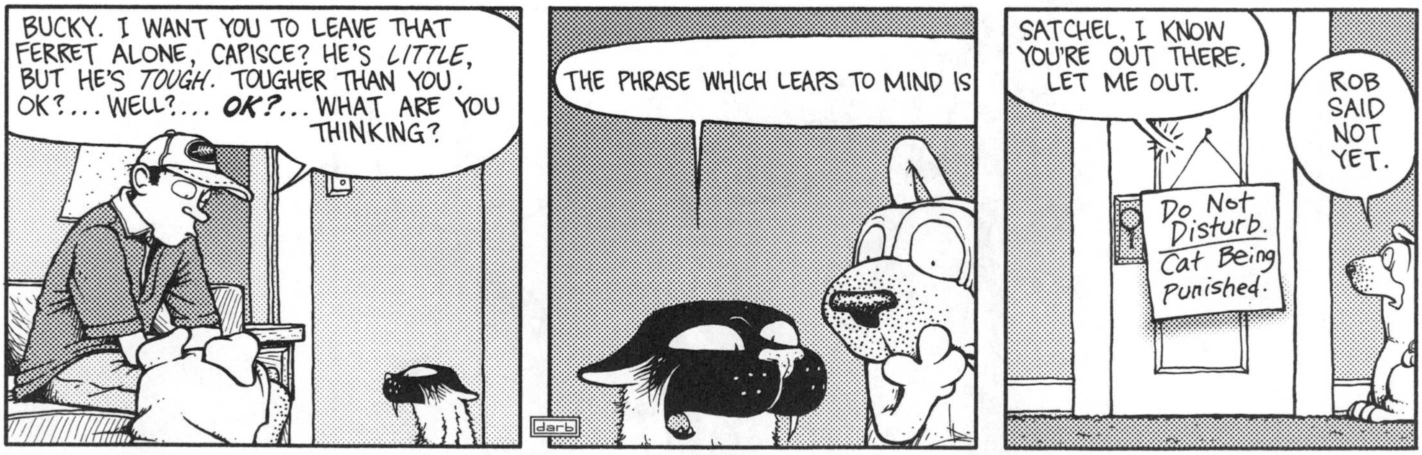
BUCKY. I WANT YOU TO LEAVE THAT FERRET ALONE, CAPISCE? HE'S *LITTLE*, BUT HE'S *TOUGH*. TOUGHER THAN YOU. OK?... WELL?... ***OK?...*** WHAT ARE YOU THINKING?
darb
THE PHRASE WHICH LEAPS TO MIND IS
SATCHEL, I KNOW YOU'RE OUT THERE. LET ME OUT.
Do Not Disturb. Cat Being Punished.
ROB SAID NOT YET.

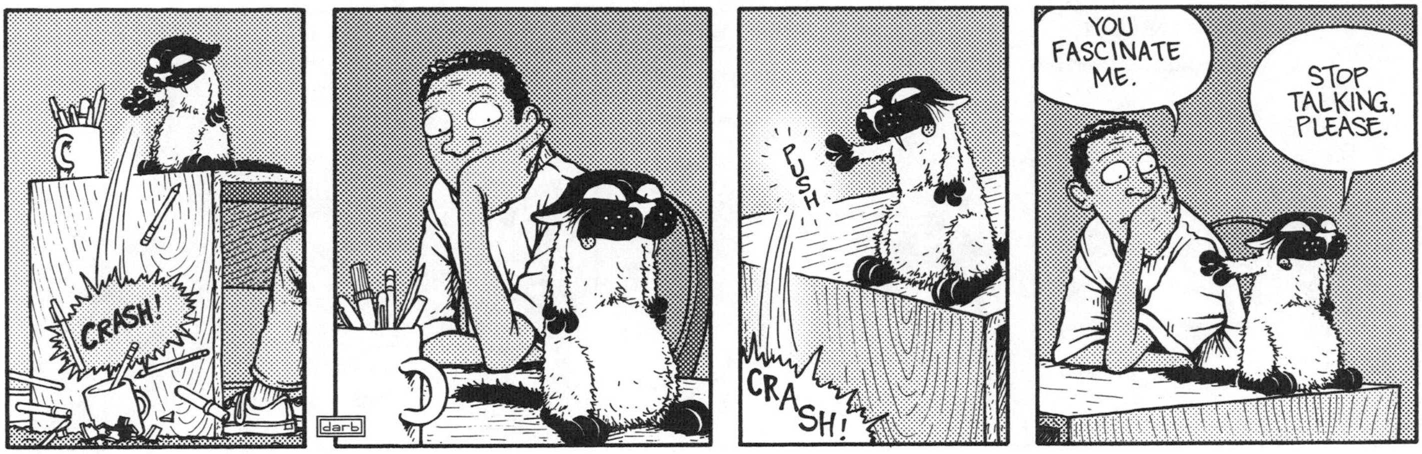
CRASH!
darb
PUSH
CRASH!
YOU FASCINATE ME.
STOP TALKING, PLEASE.

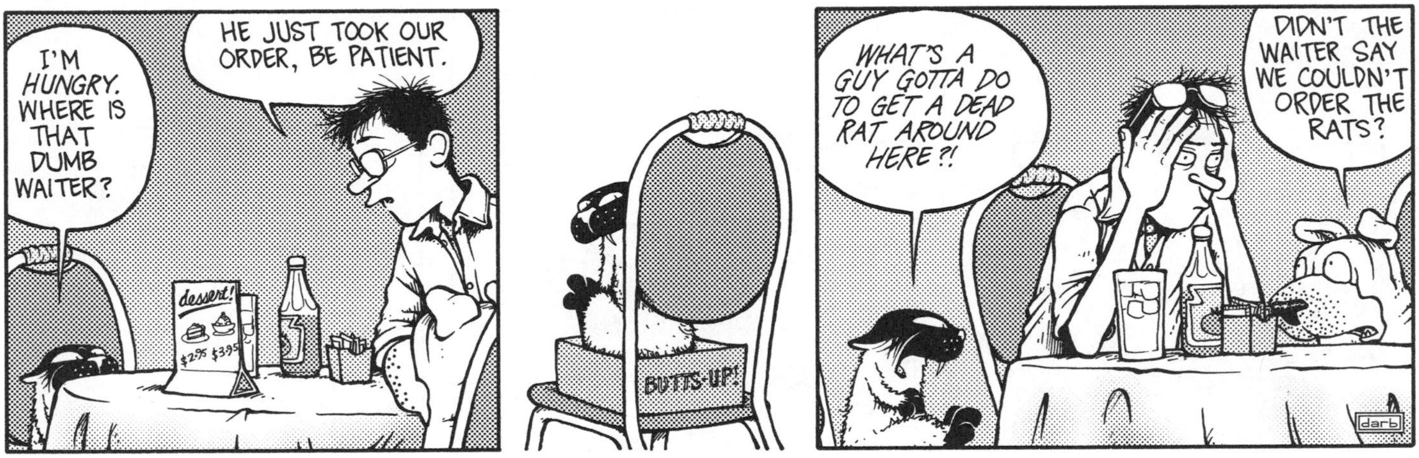
I'M HUNGRY. WHERE IS THAT DUMB WAITER?
HE JUST TOOK OUR ORDER, BE PATIENT.
dessert!
BUTTS-UP!
WHAT'S A GUY GOTTA DO TO GET A DEAD RAT AROUND HERE?!
DIDN'T THE WAITER SAY WE COULDN'T ORDER THE RATS?
darb

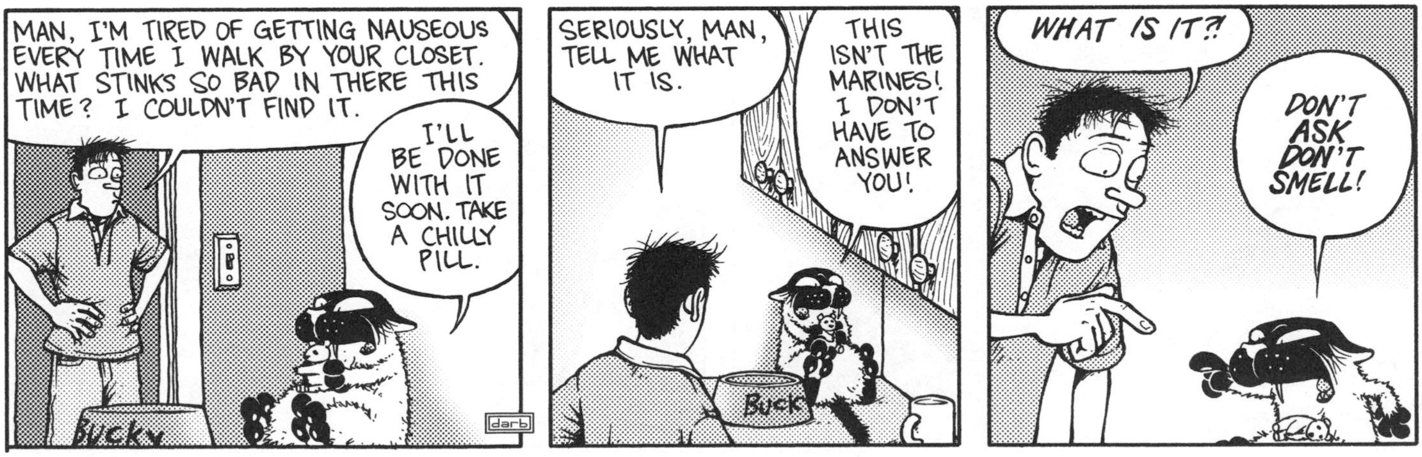
MAN, I'M TIRED OF GETTING NAUSEOUS EVERY TIME I WALK BY YOUR CLOSET. WHAT STINKS SO BAD IN THERE THIS TIME? I COULDN'T FIND IT.
I'LL BE DONE WITH IT SOON. TAKE A CHILLY PILL.
BUCKY
darb
SERIOUSLY, MAN, TELL ME WHAT IT IS.
THIS ISN'T THE MARINES! I DON'T HAVE TO ANSWER YOU!
BUCK
WHAT IS IT?!
DON'T ASK DON'T SMELL!

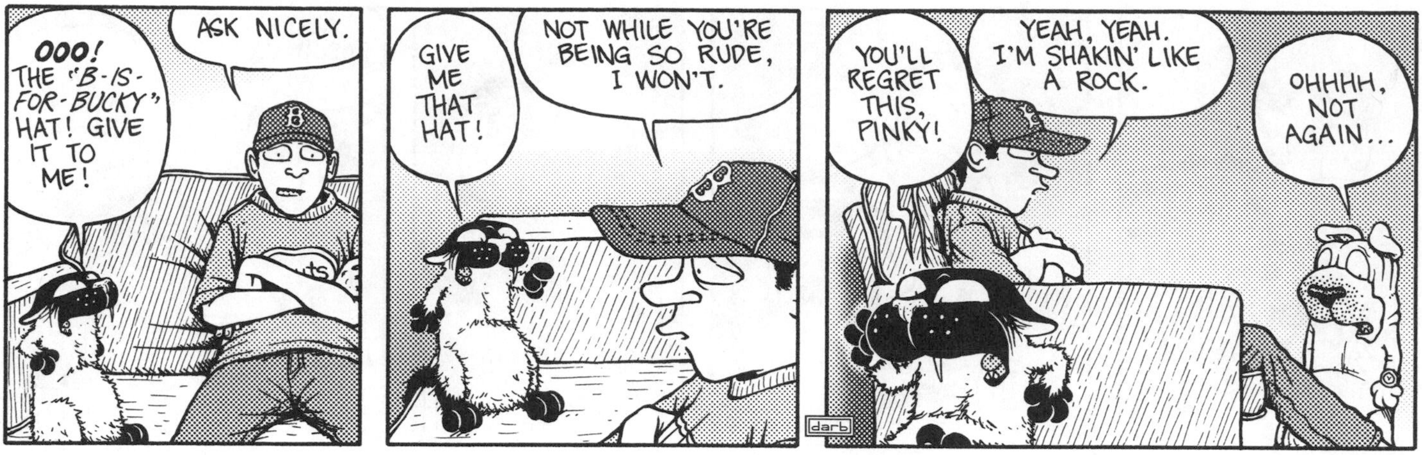
OOO! THE "B-IS-FOR-BUCKY" HAT! GIVE IT TO ME!
ASK NICELY.
GIVE ME THAT HAT!
NOT WHILE YOU'RE BEING SO RUDE, I WON'T.
YOU'LL REGRET THIS, PINKY!
YEAH, YEAH. I'M SHAKIN' LIKE A ROCK.
OHHHH, NOT AGAIN...
darb

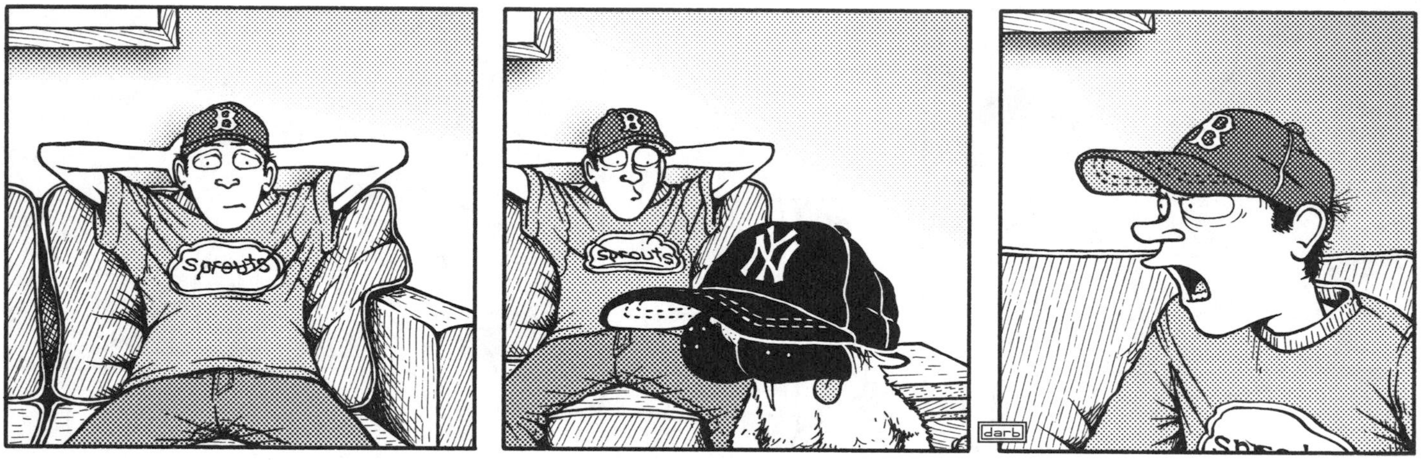
sprouts
darb

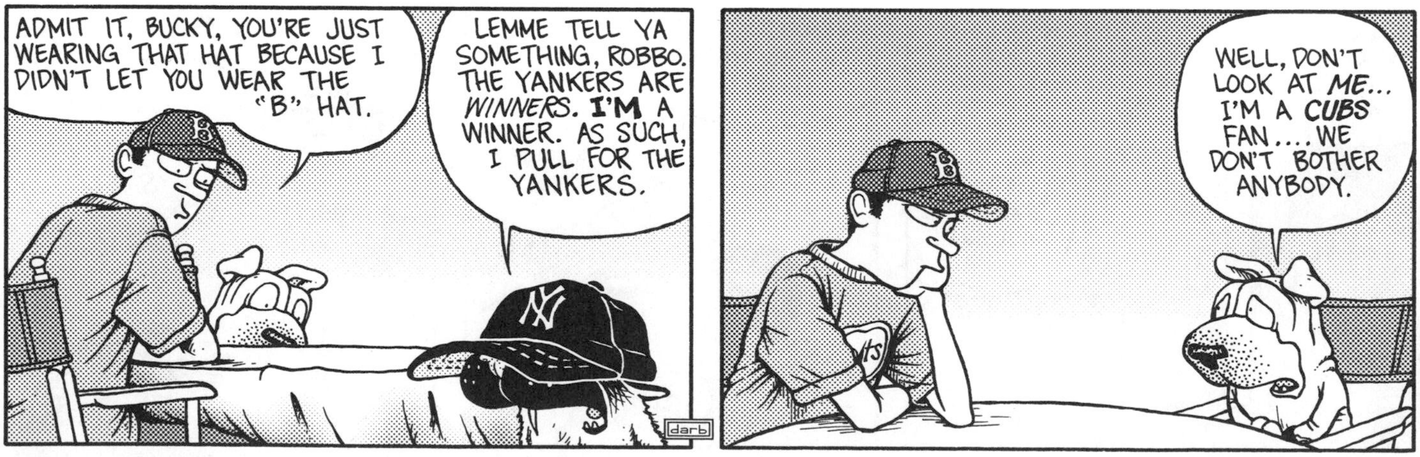
ADMIT IT, BUCKY, YOU'RE JUST WEARING THAT HAT BECAUSE I DIDN'T LET YOU WEAR THE "B" HAT.
LEMME TELL YA SOMETHING, ROBBO. THE YANKERS ARE WINNERS. I'M A WINNER. AS SUCH, I PULL FOR THE YANKERS.
darb
WELL, DON'T LOOK AT ME... I'M A CUBS FAN.... WE DON'T BOTHER ANYBODY.

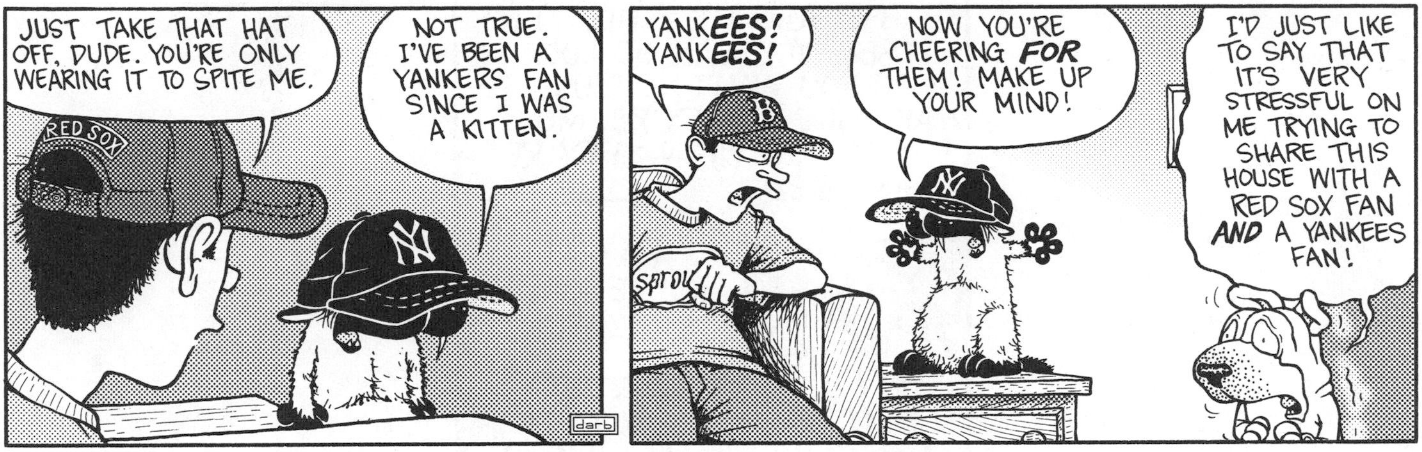
JUST TAKE THAT HAT OFF, DUDE. YOU'RE ONLY WEARING IT TO SPITE ME.
NOT TRUE. I'VE BEEN A YANKERS FAN SINCE I WAS A KITTEN.
RED SOX
YANKEES! YANKEES!
NOW YOU'RE CHEERING FOR THEM! MAKE UP YOUR MIND!
sprou
I'D JUST LIKE TO SAY THAT IT'S VERY STRESSFUL ON ME TRYING TO SHARE THIS HOUSE WITH A RED SOX FAN AND A YANKEES FAN!
darb

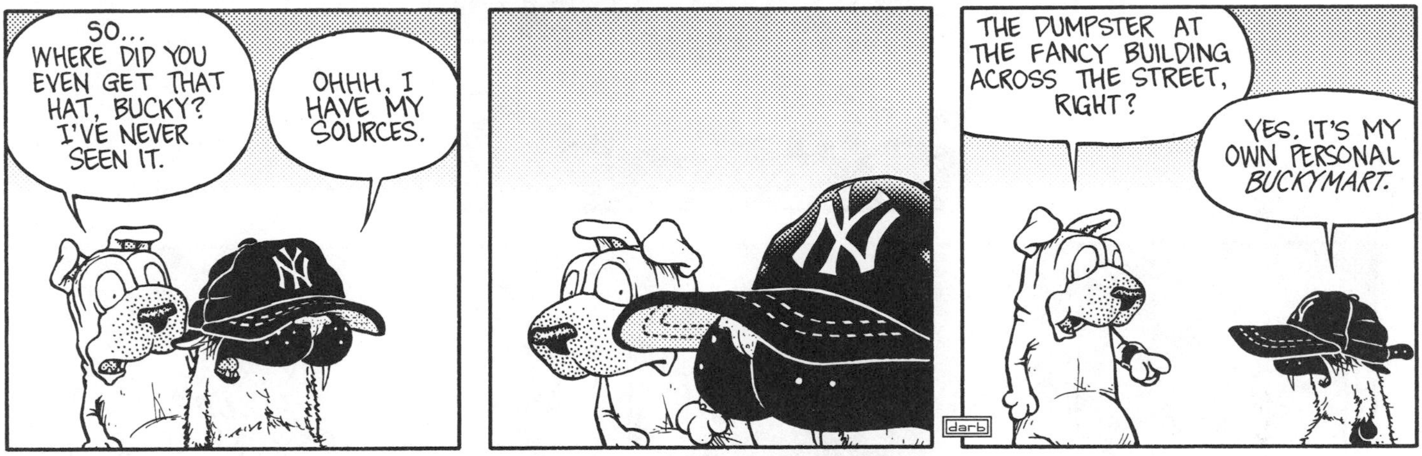
SO... WHERE DID YOU EVEN GET THAT HAT, BUCKY? I'VE NEVER SEEN IT.
OHHH, I HAVE MY SOURCES.
THE DUMPSTER AT THE FANCY BUILDING ACROSS THE STREET, RIGHT?
YES. IT'S MY OWN PERSONAL BUCKYMART.
darb

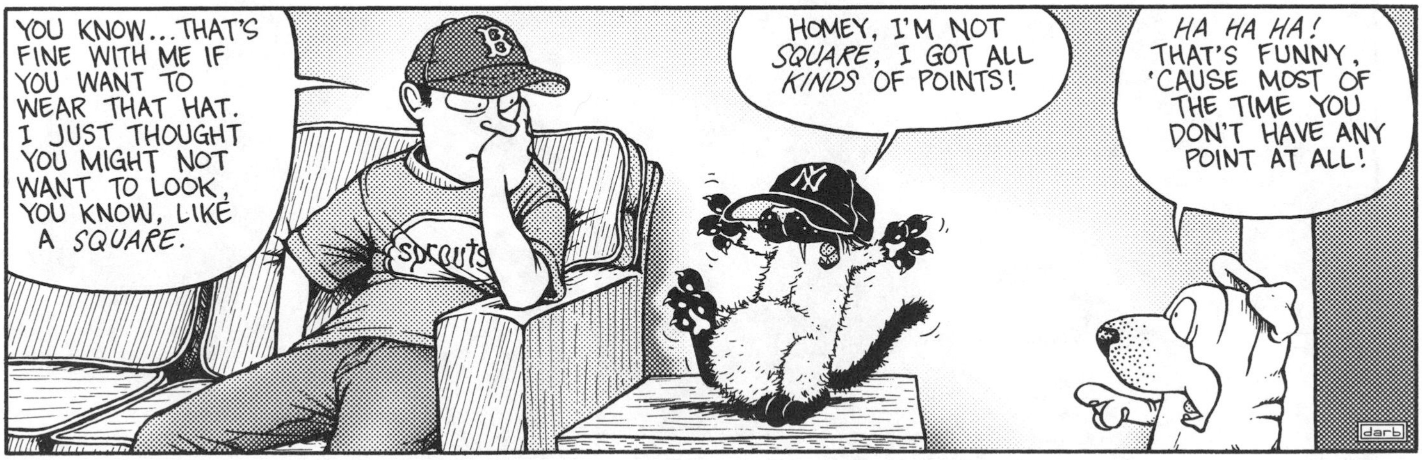
YOU KNOW...THAT'S FINE WITH ME IF YOU WANT TO WEAR THAT HAT. I JUST THOUGHT YOU MIGHT NOT WANT TO LOOK, YOU KNOW, LIKE A SQUARE.
HOMEY, I'M NOT SQUARE, I GOT ALL KINDS OF POINTS!
HA HA HA! THAT'S FUNNY, 'CAUSE MOST OF THE TIME YOU DON'T HAVE ANY POINT AT ALL!
sprouts
darb

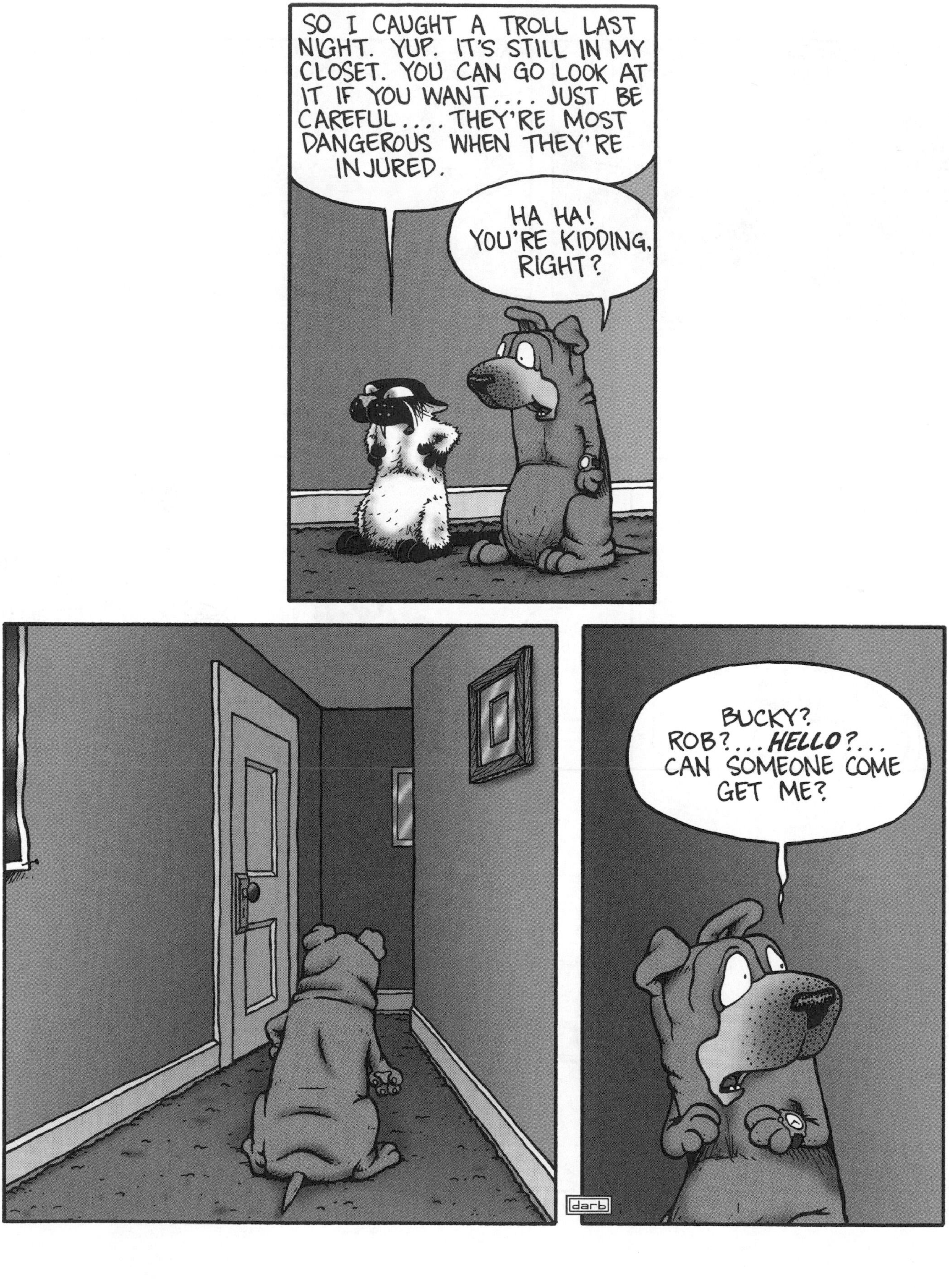
SO I CAUGHT A TROLL LAST NIGHT. YUP. IT'S STILL IN MY CLOSET. YOU CAN GO LOOK AT IT IF YOU WANT.... JUST BE CAREFUL.... THEY'RE MOST DANGEROUS WHEN THEY'RE INJURED.
HA HA! YOU'RE KIDDING, RIGHT?
BUCKY? ROB?...**HELLO**?... CAN SOMEONE COME GET ME?
darb

AW, LOOK AT THIS... SILLY YELLOW JOURNALISM...
"YELLOW JOURNALISM"? ISN'T THAT, LIKE, WHEN YOU LINE A PUPPY'S BOX WITH NEWSPA-
NO, SATCHEL.
The Daily Rag

AND AS THE LEAD SLED TEAM COMES INTO VIEW, IT'S -- CAN IT BE?!? YES! IT'S THE TEAM LED BY THE ROOKIE SATCHEL POOCH! HIS HUGE MUSCLES ARE STRAINING AS HE PULLS THE REST OF HIS TIRED TEAM TOWARD THE FINISH LINE!!
THE CROWD IS GOING WILD! HE'S ABOUT TO WIN THE 1,100 MILE-LONG IDITAROD! JUST WHO IS THIS INCREDIBLE DOG WHO'S COME OUT OF NOWHERE TO LEAD HIS RAGGED TEAM TO... TO, UM...
...HI.
MUSH!

SWOOSH
SOME PEOPLE ARE PASSIVE-AGGRESSIVE, BUCKY IS PASSING-AGGRESSIVE...
MAN...

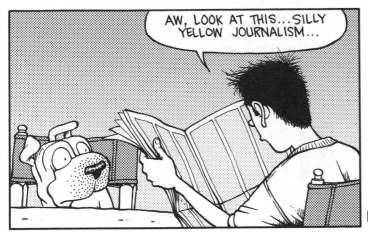

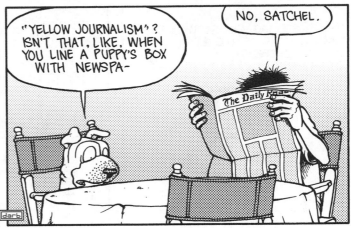

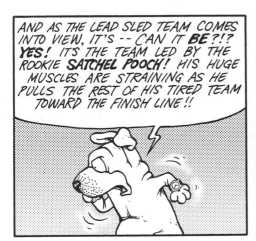

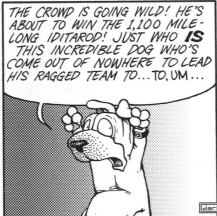

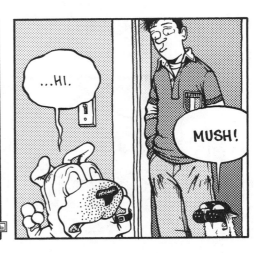

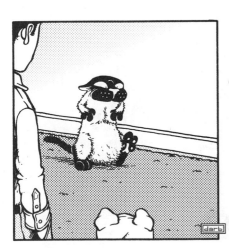

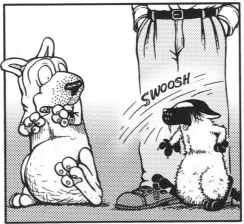

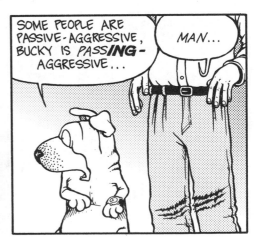

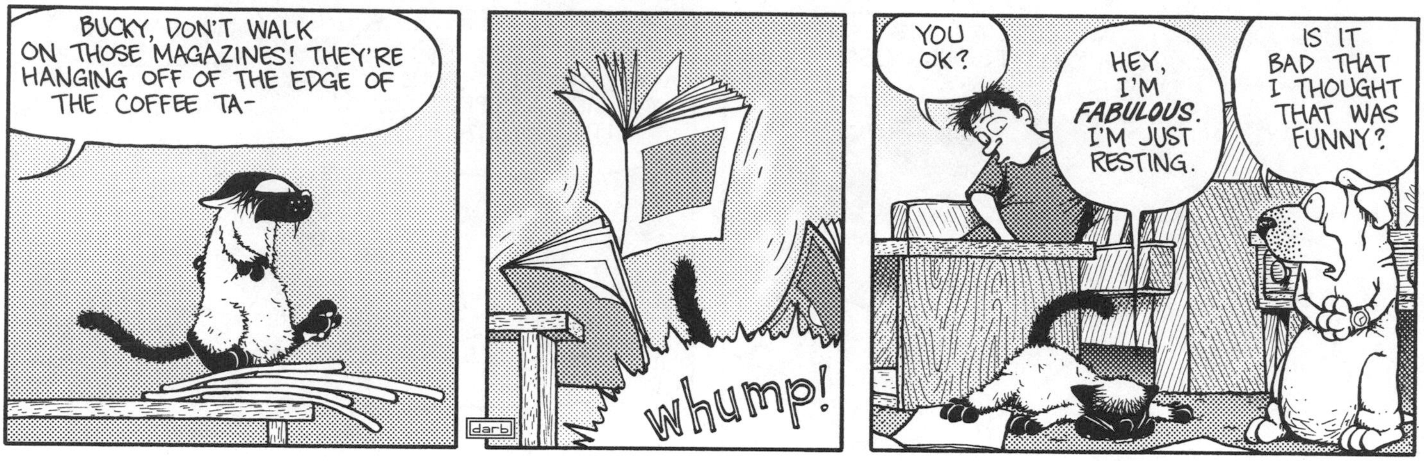
BUCKY, DON'T WALK ON THOSE MAGAZINES! THEY'RE HANGING OFF OF THE EDGE OF THE COFFEE TA-
darb
whump!
YOU OK?
HEY, I'M FABULOUS. I'M JUST RESTING.
IS IT BAD THAT I THOUGHT THAT WAS FUNNY?

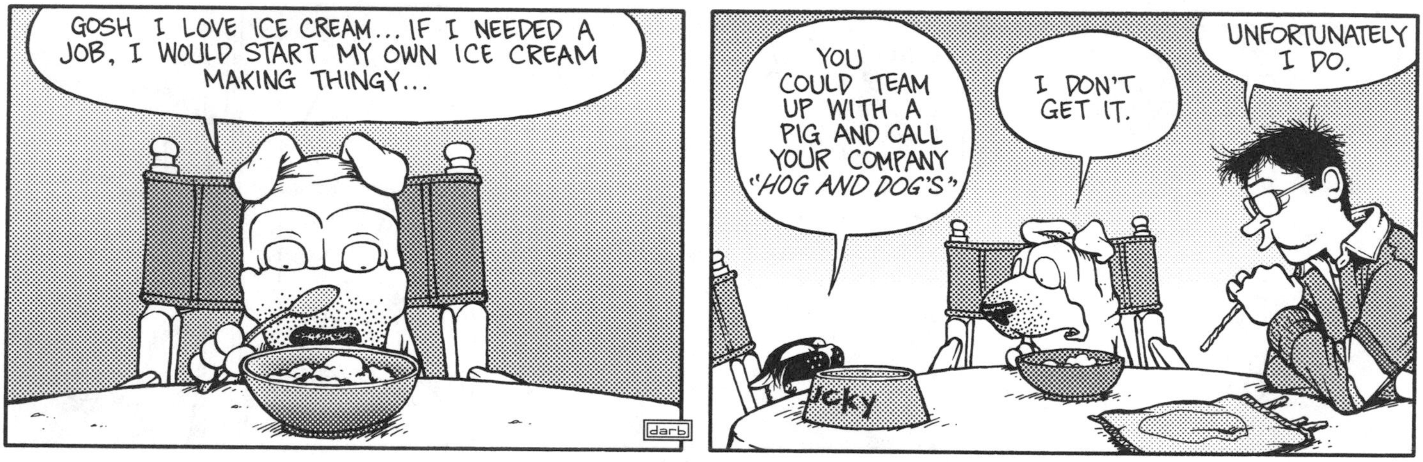
GOSH I LOVE ICE CREAM... IF I NEEDED A JOB, I WOULD START MY OWN ICE CREAM MAKING THINGY...
darb
YOU COULD TEAM UP WITH A PIG AND CALL YOUR COMPANY "HOG AND DOG'S"
I DON'T GET IT.
UNFORTUNATELY I DO.

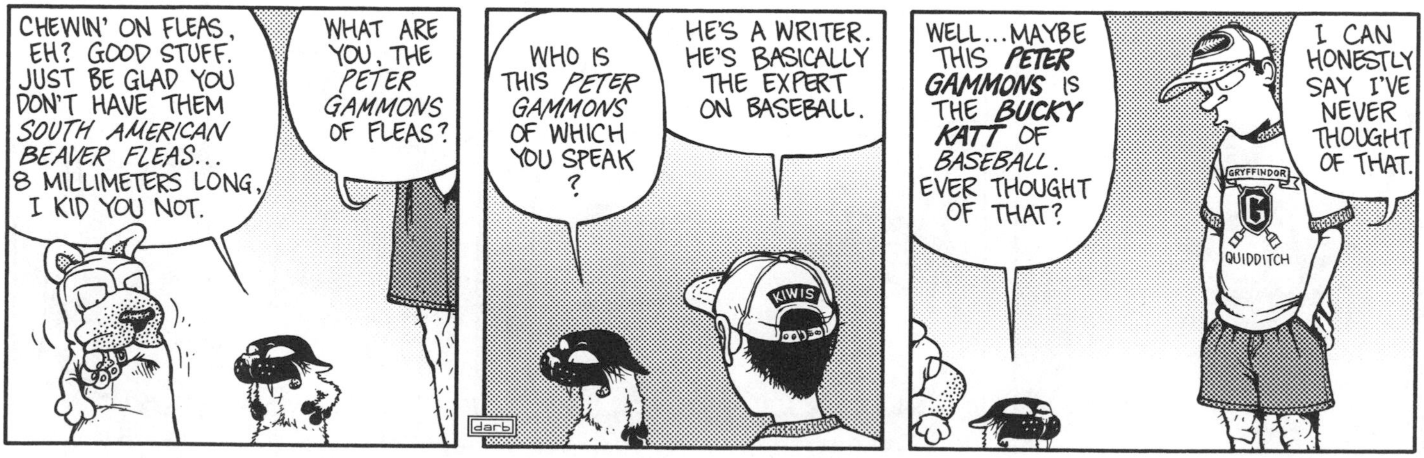
CHEWIN' ON FLEAS, EH? GOOD STUFF. JUST BE GLAD YOU DON'T HAVE THEM SOUTH AMERICAN BEAVER FLEAS... 8 MILLIMETERS LONG, I KID YOU NOT.
WHAT ARE YOU, THE PETER GAMMONS OF FLEAS?
darb
WHO IS THIS PETER GAMMONS OF WHICH YOU SPEAK ?
HE'S A WRITER. HE'S BASICALLY THE EXPERT ON BASEBALL.
KIWIS
WELL...MAYBE THIS PETER GAMMONS IS THE BUCKY KATT OF BASEBALL. EVER THOUGHT OF THAT?
I CAN HONESTLY SAY I'VE NEVER THOUGHT OF THAT.
GRYFFINDOR
G
QUIDDITCH

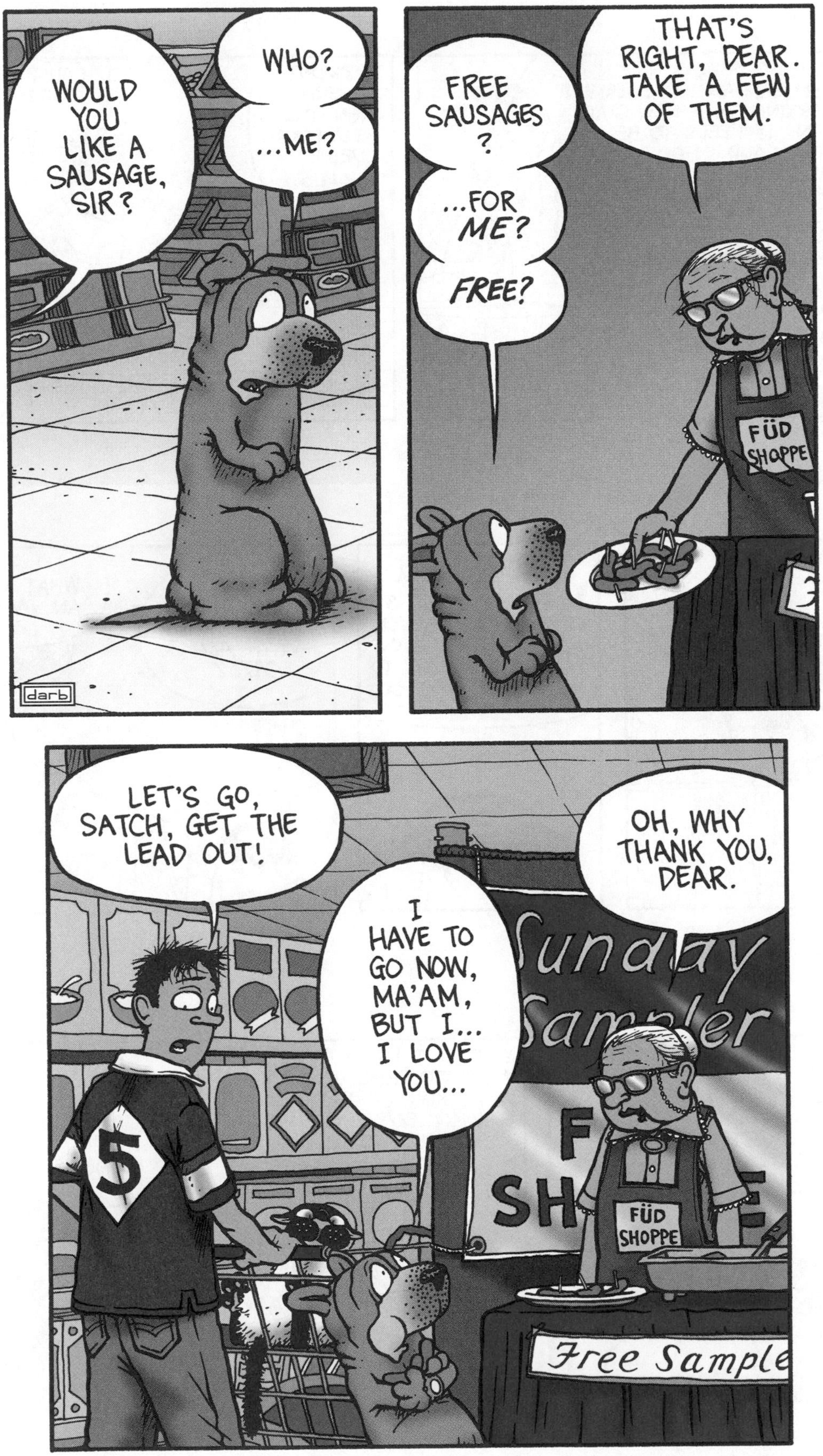
WOULD YOU LIKE A SAUSAGE, SIR?
WHO?
...ME?
darb
FREE SAUSAGES?
...FOR *ME*?
FREE?
THAT'S RIGHT, DEAR. TAKE A FEW OF THEM.
FÜD SHOPPE
LET'S GO, SATCH, GET THE LEAD OUT!
I HAVE TO GO NOW, MA'AM, BUT I... I LOVE YOU...
OH, WHY THANK YOU, DEAR.
Sunday Sampler
FÜD SHOPPE
Free Sample

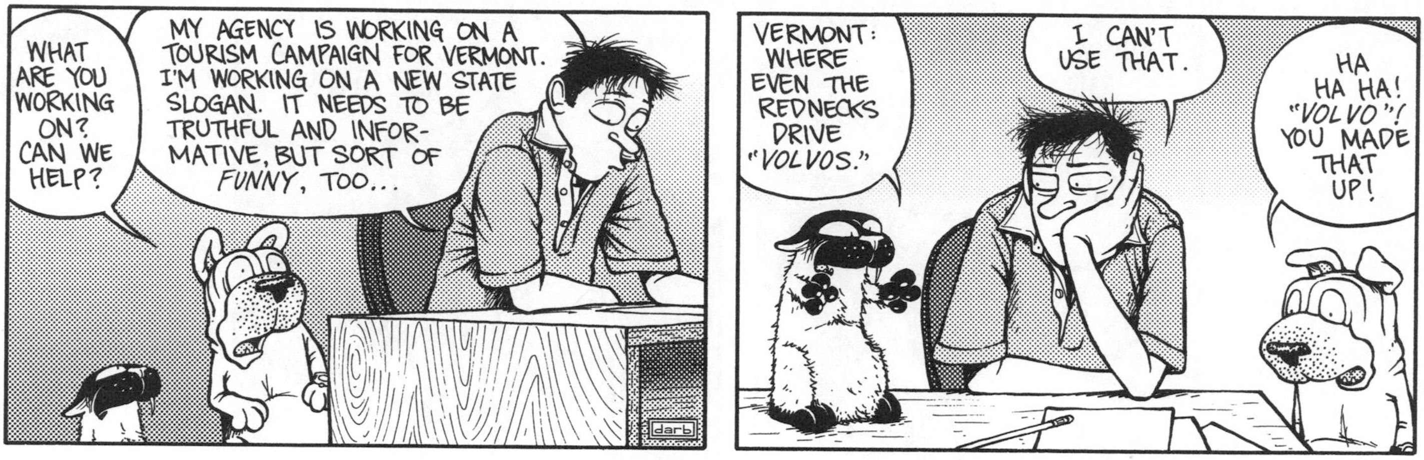
WHAT ARE YOU WORKING ON? CAN WE HELP?
MY AGENCY IS WORKING ON A TOURISM CAMPAIGN FOR VERMONT. I'M WORKING ON A NEW STATE SLOGAN. IT NEEDS TO BE TRUTHFUL AND INFORMATIVE, BUT SORT OF FUNNY, TOO...
darb
VERMONT: WHERE EVEN THE REDNECKS DRIVE "VOLVOS."
I CAN'T USE THAT.
HA HA HA! "VOLVO"! YOU MADE THAT UP!

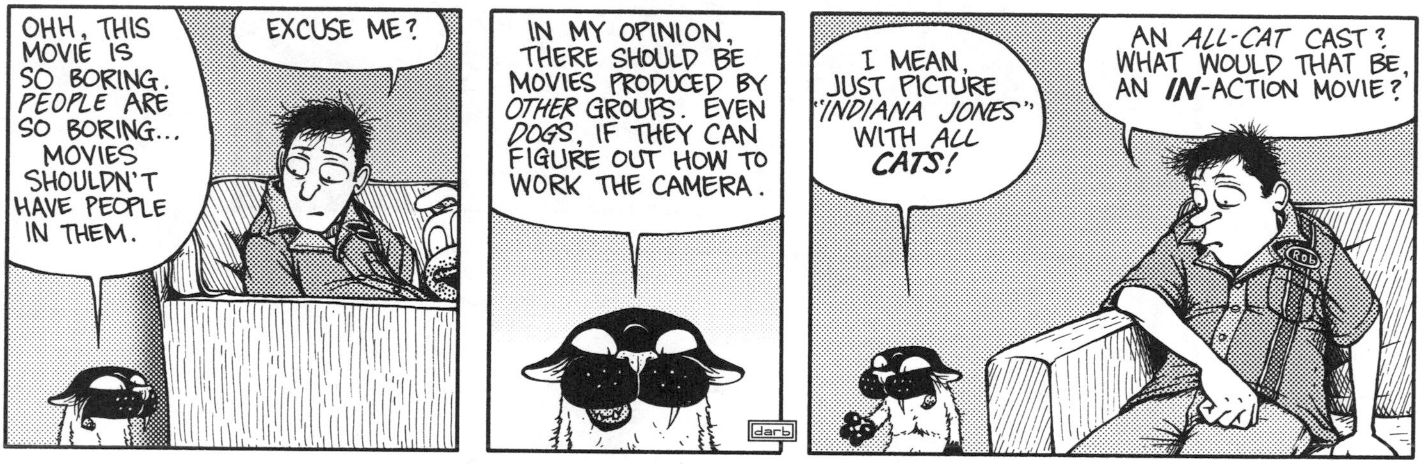
OHH, THIS MOVIE IS SO BORING. PEOPLE ARE SO BORING... MOVIES SHOULDN'T HAVE PEOPLE IN THEM.
EXCUSE ME?
IN MY OPINION, THERE SHOULD BE MOVIES PRODUCED BY OTHER GROUPS. EVEN DOGS, IF THEY CAN FIGURE OUT HOW TO WORK THE CAMERA.
darb
I MEAN, JUST PICTURE "INDIANA JONES" WITH ALL CATS!
AN ALL-CAT CAST? WHAT WOULD THAT BE, AN IN-ACTION MOVIE?
ROB

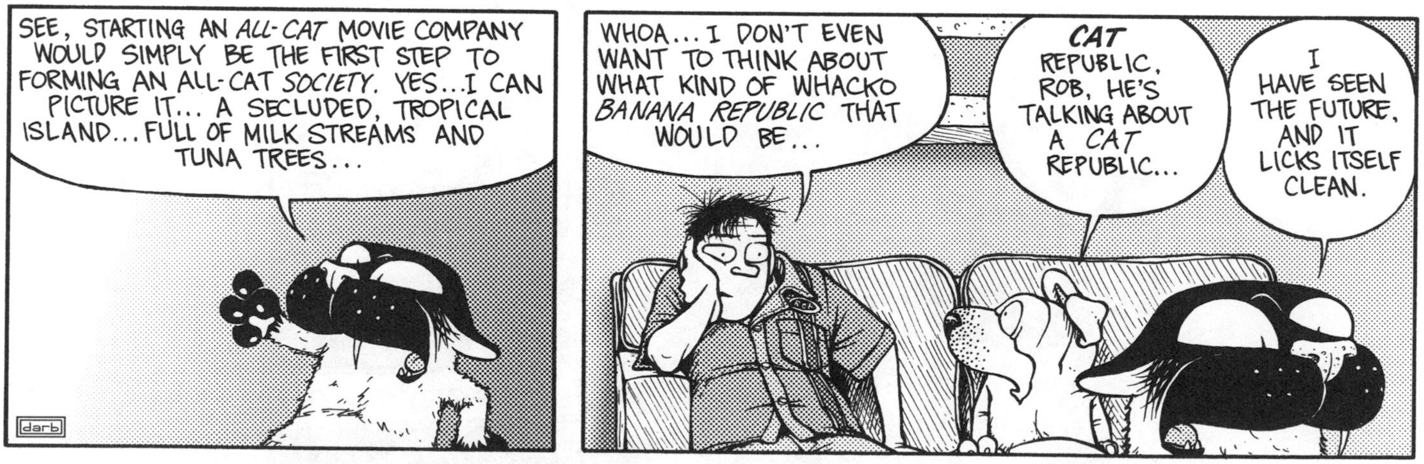
SEE, STARTING AN ALL-CAT MOVIE COMPANY WOULD SIMPLY BE THE FIRST STEP TO FORMING AN ALL-CAT SOCIETY. YES...I CAN PICTURE IT... A SECLUDED, TROPICAL ISLAND... FULL OF MILK STREAMS AND TUNA TREES...
darb
WHOA... I DON'T EVEN WANT TO THINK ABOUT WHAT KIND OF WHACKO BANANA REPUBLIC THAT WOULD BE...
CAT REPUBLIC, ROB, HE'S TALKING ABOUT A CAT REPUBLIC...
I HAVE SEEN THE FUTURE, AND IT LICKS ITSELF CLEAN.

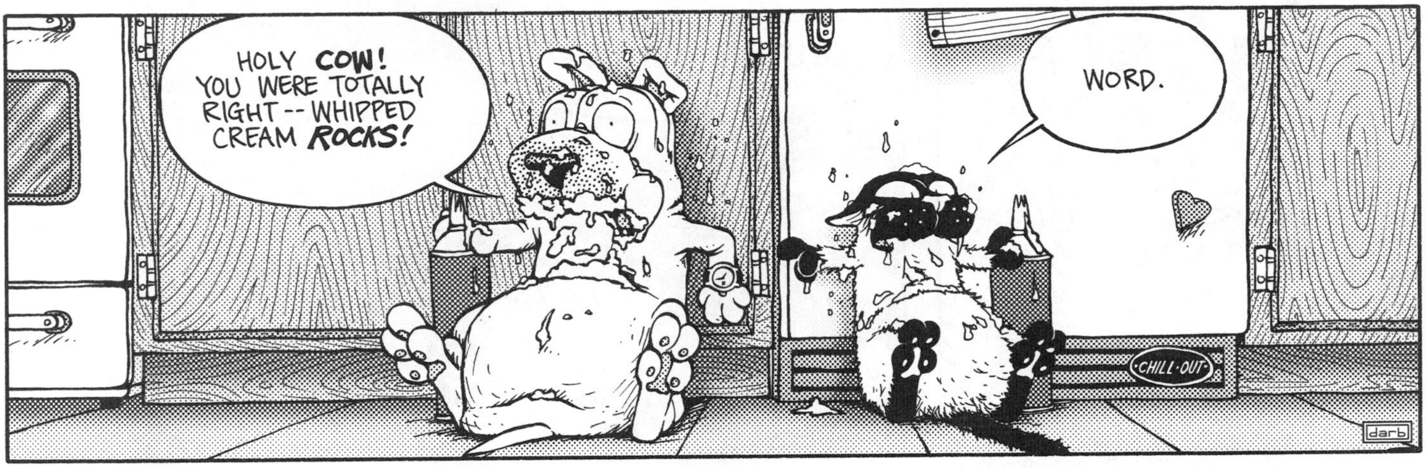
HOLY COW! YOU WERE TOTALLY RIGHT -- WHIPPED CREAM ROCKS!
WORD.
CHILL-OUT
darb

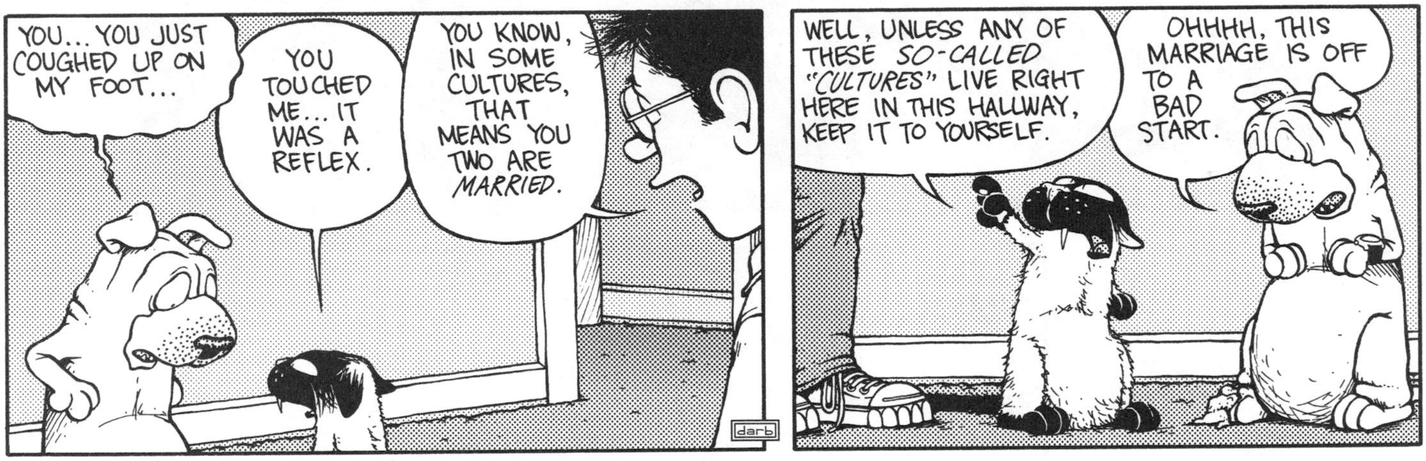
YOU... YOU JUST COUGHED UP ON MY FOOT...
YOU TOUCHED ME... IT WAS A REFLEX.
YOU KNOW, IN SOME CULTURES, THAT MEANS YOU TWO ARE MARRIED.
darb
WELL, UNLESS ANY OF THESE SO-CALLED "CULTURES" LIVE RIGHT HERE IN THIS HALLWAY, KEEP IT TO YOURSELF.
OHHHH, THIS MARRIAGE IS OFF TO A BAD START.

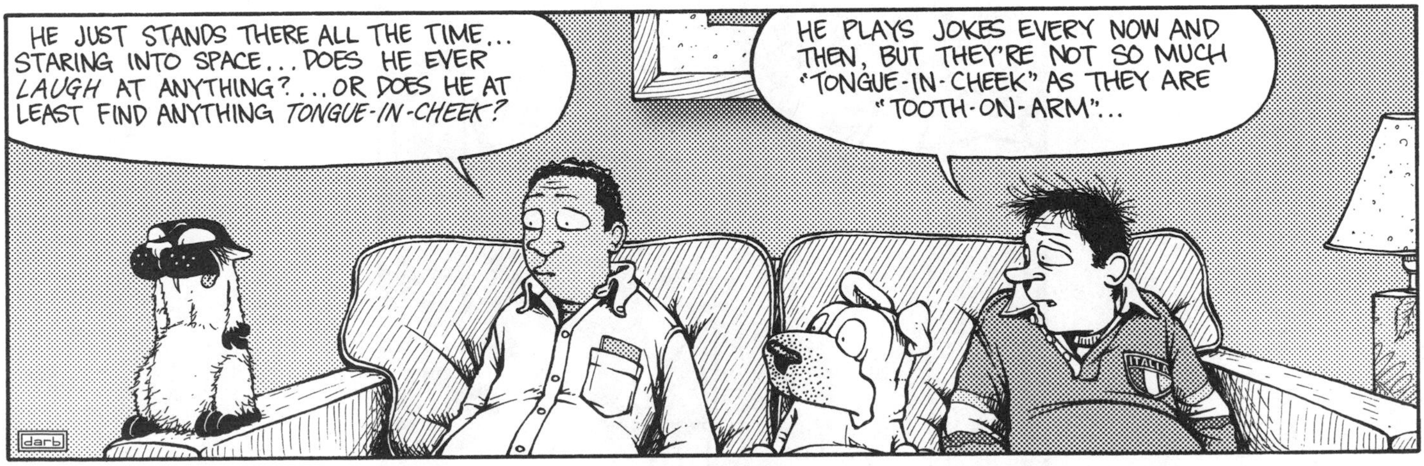
HE JUST STANDS THERE ALL THE TIME... STARING INTO SPACE... DOES HE EVER LAUGH AT ANYTHING?... OR DOES HE AT LEAST FIND ANYTHING TONGUE-IN-CHEEK?
HE PLAYS JOKES EVERY NOW AND THEN, BUT THEY'RE NOT SO MUCH "TONGUE-IN-CHEEK" AS THEY ARE "TOOTH-ON-ARM"...
ITALIA
darb

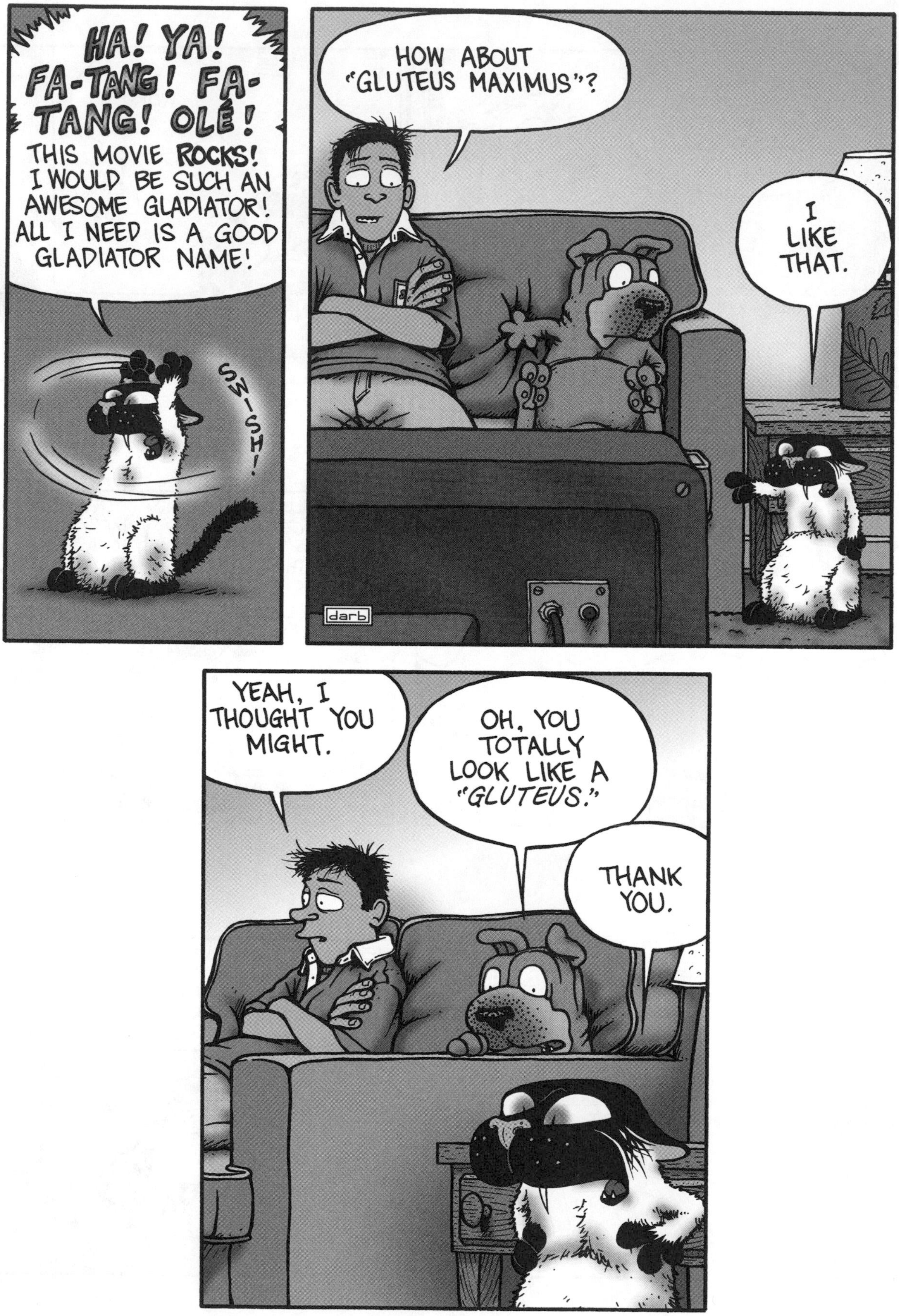
HA! YA! FA-TANG! FA-TANG! OLÉ! THIS MOVIE ROCKS! I WOULD BE SUCH AN AWESOME GLADIATOR! ALL I NEED IS A GOOD GLADIATOR NAME!
SWISH!
HOW ABOUT "GLUTEUS MAXIMUS"?
I LIKE THAT.
darb
YEAH, I THOUGHT YOU MIGHT.
OH, YOU TOTALLY LOOK LIKE A "GLUTEUS."
THANK YOU.

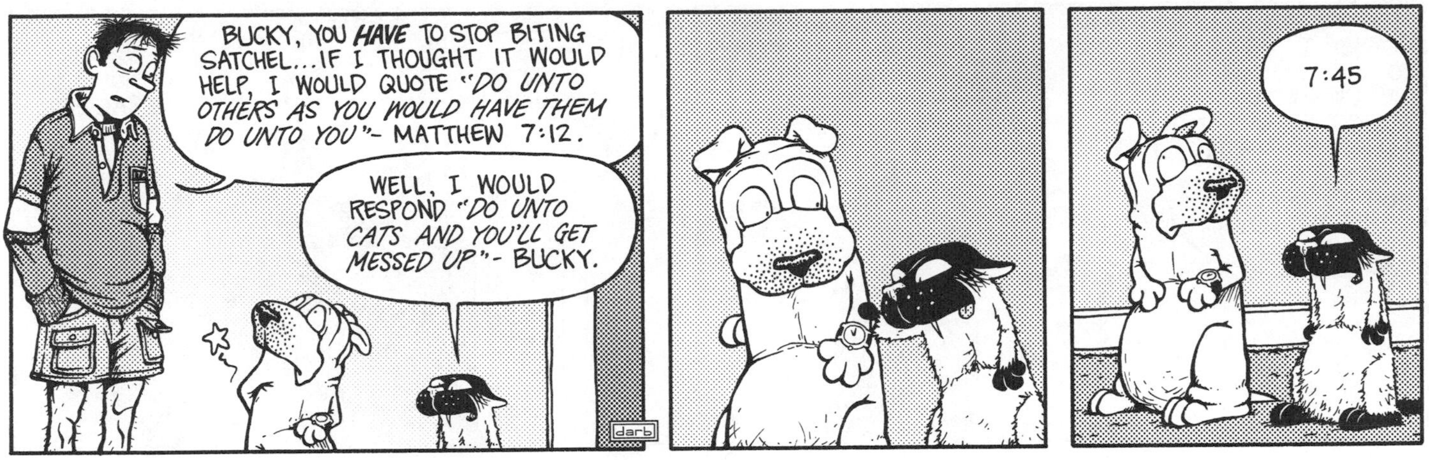
BUCKY, YOU HAVE TO STOP BITING SATCHEL... IF I THOUGHT IT WOULD HELP, I WOULD QUOTE "DO UNTO OTHERS AS YOU WOULD HAVE THEM DO UNTO YOU" - MATTHEW 7:12.
WELL, I WOULD RESPOND "DO UNTO CATS AND YOU'LL GET MESSED UP" - BUCKY.
darb
7:45

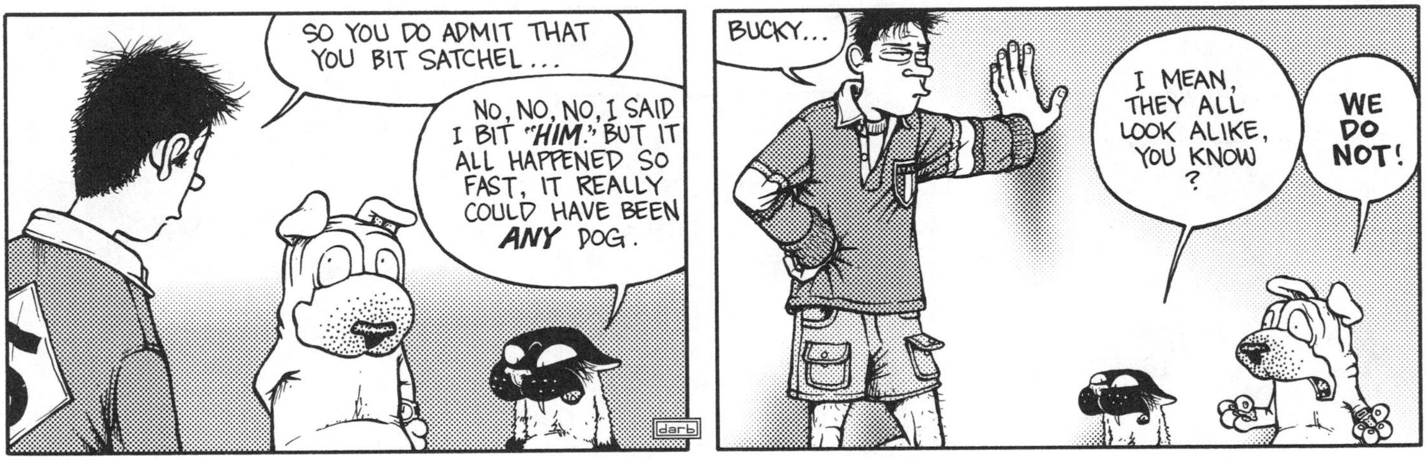
SO YOU DO ADMIT THAT YOU BIT SATCHEL...
NO, NO, NO, I SAID I BIT "HIM." BUT IT ALL HAPPENED SO FAST, IT REALLY COULD HAVE BEEN ANY DOG.
darb
BUCKY...
I MEAN, THEY ALL LOOK ALIKE, YOU KNOW?
WE DO NOT!

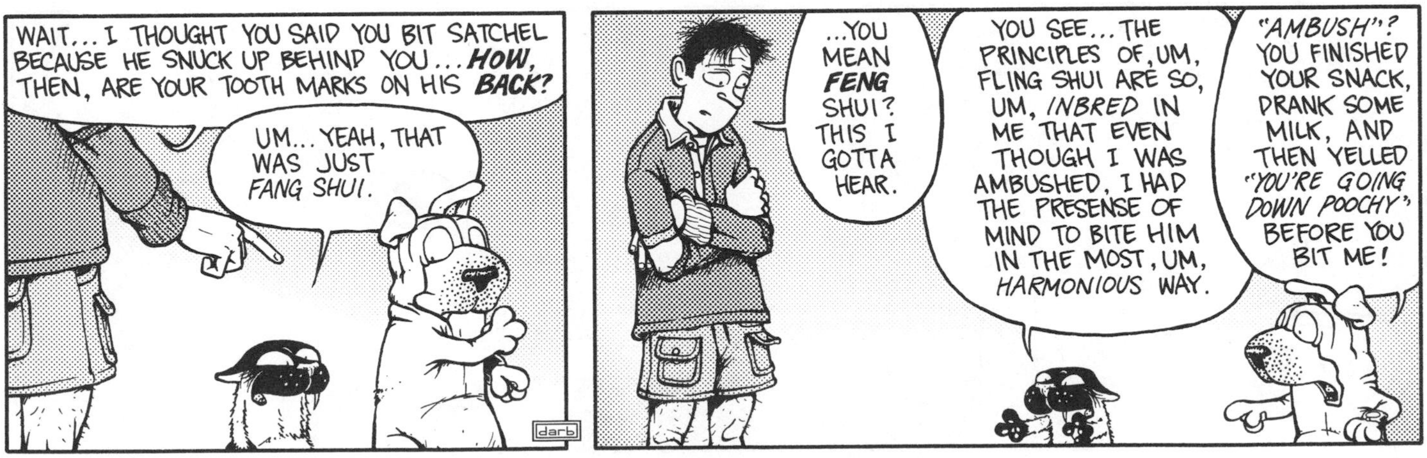
WAIT... I THOUGHT YOU SAID YOU BIT SATCHEL BECAUSE HE SNUCK UP BEHIND YOU... HOW, THEN, ARE YOUR TOOTH MARKS ON HIS BACK?
UM... YEAH, THAT WAS JUST FANG SHUI.
darb
...YOU MEAN FENG SHUI? THIS I GOTTA HEAR.
YOU SEE... THE PRINCIPLES OF, UM, FLING SHUI ARE SO, UM, INBRED IN ME THAT EVEN THOUGH I WAS AMBUSHED, I HAD THE PRESENSE OF MIND TO BITE HIM IN THE MOST, UM, HARMONIOUS WAY.
"AMBUSH"? YOU FINISHED YOUR SNACK, DRANK SOME MILK, AND THEN YELLED "YOU'RE GOING DOWN POOCHY" BEFORE YOU BIT ME!

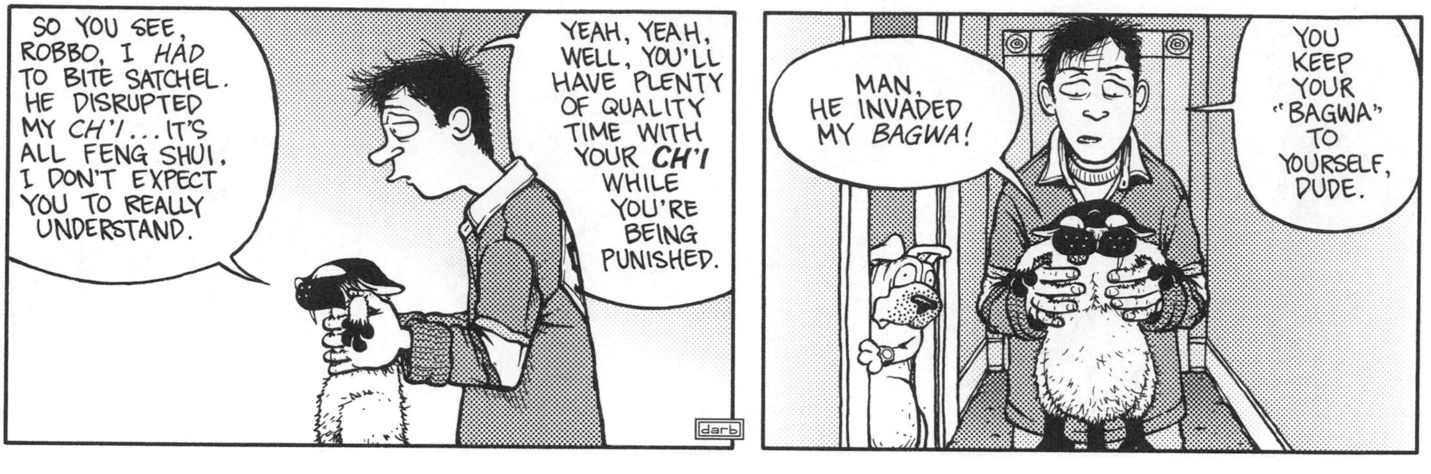
SO YOU SEE, ROBBO, I *HAD* TO BITE SATCHEL. HE DISRUPTED MY *CH'I*... IT'S ALL FENG SHUI. I DON'T EXPECT YOU TO REALLY UNDERSTAND.
YEAH, YEAH, WELL, YOU'LL HAVE PLENTY OF QUALITY TIME WITH YOUR ***CH'I*** WHILE YOU'RE BEING PUNISHED.
MAN, HE INVADED MY *BAGWA*!
YOU KEEP YOUR "BAGWA" TO YOURSELF, DUDE.
darb

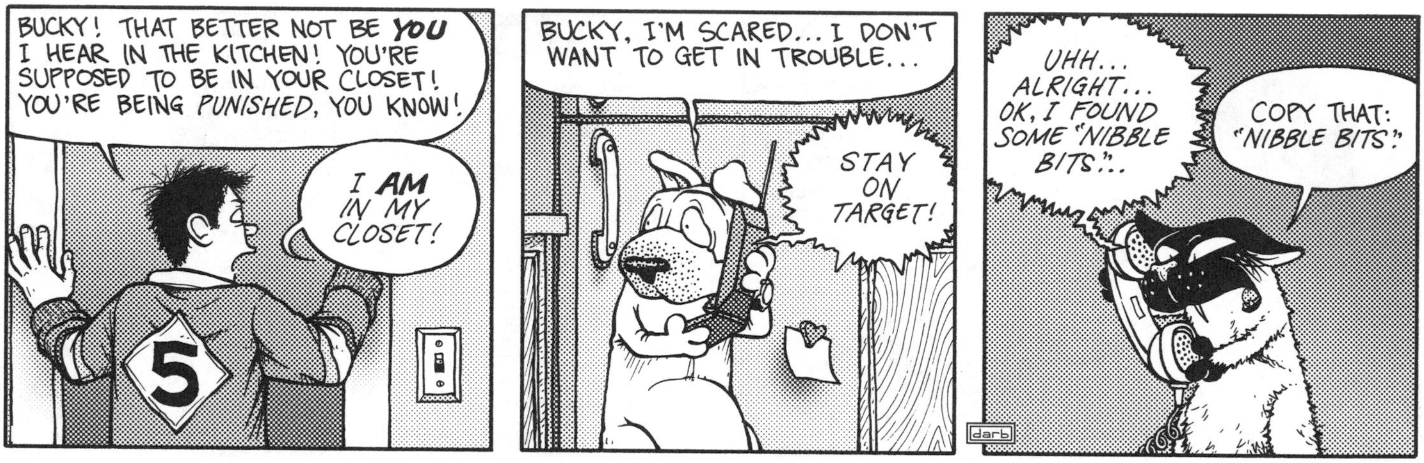
BUCKY! THAT BETTER NOT BE ***YOU*** I HEAR IN THE KITCHEN! YOU'RE SUPPOSED TO BE IN YOUR CLOSET! YOU'RE BEING *PUNISHED*, YOU KNOW!
I **AM** IN MY CLOSET!
BUCKY, I'M SCARED... I DON'T WANT TO GET IN TROUBLE...
STAY ON TARGET!
UHH... ALRIGHT... OK, I FOUND SOME "NIBBLE BITS"...
COPY THAT: "NIBBLE BITS."
darb

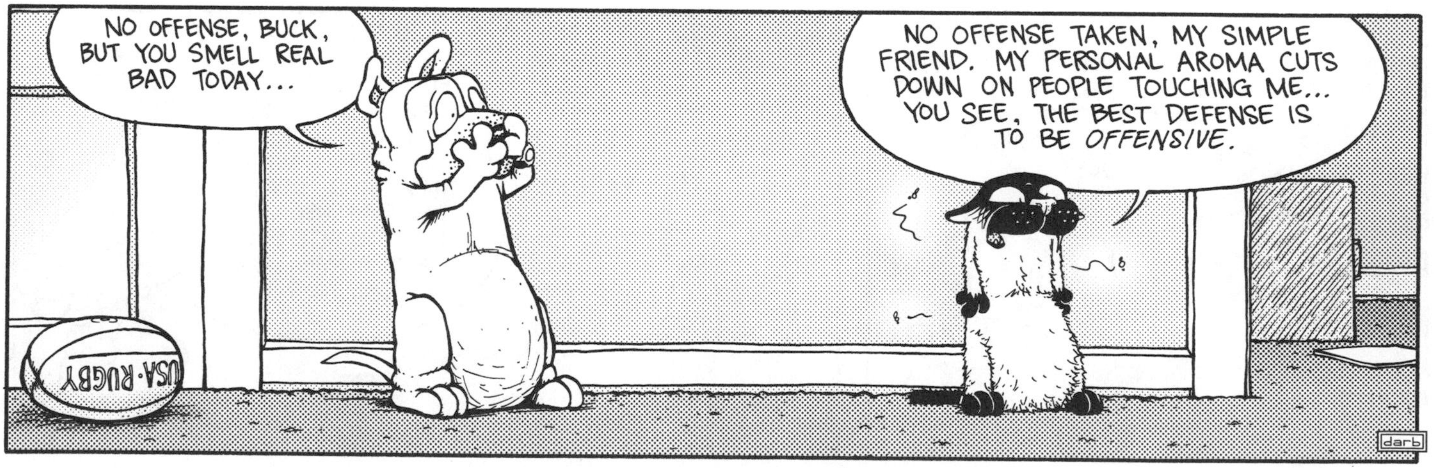
NO OFFENSE, BUCK, BUT YOU SMELL REAL BAD TODAY...
NO OFFENSE TAKEN, MY SIMPLE FRIEND. MY PERSONAL AROMA CUTS DOWN ON PEOPLE TOUCHING ME... YOU SEE, THE BEST DEFENSE IS TO BE *OFFENSIVE*.
USA·RUGBY
darb

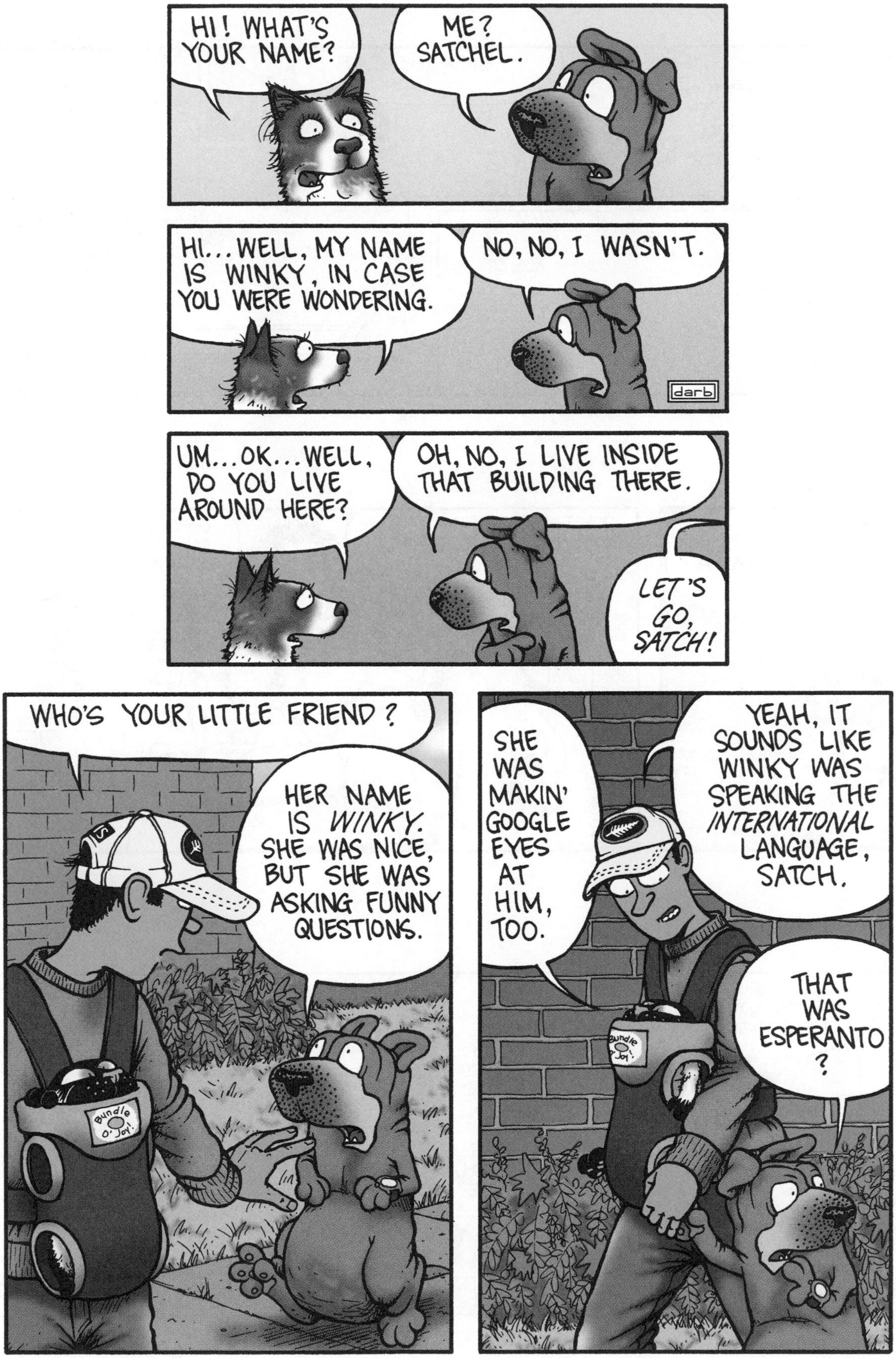
HI! WHAT'S YOUR NAME?
ME? SATCHEL.
HI...WELL, MY NAME IS WINKY, IN CASE YOU WERE WONDERING.
NO, NO, I WASN'T.
darb
UM...OK...WELL, DO YOU LIVE AROUND HERE?
OH, NO, I LIVE INSIDE THAT BUILDING THERE.
LET'S GO, SATCH!
WHO'S YOUR LITTLE FRIEND?
HER NAME IS WINKY. SHE WAS NICE, BUT SHE WAS ASKING FUNNY QUESTIONS.
Bundle O' Joy!
SHE WAS MAKIN' GOOGLE EYES AT HIM, TOO.
YEAH, IT SOUNDS LIKE WINKY WAS SPEAKING THE INTERNATIONAL LANGUAGE, SATCH.
THAT WAS ESPERANTO?

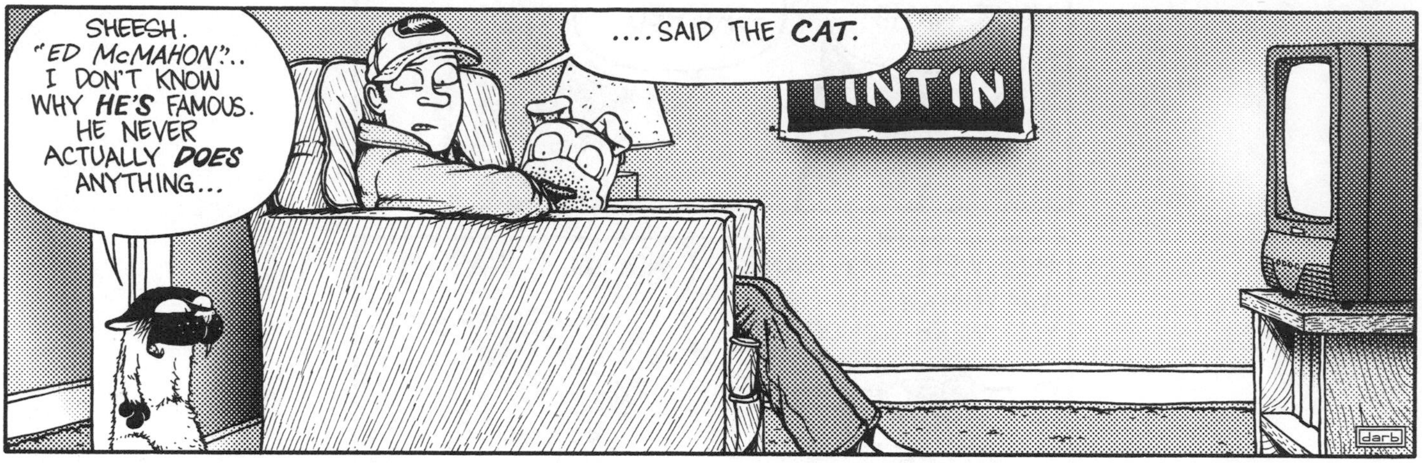
SHEESH. "ED McMAHON".. I DON'T KNOW WHY HE'S FAMOUS. HE NEVER ACTUALLY DOES ANYTHING...
....SAID THE CAT.
TINTIN
darb

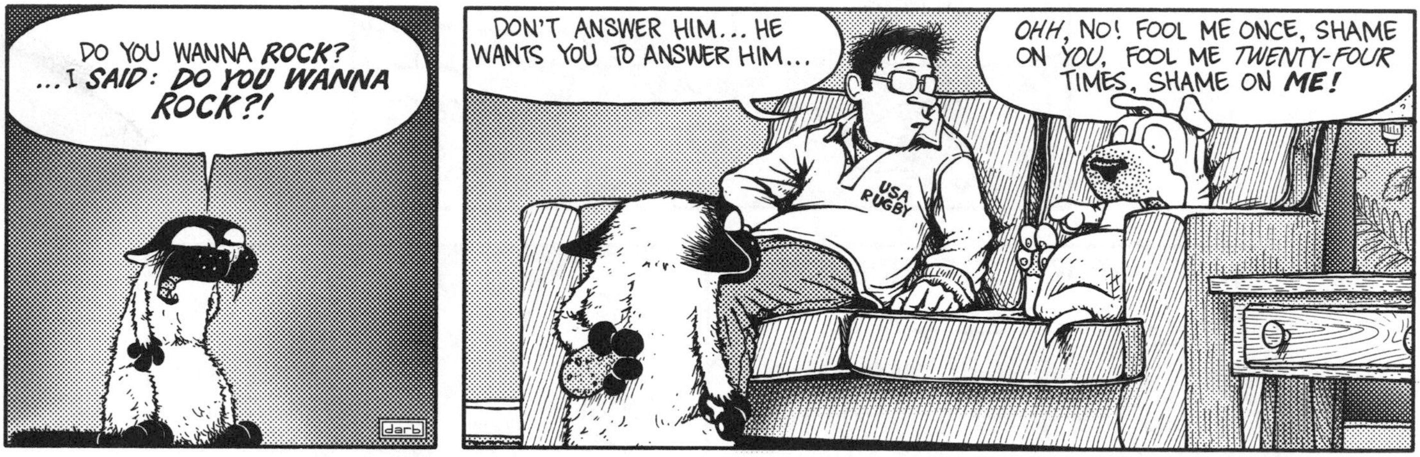
DO YOU WANNA ROCK? ...I SAID: DO YOU WANNA ROCK?!
darb
DON'T ANSWER HIM... HE WANTS YOU TO ANSWER HIM...
OHH, NO! FOOL ME ONCE, SHAME ON YOU. FOOL ME TWENTY-FOUR TIMES, SHAME ON ME!
USA RUGBY

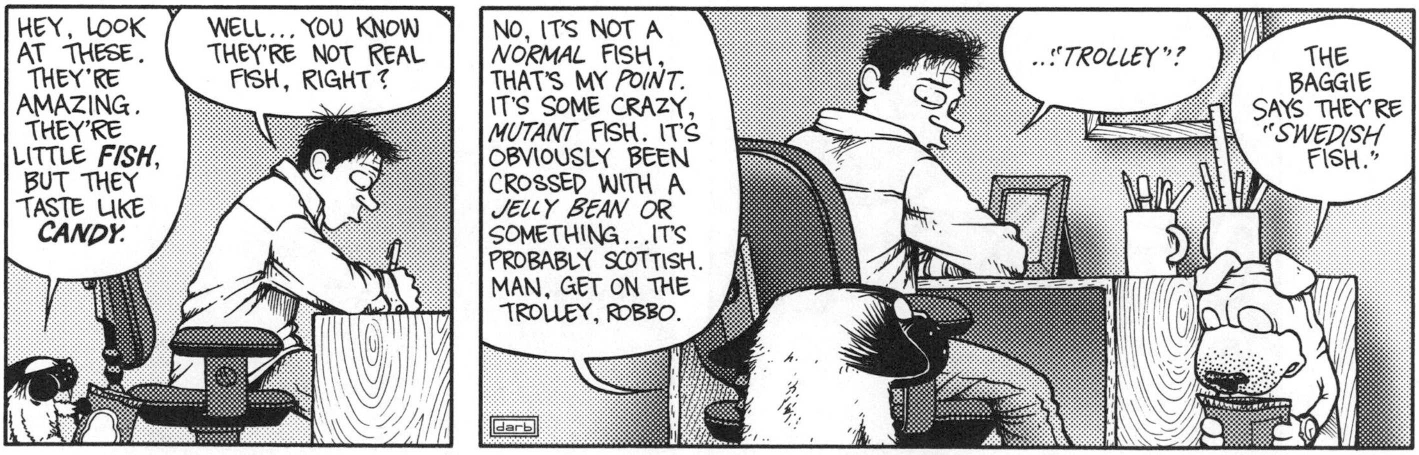
HEY, LOOK AT THESE. THEY'RE AMAZING. THEY'RE LITTLE FISH, BUT THEY TASTE LIKE CANDY.
WELL... YOU KNOW THEY'RE NOT REAL FISH, RIGHT?
NO, IT'S NOT A NORMAL FISH, THAT'S MY POINT. IT'S SOME CRAZY, MUTANT FISH. IT'S OBVIOUSLY BEEN CROSSED WITH A JELLY BEAN OR SOMETHING...IT'S PROBABLY SCOTTISH. MAN, GET ON THE TROLLEY, ROBBO.
..."TROLLEY"?
THE BAGGIE SAYS THEY'RE "SWEDISH FISH."
darb

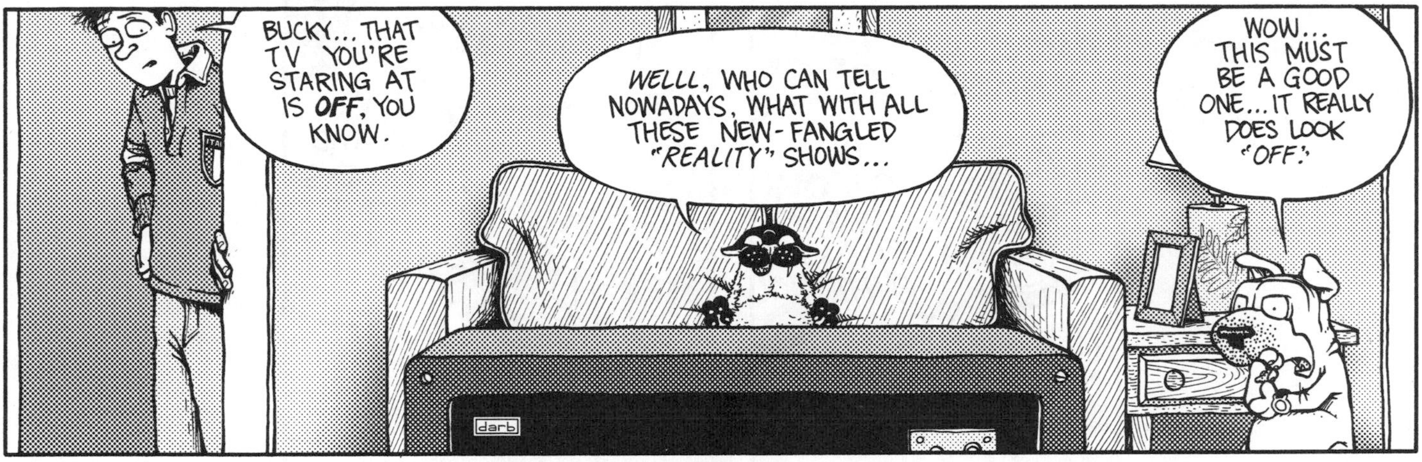
BUCKY... THAT TV YOU'RE STARING AT IS ***OFF***, YOU KNOW.
WELLL, WHO CAN TELL NOWADAYS, WHAT WITH ALL THESE NEW-FANGLED *"REALITY"* SHOWS...
WOW... THIS MUST BE A GOOD ONE... IT REALLY DOES LOOK *"OFF."*
darb

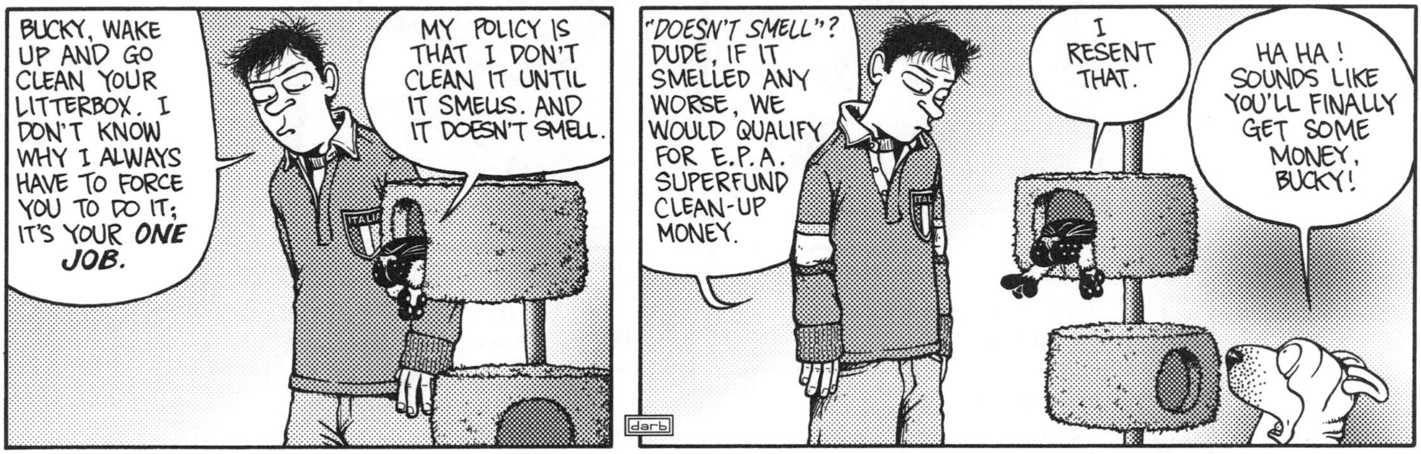
BUCKY, WAKE UP AND GO CLEAN YOUR LITTERBOX. I DON'T KNOW WHY I ALWAYS HAVE TO FORCE YOU TO DO IT; IT'S YOUR ***ONE JOB.***
MY POLICY IS THAT I DON'T CLEAN IT UNTIL IT SMELLS. AND IT DOESN'T SMELL.
"DOESN'T SMELL"? DUDE, IF IT SMELLED ANY WORSE, WE WOULD QUALIFY FOR E.P.A. SUPERFUND CLEAN-UP MONEY.
I RESENT THAT.
HA HA! SOUNDS LIKE YOU'LL FINALLY GET SOME MONEY, BUCKY!
darb

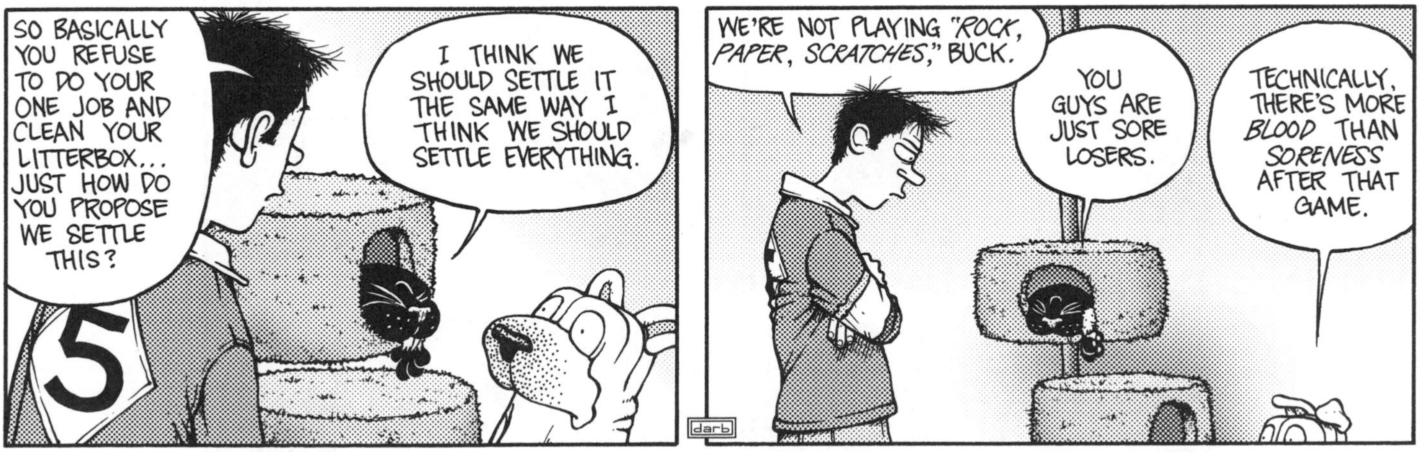
SO BASICALLY YOU REFUSE TO DO YOUR ONE JOB AND CLEAN YOUR LITTERBOX... JUST HOW DO YOU PROPOSE WE SETTLE THIS?
I THINK WE SHOULD SETTLE IT THE SAME WAY I THINK WE SHOULD SETTLE EVERYTHING.
WE'RE NOT PLAYING *"ROCK, PAPER, SCRATCHES,"* BUCK.
YOU GUYS ARE JUST SORE LOSERS.
TECHNICALLY, THERE'S MORE *BLOOD* THAN *SORENESS* AFTER THAT GAME.
darb

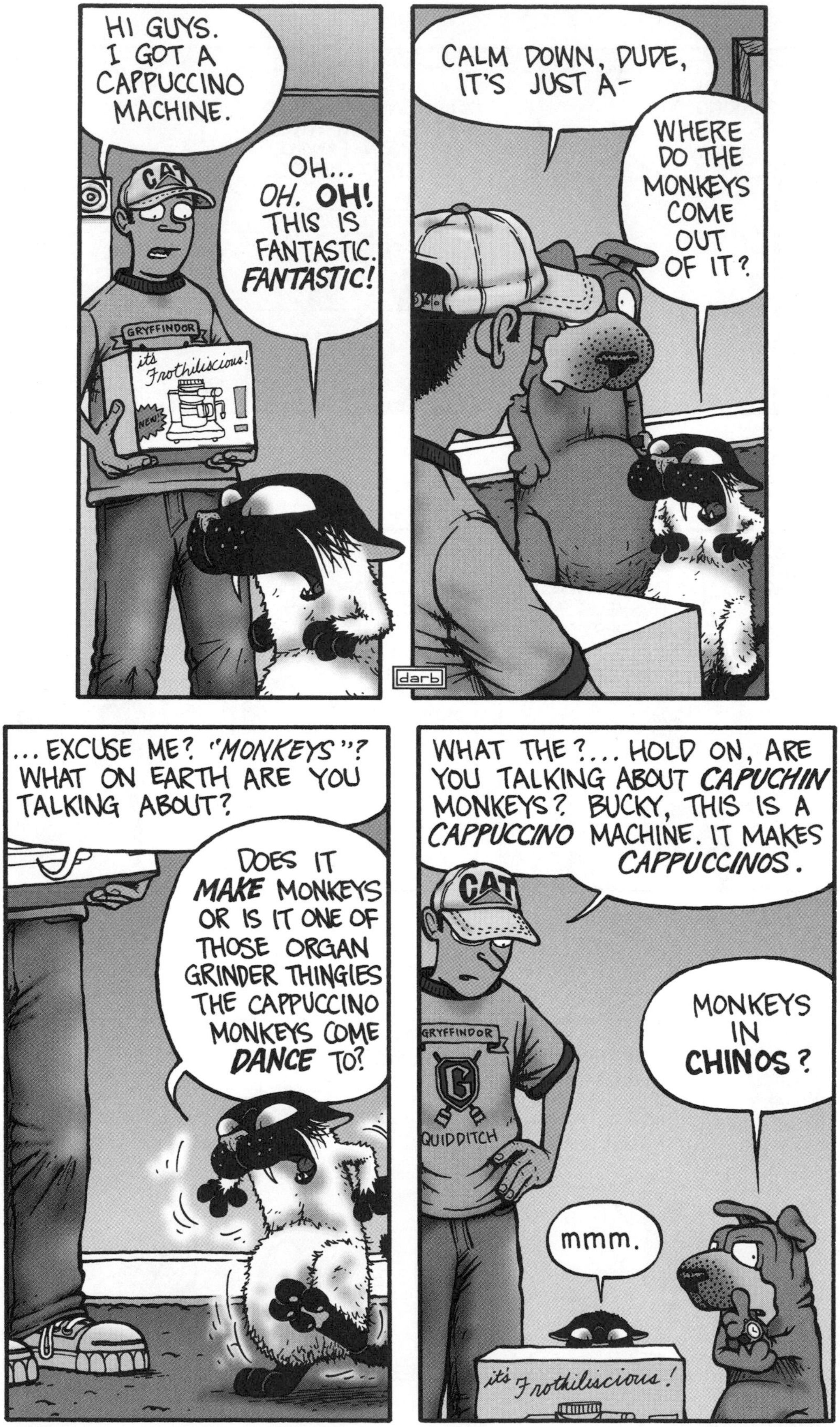
HI GUYS. I GOT A CAPPUCCINO MACHINE.
OH... OH. OH! THIS IS FANTASTIC. FANTASTIC!
it's Frothiliscious!
NEW!
GRYFFINDOR
darb
CALM DOWN, DUDE, IT'S JUST A-
WHERE DO THE MONKEYS COME OUT OF IT?
...EXCUSE ME? "MONKEYS"? WHAT ON EARTH ARE YOU TALKING ABOUT?
DOES IT MAKE MONKEYS OR IS IT ONE OF THOSE ORGAN GRINDER THINGIES THE CAPPUCCINO MONKEYS COME DANCE TO?
WHAT THE?... HOLD ON, ARE YOU TALKING ABOUT CAPUCHIN MONKEYS? BUCKY, THIS IS A CAPPUCCINO MACHINE. IT MAKES CAPPUCCINOS.
MONKEYS IN CHINOS?
mmm.
GRYFFINDOR
QUIDDITCH
it's Frothiliscious!

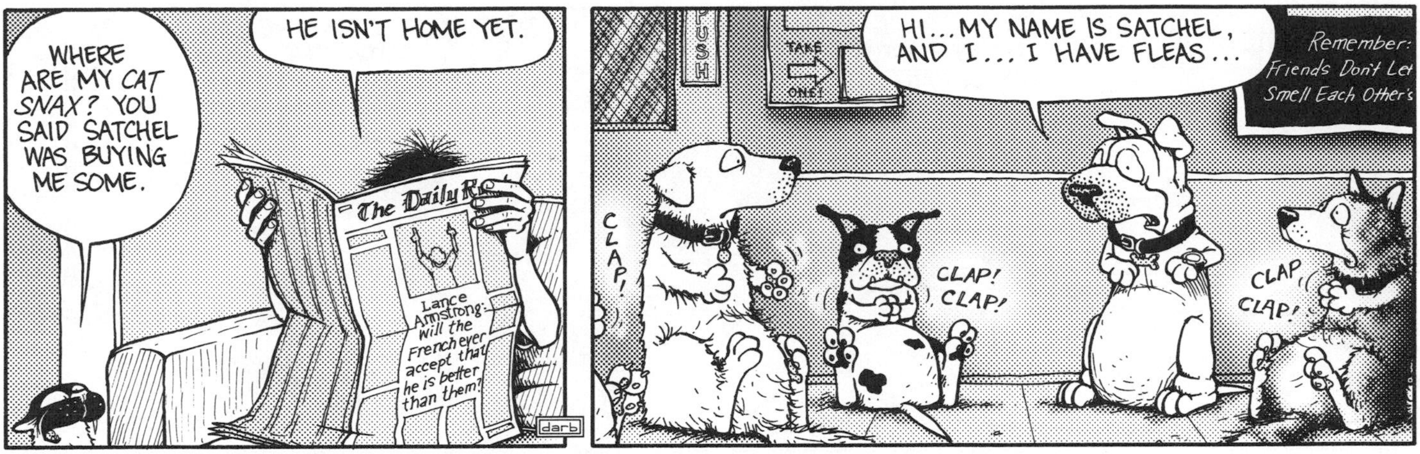
WHERE ARE MY CAT SNAX? YOU SAID SATCHEL WAS BUYING ME SOME.
HE ISN'T HOME YET.
The Daily
Lance Armstrong: will the French ever accept that he is better than them?
darb
PUSH
TAKE ONE
HI... MY NAME IS SATCHEL, AND I... I HAVE FLEAS...
Remember: Friends Don't Let
Smell Each Other's
CLAP!
CLAP! CLAP!
CLAP! CLAP!

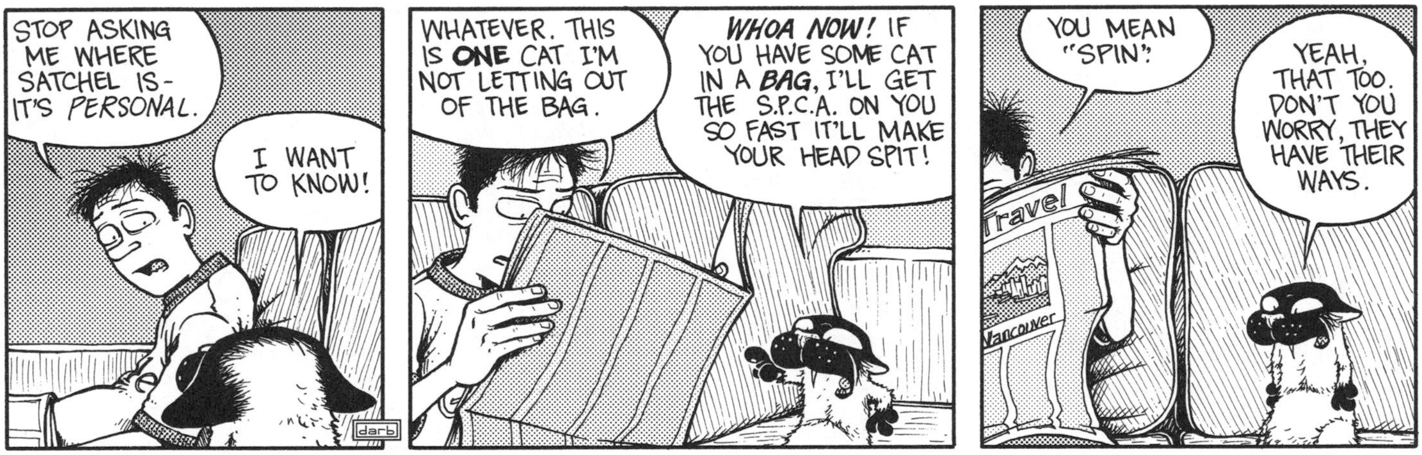
STOP ASKING ME WHERE SATCHEL IS- IT'S PERSONAL.
I WANT TO KNOW!
darb
WHATEVER. THIS IS ONE CAT I'M NOT LETTING OUT OF THE BAG.
WHOA NOW! IF YOU HAVE SOME CAT IN A BAG, I'LL GET THE S.P.C.A. ON YOU SO FAST IT'LL MAKE YOUR HEAD SPIT!
YOU MEAN "SPIN".
YEAH, THAT TOO. DON'T YOU WORRY, THEY HAVE THEIR WAYS.
Travel
Vancouver

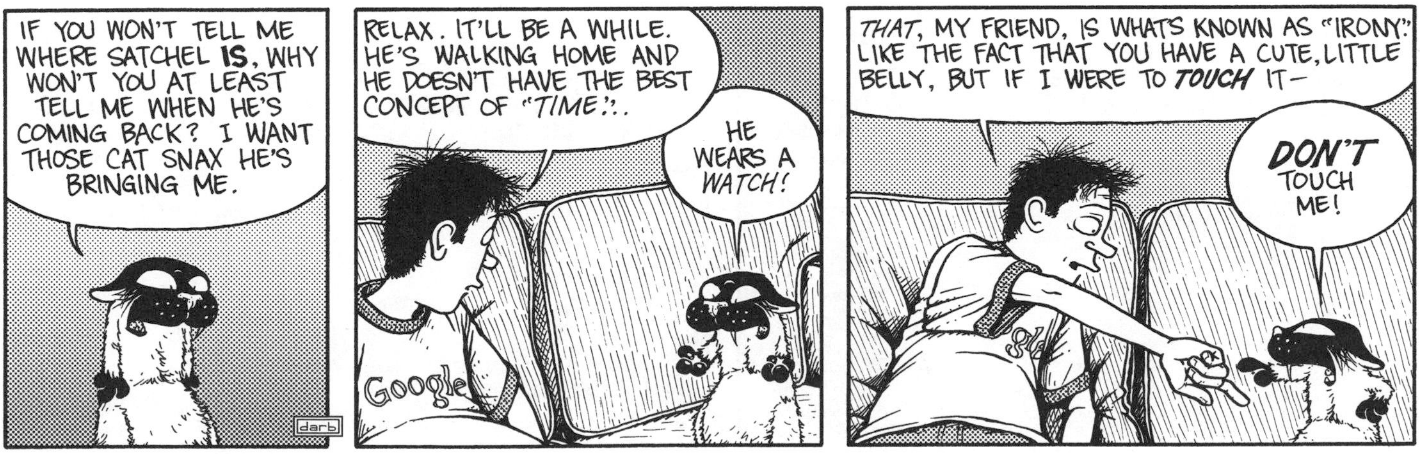
IF YOU WON'T TELL ME WHERE SATCHEL IS, WHY WON'T YOU AT LEAST TELL ME WHEN HE'S COMING BACK? I WANT THOSE CAT SNAX HE'S BRINGING ME.
darb
RELAX. IT'LL BE A WHILE. HE'S WALKING HOME AND HE DOESN'T HAVE THE BEST CONCEPT OF "TIME."
HE WEARS A WATCH!
Google
THAT, MY FRIEND, IS WHAT'S KNOWN AS "IRONY." LIKE THE FACT THAT YOU HAVE A CUTE, LITTLE BELLY, BUT IF I WERE TO TOUCH IT—
DON'T TOUCH ME!

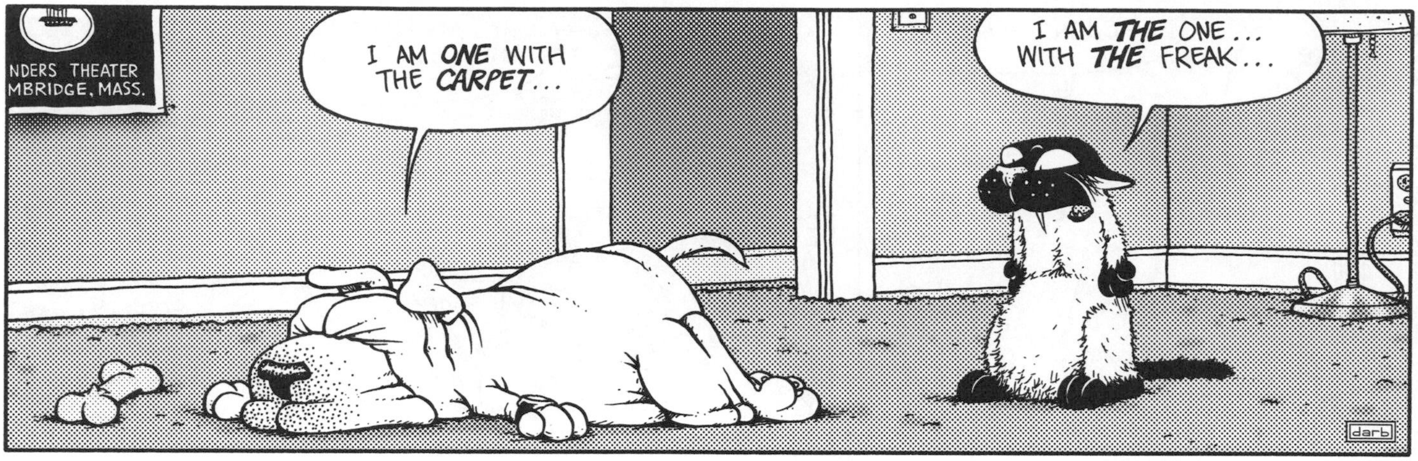
NDERS THEATER
MBRIDGE, MASS.
I AM ONE WITH THE CARPET...
I AM THE ONE... WITH THE FREAK...
darb

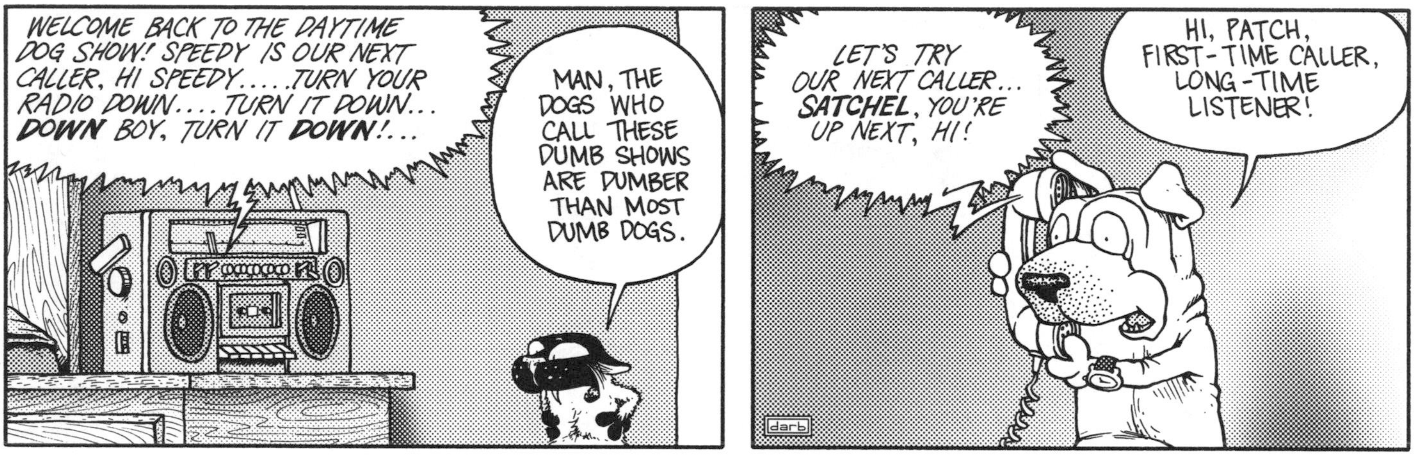
WELCOME BACK TO THE DAYTIME DOG SHOW! SPEEDY IS OUR NEXT CALLER, HI SPEEDY.....TURN YOUR RADIO DOWN....TURN IT DOWN... DOWN BOY, TURN IT DOWN!...
MAN, THE DOGS WHO CALL THESE DUMB SHOWS ARE DUMBER THAN MOST DUMB DOGS.
LET'S TRY OUR NEXT CALLER... SATCHEL, YOU'RE UP NEXT, HI!
HI, PATCH, FIRST-TIME CALLER, LONG-TIME LISTENER!
darb

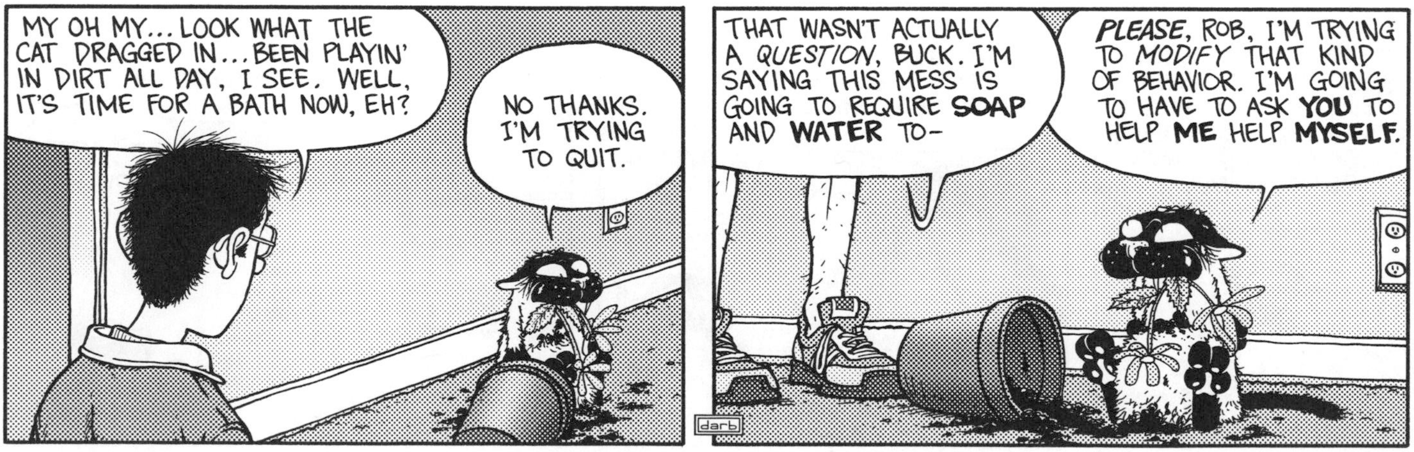
MY OH MY... LOOK WHAT THE CAT DRAGGED IN... BEEN PLAYIN' IN DIRT ALL DAY, I SEE. WELL, IT'S TIME FOR A BATH NOW, EH?
NO THANKS. I'M TRYING TO QUIT.
THAT WASN'T ACTUALLY A QUESTION, BUCK. I'M SAYING THIS MESS IS GOING TO REQUIRE SOAP AND WATER TO-
PLEASE, ROB, I'M TRYING TO MODIFY THAT KIND OF BEHAVIOR. I'M GOING TO HAVE TO ASK YOU TO HELP ME HELP MYSELF.
darb

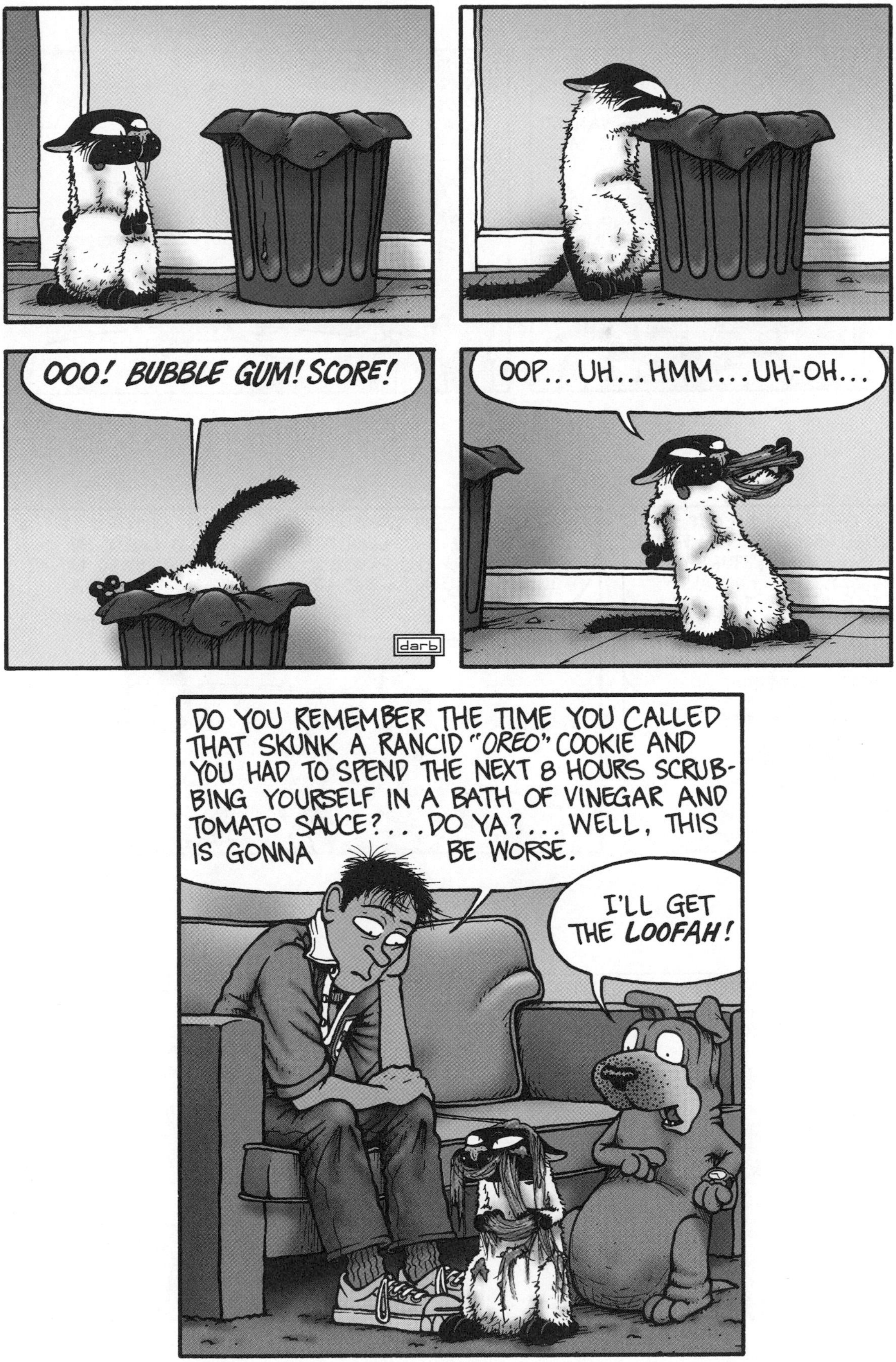
OOO! BUBBLE GUM! SCORE!
OOP... UH... HMM... UH-OH...
darb
DO YOU REMEMBER THE TIME YOU CALLED THAT SKUNK A RANCID "OREO" COOKIE AND YOU HAD TO SPEND THE NEXT 8 HOURS SCRUBBING YOURSELF IN A BATH OF VINEGAR AND TOMATO SAUCE? . . . DO YA? . . . WELL, THIS IS GONNA BE WORSE.
I'LL GET THE LOOFAH!

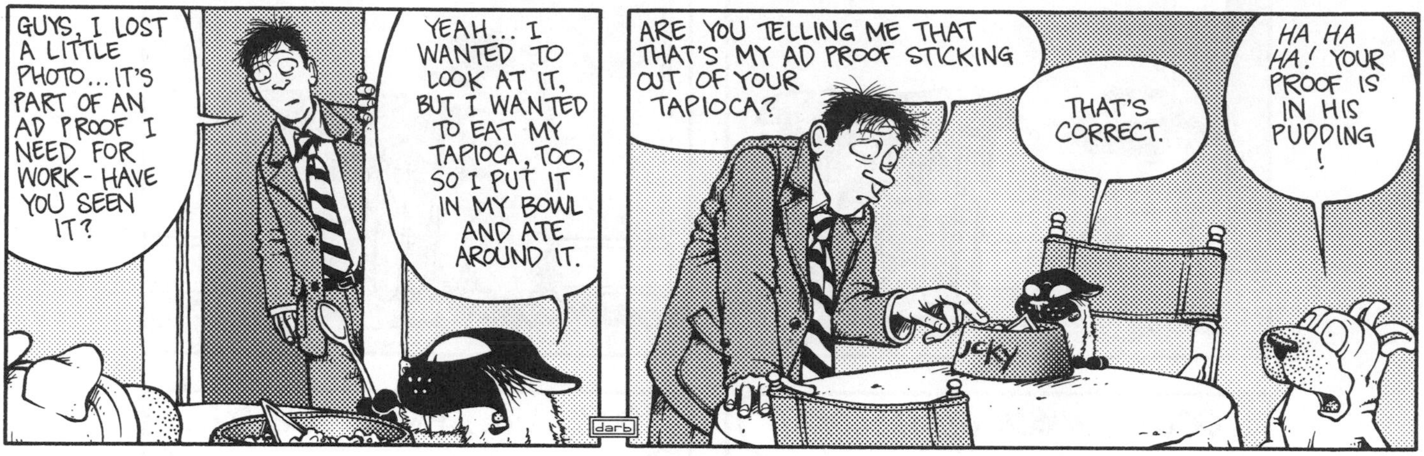
GUYS, I LOST A LITTLE PHOTO... IT'S PART OF AN AD PROOF I NEED FOR WORK- HAVE YOU SEEN IT?
YEAH... I WANTED TO LOOK AT IT, BUT I WANTED TO EAT MY TAPIOCA, TOO, SO I PUT IT IN MY BOWL AND ATE AROUND IT.
darb
ARE YOU TELLING ME THAT THAT'S MY AD PROOF STICKING OUT OF YOUR TAPIOCA?
THAT'S CORRECT.
HA HA HA! YOUR PROOF IS IN HIS PUDDING!

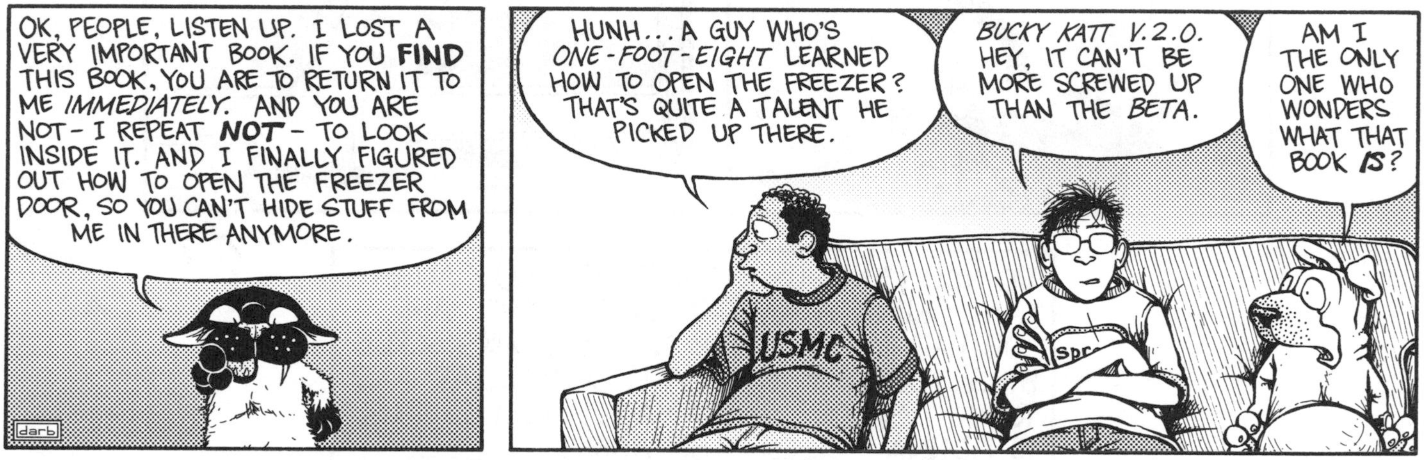
OK, PEOPLE, LISTEN UP. I LOST A VERY IMPORTANT BOOK. IF YOU **FIND** THIS BOOK, YOU ARE TO RETURN IT TO ME *IMMEDIATELY*. AND YOU ARE NOT - I REPEAT **NOT** - TO LOOK INSIDE IT. AND I FINALLY FIGURED OUT HOW TO OPEN THE FREEZER DOOR, SO YOU CAN'T HIDE STUFF FROM ME IN THERE ANYMORE.
darb
HUNH... A GUY WHO'S *ONE-FOOT-EIGHT* LEARNED HOW TO OPEN THE FREEZER? THAT'S QUITE A TALENT HE PICKED UP THERE.
USMC
BUCKY KATT V.2.0. HEY, IT CAN'T BE MORE SCREWED UP THAN THE *BETA*.
AM I THE ONLY ONE WHO WONDERS WHAT THAT BOOK ***IS***?

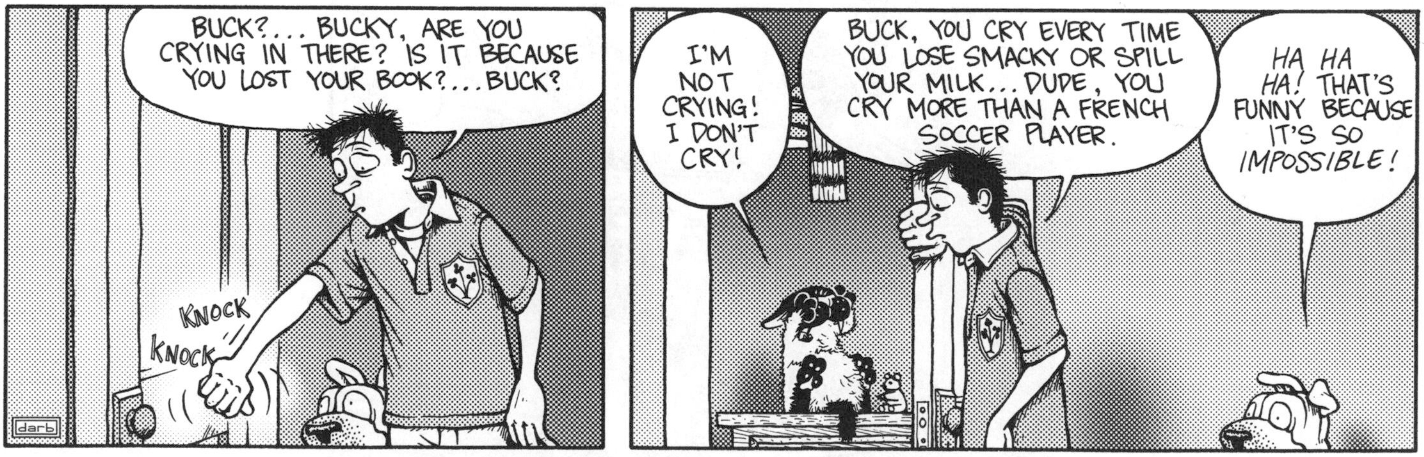
BUCK?... BUCKY, ARE YOU CRYING IN THERE? IS IT BECAUSE YOU LOST YOUR BOOK?... BUCK?
KNOCK
KNOCK
darb
I'M NOT CRYING! I DON'T CRY!
BUCK, YOU CRY EVERY TIME YOU LOSE SMACKY OR SPILL YOUR MILK... DUDE, YOU CRY MORE THAN A FRENCH SOCCER PLAYER.
HA HA HA! THAT'S FUNNY BECAUSE IT'S SO *IMPOSSIBLE*!

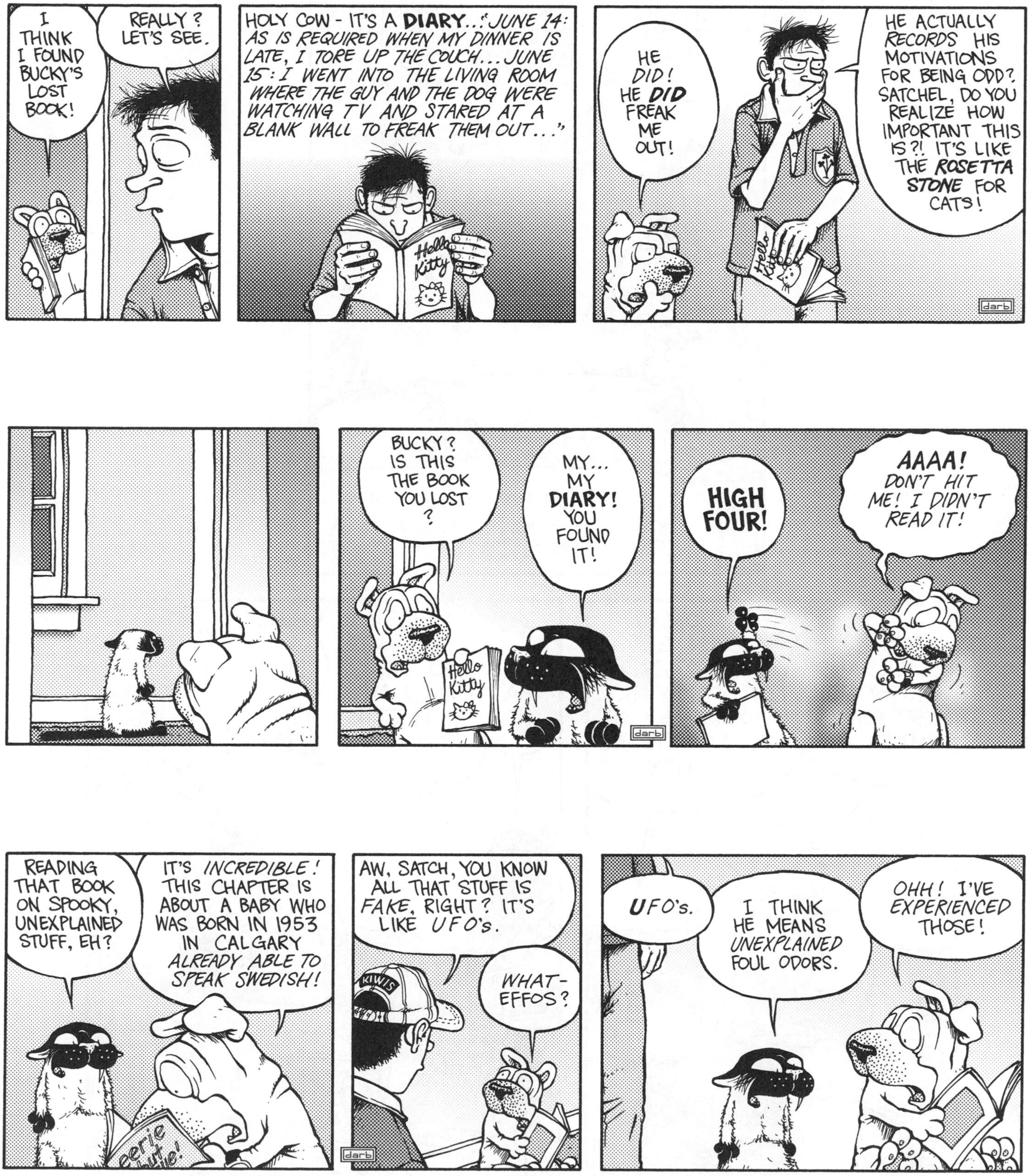
I THINK I FOUND BUCKY'S LOST BOOK!
REALLY? LET'S SEE.
HOLY COW - IT'S A **DIARY**... "JUNE 14: AS IS REQUIRED WHEN MY DINNER IS LATE, I TORE UP THE COUCH... JUNE 15: I WENT INTO THE LIVING ROOM WHERE THE GUY AND THE DOG WERE WATCHING TV AND STARED AT A BLANK WALL TO FREAK THEM OUT..."
Hello Kitty
HE DID! HE **DID** FREAK ME OUT!
HE ACTUALLY RECORDS HIS MOTIVATIONS FOR BEING ODD? SATCHEL, DO YOU REALIZE HOW IMPORTANT THIS IS?! IT'S LIKE THE **ROSETTA STONE** FOR CATS!
darb
BUCKY? IS THIS THE BOOK YOU LOST?
MY... MY **DIARY!** YOU FOUND IT!
Hello Kitty
darb
HIGH FOUR!
AAAA! DON'T HIT ME! I DIDN'T READ IT!
READING THAT BOOK ON SPOOKY, UNEXPLAINED STUFF, EH?
IT'S INCREDIBLE! THIS CHAPTER IS ABOUT A BABY WHO WAS BORN IN 1953 IN CALGARY ALREADY ABLE TO SPEAK SWEDISH!
eerie but true!
darb
AW, SATCH, YOU KNOW ALL THAT STUFF IS FAKE, RIGHT? IT'S LIKE UFO's.
KIWIS
WHAT-EFFOS?
UFO's.
I THINK HE MEANS UNEXPLAINED FOUL ODORS.
OHH! I'VE EXPERIENCED THOSE!

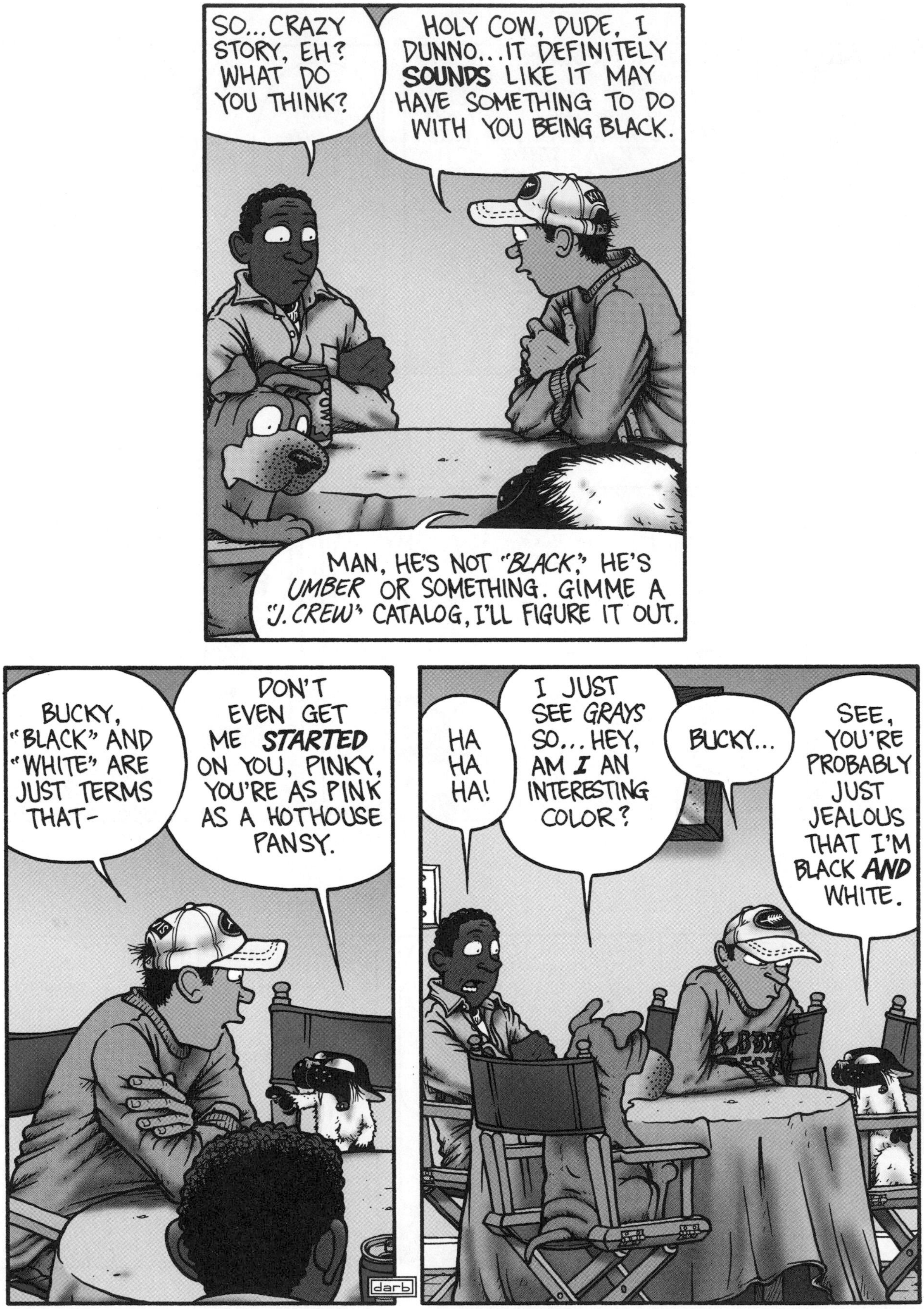
SO...CRAZY STORY, EH? WHAT DO YOU THINK?
HOLY COW, DUDE, I DUNNO...IT DEFINITELY SOUNDS LIKE IT MAY HAVE SOMETHING TO DO WITH YOU BEING BLACK.
MAN, HE'S NOT "BLACK," HE'S UMBER OR SOMETHING. GIMME A "J. CREW" CATALOG, I'LL FIGURE IT OUT.
BUCKY, "BLACK" AND "WHITE" ARE JUST TERMS THAT-
DON'T EVEN GET ME STARTED ON YOU, PINKY, YOU'RE AS PINK AS A HOTHOUSE PANSY.
darb
HA HA HA!
I JUST SEE GRAYS SO... HEY, AM I AN INTERESTING COLOR?
BUCKY...
SEE, YOU'RE PROBABLY JUST JEALOUS THAT I'M BLACK AND WHITE.

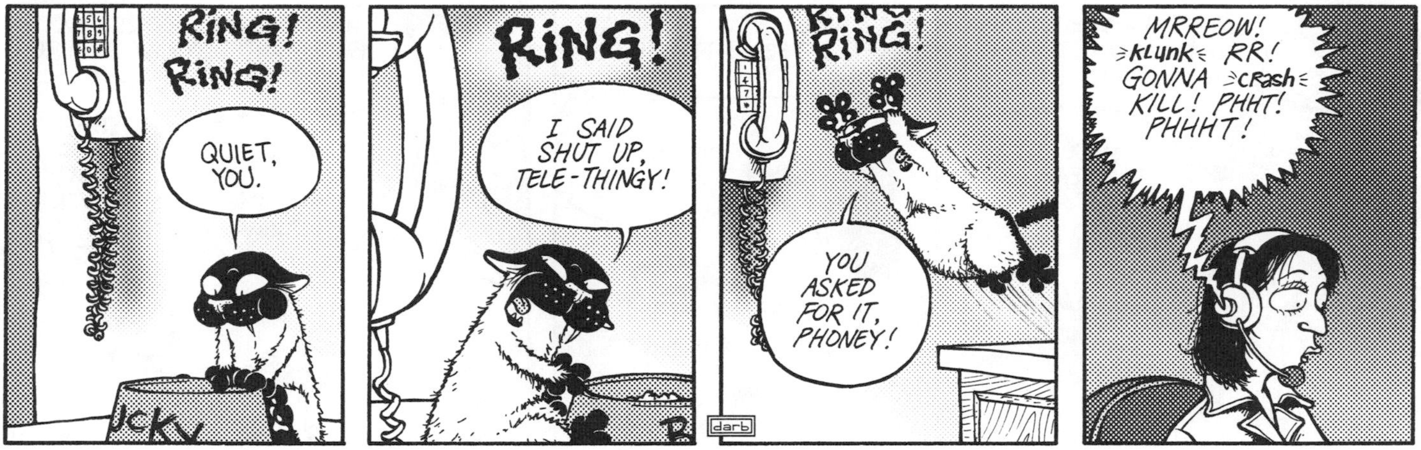
RING!
RING!
QUIET, YOU.
RING!
I SAID SHUT UP, TELE-THINGY!
RING!
YOU ASKED FOR IT, PHONEY!
darb
MRREOW! klunk RR! GONNA crash KILL! PHHT! PHHHT!

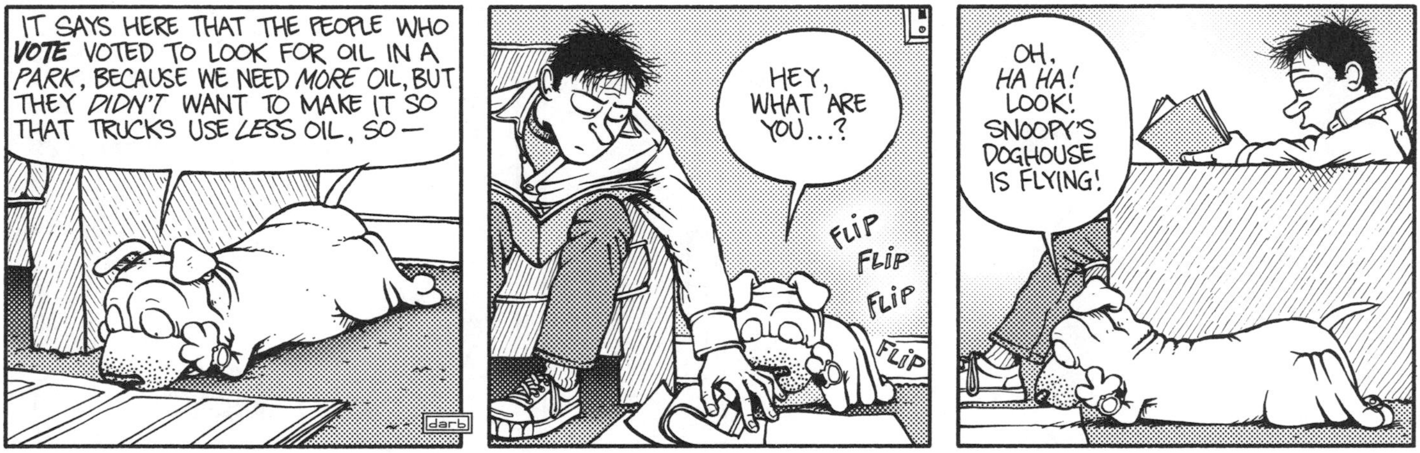
IT SAYS HERE THAT THE PEOPLE WHO VOTE VOTED TO LOOK FOR OIL IN A PARK, BECAUSE WE NEED MORE OIL, BUT THEY DIDN'T WANT TO MAKE IT SO THAT TRUCKS USE LESS OIL, SO—
darb
HEY, WHAT ARE YOU...?
FLIP
FLIP
FLIP
FLIP
OH, HA HA! LOOK! SNOOPY'S DOGHOUSE IS FLYING!

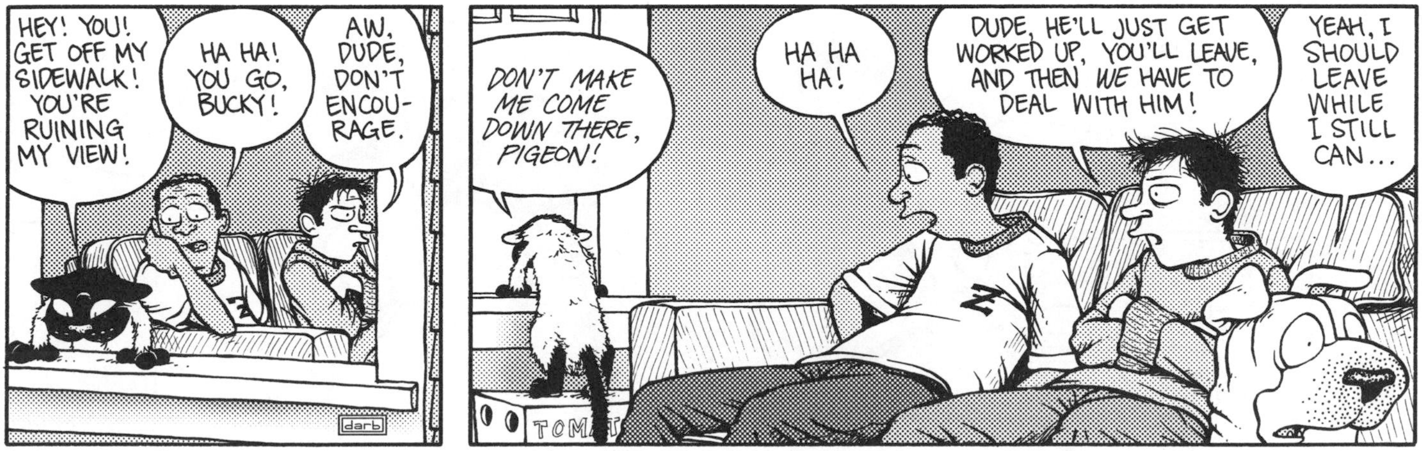
HEY! YOU! GET OFF MY SIDEWALK! YOU'RE RUINING MY VIEW!
HA HA! YOU GO, BUCKY!
AW, DUDE, DON'T ENCOU-RAGE.
darb
DON'T MAKE ME COME DOWN THERE, PIGEON!
HA HA HA!
DUDE, HE'LL JUST GET WORKED UP, YOU'LL LEAVE, AND THEN WE HAVE TO DEAL WITH HIM!
YEAH, I SHOULD LEAVE WHILE I STILL CAN...

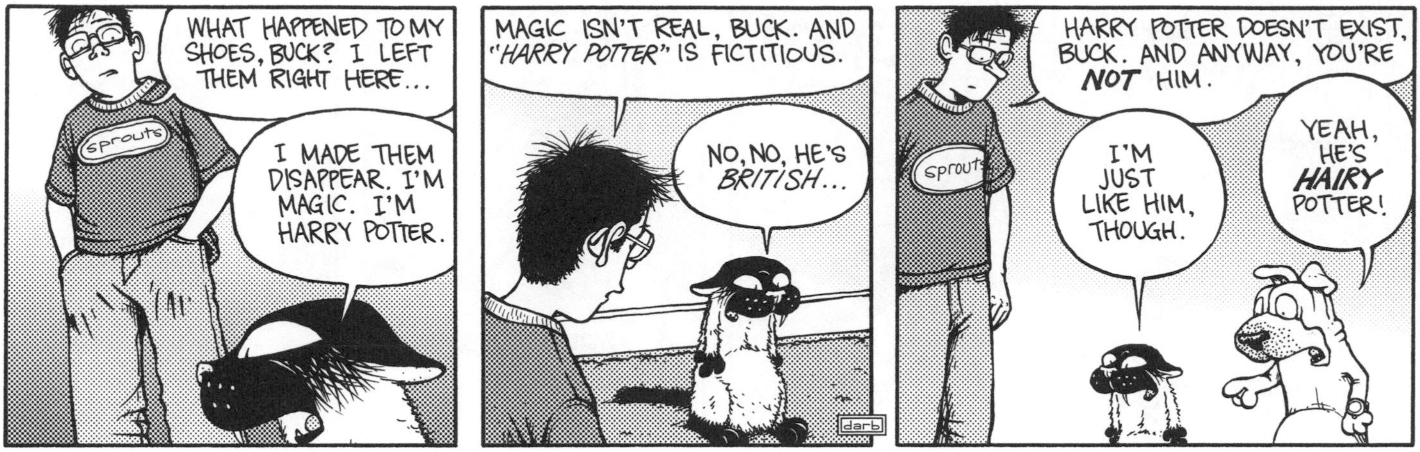
WHAT HAPPENED TO MY SHOES, BUCK? I LEFT THEM RIGHT HERE...
I MADE THEM DISAPPEAR. I'M MAGIC. I'M HARRY POTTER.
MAGIC ISN'T REAL, BUCK. AND "HARRY POTTER" IS FICTITIOUS.
NO, NO, HE'S BRITISH...
HARRY POTTER DOESN'T EXIST, BUCK. AND ANYWAY, YOU'RE NOT HIM.
I'M JUST LIKE HIM, THOUGH.
YEAH, HE'S HAIRY POTTER!
darb

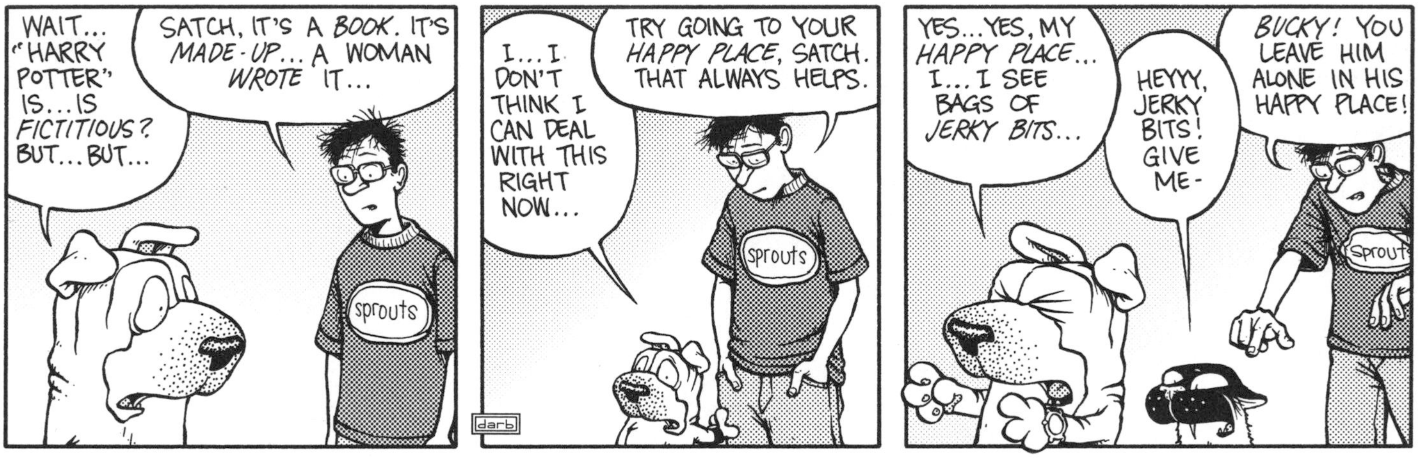
WAIT... "HARRY POTTER" IS... IS FICTITIOUS? BUT... BUT...
SATCH, IT'S A BOOK. IT'S MADE-UP... A WOMAN WROTE IT...
I... I DON'T THINK I CAN DEAL WITH THIS RIGHT NOW...
TRY GOING TO YOUR HAPPY PLACE, SATCH. THAT ALWAYS HELPS.
darb
YES... YES, MY HAPPY PLACE... I... I SEE BAGS OF JERKY BITS...
HEYYY, JERKY BITS! GIVE ME-
BUCKY! YOU LEAVE HIM ALONE IN HIS HAPPY PLACE!

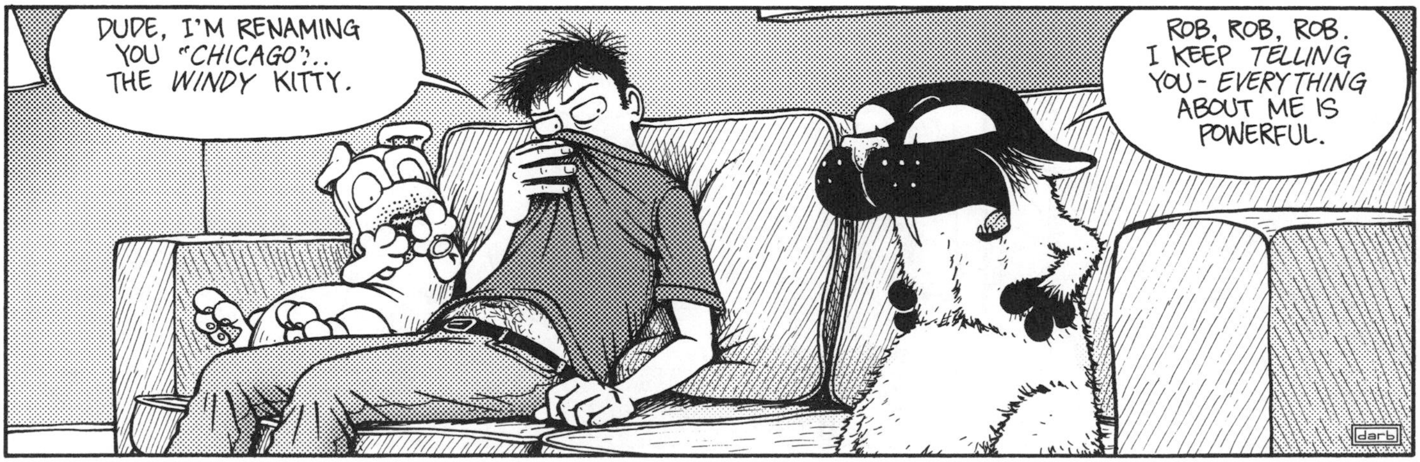
DUDE, I'M RENAMING YOU "CHICAGO"... THE WINDY KITTY.
ROB, ROB, ROB. I KEEP TELLING YOU- EVERYTHING ABOUT ME IS POWERFUL.
darb

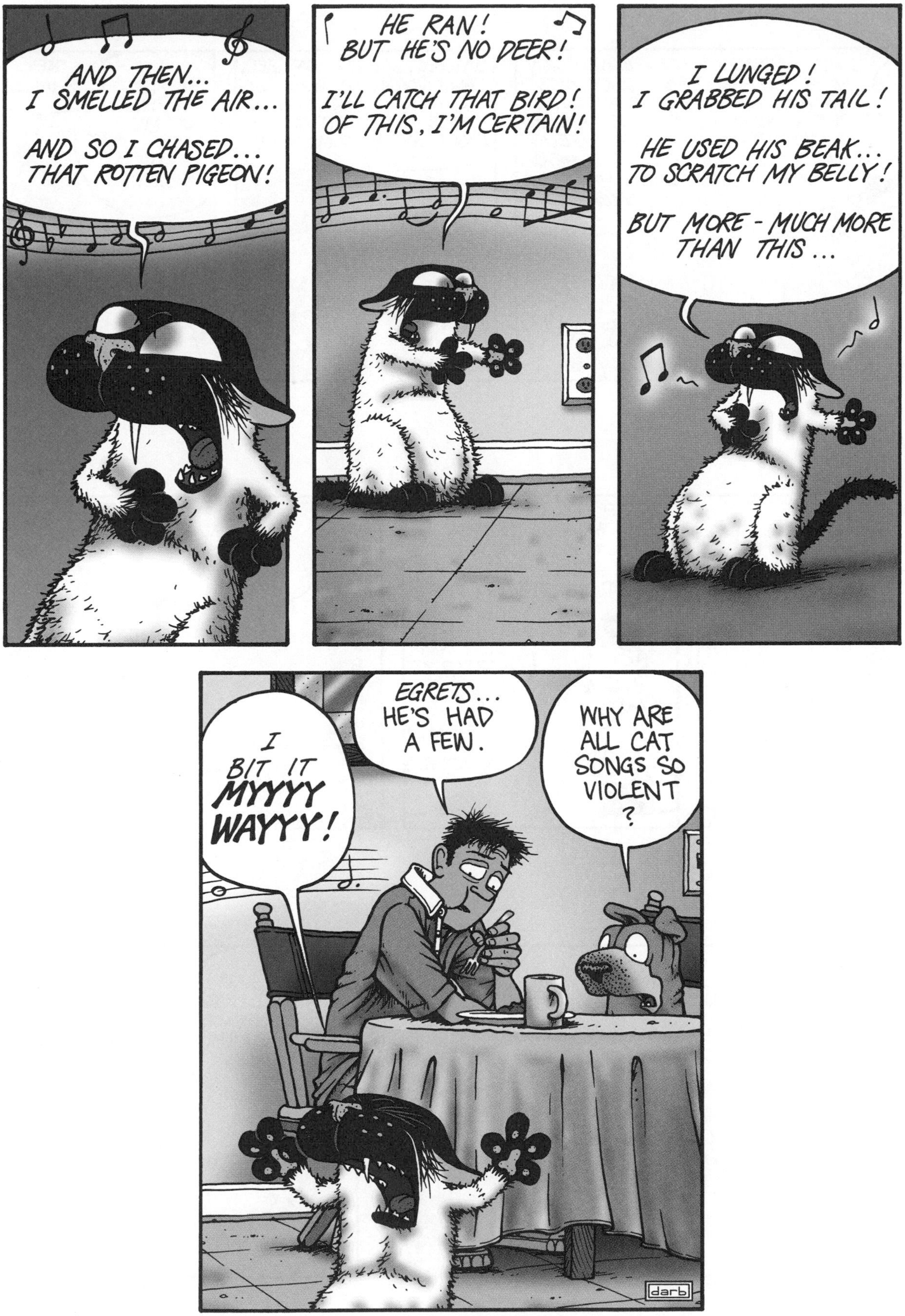
AND THEN... I SMELLED THE AIR... AND SO I CHASED... THAT ROTTEN PIGEON!
HE RAN! BUT HE'S NO DEER! I'LL CATCH THAT BIRD! OF THIS, I'M CERTAIN!
I LUNGED! I GRABBED HIS TAIL! HE USED HIS BEAK... TO SCRATCH MY BELLY! BUT MORE - MUCH MORE THAN THIS...
I BIT IT MYYYY WAYYY!
EGRETS... HE'S HAD A FEW.
WHY ARE ALL CAT SONGS SO VIOLENT ?
darb

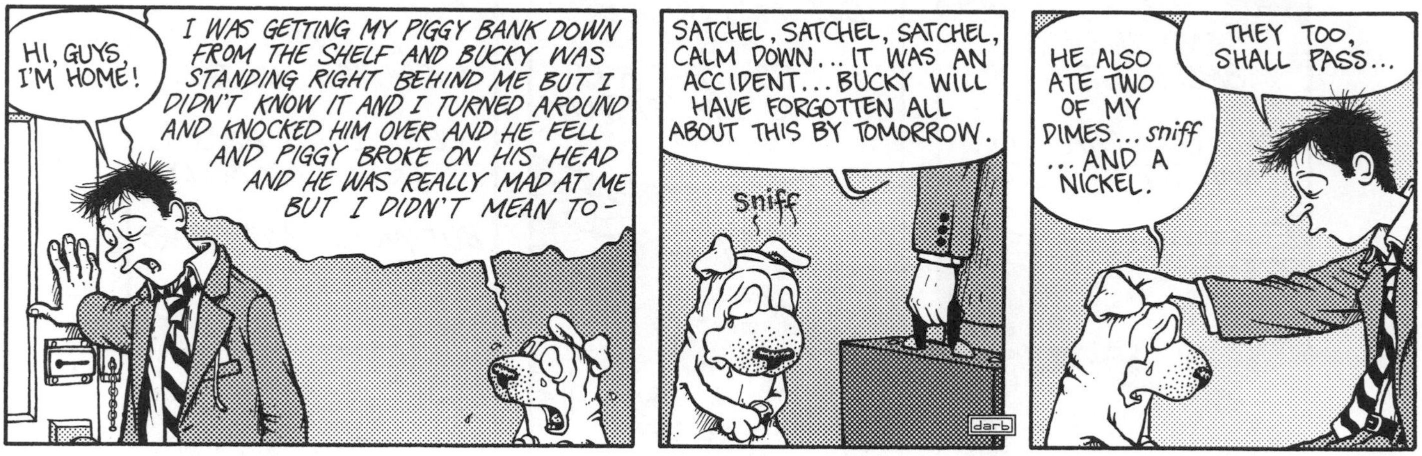
HI, GUYS, I'M HOME!
I WAS GETTING MY PIGGY BANK DOWN FROM THE SHELF AND BUCKY WAS STANDING RIGHT BEHIND ME BUT I DIDN'T KNOW IT AND I TURNED AROUND AND KNOCKED HIM OVER AND HE FELL AND PIGGY BROKE ON HIS HEAD AND HE WAS REALLY MAD AT ME BUT I DIDN'T MEAN TO-
SATCHEL, SATCHEL, SATCHEL, CALM DOWN... IT WAS AN ACCIDENT... BUCKY WILL HAVE FORGOTTEN ALL ABOUT THIS BY TOMORROW.
sniff
darb
HE ALSO ATE TWO OF MY DIMES... sniff ... AND A NICKEL.
THEY TOO, SHALL PASS...

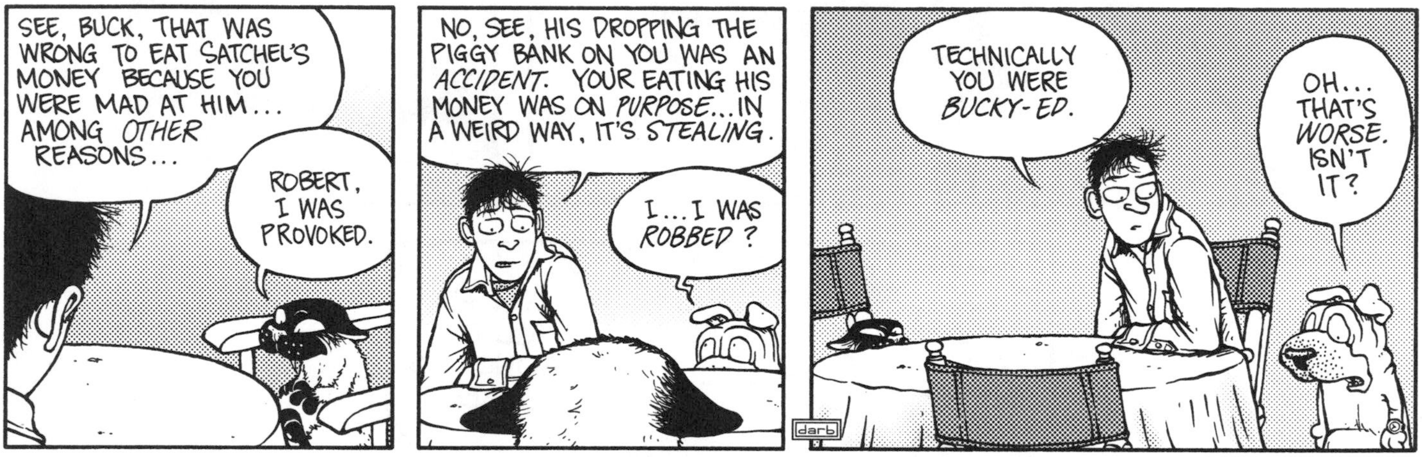
SEE, BUCK, THAT WAS WRONG TO EAT SATCHEL'S MONEY BECAUSE YOU WERE MAD AT HIM... AMONG OTHER REASONS...
ROBERT, I WAS PROVOKED.
NO, SEE, HIS DROPPING THE PIGGY BANK ON YOU WAS AN ACCIDENT. YOUR EATING HIS MONEY WAS ON PURPOSE... IN A WEIRD WAY, IT'S STEALING.
I... I WAS ROBBED?
darb
TECHNICALLY YOU WERE BUCKY-ED.
OH... THAT'S WORSE. ISN'T IT?

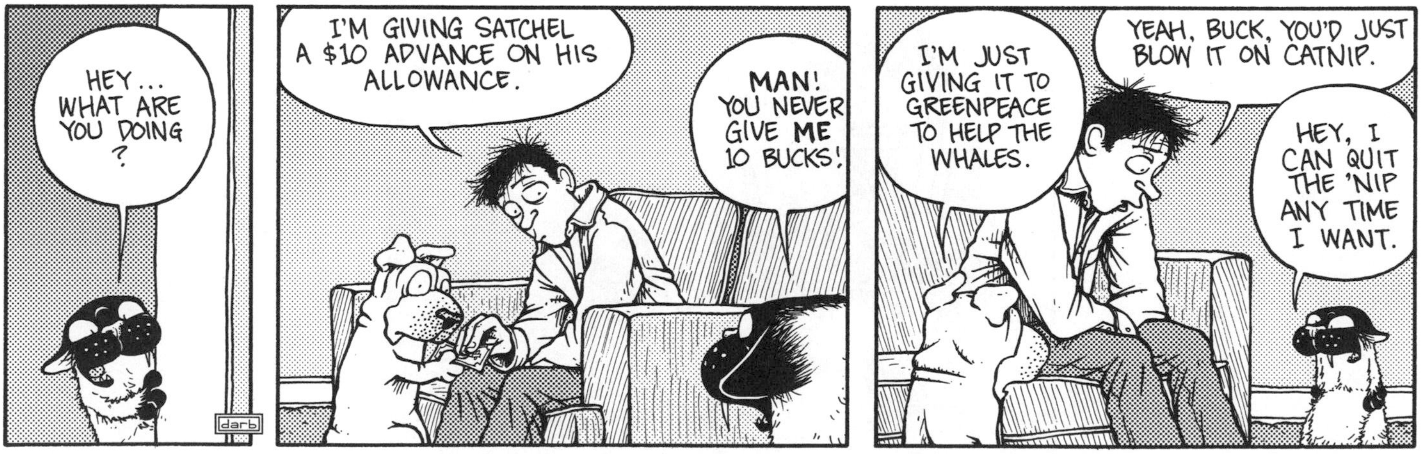
HEY... WHAT ARE YOU DOING?
darb
I'M GIVING SATCHEL A $10 ADVANCE ON HIS ALLOWANCE.
MAN! YOU NEVER GIVE ME 10 BUCKS!
I'M JUST GIVING IT TO GREENPEACE TO HELP THE WHALES.
YEAH, BUCK, YOU'D JUST BLOW IT ON CATNIP.
HEY, I CAN QUIT THE 'NIP ANY TIME I WANT.

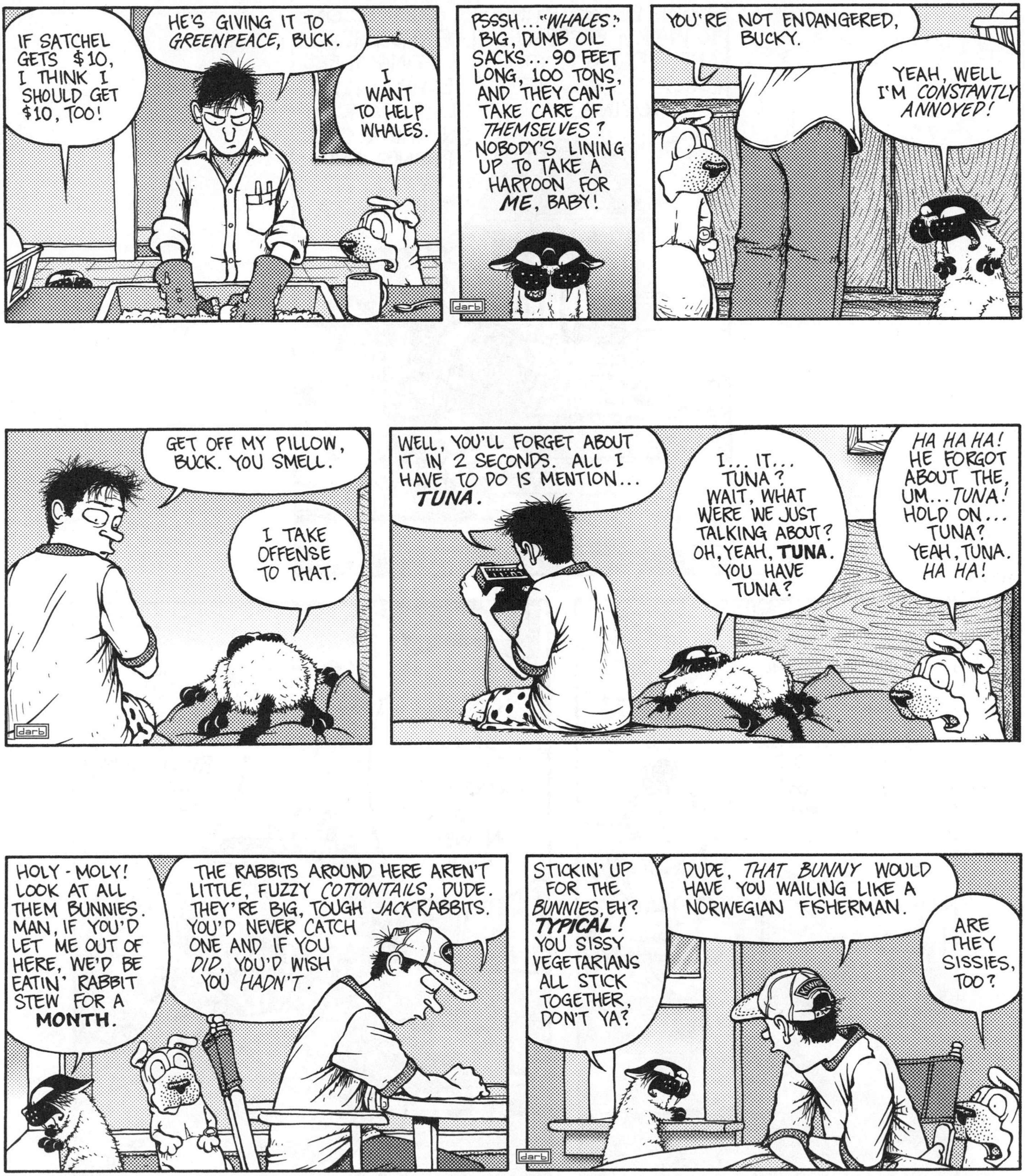

IF SATCHEL GETS $10, I THINK I SHOULD GET $10, TOO!
HE'S GIVING IT TO *GREENPEACE*, BUCK.
I WANT TO HELP WHALES.
PSSSH..."*WHALES*." BIG, DUMB OIL SACKS... 90 FEET LONG, 100 TONS, AND THEY CAN'T TAKE CARE OF *THEMSELVES*? NOBODY'S LINING UP TO TAKE A HARPOON FOR **ME**, BABY!
darb
YOU'RE NOT ENDANGERED, BUCKY.
YEAH, WELL I'M *CONSTANTLY ANNOYED!*
GET OFF MY PILLOW, BUCK. YOU SMELL.
I TAKE OFFENSE TO THAT.
darb
WELL, YOU'LL FORGET ABOUT IT IN 2 SECONDS. ALL I HAVE TO DO IS MENTION... ***TUNA***.
I... IT... TUNA? WAIT, WHAT WERE WE JUST TALKING ABOUT? OH, YEAH, **TUNA**. YOU HAVE TUNA?
HA HA HA! HE FORGOT ABOUT THE, UM... *TUNA!* HOLD ON... TUNA? YEAH, TUNA. *HA HA!*
HOLY-MOLY! LOOK AT ALL THEM BUNNIES. MAN, IF YOU'D LET ME OUT OF HERE, WE'D BE EATIN' RABBIT STEW FOR A **MONTH**.
THE RABBITS AROUND HERE AREN'T LITTLE, FUZZY *COTTONTAILS*, DUDE. THEY'RE BIG, TOUGH *JACK* RABBITS. YOU'D NEVER CATCH ONE AND IF YOU *DID*, YOU'D WISH YOU *HADN'T*.
darb
STICKIN' UP FOR THE *BUNNIES*, EH? ***TYPICAL!*** YOU SISSY VEGETARIANS ALL STICK TOGETHER, DON'T YA?
DUDE, *THAT BUNNY* WOULD HAVE YOU WAILING LIKE A NORWEGIAN FISHERMAN.
ARE THEY SISSIES, TOO?

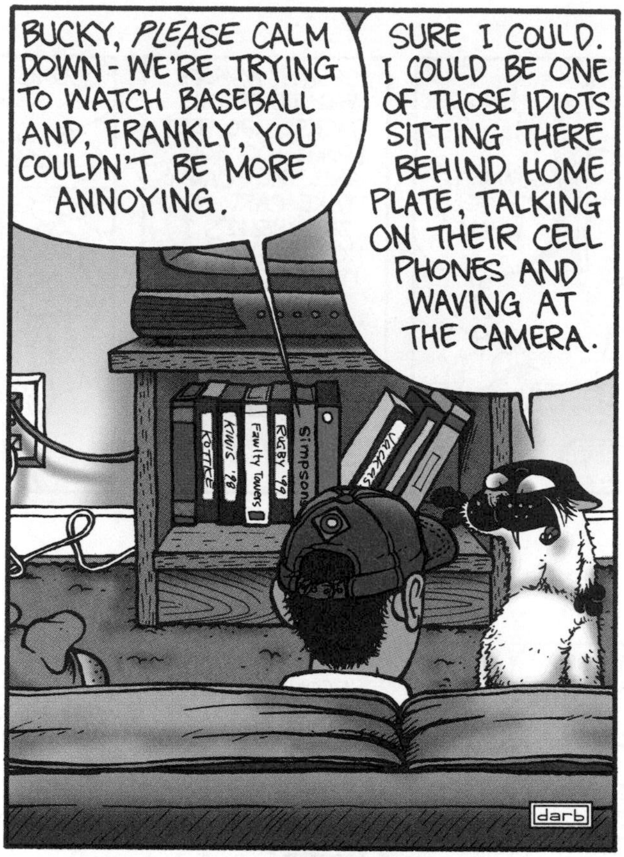
BUCKY, *PLEASE* CALM DOWN - WE'RE TRYING TO WATCH BASEBALL AND, FRANKLY, YOU COULDN'T BE MORE ANNOYING.
SURE I COULD. I COULD BE ONE OF THOSE IDIOTS SITTING THERE BEHIND HOME PLATE, TALKING ON THEIR CELL PHONES AND WAVING AT THE CAMERA.
KOTTKE
KIWIS '98
Fawlty Towers
RUGBY '99
Simpsons
Jackass
darb

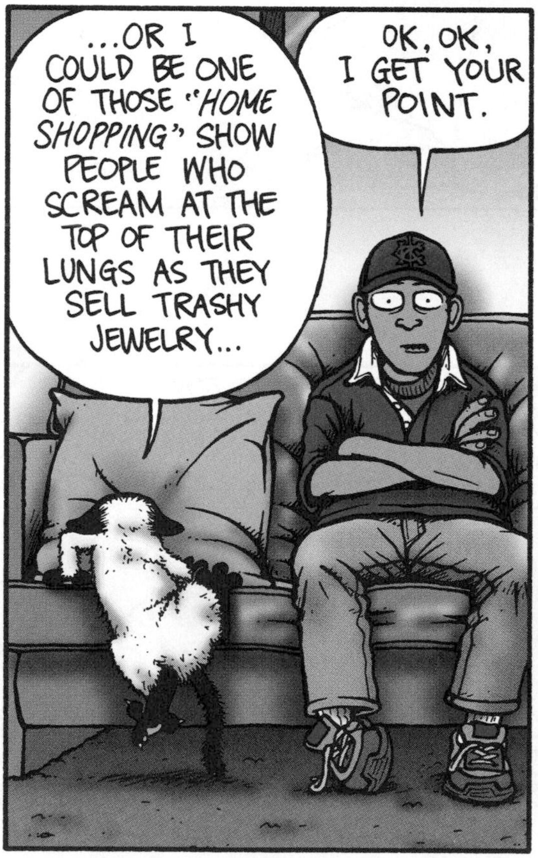
...OR I COULD BE ONE OF THOSE *"HOME SHOPPING"* SHOW PEOPLE WHO SCREAM AT THE TOP OF THEIR LUNGS AS THEY SELL TRASHY JEWELRY...
OK, OK, I GET YOUR POINT.

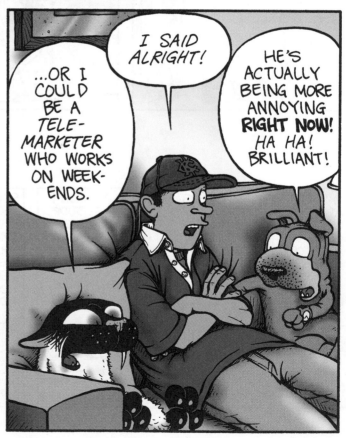

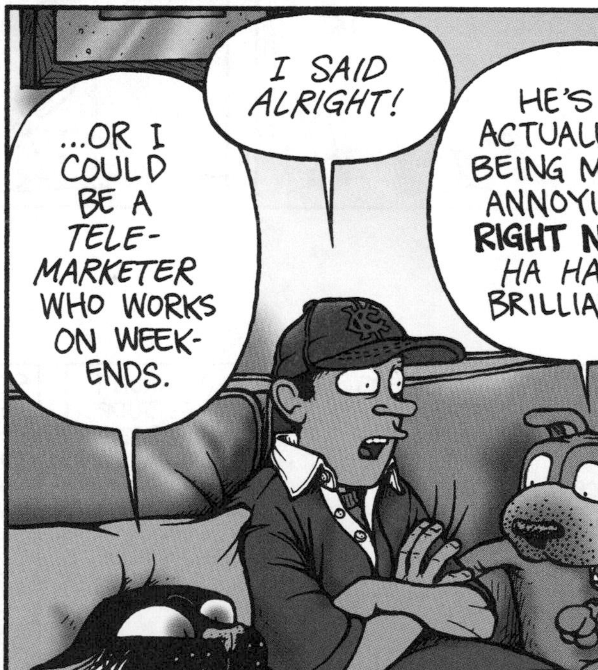
...OR I COULD BE A *TELE-MARKETER* WHO WORKS ON WEEK-ENDS.
I SAID ALRIGHT!
HE'S ACTUALLY BEING MORE ANNOYING **RIGHT NOW!** *HA HA! BRILLIANT!*

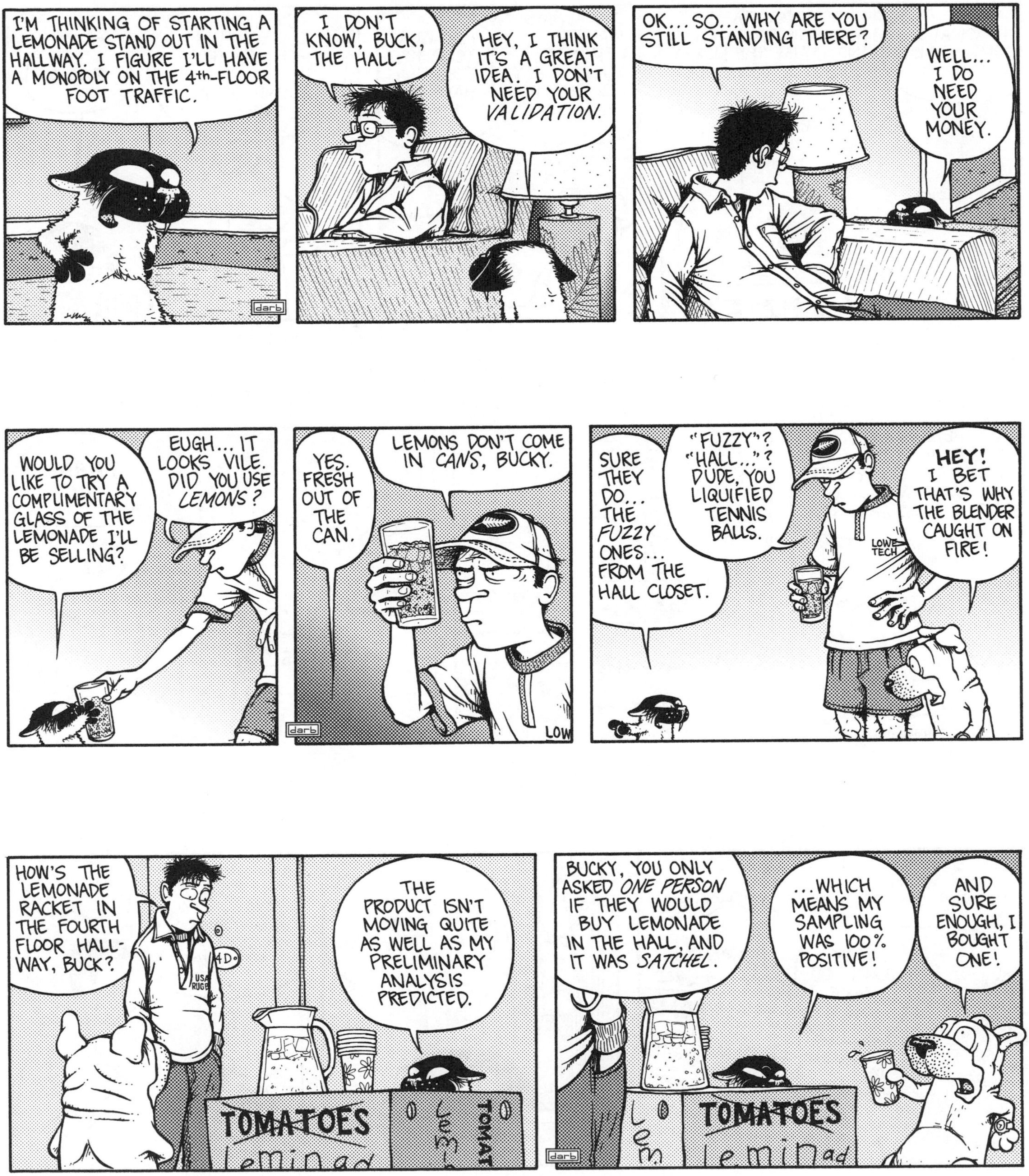
I'M THINKING OF STARTING A LEMONADE STAND OUT IN THE HALLWAY. I FIGURE I'LL HAVE A MONOPOLY ON THE 4th-FLOOR FOOT TRAFFIC.
I DON'T KNOW, BUCK, THE HALL-
HEY, I THINK IT'S A GREAT IDEA. I DON'T NEED YOUR *VALIDATION.*
OK... SO... WHY ARE YOU STILL STANDING THERE?
WELL... I DO NEED YOUR MONEY.
darb
WOULD YOU LIKE TO TRY A COMPLIMENTARY GLASS OF THE LEMONADE I'LL BE SELLING?
EUGH... IT LOOKS VILE. DID YOU USE *LEMONS?*
YES. FRESH OUT OF THE CAN.
LEMONS DON'T COME IN *CANS,* BUCKY.
SURE THEY DO... THE *FUZZY* ONES... FROM THE HALL CLOSET.
"FUZZY"? "HALL..."? DUDE, YOU LIQUIFIED TENNIS BALLS.
HEY! I BET THAT'S WHY THE BLENDER CAUGHT ON FIRE!
LOWE TECH
darb
HOW'S THE LEMONADE RACKET IN THE FOURTH FLOOR HALLWAY, BUCK?
THE PRODUCT ISN'T MOVING QUITE AS WELL AS MY PRELIMINARY ANALYSIS PREDICTED.
TOMATOES
leminad
BUCKY, YOU ONLY ASKED *ONE PERSON* IF THEY WOULD BUY LEMONADE IN THE HALL, AND IT WAS *SATCHEL.*
...WHICH MEANS MY SAMPLING WAS 100% POSITIVE!
AND SURE ENOUGH, I BOUGHT ONE!
TOMATOES
leminad
darb

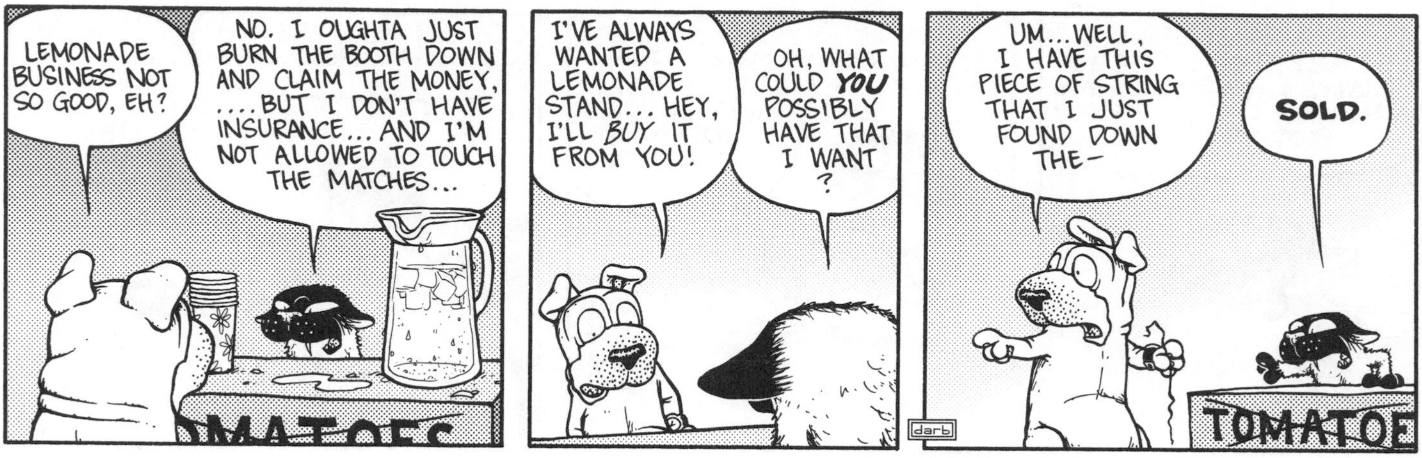
LEMONADE BUSINESS NOT SO GOOD, EH?
NO. I OUGHTA JUST BURN THE BOOTH DOWN AND CLAIM THE MONEY, ...BUT I DON'T HAVE INSURANCE... AND I'M NOT ALLOWED TO TOUCH THE MATCHES...
TOMATOES
I'VE ALWAYS WANTED A LEMONADE STAND... HEY, I'LL BUY IT FROM YOU!
OH, WHAT COULD YOU POSSIBLY HAVE THAT I WANT ?
UM...WELL, I HAVE THIS PIECE OF STRING THAT I JUST FOUND DOWN THE–
SOLD.
darb
TOMATOE

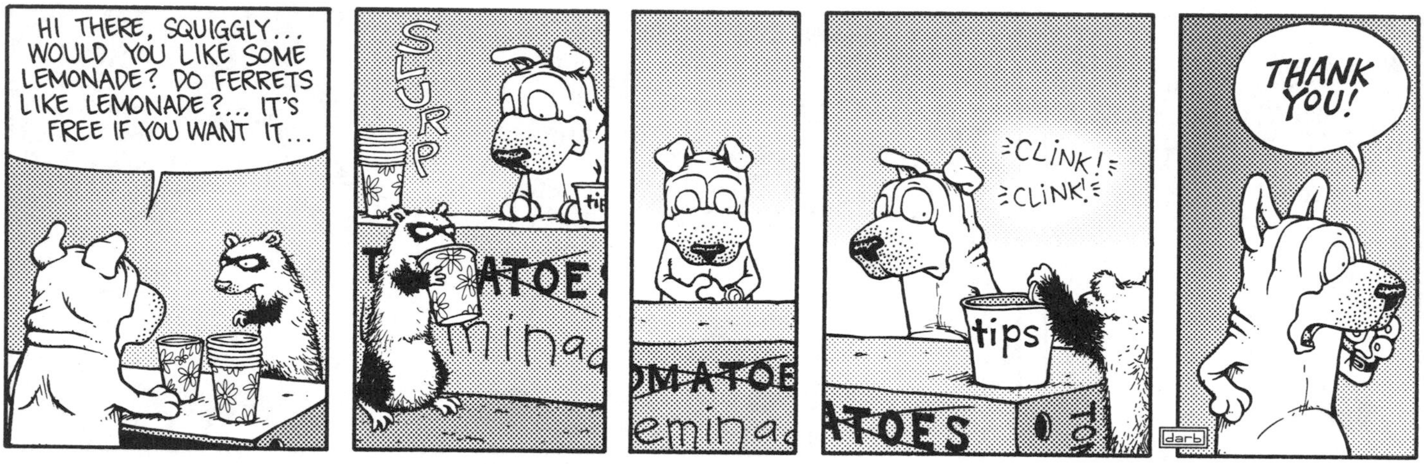
HI THERE, SQUIGGLY... WOULD YOU LIKE SOME LEMONADE? DO FERRETS LIKE LEMONADE?... IT'S FREE IF YOU WANT IT...
SLURP
CLINK! CLINK!
tips
THANK YOU!
darb

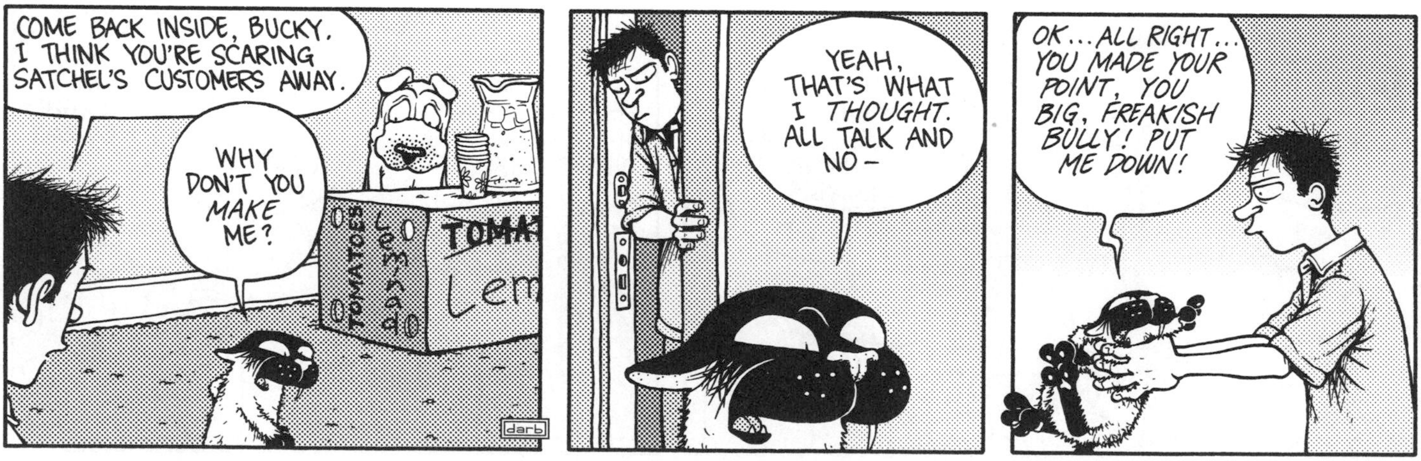
COME BACK INSIDE, BUCKY. I THINK YOU'RE SCARING SATCHEL'S CUSTOMERS AWAY.
WHY DON'T YOU MAKE ME?
TOMATOES
darb
YEAH, THAT'S WHAT I THOUGHT. ALL TALK AND NO–
OK... ALL RIGHT... YOU MADE YOUR POINT, YOU BIG, FREAKISH BULLY! PUT ME DOWN!

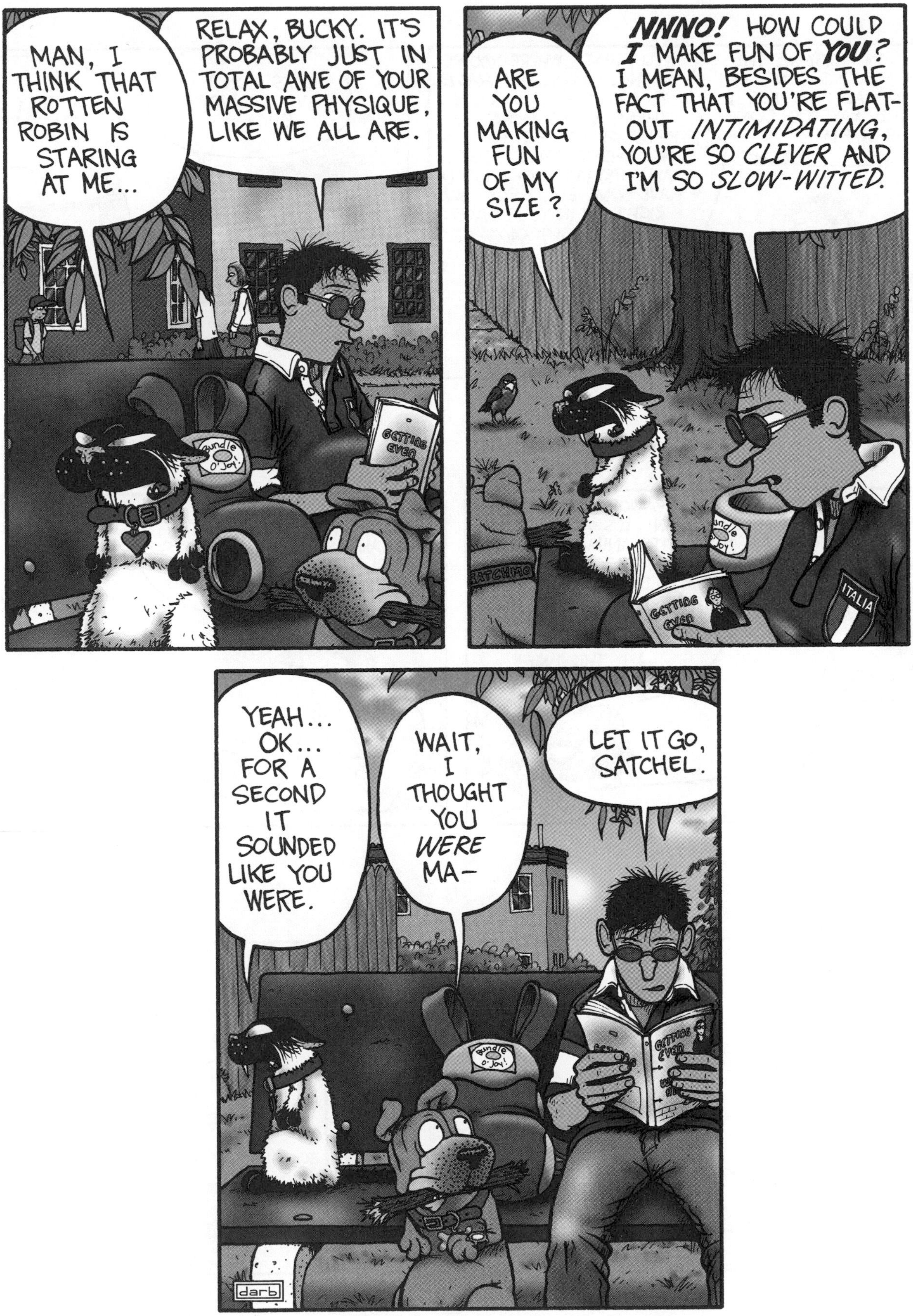
MAN, I THINK THAT ROTTEN ROBIN IS STARING AT ME...
RELAX, BUCKY. IT'S PROBABLY JUST IN TOTAL AWE OF YOUR MASSIVE PHYSIQUE, LIKE WE ALL ARE.
GETTING EVEN
BUNDLE O' JOY!
ARE YOU MAKING FUN OF MY SIZE?
NNNO! HOW COULD I MAKE FUN OF YOU? I MEAN, BESIDES THE FACT THAT YOU'RE FLAT-OUT INTIMIDATING, YOU'RE SO CLEVER AND I'M SO SLOW-WITTED.
SATCHMO
ITALIA
YEAH... OK... FOR A SECOND IT SOUNDED LIKE YOU WERE.
WAIT, I THOUGHT YOU WERE MA–
LET IT GO, SATCHEL.
darb

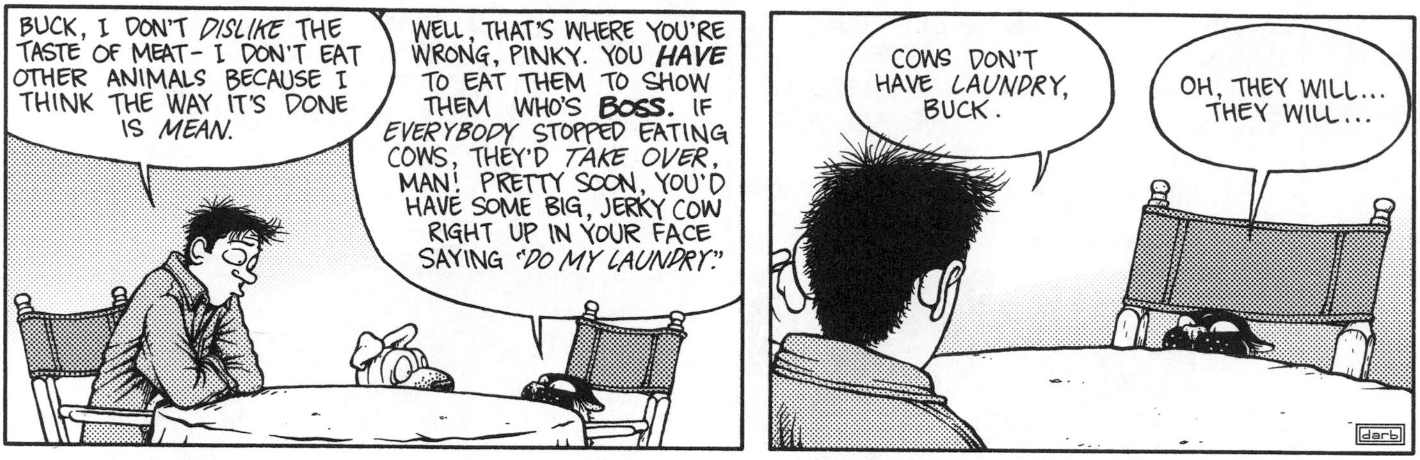
BUCK, I DON'T DISLIKE THE TASTE OF MEAT- I DON'T EAT OTHER ANIMALS BECAUSE I THINK THE WAY IT'S DONE IS MEAN.
WELL, THAT'S WHERE YOU'RE WRONG, PINKY. YOU HAVE TO EAT THEM TO SHOW THEM WHO'S BOSS. IF EVERYBODY STOPPED EATING COWS, THEY'D TAKE OVER, MAN! PRETTY SOON, YOU'D HAVE SOME BIG, JERKY COW RIGHT UP IN YOUR FACE SAYING "DO MY LAUNDRY."
COWS DON'T HAVE LAUNDRY, BUCK.
OH, THEY WILL... THEY WILL...
darb

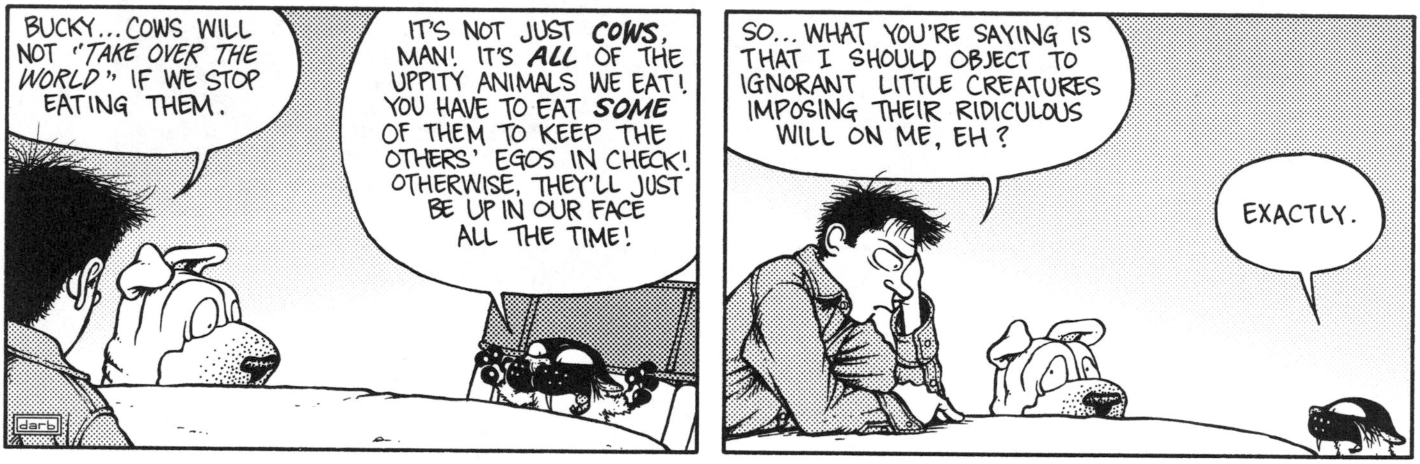
BUCKY... COWS WILL NOT "TAKE OVER THE WORLD" IF WE STOP EATING THEM.
IT'S NOT JUST COWS, MAN! IT'S ALL OF THE UPPITY ANIMALS WE EAT! YOU HAVE TO EAT SOME OF THEM TO KEEP THE OTHERS' EGOS IN CHECK! OTHERWISE, THEY'LL JUST BE UP IN OUR FACE ALL THE TIME!
darb
SO... WHAT YOU'RE SAYING IS THAT I SHOULD OBJECT TO IGNORANT LITTLE CREATURES IMPOSING THEIR RIDICULOUS WILL ON ME, EH?
EXACTLY.

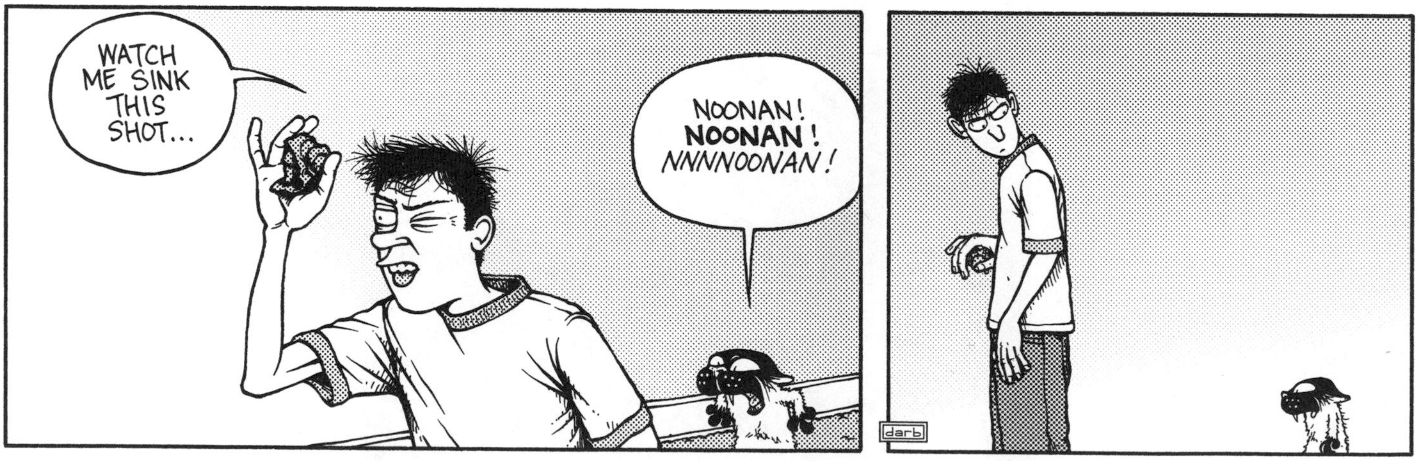
WATCH ME SINK THIS SHOT...
NOONAN! NOONAN! NNNNOONAN!
darb

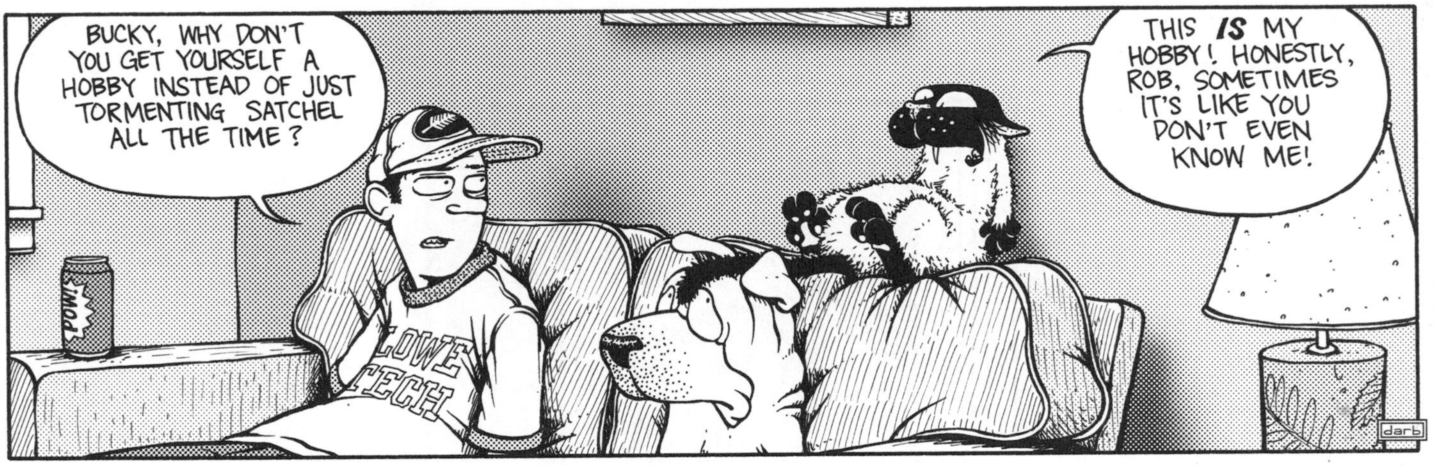
BUCKY, WHY DON'T YOU GET YOURSELF A HOBBY INSTEAD OF JUST TORMENTING SATCHEL ALL THE TIME?
THIS **IS** MY HOBBY! HONESTLY, ROB, SOMETIMES IT'S LIKE YOU DON'T EVEN KNOW ME!

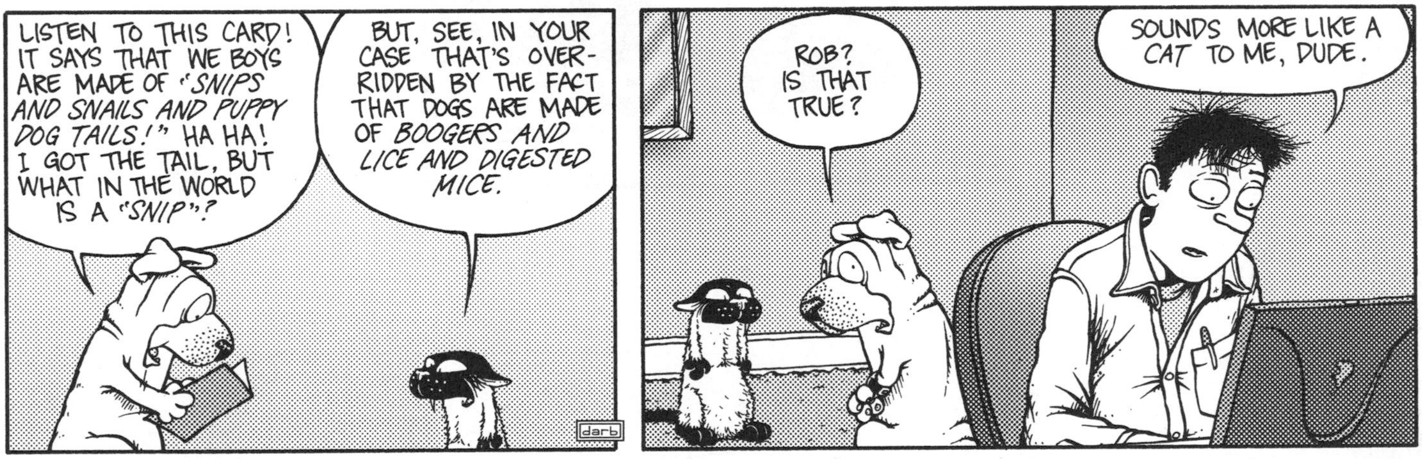
LISTEN TO THIS CARD! IT SAYS THAT WE BOYS ARE MADE OF *"SNIPS AND SNAILS AND PUPPY DOG TAILS!"* HA HA! I GOT THE TAIL, BUT WHAT IN THE WORLD IS A *"SNIP"*?
BUT, SEE, IN YOUR CASE THAT'S OVER-RIDDEN BY THE FACT THAT DOGS ARE MADE OF *BOOGERS AND LICE AND DIGESTED MICE.*
ROB? IS THAT TRUE?
SOUNDS MORE LIKE A *CAT* TO ME, DUDE.

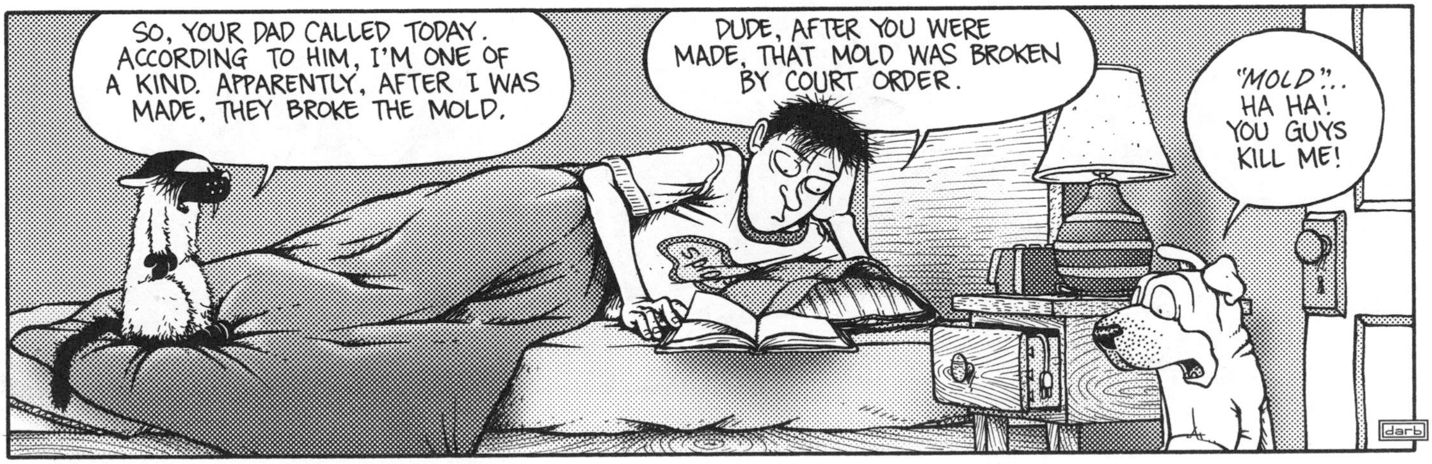
SO, YOUR DAD CALLED TODAY. ACCORDING TO HIM, I'M ONE OF A KIND. APPARENTLY, AFTER I WAS MADE, THEY BROKE THE MOLD.
DUDE, AFTER YOU WERE MADE, THAT MOLD WAS BROKEN BY COURT ORDER.
"MOLD"... HA HA! YOU GUYS KILL ME!

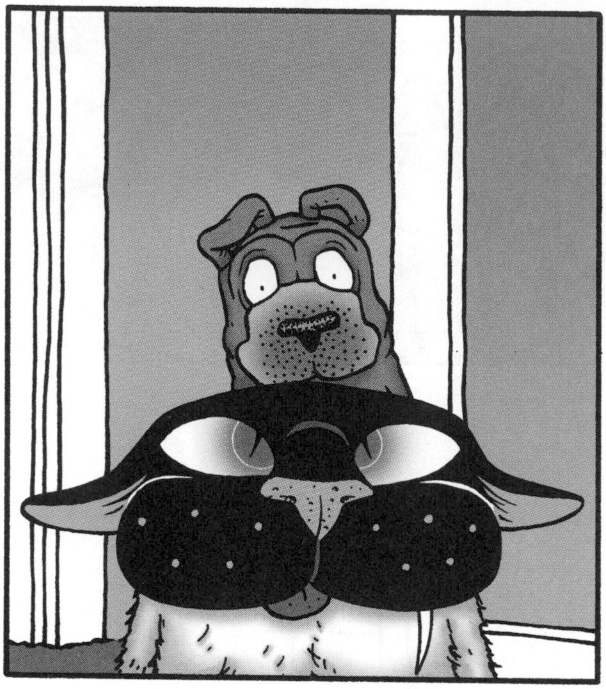

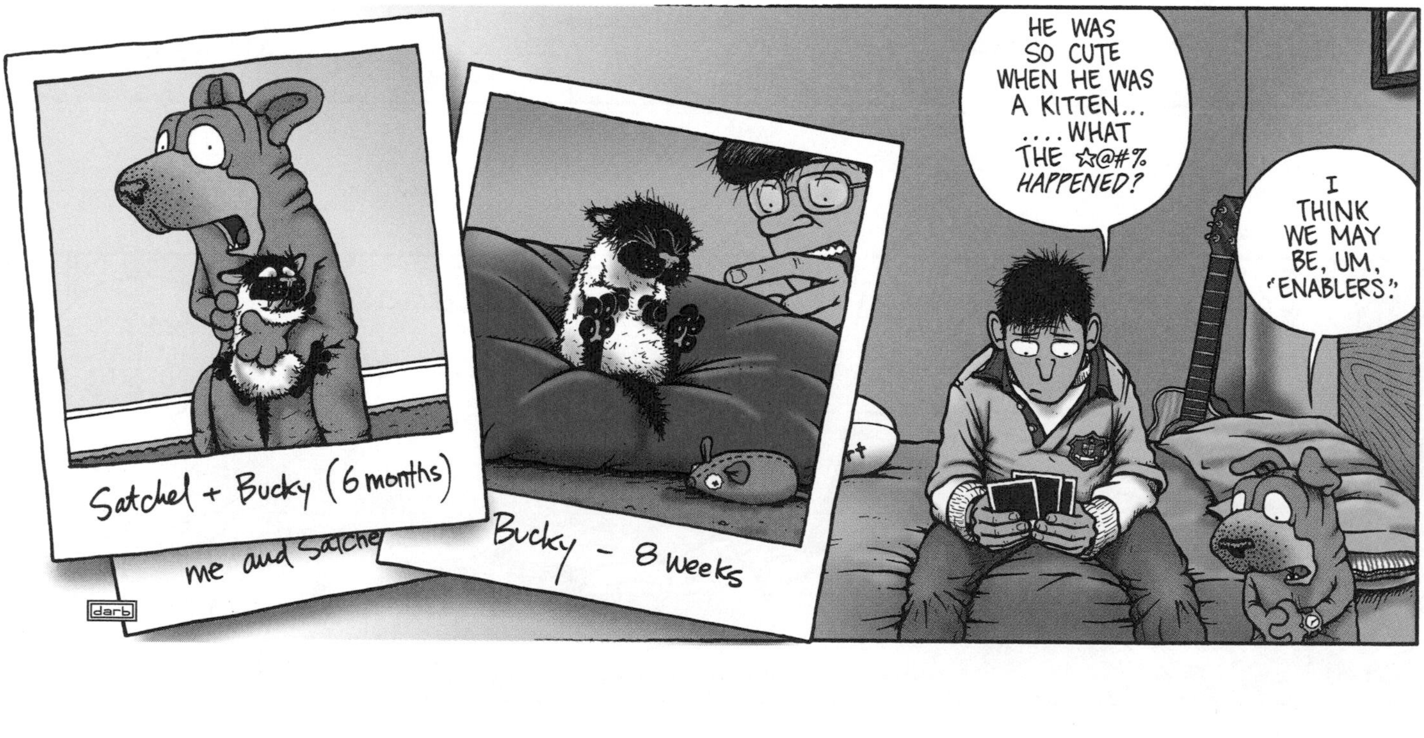
Satchel + Bucky (6 months)
me and Satche
Bucky - 8 weeks
HE WAS SO CUTE WHEN HE WAS A KITTEN... ....WHAT THE ☆@#% HAPPENED?
I THINK WE MAY BE, UM, "ENABLERS."
darb

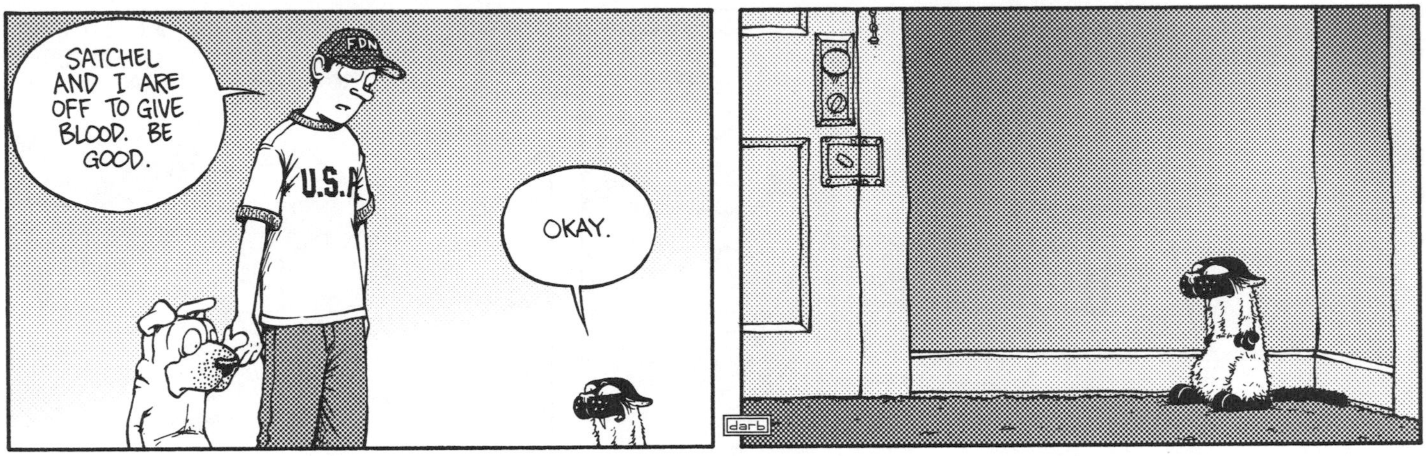
SATCHEL AND I ARE OFF TO GIVE BLOOD. BE GOOD.
OKAY.
FDNY
U.S.A.
darb

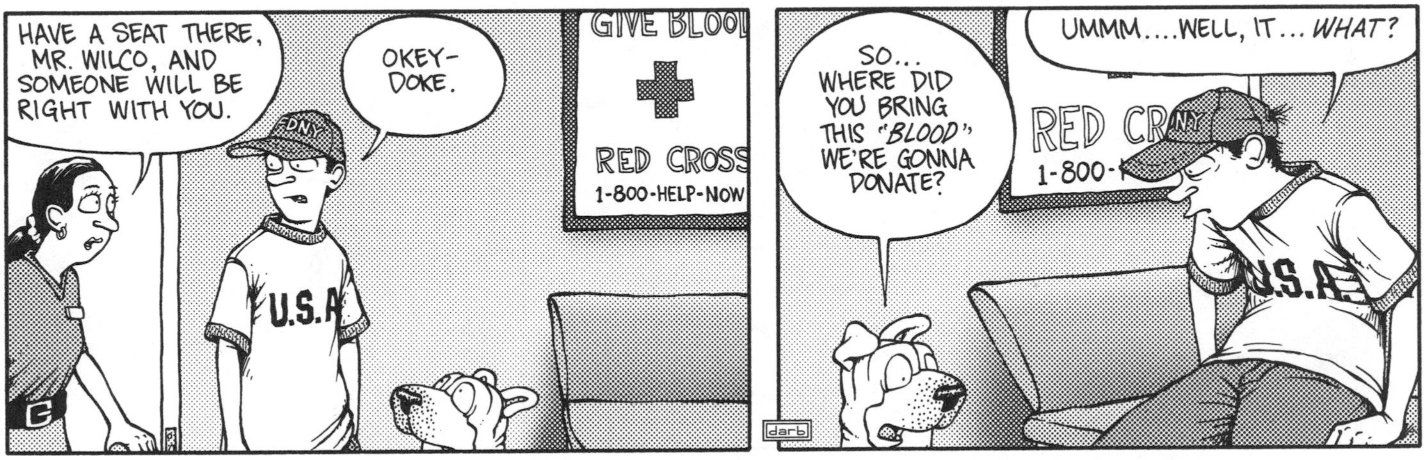
HAVE A SEAT THERE, MR. WILCO, AND SOMEONE WILL BE RIGHT WITH YOU.
OKEY-DOKE.
GIVE BLOOD
RED CROSS
1-800-HELP-NOW
FDNY
U.S.A.
SO... WHERE DID YOU BRING THIS "BLOOD" WE'RE GONNA DONATE?
UMMM....WELL, IT... WHAT?
darb

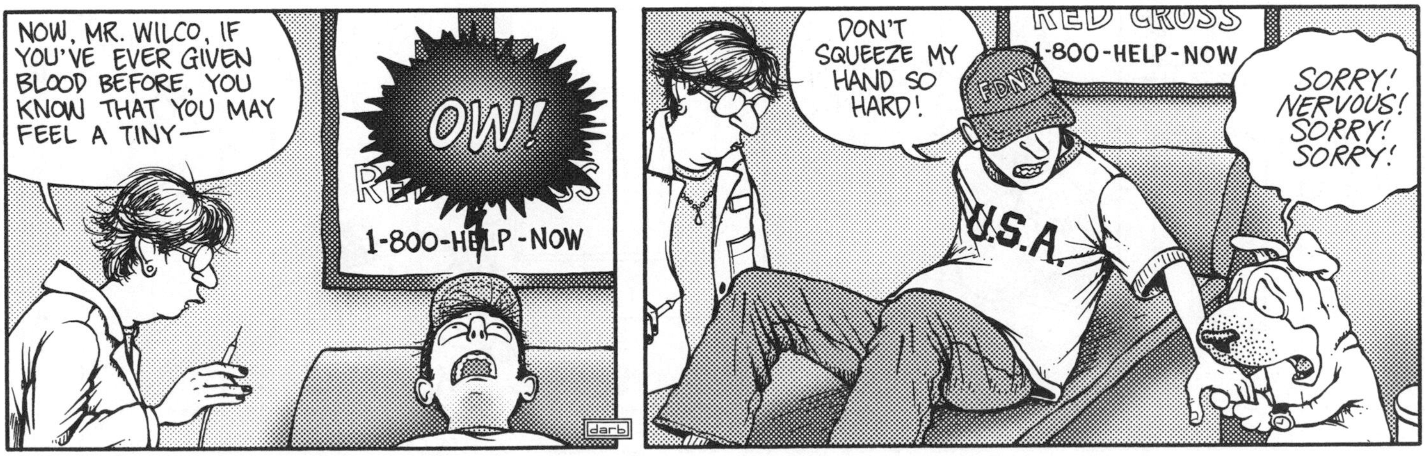
NOW, MR. WILCO, IF YOU'VE EVER GIVEN BLOOD BEFORE, YOU KNOW THAT YOU MAY FEEL A TINY—
OW!
1-800-HELP-NOW
darb
DON'T SQUEEZE MY HAND SO HARD!
SORRY! NERVOUS! SORRY! SORRY!
RED CROSS
1-800-HELP-NOW
FDNY
U.S.A.

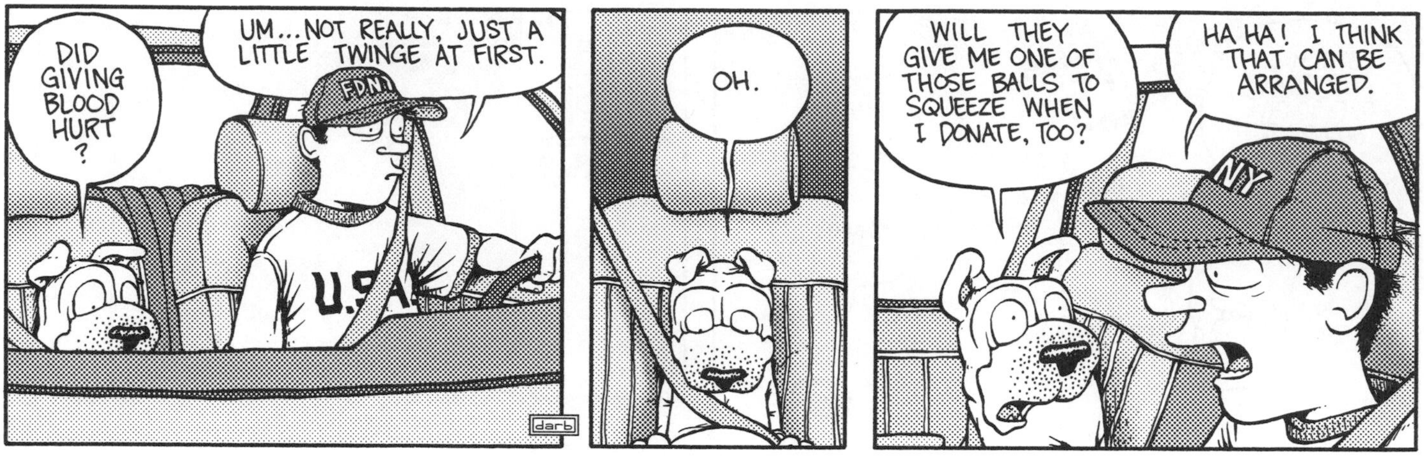
DID GIVING BLOOD HURT ?
UM... NOT REALLY, JUST A LITTLE TWINGE AT FIRST.
OH.
WILL THEY GIVE ME ONE OF THOSE BALLS TO SQUEEZE WHEN I DONATE, TOO?
HA HA! I THINK THAT CAN BE ARRANGED.

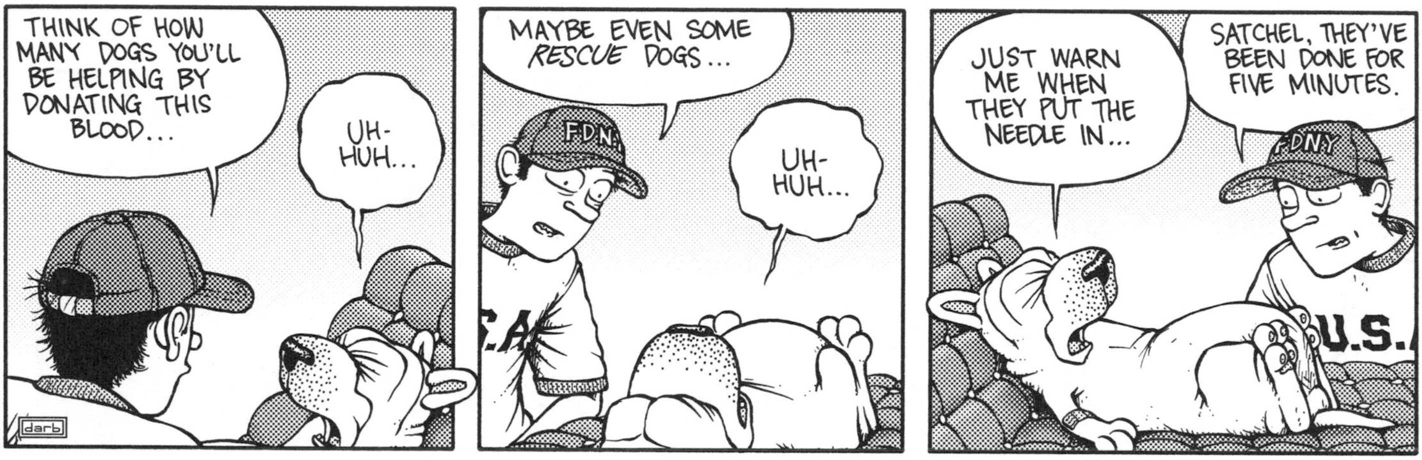
THINK OF HOW MANY DOGS YOU'LL BE HELPING BY DONATING THIS BLOOD...
UH-HUH...
MAYBE EVEN SOME *RESCUE* DOGS...
UH-HUH...
JUST WARN ME WHEN THEY PUT THE NEEDLE IN...
SATCHEL, THEY'VE BEEN DONE FOR FIVE MINUTES.

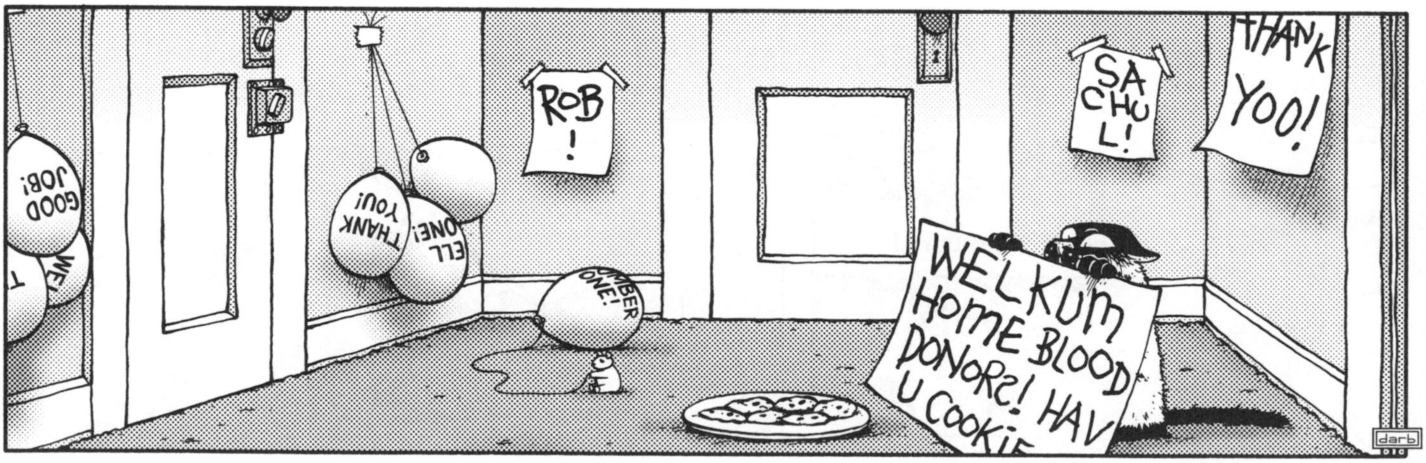
GOOD JOB!
THANK YOU!
ROB !
SA CHU L!
THANK YOO!
WELKUM HOME BLOOD DONORS! HAV U

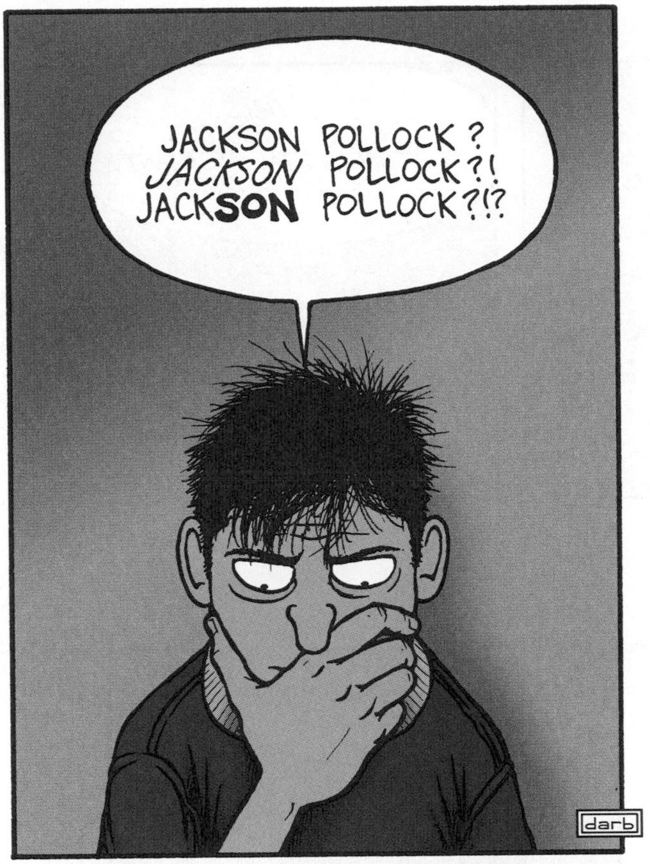
JACKSON POLLOCK?
JACKSON POLLOCK?!
JACKSON POLLOCK?!?
darb

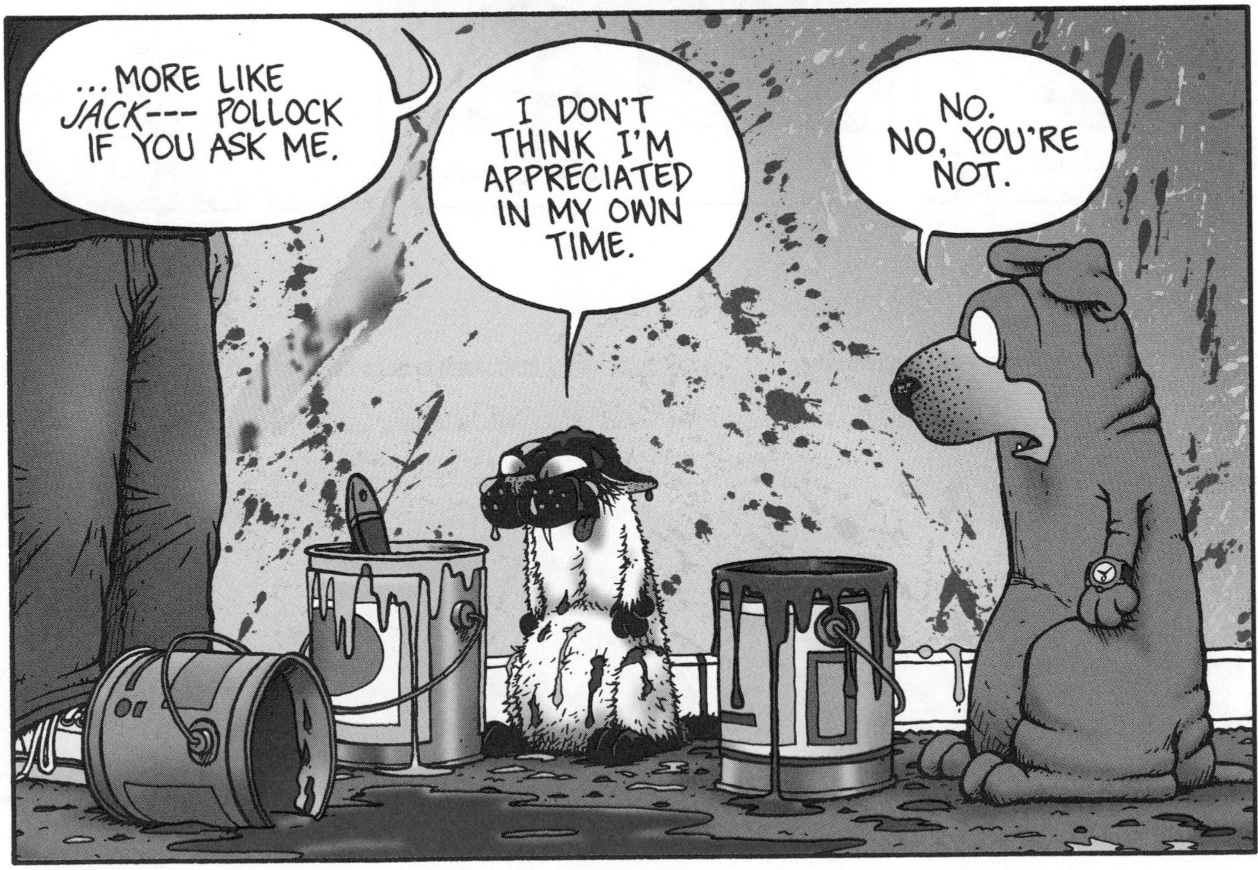
...MORE LIKE JACK--- POLLOCK IF YOU ASK ME.
I DON'T THINK I'M APPRECIATED IN MY OWN TIME.
NO. NO, YOU'RE NOT.

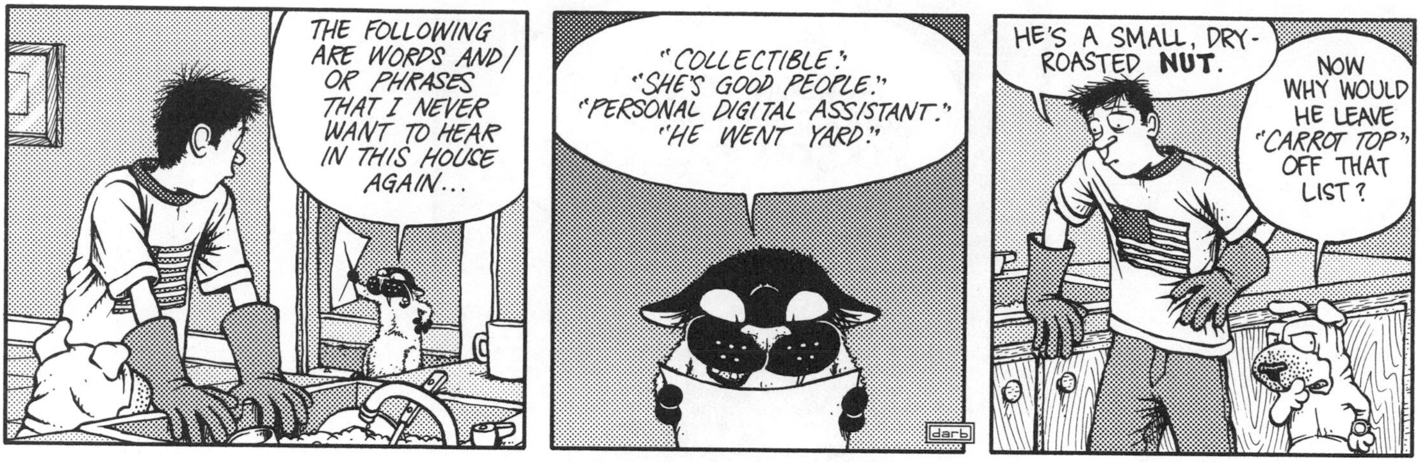
THE FOLLOWING ARE WORDS AND/ OR PHRASES THAT I NEVER WANT TO HEAR IN THIS HOUSE AGAIN...
"COLLECTIBLE." "SHE'S GOOD PEOPLE." "PERSONAL DIGITAL ASSISTANT." "HE WENT YARD."
darb
HE'S A SMALL, DRY-ROASTED **NUT**.
NOW WHY WOULD HE LEAVE "CARROT TOP" OFF THAT LIST?

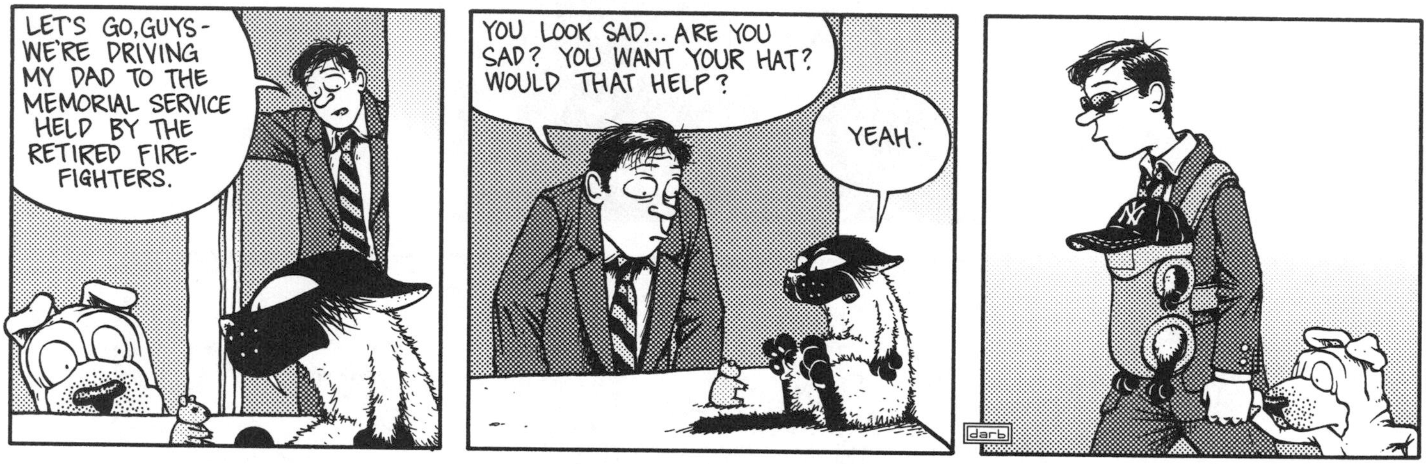
LET'S GO, GUYS- WE'RE DRIVING MY DAD TO THE MEMORIAL SERVICE HELD BY THE RETIRED FIRE-FIGHTERS.
YOU LOOK SAD... ARE YOU SAD? YOU WANT YOUR HAT? WOULD THAT HELP?
YEAH.
darb

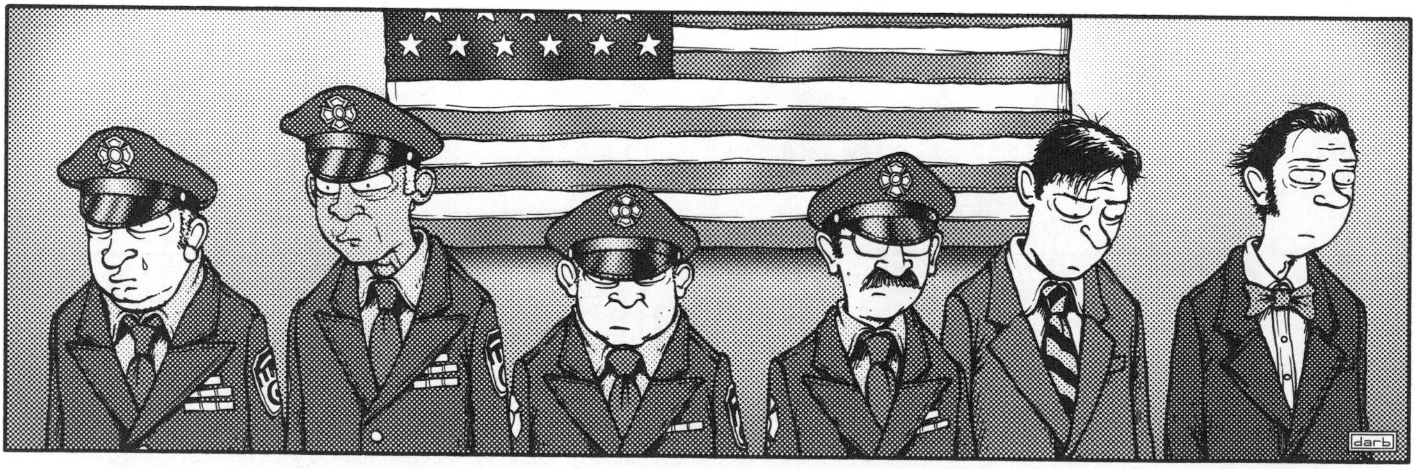
darb

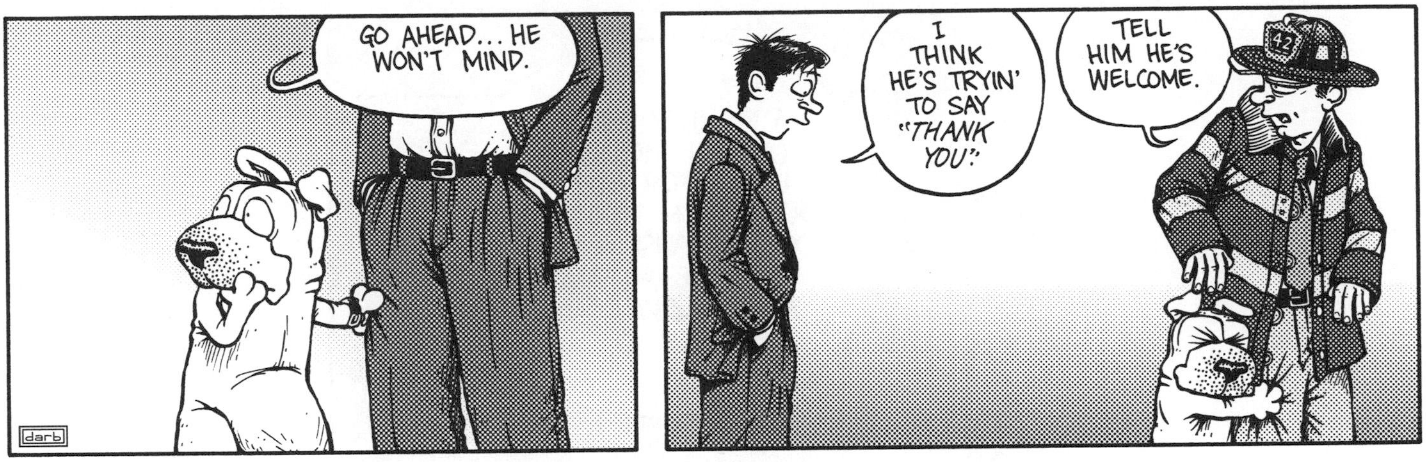
GO AHEAD... HE WON'T MIND.
I THINK HE'S TRYIN' TO SAY "THANK YOU."
TELL HIM HE'S WELCOME.

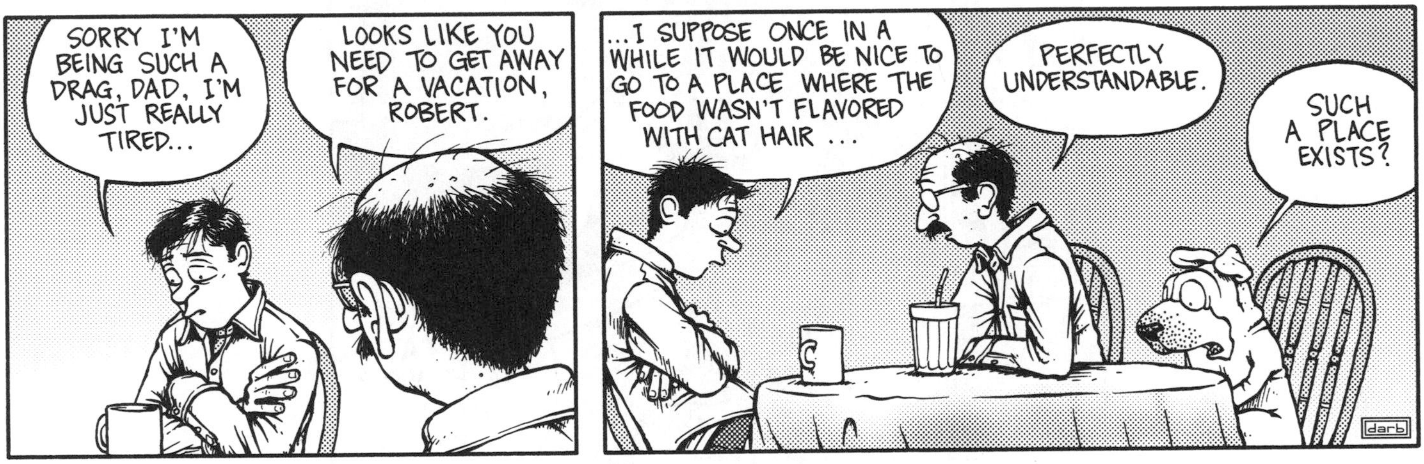
SORRY I'M BEING SUCH A DRAG, DAD. I'M JUST REALLY TIRED...
LOOKS LIKE YOU NEED TO GET AWAY FOR A VACATION, ROBERT.
...I SUPPOSE ONCE IN A WHILE IT WOULD BE NICE TO GO TO A PLACE WHERE THE FOOD WASN'T FLAVORED WITH CAT HAIR ...
PERFECTLY UNDERSTANDABLE.
SUCH A PLACE EXISTS?

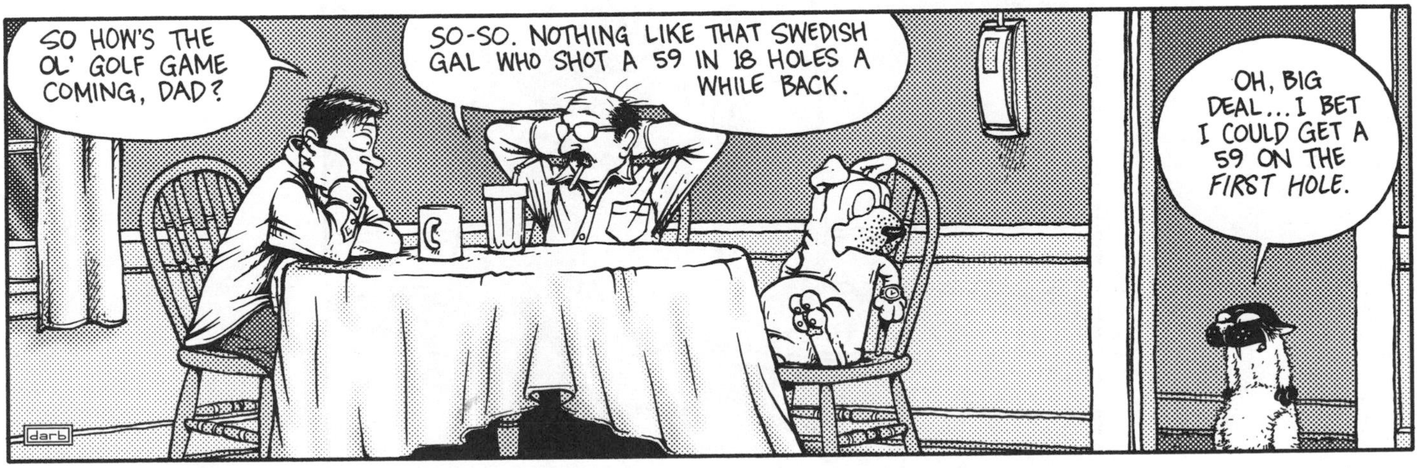
SO HOW'S THE OL' GOLF GAME COMING, DAD?
SO-SO. NOTHING LIKE THAT SWEDISH GAL WHO SHOT A 59 IN 18 HOLES A WHILE BACK.
OH, BIG DEAL... I BET I COULD GET A 59 ON THE FIRST HOLE.

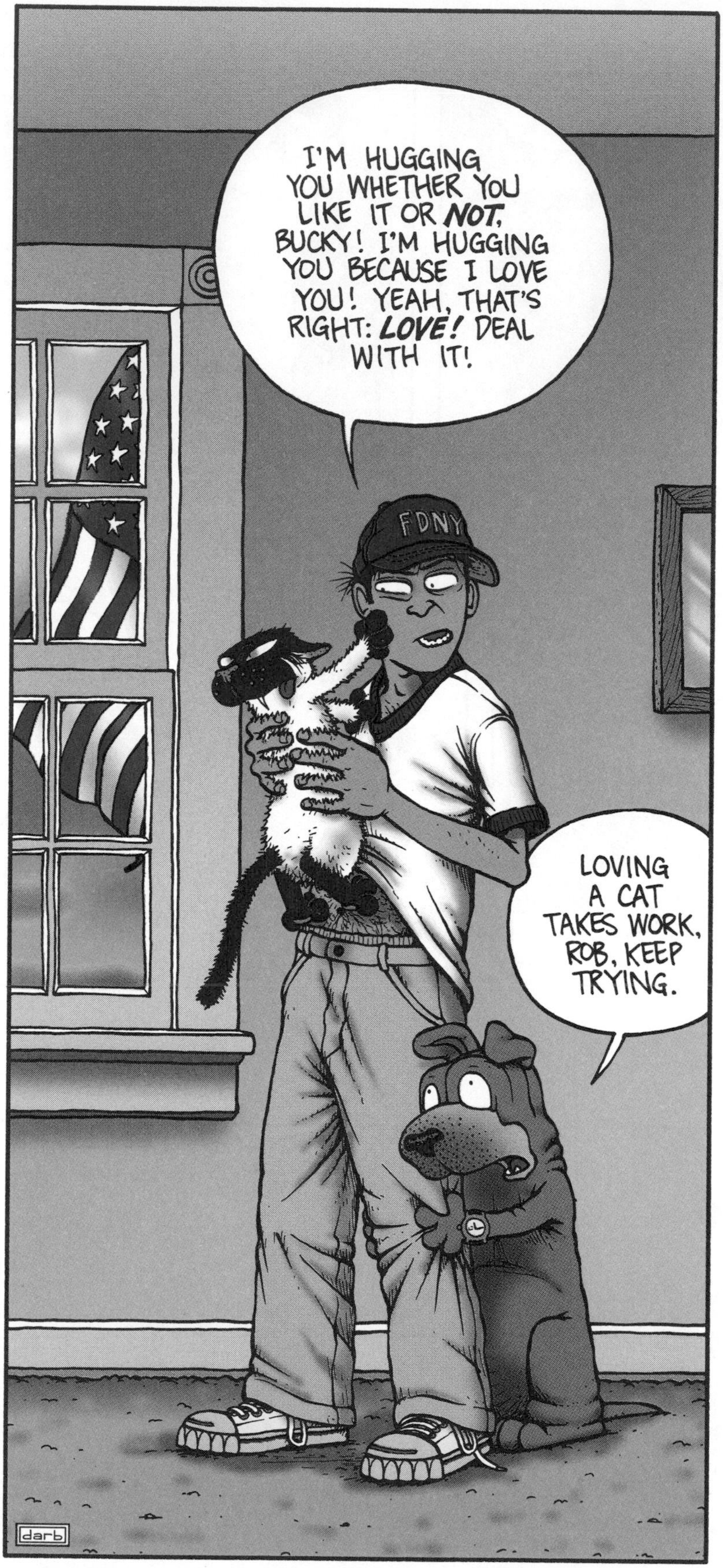
I'M HUGGING YOU WHETHER YOU LIKE IT OR **NOT**, BUCKY! I'M HUGGING YOU BECAUSE I LOVE YOU! YEAH, THAT'S RIGHT: **LOVE!** DEAL WITH IT!
FDNY
LOVING A CAT TAKES WORK, ROB, KEEP TRYING.
darb

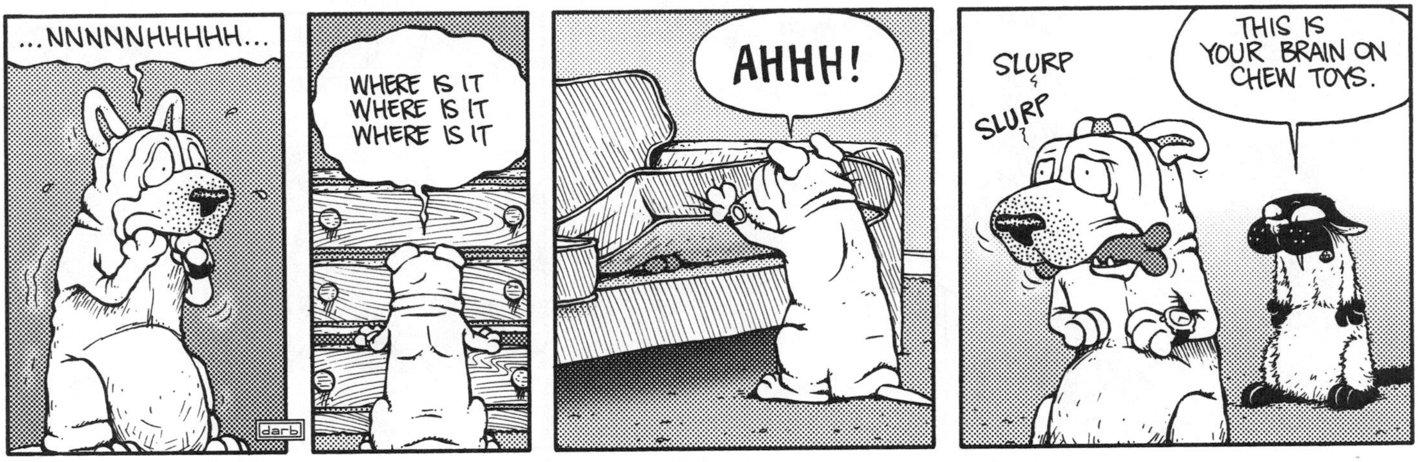

...NNNNNHHHHH...
WHERE IS IT WHERE IS IT WHERE IS IT
AHHH!
SLURP SLURP
THIS IS YOUR BRAIN ON CHEW TOYS.

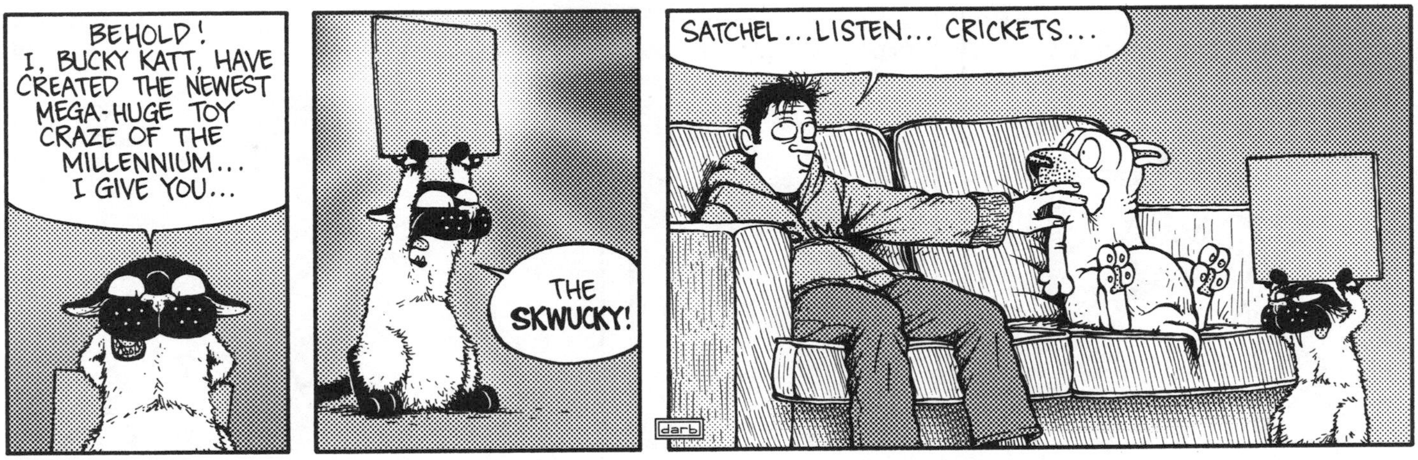

BEHOLD! I, BUCKY KATT, HAVE CREATED THE NEWEST MEGA-HUGE TOY CRAZE OF THE MILLENNIUM... I GIVE YOU...
THE SKWUCKY!
SATCHEL...LISTEN... CRICKETS...

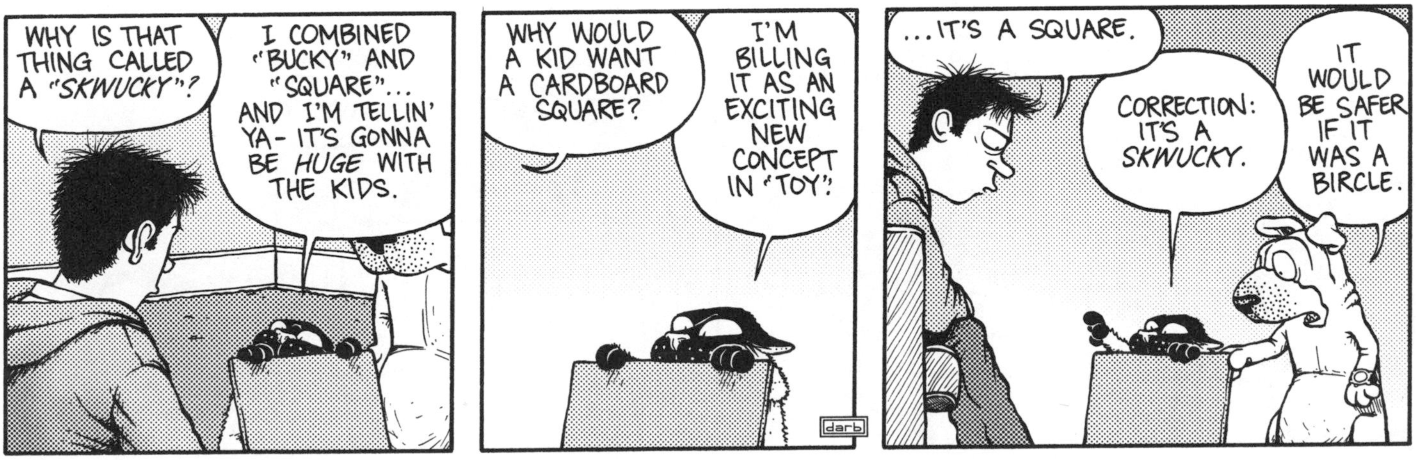

WHY IS THAT THING CALLED A "SKWUCKY"?
I COMBINED "BUCKY" AND "SQUARE"... AND I'M TELLIN' YA- IT'S GONNA BE HUGE WITH THE KIDS.
WHY WOULD A KID WANT A CARDBOARD SQUARE?
I'M BILLING IT AS AN EXCITING NEW CONCEPT IN "TOY."
...IT'S A SQUARE.
CORRECTION: IT'S A SKWUCKY.
IT WOULD BE SAFER IF IT WAS A BIRCLE.

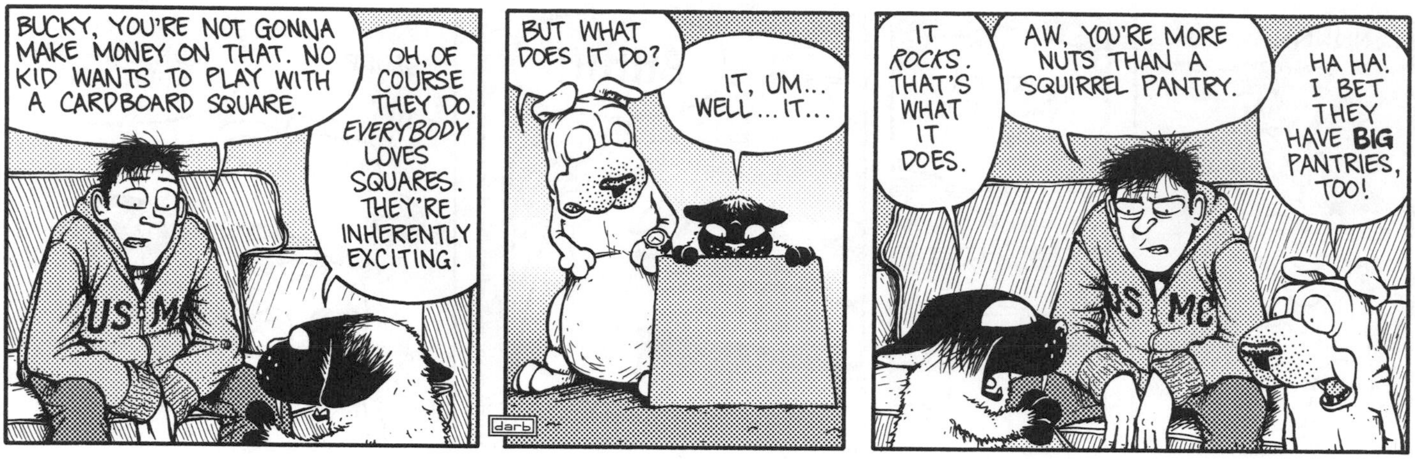
BUCKY, YOU'RE NOT GONNA MAKE MONEY ON THAT. NO KID WANTS TO PLAY WITH A CARDBOARD SQUARE.
OH, OF COURSE THEY DO. *EVERYBODY* LOVES SQUARES. THEY'RE INHERENTLY EXCITING.
BUT WHAT DOES IT DO?
IT, UM... WELL... IT...
darb
IT *ROCKS*. THAT'S WHAT IT DOES.
AW, YOU'RE MORE NUTS THAN A SQUIRREL PANTRY.
HA HA! I BET THEY HAVE **BIG** PANTRIES, TOO!
US MC

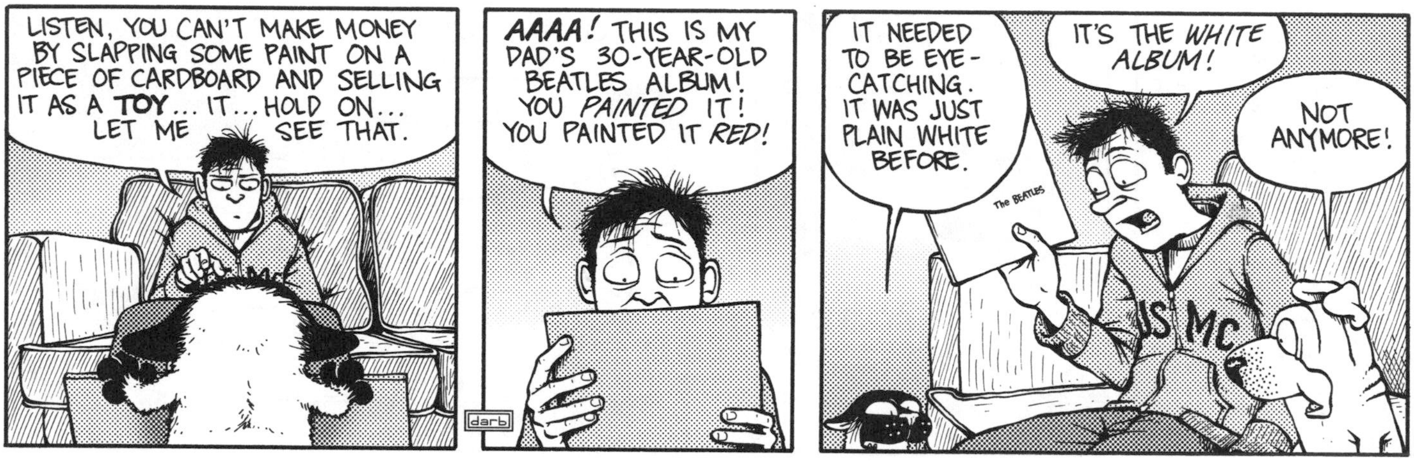
LISTEN, YOU CAN'T MAKE MONEY BY SLAPPING SOME PAINT ON A PIECE OF CARDBOARD AND SELLING IT AS A **TOY**... IT... HOLD ON... LET ME SEE THAT.
AAAA! THIS IS MY DAD'S 30-YEAR-OLD BEATLES ALBUM! YOU *PAINTED* IT! YOU PAINTED IT *RED!*
darb
IT NEEDED TO BE EYE-CATCHING. IT WAS JUST PLAIN WHITE BEFORE.
IT'S THE *WHITE ALBUM!*
NOT ANYMORE!
The BEATLES
US MC

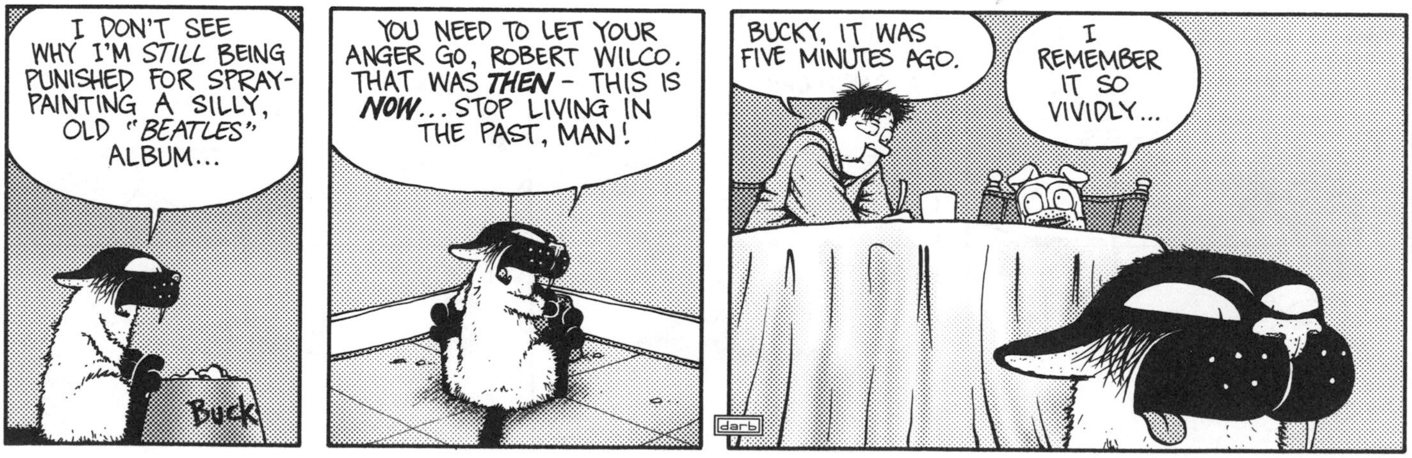
I DON'T SEE WHY I'M *STILL* BEING PUNISHED FOR SPRAY-PAINTING A SILLY, OLD "*BEATLES*" ALBUM...
Buck
YOU NEED TO LET YOUR ANGER GO, ROBERT WILCO. THAT WAS ***THEN*** - THIS IS ***NOW***... STOP LIVING IN THE PAST, MAN!
darb
BUCKY, IT WAS FIVE MINUTES AGO.
I REMEMBER IT SO VIVIDLY...

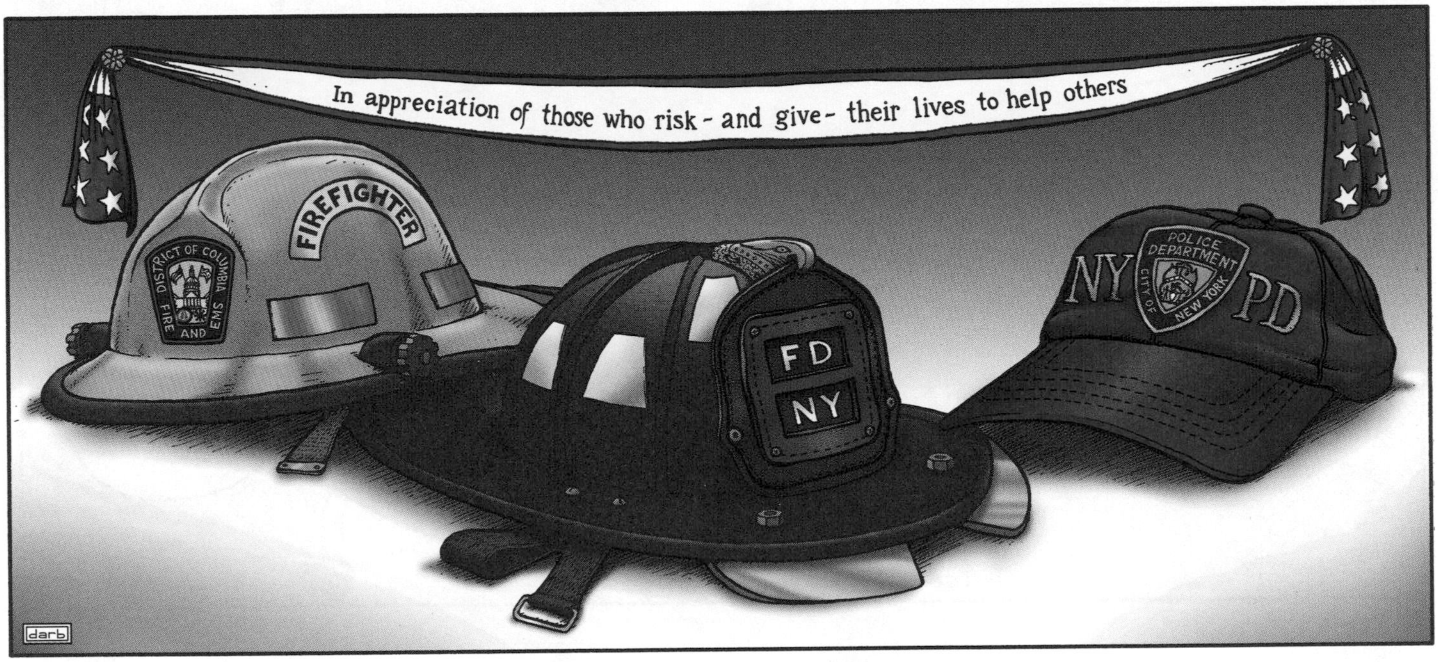
In appreciation of those who risk - and give - their lives to help others
FIREFIGHTER
DISTRICT OF COLUMBIA
FIRE AND EMS
FD
NY
NY
PD
POLICE DEPARTMENT
CITY OF NEW YORK
darb

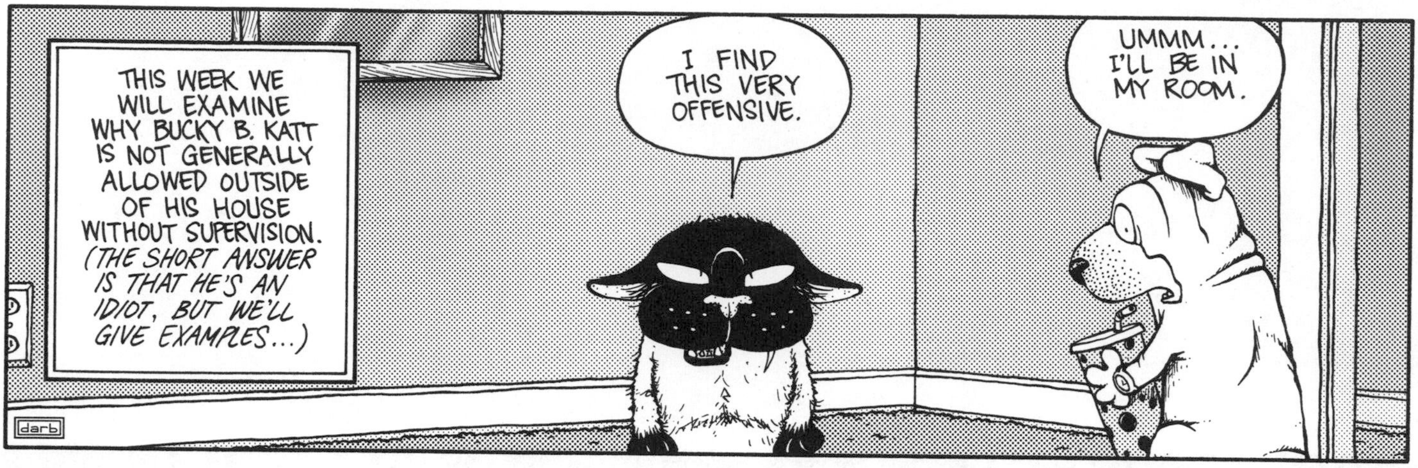

THIS WEEK WE WILL EXAMINE WHY BUCKY B. KATT IS NOT GENERALLY ALLOWED OUTSIDE OF HIS HOUSE WITHOUT SUPERVISION. (THE SHORT ANSWER IS THAT HE'S AN IDIOT, BUT WE'LL GIVE EXAMPLES...)
I FIND THIS VERY OFFENSIVE.
UMMM... I'LL BE IN MY ROOM.
darb

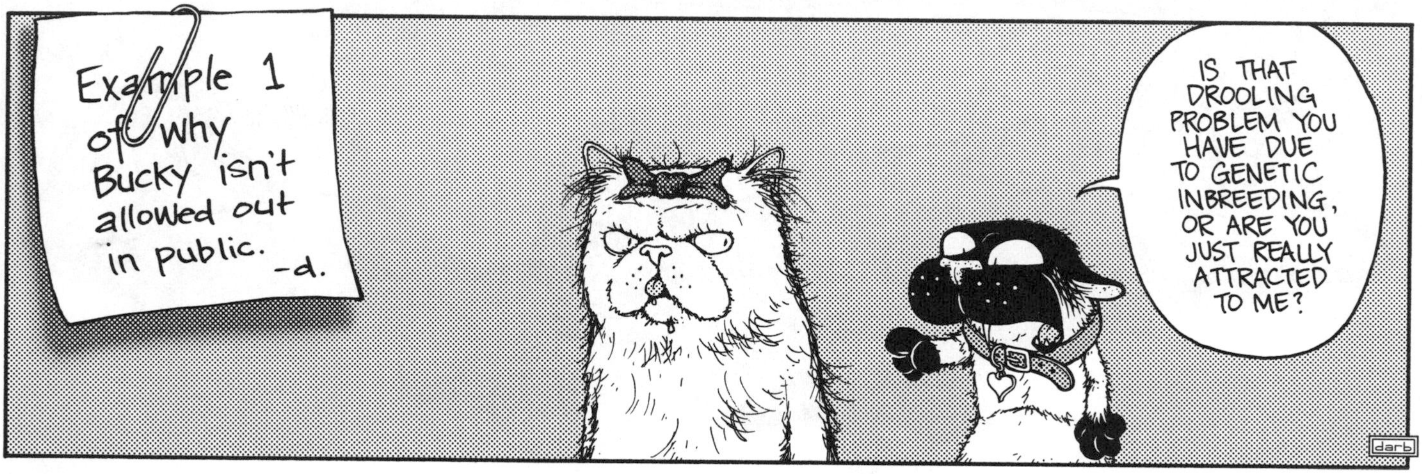

Example 1 of why Bucky isn't allowed out in public. -d.
IS THAT DROOLING PROBLEM YOU HAVE DUE TO GENETIC INBREEDING, OR ARE YOU JUST REALLY ATTRACTED TO ME?
darb

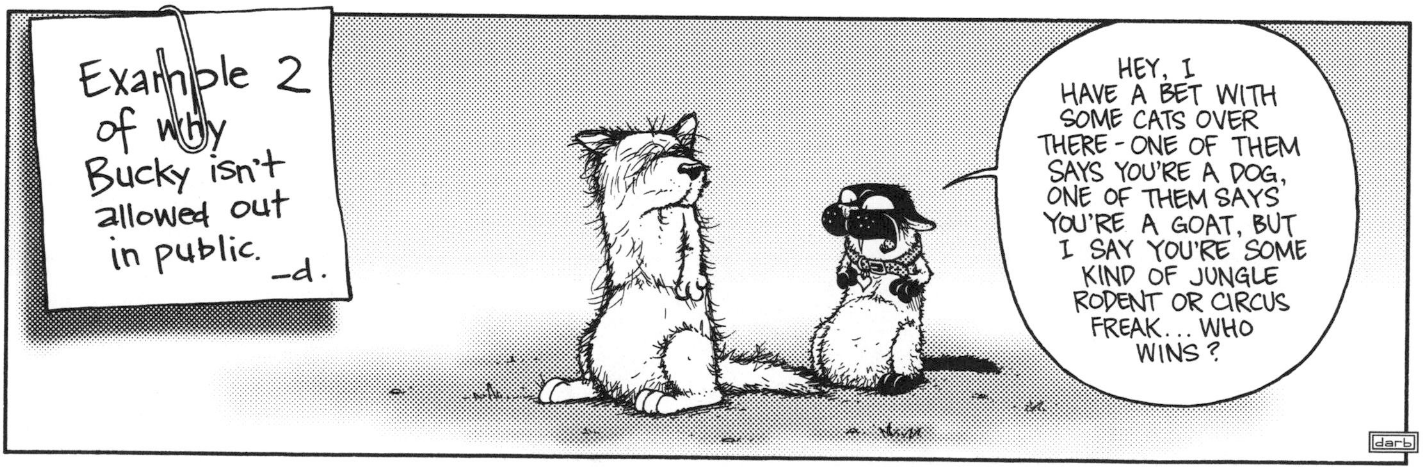

Example 2 of why Bucky isn't allowed out in public. -d.
HEY, I HAVE A BET WITH SOME CATS OVER THERE - ONE OF THEM SAYS YOU'RE A DOG, ONE OF THEM SAYS YOU'RE A GOAT, BUT I SAY YOU'RE SOME KIND OF JUNGLE RODENT OR CIRCUS FREAK... WHO WINS?
darb

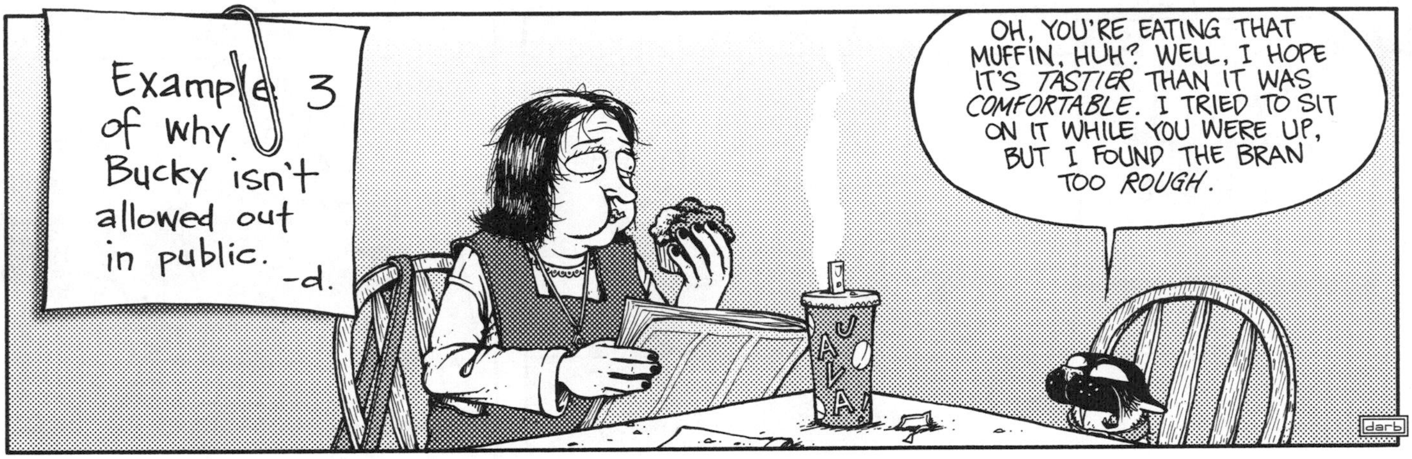
Example 3 of why Bucky isn't allowed out in public. -d.
JAVA!
OH, YOU'RE EATING THAT MUFFIN, HUH? WELL, I HOPE IT'S TASTIER THAN IT WAS COMFORTABLE. I TRIED TO SIT ON IT WHILE YOU WERE UP, BUT I FOUND THE BRAN TOO ROUGH.
darb

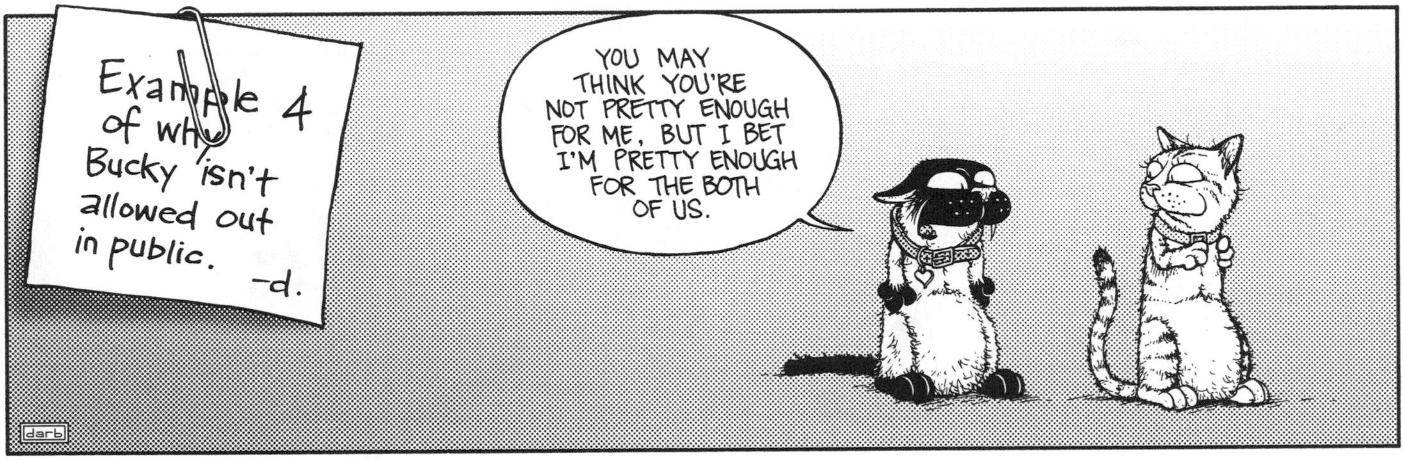
Example 4 of why Bucky isn't allowed out in public. -d.
YOU MAY THINK YOU'RE NOT PRETTY ENOUGH FOR ME, BUT I BET I'M PRETTY ENOUGH FOR THE BOTH OF US.
darb

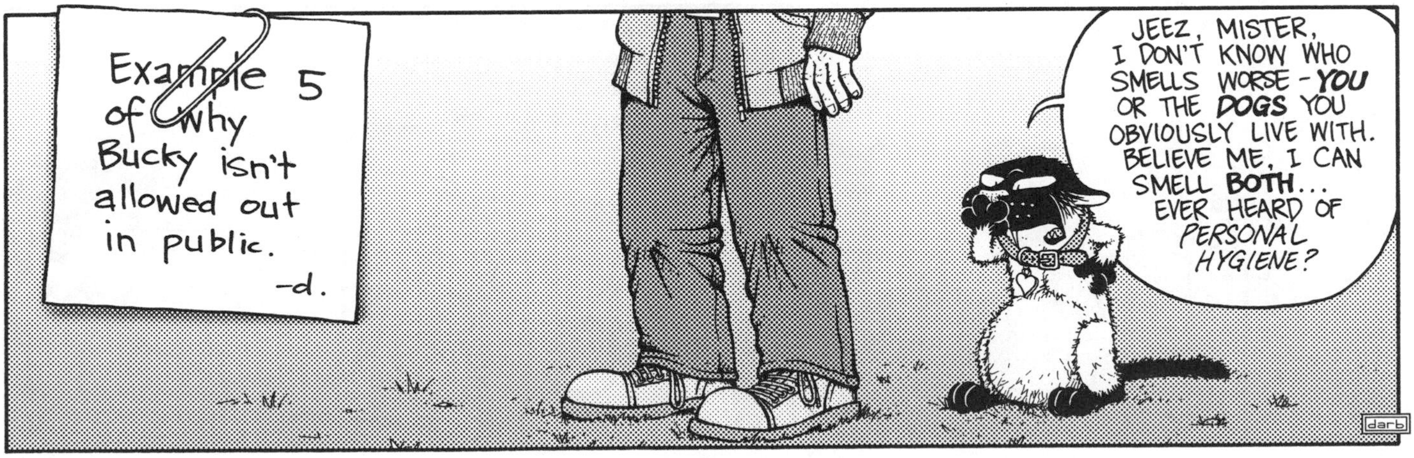
Example 5 of why Bucky isn't allowed out in public. -d.
JEEZ, MISTER, I DON'T KNOW WHO SMELLS WORSE - YOU OR THE DOGS YOU OBVIOUSLY LIVE WITH. BELIEVE ME, I CAN SMELL BOTH... EVER HEARD OF PERSONAL HYGIENE?
darb

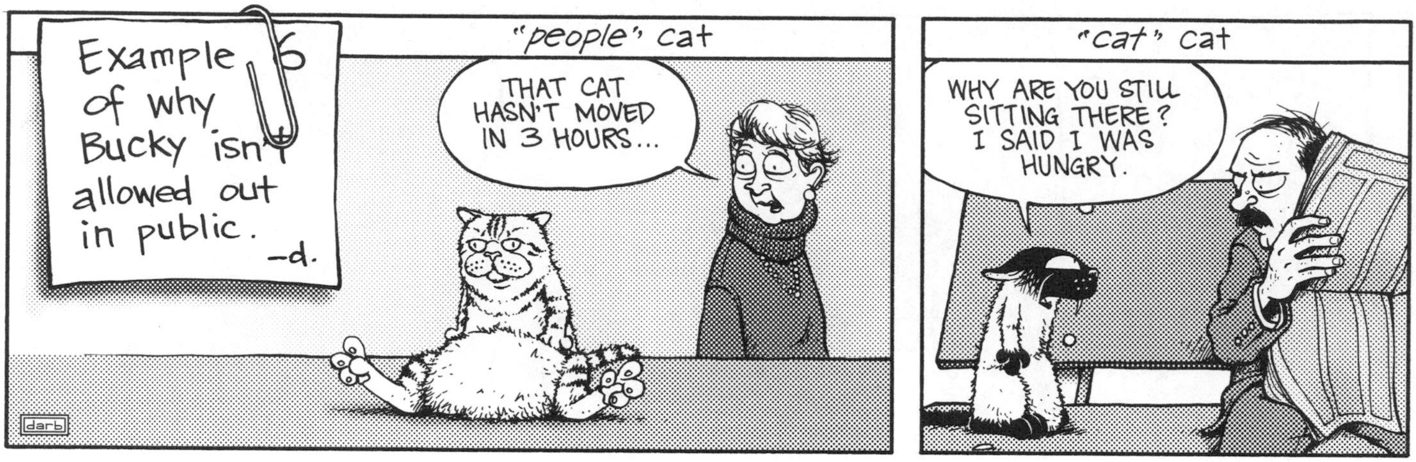
Example 6 of why Bucky isn't allowed out in public. -d.
"people" cat
THAT CAT HASN'T MOVED IN 3 HOURS...
"cat" cat
WHY ARE YOU STILL SITTING THERE? I SAID I WAS HUNGRY.

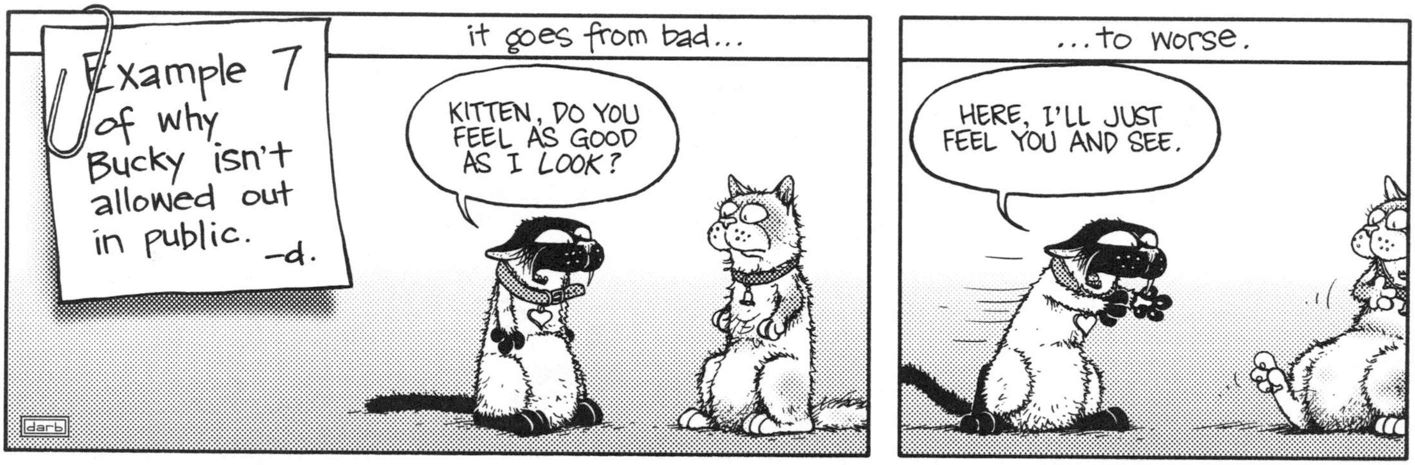
Example 7 of why Bucky isn't allowed out in public. -d.
it goes from bad...
KITTEN, DO YOU FEEL AS GOOD AS I LOOK?
...to worse.
HERE, I'LL JUST FEEL YOU AND SEE.

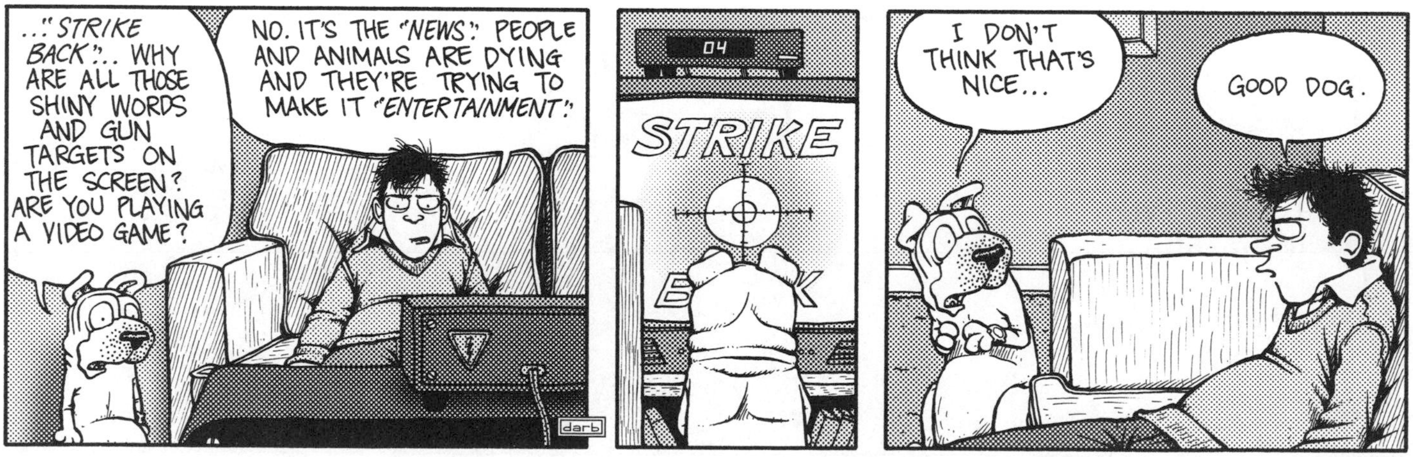
..."STRIKE BACK"... WHY ARE ALL THOSE SHINY WORDS AND GUN TARGETS ON THE SCREEN? ARE YOU PLAYING A VIDEO GAME?
NO. IT'S THE "NEWS." PEOPLE AND ANIMALS ARE DYING AND THEY'RE TRYING TO MAKE IT "ENTERTAINMENT."
04
STRIKE
I DON'T THINK THAT'S NICE...
GOOD DOG.

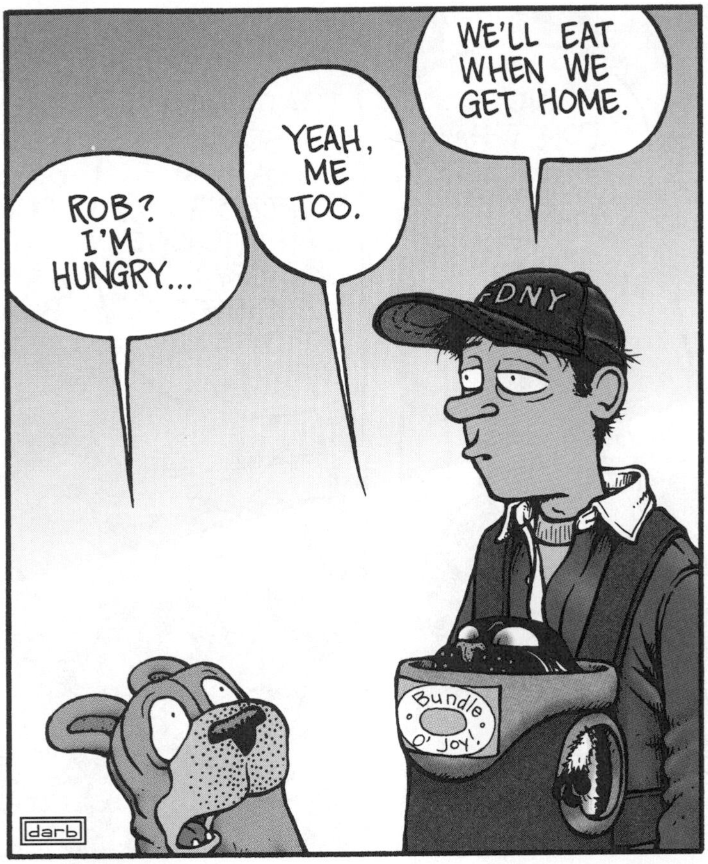
ROB? I'M HUNGRY...
YEAH, ME TOO.
WE'LL EAT WHEN WE GET HOME.
FDNY
Bundle O' Joy!
darb

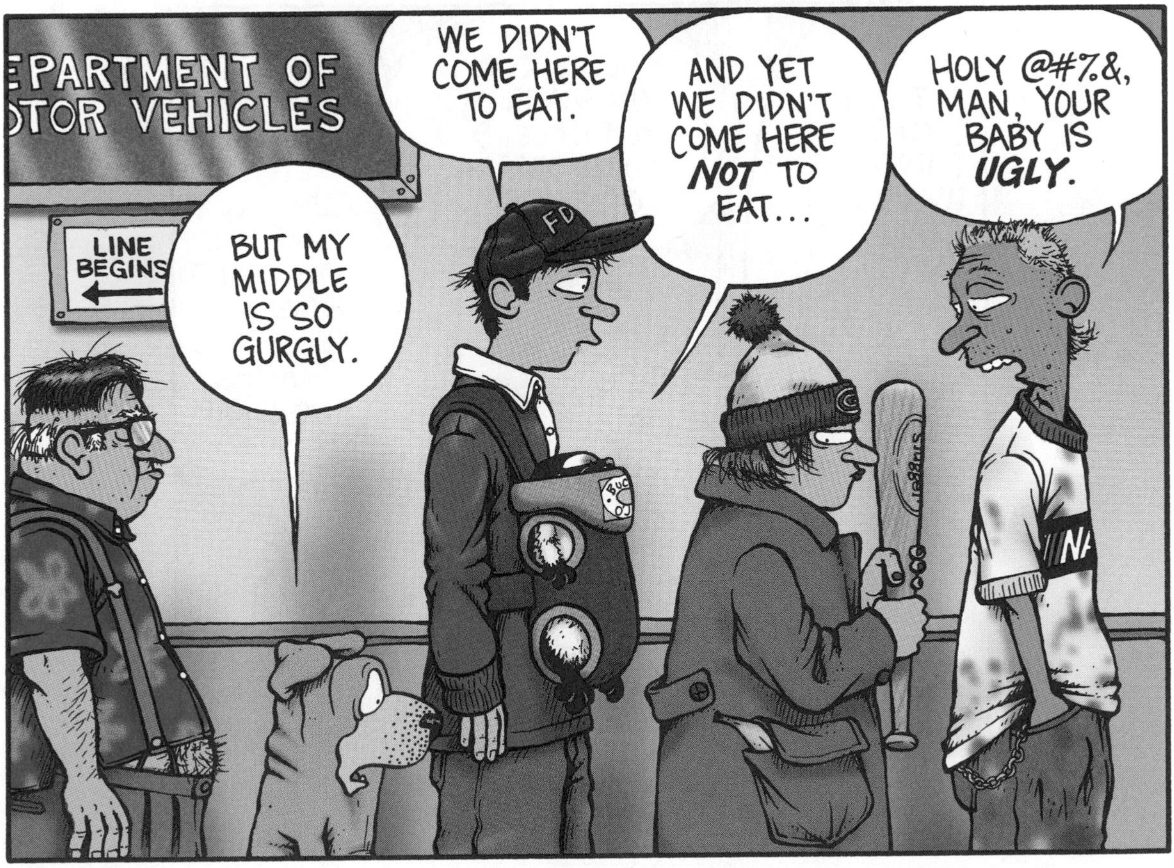
EPARTMENT OF OTOR VEHICLES
LINE BEGINS
BUT MY MIDDLE IS SO GURGLY.
WE DIDN'T COME HERE TO EAT.
AND YET WE DIDN'T COME HERE NOT TO EAT...
HOLY @#%&, MAN, YOUR BABY IS UGLY.

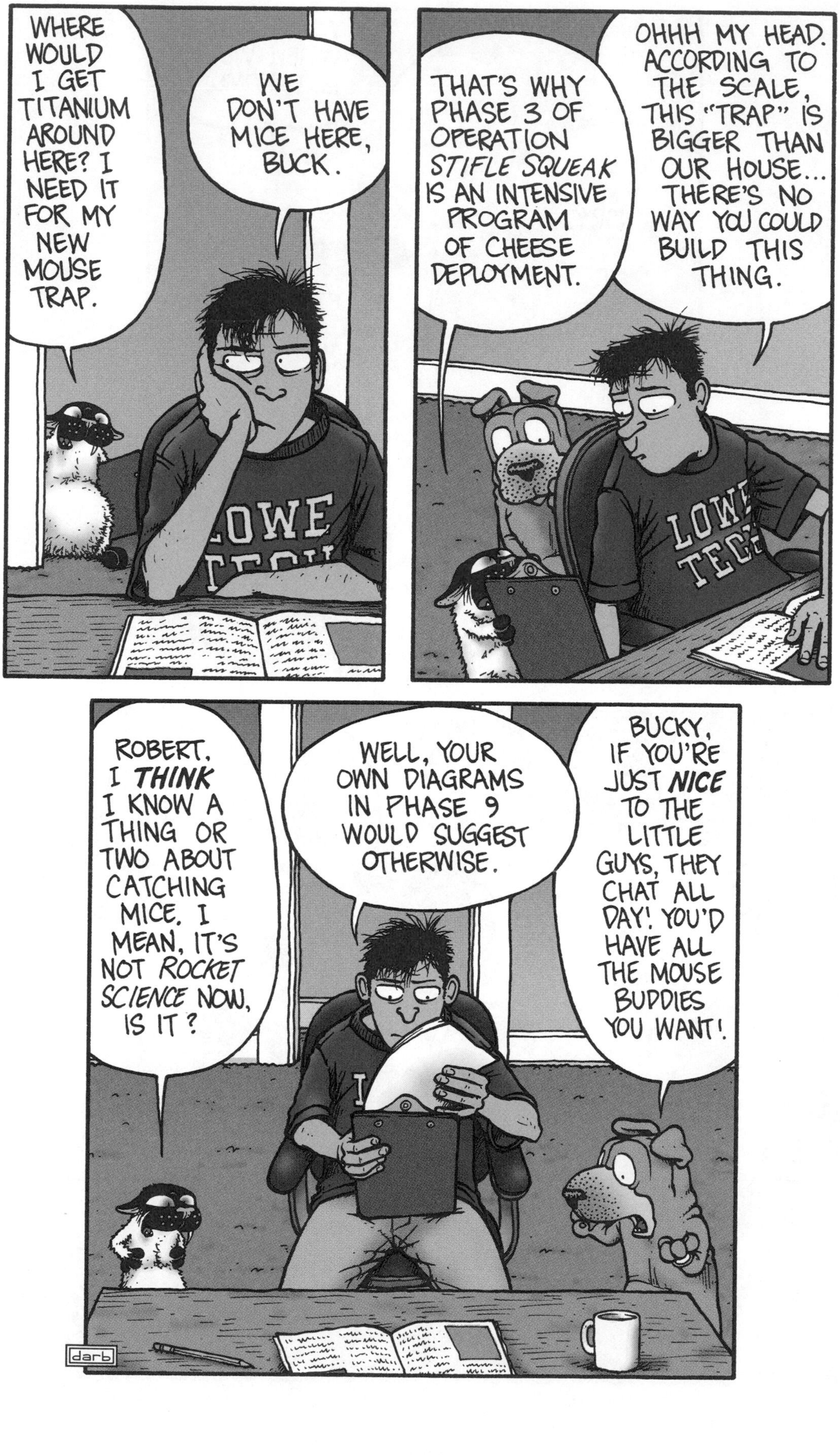
WHERE WOULD I GET TITANIUM AROUND HERE? I NEED IT FOR MY NEW MOUSE TRAP.
WE DON'T HAVE MICE HERE, BUCK.
OHHH MY HEAD. ACCORDING TO THE SCALE, THIS "TRAP" IS BIGGER THAN OUR HOUSE... THERE'S NO WAY YOU COULD BUILD THIS THING.
THAT'S WHY PHASE 3 OF OPERATION *STIFLE SQUEAK* IS AN INTENSIVE PROGRAM OF CHEESE DEPLOYMENT.
ROBERT. I **THINK** I KNOW A THING OR TWO ABOUT CATCHING MICE. I MEAN, IT'S NOT *ROCKET SCIENCE* NOW, IS IT?
WELL, YOUR OWN DIAGRAMS IN PHASE 9 WOULD SUGGEST OTHERWISE.
BUCKY, IF YOU'RE JUST **NICE** TO THE LITTLE GUYS, THEY CHAT ALL DAY! YOU'D HAVE ALL THE MOUSE BUDDIES YOU WANT!
LOWE TECH
darb

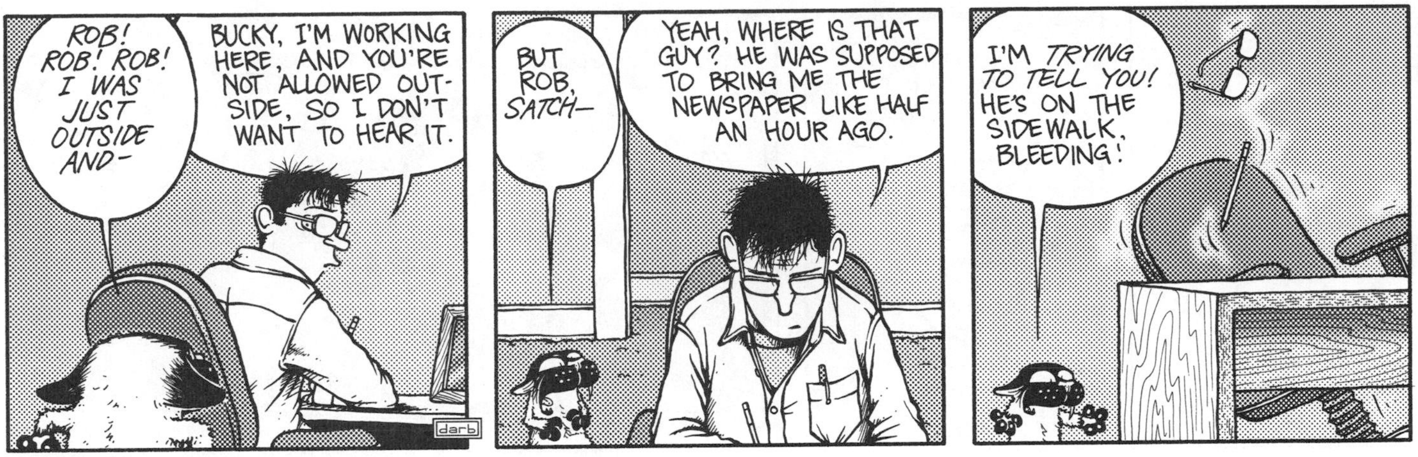
ROB! ROB! ROB! I WAS JUST OUTSIDE AND-
BUCKY, I'M WORKING HERE, AND YOU'RE NOT ALLOWED OUT-SIDE, SO I DON'T WANT TO HEAR IT.
darb
BUT ROB, SATCH-
YEAH, WHERE IS THAT GUY? HE WAS SUPPOSED TO BRING ME THE NEWSPAPER LIKE HALF AN HOUR AGO.
I'M TRYING TO TELL YOU! HE'S ON THE SIDEWALK, BLEEDING!

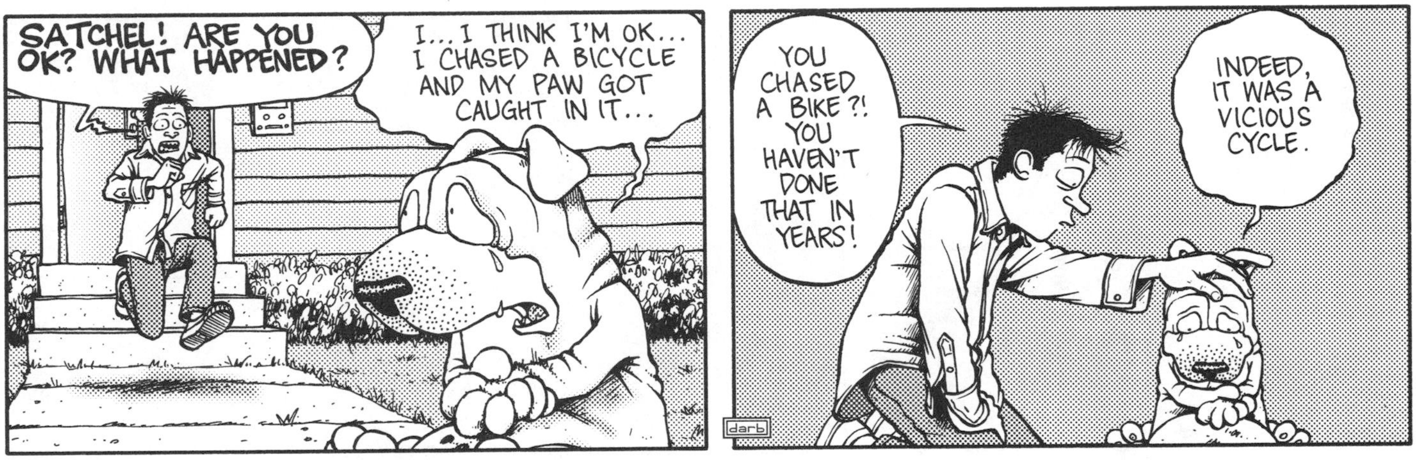
SATCHEL! ARE YOU OK? WHAT HAPPENED?
I... I THINK I'M OK... I CHASED A BICYCLE AND MY PAW GOT CAUGHT IN IT...
darb
YOU CHASED A BIKE?! YOU HAVEN'T DONE THAT IN YEARS!
INDEED, IT WAS A VICIOUS CYCLE.

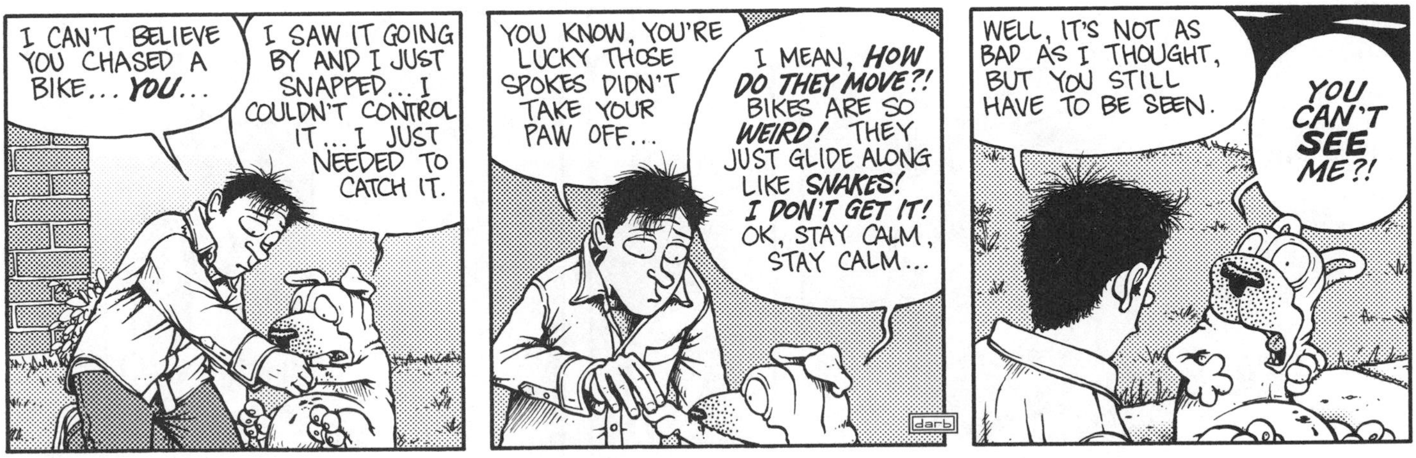
I CAN'T BELIEVE YOU CHASED A BIKE... YOU...
I SAW IT GOING BY AND I JUST SNAPPED... I COULDN'T CONTROL IT... I JUST NEEDED TO CATCH IT.
YOU KNOW, YOU'RE LUCKY THOSE SPOKES DIDN'T TAKE YOUR PAW OFF...
I MEAN, HOW DO THEY MOVE?! BIKES ARE SO WEIRD! THEY JUST GLIDE ALONG LIKE SNAKES! I DON'T GET IT! OK, STAY CALM, STAY CALM...
darb
WELL, IT'S NOT AS BAD AS I THOUGHT, BUT YOU STILL HAVE TO BE SEEN.
YOU CAN'T SEE ME?!

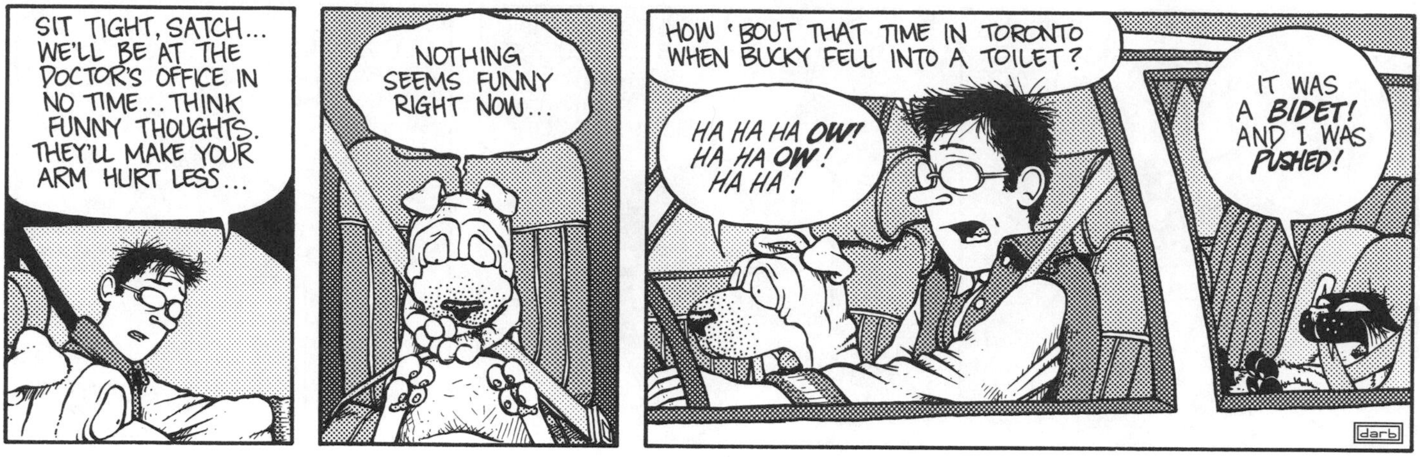
SIT TIGHT, SATCH... WE'LL BE AT THE DOCTOR'S OFFICE IN NO TIME... THINK FUNNY THOUGHTS. THEY'LL MAKE YOUR ARM HURT LESS...
NOTHING SEEMS FUNNY RIGHT NOW...
HOW 'BOUT THAT TIME IN TORONTO WHEN BUCKY FELL INTO A TOILET?
HA HA HA **OW!** HA HA **OW!** HA HA!
IT WAS A ***BIDET!*** AND I WAS ***PUSHED!***

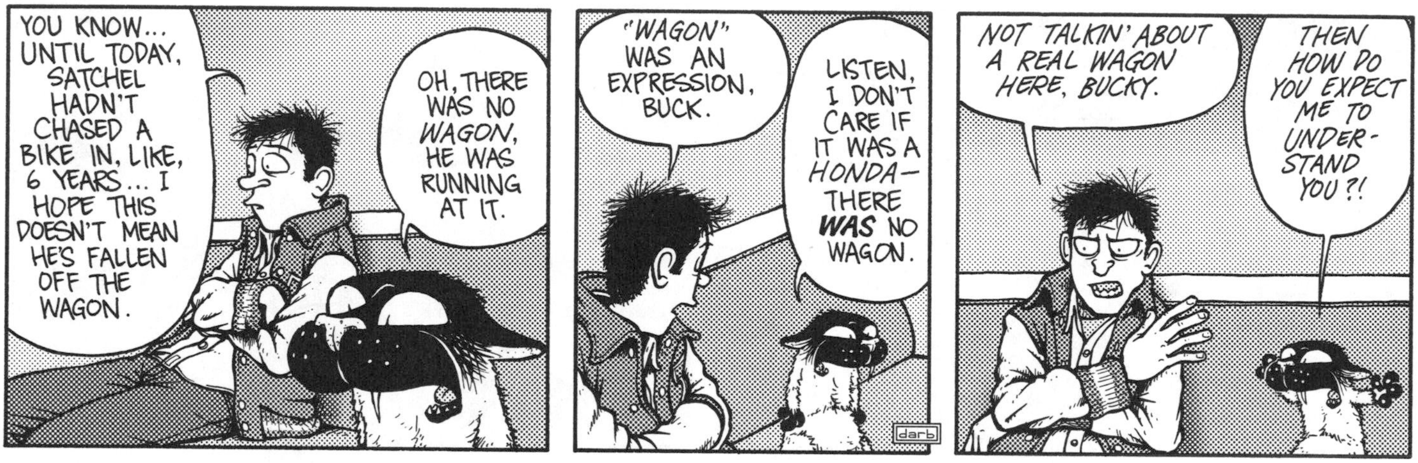
YOU KNOW... UNTIL TODAY, SATCHEL HADN'T CHASED A BIKE IN, LIKE, 6 YEARS... I HOPE THIS DOESN'T MEAN HE'S FALLEN OFF THE WAGON.
OH, THERE WAS NO *WAGON*, HE WAS RUNNING AT IT.
"WAGON" WAS AN EXPRESSION, BUCK.
LISTEN, I DON'T CARE IF IT WAS A *HONDA*– THERE **WAS** NO WAGON.
NOT TALKIN' ABOUT A REAL WAGON HERE, BUCKY.
THEN HOW DO YOU EXPECT ME TO UNDERSTAND YOU?!

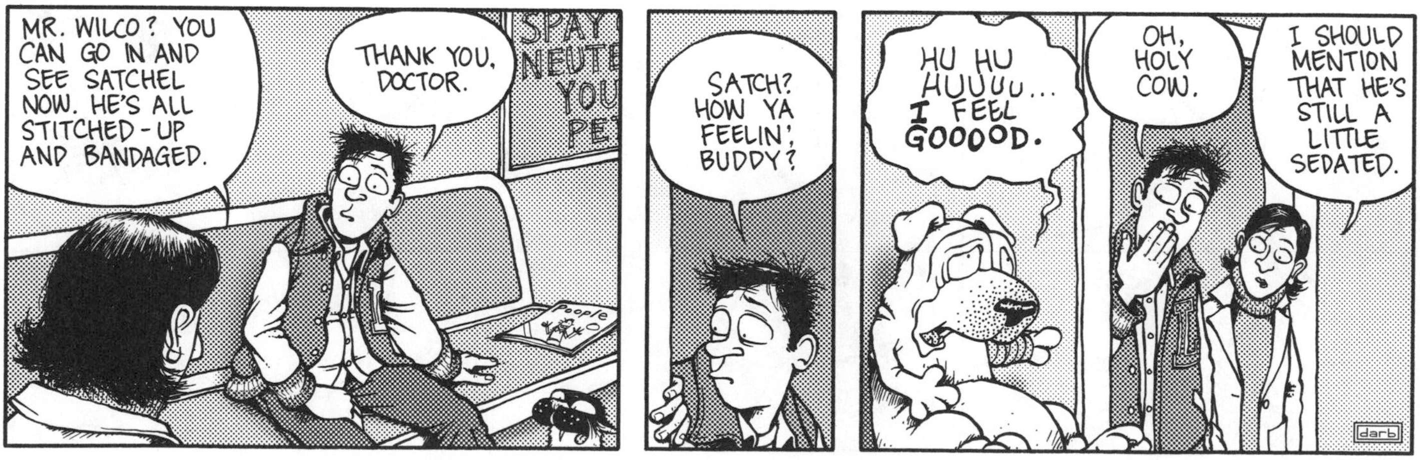
MR. WILCO? YOU CAN GO IN AND SEE SATCHEL NOW. HE'S ALL STITCHED-UP AND BANDAGED.
THANK YOU, DOCTOR.
SPAY NEUTE YOU PE
People
SATCH? HOW YA FEELIN', BUDDY?
HU HU HUUUU... **I FEEL GOOOOD.**
OH, HOLY COW.
I SHOULD MENTION THAT HE'S STILL A LITTLE SEDATED.

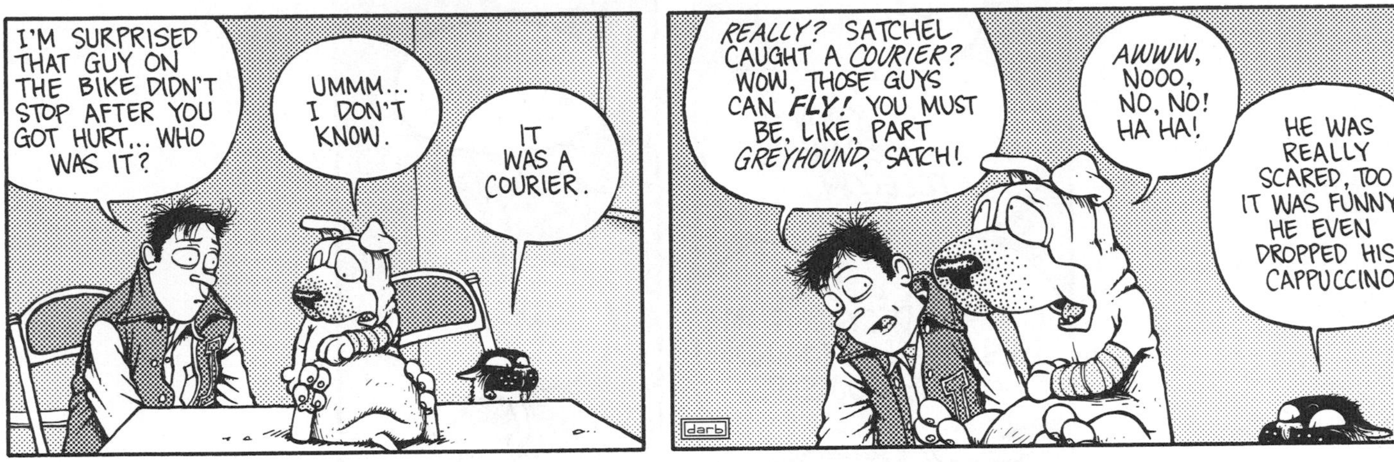
I'M SURPRISED THAT GUY ON THE BIKE DIDN'T STOP AFTER YOU GOT HURT... WHO WAS IT?
UMMM... I DON'T KNOW.
IT WAS A COURIER.
REALLY? SATCHEL CAUGHT A COURIER? WOW, THOSE GUYS CAN FLY! YOU MUST BE, LIKE, PART GREYHOUND, SATCH!
AWWW, NOOO, NO, NO! HA HA!
HE WAS REALLY SCARED, TOO. IT WAS FUNNY. HE EVEN DROPPED HIS CAPPUCCINO.
darb

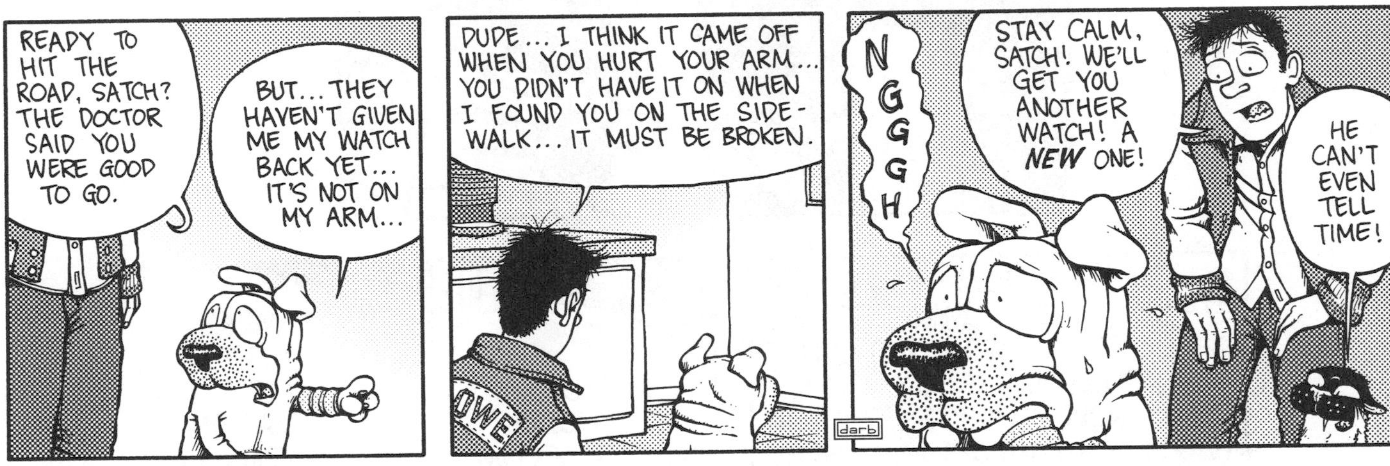
READY TO HIT THE ROAD, SATCH? THE DOCTOR SAID YOU WERE GOOD TO GO.
BUT... THEY HAVEN'T GIVEN ME MY WATCH BACK YET... IT'S NOT ON MY ARM...
DUDE... I THINK IT CAME OFF WHEN YOU HURT YOUR ARM... YOU DIDN'T HAVE IT ON WHEN I FOUND YOU ON THE SIDE-WALK... IT MUST BE BROKEN.
NGGGH
STAY CALM, SATCH! WE'LL GET YOU ANOTHER WATCH! A NEW ONE!
HE CAN'T EVEN TELL TIME!
darb

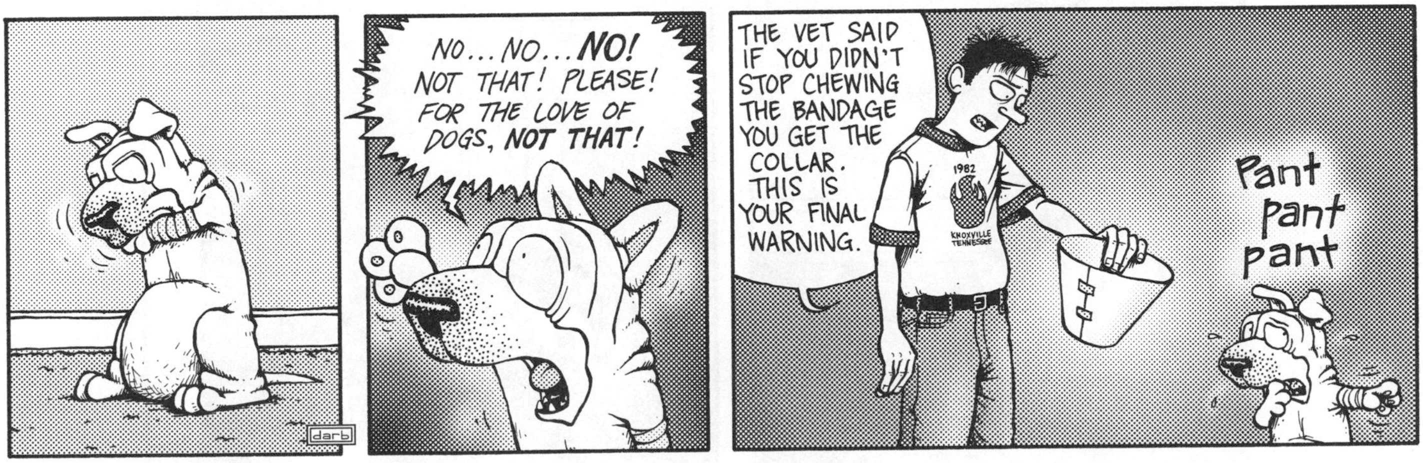
darb
NO... NO... NO! NOT THAT! PLEASE! FOR THE LOVE OF DOGS, NOT THAT!
THE VET SAID IF YOU DIDN'T STOP CHEWING THE BANDAGE YOU GET THE COLLAR. THIS IS YOUR FINAL WARNING.
1982
KNOXVILLE TENNESSEE
Pant pant pant

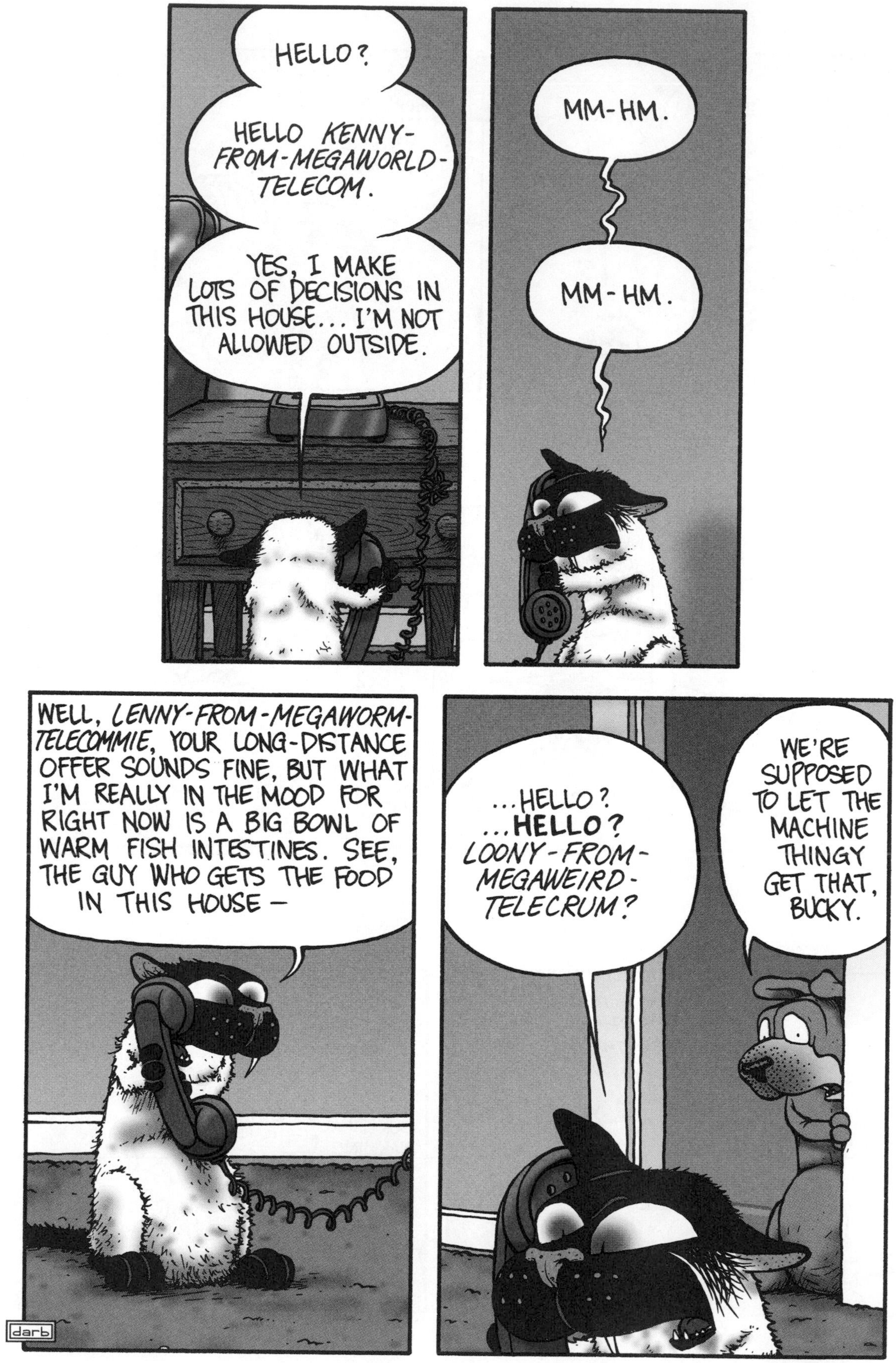
HELLO?
HELLO KENNY-FROM-MEGAWORLD-TELECOM.
YES, I MAKE LOTS OF DECISIONS IN THIS HOUSE... I'M NOT ALLOWED OUTSIDE.
MM-HM.
MM-HM.
WELL, LENNY-FROM-MEGAWORM-TELECOMMIE, YOUR LONG-DISTANCE OFFER SOUNDS FINE, BUT WHAT I'M REALLY IN THE MOOD FOR RIGHT NOW IS A BIG BOWL OF WARM FISH INTESTINES. SEE, THE GUY WHO GETS THE FOOD IN THIS HOUSE –
darb
...HELLO? ...HELLO? LOONY-FROM-MEGAWEIRD-TELECRUM?
WE'RE SUPPOSED TO LET THE MACHINE THINGY GET THAT, BUCKY.

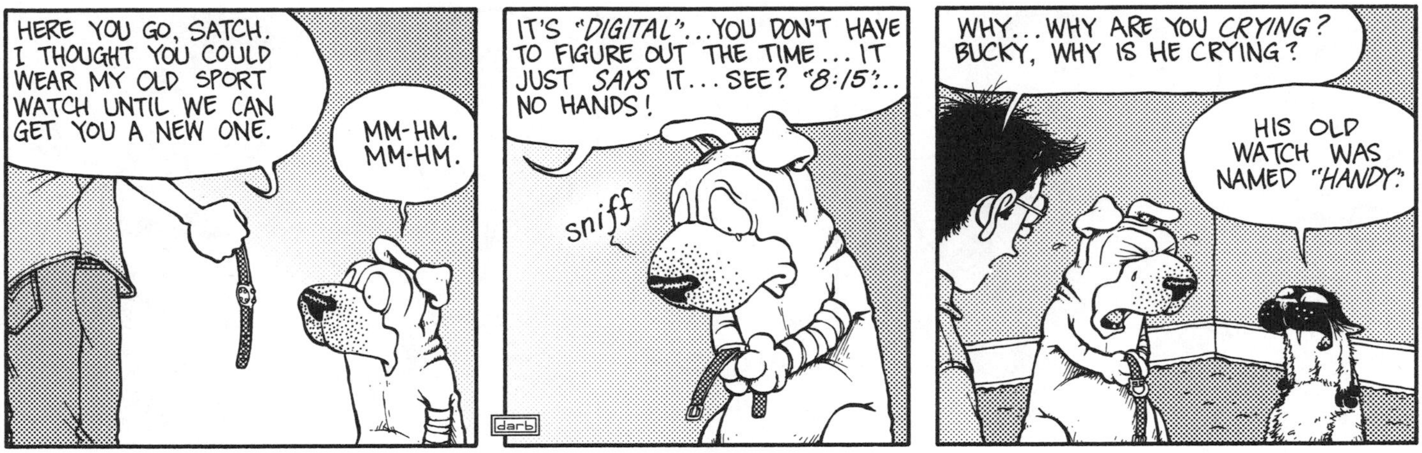
HERE YOU GO, SATCH. I THOUGHT YOU COULD WEAR MY OLD SPORT WATCH UNTIL WE CAN GET YOU A NEW ONE.
MM-HM. MM-HM.
IT'S "DIGITAL"... YOU DON'T HAVE TO FIGURE OUT THE TIME... IT JUST SAYS IT... SEE? "8:15"... NO HANDS!
sniff
WHY... WHY ARE YOU CRYING? BUCKY, WHY IS HE CRYING?
HIS OLD WATCH WAS NAMED "HANDY."

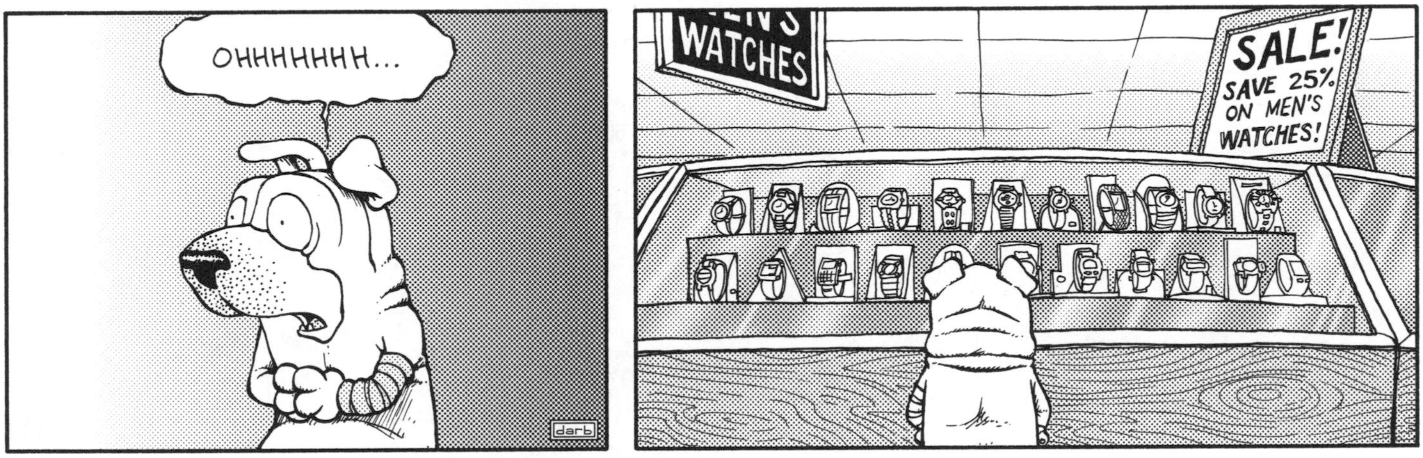
OHHHHHHH...
WATCHES
SALE! SAVE 25% ON MEN'S WATCHES!

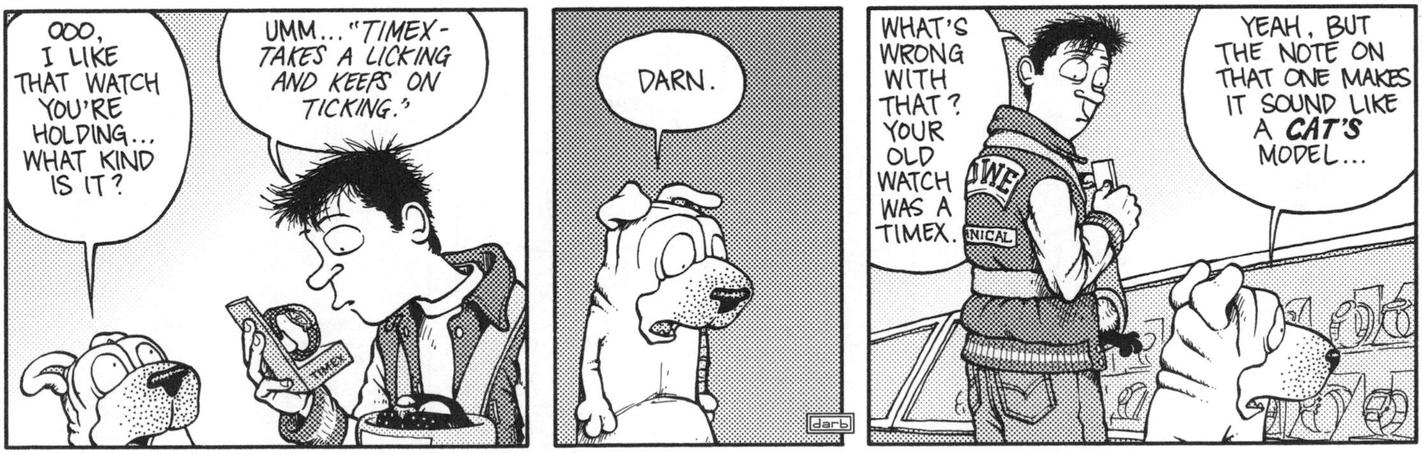
OOO, I LIKE THAT WATCH YOU'RE HOLDING... WHAT KIND IS IT?
UMM... "TIMEX - TAKES A LICKING AND KEEPS ON TICKING."
TIMEX
DARN.
WHAT'S WRONG WITH THAT? YOUR OLD WATCH WAS A TIMEX.
YEAH, BUT THE NOTE ON THAT ONE MAKES IT SOUND LIKE A CAT'S MODEL...

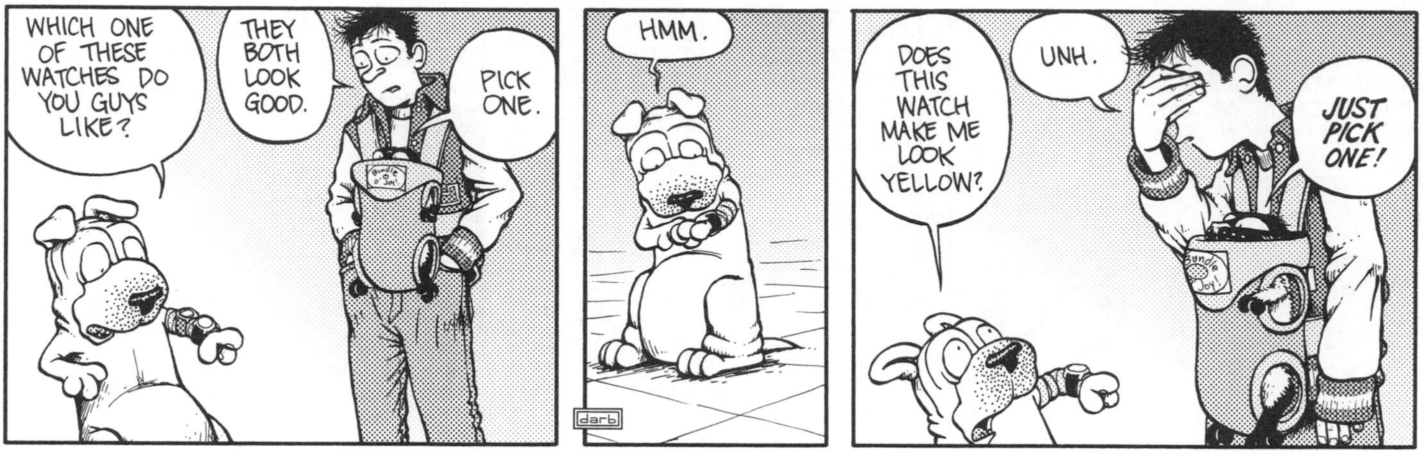
WHICH ONE OF THESE WATCHES DO YOU GUYS LIKE?
THEY BOTH LOOK GOOD.
PICK ONE.
HMM.
DOES THIS WATCH MAKE ME LOOK YELLOW?
UNH.
JUST PICK ONE!

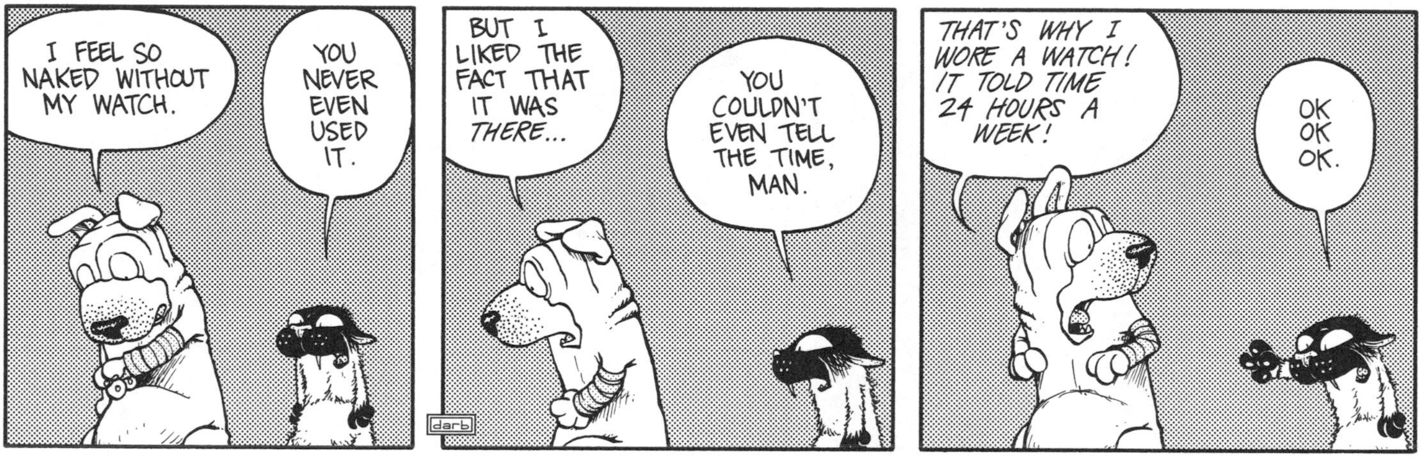
I FEEL SO NAKED WITHOUT MY WATCH.
YOU NEVER EVEN USED IT.
BUT I LIKED THE FACT THAT IT WAS THERE...
YOU COULDN'T EVEN TELL THE TIME, MAN.
THAT'S WHY I WORE A WATCH! IT TOLD TIME 24 HOURS A WEEK!
OK OK OK.

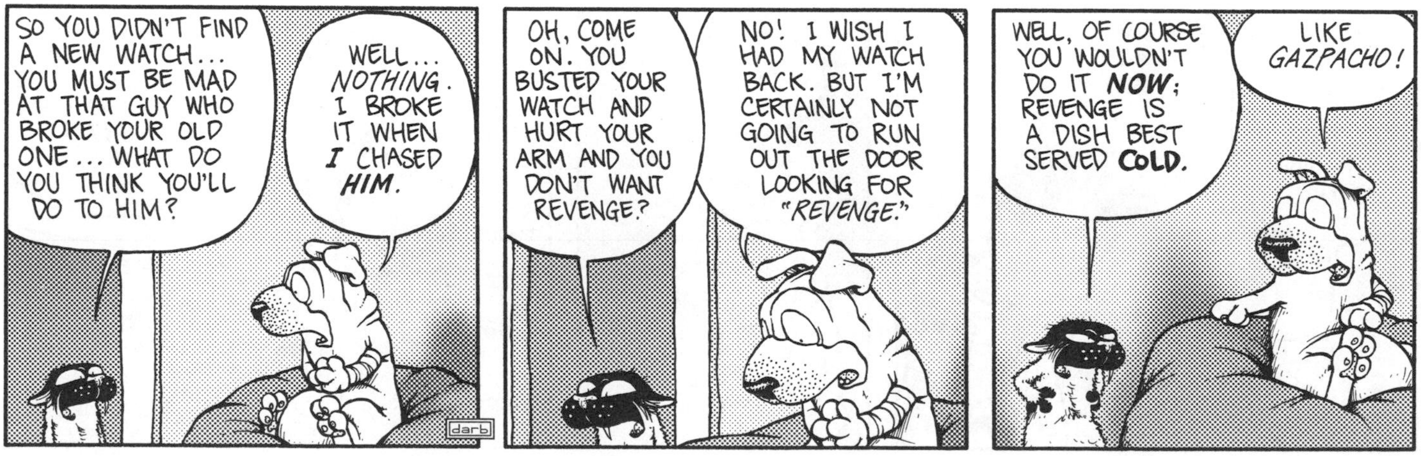
SO YOU DIDN'T FIND A NEW WATCH... YOU MUST BE MAD AT THAT GUY WHO BROKE YOUR OLD ONE... WHAT DO YOU THINK YOU'LL DO TO HIM?
WELL... NOTHING. I BROKE IT WHEN I CHASED HIM.
OH, COME ON. YOU BUSTED YOUR WATCH AND HURT YOUR ARM AND YOU DON'T WANT REVENGE?
NO! I WISH I HAD MY WATCH BACK. BUT I'M CERTAINLY NOT GOING TO RUN OUT THE DOOR LOOKING FOR "REVENGE."
WELL, OF COURSE YOU WOULDN'T DO IT NOW; REVENGE IS A DISH BEST SERVED COLD.
LIKE GAZPACHO!

WHAT WERE YOU DOING IN THE HALL?
SOMEBODY IN THIS BUILDING IS COOKING FISH -- *NORTHERN YELLOWTAIL SNAPPER*, TO BE EXACT -- AND I STARTED THINKING ABOUT HOW I NEVER GET ANY SNAPPER, AND SO I DECIDED THAT I WOULD GO **TAKE** IT WHEN THEY WEREN'T LOOKING...
darb
BUT... YOU KNOW? ULTIMATELY, SOMETHING PREVENTED ME FROM DOING THAT.
A SENSE OF RIGHT AND WRONG?
NO, IT WAS MORE OF A **DOOR**-TYPE THINGY.

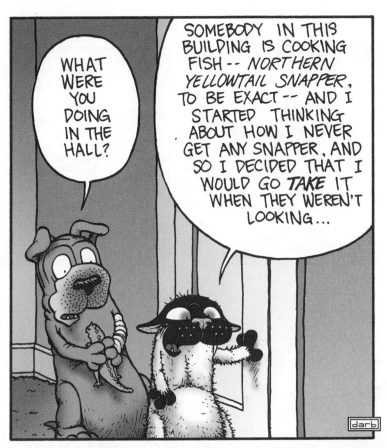

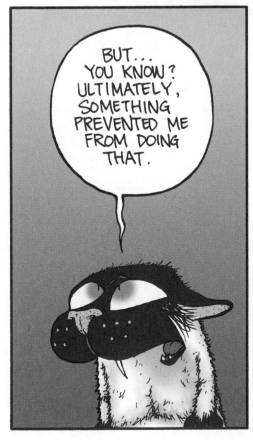

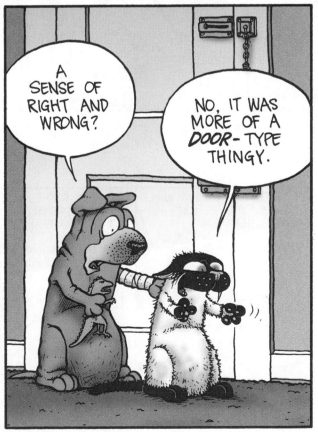

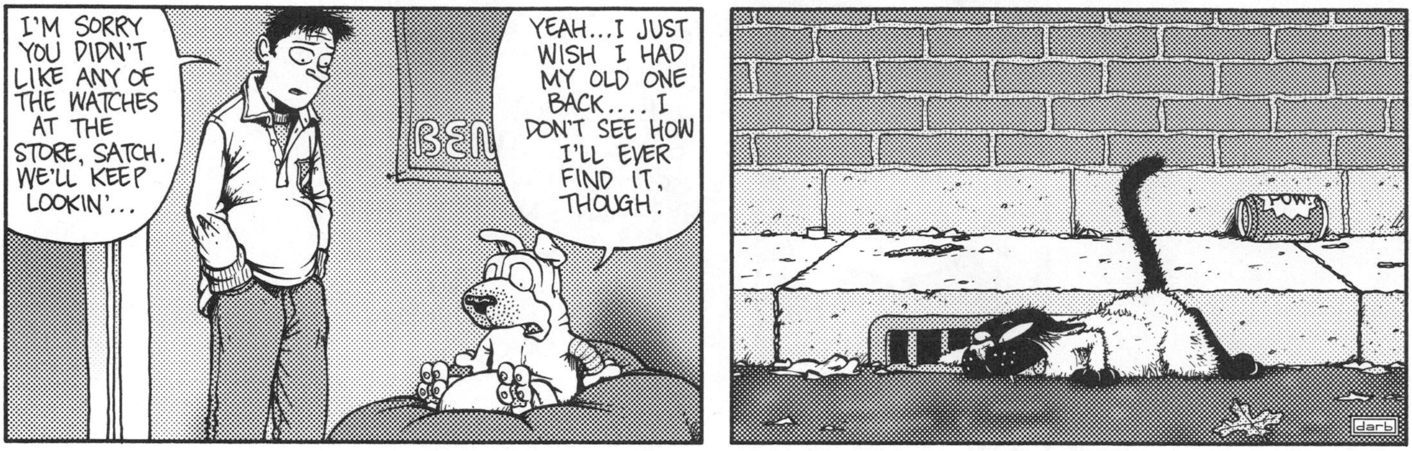
I'M SORRY YOU DIDN'T LIKE ANY OF THE WATCHES AT THE STORE, SATCH. WE'LL KEEP LOOKIN'...
YEAH... I JUST WISH I HAD MY OLD ONE BACK.... I DON'T SEE HOW I'LL EVER FIND IT, THOUGH.
POW!
darb

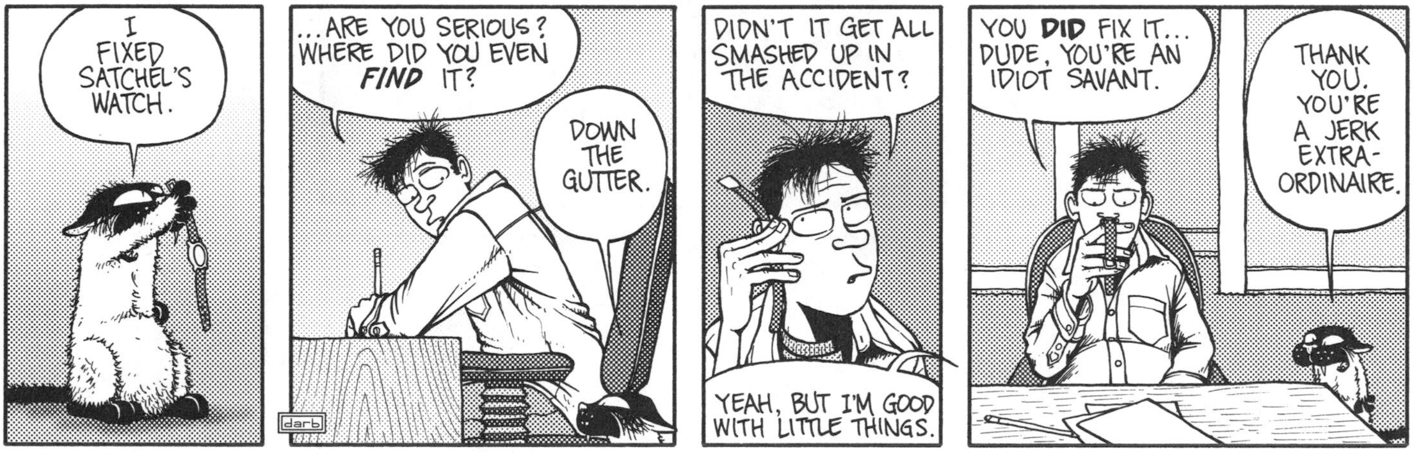
I FIXED SATCHEL'S WATCH.
darb
...ARE YOU SERIOUS? WHERE DID YOU EVEN FIND IT?
DOWN THE GUTTER.
DIDN'T IT GET ALL SMASHED UP IN THE ACCIDENT?
YEAH, BUT I'M GOOD WITH LITTLE THINGS.
YOU DID FIX IT... DUDE, YOU'RE AN IDIOT SAVANT.
THANK YOU. YOU'RE A JERK EXTRA-ORDINAIRE.

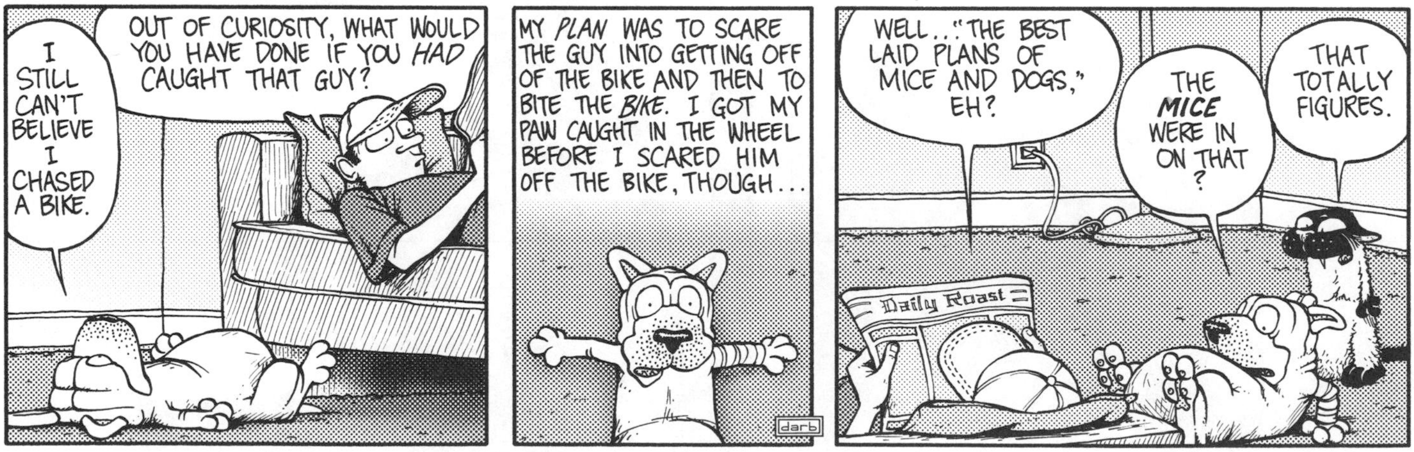
I STILL CAN'T BELIEVE I CHASED A BIKE.
OUT OF CURIOSITY, WHAT WOULD YOU HAVE DONE IF YOU HAD CAUGHT THAT GUY?
MY PLAN WAS TO SCARE THE GUY INTO GETTING OFF OF THE BIKE AND THEN TO BITE THE BIKE. I GOT MY PAW CAUGHT IN THE WHEEL BEFORE I SCARED HIM OFF THE BIKE, THOUGH...
darb
WELL..."THE BEST LAID PLANS OF MICE AND DOGS," EH?
THE MICE WERE IN ON THAT?
THAT TOTALLY FIGURES.
Daily Roast

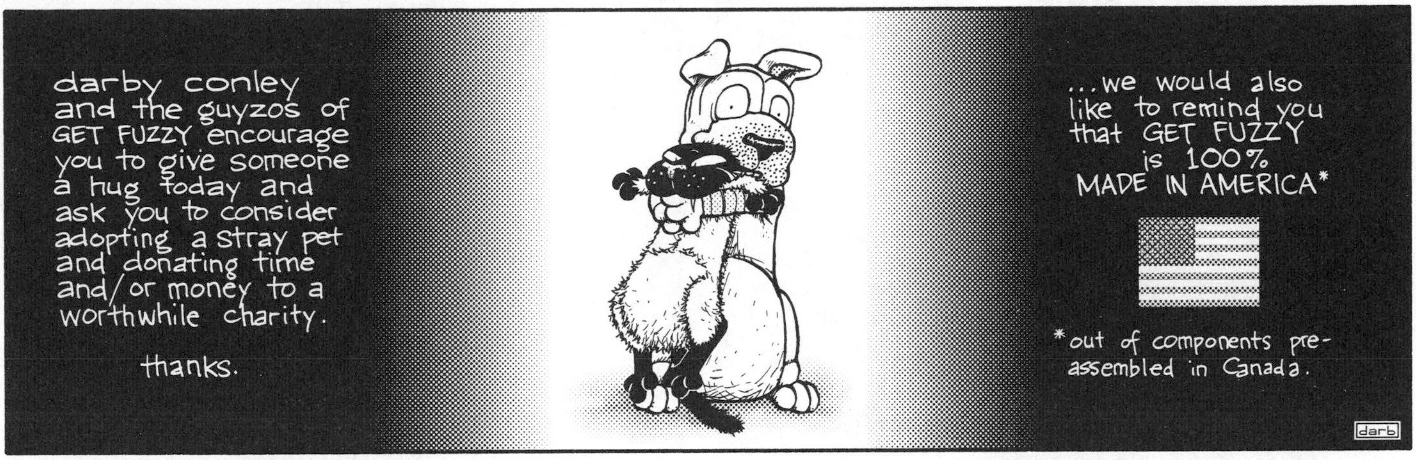
darby conley and the guyzos of GET FUZZY encourage you to give someone a hug today and ask you to consider adopting a stray pet and donating time and/or money to a worthwhile charity.
thanks.
...we would also like to remind you that GET FUZZY is 100% MADE IN AMERICA*
*out of components pre-assembled in Canada.
darb

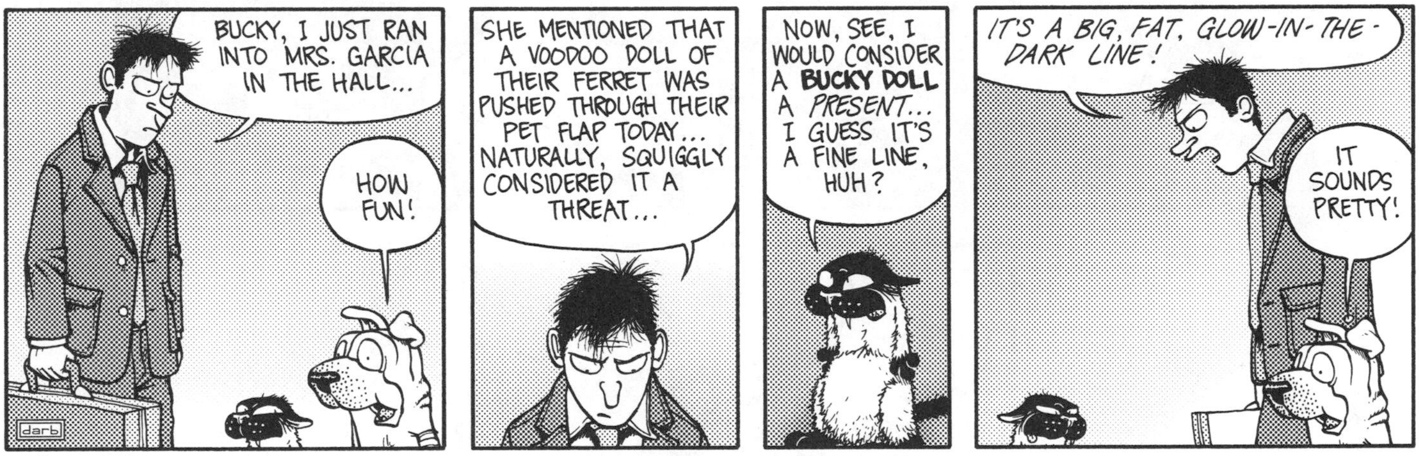
BUCKY, I JUST RAN INTO MRS. GARCIA IN THE HALL...
HOW FUN!
SHE MENTIONED THAT A VOODOO DOLL OF THEIR FERRET WAS PUSHED THROUGH THEIR PET FLAP TODAY... NATURALLY, SQUIGGLY CONSIDERED IT A THREAT...
NOW, SEE, I WOULD CONSIDER A BUCKY DOLL A PRESENT... I GUESS IT'S A FINE LINE, HUH?
IT'S A BIG, FAT, GLOW-IN-THE-DARK LINE!
IT SOUNDS PRETTY!
darb

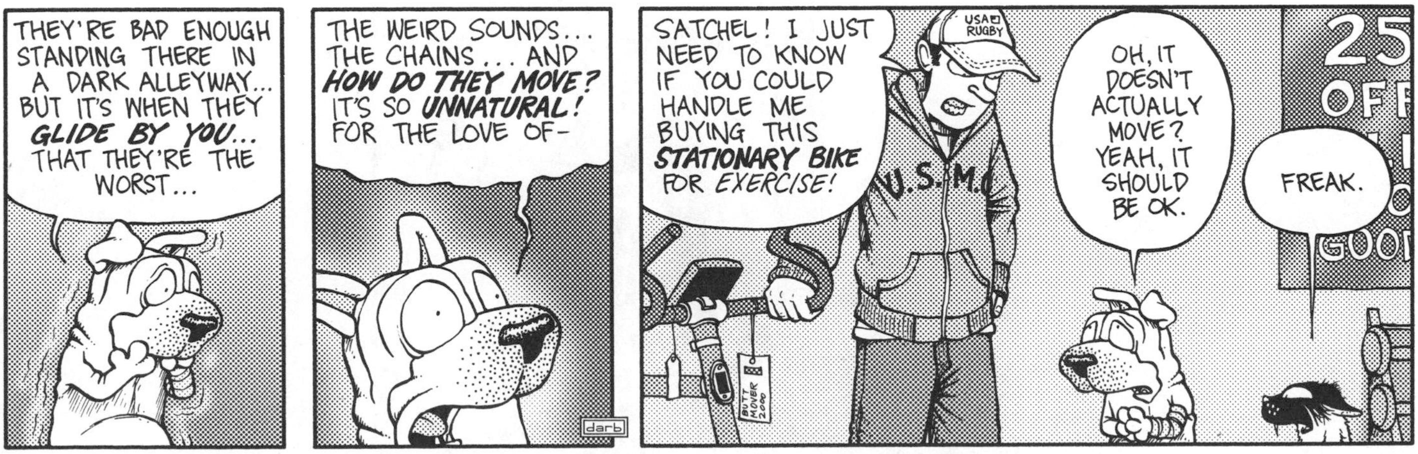
THEY'RE BAD ENOUGH STANDING THERE IN A DARK ALLEYWAY... BUT IT'S WHEN THEY GLIDE BY YOU... THAT THEY'RE THE WORST...
THE WEIRD SOUNDS... THE CHAINS... AND HOW DO THEY MOVE? IT'S SO UNNATURAL! FOR THE LOVE OF-
darb
SATCHEL! I JUST NEED TO KNOW IF YOU COULD HANDLE ME BUYING THIS STATIONARY BIKE FOR EXERCISE!
USA RUGBY
U.S.M.
BUTT MOVER 2000
OH, IT DOESN'T ACTUALLY MOVE? YEAH, IT SHOULD BE OK.
FREAK.

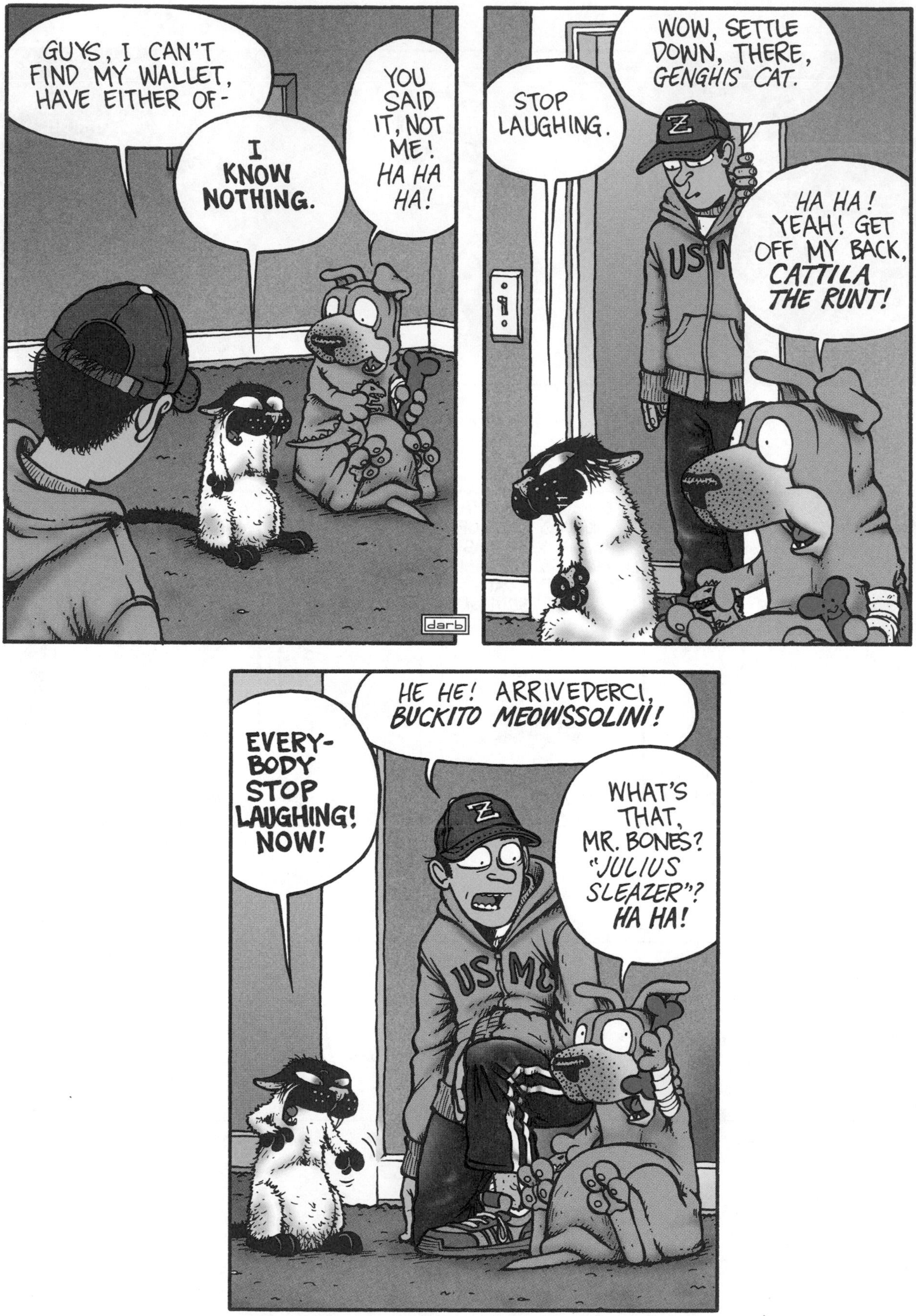
GUYS, I CAN'T FIND MY WALLET, HAVE EITHER OF-
I KNOW NOTHING.
YOU SAID IT, NOT ME! HA HA HA!
darb
WOW, SETTLE DOWN, THERE, GENGHIS CAT.
STOP LAUGHING.
HA HA! YEAH! GET OFF MY BACK, CATTILA THE RUNT!
HE HE! ARRIVEDERCI, BUCKITO MEOWSSOLINI!
EVERY-BODY STOP LAUGHING! NOW!
WHAT'S THAT, MR. BONES? "JULIUS SLEAZER"? HA HA!

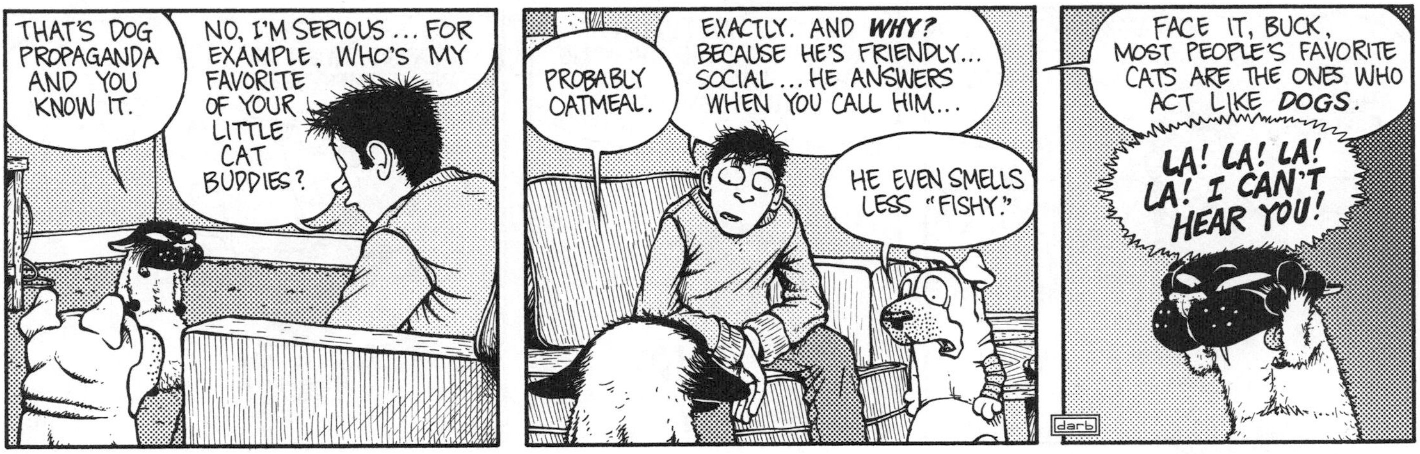
THAT'S DOG PROPAGANDA AND YOU KNOW IT.
NO, I'M SERIOUS ... FOR EXAMPLE, WHO'S MY FAVORITE OF YOUR LITTLE CAT BUDDIES?
PROBABLY OATMEAL.
EXACTLY. AND WHY? BECAUSE HE'S FRIENDLY... SOCIAL ... HE ANSWERS WHEN YOU CALL HIM...
HE EVEN SMELLS LESS "FISHY."
FACE IT, BUCK, MOST PEOPLE'S FAVORITE CATS ARE THE ONES WHO ACT LIKE DOGS.
LA! LA! LA! LA! I CAN'T HEAR YOU!
darb

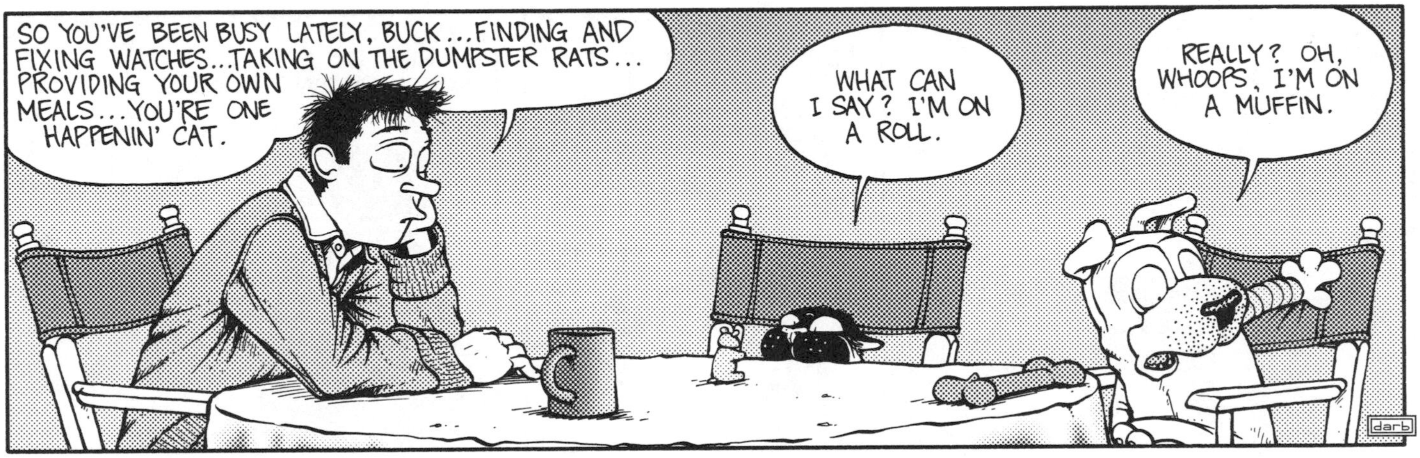
SO YOU'VE BEEN BUSY LATELY, BUCK... FINDING AND FIXING WATCHES...TAKING ON THE DUMPSTER RATS... PROVIDING YOUR OWN MEALS... YOU'RE ONE HAPPENIN' CAT.
WHAT CAN I SAY? I'M ON A ROLL.
REALLY? OH, WHOOPS, I'M ON A MUFFIN.
darb

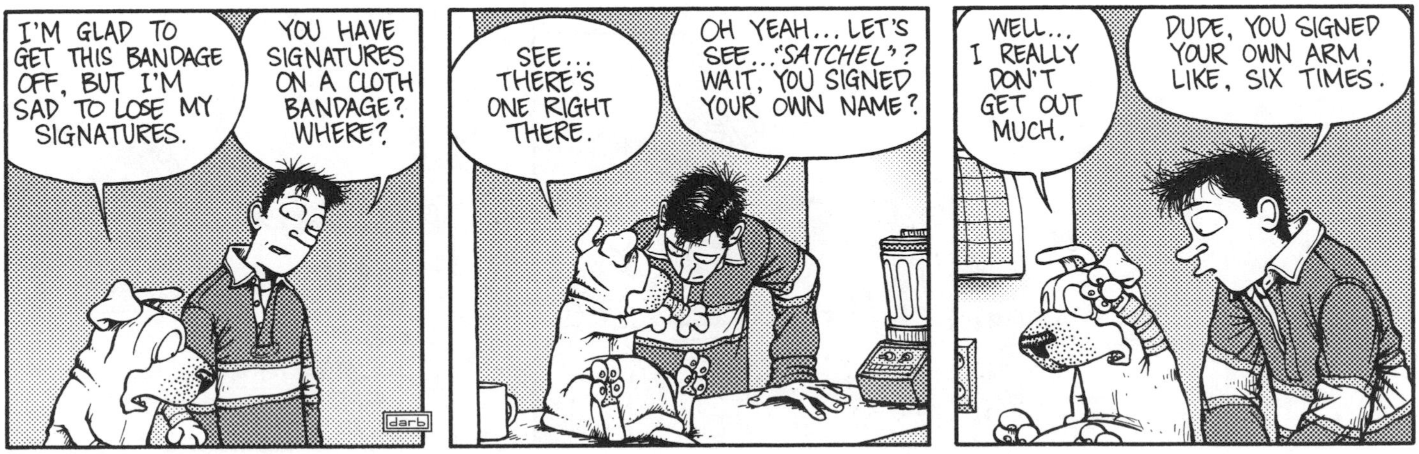
I'M GLAD TO GET THIS BANDAGE OFF, BUT I'M SAD TO LOSE MY SIGNATURES.
YOU HAVE SIGNATURES ON A CLOTH BANDAGE? WHERE?
darb
SEE... THERE'S ONE RIGHT THERE.
OH YEAH... LET'S SEE..."SATCHEL"? WAIT, YOU SIGNED YOUR OWN NAME?
WELL... I REALLY DON'T GET OUT MUCH.
DUDE, YOU SIGNED YOUR OWN ARM, LIKE, SIX TIMES.

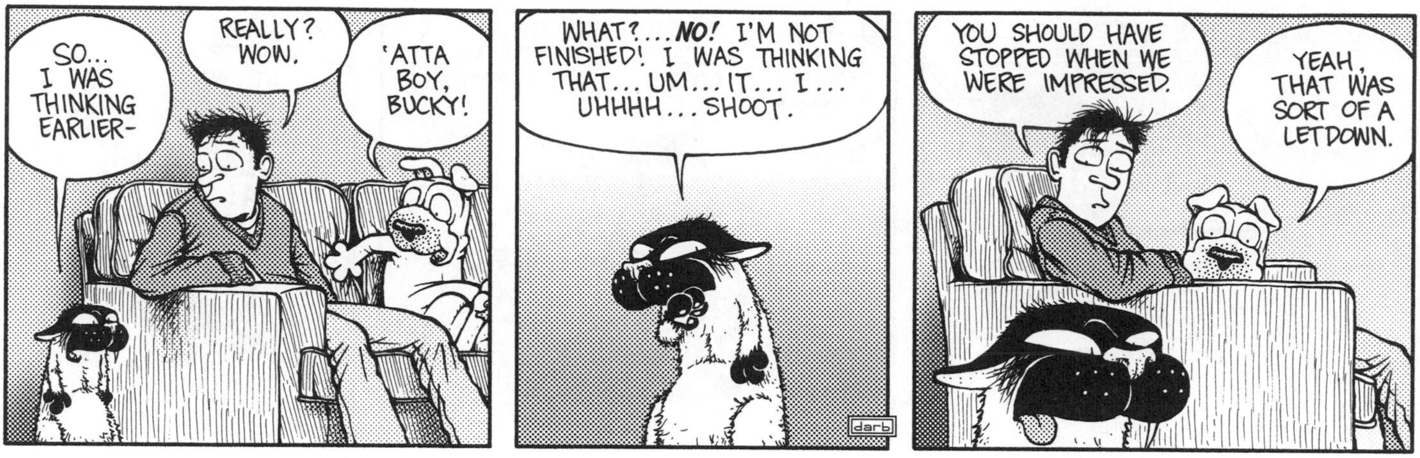

SO... I WAS THINKING EARLIER-
REALLY? WOW.
'ATTA BOY, BUCKY!
WHAT?... **NO!** I'M NOT FINISHED! I WAS THINKING THAT... UM... IT... I... UHHHH... SHOOT.
darb
YOU SHOULD HAVE STOPPED WHEN WE WERE IMPRESSED.
YEAH, THAT WAS SORT OF A LETDOWN.

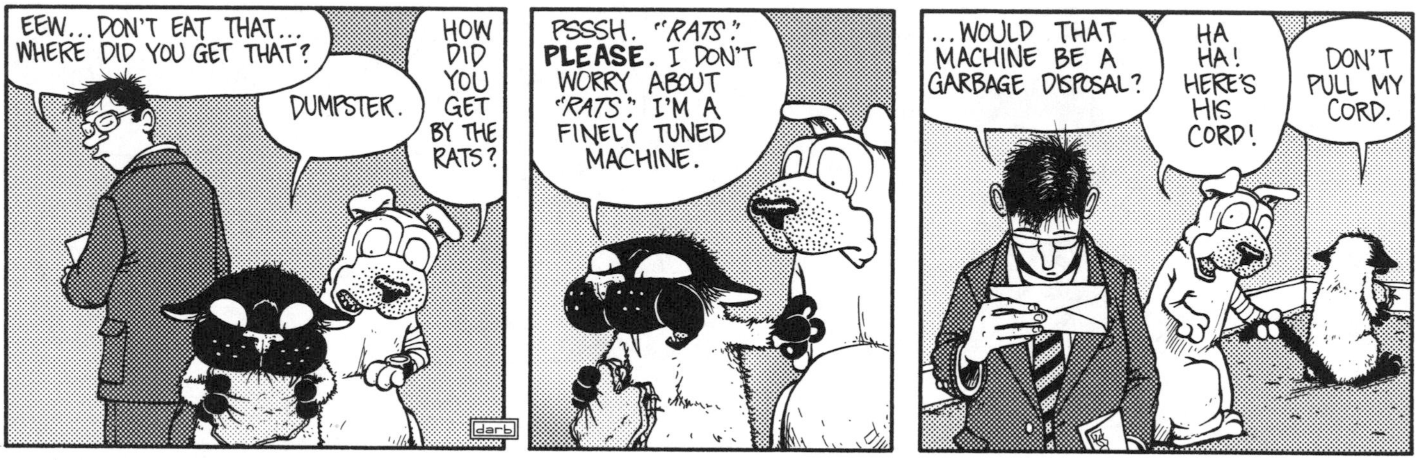

EEW... DON'T EAT THAT... WHERE DID YOU GET THAT?
DUMPSTER.
HOW DID YOU GET BY THE RATS?
darb
PSSSH. *"RATS."* **PLEASE**. I DON'T WORRY ABOUT *"RATS."* I'M A FINELY TUNED MACHINE.
...WOULD THAT MACHINE BE A GARBAGE DISPOSAL?
HA HA! HERE'S HIS CORD!
DON'T PULL MY CORD.

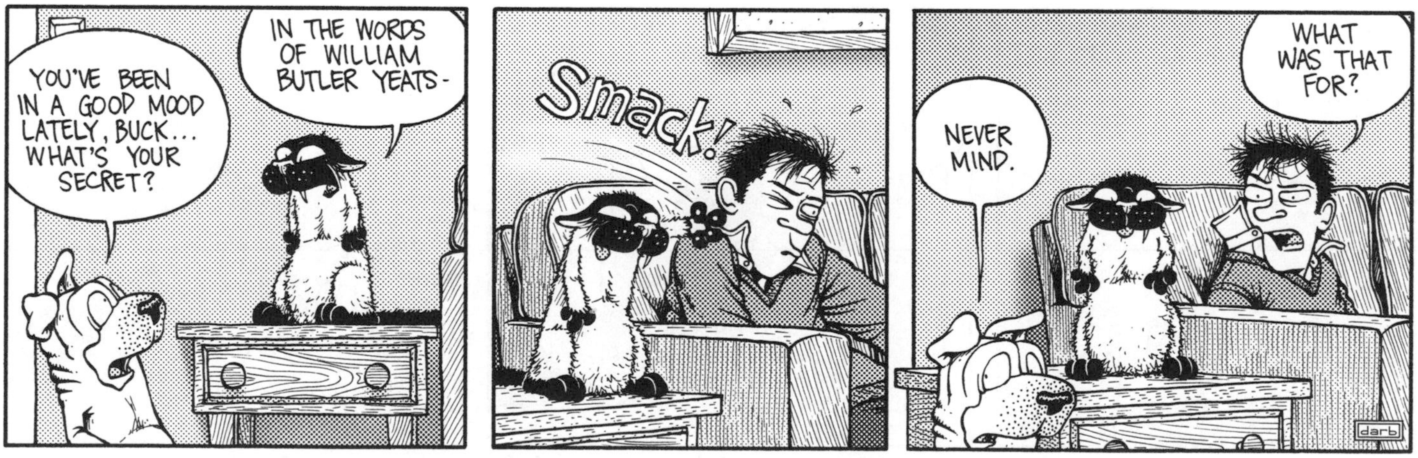

YOU'VE BEEN IN A GOOD MOOD LATELY, BUCK... WHAT'S YOUR SECRET?
IN THE WORDS OF WILLIAM BUTLER YEATS-
Smack!
WHAT WAS THAT FOR?
NEVER MIND.
darb

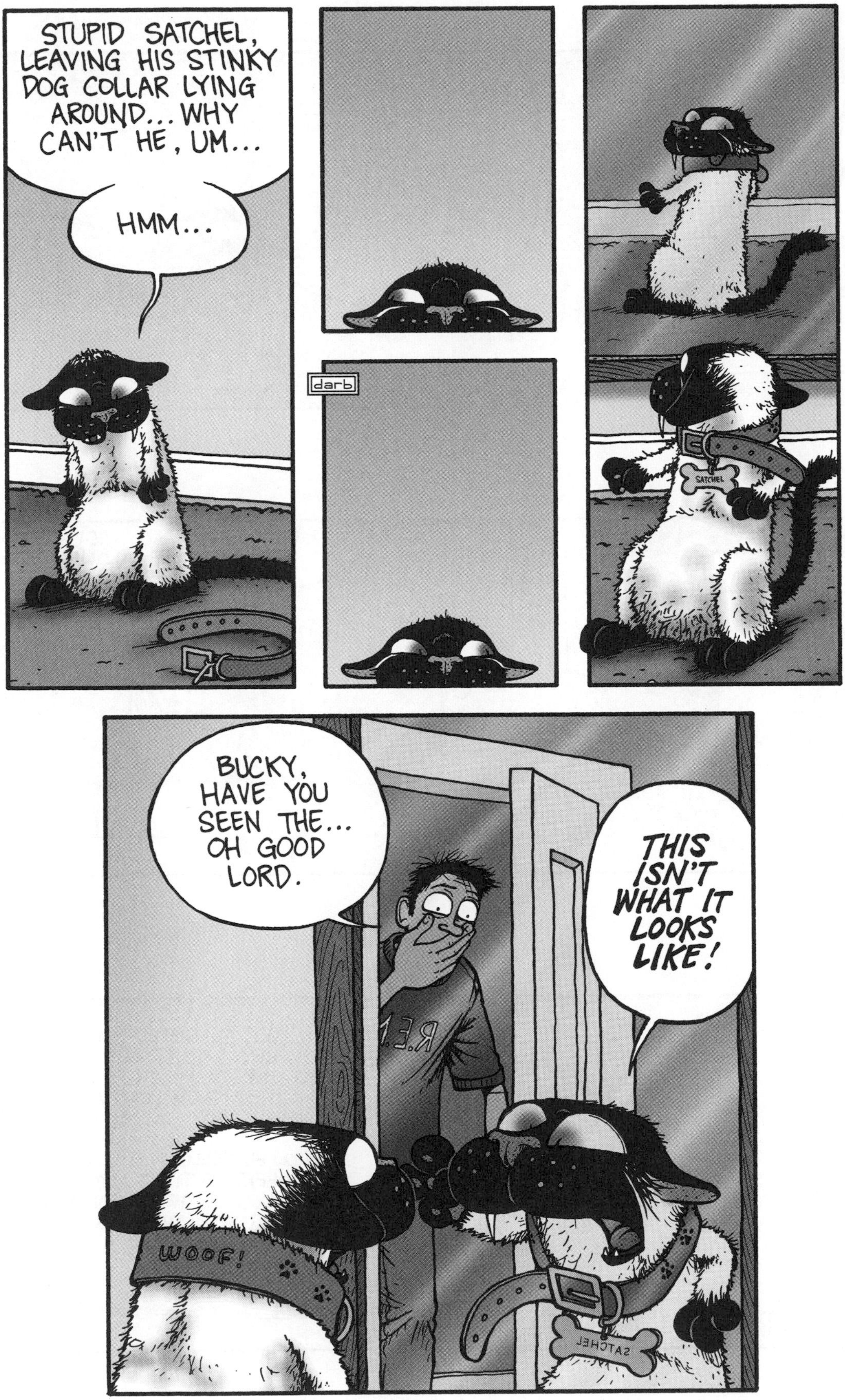
STUPID SATCHEL, LEAVING HIS STINKY DOG COLLAR LYING AROUND... WHY CAN'T HE, UM...
HMM...
darb
SATCHEL
BUCKY, HAVE YOU SEEN THE... OH GOOD LORD.
THIS ISN'T WHAT IT LOOKS LIKE!
WOOF!

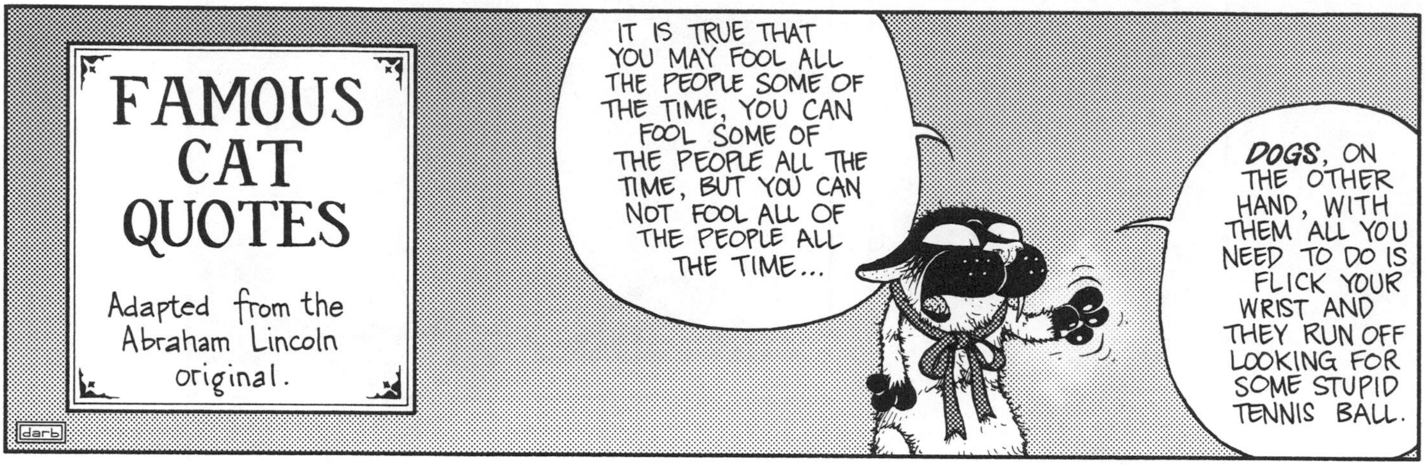
FAMOUS CAT QUOTES
Adapted from the Abraham Lincoln original.
IT IS TRUE THAT YOU MAY FOOL ALL THE PEOPLE SOME OF THE TIME, YOU CAN FOOL SOME OF THE PEOPLE ALL THE TIME, BUT YOU CAN NOT FOOL ALL OF THE PEOPLE ALL THE TIME...
DOGS, ON THE OTHER HAND, WITH THEM ALL YOU NEED TO DO IS FLICK YOUR WRIST AND THEY RUN OFF LOOKING FOR SOME STUPID TENNIS BALL.
darb

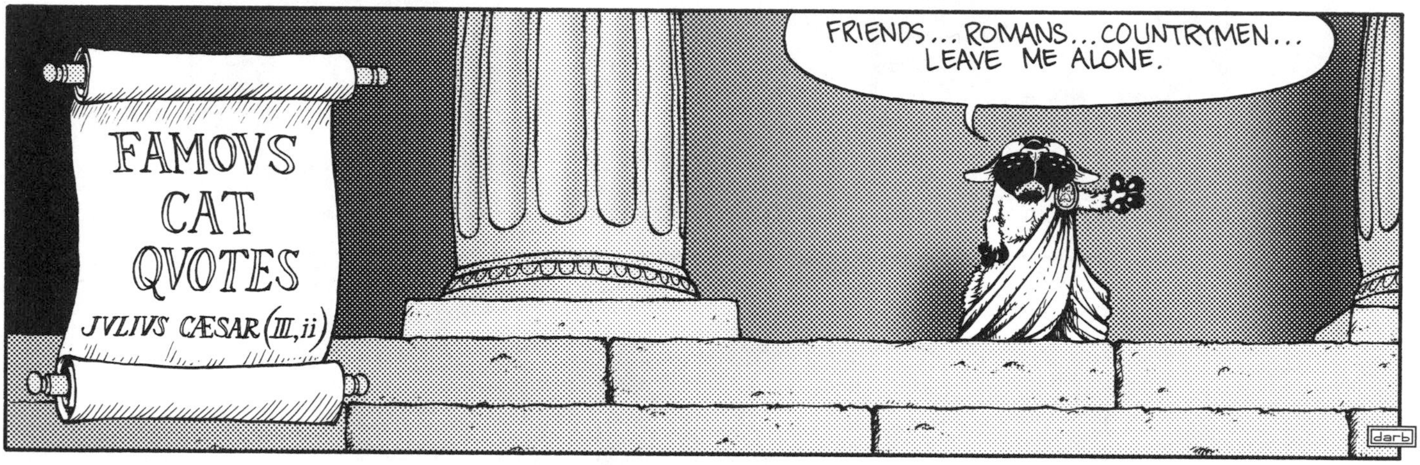
FAMOVS CAT QVOTES
JVLIVS CÆSAR (III,ii)
FRIENDS... ROMANS... COUNTRYMEN... LEAVE ME ALONE.
darb

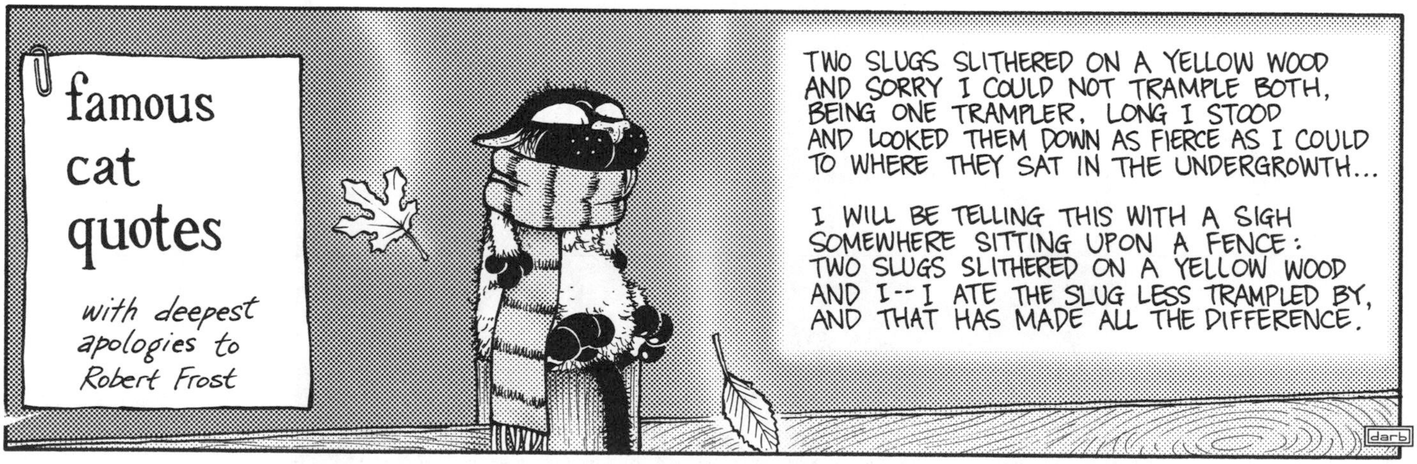
famous cat quotes
with deepest apologies to Robert Frost
TWO SLUGS SLITHERED ON A YELLOW WOOD AND SORRY I COULD NOT TRAMPLE BOTH, BEING ONE TRAMPLER. LONG I STOOD AND LOOKED THEM DOWN AS FIERCE AS I COULD TO WHERE THEY SAT IN THE UNDERGROWTH...
I WILL BE TELLING THIS WITH A SIGH SOMEWHERE SITTING UPON A FENCE: TWO SLUGS SLITHERED ON A YELLOW WOOD AND I-- I ATE THE SLUG LESS TRAMPLED BY, AND THAT HAS MADE ALL THE DIFFERENCE.
darb

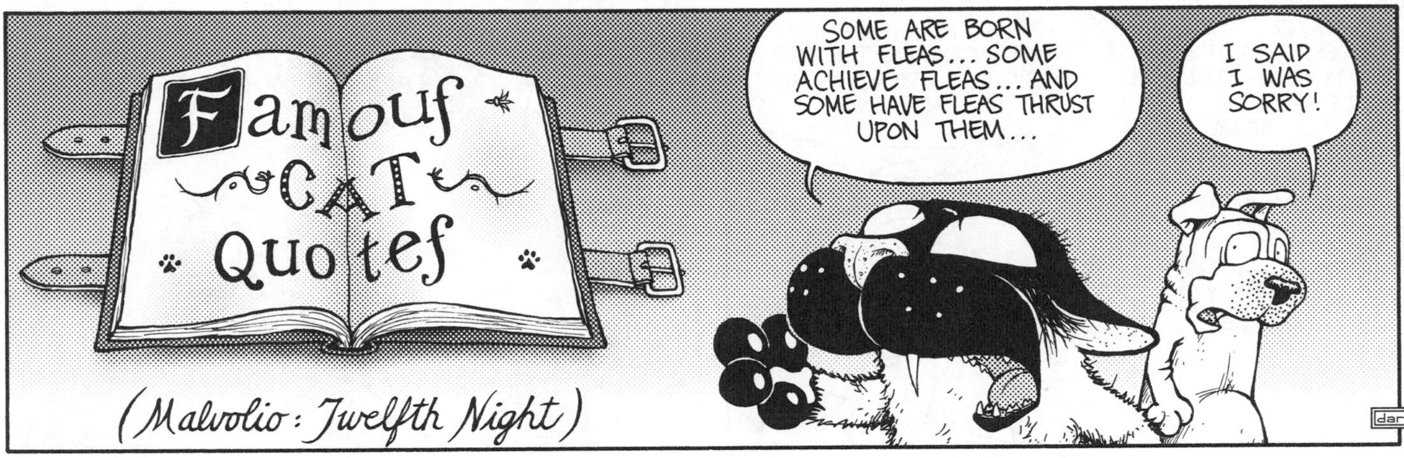
Famouf CAT Quotef
(Malvolio: Twelfth Night)
SOME ARE BORN WITH FLEAS... SOME ACHIEVE FLEAS... AND SOME HAVE FLEAS THRUST UPON THEM...
I SAID I WAS SORRY!
darb

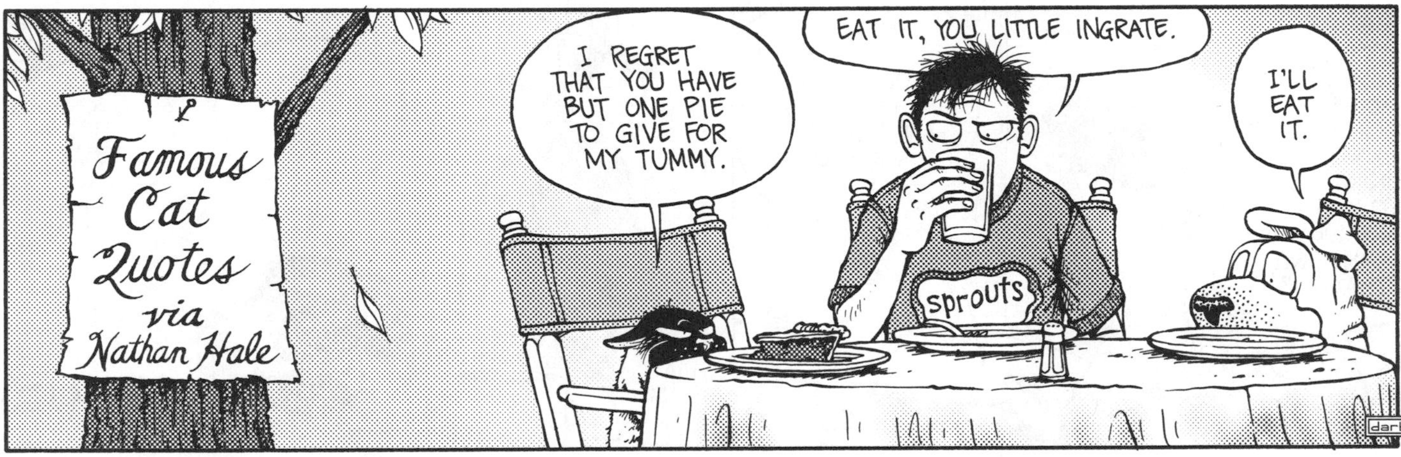
Famous Cat Quotes via Nathan Hale
I REGRET THAT YOU HAVE BUT ONE PIE TO GIVE FOR MY TUMMY.
EAT IT, YOU LITTLE INGRATE.
I'LL EAT IT.
sprouts
darb

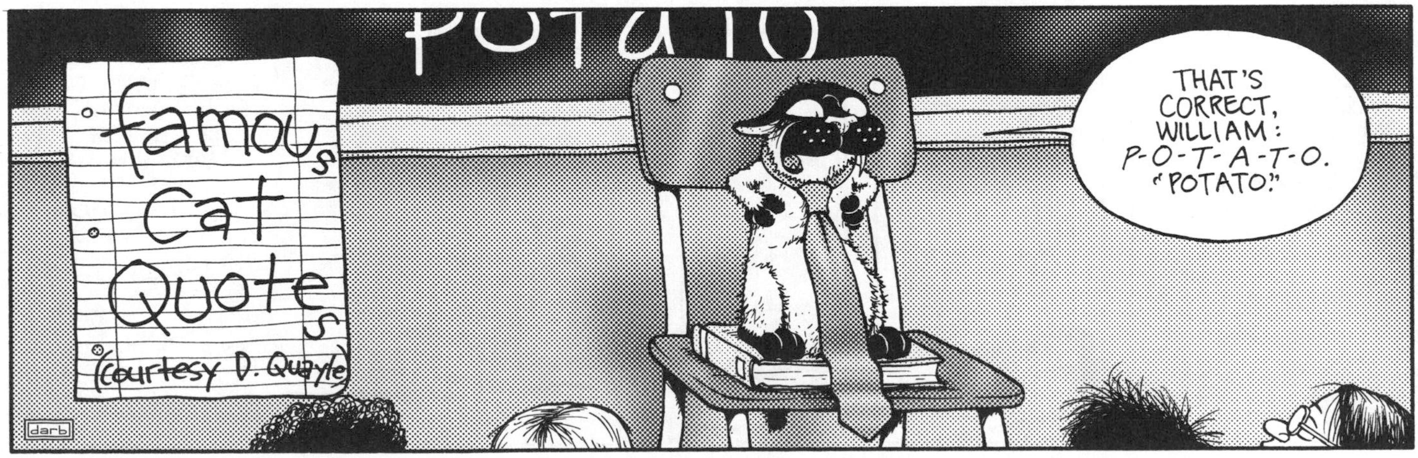
famous Cat Quotes
(courtesy D. Quayle)
POTATO
THAT'S CORRECT, WILLIAM: P-O-T-A-T-O. "POTATO."
darb

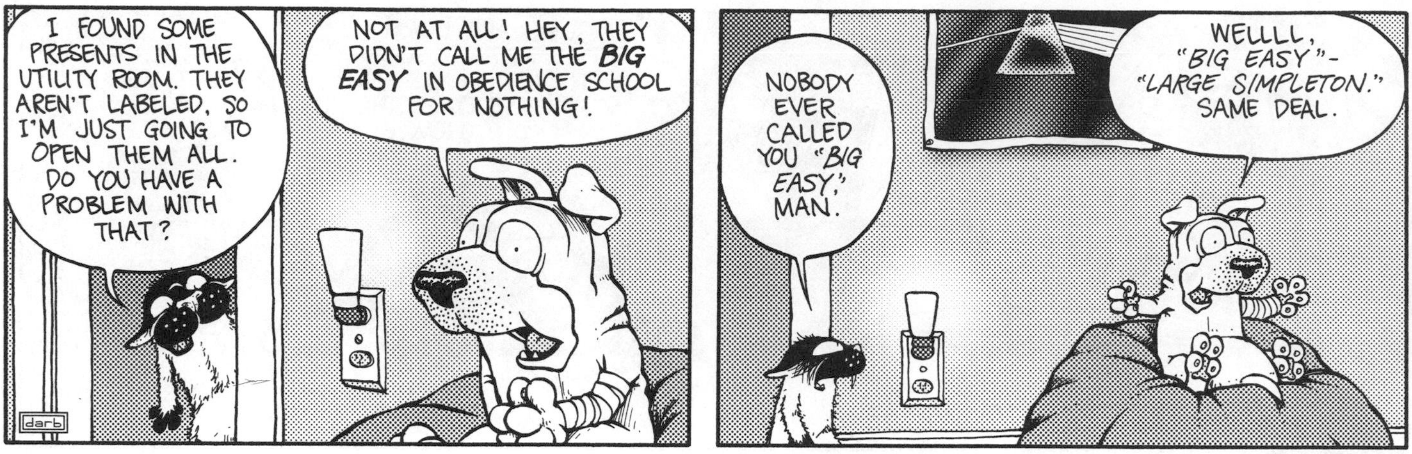
I FOUND SOME PRESENTS IN THE UTILITY ROOM. THEY AREN'T LABELED, SO I'M JUST GOING TO OPEN THEM ALL. DO YOU HAVE A PROBLEM WITH THAT?
NOT AT ALL! HEY, THEY DIDN'T CALL ME THE *BIG EASY* IN OBEDIENCE SCHOOL FOR NOTHING!
NOBODY EVER CALLED YOU "*BIG EASY*," MAN.
WELLLL, "*BIG EASY*"- "*LARGE SIMPLETON*." SAME DEAL.

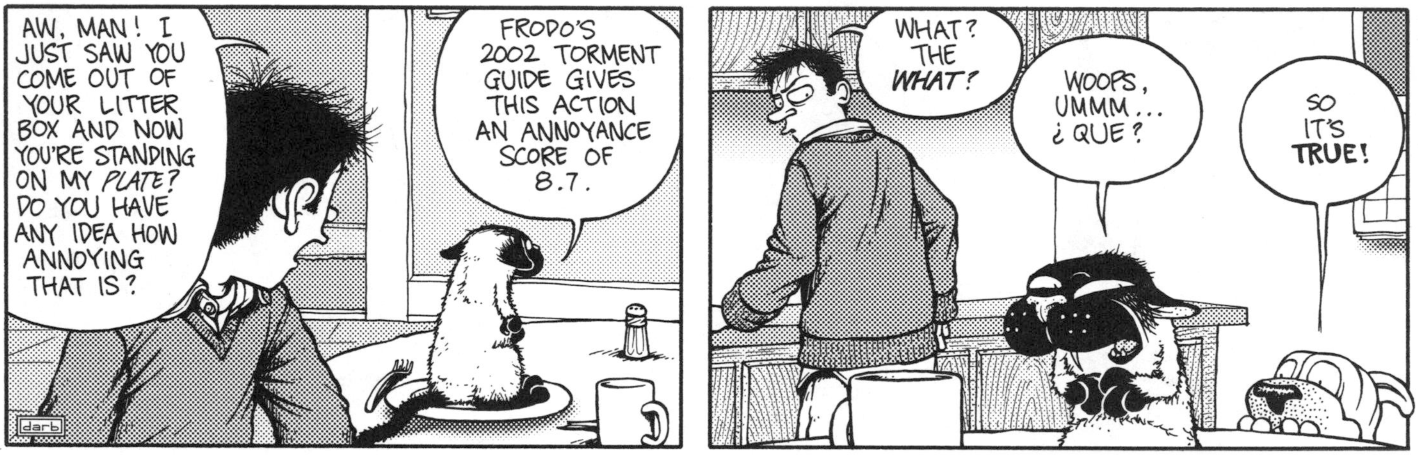
AW, MAN! I JUST SAW YOU COME OUT OF YOUR LITTER BOX AND NOW YOU'RE STANDING ON MY *PLATE*? DO YOU HAVE ANY IDEA HOW ANNOYING THAT IS?
FRODO'S 2002 TORMENT GUIDE GIVES THIS ACTION AN ANNOYANCE SCORE OF 8.7.
WHAT? THE *WHAT*?
WOOPS, UMMM... ¿QUE?
SO IT'S **TRUE**!

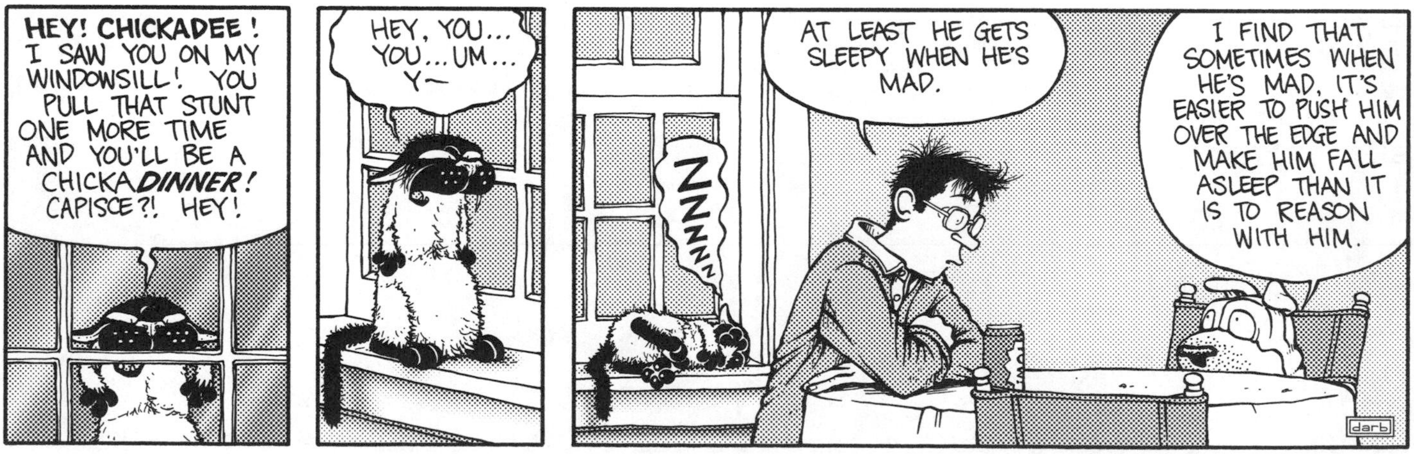
HEY! CHICKADEE! I SAW YOU ON MY WINDOWSILL! YOU PULL THAT STUNT ONE MORE TIME AND YOU'LL BE A CHICKA*DINNER*! CAPISCE?! HEY!
HEY, YOU... YOU...UM... Y~
AT LEAST HE GETS SLEEPY WHEN HE'S MAD.
ZZZZZ
I FIND THAT SOMETIMES WHEN HE'S MAD, IT'S EASIER TO PUSH HIM OVER THE EDGE AND MAKE HIM FALL ASLEEP THAN IT IS TO REASON WITH HIM.

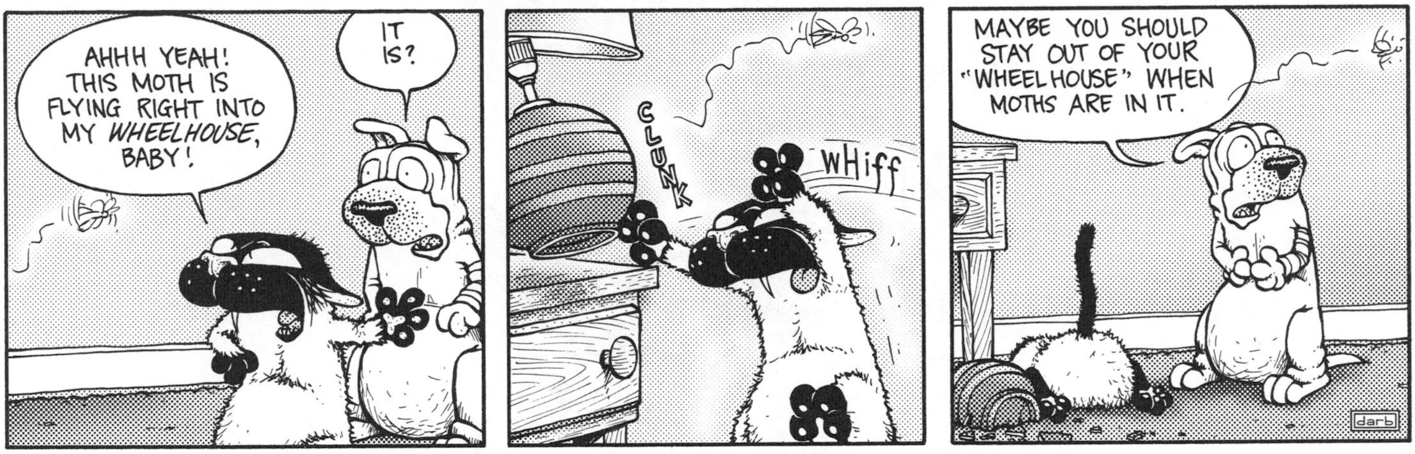
AHHH YEAH! THIS MOTH IS FLYING RIGHT INTO MY *WHEELHOUSE*, BABY!
IT IS?
CLUNK
WHiff
MAYBE YOU SHOULD STAY OUT OF YOUR "WHEELHOUSE" WHEN MOTHS ARE IN IT.
darb

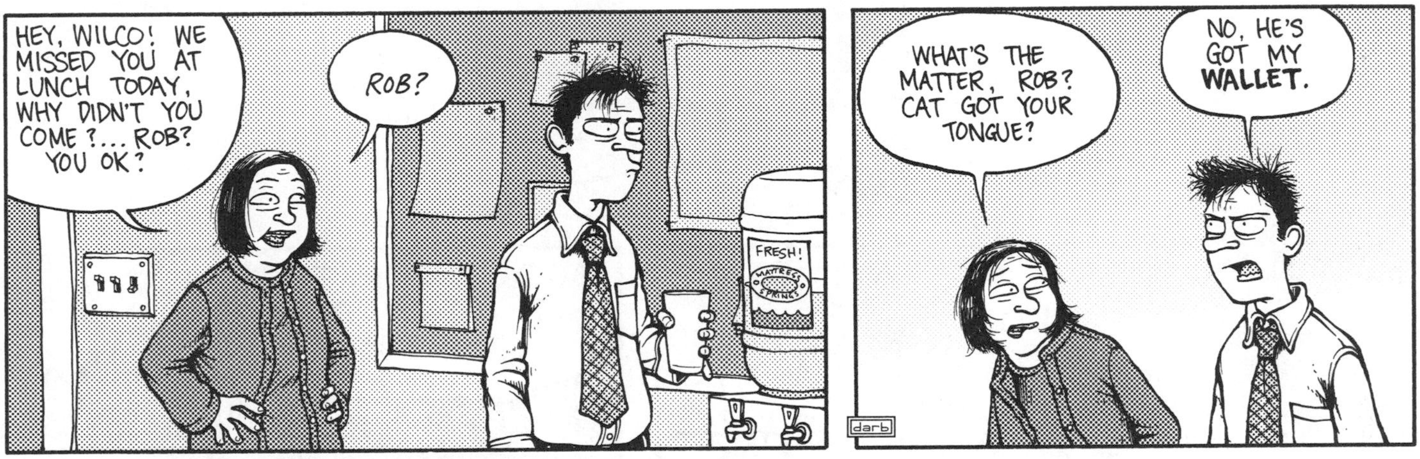
HEY, WILCO! WE MISSED YOU AT LUNCH TODAY, WHY DIDN'T YOU COME?... ROB? YOU OK?
ROB?
FRESH!
MATTRESS SPRINGS
darb
WHAT'S THE MATTER, ROB? CAT GOT YOUR TONGUE?
NO, HE'S GOT MY **WALLET**.

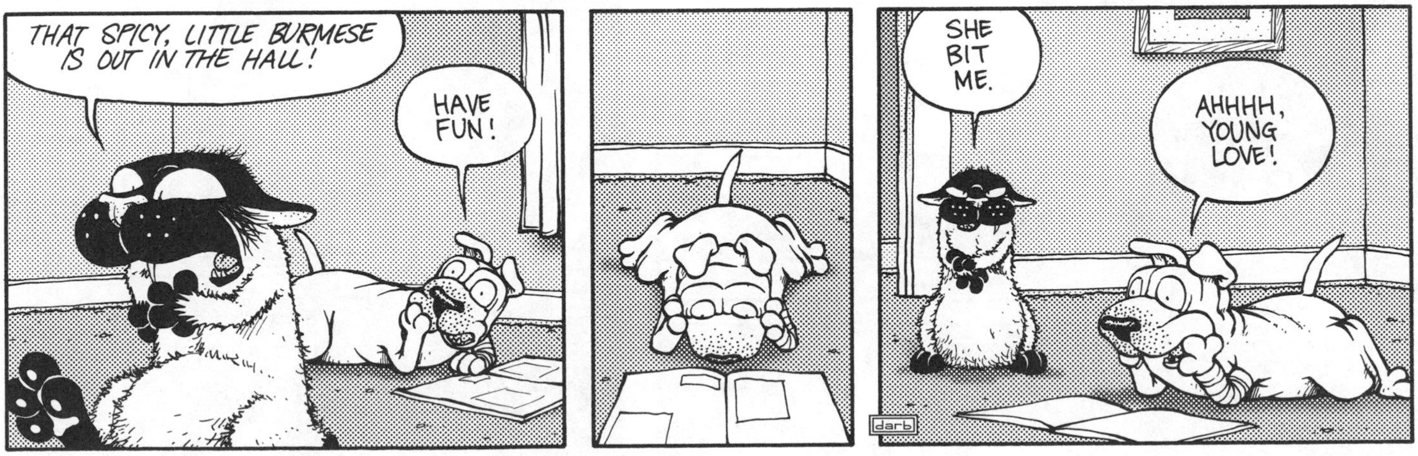
THAT SPICY, LITTLE BURMESE IS OUT IN THE HALL!
HAVE FUN!
darb
SHE BIT ME.
AHHHH, YOUNG LOVE!

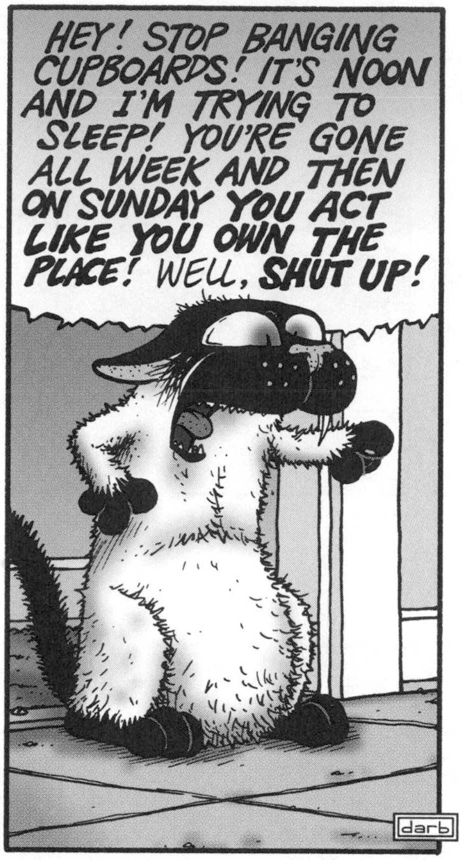
HEY! STOP BANGING CUPBOARDS! IT'S NOON AND I'M TRYING TO SLEEP! YOU'RE GONE ALL WEEK AND THEN ON SUNDAY YOU ACT LIKE YOU OWN THE PLACE! WELL, SHUT UP!
darb

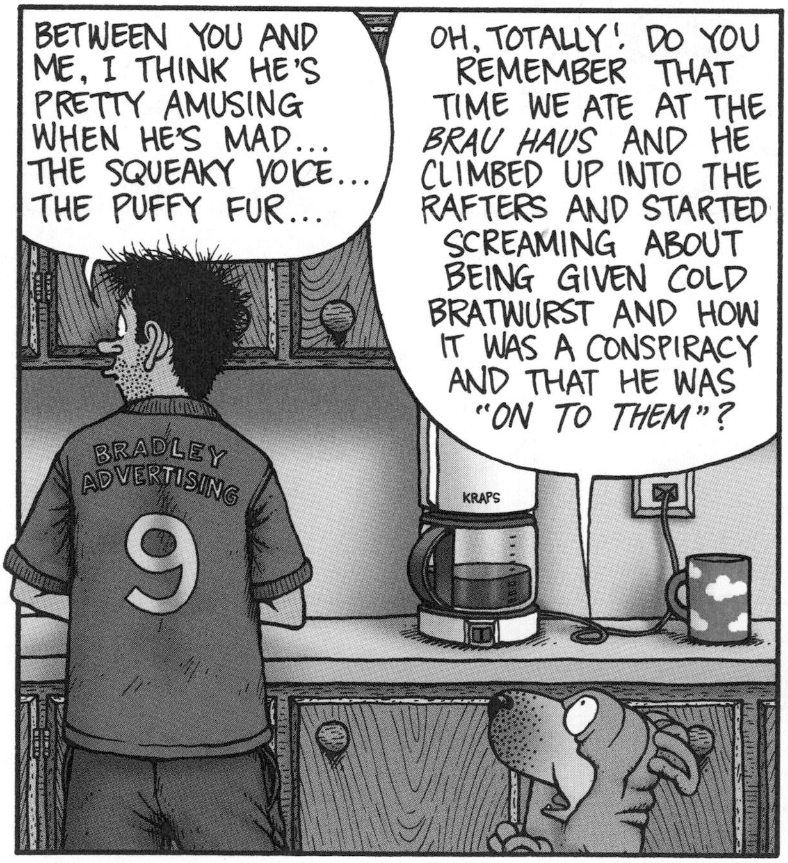
BETWEEN YOU AND ME, I THINK HE'S PRETTY AMUSING WHEN HE'S MAD... THE SQUEAKY VOICE... THE PUFFY FUR...
OH, TOTALLY! DO YOU REMEMBER THAT TIME WE ATE AT THE *BRAU HAUS* AND HE CLIMBED UP INTO THE RAFTERS AND STARTED SCREAMING ABOUT BEING GIVEN COLD BRATWURST AND HOW IT WAS A CONSPIRACY AND THAT HE WAS *"ON TO THEM"*?
BRADLEY ADVERTISING
9
KRAPS

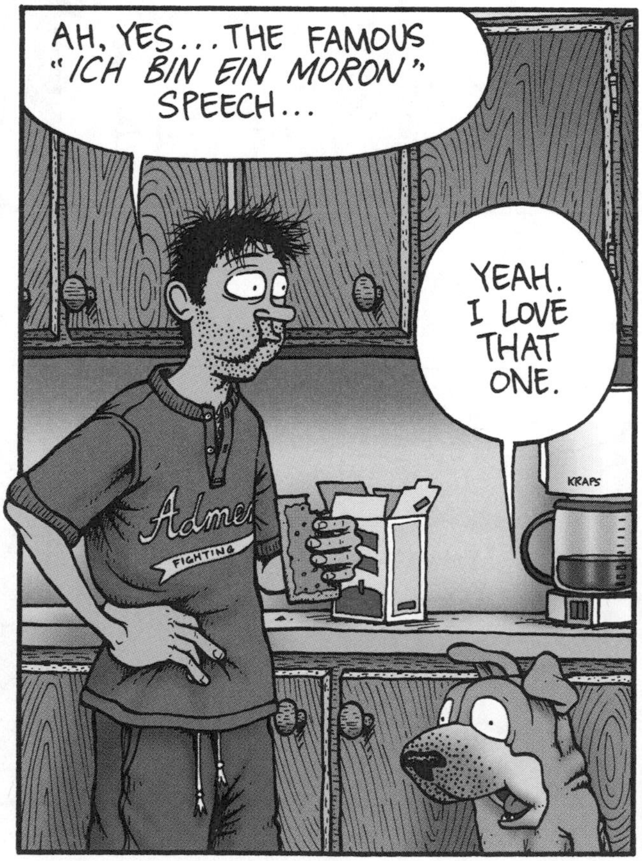
AH, YES... THE FAMOUS *"ICH BIN EIN MORON"* SPEECH...
YEAH. I LOVE THAT ONE.
Admen
FIGHTING
KRAPS

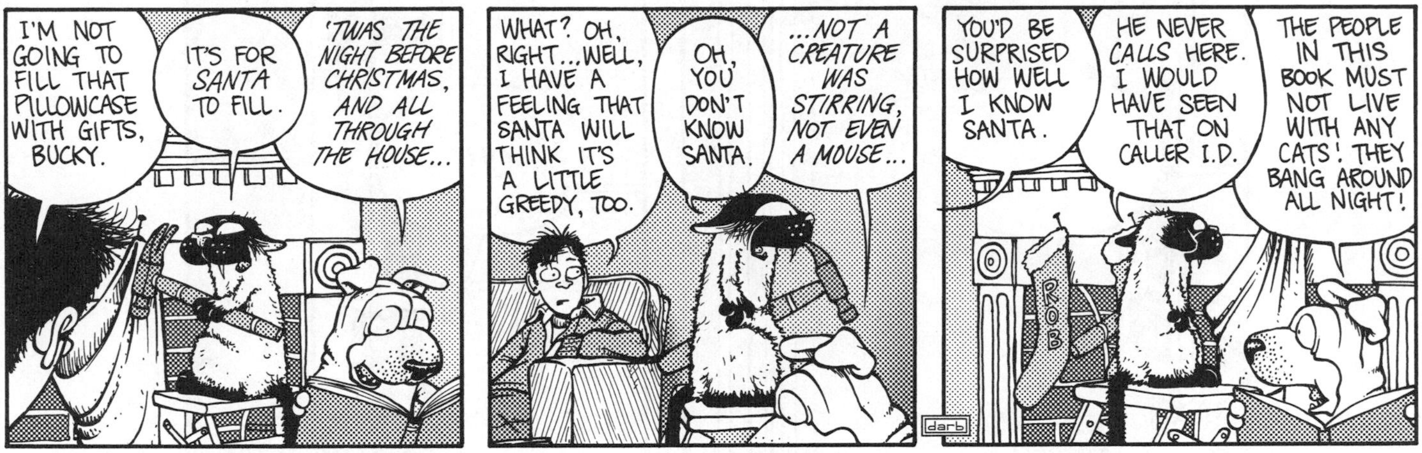

I'M NOT GOING TO FILL THAT PILLOWCASE WITH GIFTS, BUCKY.
IT'S FOR SANTA TO FILL.
'TWAS THE NIGHT BEFORE CHRISTMAS, AND ALL THROUGH THE HOUSE...
WHAT? OH, RIGHT...WELL, I HAVE A FEELING THAT SANTA WILL THINK IT'S A LITTLE GREEDY, TOO.
OH, YOU DON'T KNOW SANTA.
...NOT A CREATURE WAS STIRRING, NOT EVEN A MOUSE...
YOU'D BE SURPRISED HOW WELL I KNOW SANTA.
HE NEVER CALLS HERE. I WOULD HAVE SEEN THAT ON CALLER I.D.
THE PEOPLE IN THIS BOOK MUST NOT LIVE WITH ANY CATS! THEY BANG AROUND ALL NIGHT!
ROB
darb

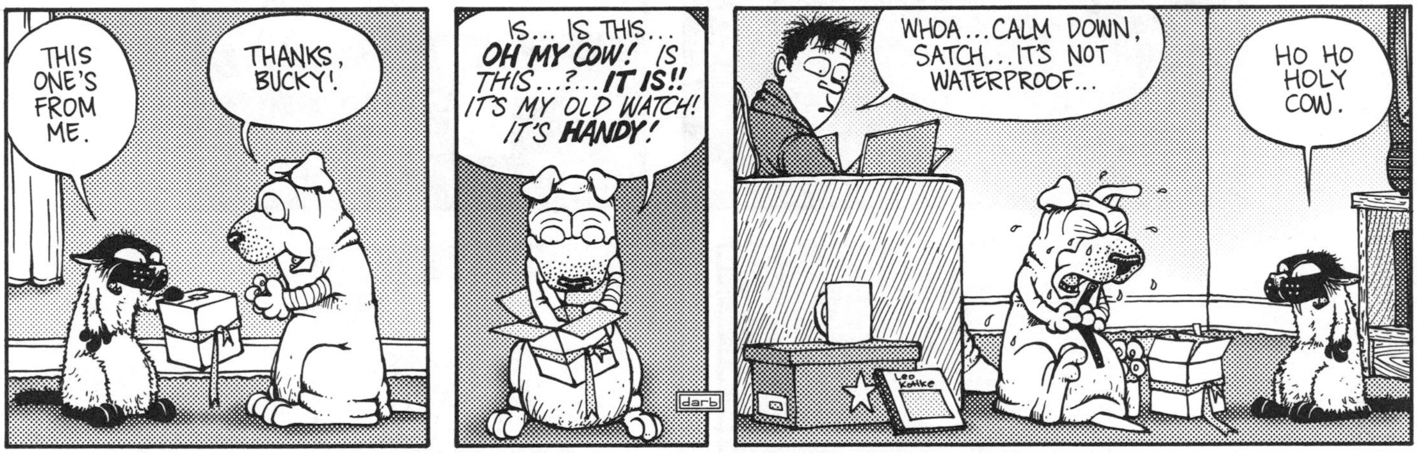

THIS ONE'S FROM ME.
THANKS, BUCKY!
IS... IS THIS... OH MY COW! IS THIS...?...IT IS!! IT'S MY OLD WATCH! IT'S HANDY!
darb
WHOA...CALM DOWN, SATCH...IT'S NOT WATERPROOF...
HO HO HOLY COW.
LEO KOTTKE

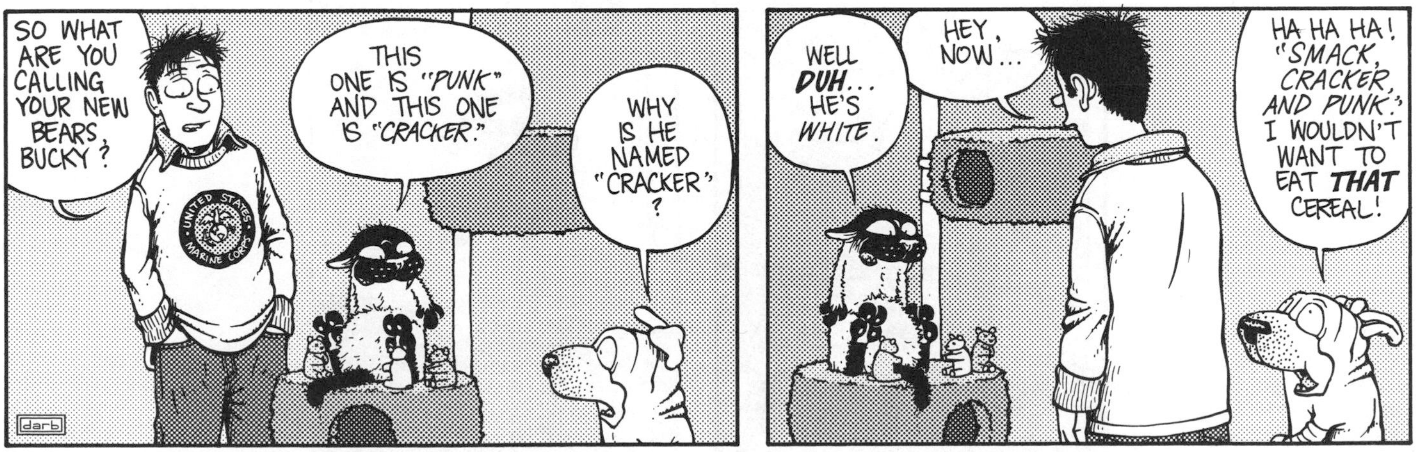

SO WHAT ARE YOU CALLING YOUR NEW BEARS, BUCKY?
THIS ONE IS "PUNK" AND THIS ONE IS "CRACKER."
WHY IS HE NAMED "CRACKER"?
UNITED STATES MARINE CORPS
darb
WELL DUH... HE'S WHITE.
HEY, NOW...
HA HA HA! "SMACK, CRACKER, AND PUNK." I WOULDN'T WANT TO EAT THAT CEREAL!

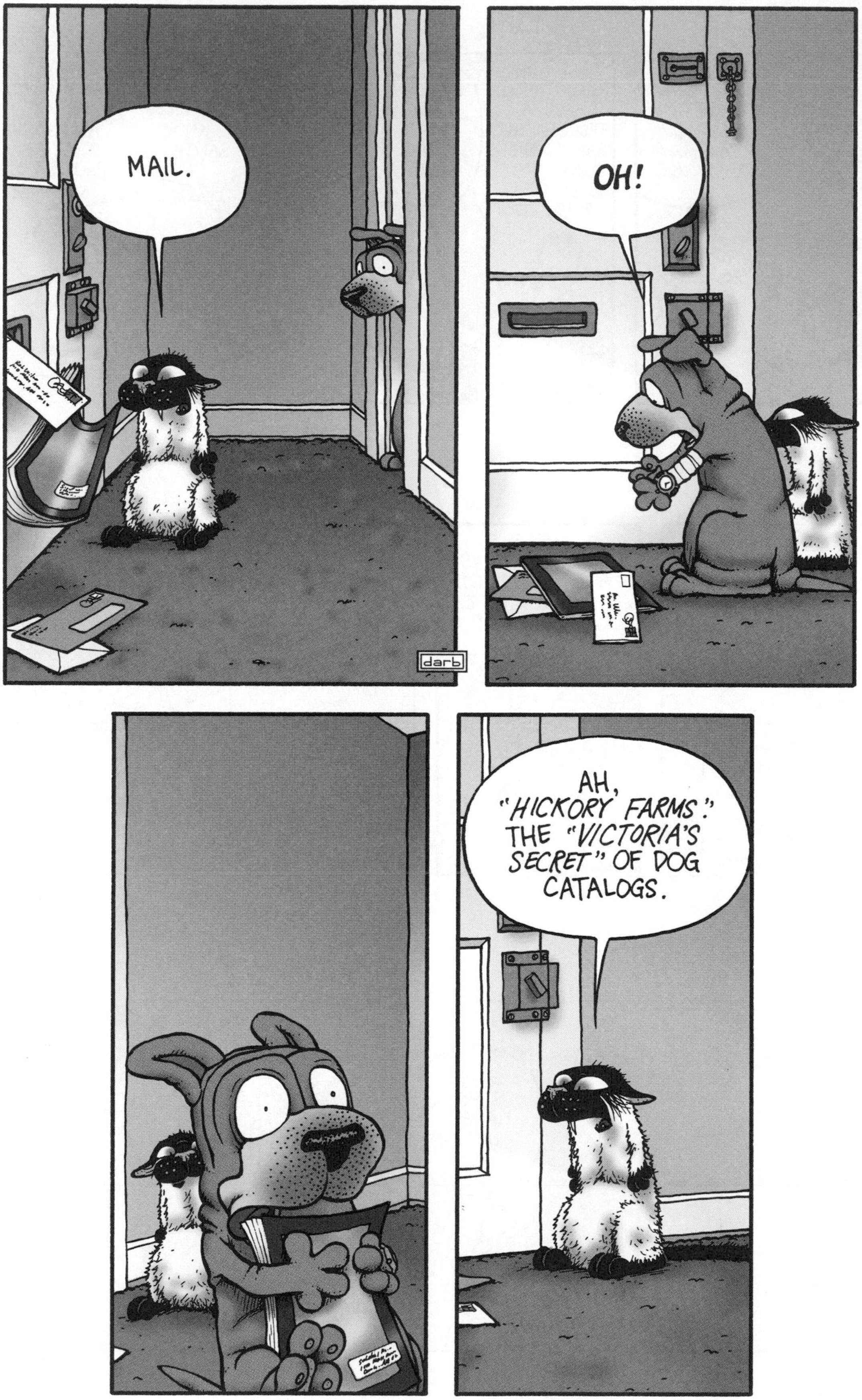
MAIL.
OH!
AH, "HICKORY FARMS." THE "VICTORIA'S SECRET" OF DOG CATALOGS.
darb

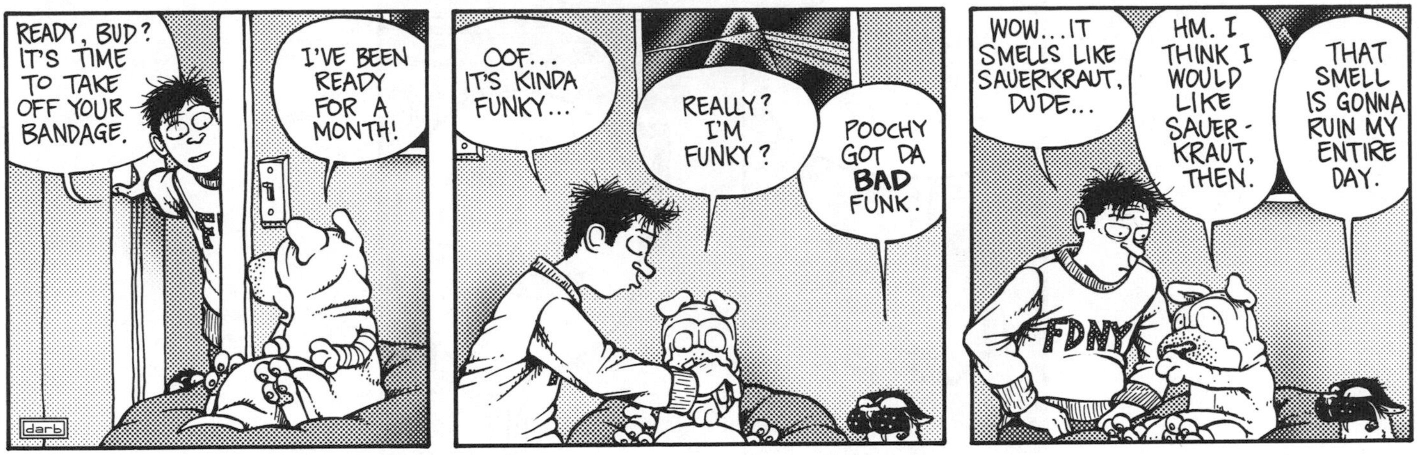
READY, BUD? IT'S TIME TO TAKE OFF YOUR BANDAGE.
I'VE BEEN READY FOR A MONTH!
darb
OOF... IT'S KINDA FUNKY...
REALLY? I'M FUNKY?
POOCHY GOT DA **BAD** FUNK.
WOW...IT SMELLS LIKE SAUERKRAUT, DUDE...
HM. I THINK I WOULD LIKE SAUER-KRAUT, THEN.
THAT SMELL IS GONNA RUIN MY ENTIRE DAY.
FDNY

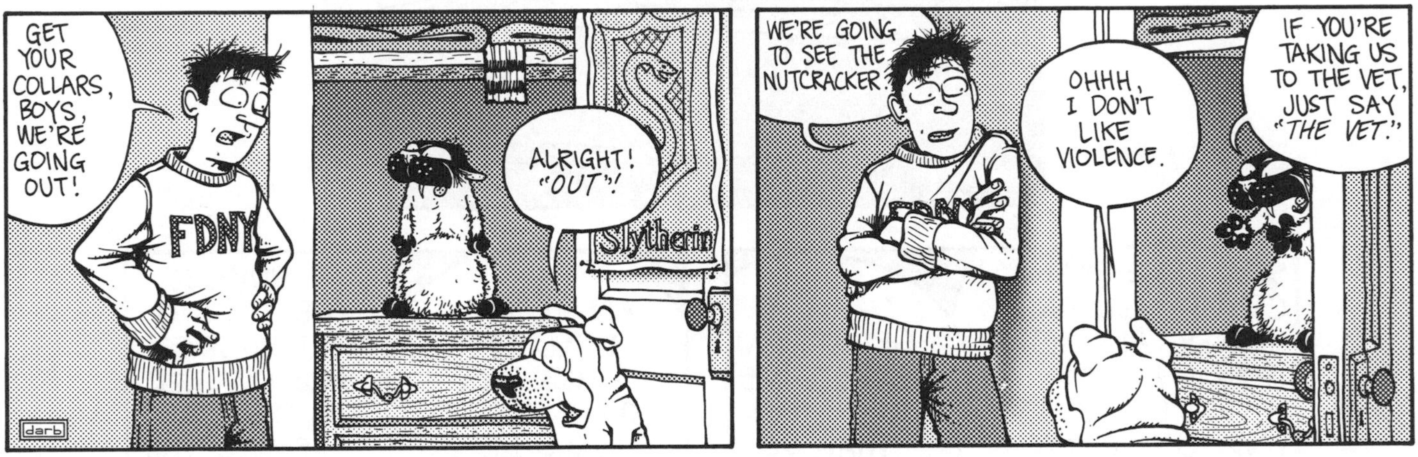
GET YOUR COLLARS, BOYS, WE'RE GOING OUT!
FDNY
ALRIGHT! "OUT"!
Slytherin
darb
WE'RE GOING TO SEE THE NUTCRACKER.
OHHH, I DON'T LIKE VIOLENCE.
IF YOU'RE TAKING US TO THE VET, JUST SAY "THE VET."

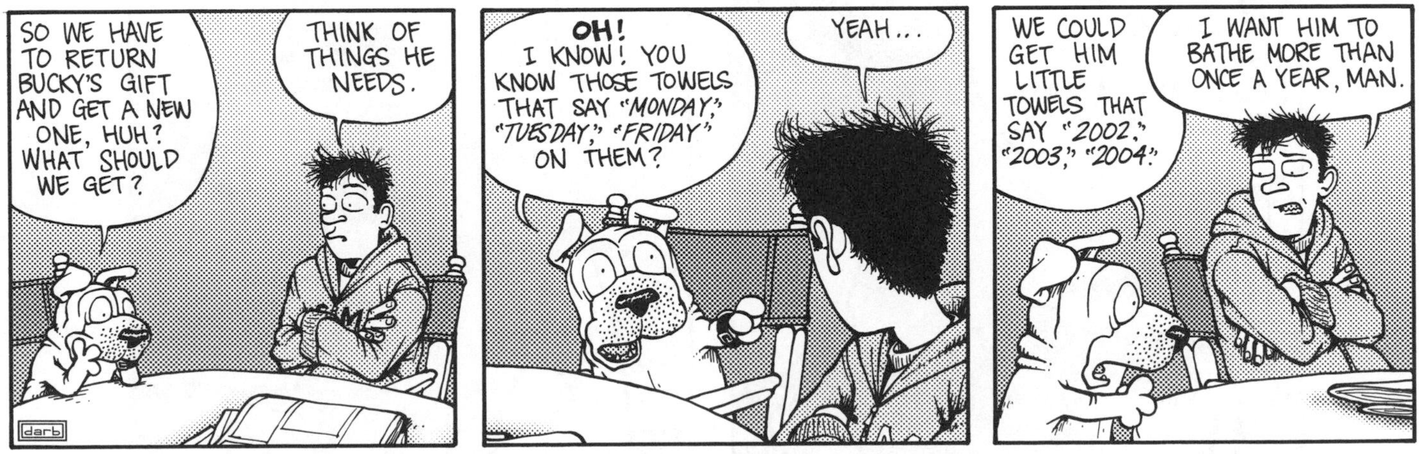
SO WE HAVE TO RETURN BUCKY'S GIFT AND GET A NEW ONE, HUH? WHAT SHOULD WE GET?
THINK OF THINGS HE NEEDS.
darb
OH! I KNOW! YOU KNOW THOSE TOWELS THAT SAY "MONDAY," "TUESDAY," "FRIDAY" ON THEM?
YEAH...
WE COULD GET HIM LITTLE TOWELS THAT SAY "2002," "2003," "2004."
I WANT HIM TO BATHE MORE THAN ONCE A YEAR, MAN.

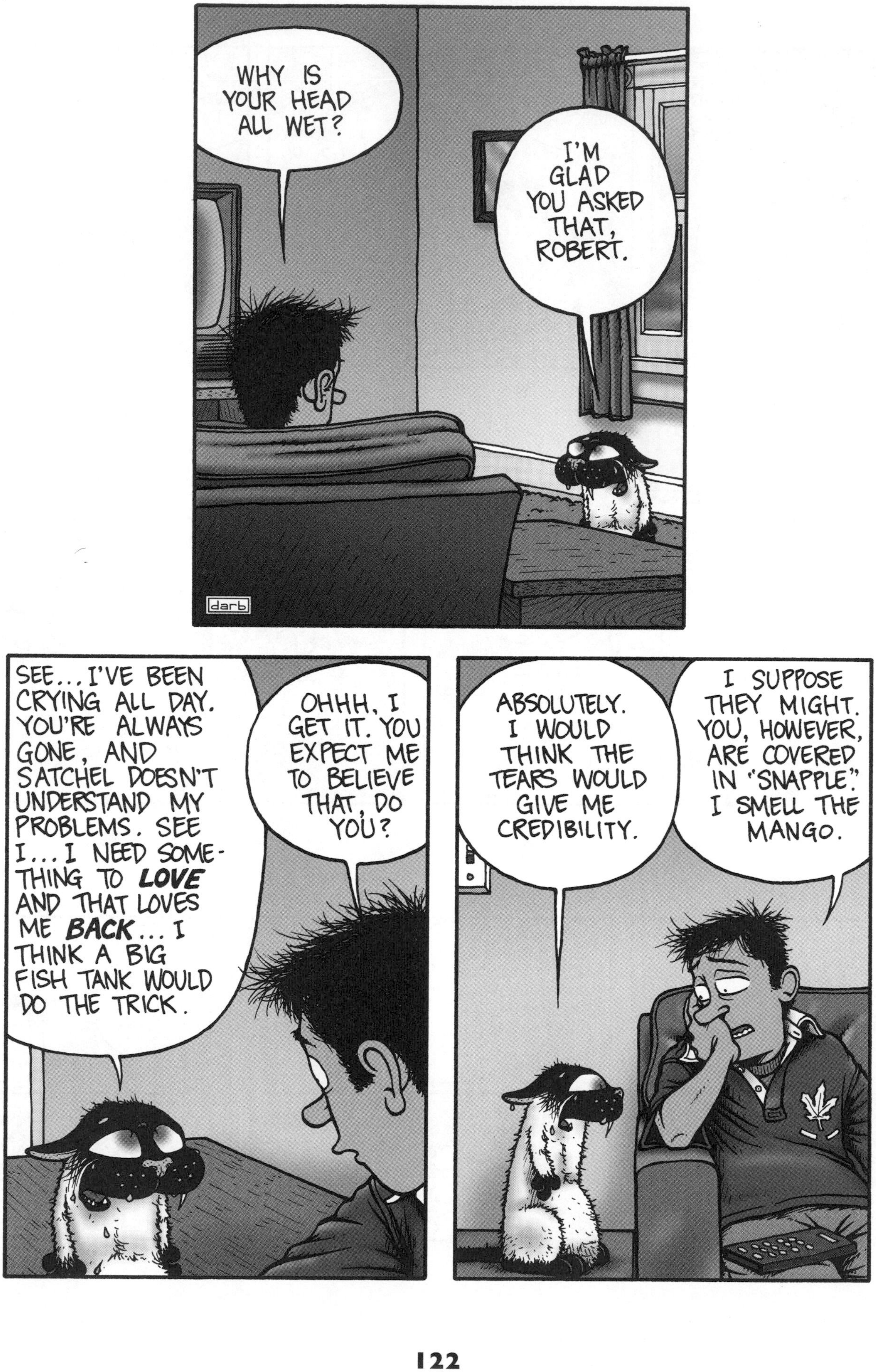
WHY IS YOUR HEAD ALL WET?
I'M GLAD YOU ASKED THAT, ROBERT.
darb
SEE... I'VE BEEN CRYING ALL DAY. YOU'RE ALWAYS GONE, AND SATCHEL DOESN'T UNDERSTAND MY PROBLEMS. SEE I... I NEED SOME-THING TO LOVE AND THAT LOVES ME BACK... I THINK A BIG FISH TANK WOULD DO THE TRICK.
OHHH, I GET IT. YOU EXPECT ME TO BELIEVE THAT, DO YOU?
ABSOLUTELY. I WOULD THINK THE TEARS WOULD GIVE ME CREDIBILITY.
I SUPPOSE THEY MIGHT. YOU, HOWEVER, ARE COVERED IN "SNAPPLE." I SMELL THE MANGO.

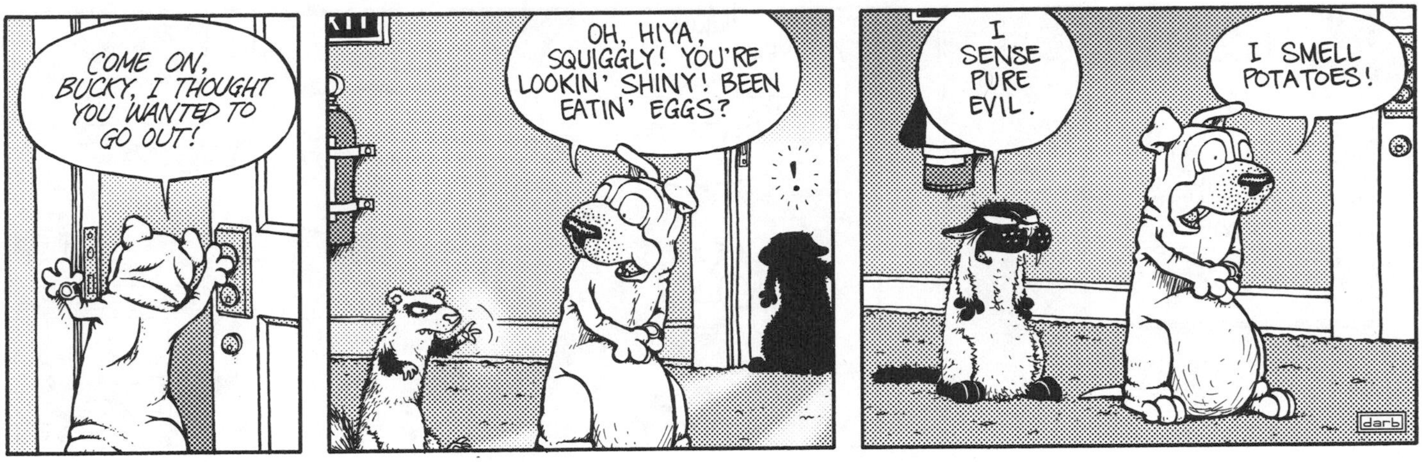
COME ON, BUCKY, I THOUGHT YOU WANTED TO GO OUT!
OH, HIYA, SQUIGGLY! YOU'RE LOOKIN' SHINY! BEEN EATIN' EGGS?
!
I SENSE PURE EVIL.
I SMELL POTATOES!
darb

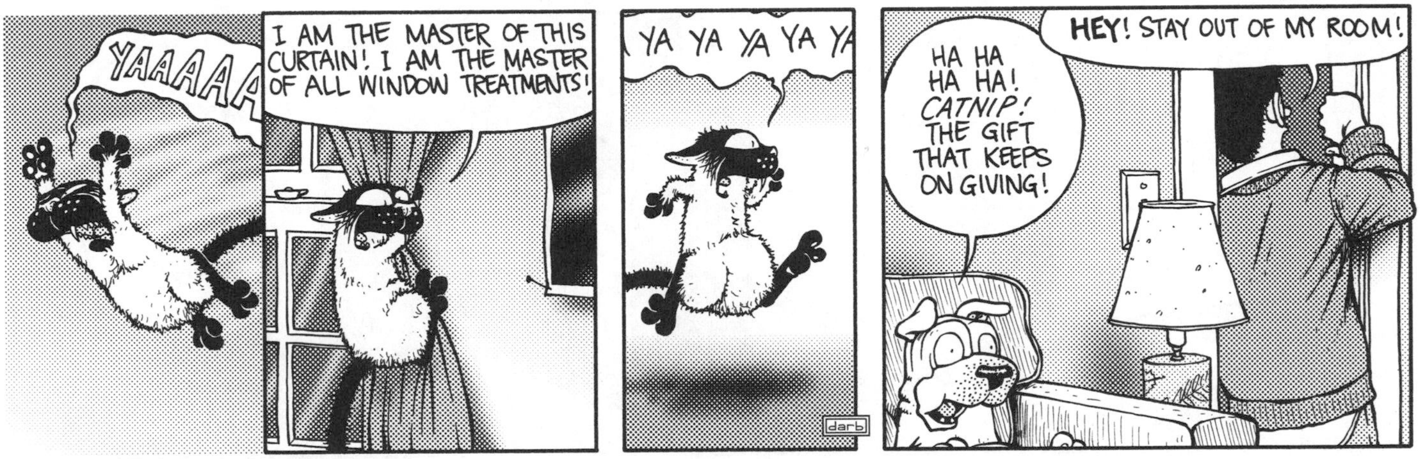
YAAAAAA
I AM THE MASTER OF THIS CURTAIN! I AM THE MASTER OF ALL WINDOW TREATMENTS!
YA YA YA YA YA
darb
HEY! STAY OUT OF MY ROOM!
HA HA HA HA! CATNIP! THE GIFT THAT KEEPS ON GIVING!

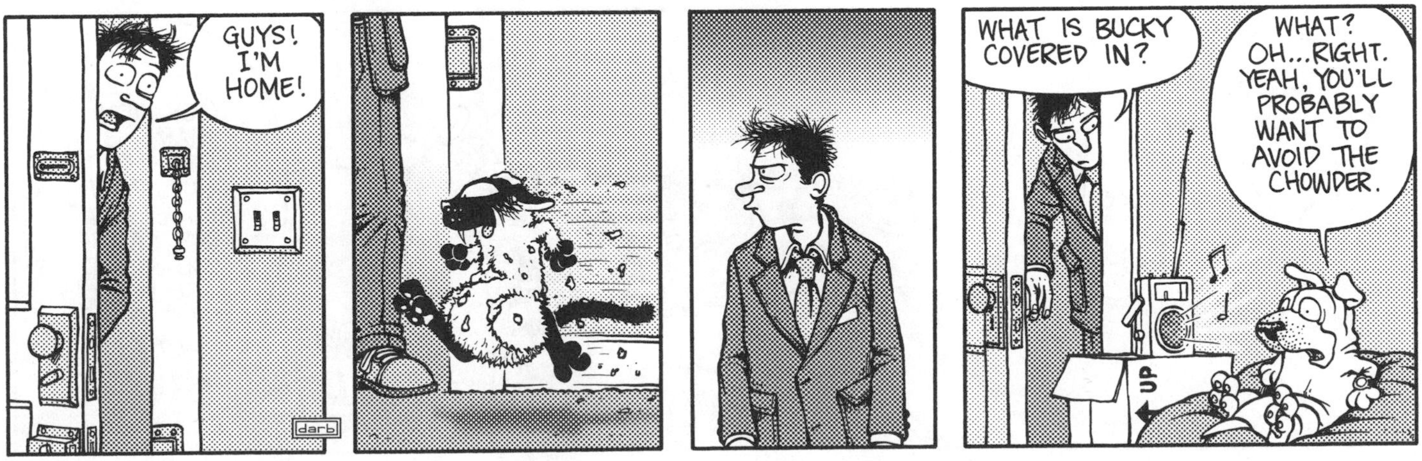
GUYS! I'M HOME!
darb
WHAT IS BUCKY COVERED IN?
WHAT? OH...RIGHT. YEAH, YOU'LL PROBABLY WANT TO AVOID THE CHOWDER.
UP

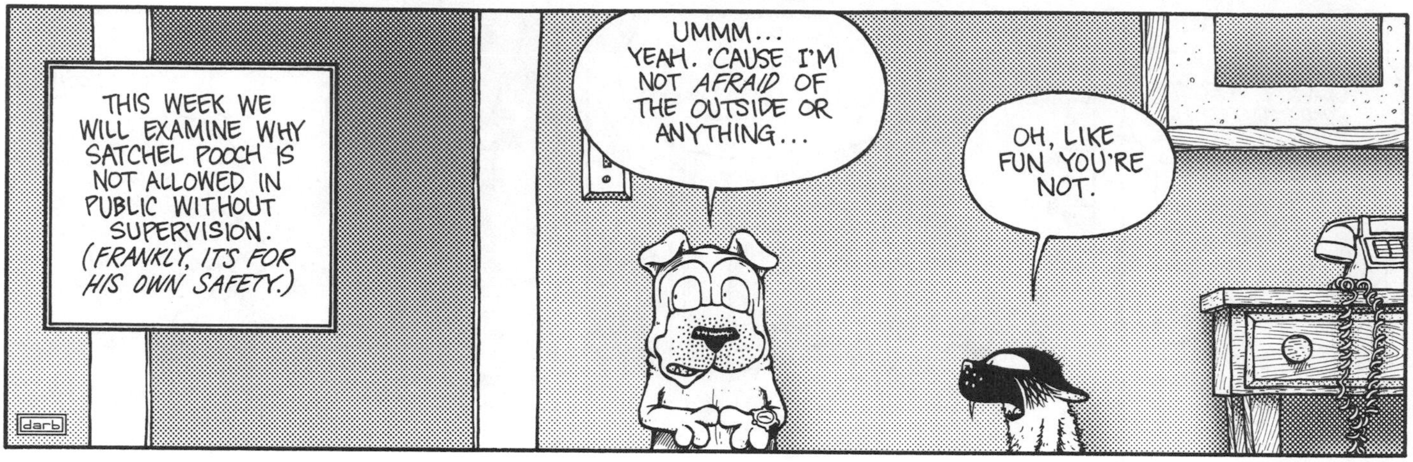
THIS WEEK WE WILL EXAMINE WHY SATCHEL POOCH IS NOT ALLOWED IN PUBLIC WITHOUT SUPERVISION. (FRANKLY, IT'S FOR HIS OWN SAFETY.)
UMMM... YEAH. 'CAUSE I'M NOT AFRAID OF THE OUTSIDE OR ANYTHING...
OH, LIKE FUN YOU'RE NOT.

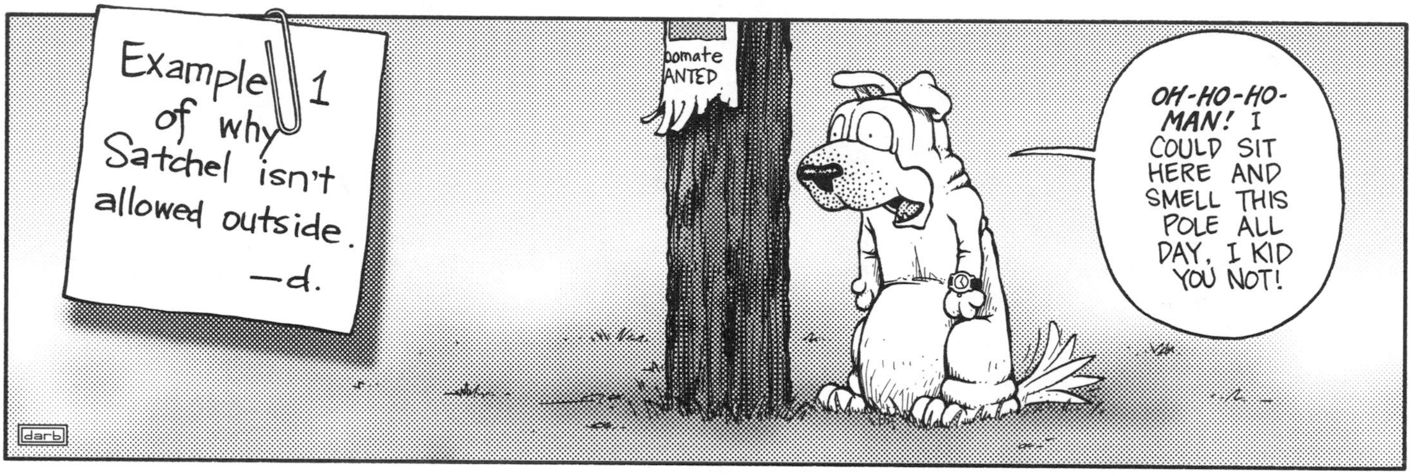
Example 1 of why Satchel isn't allowed outside. —d.
OH-HO-HO-MAN! I COULD SIT HERE AND SMELL THIS POLE ALL DAY, I KID YOU NOT!

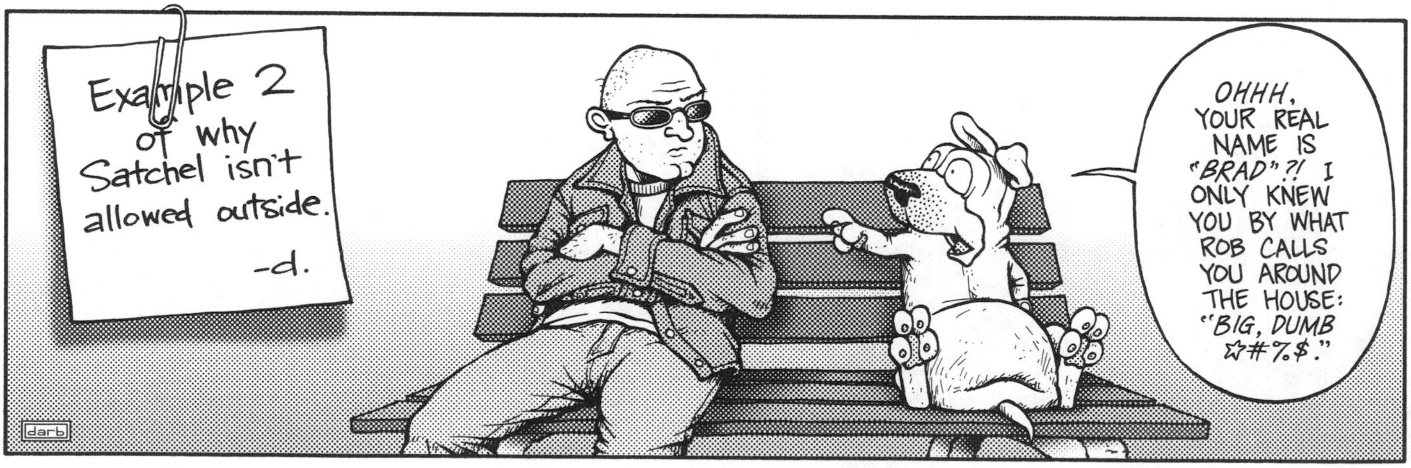
Example 2 of why Satchel isn't allowed outside. -d.
OHHH, YOUR REAL NAME IS "BRAD"?! I ONLY KNEW YOU BY WHAT ROB CALLS YOU AROUND THE HOUSE: "BIG, DUMB ☆#%$."

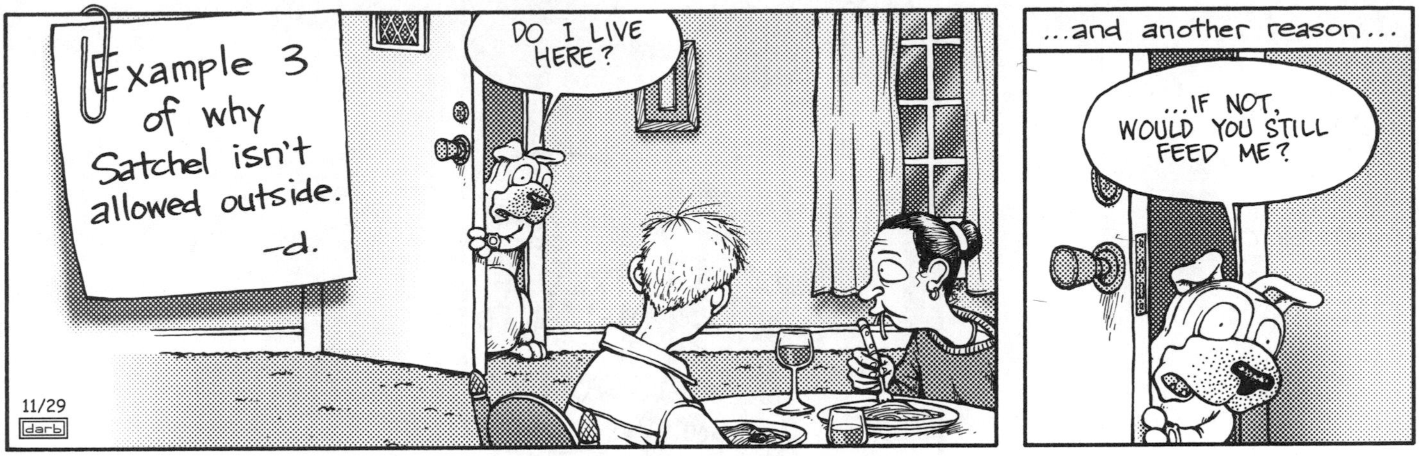
Example 3 of why Satchel isn't allowed outside. –d.
DO I LIVE HERE?
11/29
darb
...and another reason...
...IF NOT, WOULD YOU STILL FEED ME?

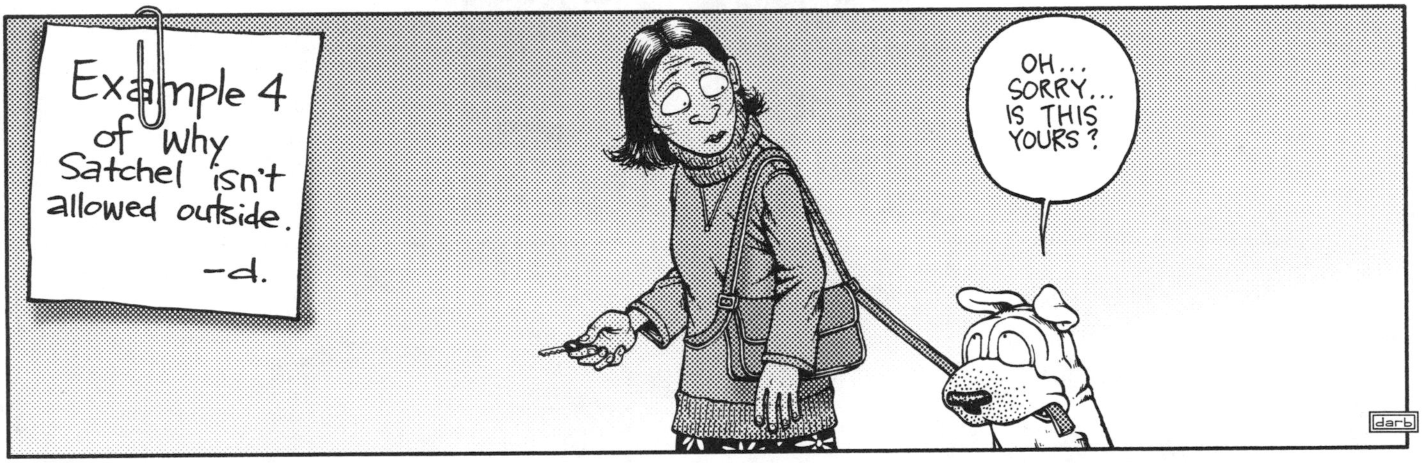
Example 4 of why Satchel isn't allowed outside. –d.
OH... SORRY... IS THIS YOURS?
darb

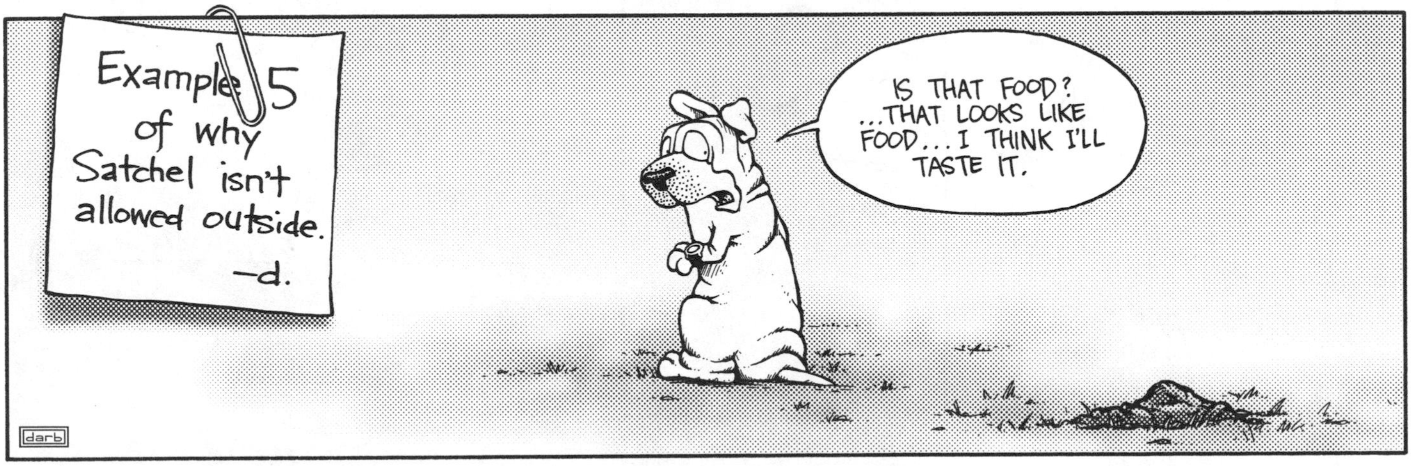
Example 5 of why Satchel isn't allowed outside. –d.
IS THAT FOOD? ...THAT LOOKS LIKE FOOD... I THINK I'LL TASTE IT.
darb

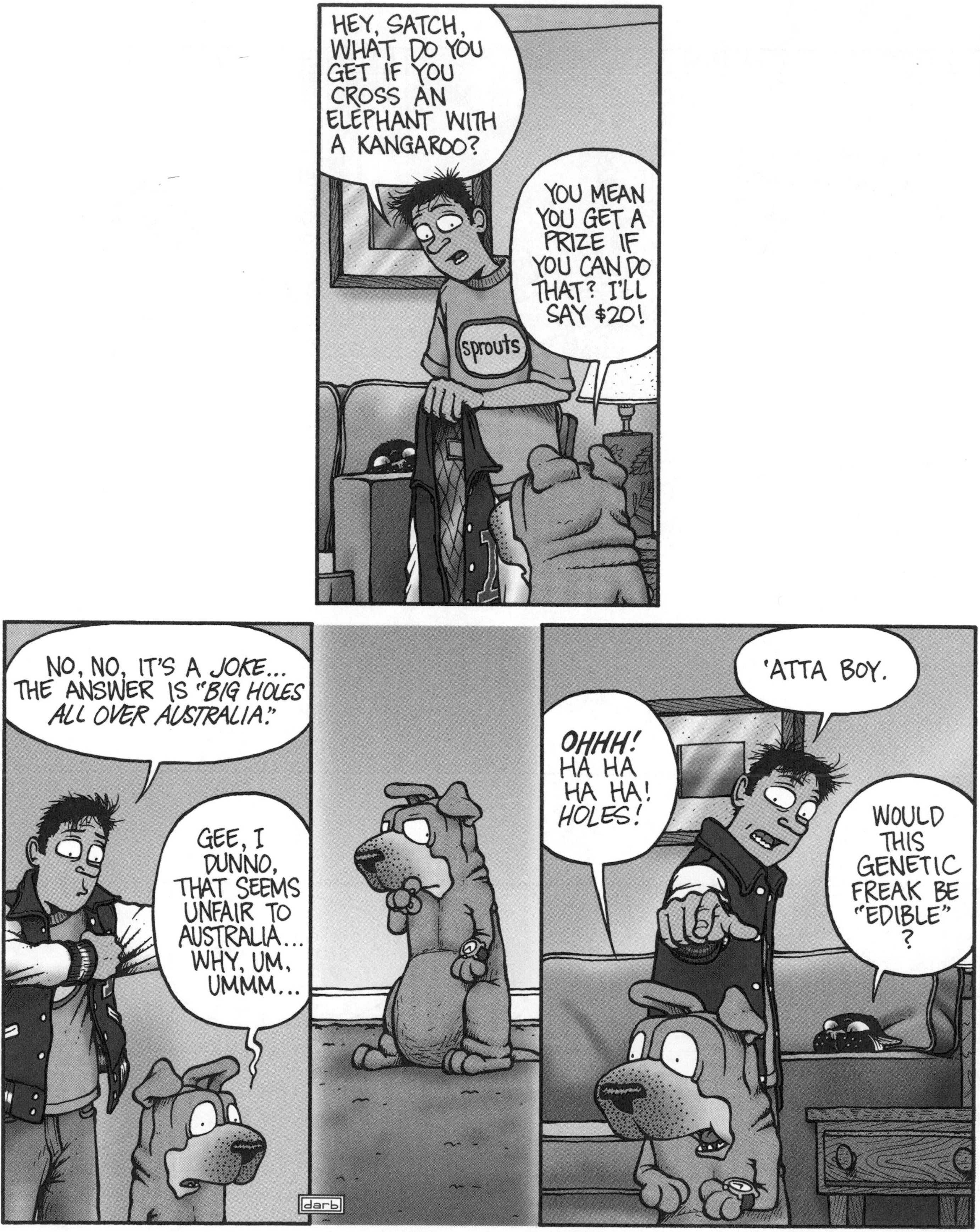
HEY, SATCH, WHAT DO YOU GET IF YOU CROSS AN ELEPHANT WITH A KANGAROO?
YOU MEAN YOU GET A PRIZE IF YOU CAN DO THAT? I'LL SAY $20!
sprouts
NO, NO, IT'S A JOKE... THE ANSWER IS *"BIG HOLES ALL OVER AUSTRALIA."*
GEE, I DUNNO, THAT SEEMS UNFAIR TO AUSTRALIA... WHY, UM, UMMM...
darb
'ATTA BOY.
OHHH! HA HA HA HA! *HOLES!*
WOULD THIS GENETIC FREAK BE "EDIBLE"?

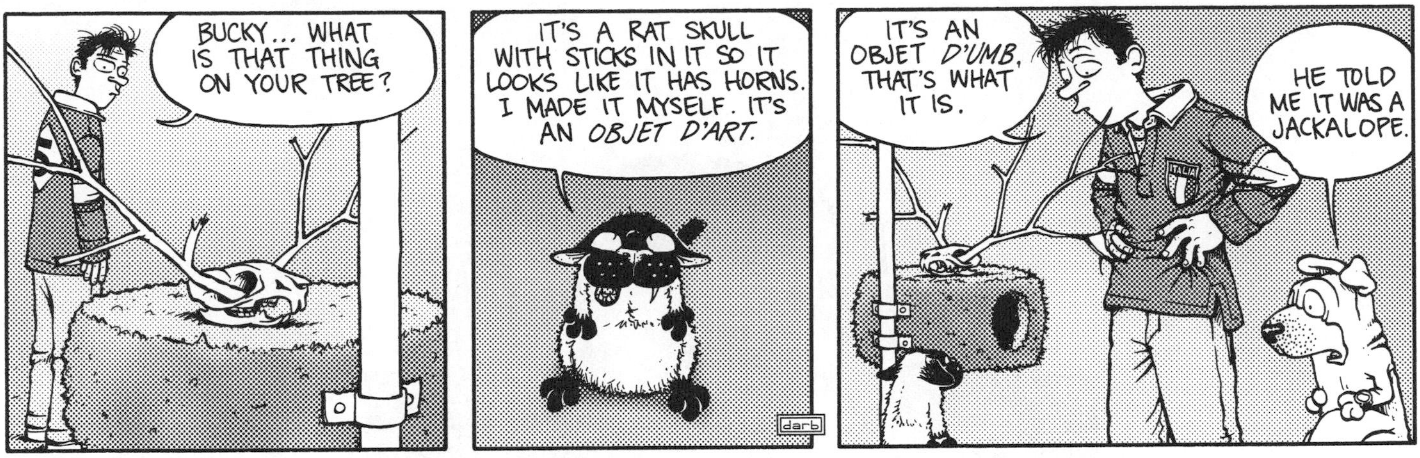
BUCKY... WHAT IS THAT THING ON YOUR TREE?
IT'S A RAT SKULL WITH STICKS IN IT SO IT LOOKS LIKE IT HAS HORNS. I MADE IT MYSELF. IT'S AN *OBJET D'ART.*
IT'S AN OBJET *D'UMB,* THAT'S WHAT IT IS.
HE TOLD ME IT WAS A JACKALOPE.
ITALIA

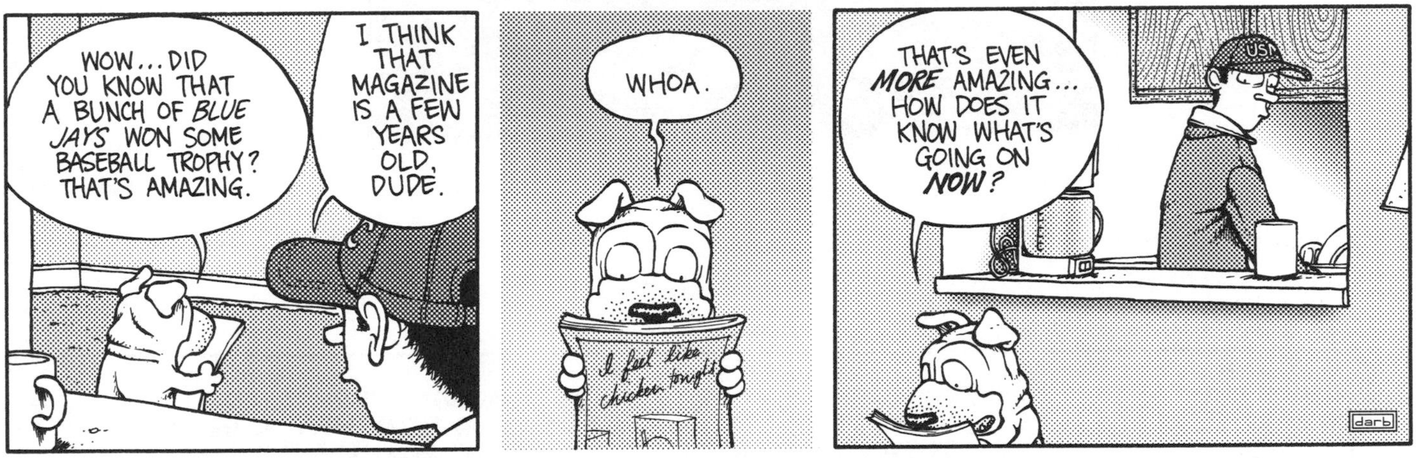
WOW... DID YOU KNOW THAT A BUNCH OF *BLUE JAYS* WON SOME BASEBALL TROPHY? THAT'S AMAZING.
I THINK THAT MAGAZINE IS A FEW YEARS OLD, DUDE.
WHOA.
I feel like chicken tonight
THAT'S EVEN ***MORE*** AMAZING... HOW DOES IT KNOW WHAT'S GOING ON ***NOW***?

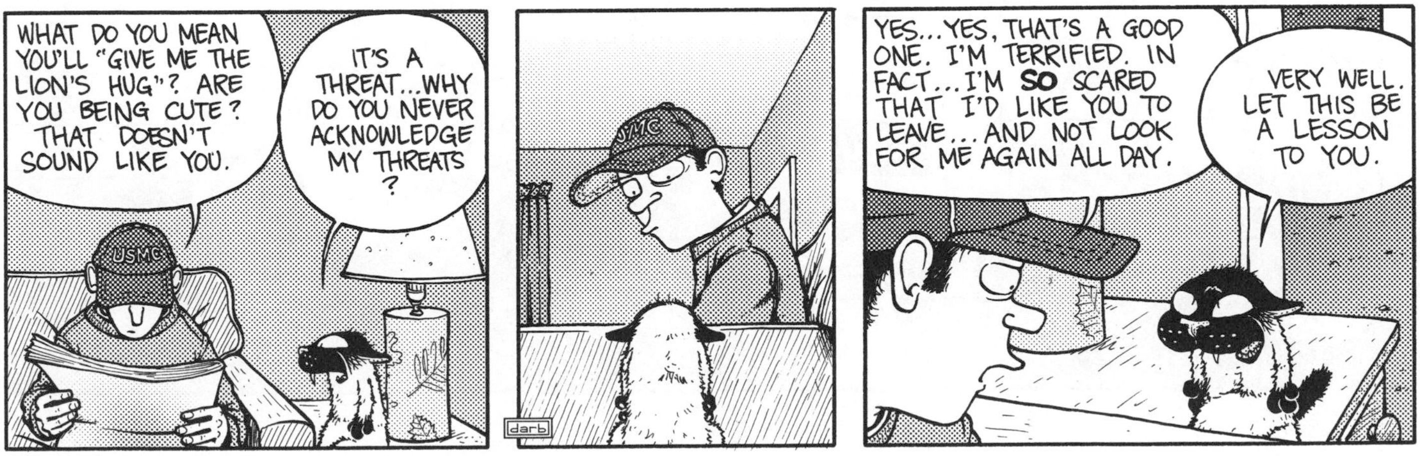
WHAT DO YOU MEAN YOU'LL "GIVE ME THE LION'S HUG"? ARE YOU BEING CUTE? THAT DOESN'T SOUND LIKE YOU.
IT'S A THREAT...WHY DO YOU NEVER ACKNOWLEDGE MY THREATS?
USMC
YES...YES, THAT'S A GOOD ONE. I'M TERRIFIED. IN FACT...I'M **SO** SCARED THAT I'D LIKE YOU TO LEAVE... AND NOT LOOK FOR ME AGAIN ALL DAY.
VERY WELL. LET THIS BE A LESSON TO YOU.

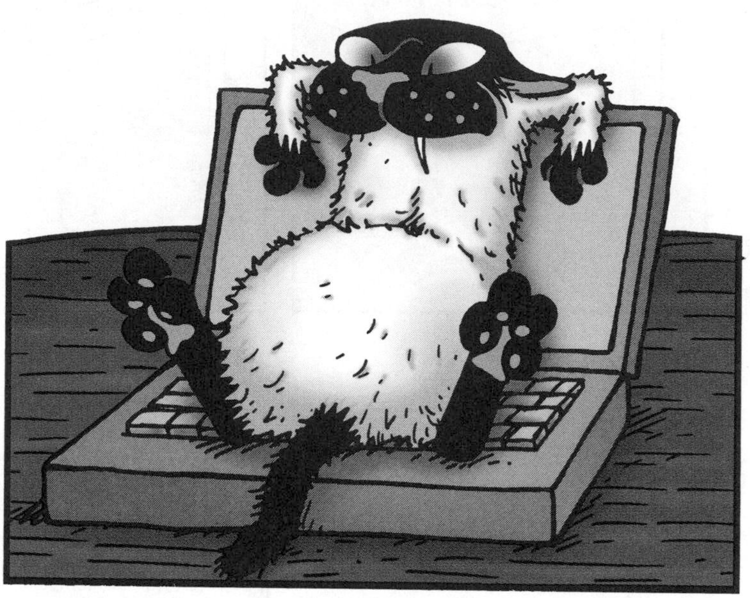

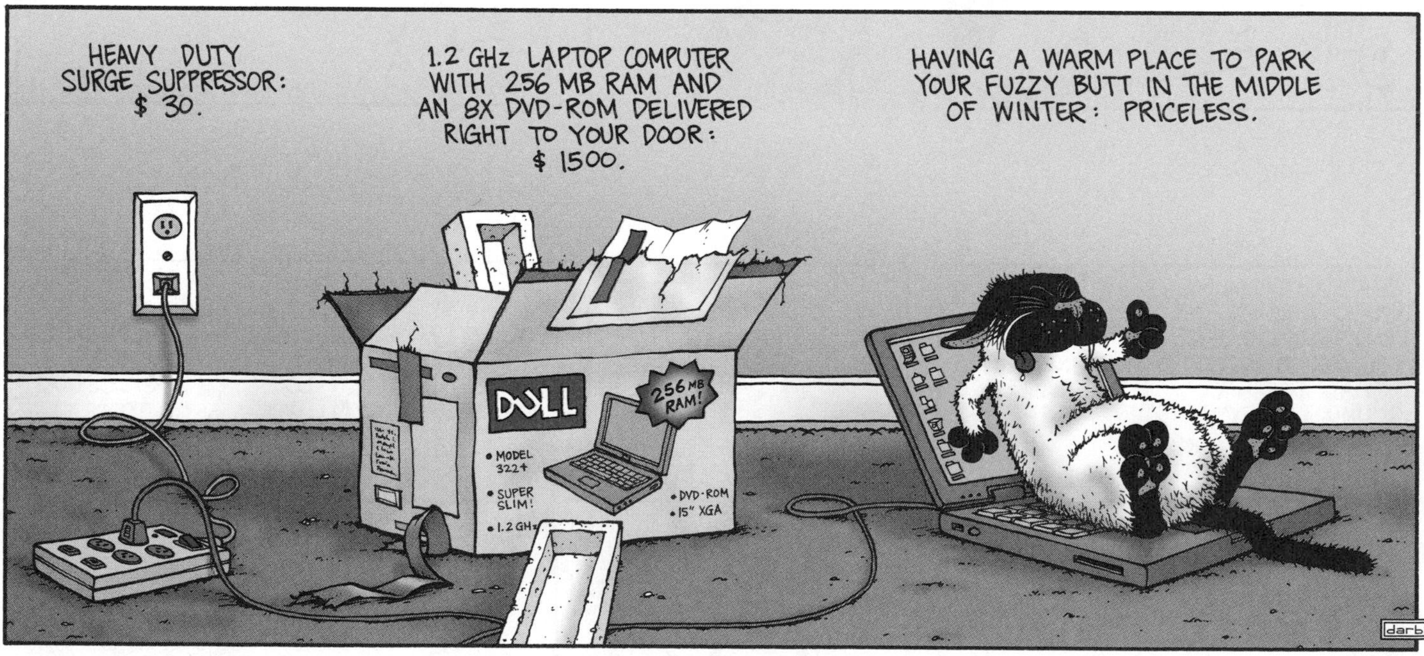

HEAVY DUTY SURGE SUPPRESSOR: $ 30.
1.2 GHz LAPTOP COMPUTER WITH 256 MB RAM AND AN 8X DVD-ROM DELIVERED RIGHT TO YOUR DOOR: $ 1500.
HAVING A WARM PLACE TO PARK YOUR FUZZY BUTT IN THE MIDDLE OF WINTER: PRICELESS.
256 MB RAM!
• MODEL 322+
• SUPER SLIM!
• DVD-ROM
• 15" XGA
darb

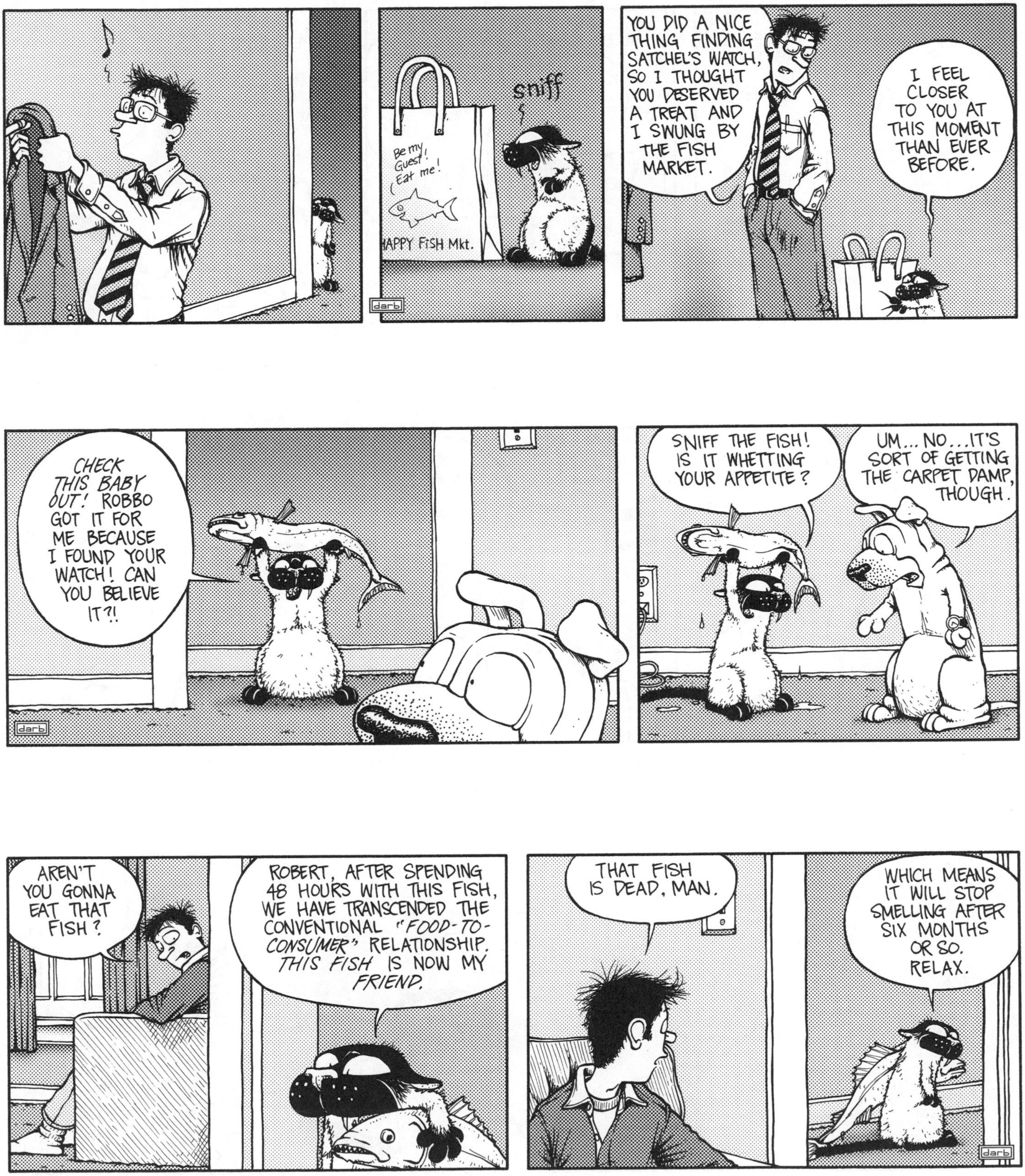
sniff
Be my Guest! Eat me!
HAPPY FISH Mkt.
darb
YOU DID A NICE THING FINDING SATCHEL'S WATCH, SO I THOUGHT YOU DESERVED A TREAT AND I SWUNG BY THE FISH MARKET.
I FEEL CLOSER TO YOU AT THIS MOMENT THAN EVER BEFORE.
CHECK THIS BABY OUT! ROBBO GOT IT FOR ME BECAUSE I FOUND YOUR WATCH! CAN YOU BELIEVE IT?!
darb
SNIFF THE FISH! IS IT WHETTING YOUR APPETITE?
UM... NO... IT'S SORT OF GETTING THE CARPET DAMP, THOUGH.
AREN'T YOU GONNA EAT THAT FISH?
ROBERT, AFTER SPENDING 48 HOURS WITH THIS FISH, WE HAVE TRANSCENDED THE CONVENTIONAL "FOOD-TO-CONSUMER" RELATIONSHIP. THIS FISH IS NOW MY FRIEND.
THAT FISH IS DEAD, MAN.
WHICH MEANS IT WILL STOP SMELLING AFTER SIX MONTHS OR SO. RELAX.
darb

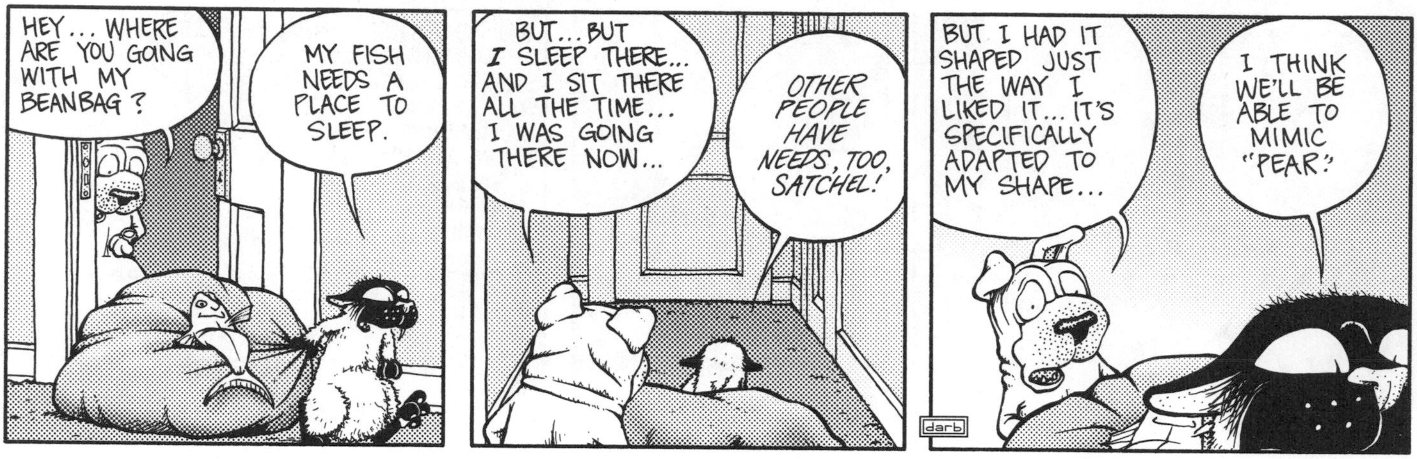
HEY... WHERE ARE YOU GOING WITH MY BEANBAG?
MY FISH NEEDS A PLACE TO SLEEP.
BUT... BUT *I* SLEEP THERE... AND I SIT THERE ALL THE TIME... I WAS GOING THERE NOW...
OTHER PEOPLE HAVE NEEDS, TOO, SATCHEL!
BUT I HAD IT SHAPED JUST THE WAY I LIKED IT... IT'S SPECIFICALLY ADAPTED TO MY SHAPE...
I THINK WE'LL BE ABLE TO MIMIC "PEAR."
darb

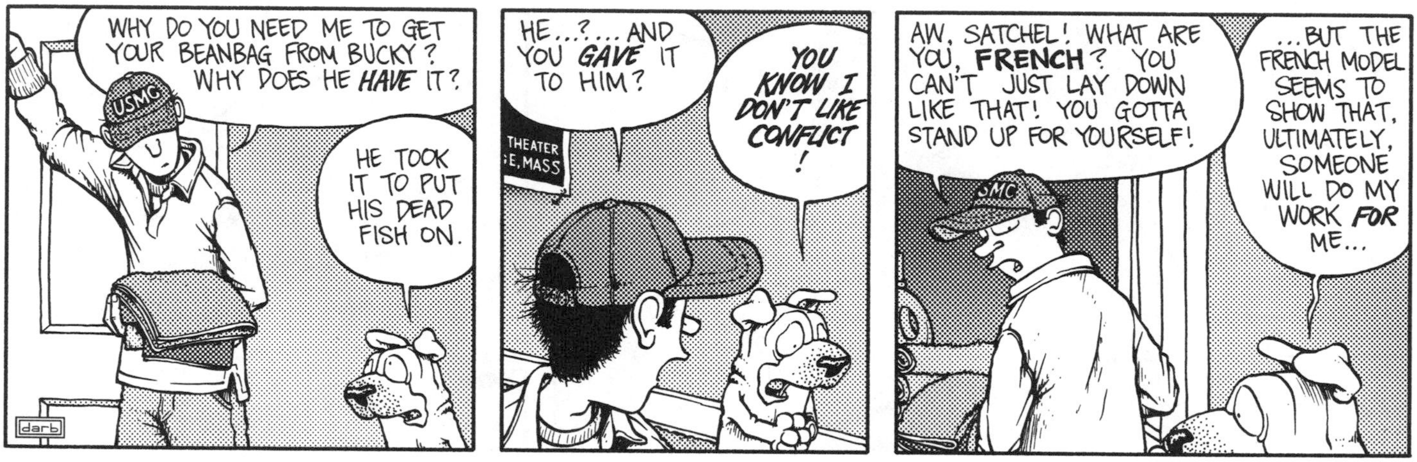
WHY DO YOU NEED ME TO GET YOUR BEANBAG FROM BUCKY? WHY DOES HE ***HAVE*** IT?
USMC
HE TOOK IT TO PUT HIS DEAD FISH ON.
darb
HE...?... AND YOU ***GAVE*** IT TO HIM?
THEATER
E, MASS
YOU KNOW I DON'T LIKE CONFLICT!
AW, SATCHEL! WHAT ARE YOU, **FRENCH**? YOU CAN'T JUST LAY DOWN LIKE THAT! YOU GOTTA STAND UP FOR YOURSELF!
...BUT THE FRENCH MODEL SEEMS TO SHOW THAT, ULTIMATELY, SOMEONE WILL DO MY WORK ***FOR*** ME...

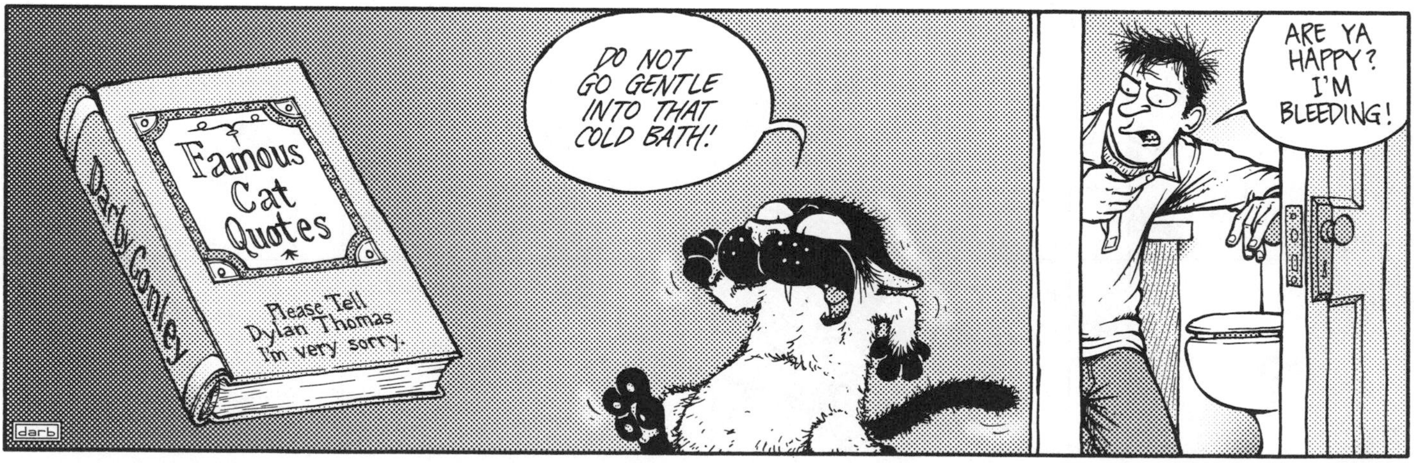
Famous Cat Quotes
Darby Conley
Please Tell Dylan Thomas I'm very sorry.
DO NOT GO GENTLE INTO THAT COLD BATH!
ARE YA HAPPY? I'M BLEEDING!
darb

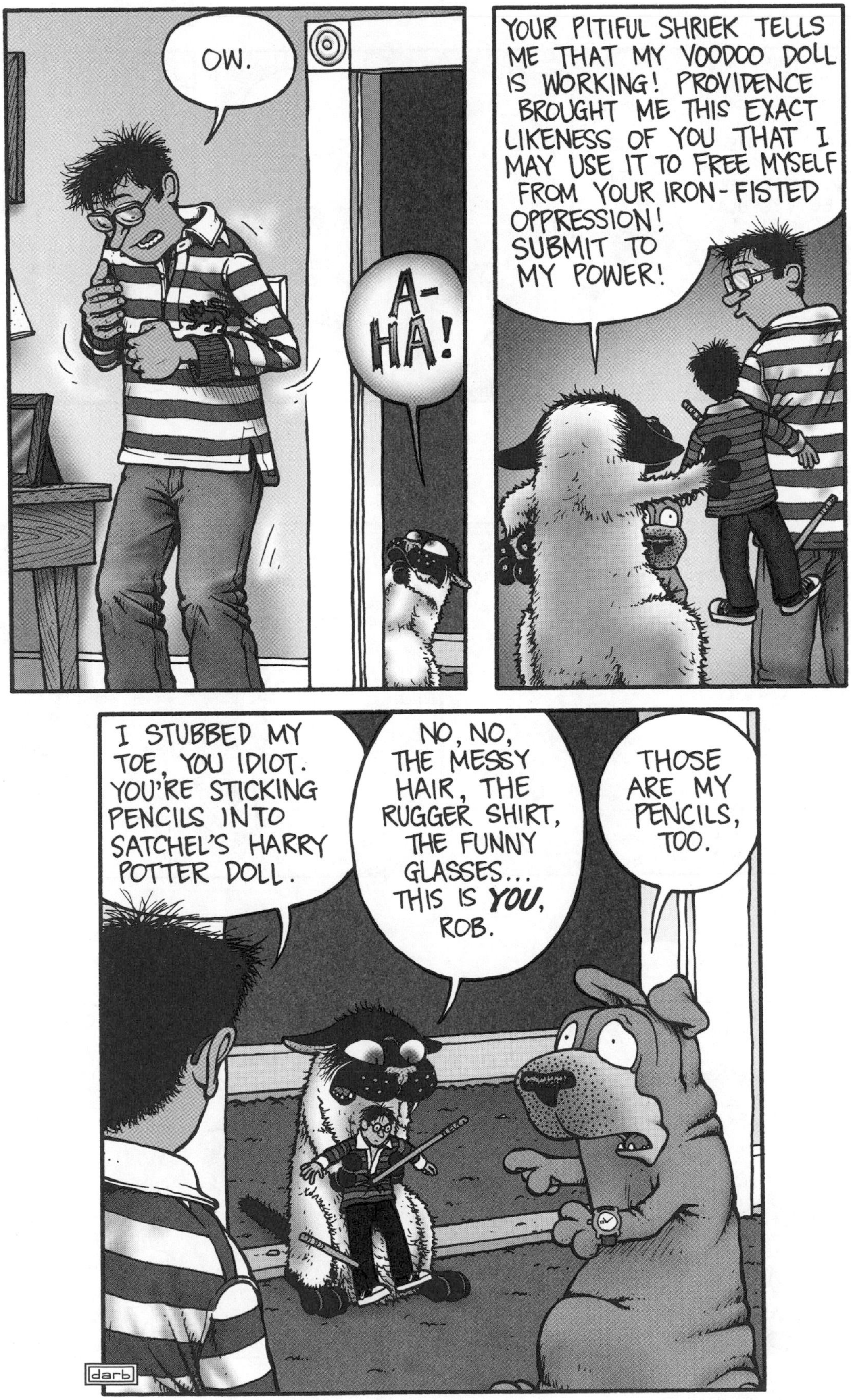
OW.
A-HA!
YOUR PITIFUL SHRIEK TELLS ME THAT MY VOODOO DOLL IS WORKING! PROVIDENCE BROUGHT ME THIS EXACT LIKENESS OF YOU THAT I MAY USE IT TO FREE MYSELF FROM YOUR IRON-FISTED OPPRESSION! SUBMIT TO MY POWER!
I STUBBED MY TOE, YOU IDIOT. YOU'RE STICKING PENCILS INTO SATCHEL'S HARRY POTTER DOLL.
NO, NO, THE MESSY HAIR, THE RUGGER SHIRT, THE FUNNY GLASSES... THIS IS *YOU*, ROB.
THOSE ARE MY PENCILS, TOO.
darb

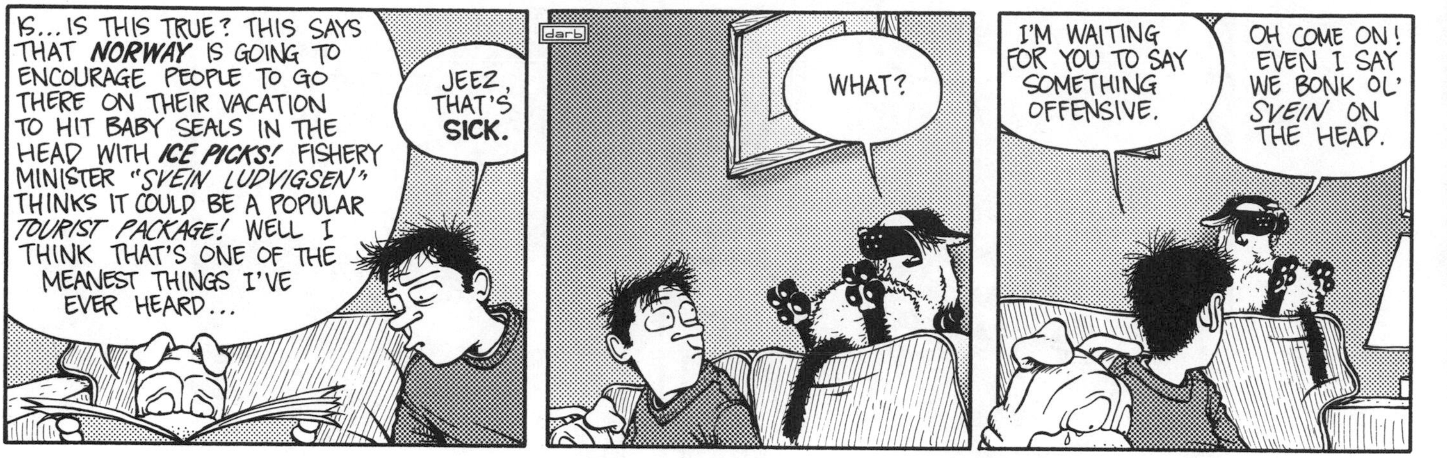
IS... IS THIS TRUE? THIS SAYS THAT NORWAY IS GOING TO ENCOURAGE PEOPLE TO GO THERE ON THEIR VACATION TO HIT BABY SEALS IN THE HEAD WITH ICE PICKS! FISHERY MINISTER "SVEIN LUDVIGSEN" THINKS IT COULD BE A POPULAR TOURIST PACKAGE! WELL I THINK THAT'S ONE OF THE MEANEST THINGS I'VE EVER HEARD...
JEEZ, THAT'S SICK.
darb
WHAT?
I'M WAITING FOR YOU TO SAY SOMETHING OFFENSIVE.
OH COME ON! EVEN I SAY WE BONK OL' SVEIN ON THE HEAD.

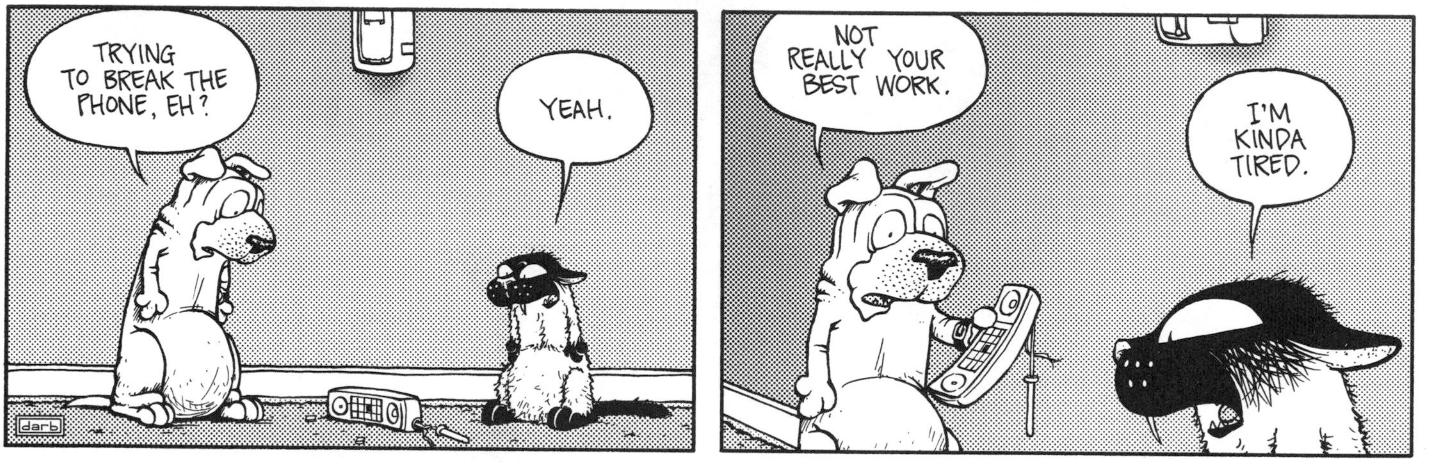
TRYING TO BREAK THE PHONE, EH?
YEAH.
darb
NOT REALLY YOUR BEST WORK.
I'M KINDA TIRED.

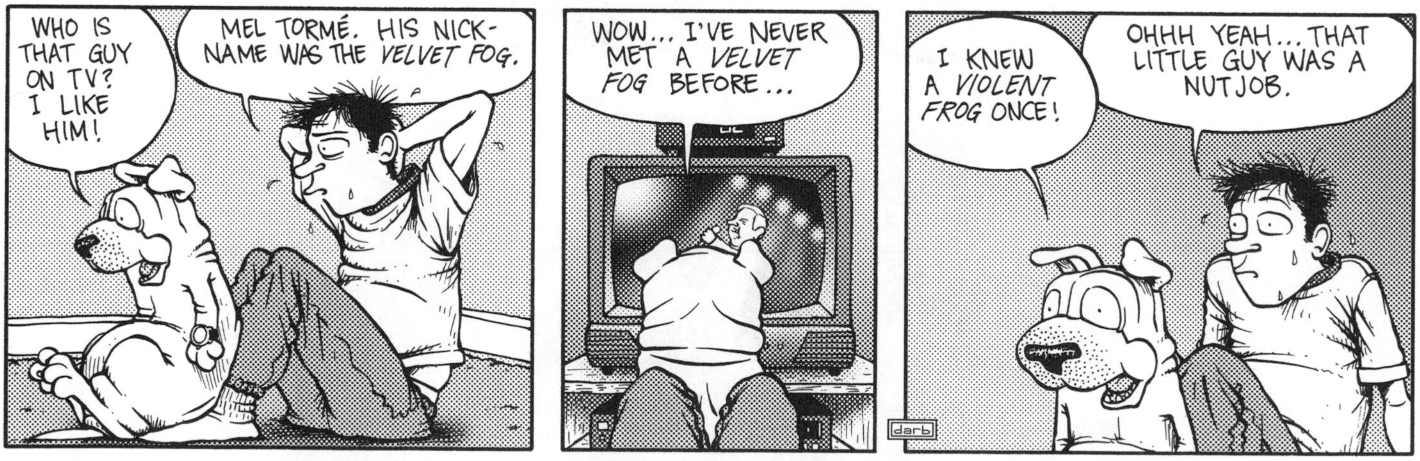
WHO IS THAT GUY ON TV? I LIKE HIM!
MEL TORMÉ. HIS NICK-NAME WAS THE VELVET FOG.
WOW... I'VE NEVER MET A VELVET FOG BEFORE...
darb
I KNEW A VIOLENT FROG ONCE!
OHHH YEAH... THAT LITTLE GUY WAS A NUTJOB.

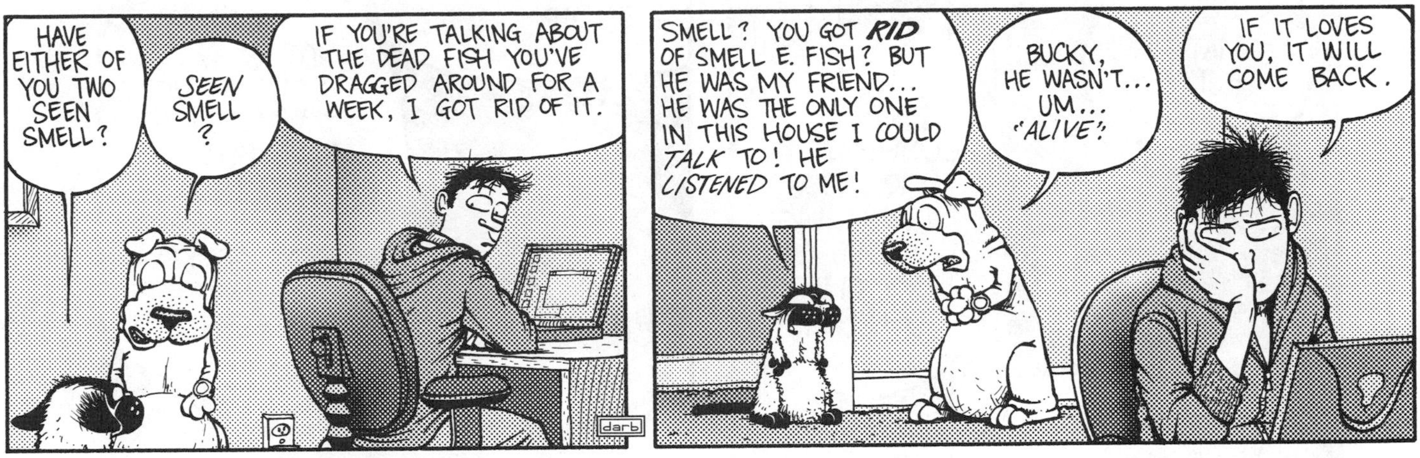
HAVE EITHER OF YOU TWO SEEN SMELL?
SEEN SMELL?
IF YOU'RE TALKING ABOUT THE DEAD FISH YOU'VE DRAGGED AROUND FOR A WEEK, I GOT RID OF IT.
SMELL? YOU GOT RID OF SMELL E. FISH? BUT HE WAS MY FRIEND... HE WAS THE ONLY ONE IN THIS HOUSE I COULD TALK TO! HE LISTENED TO ME!
BUCKY, HE WASN'T... UM... "ALIVE".
IF IT LOVES YOU, IT WILL COME BACK.

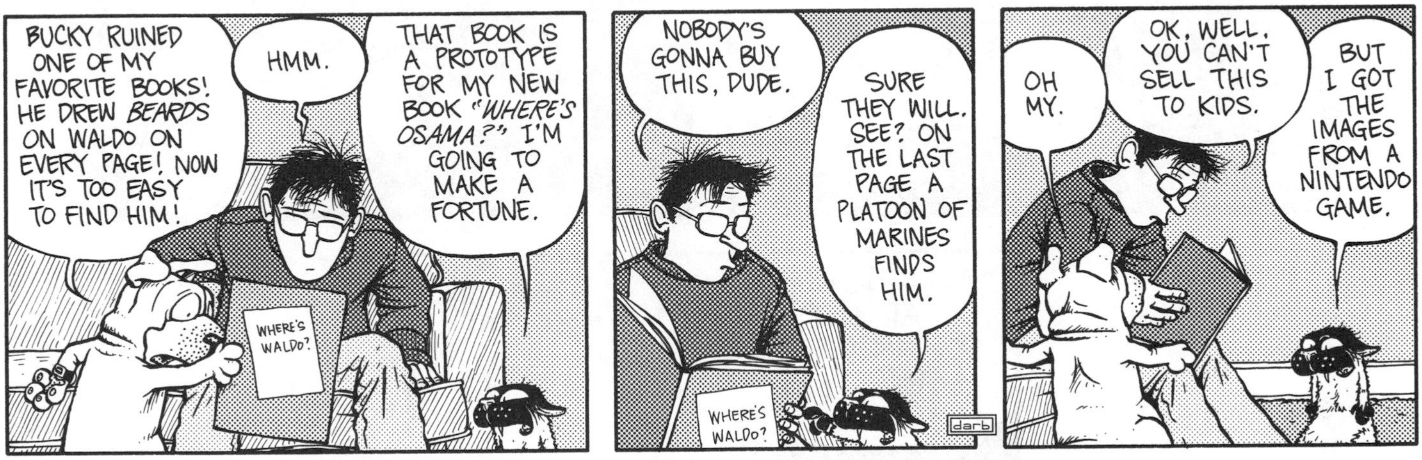
BUCKY RUINED ONE OF MY FAVORITE BOOKS! HE DREW BEARDS ON WALDO ON EVERY PAGE! NOW IT'S TOO EASY TO FIND HIM!
HMM.
THAT BOOK IS A PROTOTYPE FOR MY NEW BOOK "WHERE'S OSAMA?" I'M GOING TO MAKE A FORTUNE.
WHERE'S WALDO?
NOBODY'S GONNA BUY THIS, DUDE.
SURE THEY WILL. SEE? ON THE LAST PAGE A PLATOON OF MARINES FINDS HIM.
WHERE'S WALDO?
OH MY.
OK, WELL, YOU CAN'T SELL THIS TO KIDS.
BUT I GOT THE IMAGES FROM A NINTENDO GAME.

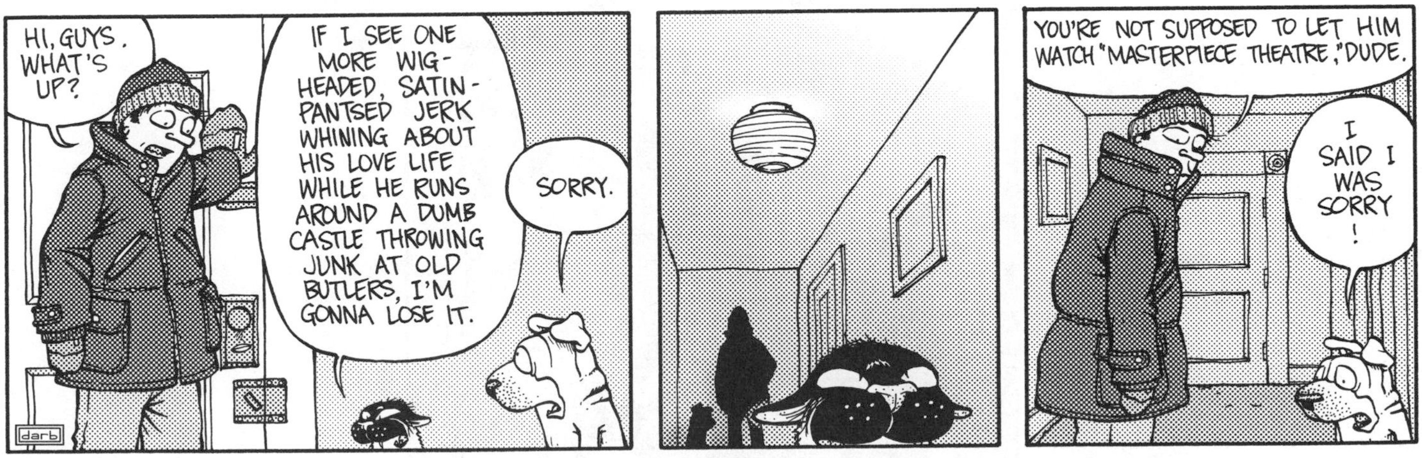
HI, GUYS. WHAT'S UP?
IF I SEE ONE MORE WIG-HEADED, SATIN-PANTSED JERK WHINING ABOUT HIS LOVE LIFE WHILE HE RUNS AROUND A DUMB CASTLE THROWING JUNK AT OLD BUTLERS, I'M GONNA LOSE IT.
SORRY.
YOU'RE NOT SUPPOSED TO LET HIM WATCH "MASTERPIECE THEATRE," DUDE.
I SAID I WAS SORRY!

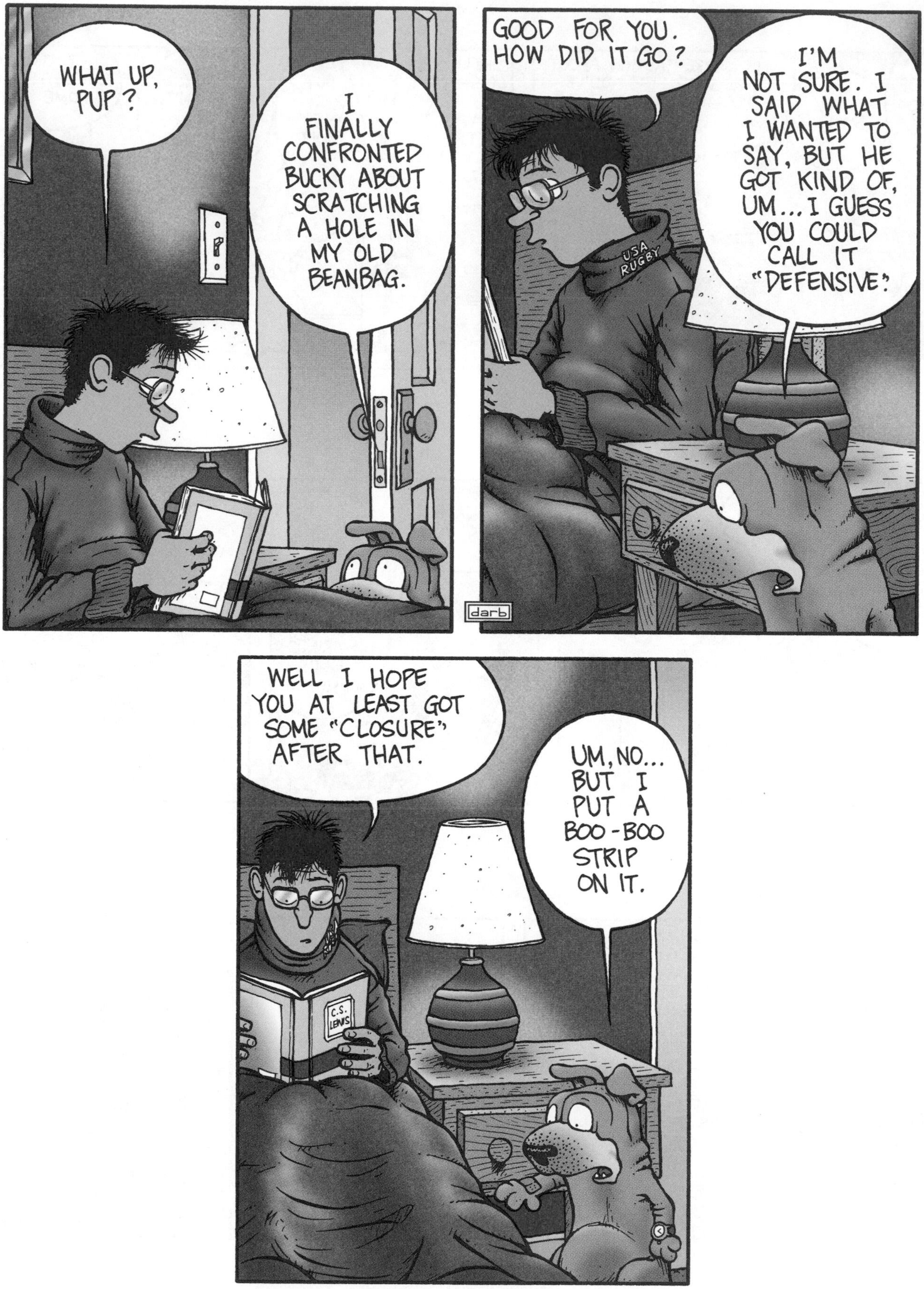
WHAT UP, PUP?
I FINALLY CONFRONTED BUCKY ABOUT SCRATCHING A HOLE IN MY OLD BEANBAG.
darb
GOOD FOR YOU. HOW DID IT GO?
I'M NOT SURE. I SAID WHAT I WANTED TO SAY, BUT HE GOT KIND OF, UM... I GUESS YOU COULD CALL IT "DEFENSIVE."
USA RUGBY
WELL I HOPE YOU AT LEAST GOT SOME "CLOSURE" AFTER THAT.
UM, NO... BUT I PUT A BOO-BOO STRIP ON IT.
C.S. LEWIS

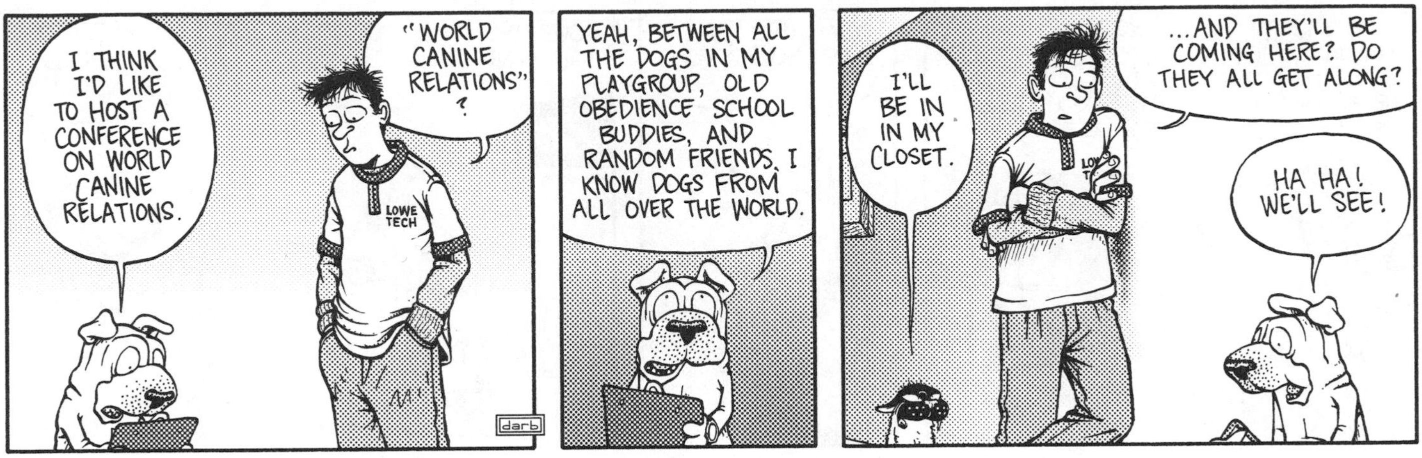
I THINK I'D LIKE TO HOST A CONFERENCE ON WORLD CANINE RELATIONS.
"WORLD CANINE RELATIONS"?
YEAH, BETWEEN ALL THE DOGS IN MY PLAYGROUP, OLD OBEDIENCE SCHOOL BUDDIES, AND RANDOM FRIENDS, I KNOW DOGS FROM ALL OVER THE WORLD.
...AND THEY'LL BE COMING HERE? DO THEY ALL GET ALONG?
I'LL BE IN IN MY CLOSET.
HA HA! WE'LL SEE!
LOWE TECH
darb

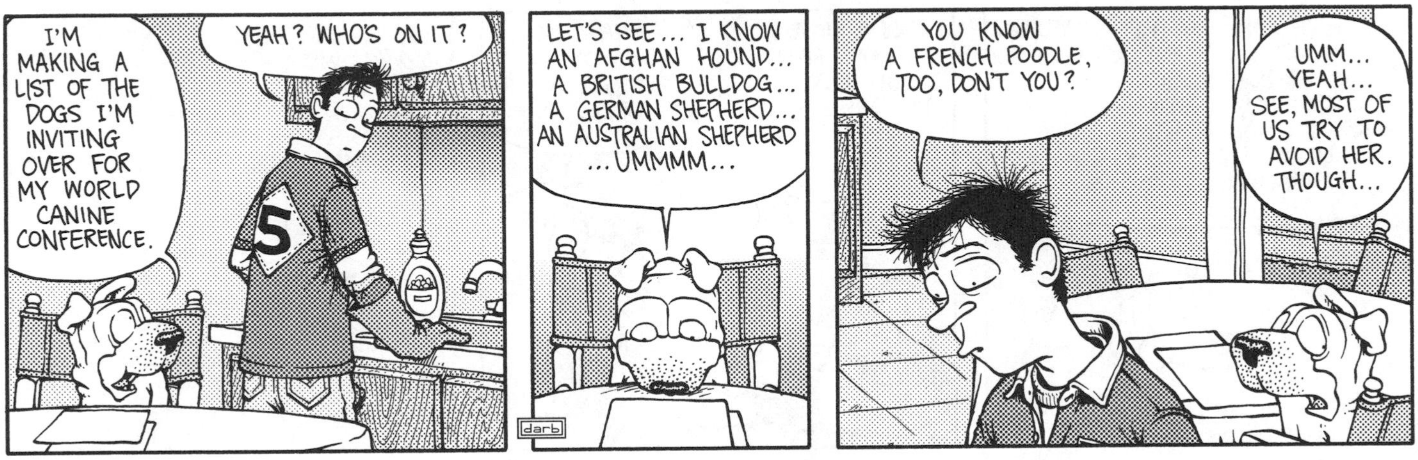
I'M MAKING A LIST OF THE DOGS I'M INVITING OVER FOR MY WORLD CANINE CONFERENCE.
YEAH? WHO'S ON IT?
LET'S SEE... I KNOW AN AFGHAN HOUND... A BRITISH BULLDOG... A GERMAN SHEPHERD... AN AUSTRALIAN SHEPHERD ...UMMMM...
YOU KNOW A FRENCH POODLE, TOO, DON'T YOU?
UMM... YEAH... SEE, MOST OF US TRY TO AVOID HER. THOUGH...
5
darb

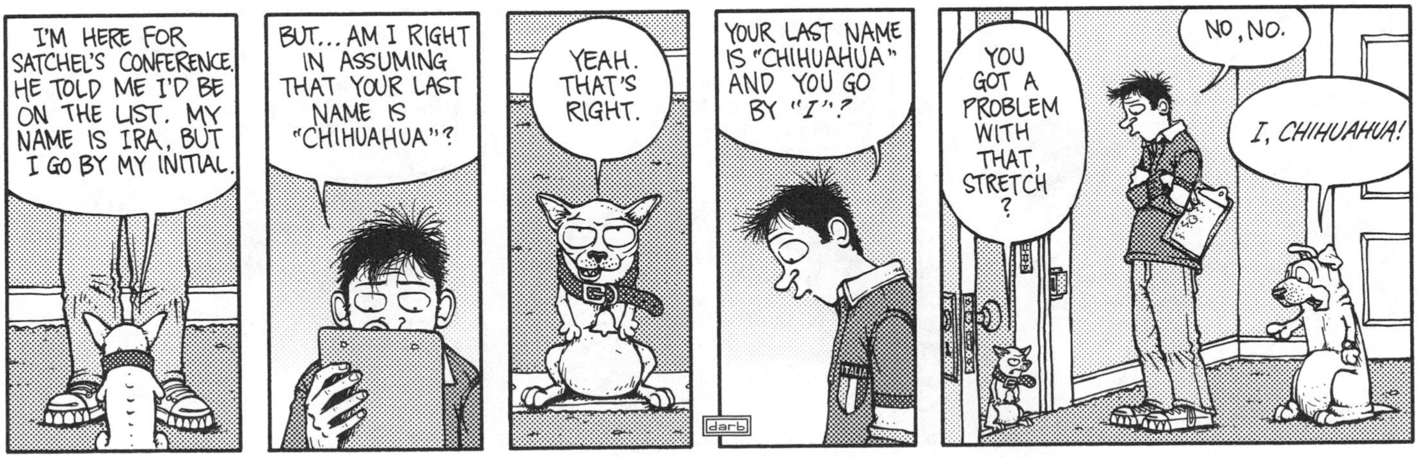
I'M HERE FOR SATCHEL'S CONFERENCE. HE TOLD ME I'D BE ON THE LIST. MY NAME IS IRA, BUT I GO BY MY INITIAL.
BUT... AM I RIGHT IN ASSUMING THAT YOUR LAST NAME IS "CHIHUAHUA"?
YEAH. THAT'S RIGHT.
YOUR LAST NAME IS "CHIHUAHUA" AND YOU GO BY "I"?
YOU GOT A PROBLEM WITH THAT, STRETCH?
NO, NO.
I, CHIHUAHUA!
darb

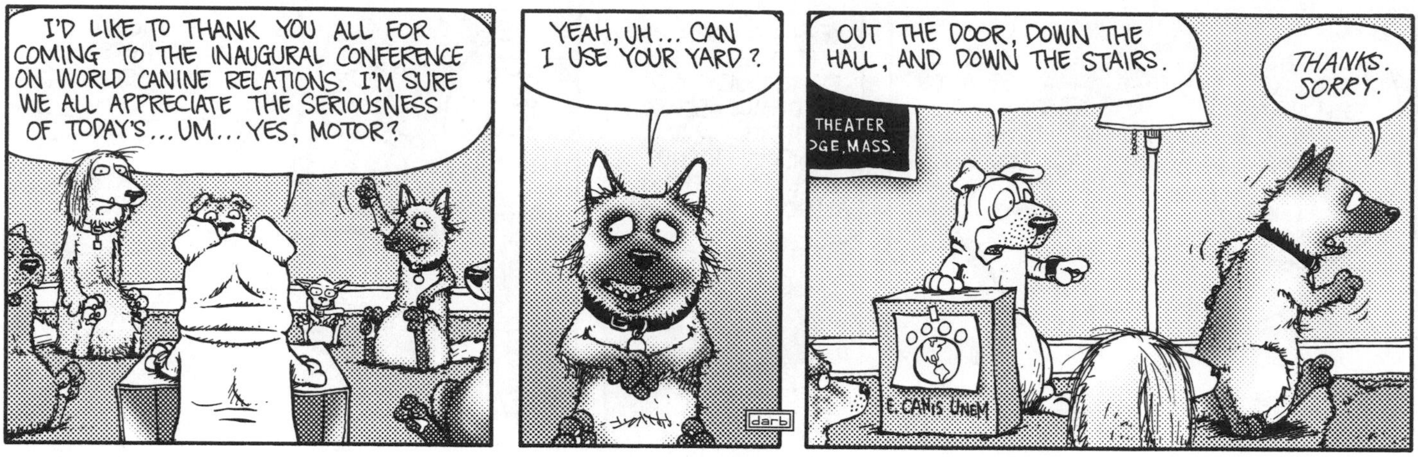
I'D LIKE TO THANK YOU ALL FOR COMING TO THE INAUGURAL CONFERENCE ON WORLD CANINE RELATIONS. I'M SURE WE ALL APPRECIATE THE SERIOUSNESS OF TODAY'S... UM... YES, MOTOR?
YEAH, UH... CAN I USE YOUR YARD?
darb
THEATER
DGE, MASS.
OUT THE DOOR, DOWN THE HALL, AND DOWN THE STAIRS.
THANKS. SORRY.
E. CANIS UNEM

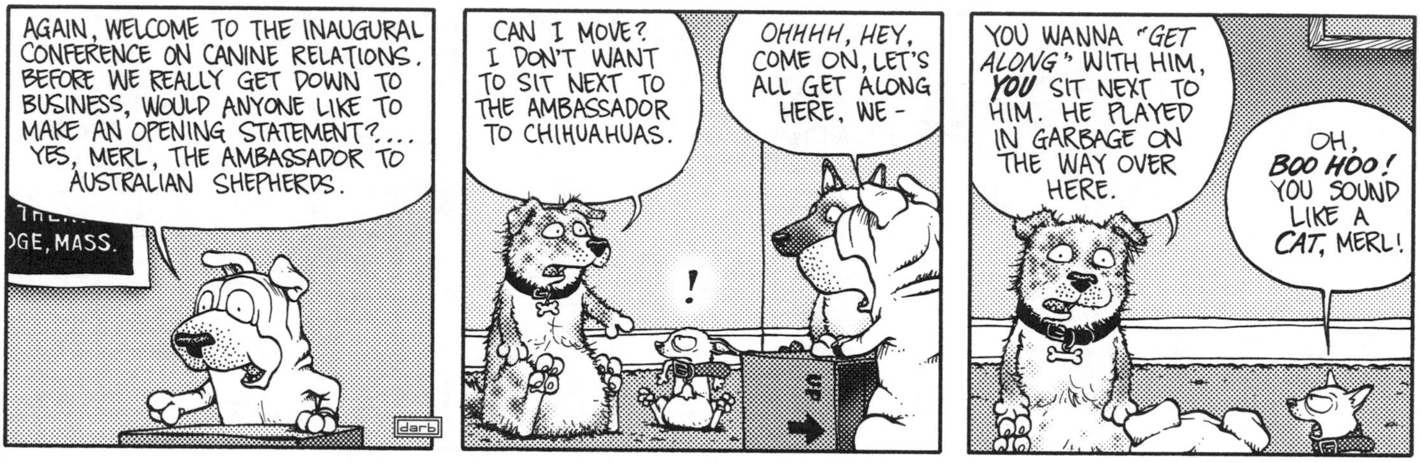
AGAIN, WELCOME TO THE INAUGURAL CONFERENCE ON CANINE RELATIONS. BEFORE WE REALLY GET DOWN TO BUSINESS, WOULD ANYONE LIKE TO MAKE AN OPENING STATEMENT?.... YES, MERL, THE AMBASSADOR TO AUSTRALIAN SHEPHERDS.
DGE, MASS.
darb
CAN I MOVE? I DON'T WANT TO SIT NEXT TO THE AMBASSADOR TO CHIHUAHUAS.
OHHHH, HEY, COME ON, LET'S ALL GET ALONG HERE, WE-
!
UP
YOU WANNA "GET ALONG" WITH HIM, YOU SIT NEXT TO HIM. HE PLAYED IN GARBAGE ON THE WAY OVER HERE.
OH, BOO HOO! YOU SOUND LIKE A CAT, MERL!

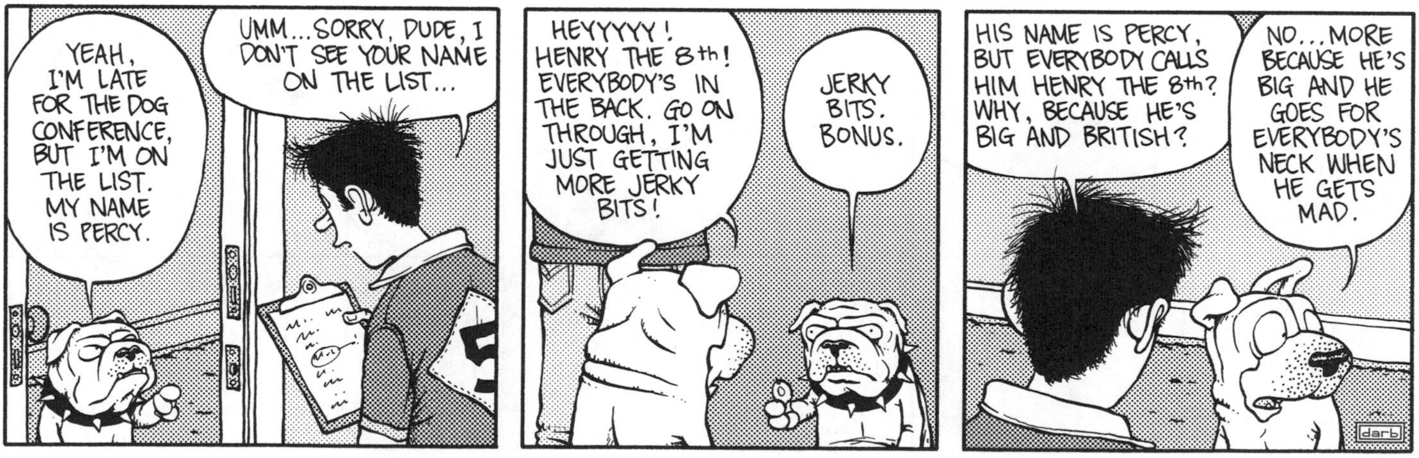
YEAH, I'M LATE FOR THE DOG CONFERENCE, BUT I'M ON THE LIST. MY NAME IS PERCY.
UMM... SORRY, DUDE, I DON'T SEE YOUR NAME ON THE LIST...
5
HEYYYYY! HENRY THE 8th! EVERYBODY'S IN THE BACK. GO ON THROUGH, I'M JUST GETTING MORE JERKY BITS!
JERKY BITS. BONUS.
HIS NAME IS PERCY, BUT EVERYBODY CALLS HIM HENRY THE 8th? WHY, BECAUSE HE'S BIG AND BRITISH?
NO... MORE BECAUSE HE'S BIG AND HE GOES FOR EVERYBODY'S NECK WHEN HE GETS MAD.
darb

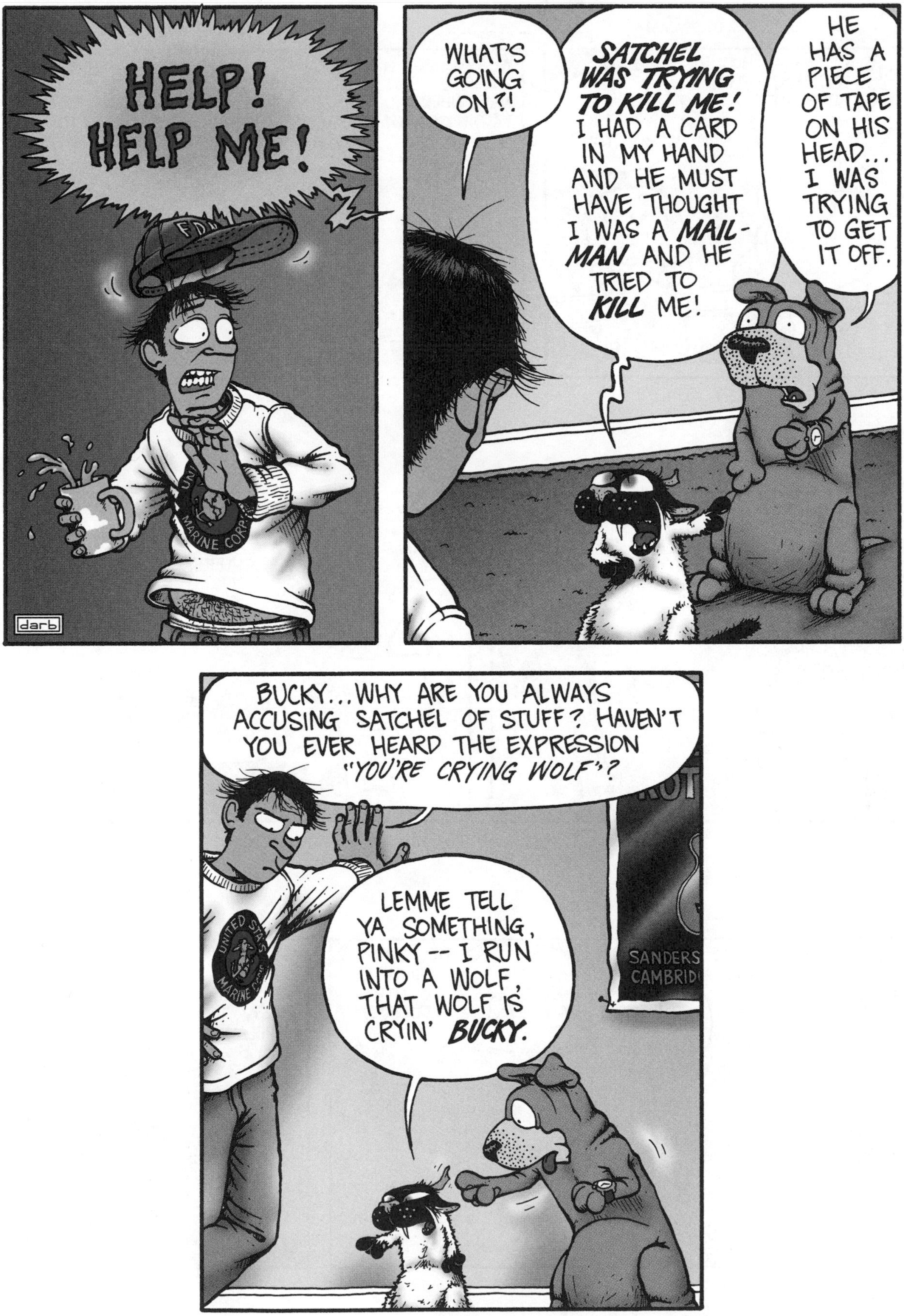
HELP! HELP ME!
darb
WHAT'S GOING ON?!
SATCHEL WAS TRYING TO KILL ME! I HAD A CARD IN MY HAND AND HE MUST HAVE THOUGHT I WAS A MAIL-MAN AND HE TRIED TO KILL ME!
HE HAS A PIECE OF TAPE ON HIS HEAD... I WAS TRYING TO GET IT OFF.
BUCKY...WHY ARE YOU ALWAYS ACCUSING SATCHEL OF STUFF? HAVEN'T YOU EVER HEARD THE EXPRESSION "YOU'RE CRYING WOLF"?
LEMME TELL YA SOMETHING, PINKY -- I RUN INTO A WOLF, THAT WOLF IS CRYIN' BUCKY.

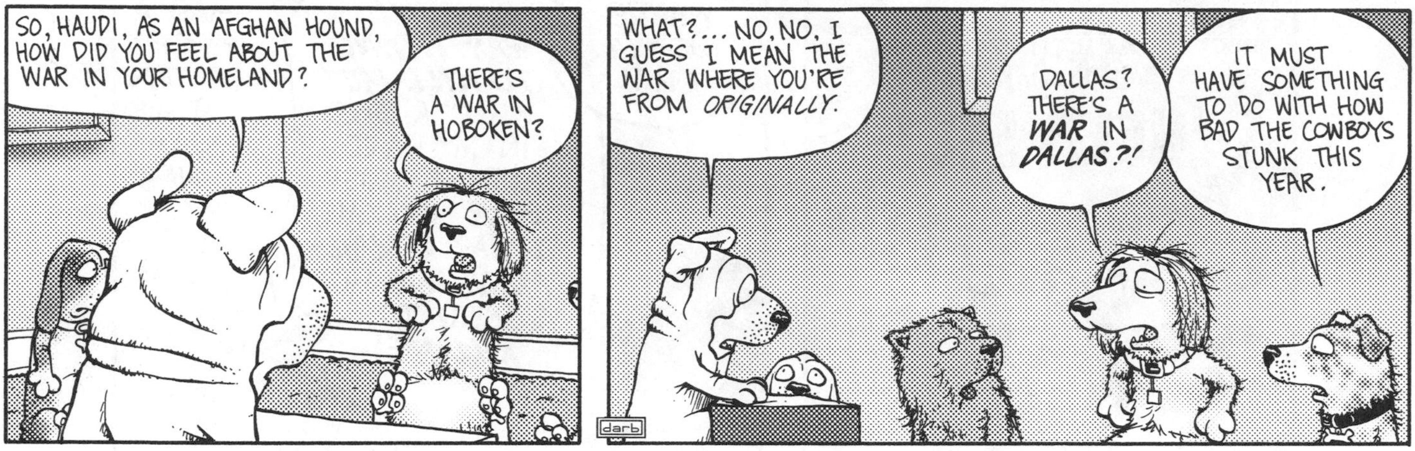
SO, HAUDI, AS AN AFGHAN HOUND, HOW DID YOU FEEL ABOUT THE WAR IN YOUR HOMELAND?
THERE'S A WAR IN HOBOKEN?
WHAT?... NO, NO, I GUESS I MEAN THE WAR WHERE YOU'RE FROM *ORIGINALLY*.
DALLAS? THERE'S A ***WAR*** IN ***DALLAS?!***
IT MUST HAVE SOMETHING TO DO WITH HOW BAD THE COWBOYS STUNK THIS YEAR.
darb

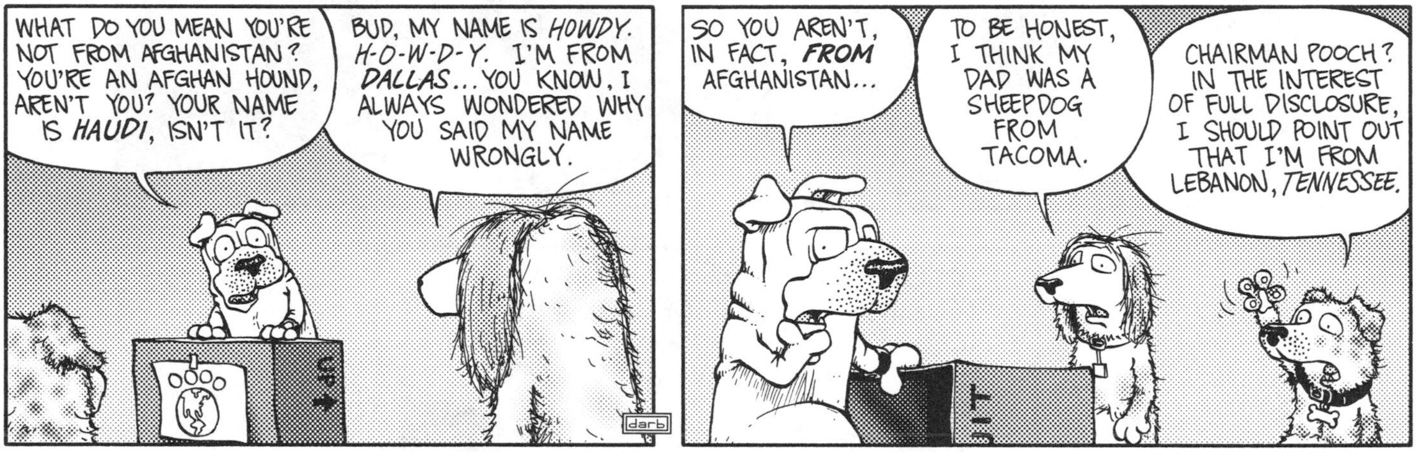
WHAT DO YOU MEAN YOU'RE NOT FROM AFGHANISTAN? YOU'RE AN AFGHAN HOUND, AREN'T YOU? YOUR NAME IS ***HAUDI***, ISN'T IT?
BUD, MY NAME IS *HOWDY*. *H-O-W-D-Y*. I'M FROM ***DALLAS***... YOU KNOW, I ALWAYS WONDERED WHY YOU SAID MY NAME WRONGLY.
UP
darb
SO YOU AREN'T, IN FACT, ***FROM*** AFGHANISTAN...
TO BE HONEST, I THINK MY DAD WAS A SHEEPDOG FROM TACOMA.
CHAIRMAN POOCH? IN THE INTEREST OF FULL DISCLOSURE, I SHOULD POINT OUT THAT I'M FROM LEBANON, *TENNESSEE*.

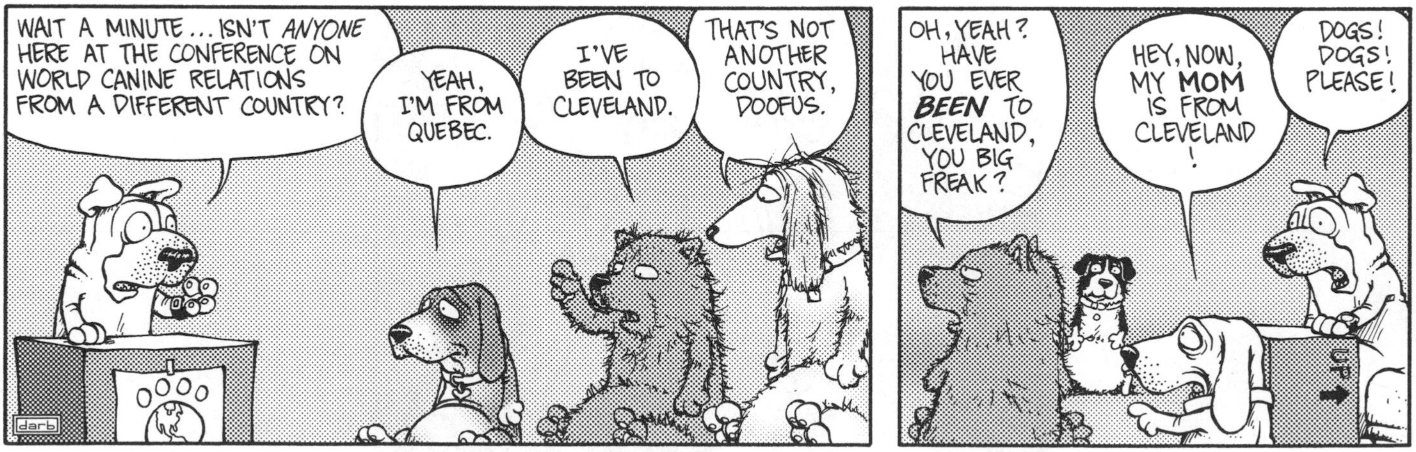
WAIT A MINUTE... ISN'T *ANYONE* HERE AT THE CONFERENCE ON WORLD CANINE RELATIONS FROM A DIFFERENT COUNTRY?
YEAH, I'M FROM QUEBEC.
I'VE BEEN TO CLEVELAND.
THAT'S NOT ANOTHER COUNTRY, DOOFUS.
darb
OH, YEAH? HAVE YOU EVER ***BEEN*** TO CLEVELAND, YOU BIG FREAK?
HEY, NOW, MY **MOM** IS FROM CLEVELAND!
DOGS! DOGS! PLEASE!
UP

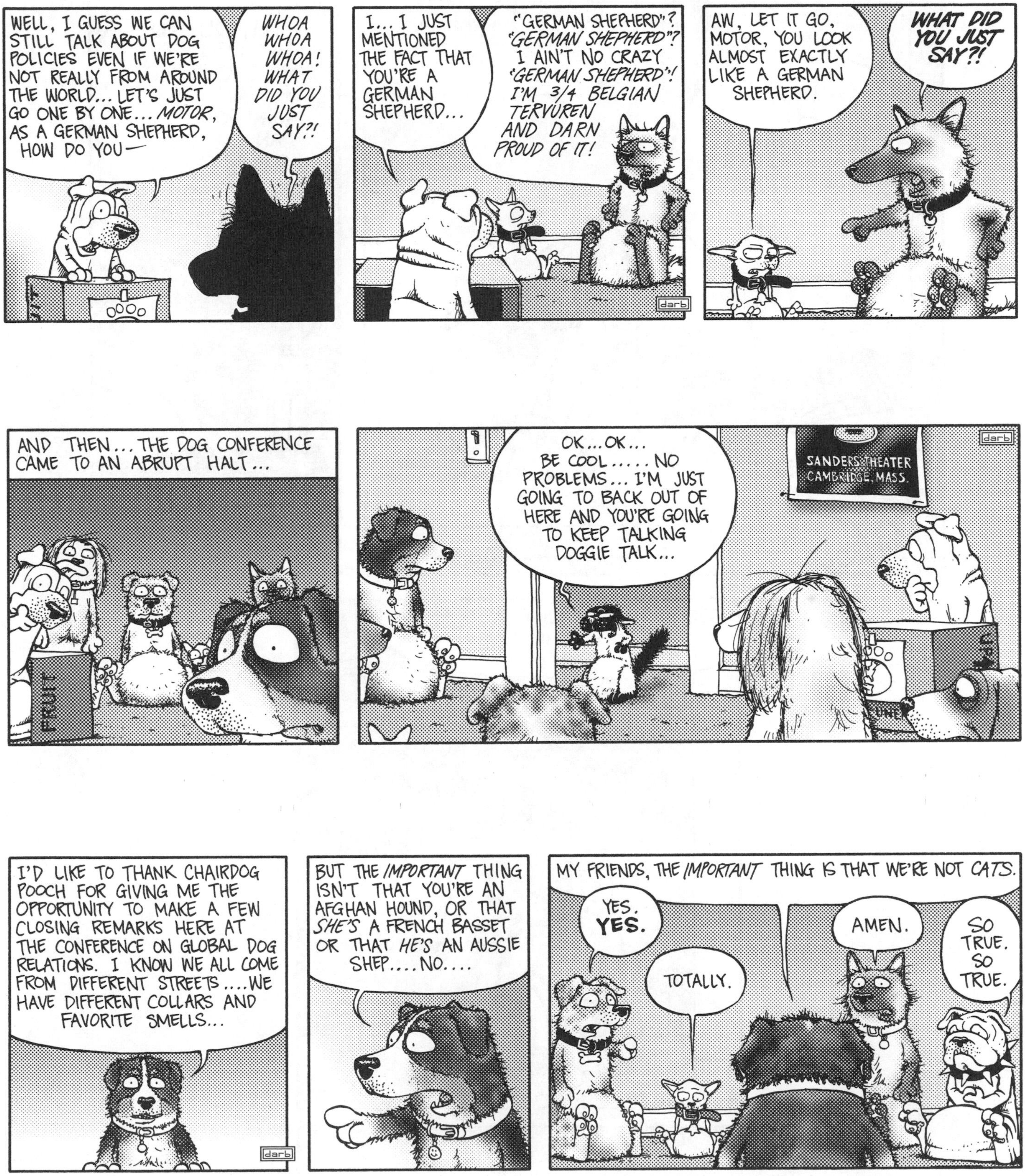

WELL, I GUESS WE CAN STILL TALK ABOUT DOG POLICIES EVEN IF WE'RE NOT REALLY FROM AROUND THE WORLD... LET'S JUST GO ONE BY ONE... MOTOR, AS A GERMAN SHEPHERD, HOW DO YOU—
WHOA WHOA WHOA! WHAT DID YOU JUST SAY?!
I... I JUST MENTIONED THE FACT THAT YOU'RE A GERMAN SHEPHERD...
"GERMAN SHEPHERD"? "GERMAN SHEPHERD"? I AIN'T NO CRAZY "GERMAN SHEPHERD"! I'M 3/4 BELGIAN TERVUREN AND DARN PROUD OF IT!
darb
AW, LET IT GO, MOTOR, YOU LOOK ALMOST EXACTLY LIKE A GERMAN SHEPHERD.
WHAT DID YOU JUST SAY?!
AND THEN... THE DOG CONFERENCE CAME TO AN ABRUPT HALT...
FRUIT
darb
SANDERS THEATER CAMBRIDGE, MASS.
OK...OK... BE COOL..... NO PROBLEMS... I'M JUST GOING TO BACK OUT OF HERE AND YOU'RE GOING TO KEEP TALKING DOGGIE TALK...
I'D LIKE TO THANK CHAIRDOG POOCH FOR GIVING ME THE OPPORTUNITY TO MAKE A FEW CLOSING REMARKS HERE AT THE CONFERENCE ON GLOBAL DOG RELATIONS. I KNOW WE ALL COME FROM DIFFERENT STREETS.... WE HAVE DIFFERENT COLLARS AND FAVORITE SMELLS...
darb
BUT THE IMPORTANT THING ISN'T THAT YOU'RE AN AFGHAN HOUND, OR THAT SHE'S A FRENCH BASSET OR THAT HE'S AN AUSSIE SHEP.... NO....
MY FRIENDS, THE IMPORTANT THING IS THAT WE'RE NOT CATS.
YES. YES.
TOTALLY.
AMEN.
SO TRUE. SO TRUE.

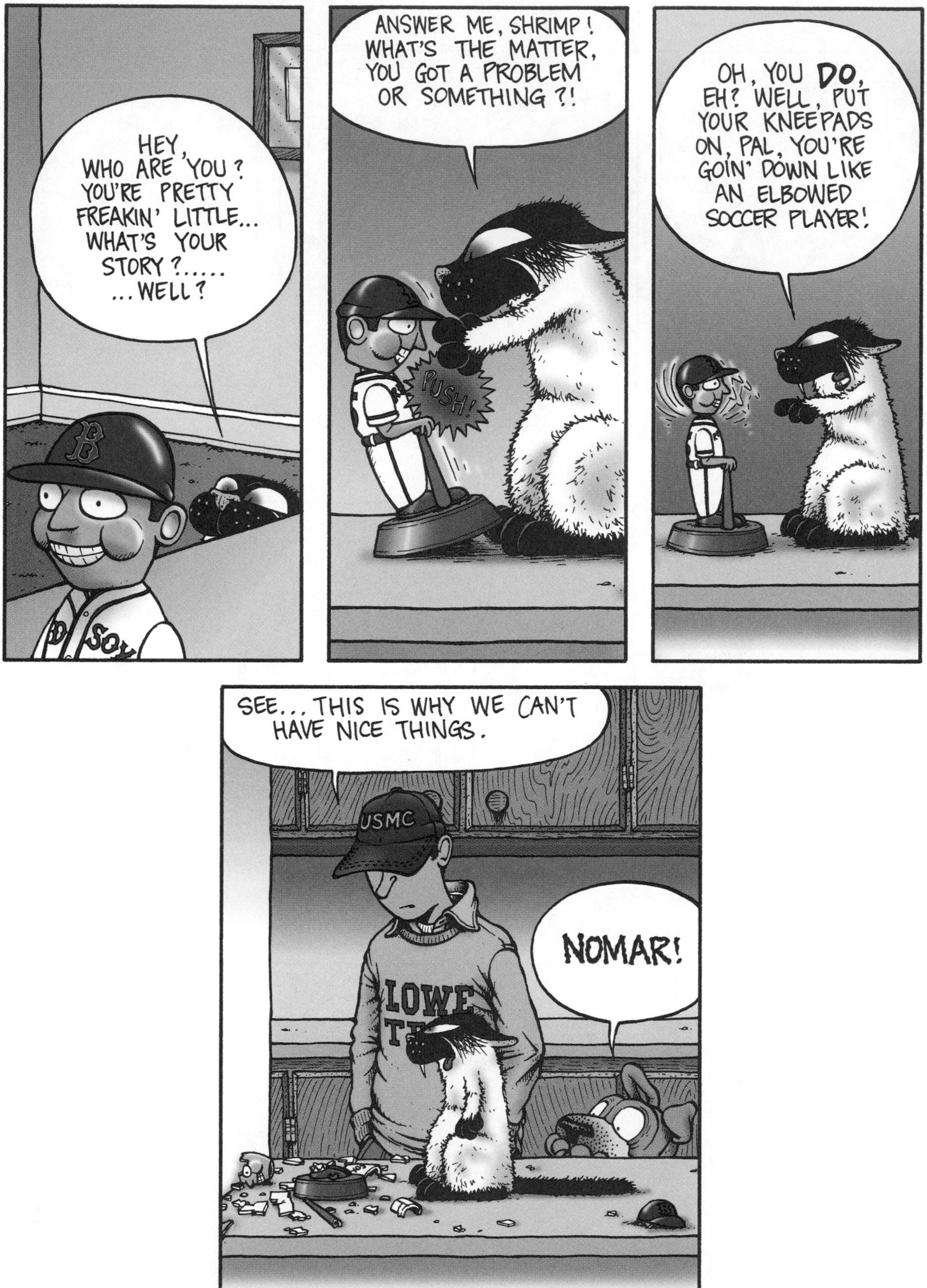
HEY, WHO ARE YOU? YOU'RE PRETTY FREAKIN' LITTLE... WHAT'S YOUR STORY?..... ...WELL?
ANSWER ME, SHRIMP! WHAT'S THE MATTER, YOU GOT A PROBLEM OR SOMETHING?!
PUSH!
OH, YOU **DO**, EH? WELL, PUT YOUR KNEEPADS ON, PAL, YOU'RE GOIN' DOWN LIKE AN ELBOWED SOCCER PLAYER!
SEE... THIS IS WHY WE CAN'T HAVE NICE THINGS.
NOMAR!
darb

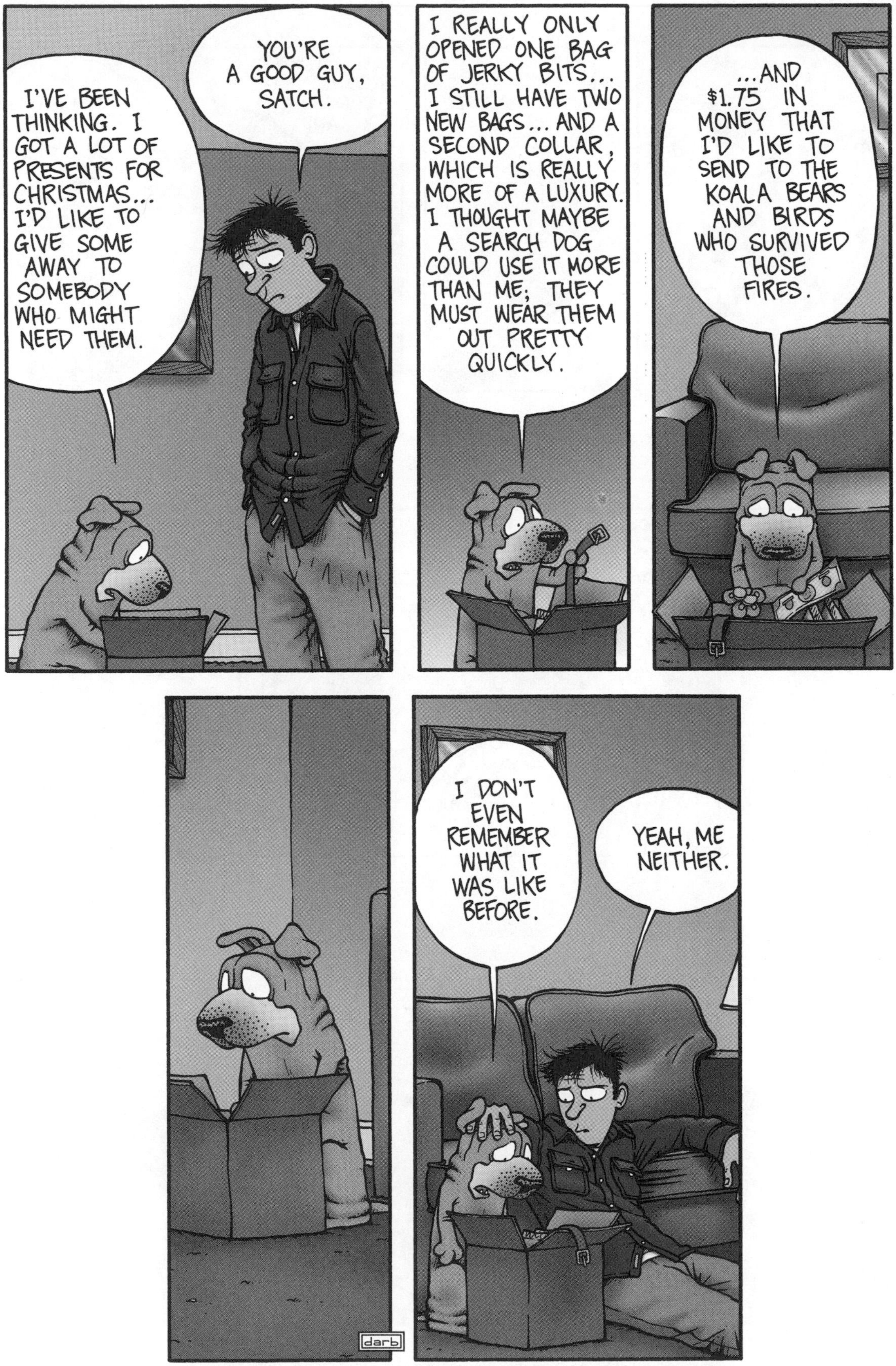
I'VE BEEN THINKING. I GOT A LOT OF PRESENTS FOR CHRISTMAS... I'D LIKE TO GIVE SOME AWAY TO SOMEBODY WHO MIGHT NEED THEM.
YOU'RE A GOOD GUY, SATCH.
I REALLY ONLY OPENED ONE BAG OF JERKY BITS... I STILL HAVE TWO NEW BAGS... AND A SECOND COLLAR, WHICH IS REALLY MORE OF A LUXURY. I THOUGHT MAYBE A SEARCH DOG COULD USE IT MORE THAN ME; THEY MUST WEAR THEM OUT PRETTY QUICKLY.
...AND $1.75 IN MONEY THAT I'D LIKE TO SEND TO THE KOALA BEARS AND BIRDS WHO SURVIVED THOSE FIRES.
darb
I DON'T EVEN REMEMBER WHAT IT WAS LIKE BEFORE.
YEAH, ME NEITHER.

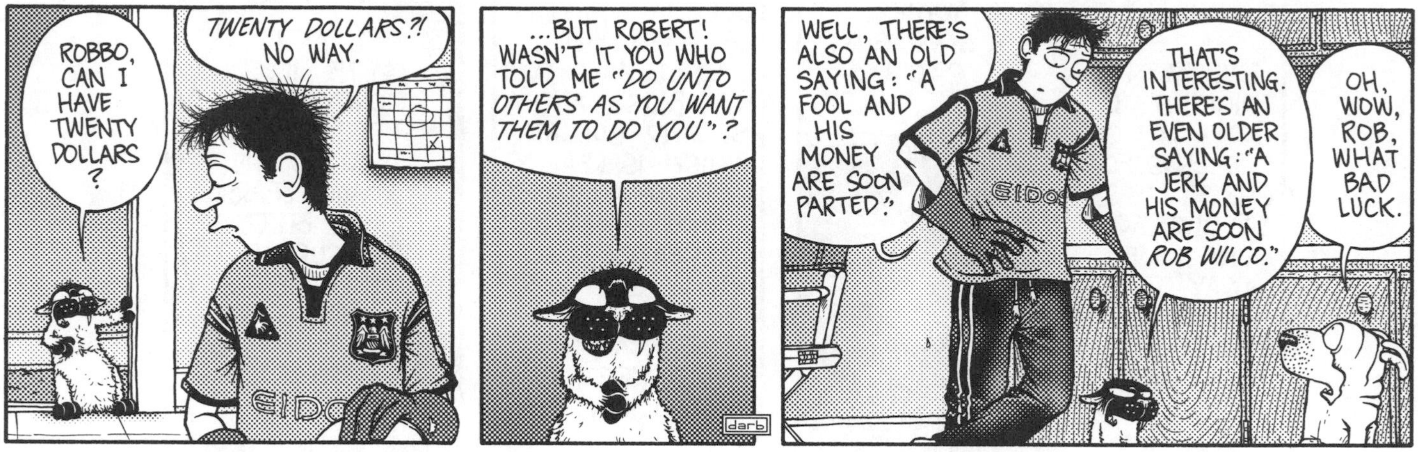
ROBBO, CAN I HAVE TWENTY DOLLARS ?
TWENTY DOLLARS?! NO WAY.
...BUT ROBERT! WASN'T IT YOU WHO TOLD ME "DO UNTO OTHERS AS YOU WANT THEM TO DO YOU"?
WELL, THERE'S ALSO AN OLD SAYING: "A FOOL AND HIS MONEY ARE SOON PARTED."
THAT'S INTERESTING. THERE'S AN EVEN OLDER SAYING: "A JERK AND HIS MONEY ARE SOON ROB WILCO."
OH, WOW, ROB, WHAT BAD LUCK.

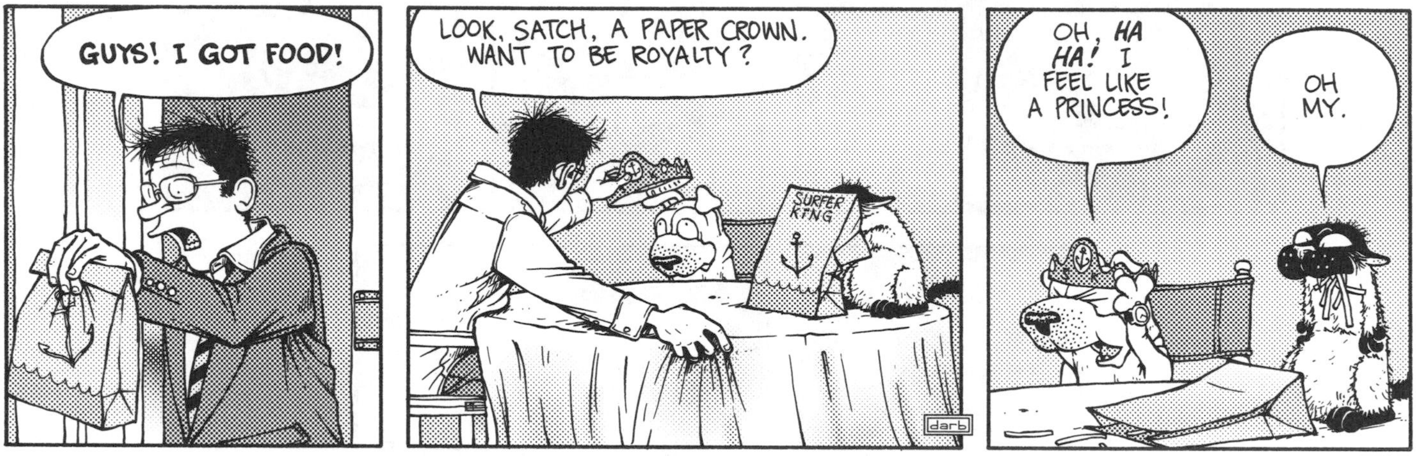
GUYS! I GOT FOOD!
LOOK, SATCH, A PAPER CROWN. WANT TO BE ROYALTY?
SURFER KING
OH, HA HA! I FEEL LIKE A PRINCESS!
OH MY.

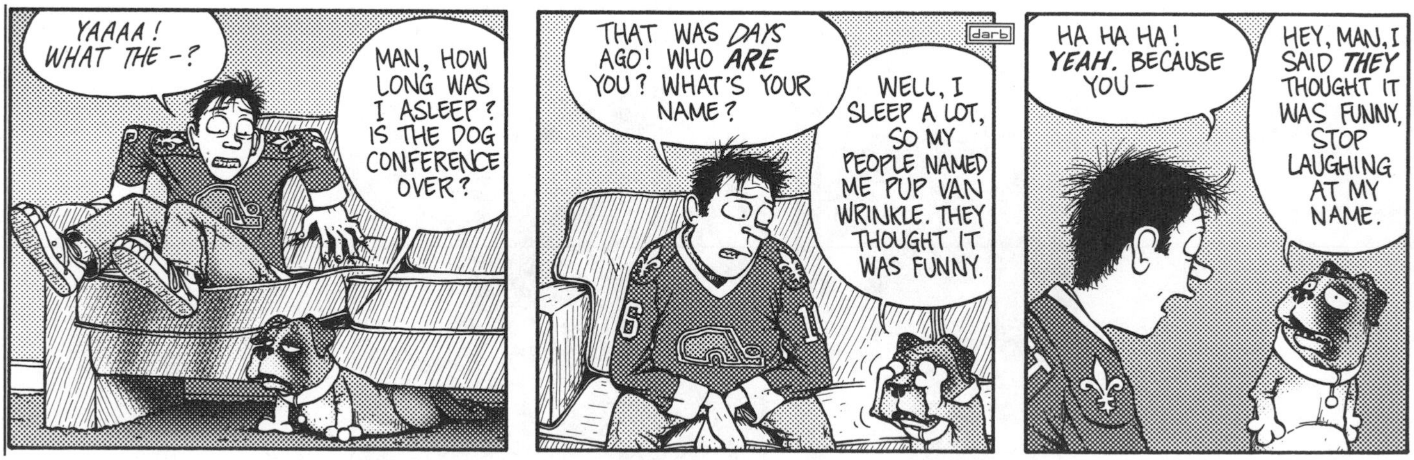
YAAAA! WHAT THE -?
MAN, HOW LONG WAS I ASLEEP? IS THE DOG CONFERENCE OVER?
THAT WAS DAYS AGO! WHO ARE YOU? WHAT'S YOUR NAME?
WELL, I SLEEP A LOT, SO MY PEOPLE NAMED ME PUP VAN WRINKLE. THEY THOUGHT IT WAS FUNNY.
HA HA HA! YEAH. BECAUSE YOU —
HEY, MAN, I SAID THEY THOUGHT IT WAS FUNNY, STOP LAUGHING AT MY NAME.

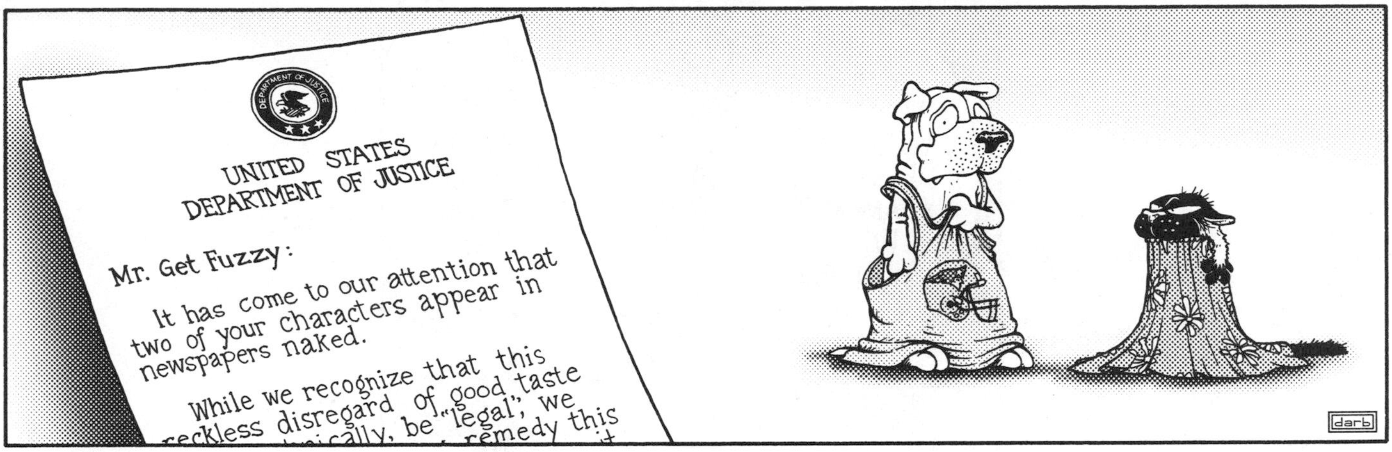
UNITED STATES
DEPARTMENT OF JUSTICE
Mr. Get Fuzzy:
It has come to our attention that two of your characters appear in newspapers naked.
While we recognize that this reckless disregard of good taste
darb

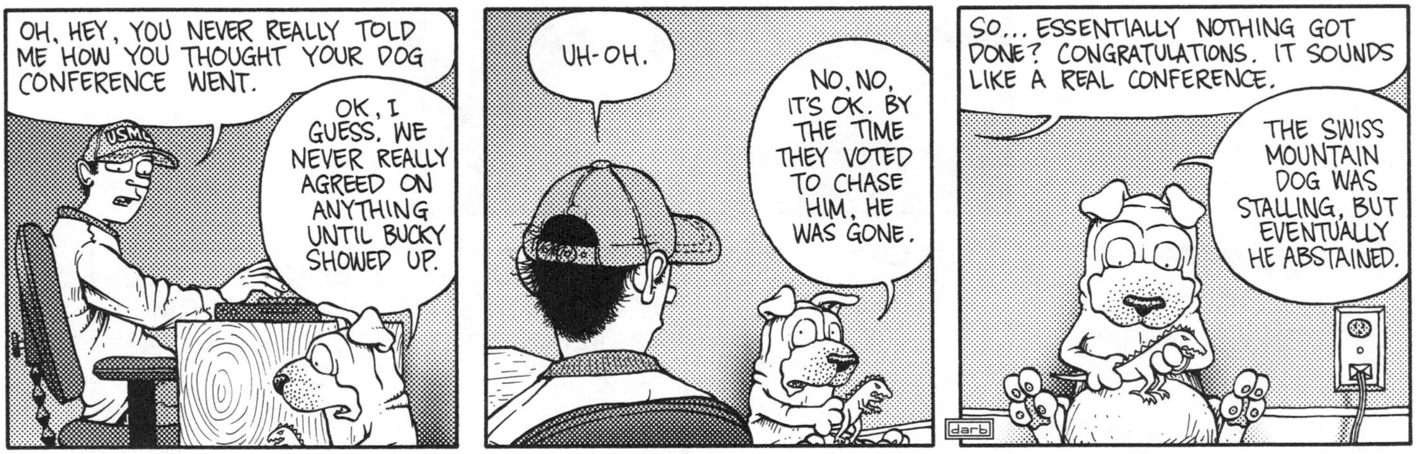
OH, HEY, YOU NEVER REALLY TOLD ME HOW YOU THOUGHT YOUR DOG CONFERENCE WENT.
OK, I GUESS. WE NEVER REALLY AGREED ON ANYTHING UNTIL BUCKY SHOWED UP.
USMC
UH-OH.
NO, NO, IT'S OK. BY THE TIME THEY VOTED TO CHASE HIM, HE WAS GONE.
SO... ESSENTIALLY NOTHING GOT DONE? CONGRATULATIONS. IT SOUNDS LIKE A REAL CONFERENCE.
THE SWISS MOUNTAIN DOG WAS STALLING, BUT EVENTUALLY HE ABSTAINED.
darb

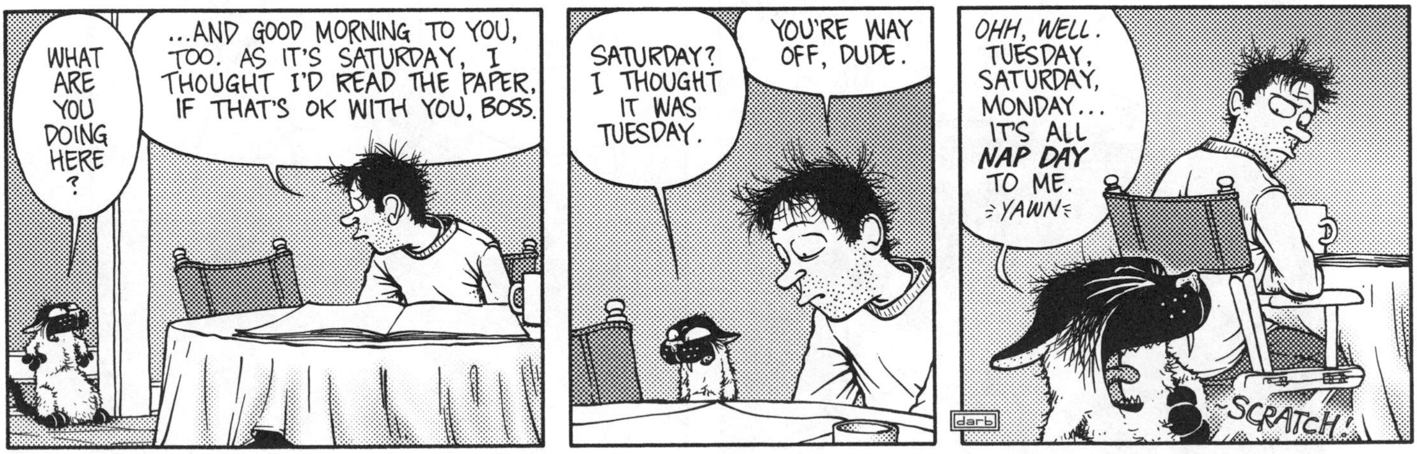
WHAT ARE YOU DOING HERE?
...AND GOOD MORNING TO YOU, TOO. AS IT'S SATURDAY, I THOUGHT I'D READ THE PAPER, IF THAT'S OK WITH YOU, BOSS.
SATURDAY? I THOUGHT IT WAS TUESDAY.
YOU'RE WAY OFF, DUDE.
OHH, WELL. TUESDAY, SATURDAY, MONDAY... IT'S ALL NAP DAY TO ME.
YAWN
SCRATCH!
darb

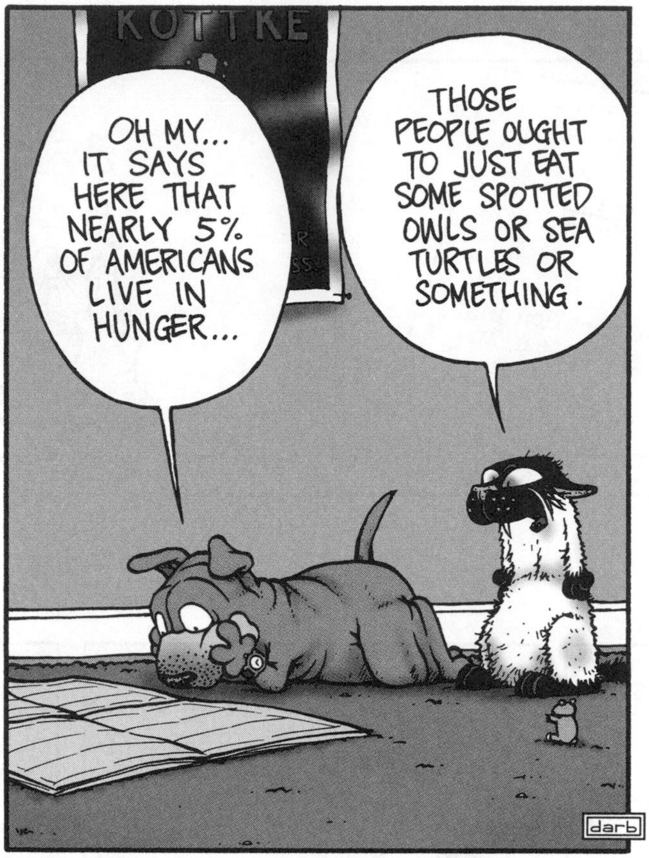
KOTTKE
OH MY... IT SAYS HERE THAT NEARLY 5% OF AMERICANS LIVE IN HUNGER...
THOSE PEOPLE OUGHT TO JUST EAT SOME SPOTTED OWLS OR SEA TURTLES OR SOMETHING.
darb

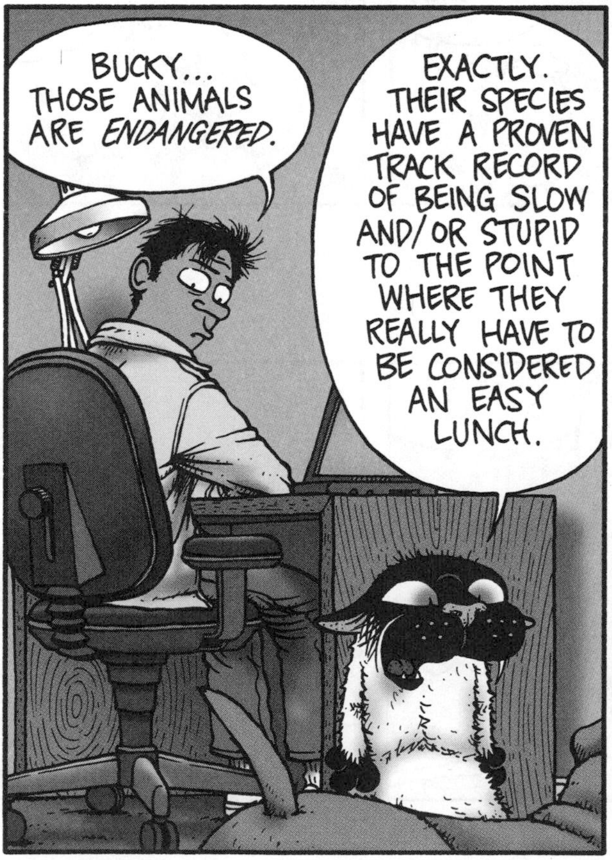
BUCKY... THOSE ANIMALS ARE *ENDANGERED*.
EXACTLY. THEIR SPECIES HAVE A PROVEN TRACK RECORD OF BEING SLOW AND/OR STUPID TO THE POINT WHERE THEY REALLY HAVE TO BE CONSIDERED AN EASY LUNCH.

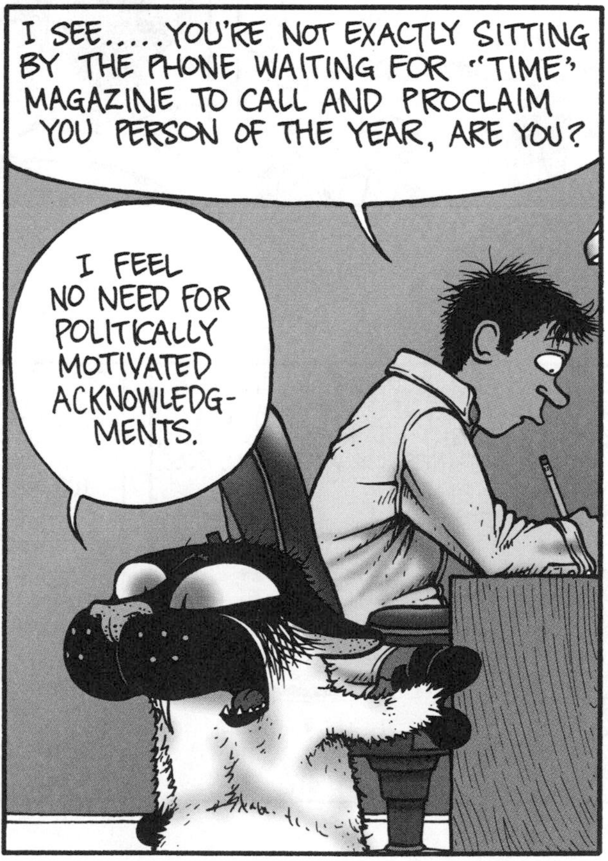
I SEE..... YOU'RE NOT EXACTLY SITTING BY THE PHONE WAITING FOR "TIME" MAGAZINE TO CALL AND PROCLAIM YOU PERSON OF THE YEAR, ARE YOU?
I FEEL NO NEED FOR POLITICALLY MOTIVATED ACKNOWLEDG- MENTS.

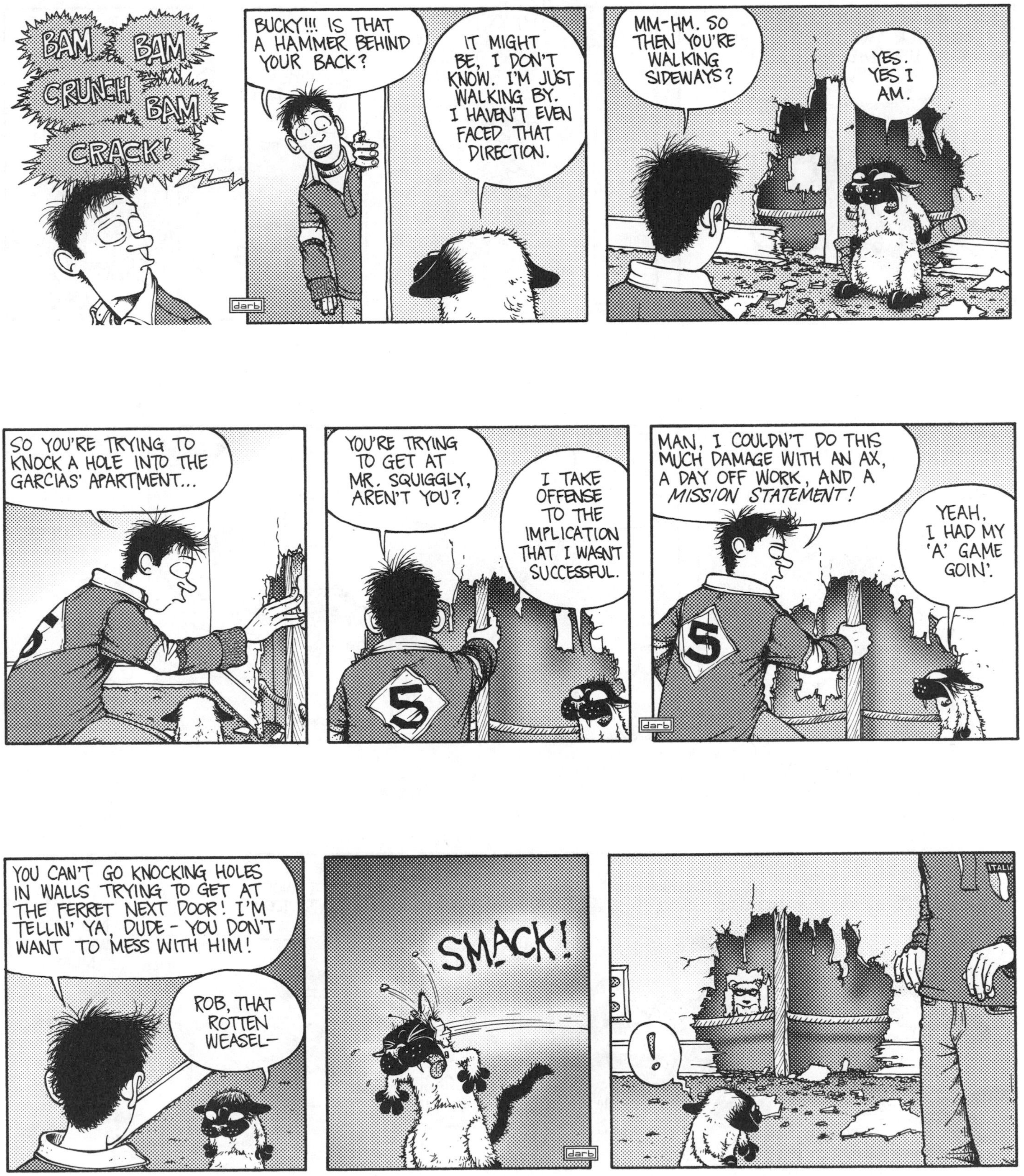
BAM BAM
CRUNCH BAM
CRACK!
BUCKY!!! IS THAT A HAMMER BEHIND YOUR BACK?
IT MIGHT BE, I DON'T KNOW. I'M JUST WALKING BY. I HAVEN'T EVEN FACED THAT DIRECTION.
MM-HM. SO THEN YOU'RE WALKING SIDEWAYS?
YES. YES I AM.
SO YOU'RE TRYING TO KNOCK A HOLE INTO THE GARCIAS' APARTMENT...
YOU'RE TRYING TO GET AT MR. SQUIGGLY, AREN'T YOU?
I TAKE OFFENSE TO THE IMPLICATION THAT I WASN'T SUCCESSFUL.
MAN, I COULDN'T DO THIS MUCH DAMAGE WITH AN AX, A DAY OFF WORK, AND A MISSION STATEMENT!
YEAH, I HAD MY 'A' GAME GOIN'.
YOU CAN'T GO KNOCKING HOLES IN WALLS TRYING TO GET AT THE FERRET NEXT DOOR! I'M TELLIN' YA, DUDE - YOU DON'T WANT TO MESS WITH HIM!
ROB, THAT ROTTEN WEASEL-
SMACK!
!

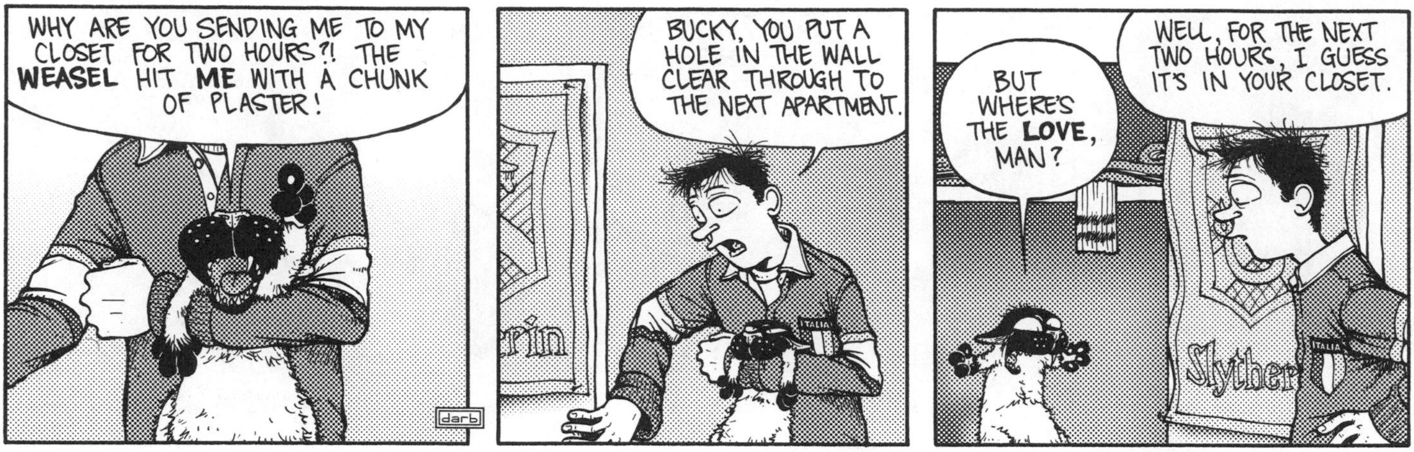
WHY ARE YOU SENDING ME TO MY CLOSET FOR TWO HOURS?! THE **WEASEL** HIT **ME** WITH A CHUNK OF PLASTER!
darb
BUCKY, YOU PUT A HOLE IN THE WALL CLEAR THROUGH TO THE NEXT APARTMENT.
BUT WHERE'S THE **LOVE**, MAN?
WELL, FOR THE NEXT TWO HOURS, I GUESS IT'S IN YOUR CLOSET.

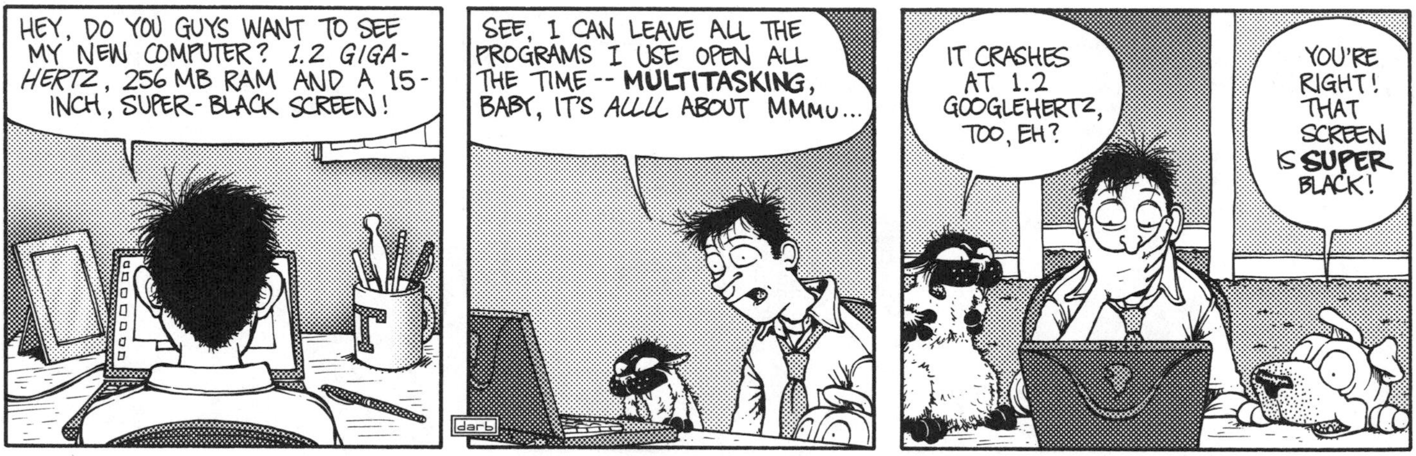
HEY, DO YOU GUYS WANT TO SEE MY NEW COMPUTER? *1.2 GIGA-HERTZ*, 256 MB RAM AND A 15-INCH, SUPER-BLACK SCREEN!
SEE, I CAN LEAVE ALL THE PROGRAMS I USE OPEN ALL THE TIME -- **MULTITASKING**, BABY, IT'S *ALLLL* ABOUT MMMU...
darb
IT CRASHES AT 1.2 GOOGLEHERTZ, TOO, EH?
YOU'RE RIGHT! THAT SCREEN IS **SUPER** BLACK!

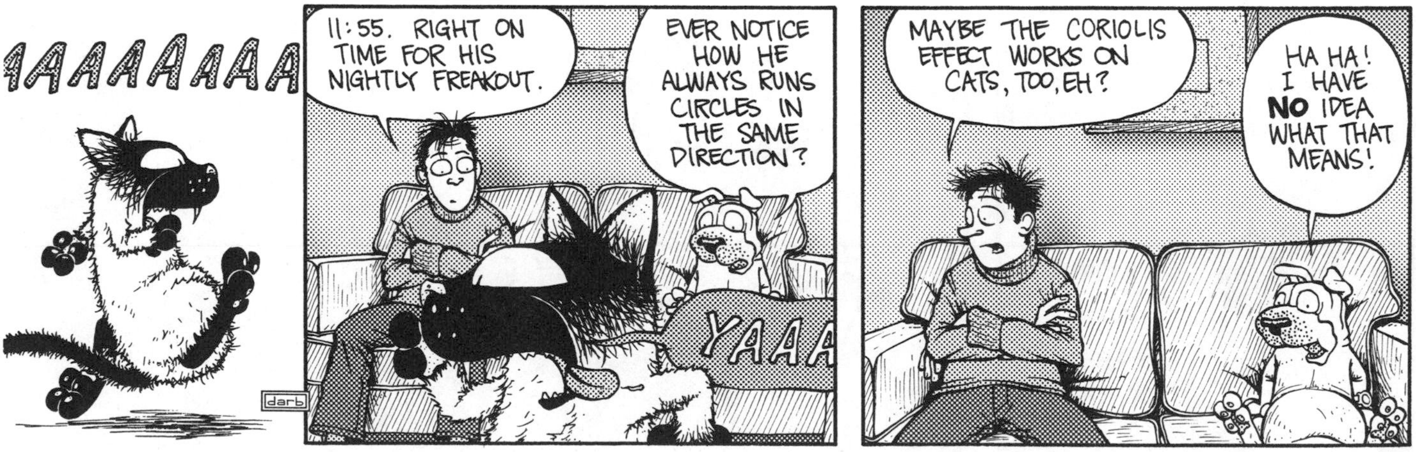
AAAAAAAAA
darb
11:55. RIGHT ON TIME FOR HIS NIGHTLY FREAKOUT.
EVER NOTICE HOW HE ALWAYS RUNS CIRCLES IN THE SAME DIRECTION?
YAAA
MAYBE THE CORIOLIS EFFECT WORKS ON CATS, TOO, EH?
HA HA! I HAVE **NO** IDEA WHAT THAT MEANS!

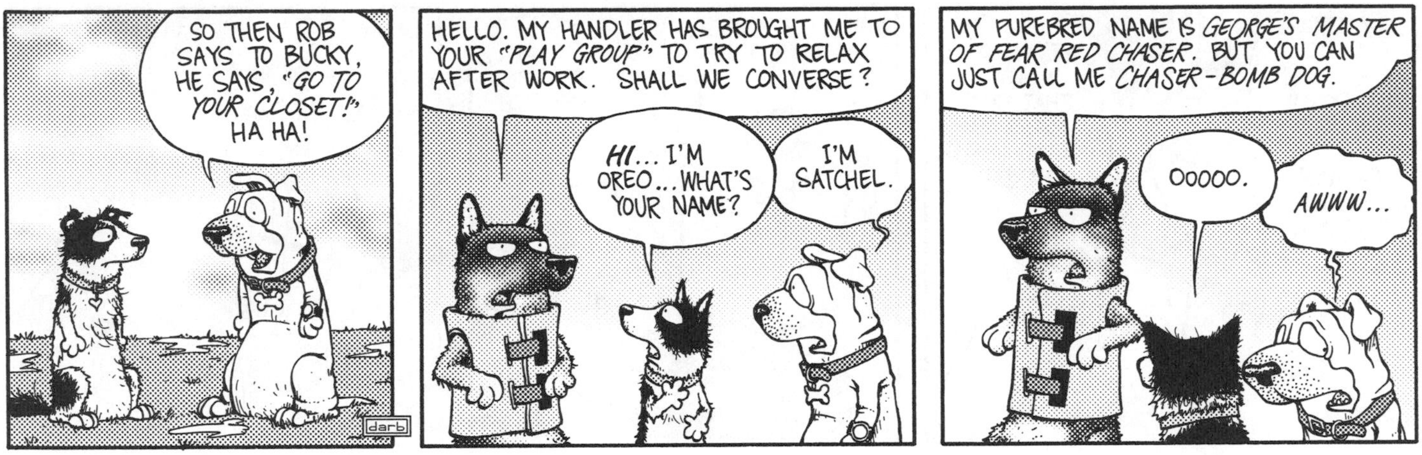
SO THEN ROB SAYS TO BUCKY, HE SAYS, "GO TO YOUR CLOSET!" HA HA!
darb
HELLO. MY HANDLER HAS BROUGHT ME TO YOUR "PLAY GROUP" TO TRY TO RELAX AFTER WORK. SHALL WE CONVERSE?
HI... I'M OREO... WHAT'S YOUR NAME?
I'M SATCHEL.
MY PUREBRED NAME IS GEORGE'S MASTER OF FEAR RED CHASER. BUT YOU CAN JUST CALL ME CHASER-BOMB DOG.
OOOOO.
AWWW...

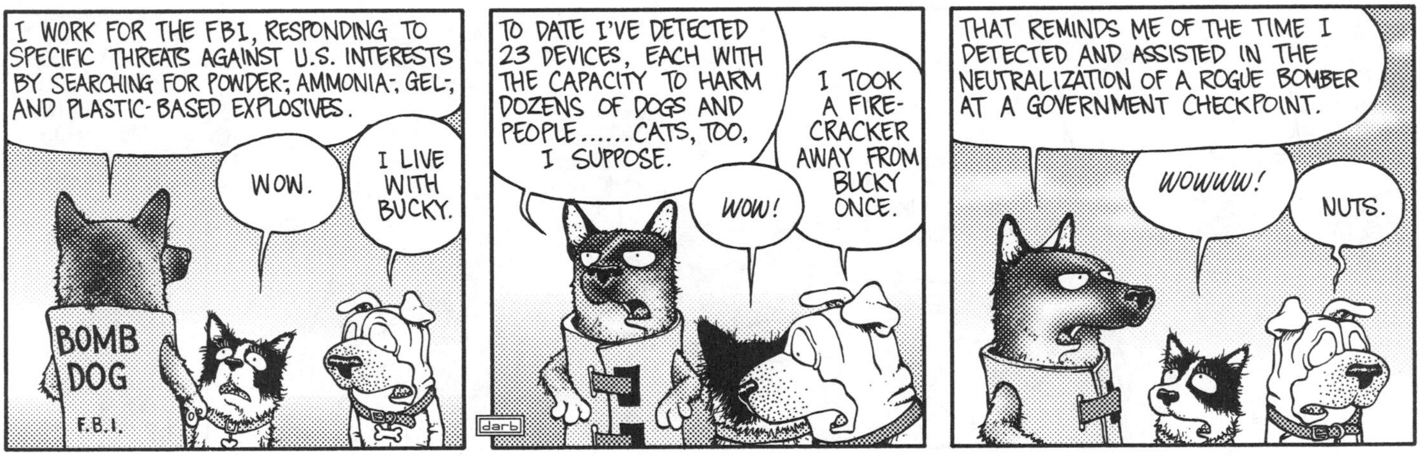
I WORK FOR THE FBI, RESPONDING TO SPECIFIC THREATS AGAINST U.S. INTERESTS BY SEARCHING FOR POWDER-, AMMONIA-, GEL-, AND PLASTIC-BASED EXPLOSIVES.
WOW.
I LIVE WITH BUCKY.
BOMB DOG
F.B.I.
darb
TO DATE I'VE DETECTED 23 DEVICES, EACH WITH THE CAPACITY TO HARM DOZENS OF DOGS AND PEOPLE......CATS, TOO, I SUPPOSE.
WOW!
I TOOK A FIRE-CRACKER AWAY FROM BUCKY ONCE.
THAT REMINDS ME OF THE TIME I DETECTED AND ASSISTED IN THE NEUTRALIZATION OF A ROGUE BOMBER AT A GOVERNMENT CHECKPOINT.
WOWWW!
NUTS.

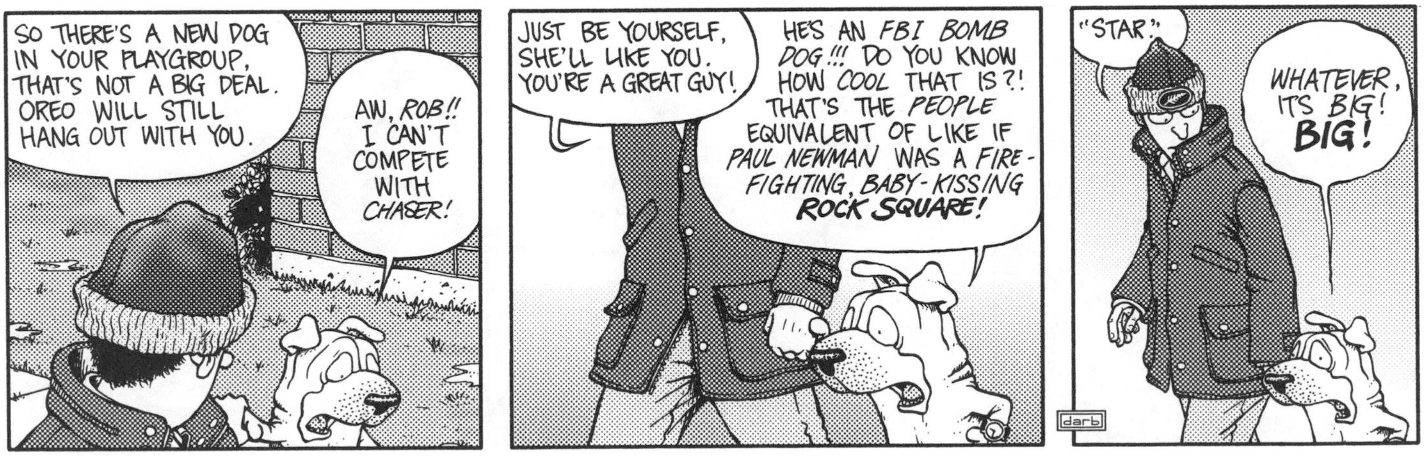
SO THERE'S A NEW DOG IN YOUR PLAYGROUP, THAT'S NOT A BIG DEAL. OREO WILL STILL HANG OUT WITH YOU.
AW, ROB!! I CAN'T COMPETE WITH CHASER!
JUST BE YOURSELF, SHE'LL LIKE YOU. YOU'RE A GREAT GUY!
HE'S AN FBI BOMB DOG!!! DO YOU KNOW HOW COOL THAT IS?! THAT'S THE PEOPLE EQUIVALENT OF LIKE IF PAUL NEWMAN WAS A FIRE-FIGHTING, BABY-KISSING ROCK SQUARE!
darb
"STAR."
WHATEVER, ITS BIG! BIG!

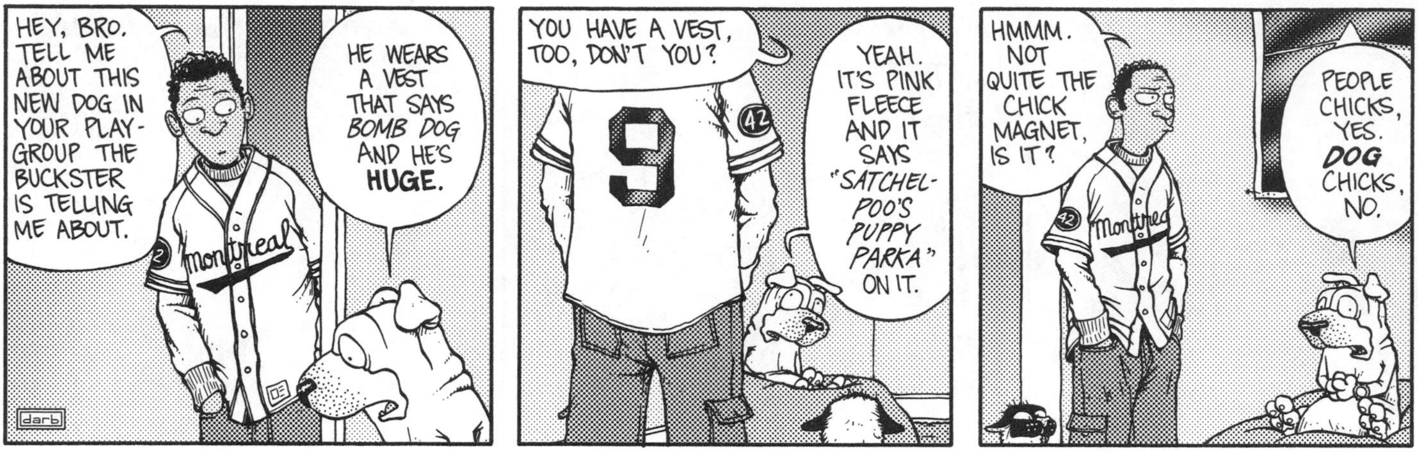
HEY, BRO. TELL ME ABOUT THIS NEW DOG IN YOUR PLAY-GROUP THE BUCKSTER IS TELLING ME ABOUT.
HE WEARS A VEST THAT SAYS *BOMB DOG* AND HE'S **HUGE**.
YOU HAVE A VEST, TOO, DON'T YOU?
YEAH. IT'S PINK FLEECE AND IT SAYS "*SATCHEL-POO'S PUPPY PARKA*" ON IT.
HMMM. NOT QUITE THE CHICK MAGNET, IS IT?
PEOPLE CHICKS, YES. ***DOG*** CHICKS, NO.

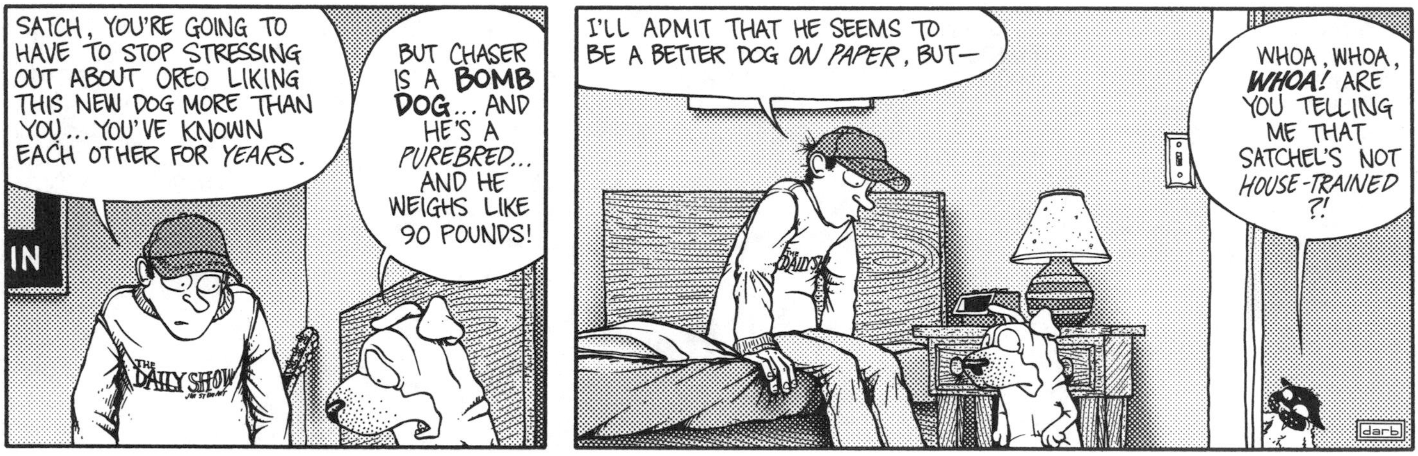
SATCH, YOU'RE GOING TO HAVE TO STOP STRESSING OUT ABOUT OREO LIKING THIS NEW DOG MORE THAN YOU... YOU'VE KNOWN EACH OTHER FOR *YEARS*.
BUT CHASER IS A **BOMB DOG**... AND HE'S A *PUREBRED*... AND HE WEIGHS LIKE 90 POUNDS!
I'LL ADMIT THAT HE SEEMS TO BE A BETTER DOG *ON PAPER*, BUT—
WHOA, WHOA, ***WHOA!*** ARE YOU TELLING ME THAT SATCHEL'S NOT *HOUSE-TRAINED* ?!

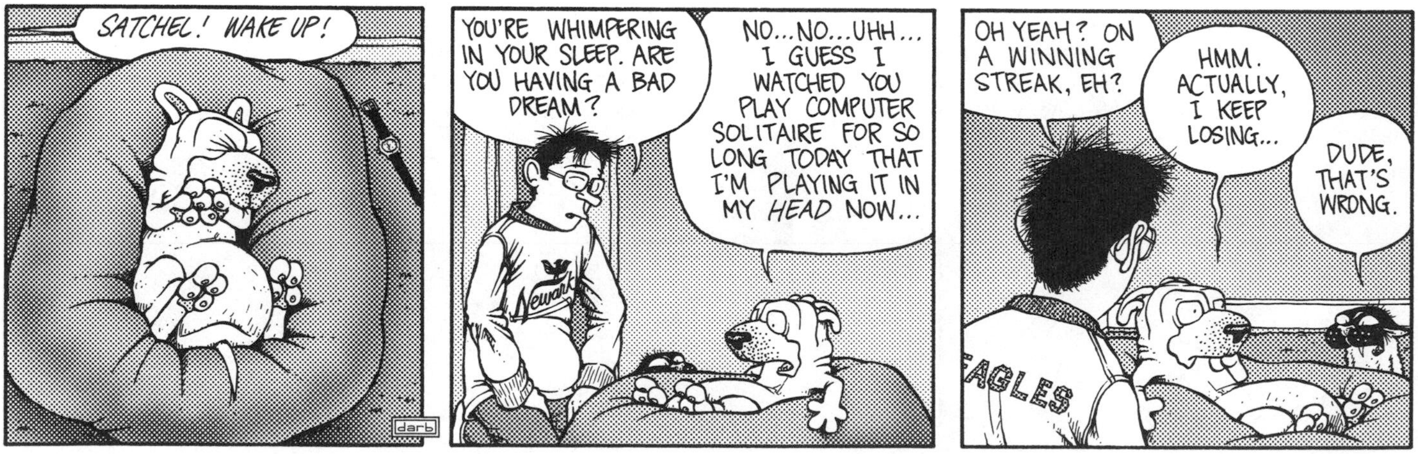
SATCHEL! WAKE UP!
YOU'RE WHIMPERING IN YOUR SLEEP. ARE YOU HAVING A BAD DREAM?
NO...NO...UHH... I GUESS I WATCHED YOU PLAY COMPUTER SOLITAIRE FOR SO LONG TODAY THAT I'M PLAYING IT IN MY *HEAD* NOW...
OH YEAH? ON A WINNING STREAK, EH?
HMM. ACTUALLY, I KEEP LOSING...
DUDE, THAT'S WRONG.

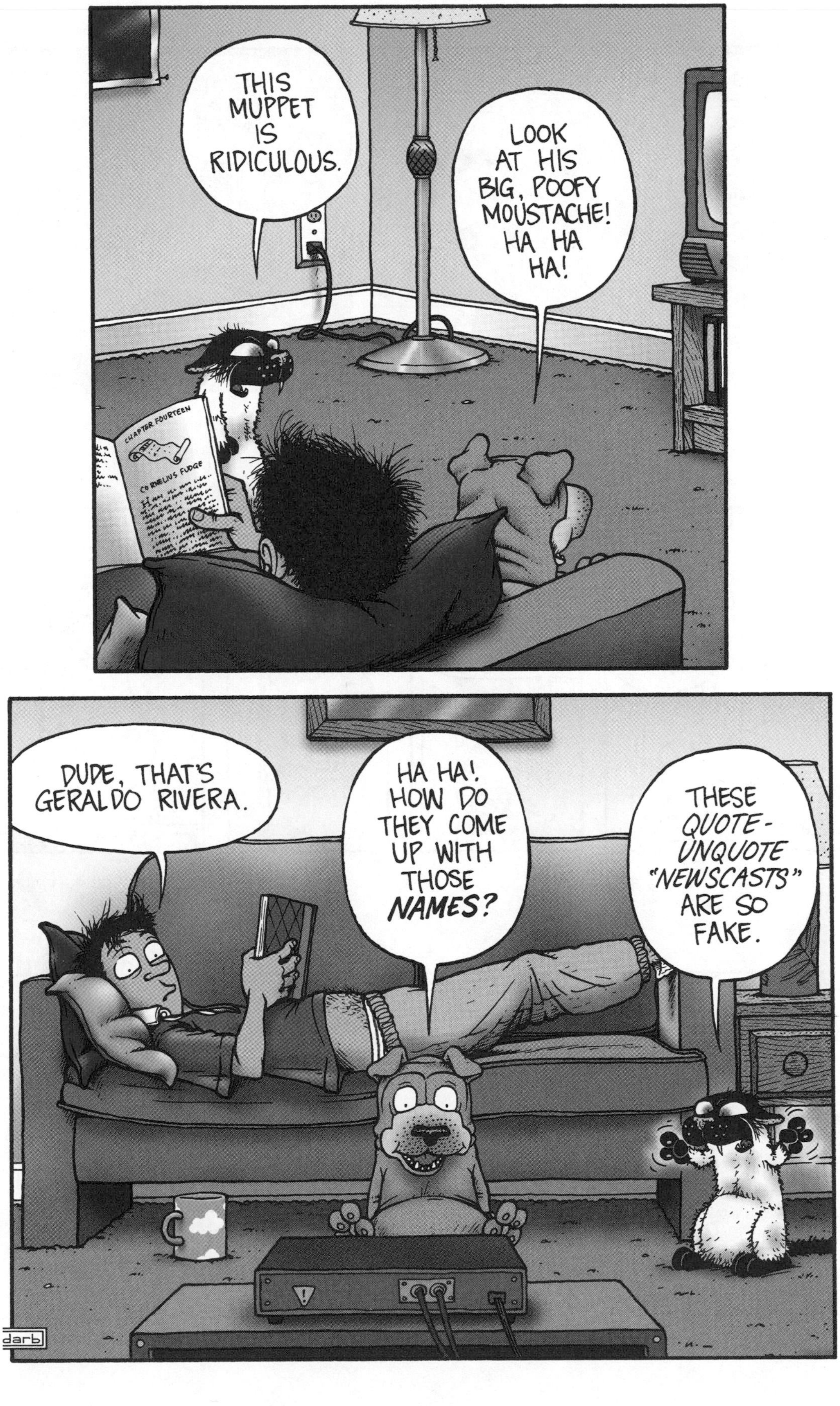
THIS MUPPET IS RIDICULOUS.
LOOK AT HIS BIG, POOFY MOUSTACHE! HA HA HA!
CHAPTER FOURTEEN
CORNELIUS FUDGE
DUDE, THAT'S GERALDO RIVERA.
HA HA! HOW DO THEY COME UP WITH THOSE *NAMES?*
THESE *QUOTE-UNQUOTE "NEWSCASTS"* ARE SO FAKE.
darb

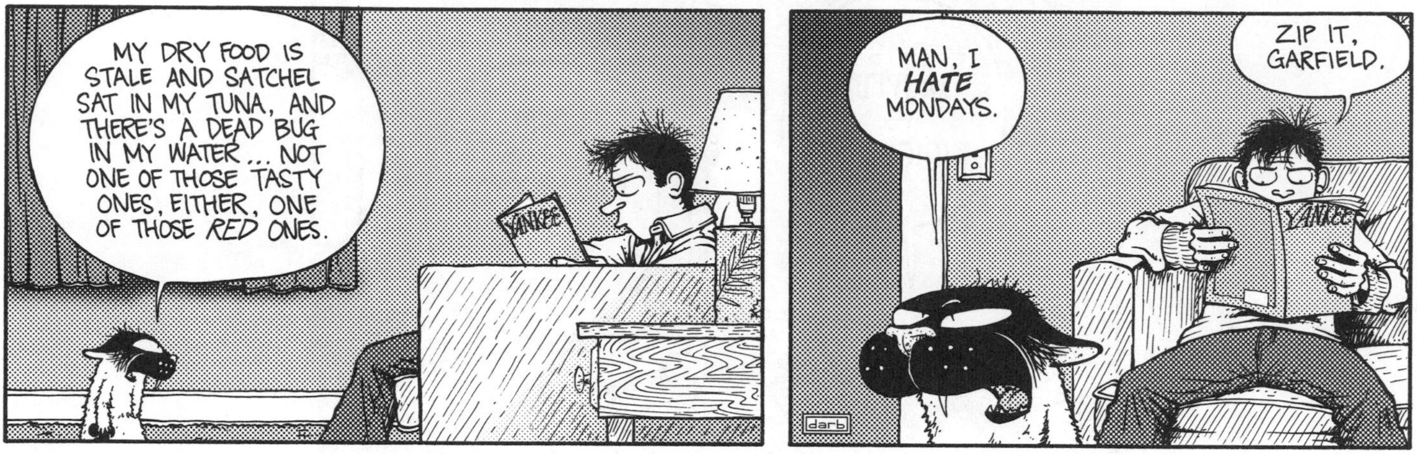
MY DRY FOOD IS STALE AND SATCHEL SAT IN MY TUNA, AND THERE'S A DEAD BUG IN MY WATER... NOT ONE OF THOSE TASTY ONES, EITHER. ONE OF THOSE *RED* ONES.
YANKEE
MAN, I **HATE** MONDAYS.
ZIP IT, GARFIELD.
YANKEE
darb

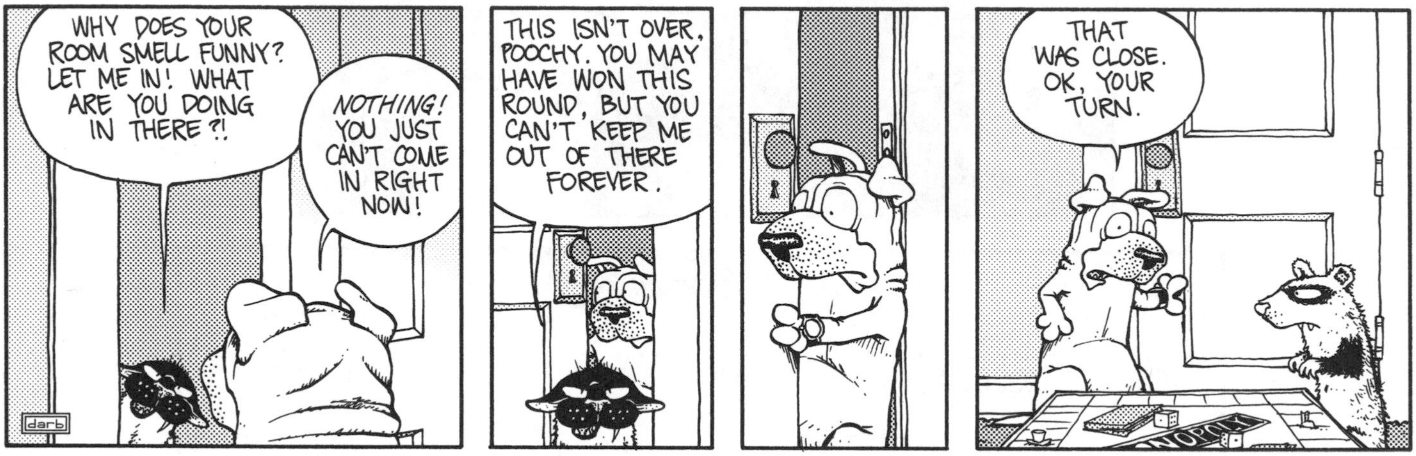
WHY DOES YOUR ROOM SMELL FUNNY? LET ME IN! WHAT ARE YOU DOING IN THERE?!
NOTHING! YOU JUST CAN'T COME IN RIGHT NOW!
darb
THIS ISN'T OVER, POOCHY. YOU MAY HAVE WON THIS ROUND, BUT YOU CAN'T KEEP ME OUT OF THERE FOREVER.
THAT WAS CLOSE. OK, YOUR TURN.
NOPOLY

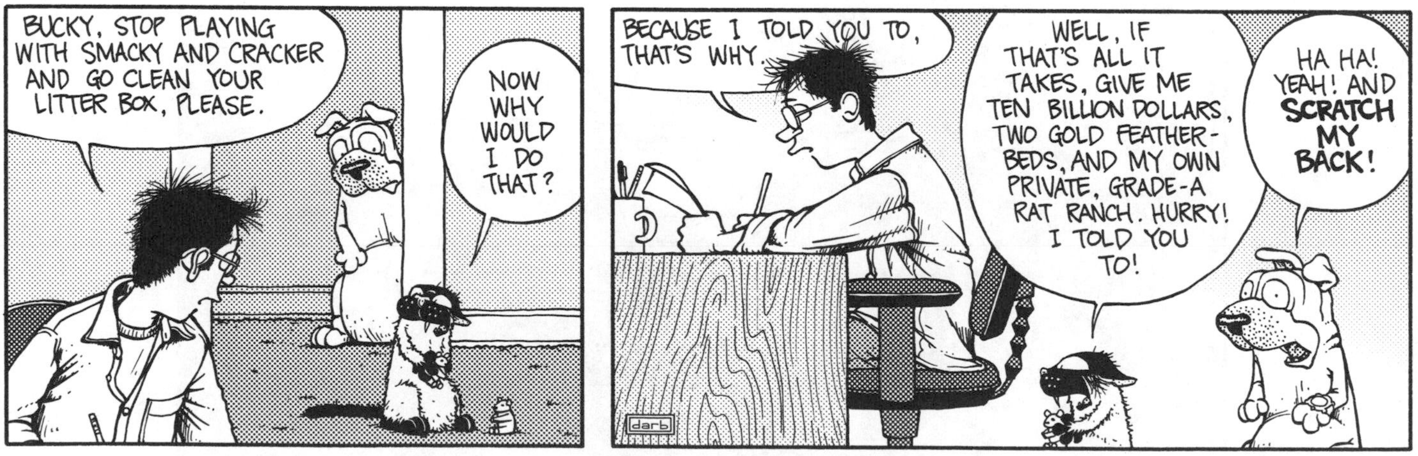
BUCKY, STOP PLAYING WITH SMACKY AND CRACKER AND GO CLEAN YOUR LITTER BOX, PLEASE.
NOW WHY WOULD I DO THAT?
BECAUSE I TOLD YOU TO, THAT'S WHY.
WELL, IF THAT'S ALL IT TAKES, GIVE ME TEN BILLION DOLLARS, TWO GOLD FEATHER-BEDS, AND MY OWN PRIVATE, GRADE-A RAT RANCH. HURRY! I TOLD YOU TO!
HA HA! YEAH! AND **SCRATCH MY BACK!**
darb

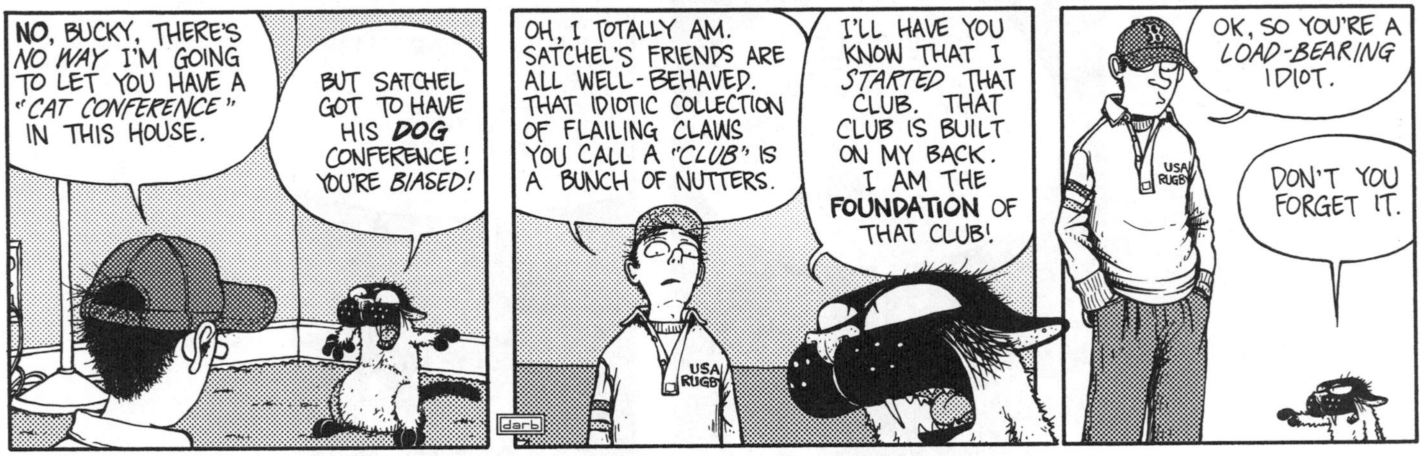
NO, BUCKY, THERE'S *NO WAY* I'M GOING TO LET YOU HAVE A "*CAT CONFERENCE*" IN THIS HOUSE.
BUT SATCHEL GOT TO HAVE HIS **DOG** CONFERENCE! YOU'RE *BIASED*!
OH, I TOTALLY AM. SATCHEL'S FRIENDS ARE ALL WELL-BEHAVED. THAT IDIOTIC COLLECTION OF FLAILING CLAWS YOU CALL A "*CLUB*" IS A BUNCH OF NUTTERS.
I'LL HAVE YOU KNOW THAT I *STARTED* THAT CLUB. THAT CLUB IS BUILT ON MY BACK. I AM THE **FOUNDATION** OF THAT CLUB!
OK, SO YOU'RE A *LOAD-BEARING* IDIOT.
DON'T YOU FORGET IT.

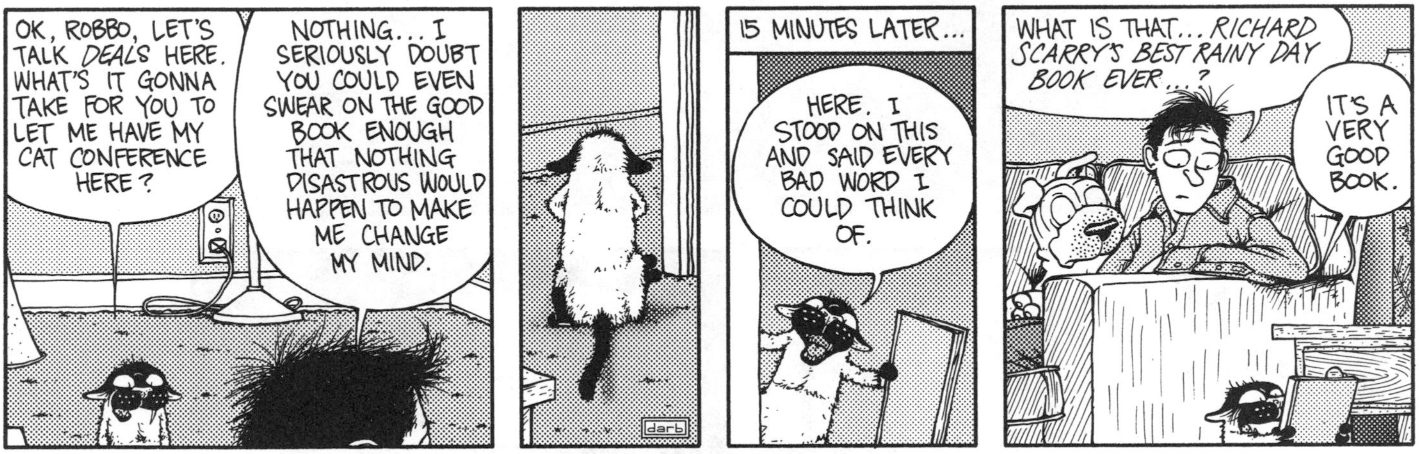
OK, ROBBO, LET'S TALK *DEALS* HERE. WHAT'S IT GONNA TAKE FOR YOU TO LET ME HAVE MY CAT CONFERENCE HERE?
NOTHING... I SERIOUSLY DOUBT YOU COULD EVEN SWEAR ON THE GOOD BOOK ENOUGH THAT NOTHING DISASTROUS WOULD HAPPEN TO MAKE ME CHANGE MY MIND.
15 MINUTES LATER...
HERE. I STOOD ON THIS AND SAID EVERY BAD WORD I COULD THINK OF.
WHAT IS THAT... *RICHARD SCARRY'S BEST RAINY DAY BOOK EVER*...?
IT'S A VERY GOOD BOOK.

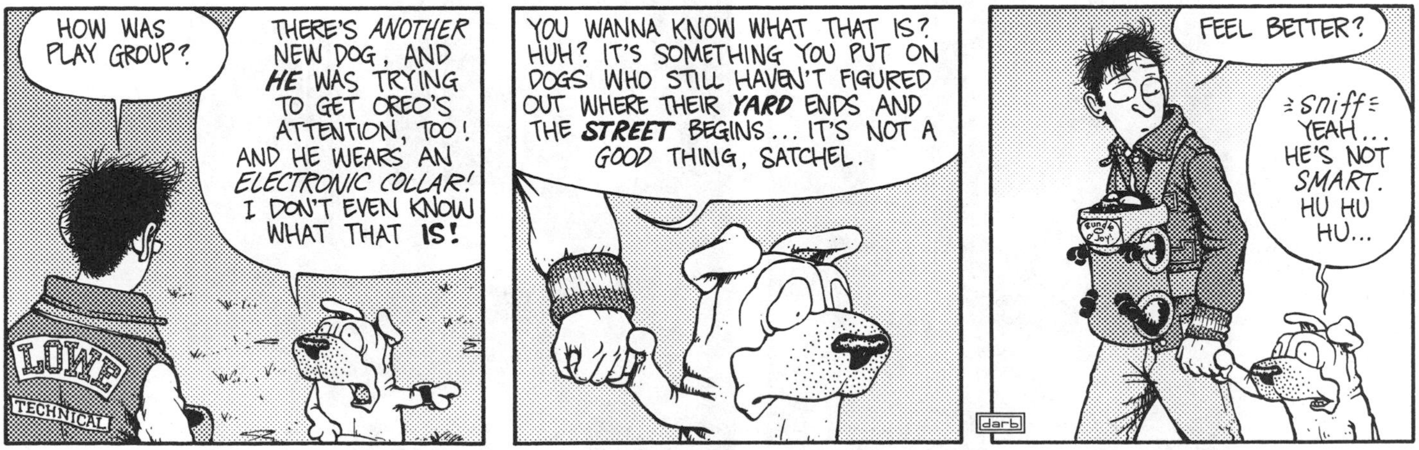
HOW WAS PLAY GROUP?
THERE'S *ANOTHER* NEW DOG, AND ***HE*** WAS TRYING TO GET OREO'S ATTENTION, TOO! AND HE WEARS AN *ELECTRONIC COLLAR*! I DON'T EVEN KNOW WHAT THAT **IS**!
LOWE
TECHNICAL
YOU WANNA KNOW WHAT THAT IS? HUH? IT'S SOMETHING YOU PUT ON DOGS WHO STILL HAVEN'T FIGURED OUT WHERE THEIR ***YARD*** ENDS AND THE ***STREET*** BEGINS... IT'S NOT A *GOOD* THING, SATCHEL.
FEEL BETTER?
sniff YEAH... HE'S NOT *SMART*. HU HU HU...

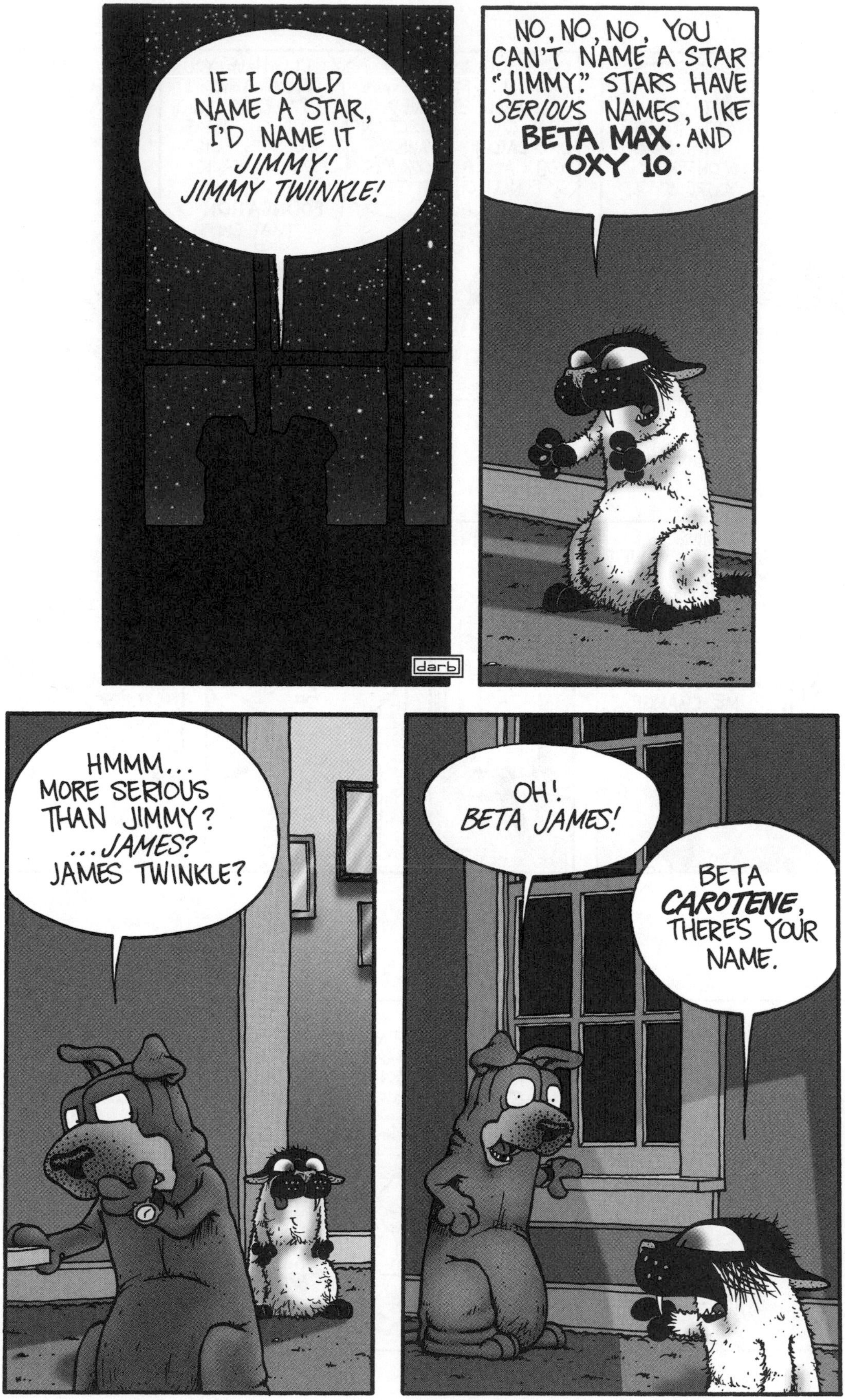
IF I COULD NAME A STAR, I'D NAME IT *JIMMY!* *JIMMY TWINKLE!*
darb
NO, NO, NO, YOU CAN'T NAME A STAR "JIMMY." STARS HAVE *SERIOUS* NAMES, LIKE **BETA MAX**. AND **OXY 10**.
HMMM... MORE SERIOUS THAN JIMMY? ...*JAMES?* JAMES TWINKLE?
OH! *BETA JAMES!*
BETA ***CAROTENE***, THERE'S YOUR NAME.

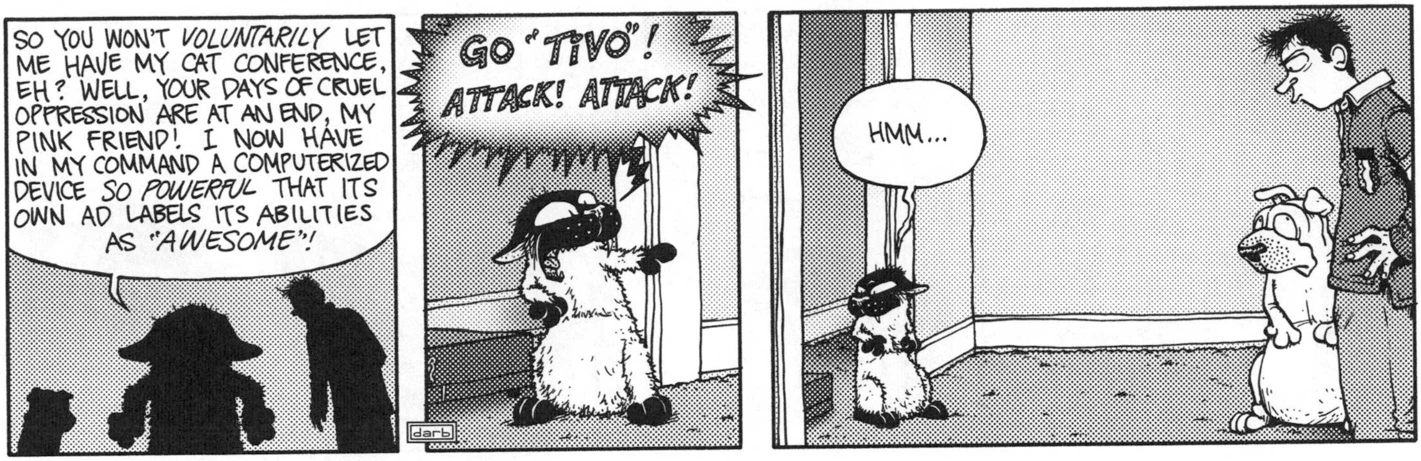
SO YOU WON'T *VOLUNTARILY* LET ME HAVE MY CAT CONFERENCE, EH? WELL, YOUR DAYS OF CRUEL OPPRESSION ARE AT AN END, MY PINK FRIEND! I NOW HAVE IN MY COMMAND A COMPUTERIZED DEVICE *SO POWERFUL* THAT ITS OWN AD LABELS ITS ABILITIES AS "*AWESOME*"!
GO "TIVO"! ATTACK! ATTACK!
darb
HMM...

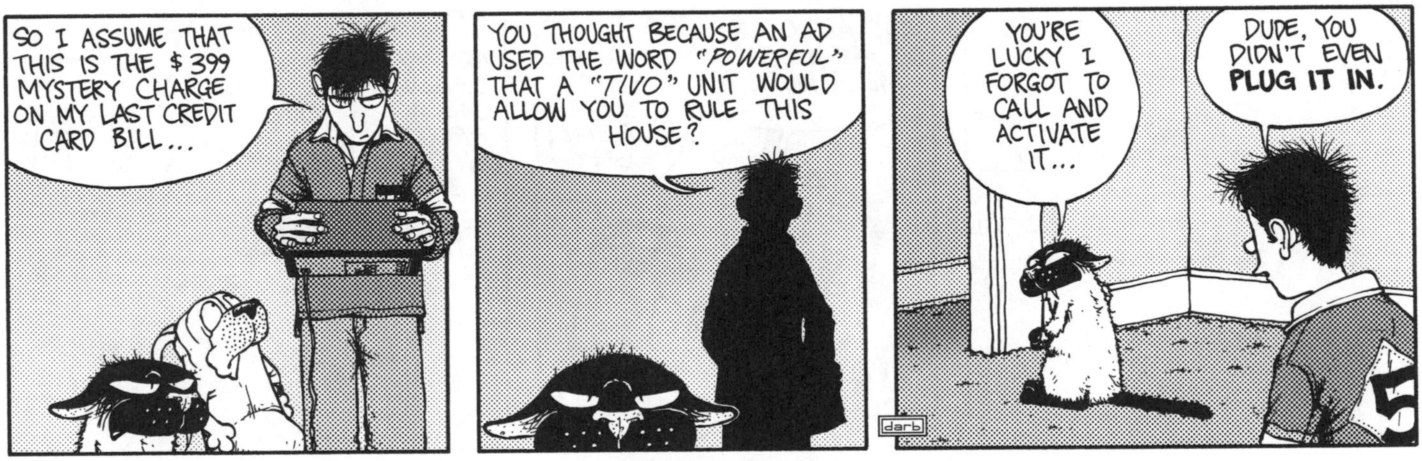
SO I ASSUME THAT THIS IS THE $399 MYSTERY CHARGE ON MY LAST CREDIT CARD BILL...
YOU THOUGHT BECAUSE AN AD USED THE WORD "*POWERFUL*" THAT A "*TIVO*" UNIT WOULD ALLOW YOU TO RULE THIS HOUSE?
darb
YOU'RE LUCKY I FORGOT TO CALL AND ACTIVATE IT...
DUDE, YOU DIDN'T EVEN **PLUG IT IN**.

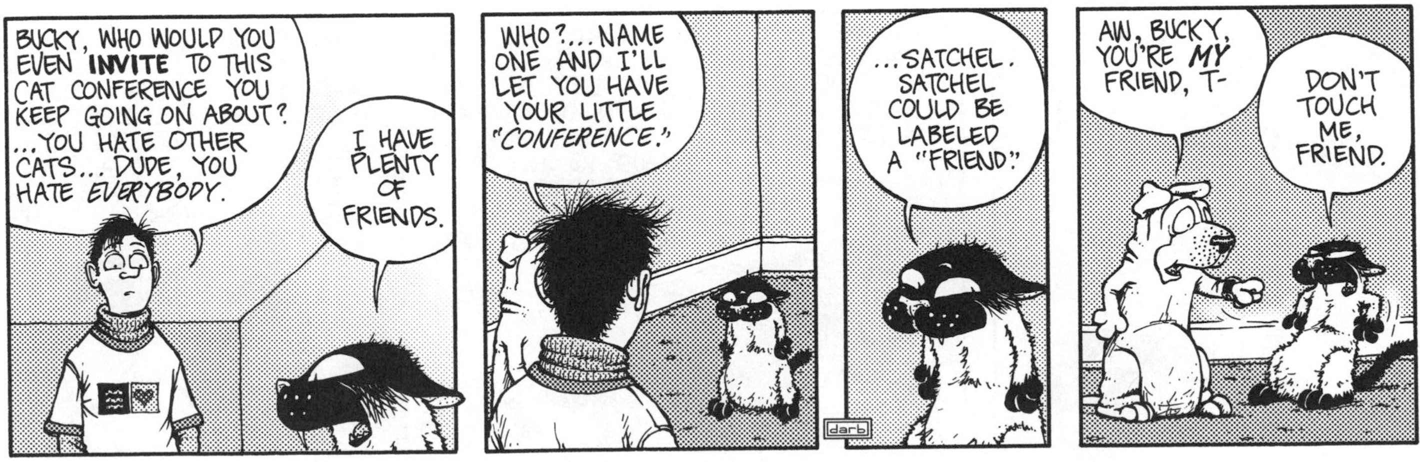
BUCKY, WHO WOULD YOU EVEN **INVITE** TO THIS CAT CONFERENCE YOU KEEP GOING ON ABOUT? ...YOU HATE OTHER CATS... DUDE, YOU HATE *EVERYBODY*.
I HAVE PLENTY OF FRIENDS.
WHO?... NAME ONE AND I'LL LET YOU HAVE YOUR LITTLE "*CONFERENCE*."
...SATCHEL. SATCHEL COULD BE LABELED A "FRIEND."
darb
AW, BUCKY, YOU'RE *MY* FRIEND, T-
DON'T TOUCH ME, FRIEND.

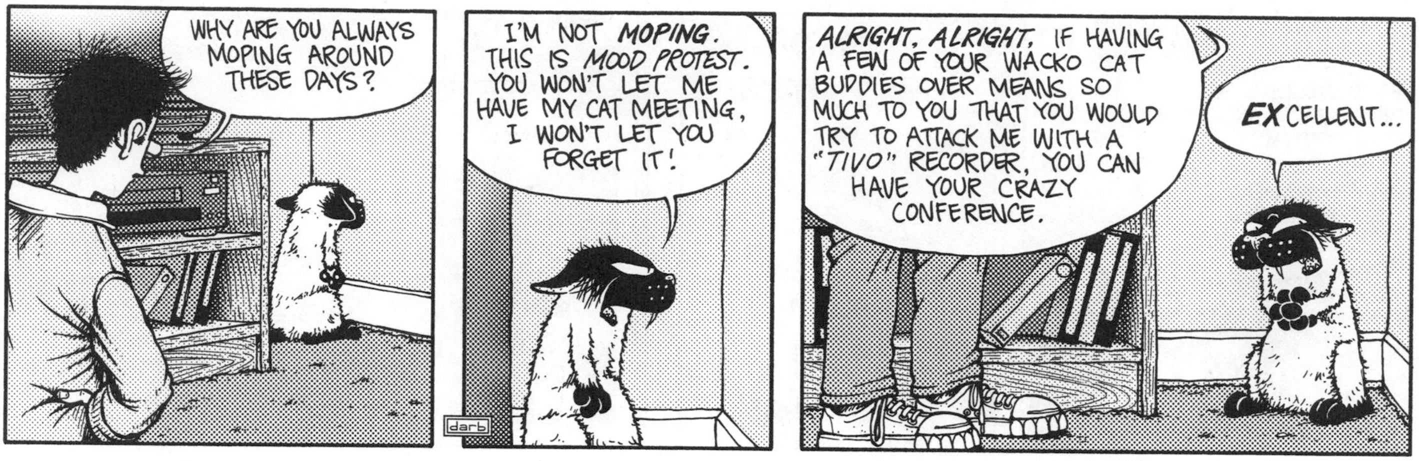
WHY ARE YOU ALWAYS MOPING AROUND THESE DAYS?
I'M NOT MOPING. THIS IS MOOD PROTEST. YOU WON'T LET ME HAVE MY CAT MEETING, I WON'T LET YOU FORGET IT!
darb
ALRIGHT, ALRIGHT. IF HAVING A FEW OF YOUR WACKO CAT BUDDIES OVER MEANS SO MUCH TO YOU THAT YOU WOULD TRY TO ATTACK ME WITH A "TIVO" RECORDER, YOU CAN HAVE YOUR CRAZY CONFERENCE.
EXCELLENT...

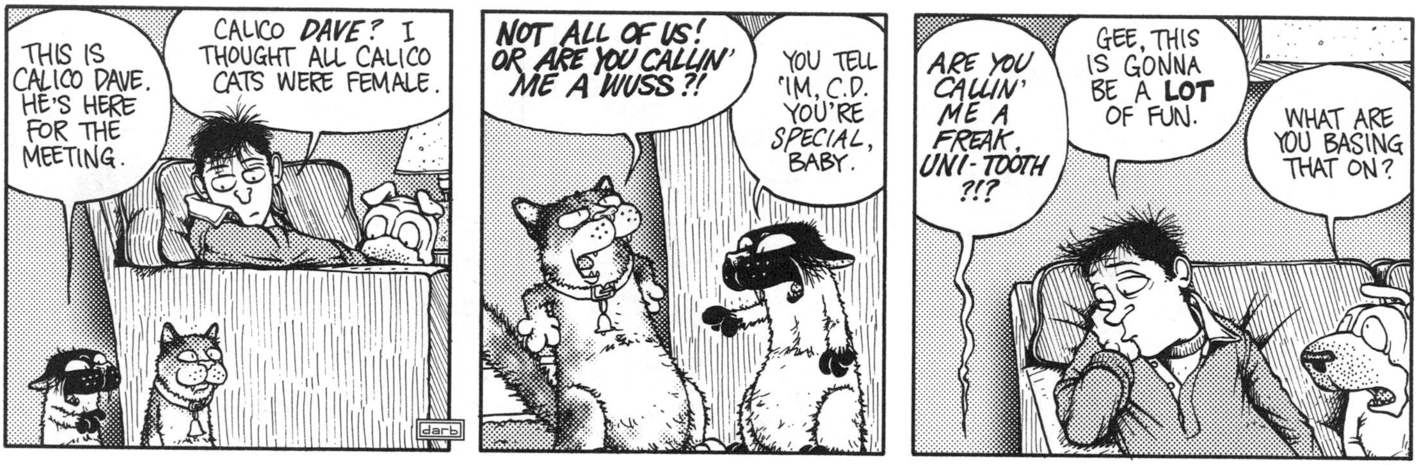
THIS IS CALICO DAVE. HE'S HERE FOR THE MEETING.
CALICO DAVE? I THOUGHT ALL CALICO CATS WERE FEMALE.
darb
NOT ALL OF US! OR ARE YOU CALLIN' ME A WUSS?!
YOU TELL 'IM, C.D. YOU'RE SPECIAL, BABY.
ARE YOU CALLIN' ME A FREAK, UNI-TOOTH ?!?
GEE, THIS IS GONNA BE A LOT OF FUN.
WHAT ARE YOU BASING THAT ON?

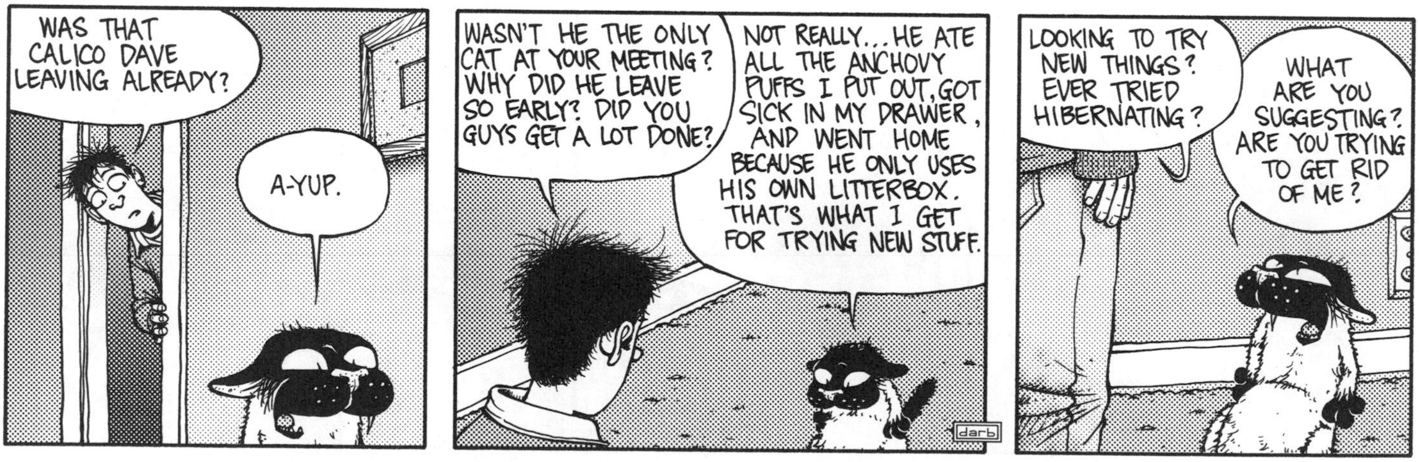
WAS THAT CALICO DAVE LEAVING ALREADY?
A-YUP.
WASN'T HE THE ONLY CAT AT YOUR MEETING? WHY DID HE LEAVE SO EARLY? DID YOU GUYS GET A LOT DONE?
NOT REALLY... HE ATE ALL THE ANCHOVY PUFFS I PUT OUT, GOT SICK IN MY DRAWER, AND WENT HOME BECAUSE HE ONLY USES HIS OWN LITTERBOX. THAT'S WHAT I GET FOR TRYING NEW STUFF.
darb
LOOKING TO TRY NEW THINGS? EVER TRIED HIBERNATING?
WHAT ARE YOU SUGGESTING? ARE YOU TRYING TO GET RID OF ME?

WHY HAVEN'T YOU OPENED THIS YET?
...OPENED?
YEAH, THE COVER IS JUST A PICTURE; THE ACTUAL "LITE BRITE" IS INSIDE.
YOU MEAN THERE'S MORE TO THIS BOX THAN A FANTASTIC PICTURE OF A GLOWING CLOWN? OH MY HEAD!
AHHHH, THAT'S WHAT I LOVE ABOUT YOU, SATCH.
YOU LOVE THE FACT THAT HE'S DIMMER THAN A ONE-STAR RESTAURANT, EH?
I.... I'M SO **HAPPY**...

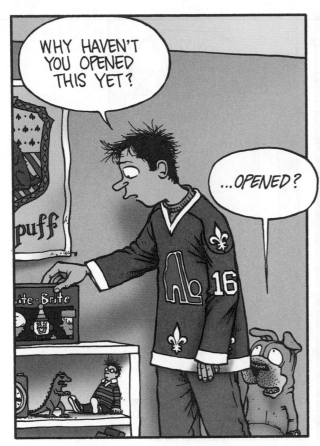

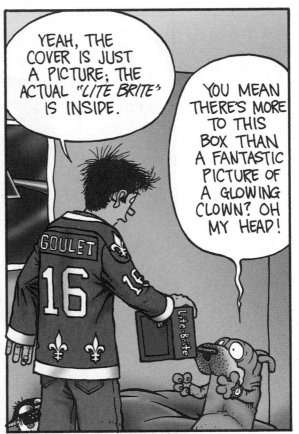

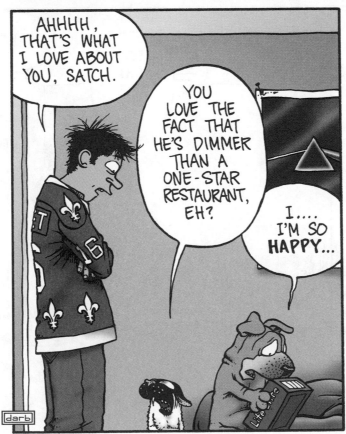

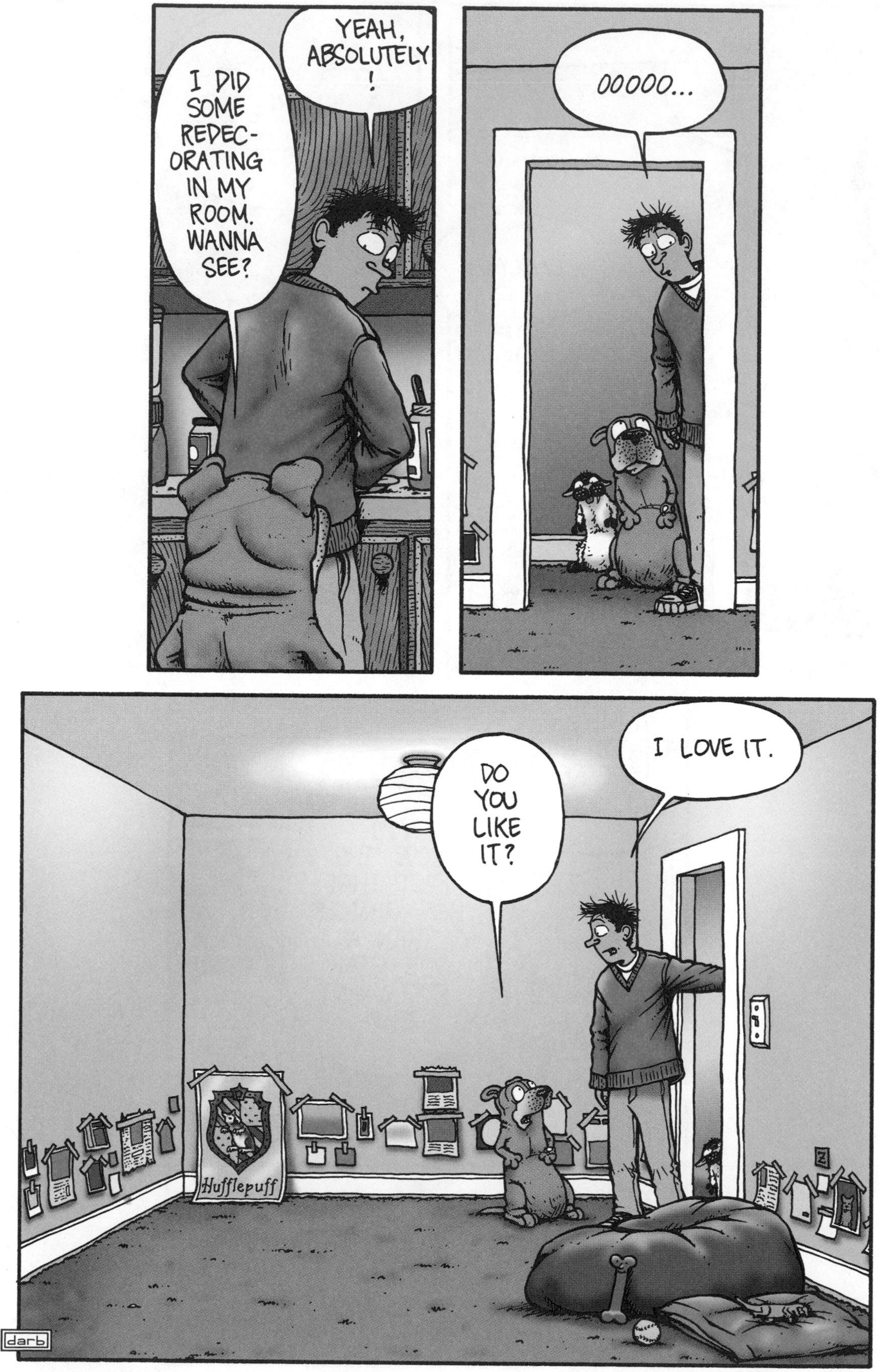

I DID SOME REDEC-ORATING IN MY ROOM. WANNA SEE?
YEAH, ABSOLUTELY!
OOOOO...
DO YOU LIKE IT?
I LOVE IT.
Hufflepuff
darb

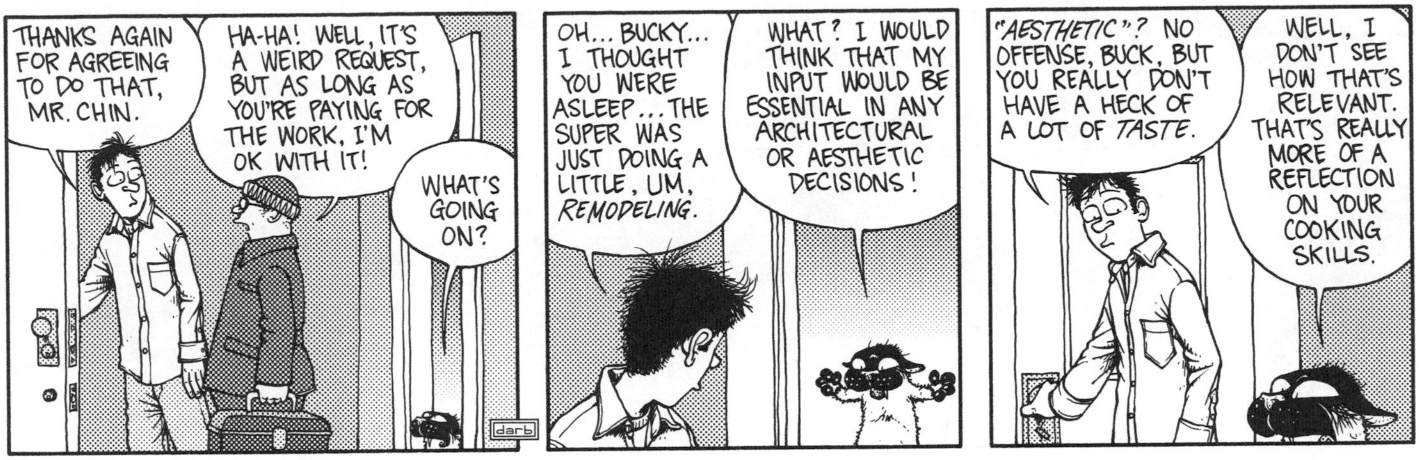
THANKS AGAIN FOR AGREEING TO DO THAT, MR. CHIN.
HA-HA! WELL, IT'S A WEIRD REQUEST, BUT AS LONG AS YOU'RE PAYING FOR THE WORK, I'M OK WITH IT!
WHAT'S GOING ON?
darb
OH... BUCKY... I THOUGHT YOU WERE ASLEEP... THE SUPER WAS JUST DOING A LITTLE, UM, *REMODELING*.
WHAT? I WOULD THINK THAT MY INPUT WOULD BE ESSENTIAL IN ANY ARCHITECTURAL OR AESTHETIC DECISIONS!
"*AESTHETIC*"? NO OFFENSE, BUCK, BUT YOU REALLY DON'T HAVE A HECK OF A LOT OF *TASTE*.
WELL, I DON'T SEE HOW THAT'S RELEVANT. THAT'S REALLY MORE OF A REFLECTION ON YOUR COOKING SKILLS.

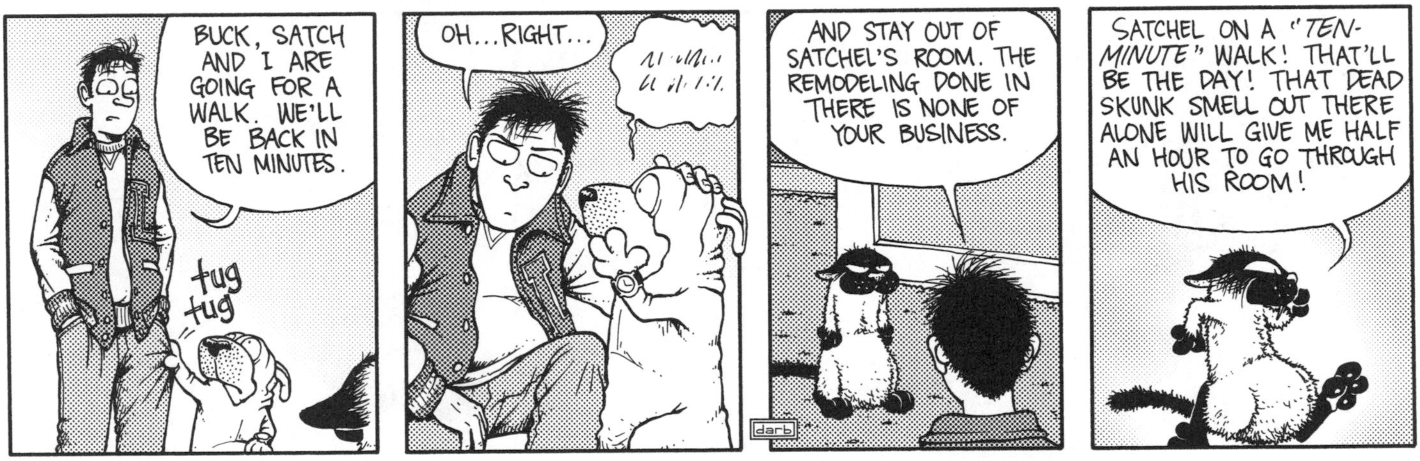
BUCK, SATCH AND I ARE GOING FOR A WALK. WE'LL BE BACK IN TEN MINUTES.
tug tug
OH... RIGHT...
darb
AND STAY OUT OF SATCHEL'S ROOM. THE REMODELING DONE IN THERE IS NONE OF YOUR BUSINESS.
SATCHEL ON A "*TEN-MINUTE*" WALK! THAT'LL BE THE DAY! THAT DEAD SKUNK SMELL OUT THERE ALONE WILL GIVE ME HALF AN HOUR TO GO THROUGH HIS ROOM!

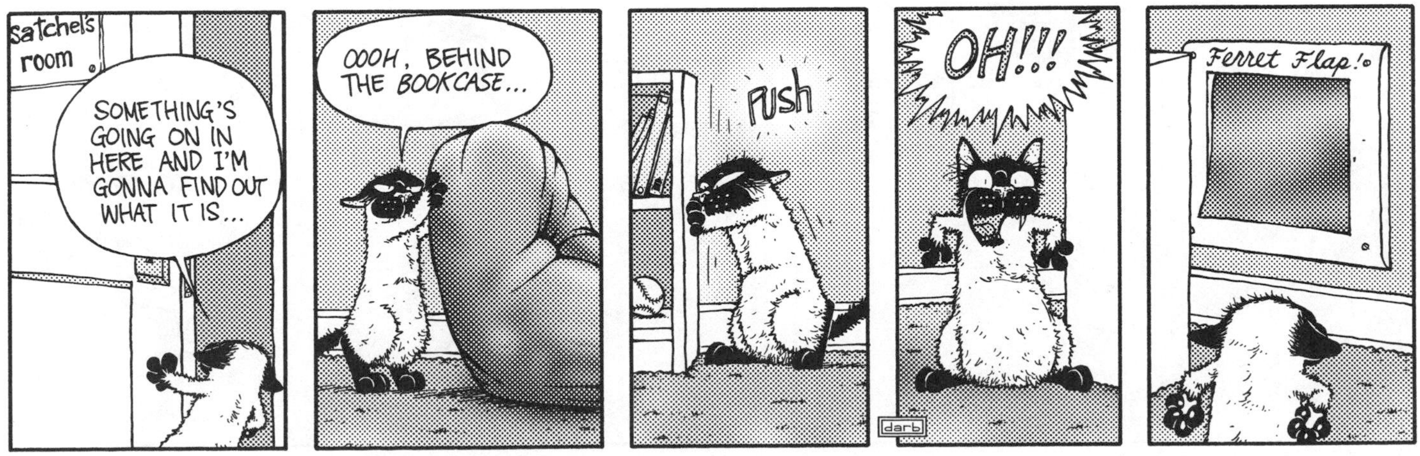
satchel's room
SOMETHING'S GOING ON IN HERE AND I'M GONNA FIND OUT WHAT IT IS...
OOOH, BEHIND THE *BOOKCASE*...
PUSH
OH!!!
darb
Ferret Flap!

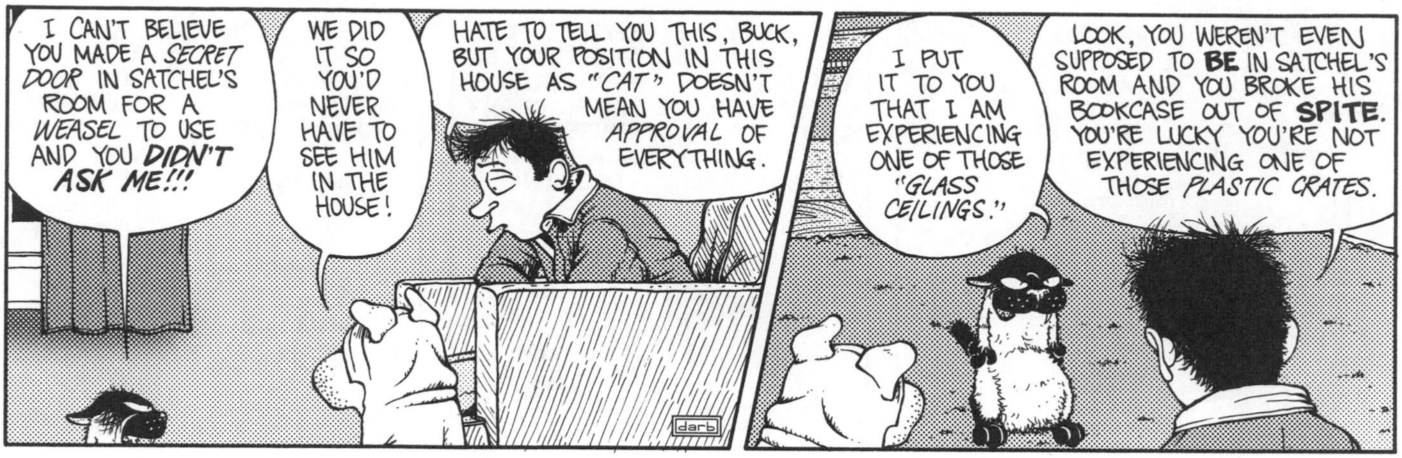
I CAN'T BELIEVE YOU MADE A *SECRET DOOR* IN SATCHEL'S ROOM FOR A *WEASEL* TO USE AND YOU **DIDN'T ASK ME!!!**
WE DID IT SO YOU'D NEVER HAVE TO SEE HIM IN THE HOUSE!
HATE TO TELL YOU THIS, BUCK, BUT YOUR POSITION IN THIS HOUSE AS "CAT" DOESN'T MEAN YOU HAVE *APPROVAL* OF EVERYTHING.
I PUT IT TO YOU THAT I AM EXPERIENCING ONE OF THOSE *"GLASS CEILINGS."*
LOOK, YOU WEREN'T EVEN SUPPOSED TO **BE** IN SATCHEL'S ROOM AND YOU BROKE HIS BOOKCASE OUT OF **SPITE**. YOU'RE LUCKY YOU'RE NOT EXPERIENCING ONE OF THOSE *PLASTIC CRATES*.

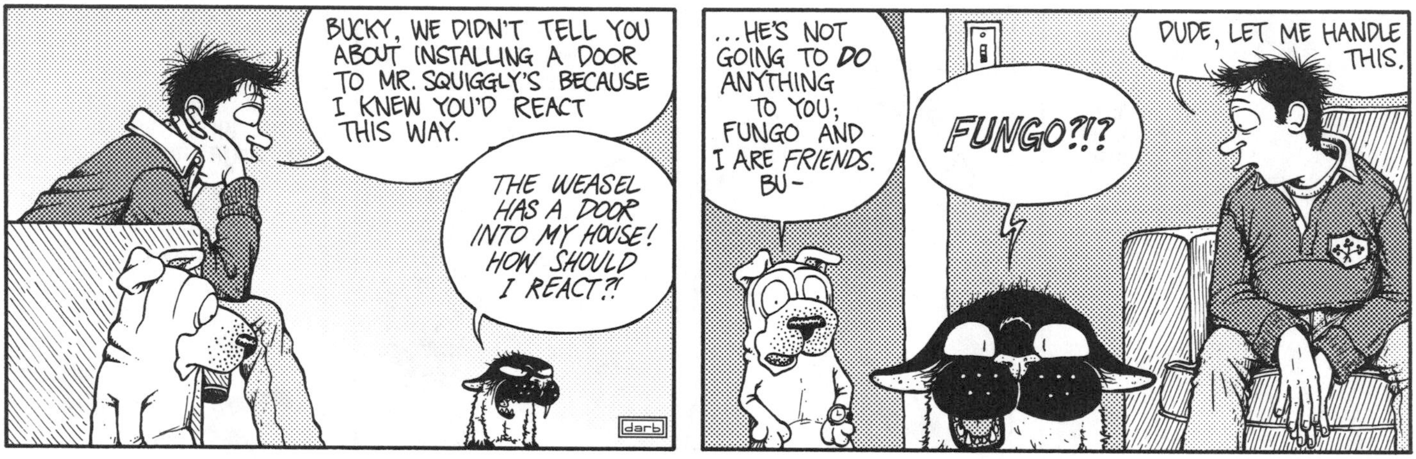
BUCKY, WE DIDN'T TELL YOU ABOUT INSTALLING A DOOR TO MR. SQUIGGLY'S BECAUSE I KNEW YOU'D REACT THIS WAY.
THE WEASEL HAS A DOOR INTO MY HOUSE! HOW SHOULD I REACT?!
...HE'S NOT GOING TO **DO** ANYTHING TO YOU; FUNGO AND I ARE *FRIENDS*. BU-
FUNGO?!?
DUDE, LET ME HANDLE THIS.

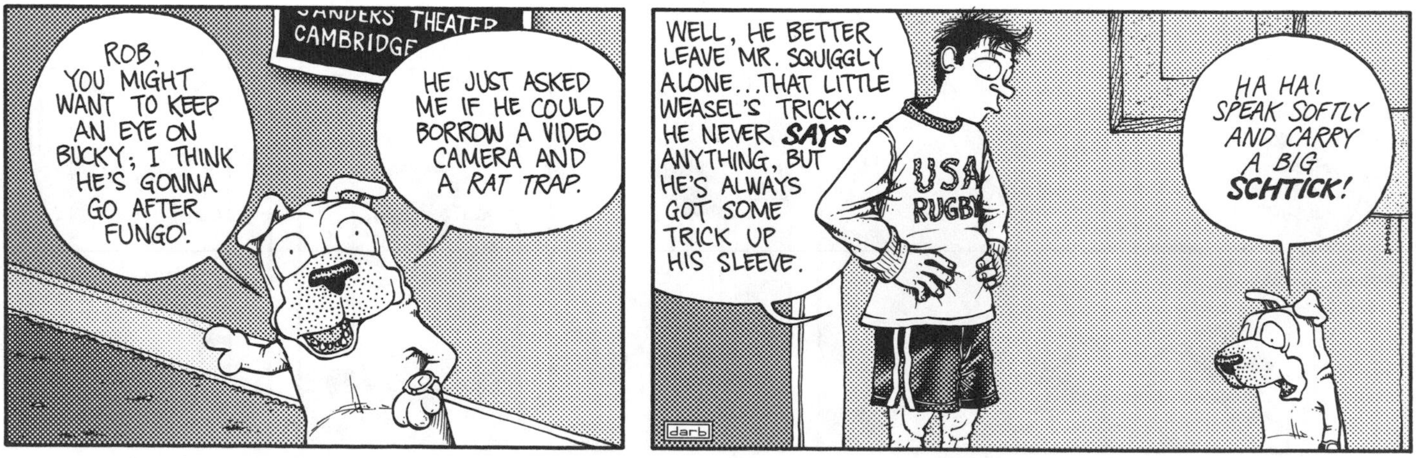
SANDERS THEATER CAMBRIDGE
ROB, YOU MIGHT WANT TO KEEP AN EYE ON BUCKY; I THINK HE'S GONNA GO AFTER FUNGO!
HE JUST ASKED ME IF HE COULD BORROW A VIDEO CAMERA AND A *RAT TRAP*.
WELL, HE BETTER LEAVE MR. SQUIGGLY ALONE...THAT LITTLE WEASEL'S TRICKY... HE NEVER ***SAYS*** ANYTHING, BUT HE'S ALWAYS GOT SOME TRICK UP HIS SLEEVE.
USA RUGBY
HA HA! SPEAK SOFTLY AND CARRY A BIG ***SCHTICK!***

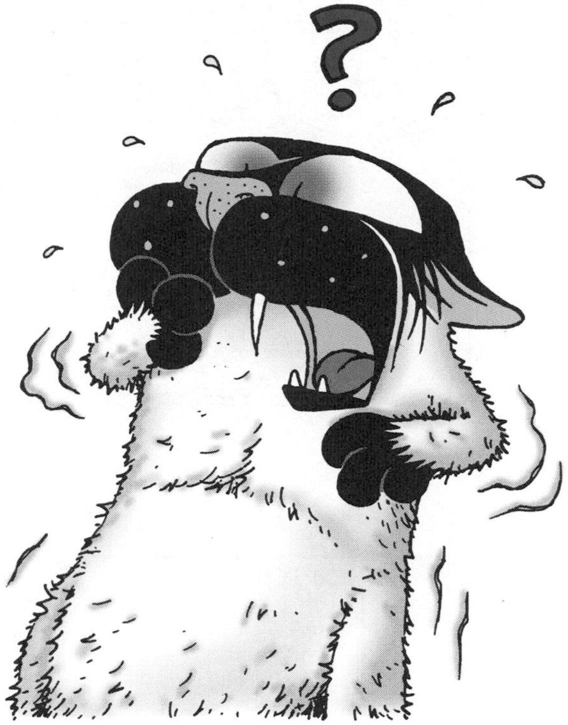

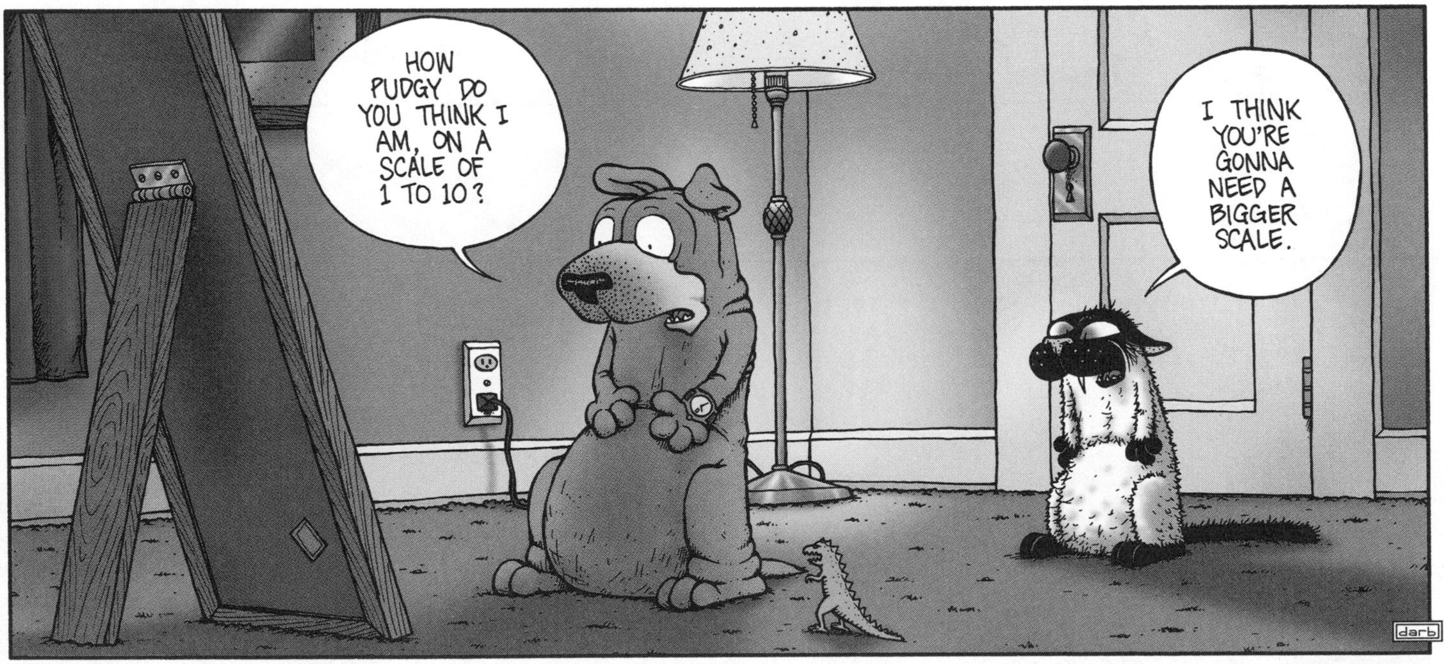
HOW PUDGY DO YOU THINK I AM, ON A SCALE OF 1 TO 10?
I THINK YOU'RE GONNA NEED A BIGGER SCALE.
darb

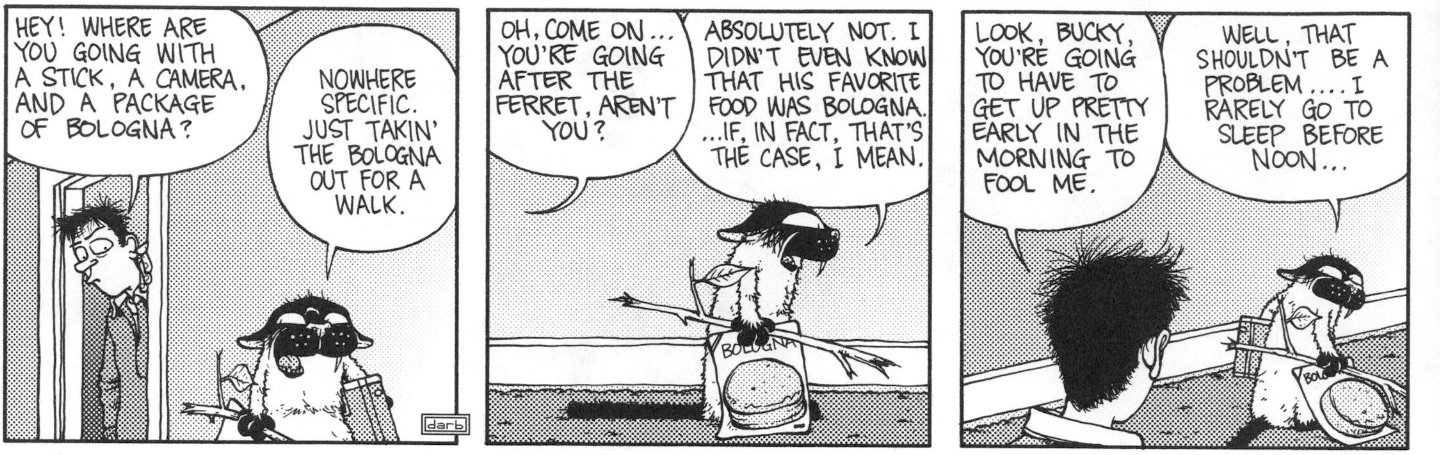
HEY! WHERE ARE YOU GOING WITH A STICK, A CAMERA, AND A PACKAGE OF BOLOGNA?
NOWHERE SPECIFIC. JUST TAKIN' THE BOLOGNA OUT FOR A WALK.
OH, COME ON... YOU'RE GOING AFTER THE FERRET, AREN'T YOU?
ABSOLUTELY NOT. I DIDN'T EVEN KNOW THAT HIS FAVORITE FOOD WAS BOLOGNA. ...IF, IN FACT, THAT'S THE CASE, I MEAN.
BOLOGNA
LOOK, BUCKY, YOU'RE GOING TO HAVE TO GET UP PRETTY EARLY IN THE MORNING TO FOOL ME.
WELL, THAT SHOULDN'T BE A PROBLEM.... I RARELY GO TO SLEEP BEFORE NOON...
darb

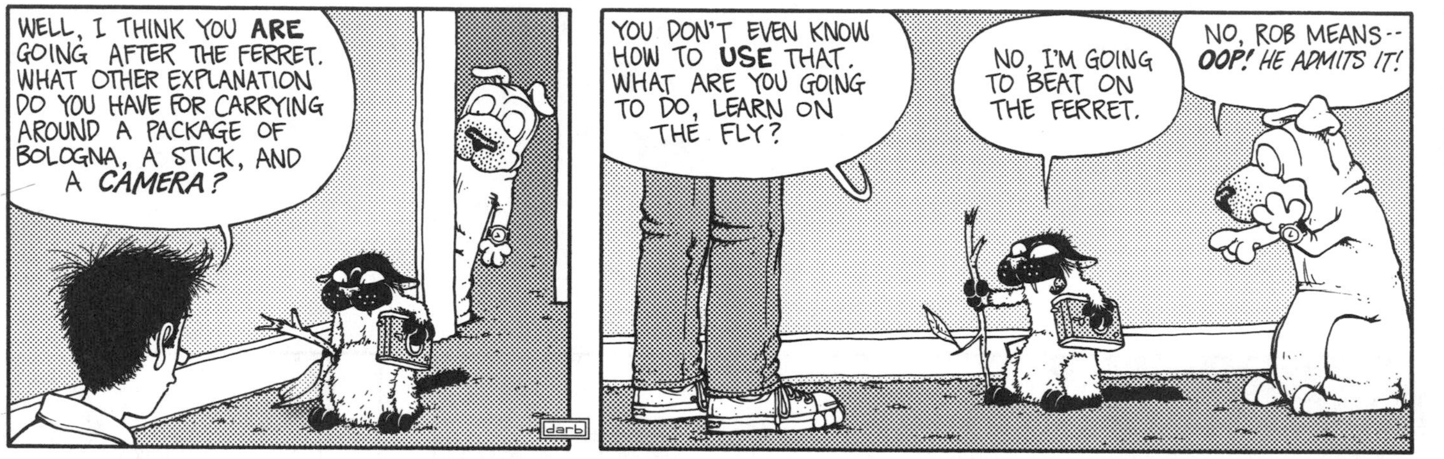
WELL, I THINK YOU **ARE** GOING AFTER THE FERRET. WHAT OTHER EXPLANATION DO YOU HAVE FOR CARRYING AROUND A PACKAGE OF BOLOGNA, A STICK, AND A ***CAMERA?***
darb
YOU DON'T EVEN KNOW HOW TO **USE** THAT. WHAT ARE YOU GOING TO DO, LEARN ON THE FLY?
NO, I'M GOING TO BEAT ON THE FERRET.
NO, ROB MEANS-- ***OOP!*** *HE ADMITS IT!*

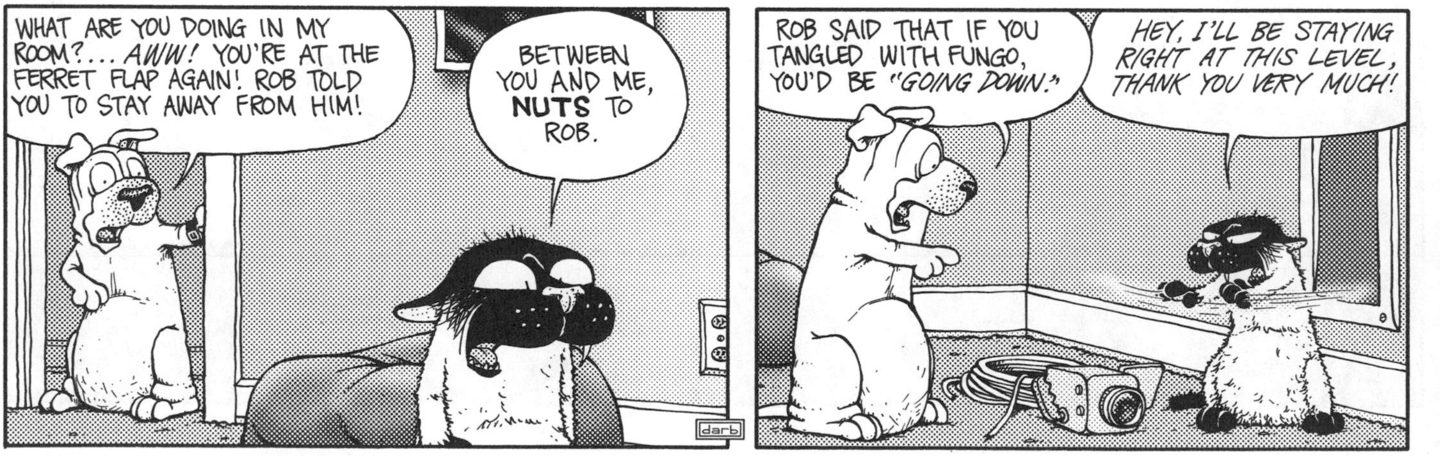
WHAT ARE YOU DOING IN MY ROOM?... *AWW!* YOU'RE AT THE FERRET FLAP AGAIN! ROB TOLD YOU TO STAY AWAY FROM HIM!
BETWEEN YOU AND ME, **NUTS** TO ROB.
darb
ROB SAID THAT IF YOU TANGLED WITH FUNGO, YOU'D BE *"GOING DOWN."*
HEY, I'LL BE STAYING RIGHT AT THIS LEVEL, THANK YOU VERY MUCH!

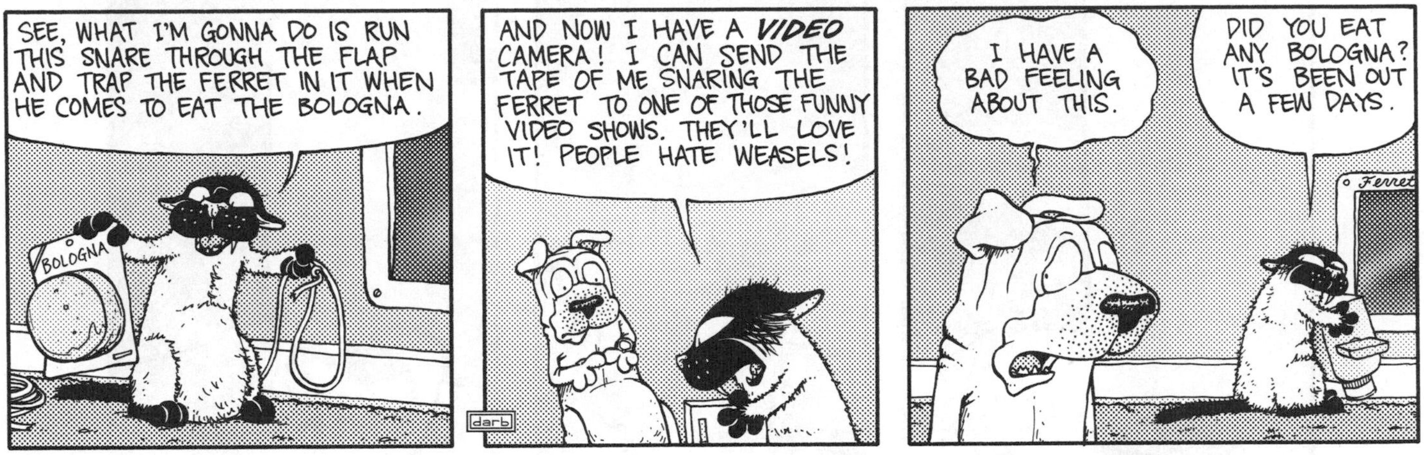
SEE, WHAT I'M GONNA DO IS RUN THIS SNARE THROUGH THE FLAP AND TRAP THE FERRET IN IT WHEN HE COMES TO EAT THE BOLOGNA.
BOLOGNA
AND NOW I HAVE A VIDEO CAMERA! I CAN SEND THE TAPE OF ME SNARING THE FERRET TO ONE OF THOSE FUNNY VIDEO SHOWS. THEY'LL LOVE IT! PEOPLE HATE WEASELS!
darb
I HAVE A BAD FEELING ABOUT THIS.
DID YOU EAT ANY BOLOGNA? IT'S BEEN OUT A FEW DAYS.
Ferret

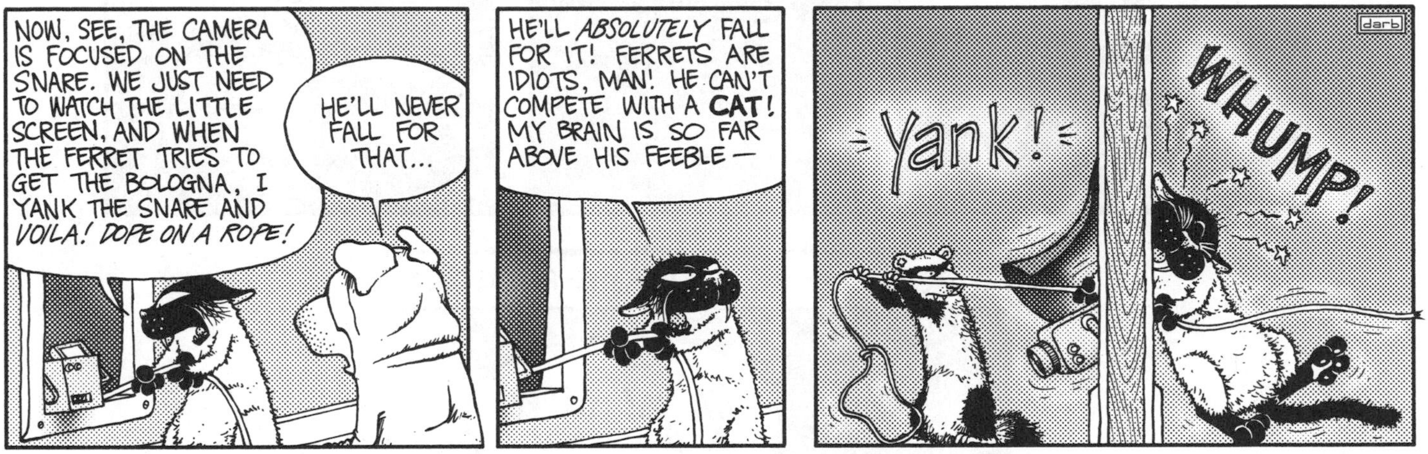
NOW, SEE, THE CAMERA IS FOCUSED ON THE SNARE. WE JUST NEED TO WATCH THE LITTLE SCREEN, AND WHEN THE FERRET TRIES TO GET THE BOLOGNA, I YANK THE SNARE AND VOILA! DOPE ON A ROPE!
HE'LL NEVER FALL FOR THAT...
HE'LL ABSOLUTELY FALL FOR IT! FERRETS ARE IDIOTS, MAN! HE CAN'T COMPETE WITH A CAT! MY BRAIN IS SO FAR ABOVE HIS FEEBLE—
darb
Yank!
WHUMP!

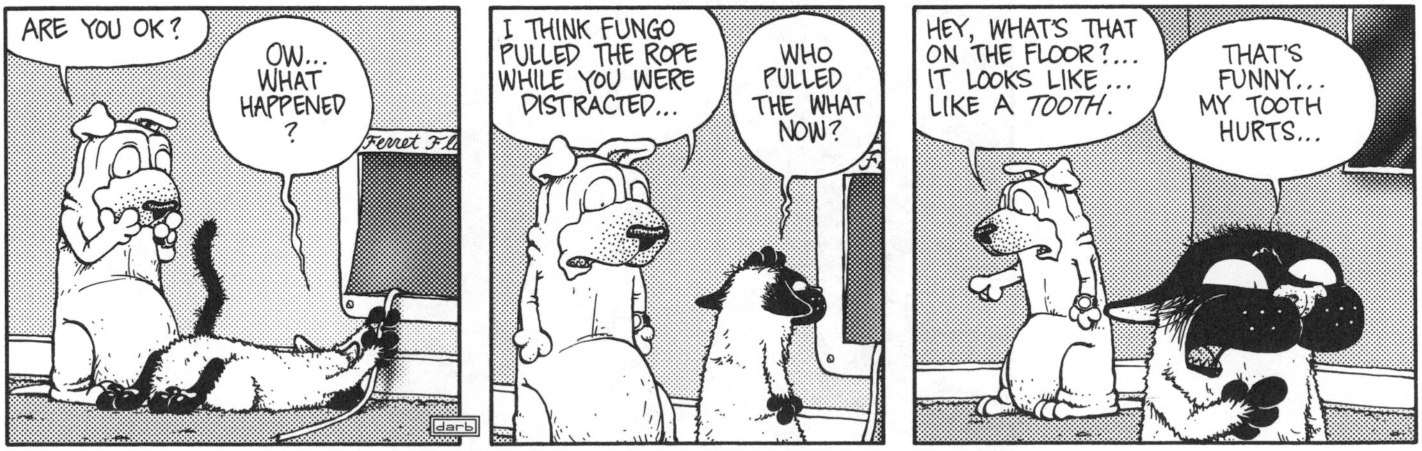
ARE YOU OK?
OW... WHAT HAPPENED?
Ferret Fl
darb
I THINK FUNGO PULLED THE ROPE WHILE YOU WERE DISTRACTED...
WHO PULLED THE WHAT NOW?
HEY, WHAT'S THAT ON THE FLOOR?... IT LOOKS LIKE... LIKE A TOOTH.
THAT'S FUNNY... MY TOOTH HURTS...

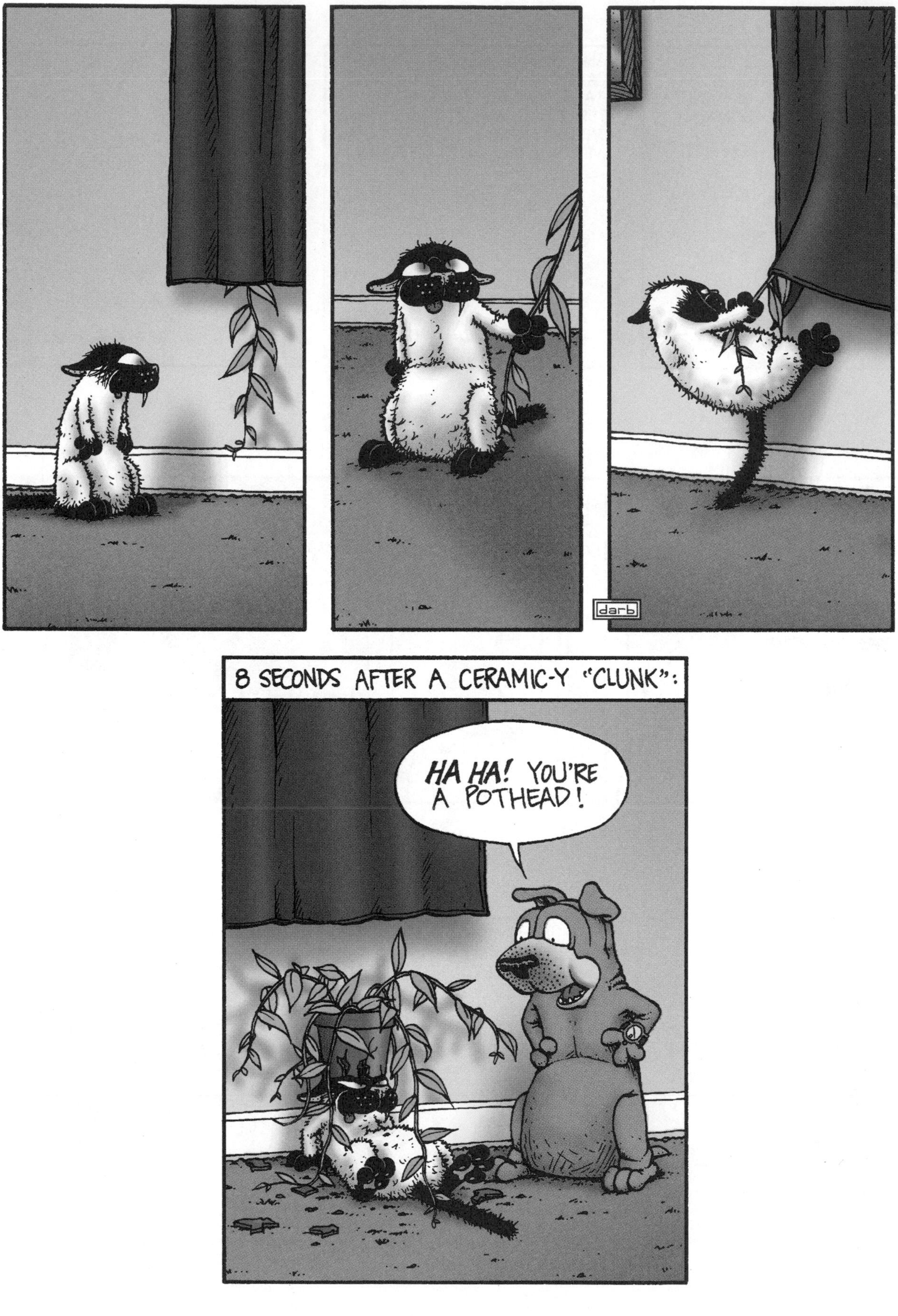
darb
8 SECONDS AFTER A CERAMIC-Y "CLUNK":
HA HA! YOU'RE A POTHEAD!

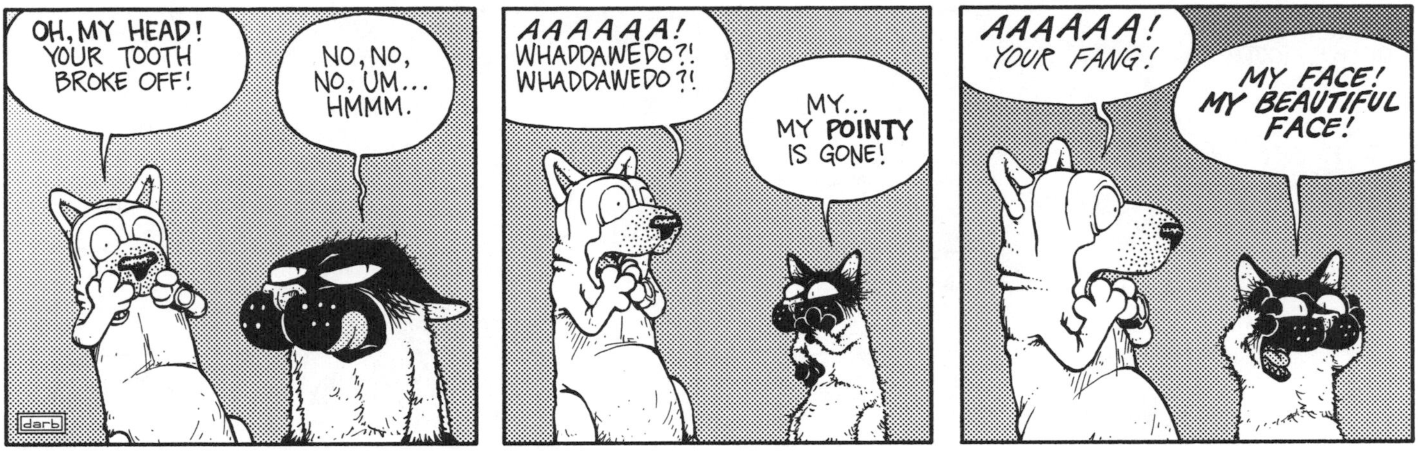
OH, MY HEAD! YOUR TOOTH BROKE OFF!
NO, NO, NO, UM... HMMM.
AAAAAA! WHADDAWEDO?! WHADDAWEDO?!
MY... MY POINTY IS GONE!
AAAAAA! YOUR FANG!
MY FACE! MY BEAUTIFUL FACE!

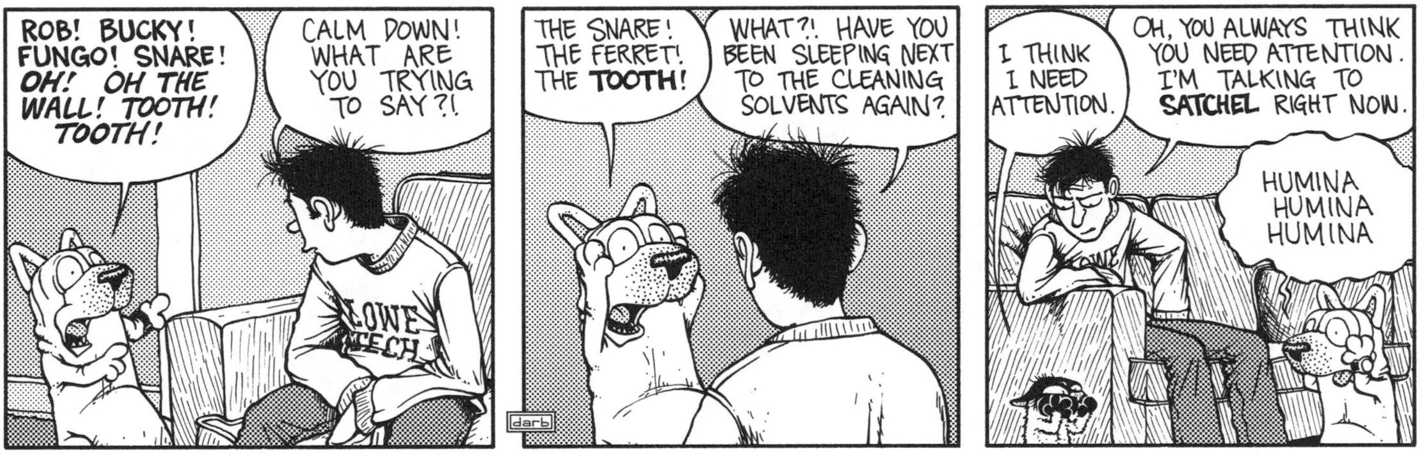
ROB! BUCKY! FUNGO! SNARE! OH! OH THE WALL! TOOTH! TOOTH!
CALM DOWN! WHAT ARE YOU TRYING TO SAY?!
LOWE TECH
THE SNARE! THE FERRET! THE TOOTH!
WHAT?! HAVE YOU BEEN SLEEPING NEXT TO THE CLEANING SOLVENTS AGAIN?
I THINK I NEED ATTENTION.
OH, YOU ALWAYS THINK YOU NEED ATTENTION. I'M TALKING TO SATCHEL RIGHT NOW.
HUMINA HUMINA HUMINA

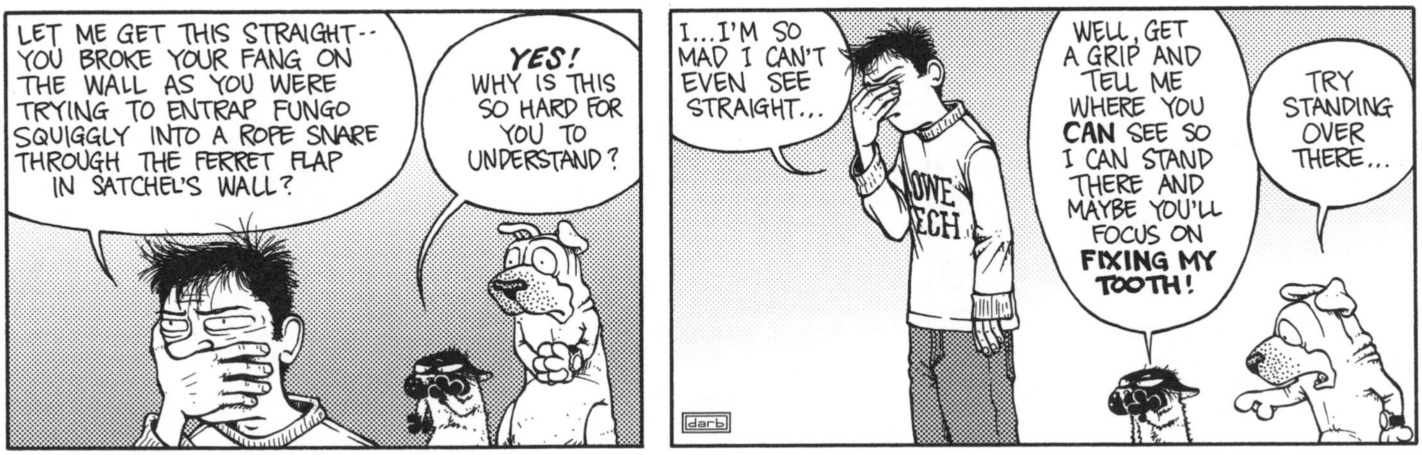
LET ME GET THIS STRAIGHT-- YOU BROKE YOUR FANG ON THE WALL AS YOU WERE TRYING TO ENTRAP FUNGO SQUIGGLY INTO A ROPE SNARE THROUGH THE FERRET FLAP IN SATCHEL'S WALL?
YES! WHY IS THIS SO HARD FOR YOU TO UNDERSTAND?
I...I'M SO MAD I CAN'T EVEN SEE STRAIGHT...
LOWE TECH
WELL, GET A GRIP AND TELL ME WHERE YOU CAN SEE SO I CAN STAND THERE AND MAYBE YOU'LL FOCUS ON FIXING MY TOOTH!
TRY STANDING OVER THERE...

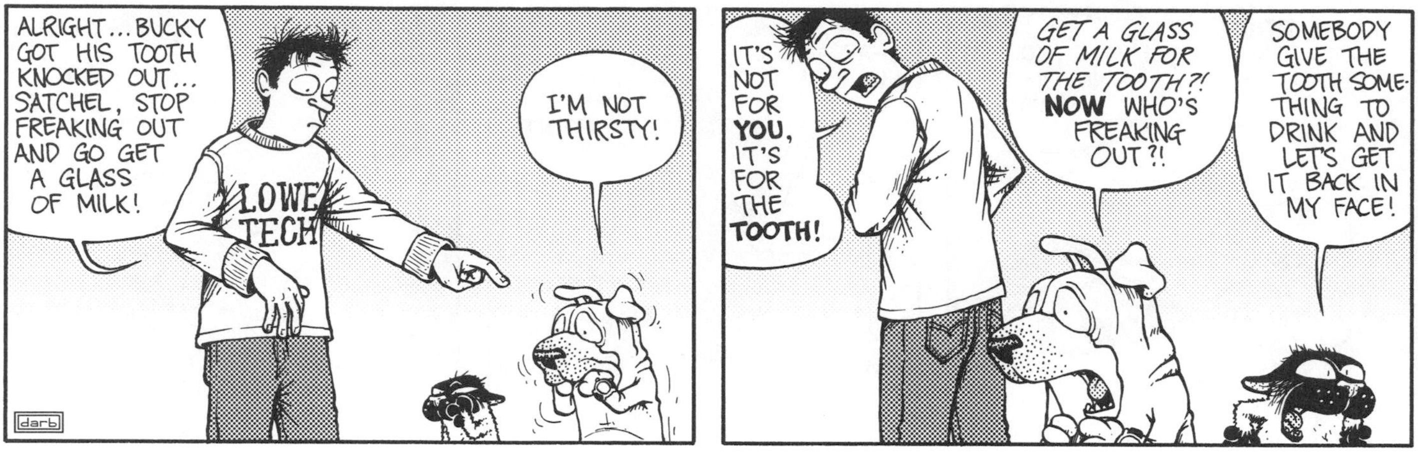
ALRIGHT... BUCKY GOT HIS TOOTH KNOCKED OUT... SATCHEL, STOP FREAKING OUT AND GO GET A GLASS OF MILK!
LOWE TECH
I'M NOT THIRSTY!
darb
IT'S NOT FOR **YOU**, IT'S FOR THE **TOOTH!**
GET A GLASS OF MILK FOR THE TOOTH?! **NOW** WHO'S FREAKING OUT?!
SOMEBODY GIVE THE TOOTH SOMETHING TO DRINK AND LET'S GET IT BACK IN MY FACE!

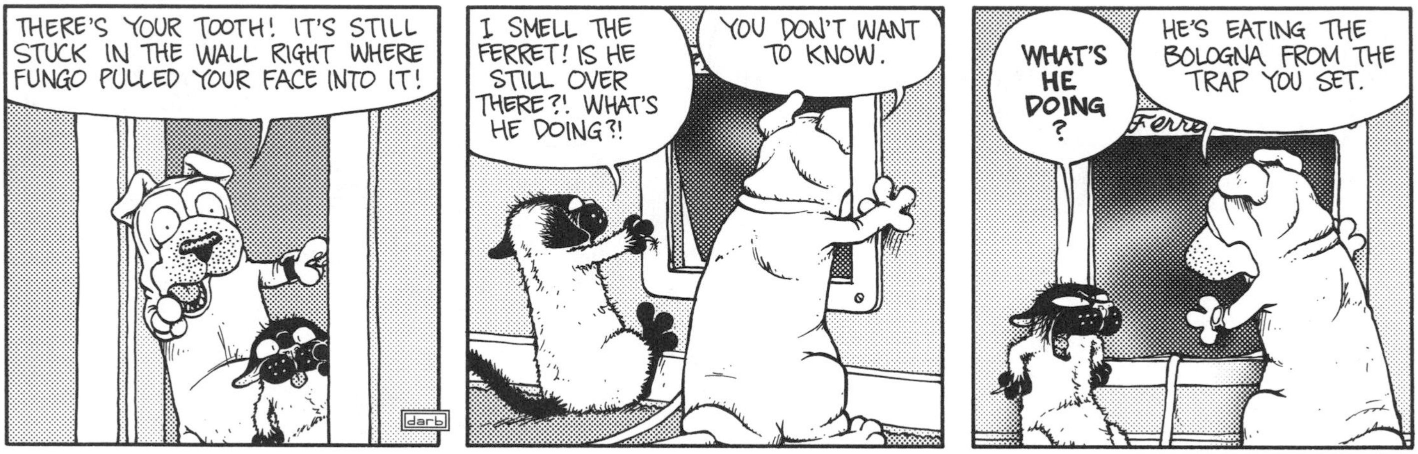
THERE'S YOUR TOOTH! IT'S STILL STUCK IN THE WALL RIGHT WHERE FUNGO PULLED YOUR FACE INTO IT!
darb
I SMELL THE FERRET! IS HE STILL OVER THERE?! WHAT'S HE DOING?!
YOU DON'T WANT TO KNOW.
WHAT'S HE DOING?
HE'S EATING THE BOLOGNA FROM THE TRAP YOU SET.

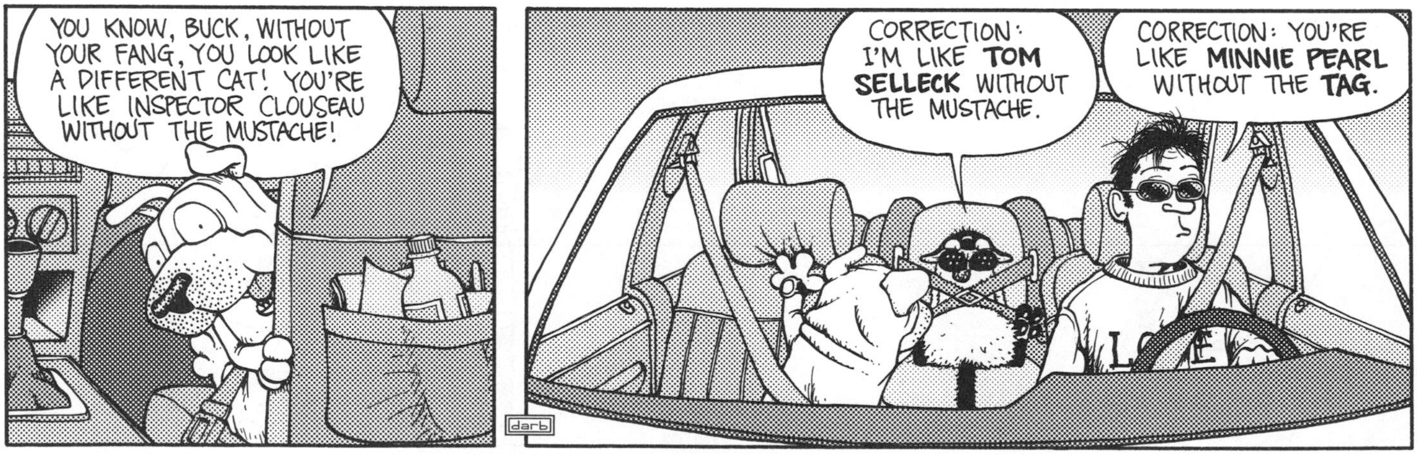
YOU KNOW, BUCK, WITHOUT YOUR FANG, YOU LOOK LIKE A DIFFERENT CAT! YOU'RE LIKE INSPECTOR CLOUSEAU WITHOUT THE MUSTACHE!
darb
CORRECTION: I'M LIKE **TOM SELLECK** WITHOUT THE MUSTACHE.
CORRECTION: YOU'RE LIKE **MINNIE PEARL** WITHOUT THE **TAG**.

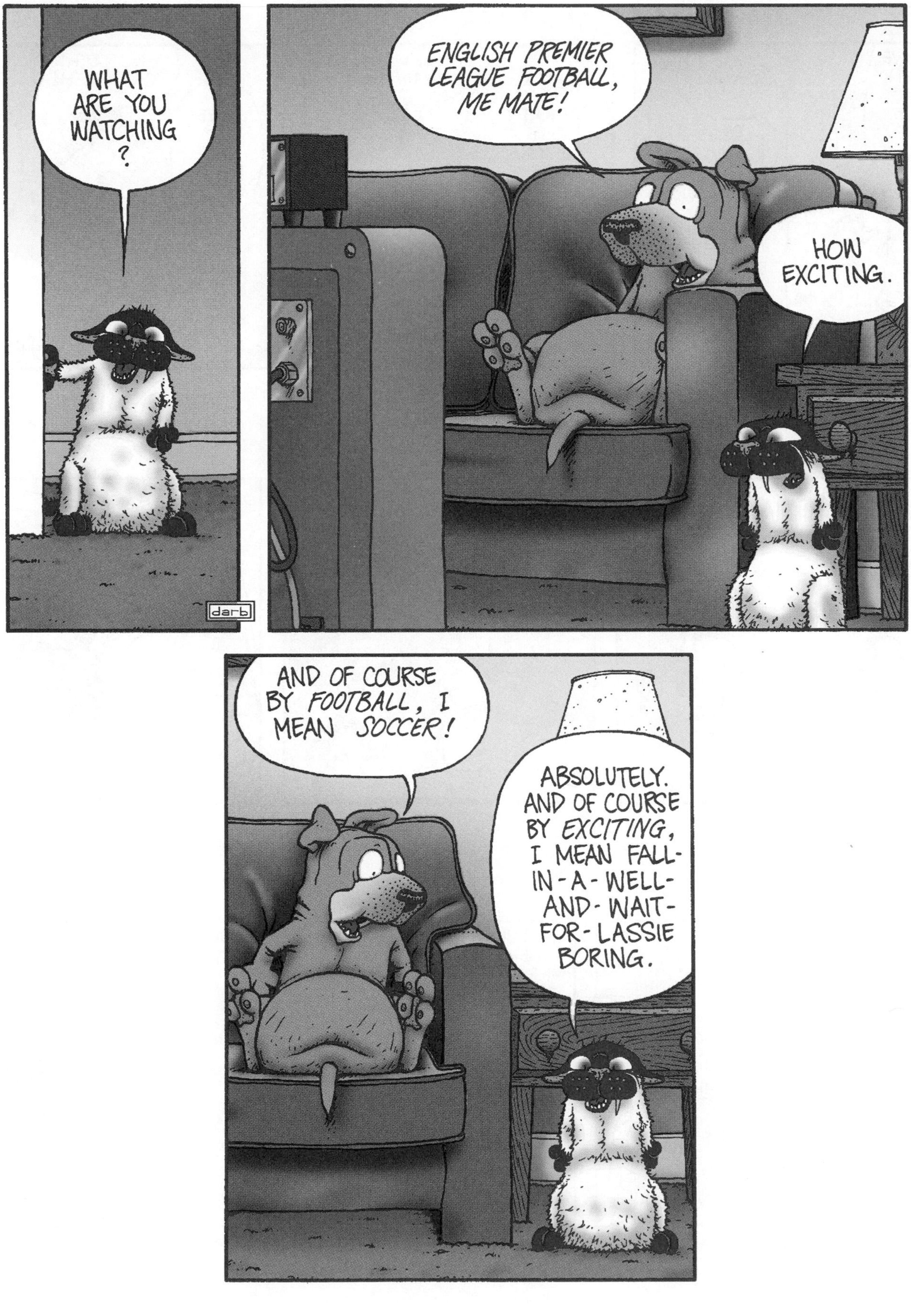
WHAT ARE YOU WATCHING ?
ENGLISH PREMIER LEAGUE FOOTBALL, ME MATE!
HOW EXCITING.
darb
AND OF COURSE BY FOOTBALL, I MEAN SOCCER!
ABSOLUTELY. AND OF COURSE BY EXCITING, I MEAN FALL-IN-A-WELL-AND-WAIT-FOR-LASSIE BORING.

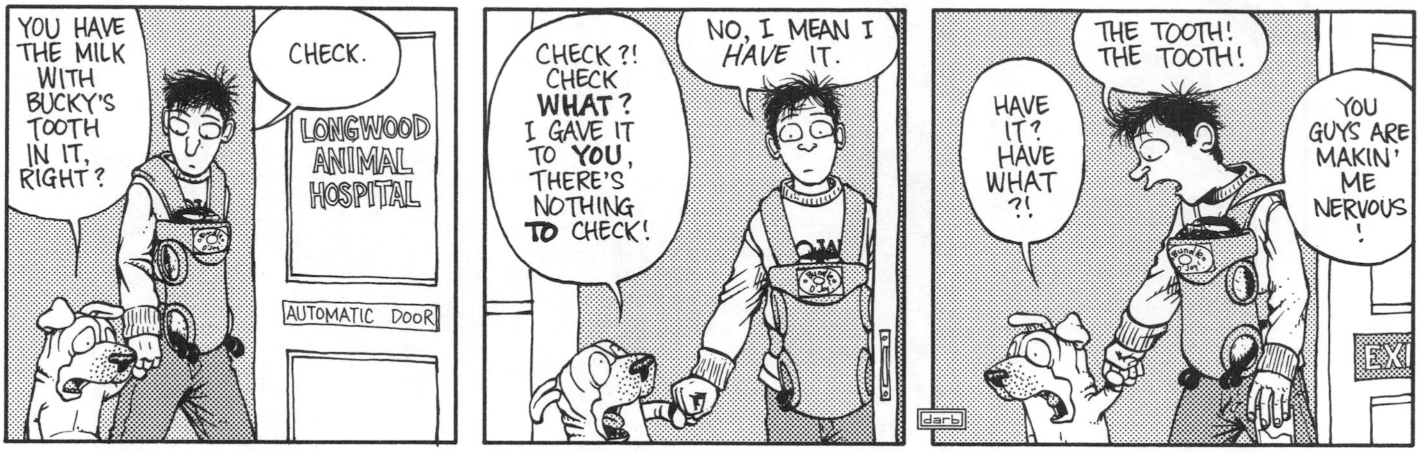
YOU HAVE THE MILK WITH BUCKY'S TOOTH IN IT, RIGHT?
CHECK.
LONGWOOD ANIMAL HOSPITAL
AUTOMATIC DOOR
CHECK?! CHECK WHAT? I GAVE IT TO YOU, THERE'S NOTHING TO CHECK!
NO, I MEAN I HAVE IT.
HAVE IT? HAVE WHAT?!
THE TOOTH! THE TOOTH!
YOU GUYS ARE MAKIN' ME NERVOUS!

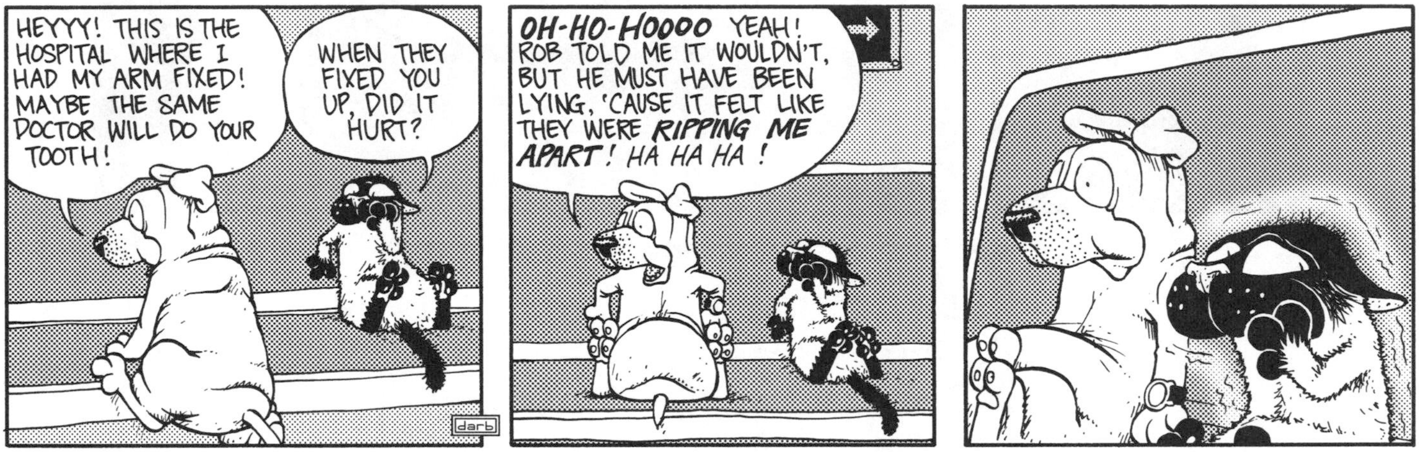
HEYYY! THIS IS THE HOSPITAL WHERE I HAD MY ARM FIXED! MAYBE THE SAME DOCTOR WILL DO YOUR TOOTH!
WHEN THEY FIXED YOU UP, DID IT HURT?
OH-HO-HOOOO YEAH! ROB TOLD ME IT WOULDN'T, BUT HE MUST HAVE BEEN LYING, 'CAUSE IT FELT LIKE THEY WERE RIPPING ME APART! HA HA HA!

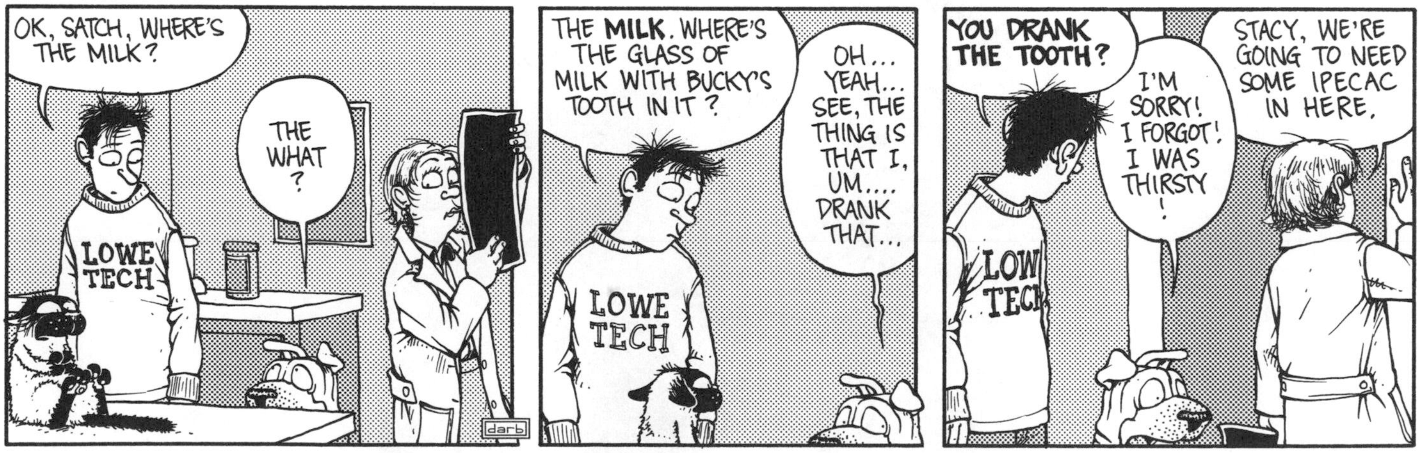
OK, SATCH, WHERE'S THE MILK?
THE WHAT?
LOWE TECH
THE MILK. WHERE'S THE GLASS OF MILK WITH BUCKY'S TOOTH IN IT?
OH... YEAH... SEE, THE THING IS THAT I, UM.... DRANK THAT...
YOU DRANK THE TOOTH?
I'M SORRY! I FORGOT! I WAS THIRSTY!
STACY, WE'RE GOING TO NEED SOME IPECAC IN HERE.

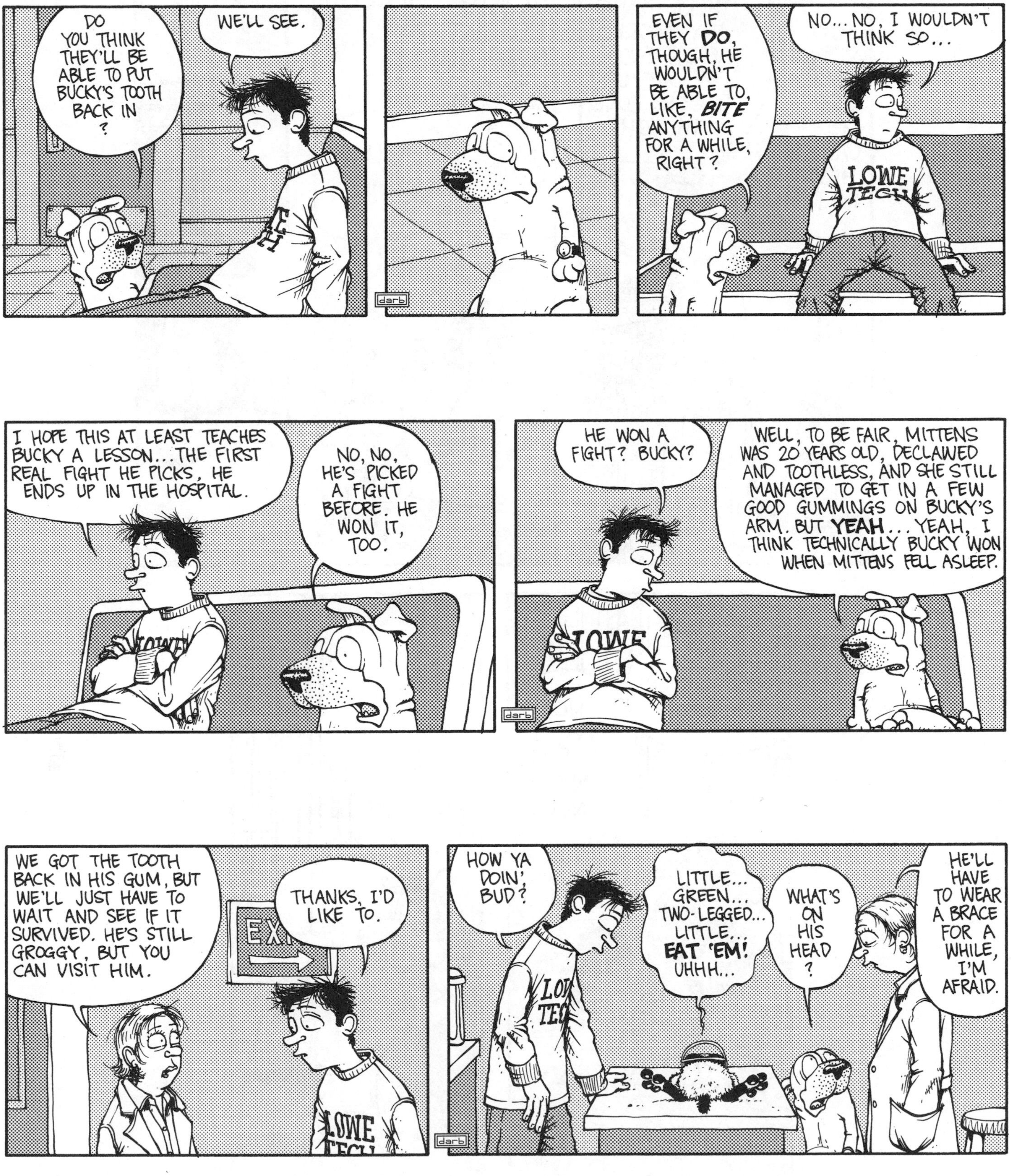
DO YOU THINK THEY'LL BE ABLE TO PUT BUCKY'S TOOTH BACK IN ?
WE'LL SEE.
darb
EVEN IF THEY **DO**, THOUGH, HE WOULDN'T BE ABLE TO, LIKE, ***BITE*** ANYTHING FOR A WHILE, RIGHT ?
NO... NO, I WOULDN'T THINK SO...
LOWE TECH
I HOPE THIS AT LEAST TEACHES BUCKY A LESSON... THE FIRST REAL FIGHT HE PICKS, HE ENDS UP IN THE HOSPITAL.
NO, NO, HE'S PICKED A FIGHT BEFORE. HE WON IT, TOO.
darb
HE WON A FIGHT? BUCKY?
WELL, TO BE FAIR, MITTENS WAS 20 YEARS OLD, DECLAWED AND TOOTHLESS, AND SHE STILL MANAGED TO GET IN A FEW GOOD GUMMINGS ON BUCKY'S ARM. BUT **YEAH**... YEAH, I THINK TECHNICALLY BUCKY WON WHEN MITTENS FELL ASLEEP.
WE GOT THE TOOTH BACK IN HIS GUM, BUT WE'LL JUST HAVE TO WAIT AND SEE IF IT SURVIVED. HE'S STILL GROGGY, BUT YOU CAN VISIT HIM.
THANKS, I'D LIKE TO.
LOWE
darb
HOW YA DOIN', BUD?
LITTLE... GREEN... TWO-LEGGED... LITTLE... **EAT 'EM!** UHHH...
WHAT'S ON HIS HEAD ?
HE'LL HAVE TO WEAR A BRACE FOR A WHILE, I'M AFRAID.

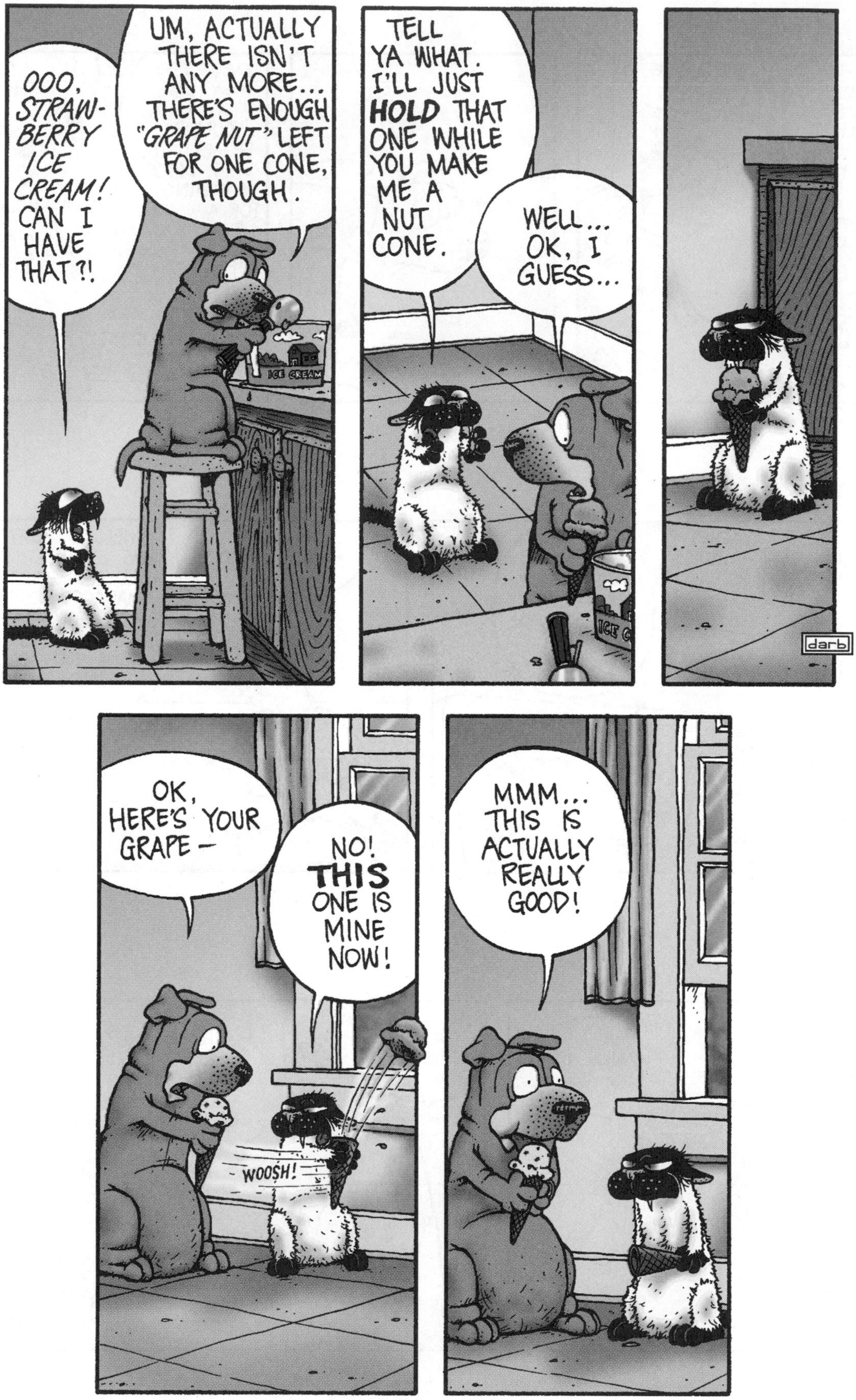

OOO, STRAW-BERRY ICE CREAM! CAN I HAVE THAT?!
UM, ACTUALLY THERE ISN'T ANY MORE... THERE'S ENOUGH "GRAPE NUT" LEFT FOR ONE CONE, THOUGH.
ICE CREAM
TELL YA WHAT. I'LL JUST HOLD THAT ONE WHILE YOU MAKE ME A NUT CONE.
WELL... OK, I GUESS...
darb
OK, HERE'S YOUR GRAPE –
NO! THIS ONE IS MINE NOW!
WOOSH!
MMM... THIS IS ACTUALLY REALLY GOOD!

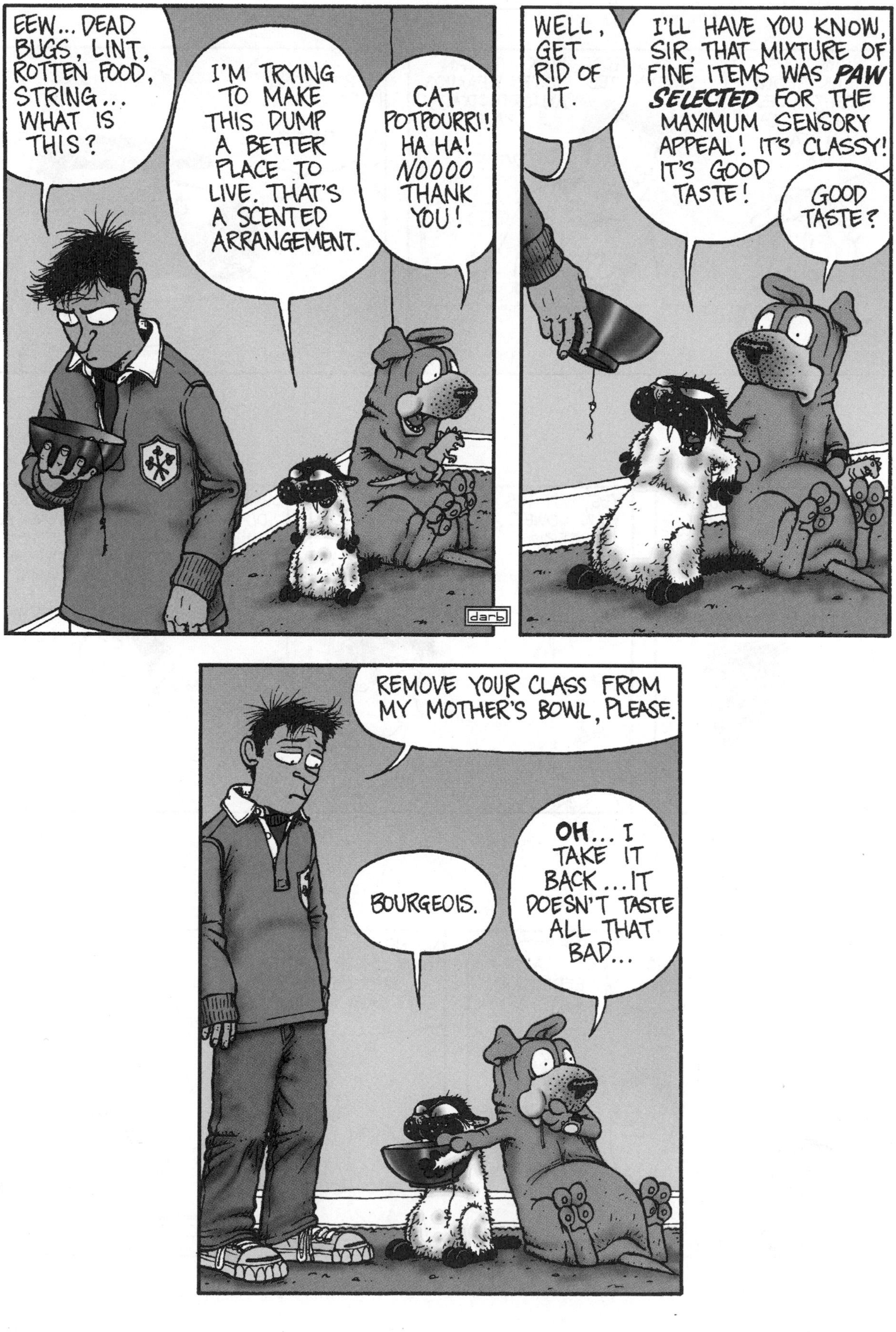
EEW... DEAD BUGS, LINT, ROTTEN FOOD, STRING... WHAT IS THIS?
I'M TRYING TO MAKE THIS DUMP A BETTER PLACE TO LIVE. THAT'S A SCENTED ARRANGEMENT.
CAT POTPOURRI! HA HA! NOOOO THANK YOU!
darb
WELL, GET RID OF IT.
I'LL HAVE YOU KNOW, SIR, THAT MIXTURE OF FINE ITEMS WAS PAW SELECTED FOR THE MAXIMUM SENSORY APPEAL! IT'S CLASSY! IT'S GOOD TASTE!
GOOD TASTE?
REMOVE YOUR CLASS FROM MY MOTHER'S BOWL, PLEASE.
BOURGEOIS.
OH... I TAKE IT BACK... IT DOESN'T TASTE ALL THAT BAD...

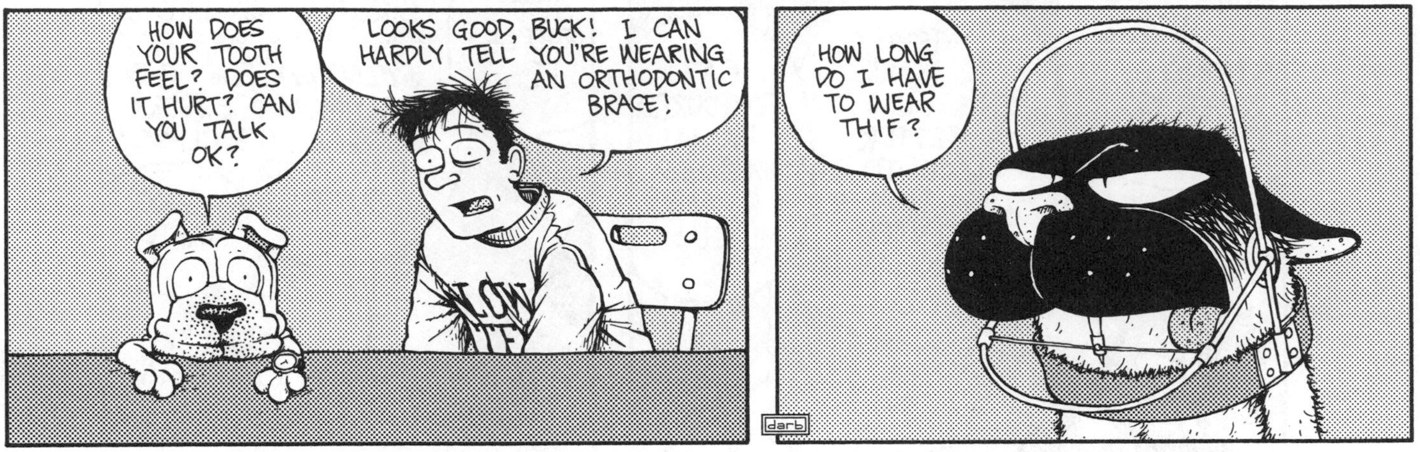
HOW DOES YOUR TOOTH FEEL? DOES IT HURT? CAN YOU TALK OK?
LOOKS GOOD, BUCK! I CAN HARDLY TELL YOU'RE WEARING AN ORTHODONTIC BRACE!
HOW LONG DO I HAVE TO WEAR THIF?
darb

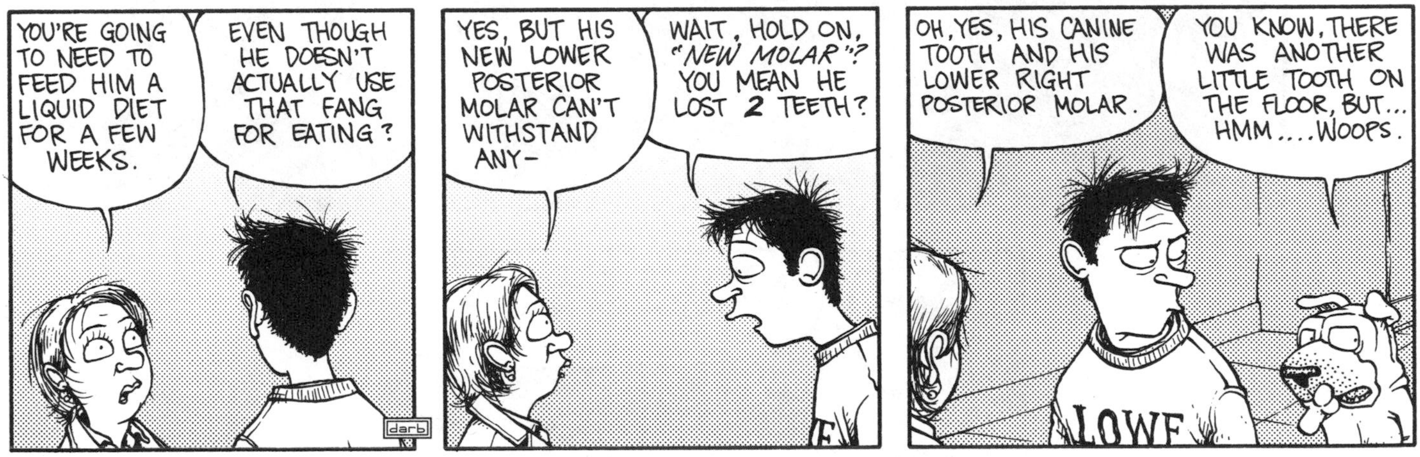
YOU'RE GOING TO NEED TO FEED HIM A LIQUID DIET FOR A FEW WEEKS.
EVEN THOUGH HE DOESN'T ACTUALLY USE THAT FANG FOR EATING?
darb
YES, BUT HIS NEW LOWER POSTERIOR MOLAR CAN'T WITHSTAND ANY-
WAIT, HOLD ON, "NEW MOLAR"? YOU MEAN HE LOST 2 TEETH?
OH, YES, HIS CANINE TOOTH AND HIS LOWER RIGHT POSTERIOR MOLAR.
YOU KNOW, THERE WAS ANOTHER LITTLE TOOTH ON THE FLOOR, BUT... HMM.... WOOPS.

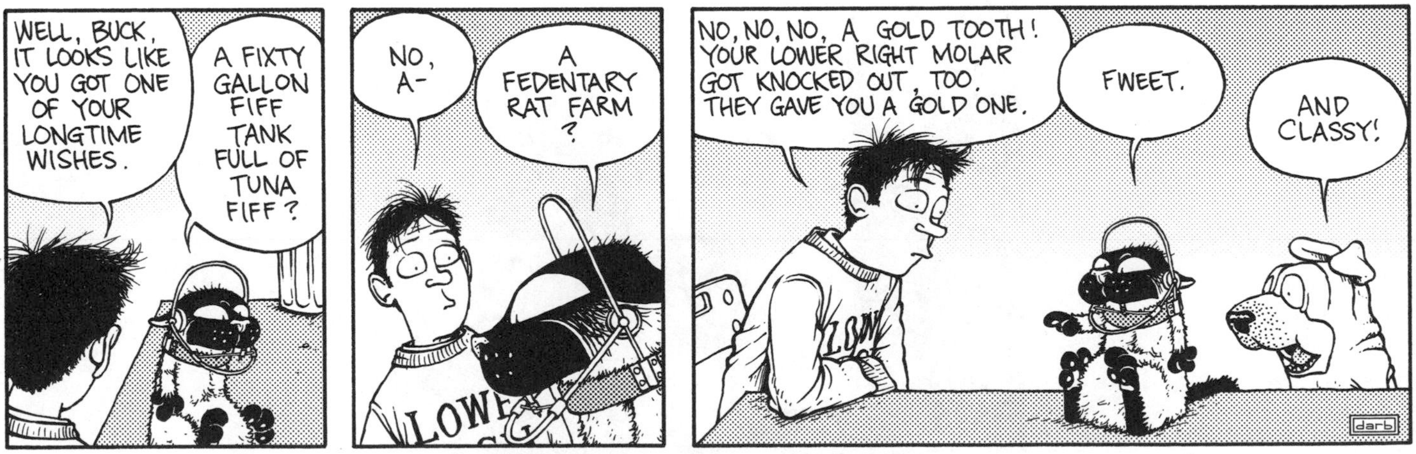
WELL, BUCK, IT LOOKS LIKE YOU GOT ONE OF YOUR LONGTIME WISHES.
A FIXTY GALLON FIFF TANK FULL OF TUNA FIFF?
NO, A-
A FEDENTARY RAT FARM?
NO, NO, NO, A GOLD TOOTH! YOUR LOWER RIGHT MOLAR GOT KNOCKED OUT, TOO. THEY GAVE YOU A GOLD ONE.
FWEET.
AND CLASSY!
darb

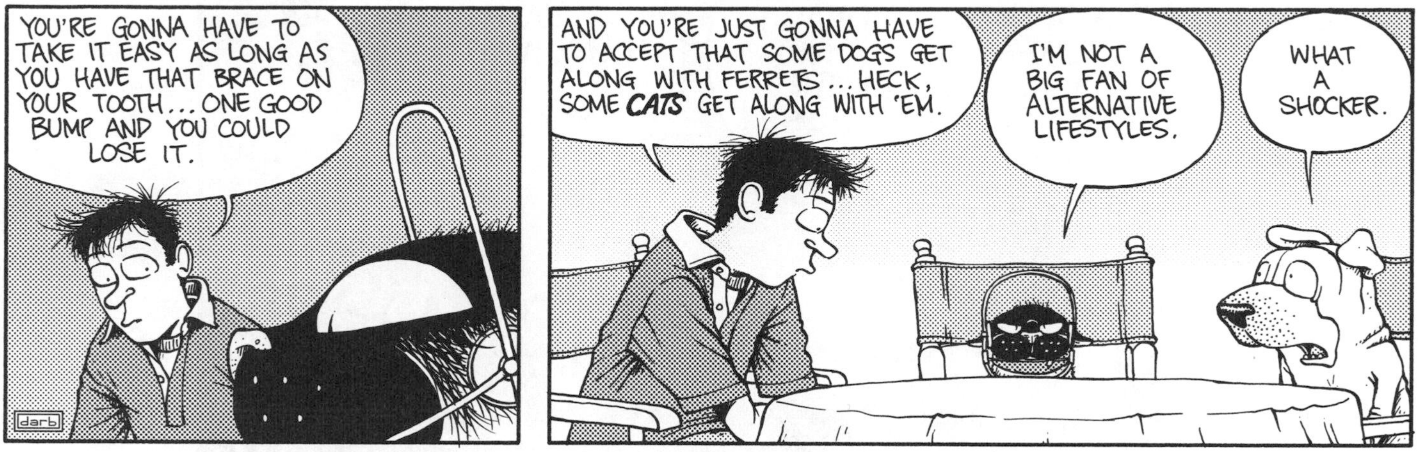
YOU'RE GONNA HAVE TO TAKE IT EASY AS LONG AS YOU HAVE THAT BRACE ON YOUR TOOTH... ONE GOOD BUMP AND YOU COULD LOSE IT.
AND YOU'RE JUST GONNA HAVE TO ACCEPT THAT SOME DOGS GET ALONG WITH FERRETS... HECK, SOME CATS GET ALONG WITH 'EM.
I'M NOT A BIG FAN OF ALTERNATIVE LIFESTYLES.
WHAT A SHOCKER.
darb

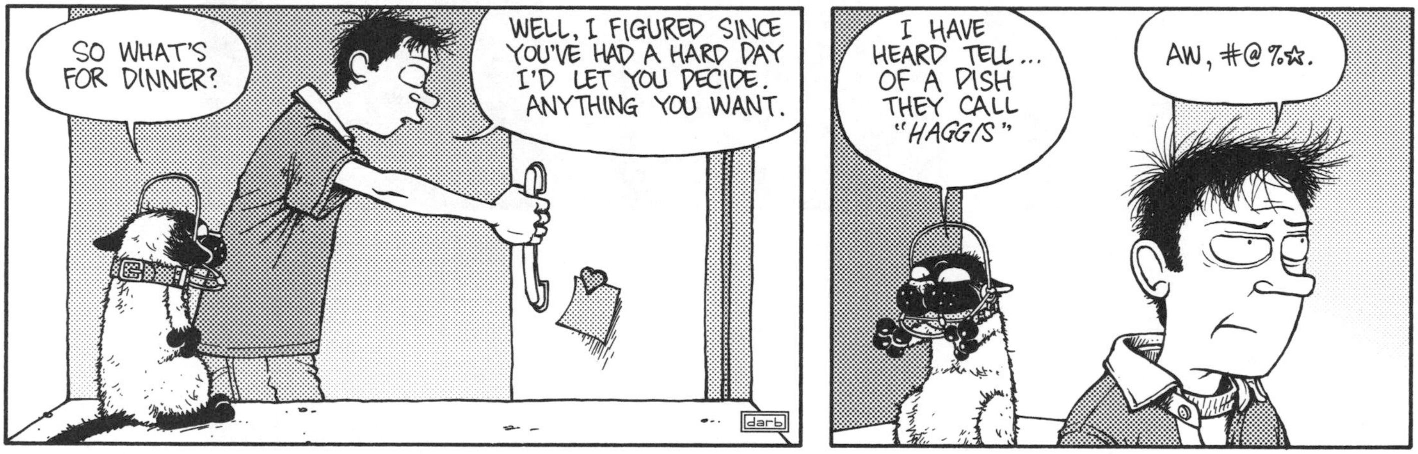
SO WHAT'S FOR DINNER?
WELL, I FIGURED SINCE YOU'VE HAD A HARD DAY I'D LET YOU DECIDE. ANYTHING YOU WANT.
I HAVE HEARD TELL... OF A DISH THEY CALL "HAGGIS"
AW, #@%☆.
darb

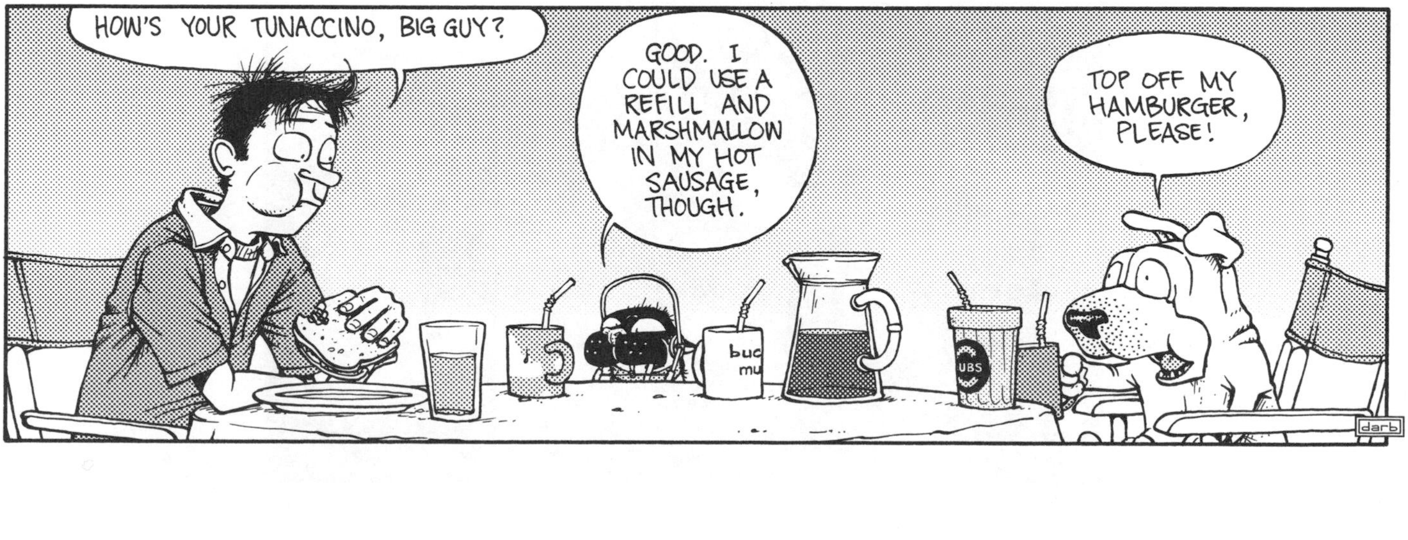
HOW'S YOUR TUNACCINO, BIG GUY?
GOOD. I COULD USE A REFILL AND MARSHMALLOW IN MY HOT SAUSAGE, THOUGH.
TOP OFF MY HAMBURGER, PLEASE!
darb

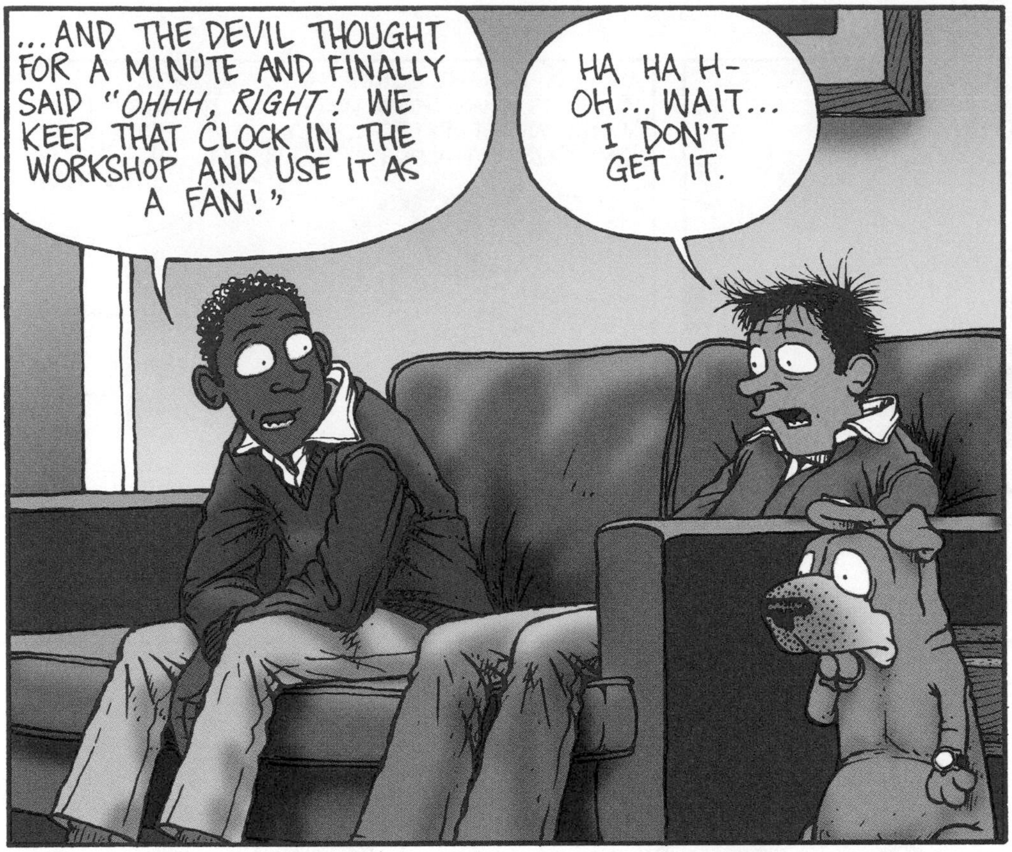
...AND THE DEVIL THOUGHT FOR A MINUTE AND FINALLY SAID "OHHH, RIGHT! WE KEEP THAT CLOCK IN THE WORKSHOP AND USE IT AS A FAN!"
HA HA H- OH... WAIT... I DON'T GET IT.

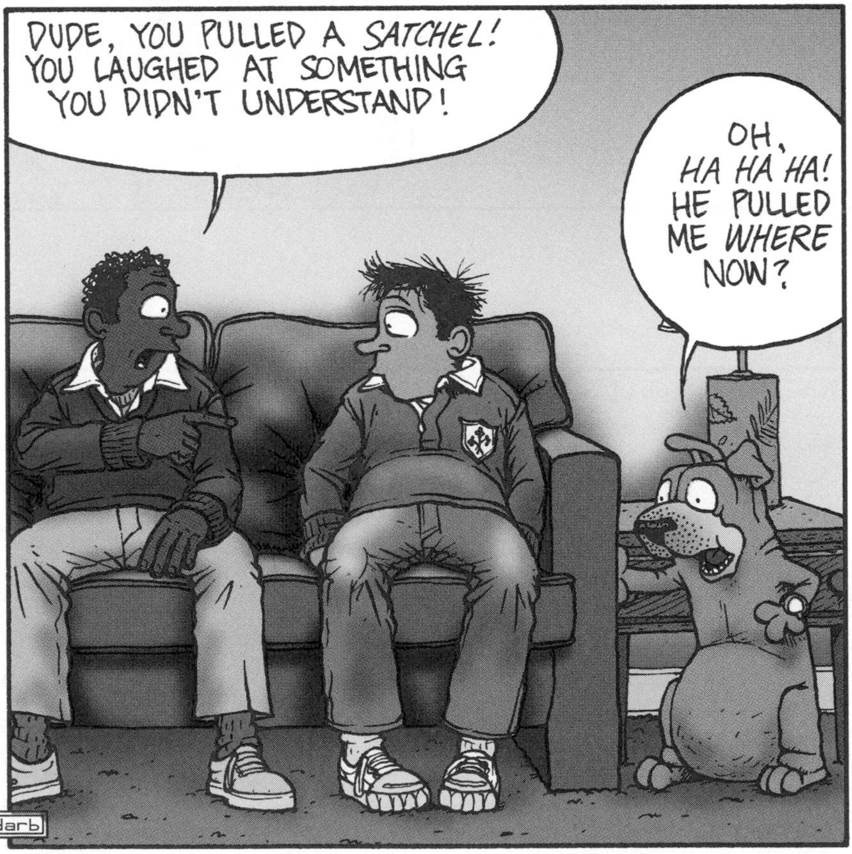
DUDE, YOU PULLED A SATCHEL! YOU LAUGHED AT SOMETHING YOU DIDN'T UNDERSTAND!
OH, HA HA HA! HE PULLED ME WHERE NOW?
darb

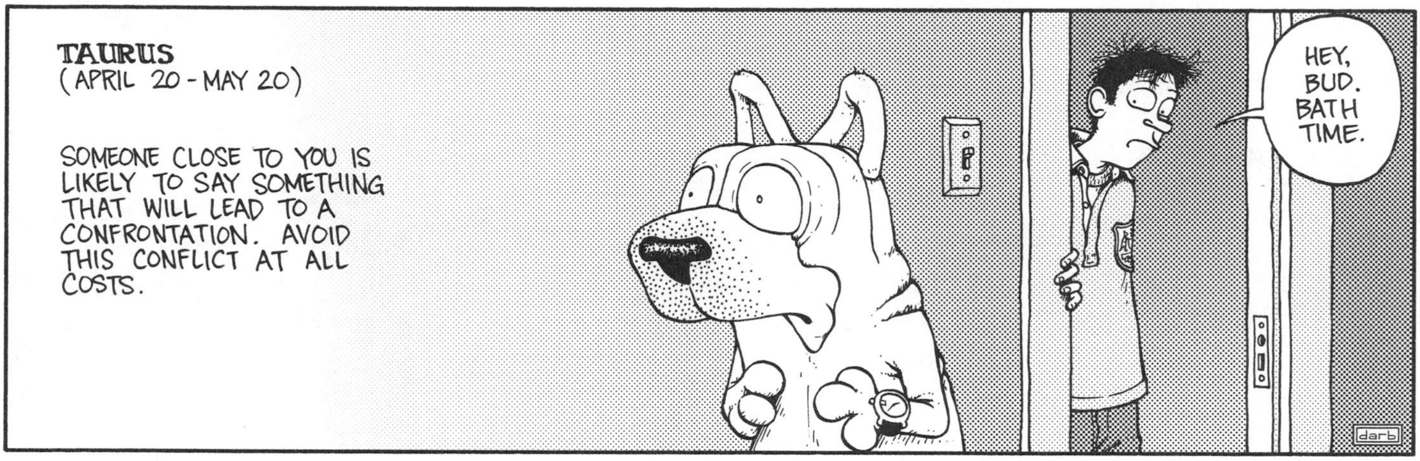
TAURUS
(APRIL 20 - MAY 20)
SOMEONE CLOSE TO YOU IS LIKELY TO SAY SOMETHING THAT WILL LEAD TO A CONFRONTATION. AVOID THIS CONFLICT AT ALL COSTS.
HEY, BUD. BATH TIME.
darb

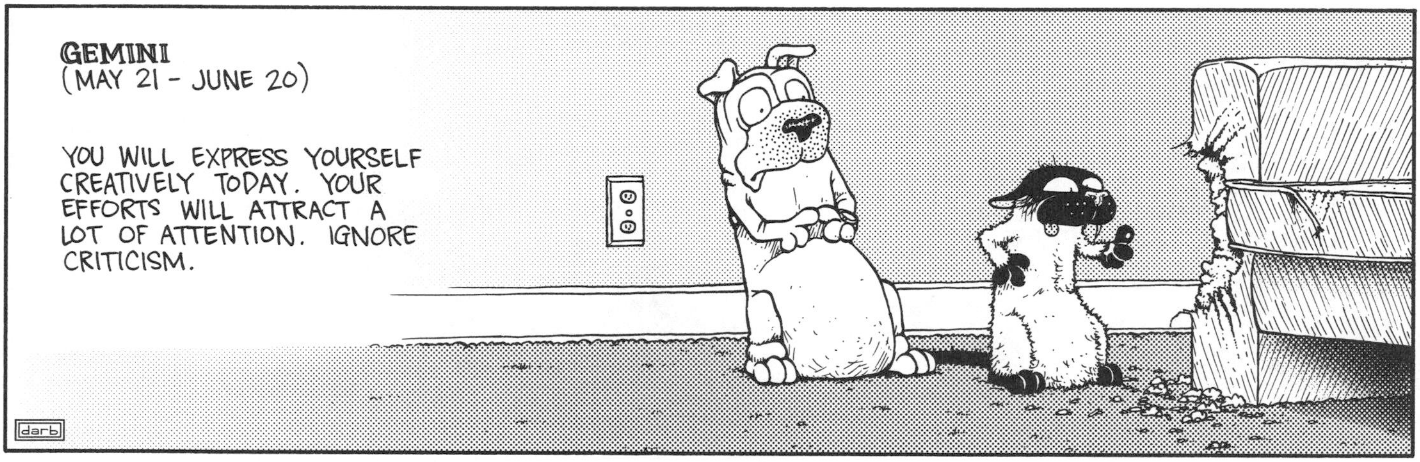
GEMINI
(MAY 21 - JUNE 20)
YOU WILL EXPRESS YOURSELF CREATIVELY TODAY. YOUR EFFORTS WILL ATTRACT A LOT OF ATTENTION. IGNORE CRITICISM.
darb

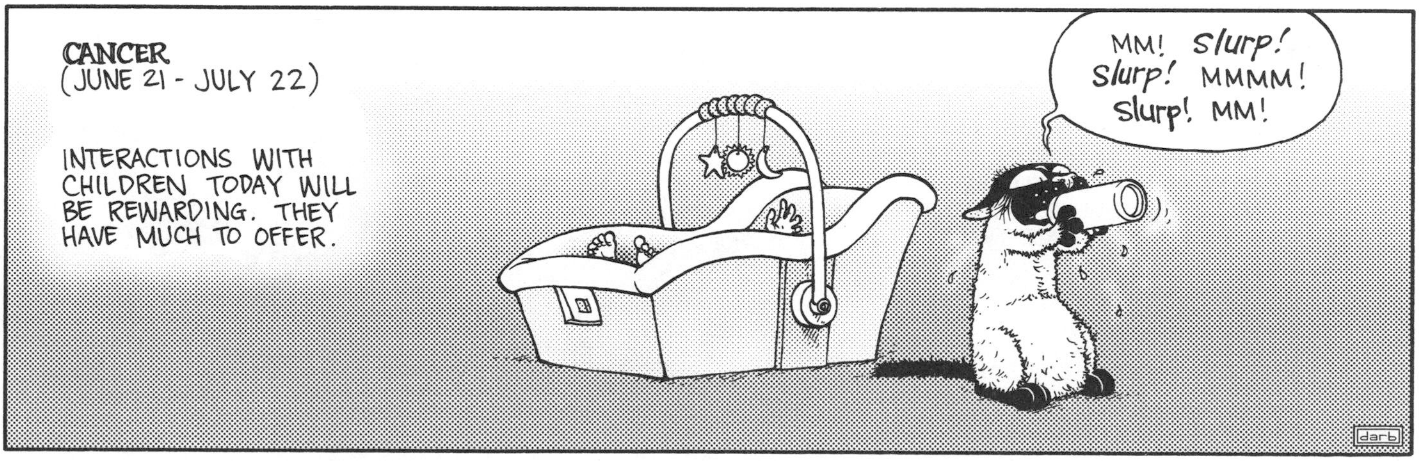
CANCER
(JUNE 21 - JULY 22)
INTERACTIONS WITH CHILDREN TODAY WILL BE REWARDING. THEY HAVE MUCH TO OFFER.
MM! slurp! slurp! MMMM! slurp! MM!
darb

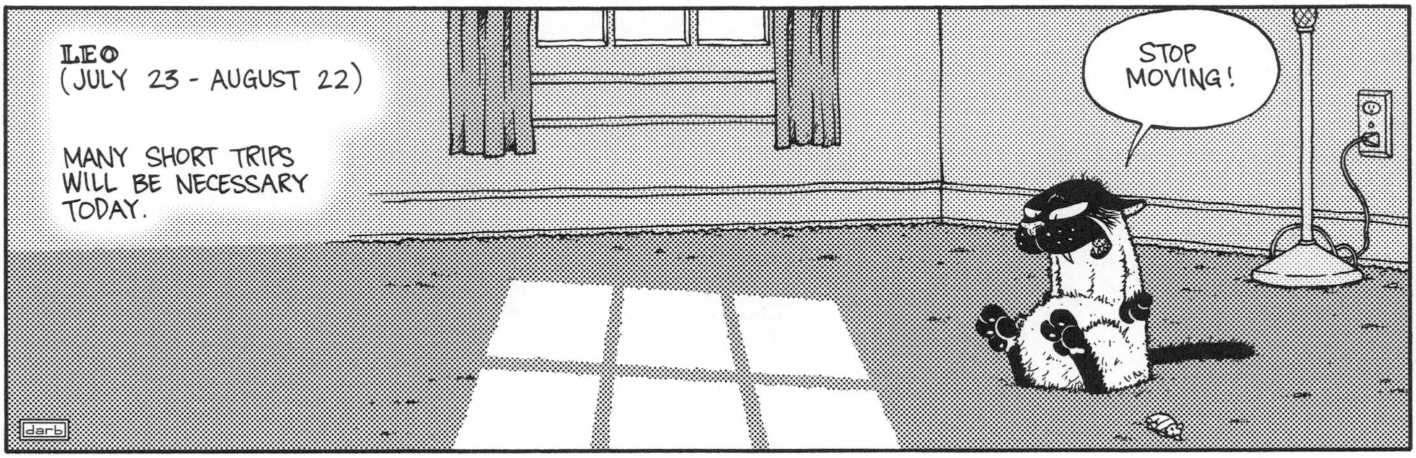
LEO
(JULY 23 - AUGUST 22)
MANY SHORT TRIPS WILL BE NECESSARY TODAY.
STOP MOVING!
darb

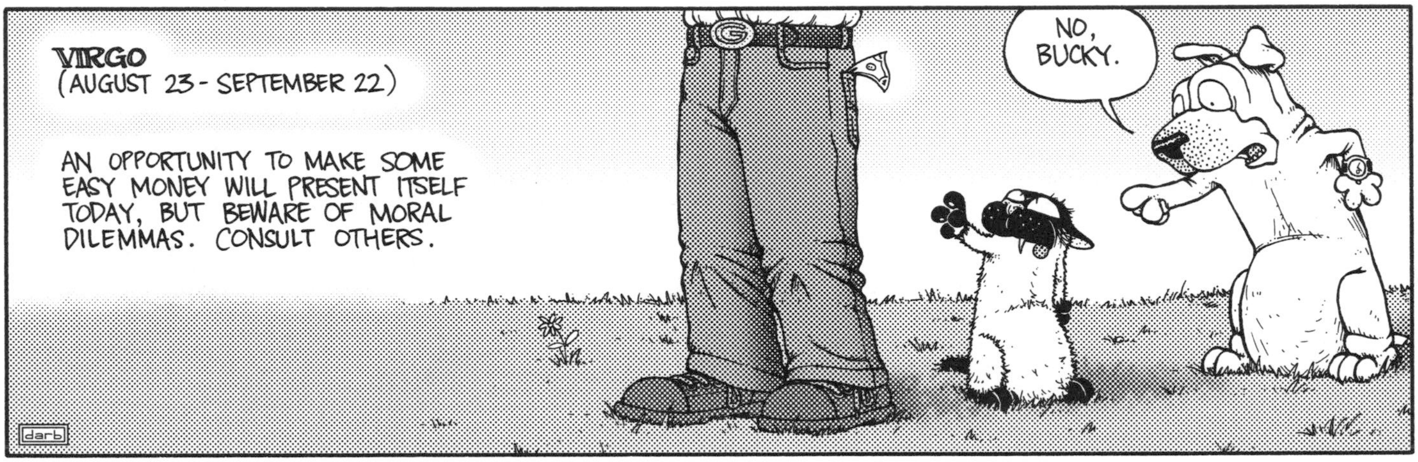
VIRGO
(AUGUST 23 - SEPTEMBER 22)
AN OPPORTUNITY TO MAKE SOME EASY MONEY WILL PRESENT ITSELF TODAY, BUT BEWARE OF MORAL DILEMMAS. CONSULT OTHERS.
NO, BUCKY.
darb

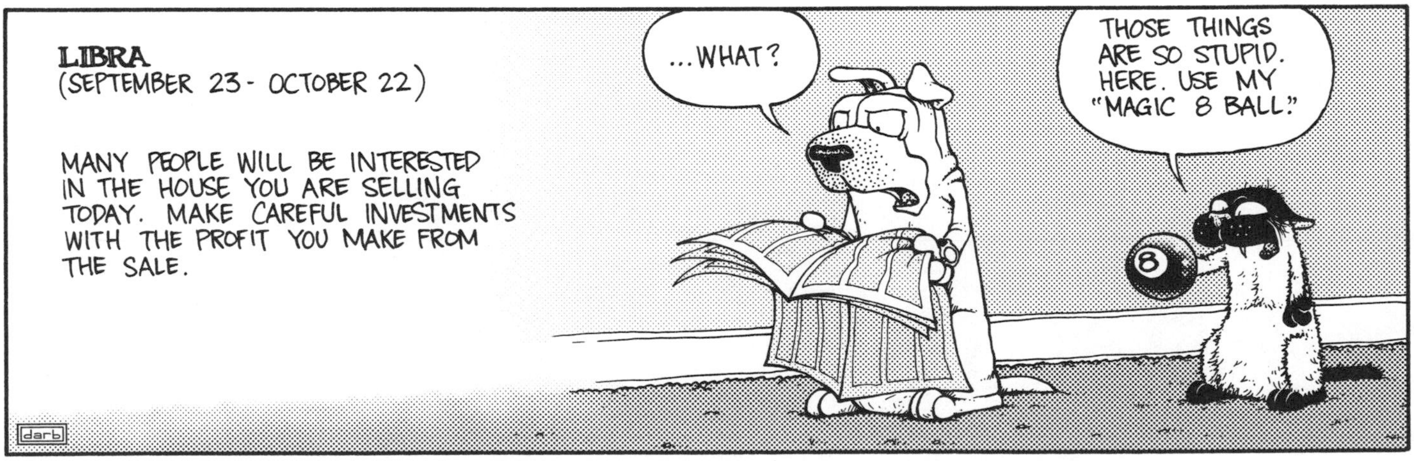
LIBRA
(SEPTEMBER 23 - OCTOBER 22)
MANY PEOPLE WILL BE INTERESTED IN THE HOUSE YOU ARE SELLING TODAY. MAKE CAREFUL INVESTMENTS WITH THE PROFIT YOU MAKE FROM THE SALE.
...WHAT?
THOSE THINGS ARE SO STUPID. HERE. USE MY "MAGIC 8 BALL."
darb

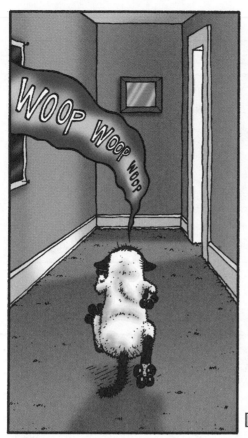

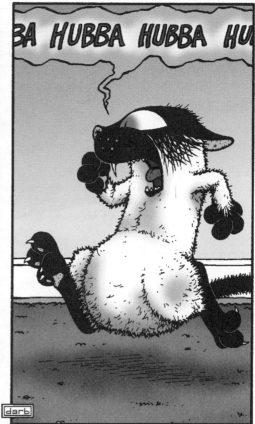

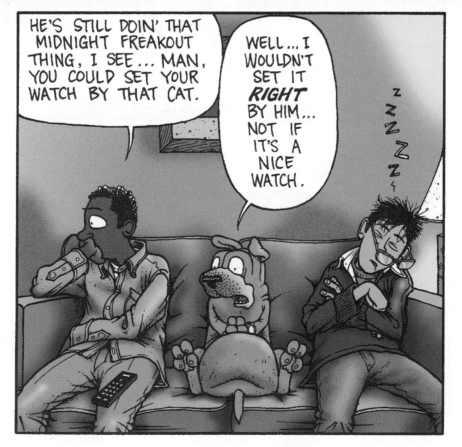

WOOP WOOP WOOP WOOP
BA HUBBA HUBBA HU
darb
HE'S STILL DOIN' THAT MIDNIGHT FREAKOUT THING, I SEE... MAN, YOU COULD SET YOUR WATCH BY THAT CAT.
WELL... I WOULDN'T SET IT RIGHT BY HIM... NOT IF IT'S A NICE WATCH.
Z Z Z Z Z

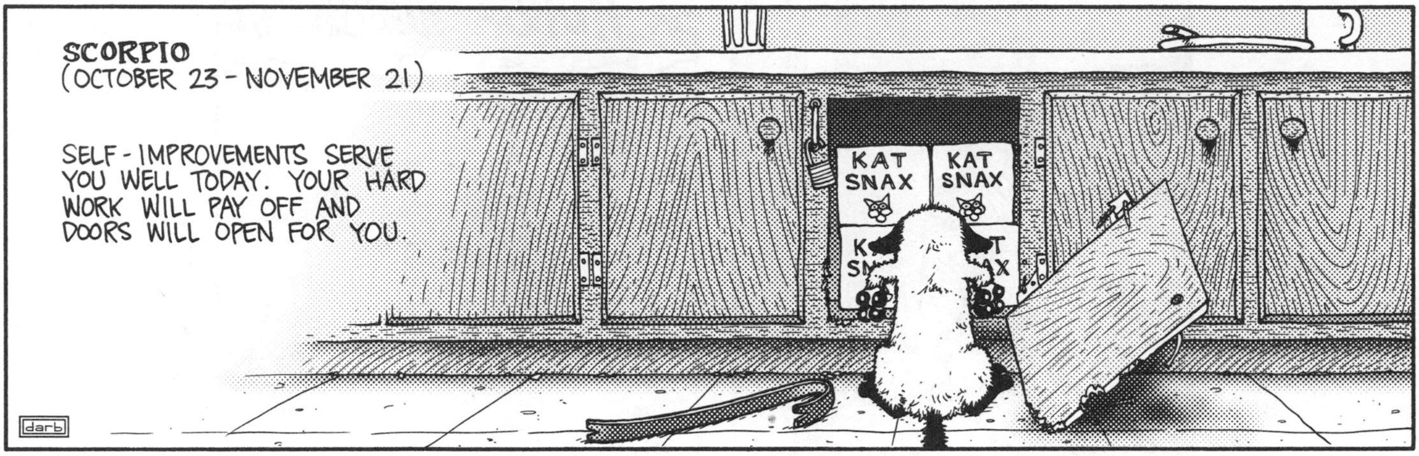
SCORPIO
(OCTOBER 23 - NOVEMBER 21)
SELF-IMPROVEMENTS SERVE YOU WELL TODAY. YOUR HARD WORK WILL PAY OFF AND DOORS WILL OPEN FOR YOU.
KAT SNAX
KAT SNAX
darb

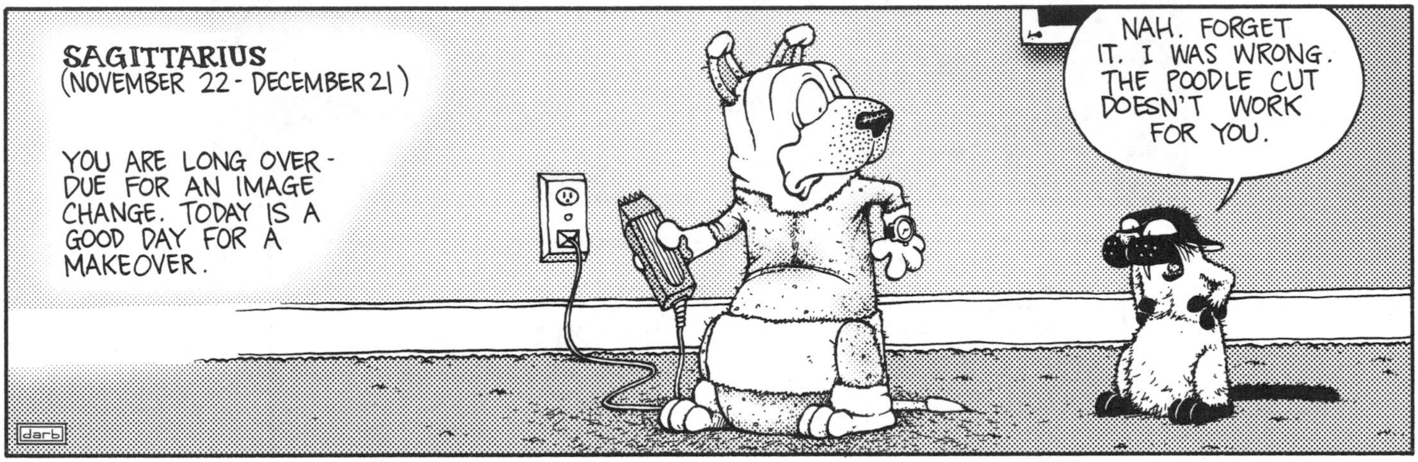
SAGITTARIUS
(NOVEMBER 22 - DECEMBER 21)
YOU ARE LONG OVER-DUE FOR AN IMAGE CHANGE. TODAY IS A GOOD DAY FOR A MAKEOVER.
NAH. FORGET IT. I WAS WRONG. THE POODLE CUT DOESN'T WORK FOR YOU.
darb

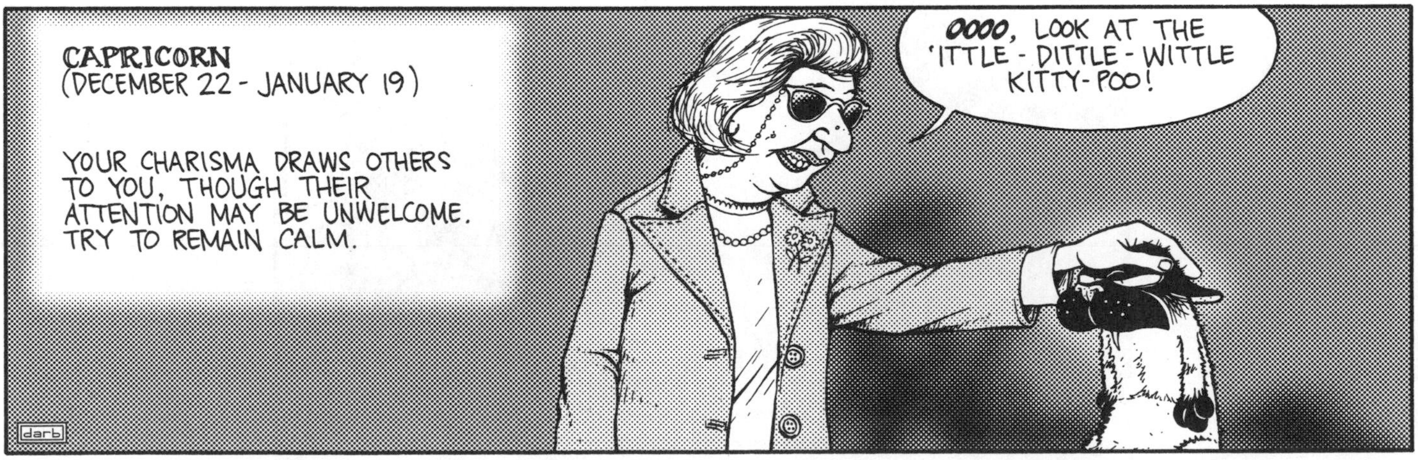
CAPRICORN
(DECEMBER 22 - JANUARY 19)
YOUR CHARISMA DRAWS OTHERS TO YOU, THOUGH THEIR ATTENTION MAY BE UNWELCOME. TRY TO REMAIN CALM.
OOOO, LOOK AT THE 'ITTLE-DITTLE-WITTLE KITTY-POO!
darb

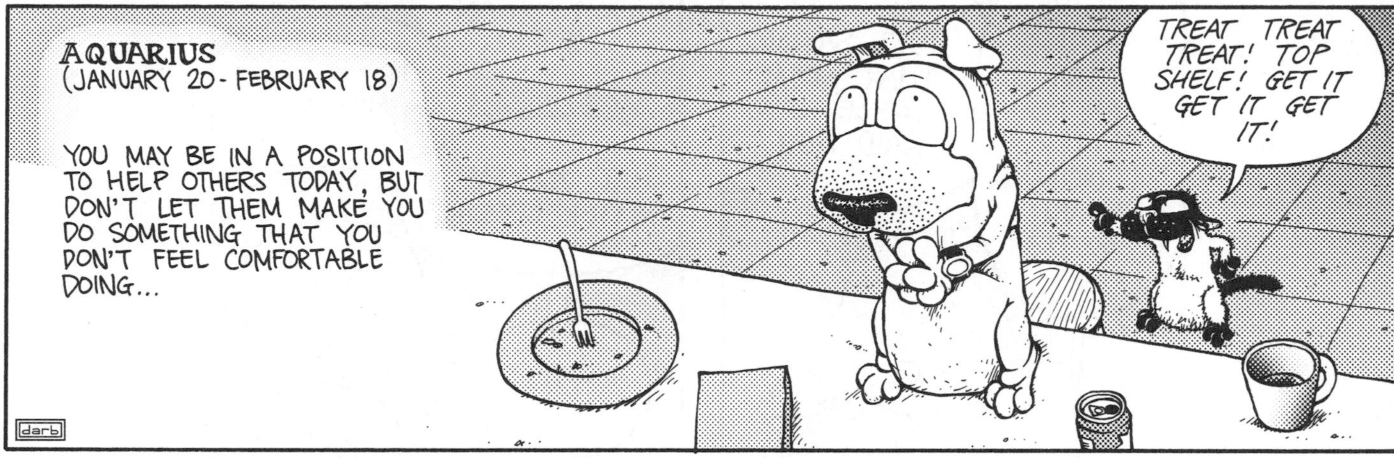
AQUARIUS
(JANUARY 20 - FEBRUARY 18)
YOU MAY BE IN A POSITION TO HELP OTHERS TODAY, BUT DON'T LET THEM MAKE YOU DO SOMETHING THAT YOU DON'T FEEL COMFORTABLE DOING...
TREAT TREAT TREAT! TOP SHELF! GET IT GET IT GET IT!
darb

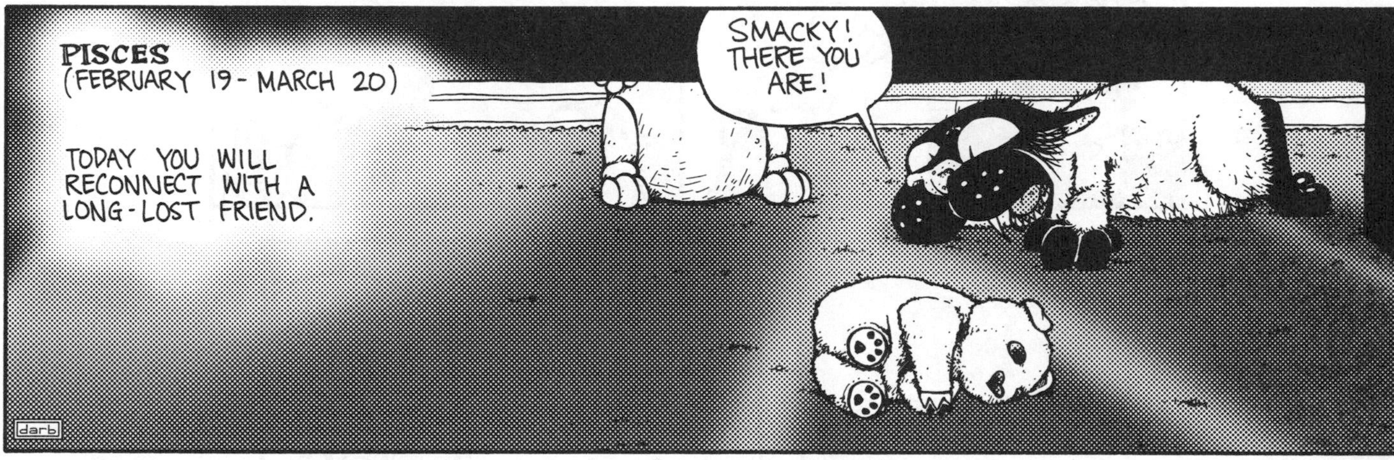
PISCES
(FEBRUARY 19 - MARCH 20)
TODAY YOU WILL RECONNECT WITH A LONG-LOST FRIEND.
SMACKY! THERE YOU ARE!
darb

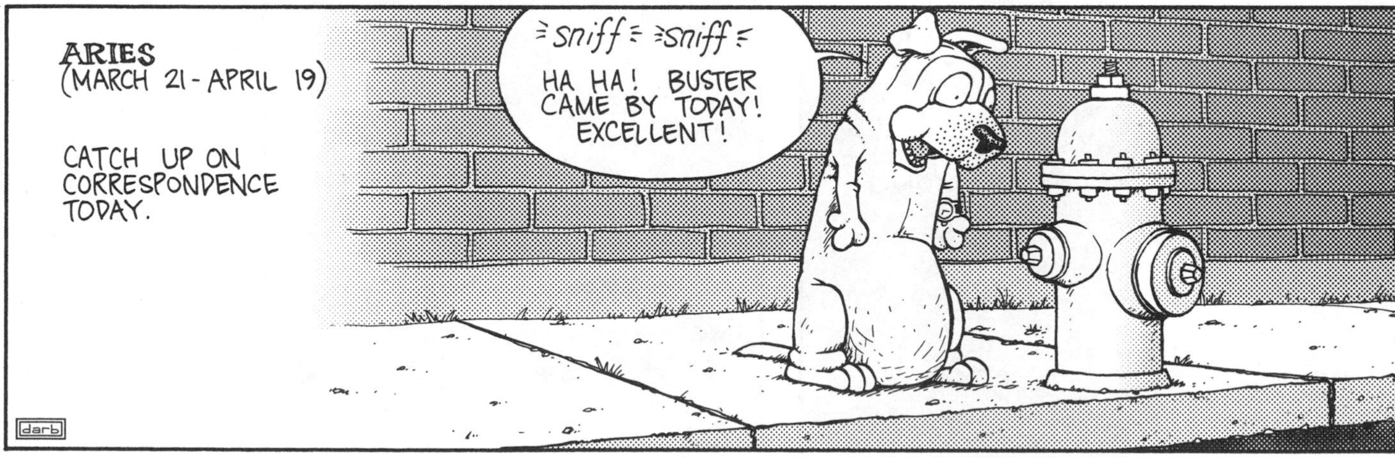
ARIES
(MARCH 21 - APRIL 19)
CATCH UP ON CORRESPONDENCE TODAY.
sniff sniff
HA HA! BUSTER CAME BY TODAY! EXCELLENT!
darb

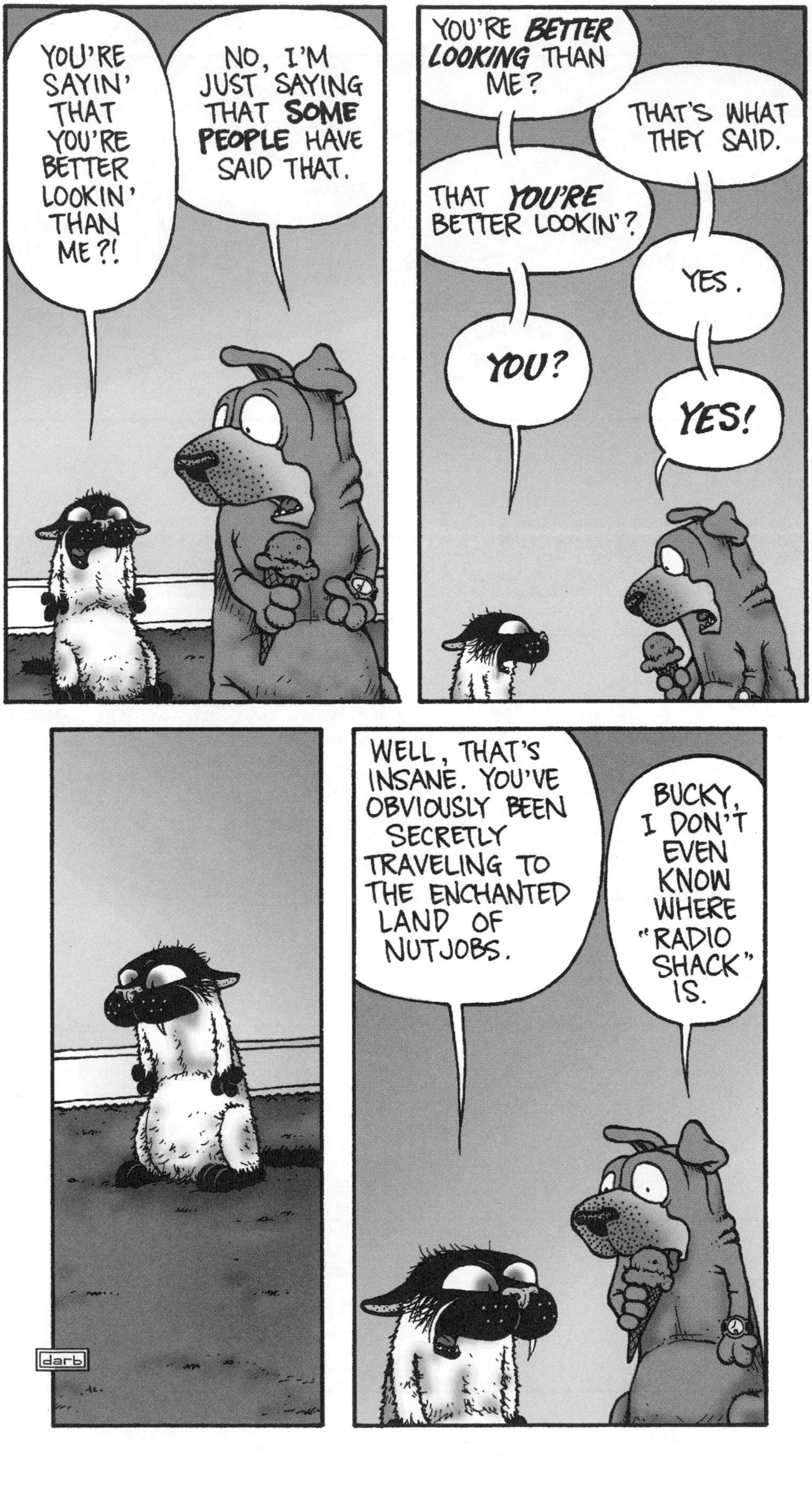
YOU'RE SAYIN' THAT YOU'RE BETTER LOOKIN' THAN ME?!
NO, I'M JUST SAYING THAT **SOME PEOPLE** HAVE SAID THAT.
YOU'RE ***BETTER LOOKING*** THAN ME?
THAT'S WHAT THEY SAID.
THAT ***YOU'RE*** BETTER LOOKIN'?
YES.
YOU?
YES!
darb
WELL, THAT'S INSANE. YOU'VE OBVIOUSLY BEEN SECRETLY TRAVELING TO THE ENCHANTED LAND OF NUTJOBS.
BUCKY, I DON'T EVEN KNOW WHERE "RADIO SHACK" IS.

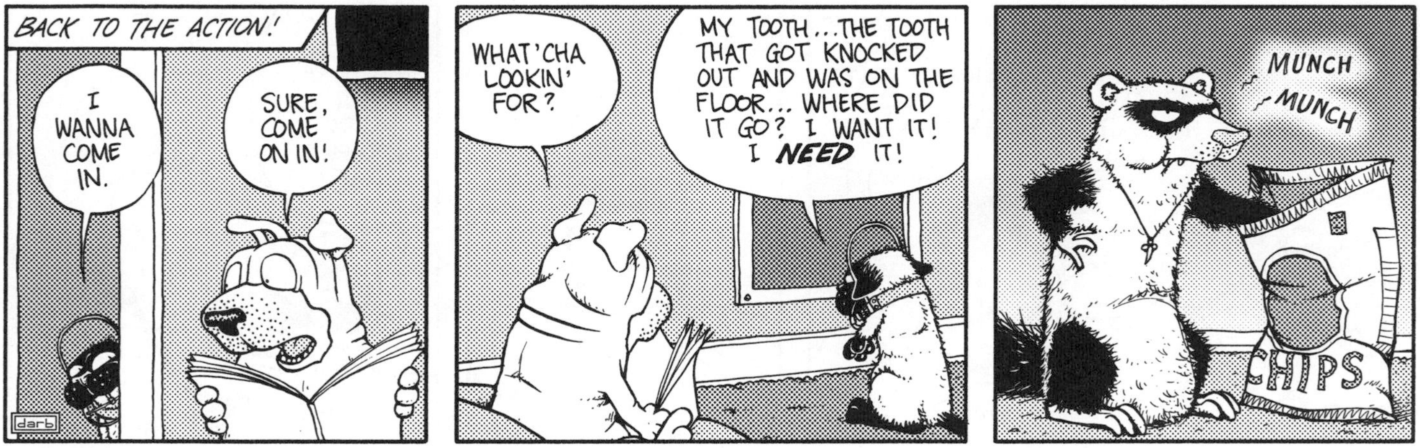
BACK TO THE ACTION!
I WANNA COME IN.
SURE, COME ON IN!
WHAT'CHA LOOKIN' FOR?
MY TOOTH... THE TOOTH THAT GOT KNOCKED OUT AND WAS ON THE FLOOR... WHERE DID IT GO? I WANT IT! I NEED IT!
MUNCH
MUNCH
CHIPS

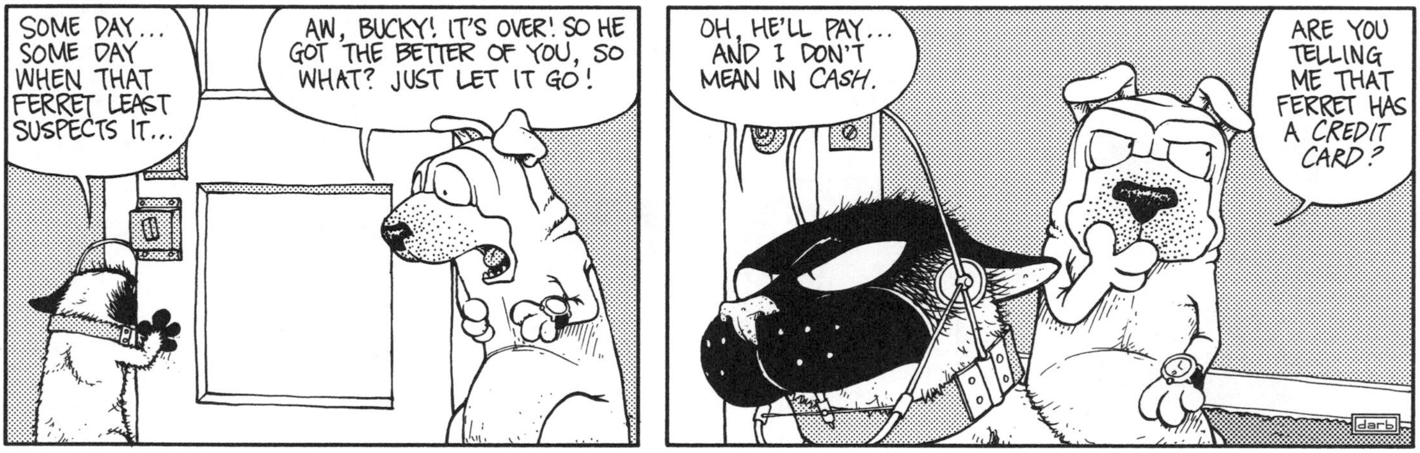
SOME DAY... SOME DAY WHEN THAT FERRET LEAST SUSPECTS IT...
AW, BUCKY! IT'S OVER! SO HE GOT THE BETTER OF YOU, SO WHAT? JUST LET IT GO!
OH, HE'LL PAY... AND I DON'T MEAN IN CASH.
ARE YOU TELLING ME THAT FERRET HAS A CREDIT CARD?

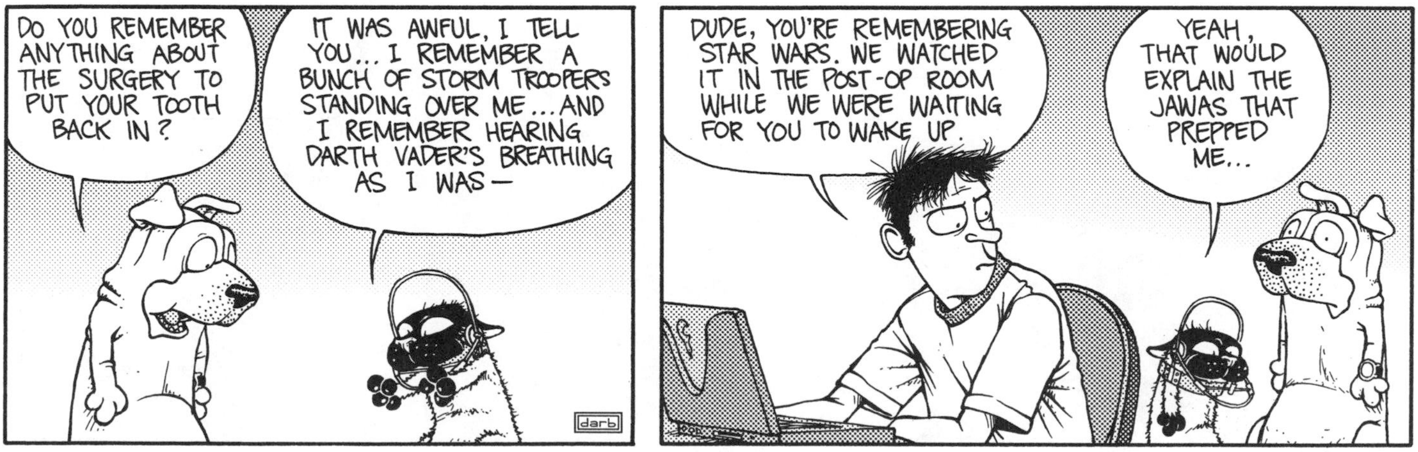
DO YOU REMEMBER ANYTHING ABOUT THE SURGERY TO PUT YOUR TOOTH BACK IN?
IT WAS AWFUL, I TELL YOU... I REMEMBER A BUNCH OF STORM TROOPERS STANDING OVER ME... AND I REMEMBER HEARING DARTH VADER'S BREATHING AS I WAS—
DUDE, YOU'RE REMEMBERING STAR WARS. WE WATCHED IT IN THE POST-OP ROOM WHILE WE WERE WAITING FOR YOU TO WAKE UP.
YEAH, THAT WOULD EXPLAIN THE JAWAS THAT PREPPED ME...

I HAVE SOME PURCHASES TO MAKE. I WAS WONDERING IF I COULD HAVE MY ALLOWANCE.
ALLOWANCE?! YOU KNOCKED YOUR TOOTH OUT TRYING TO SNARE THE NEIGHBOR'S PET AND IT COST ME $525 TO PUT IT BACK IN YOUR HEAD.
DOES MY POSITION OF HOUSE CAT ENTITLE ME TO WORKER'S COMP?
NO.

SO HOW DID HE GET HURT TO BEGIN WITH?
HE WAS TRYING TO TRAP A FERRET.
I WISH I'D SEEN HIM WITHOUT THE FANG...THAT WOULD HAVE LOOKED SO WEIRD...
YEAH, IT DID.
I MEAN, WITHOUT THAT FANG, HE'S LIKE AN UPSIDE-DOWN WEDGE-BOT ON BATTLEBOTS... HE'S GOT NOTHIN'...
GOOD ANALOGY, DUDE.
LOWE TECH
LOWE

AHHH, THE TOP OF THE TELEVISION... TO BOLDLY GO WHERE NO CAT HAS GONE BEFORE...
WHAT WITH BUCKY'S HEAD-GEAR, SATCHEL'S OVERACTING, AND ALL THE INTERSPECIES TENSION, IT'S BEEN LIKE A STAR TREK EPISODE AROUND HERE.
LOWE TECH
I GUESS I SHOULD GET OUTTA HERE, THEN, EH? HA HA!
MY BUG... IT'S DEAD, JOE...

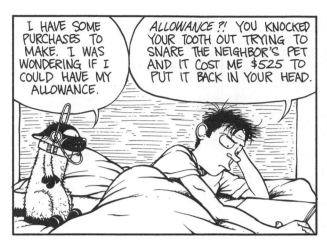

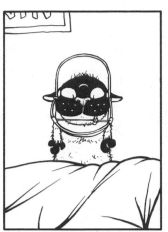

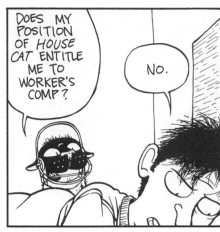

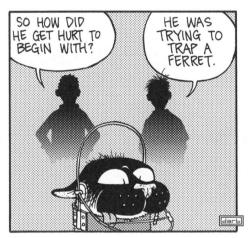

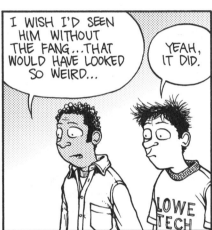

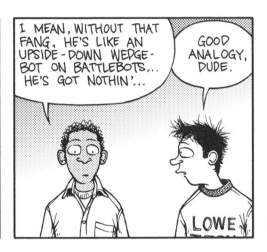

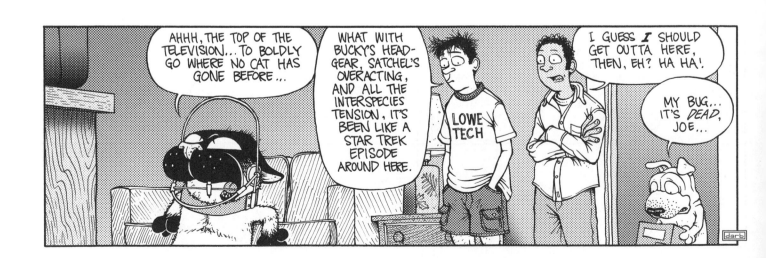

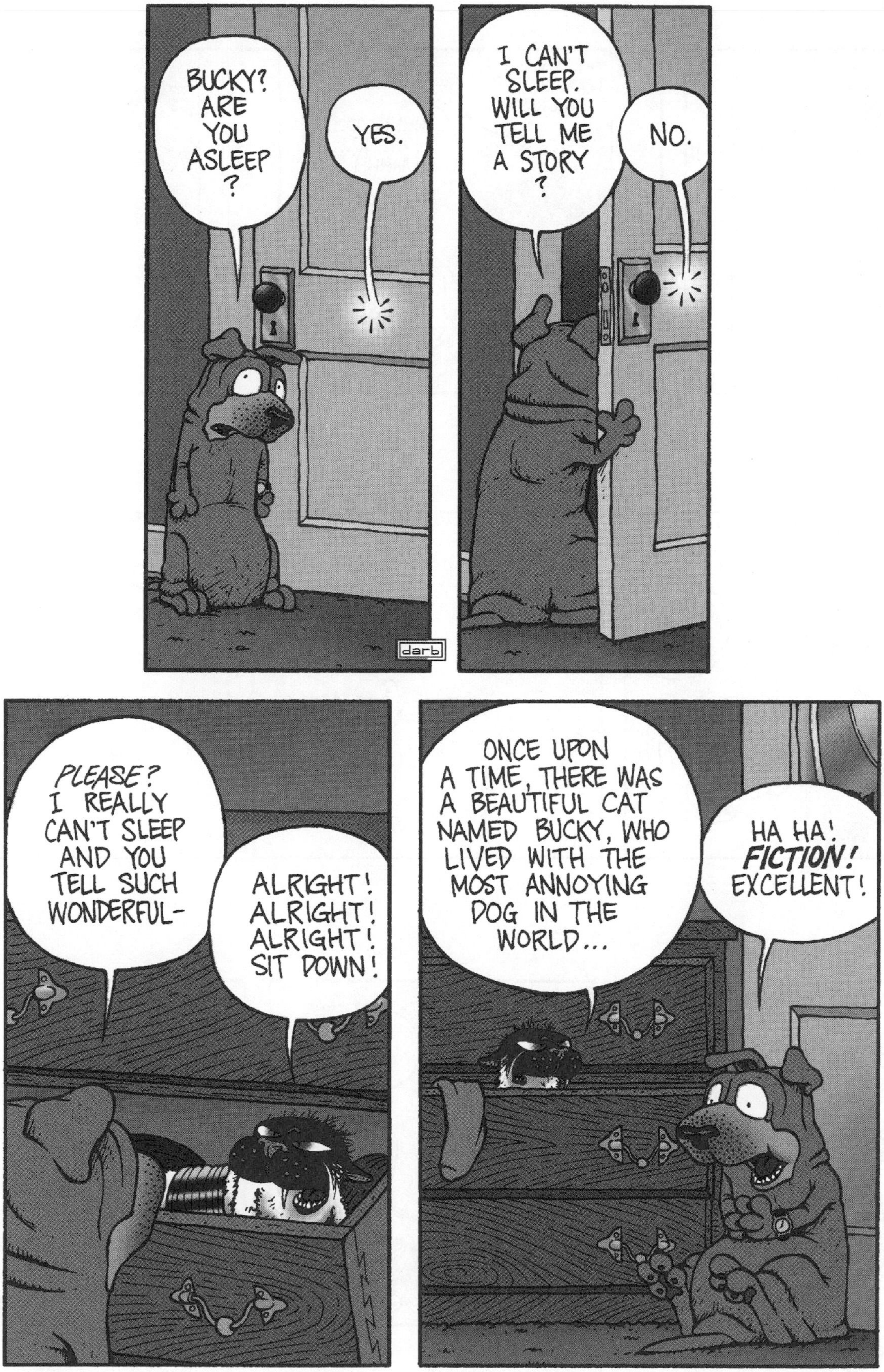
BUCKY? ARE YOU ASLEEP ?
YES.
I CAN'T SLEEP. WILL YOU TELL ME A STORY ?
NO.
darb
PLEASE? I REALLY CAN'T SLEEP AND YOU TELL SUCH WONDERFUL-
ALRIGHT! ALRIGHT! ALRIGHT! SIT DOWN!
ONCE UPON A TIME, THERE WAS A BEAUTIFUL CAT NAMED BUCKY, WHO LIVED WITH THE MOST ANNOYING DOG IN THE WORLD...
HA HA! **FICTION!** EXCELLENT!

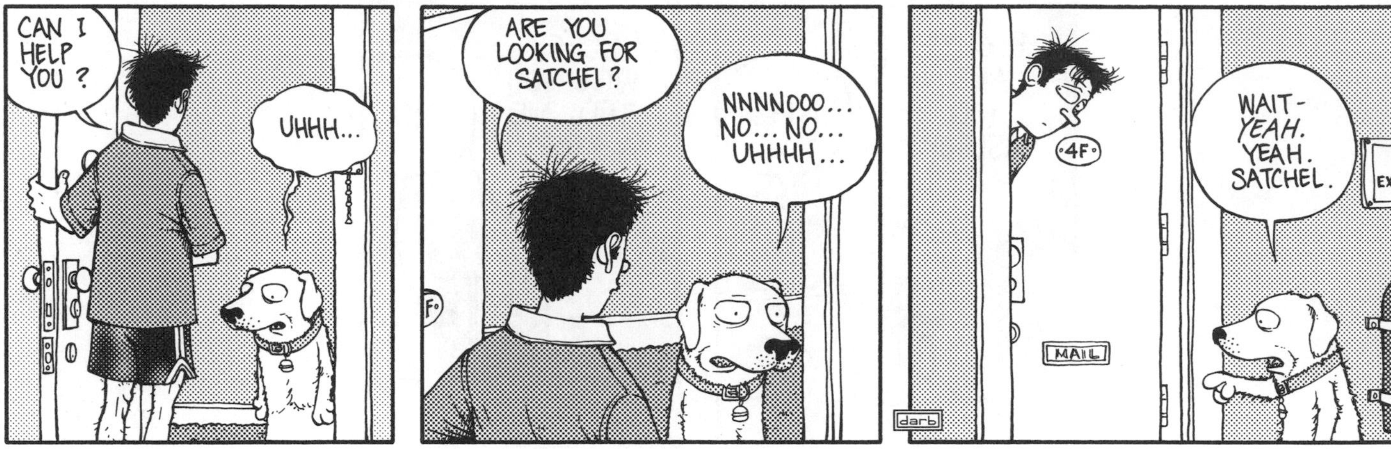
CAN I HELP YOU ?
UHHH...
ARE YOU LOOKING FOR SATCHEL ?
NNNNOOO... NO... NO... UHHHH...
4F
MAIL
WAIT- *YEAH*. YEAH. SATCHEL.
darb

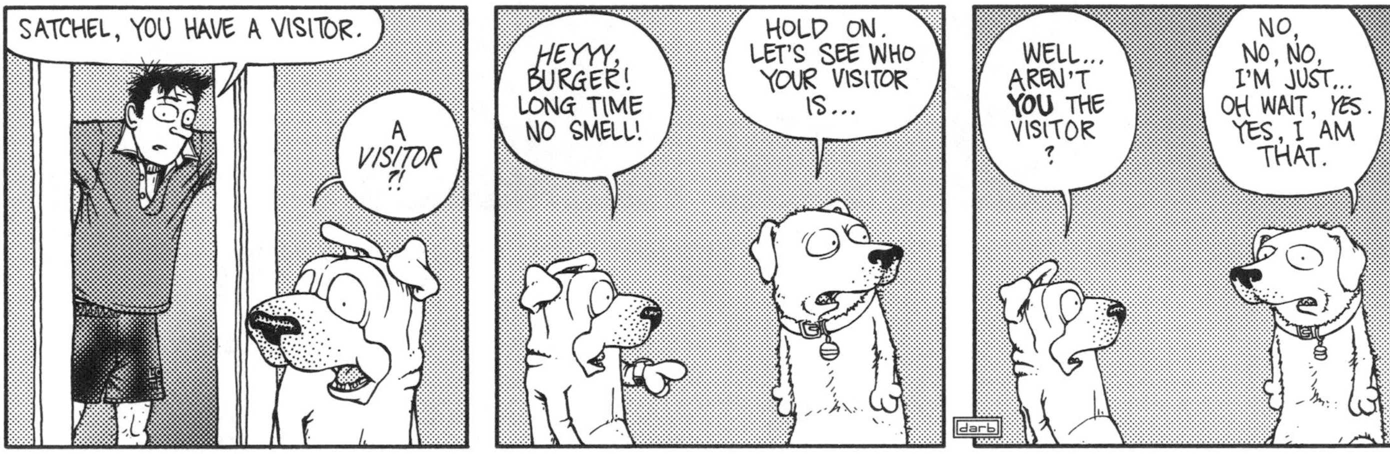
SATCHEL, YOU HAVE A VISITOR.
A *VISITOR* ?!
HEYYY, BURGER! LONG TIME NO SMELL!
HOLD ON. LET'S SEE WHO YOUR VISITOR IS...
WELL... AREN'T **YOU** THE VISITOR ?
NO, NO, NO, I'M JUST... OH WAIT, *YES*. YES, I AM THAT.
darb

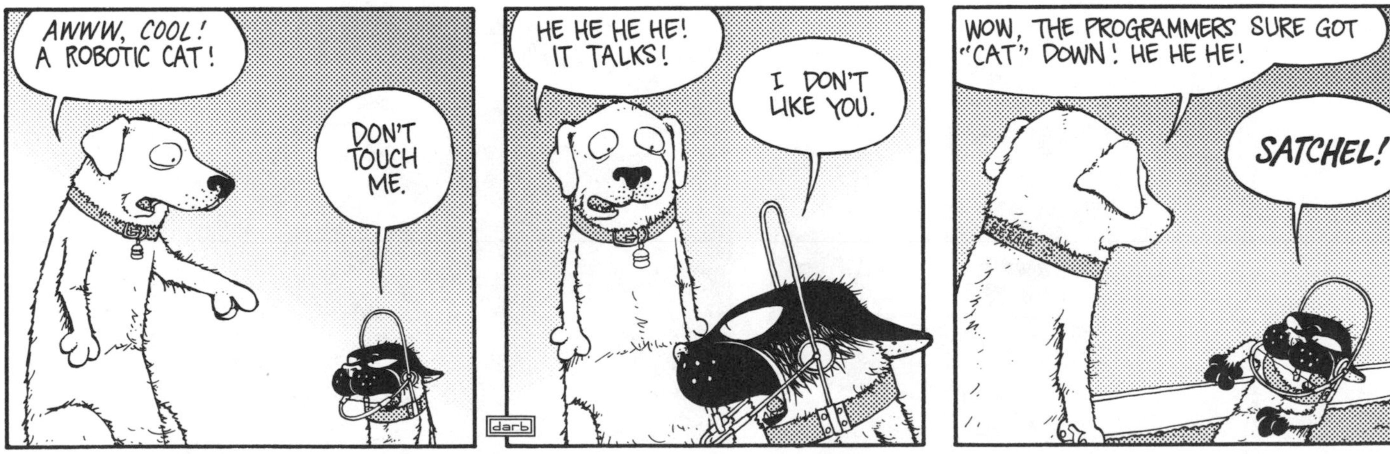
AWWW, COOL! A ROBOTIC CAT!
DON'T TOUCH ME.
HE HE HE HE! IT TALKS!
I DON'T LIKE YOU.
WOW, THE PROGRAMMERS SURE GOT "CAT" DOWN! HE HE HE!
SATCHEL!
darb

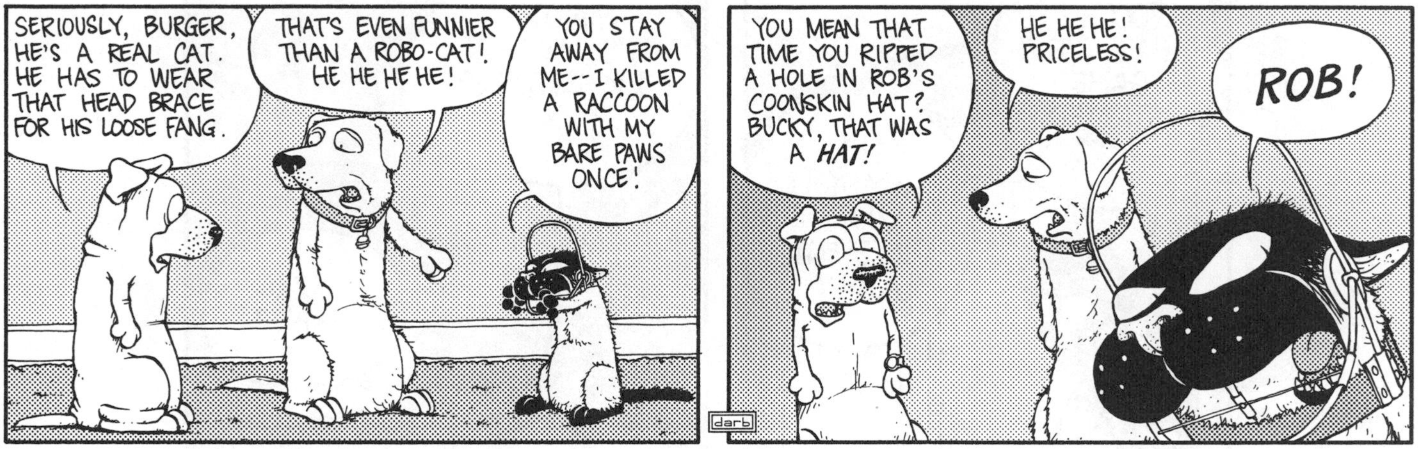
SERIOUSLY, BURGER, HE'S A REAL CAT. HE HAS TO WEAR THAT HEAD BRACE FOR HIS LOOSE FANG.
THAT'S EVEN FUNNIER THAN A ROBO-CAT! HE HE HE HE!
YOU STAY AWAY FROM ME--I KILLED A RACCOON WITH MY BARE PAWS ONCE!
YOU MEAN THAT TIME YOU RIPPED A HOLE IN ROB'S COONSKIN HAT? BUCKY, THAT WAS A *HAT!*
HE HE HE! PRICELESS!
ROB!
darb

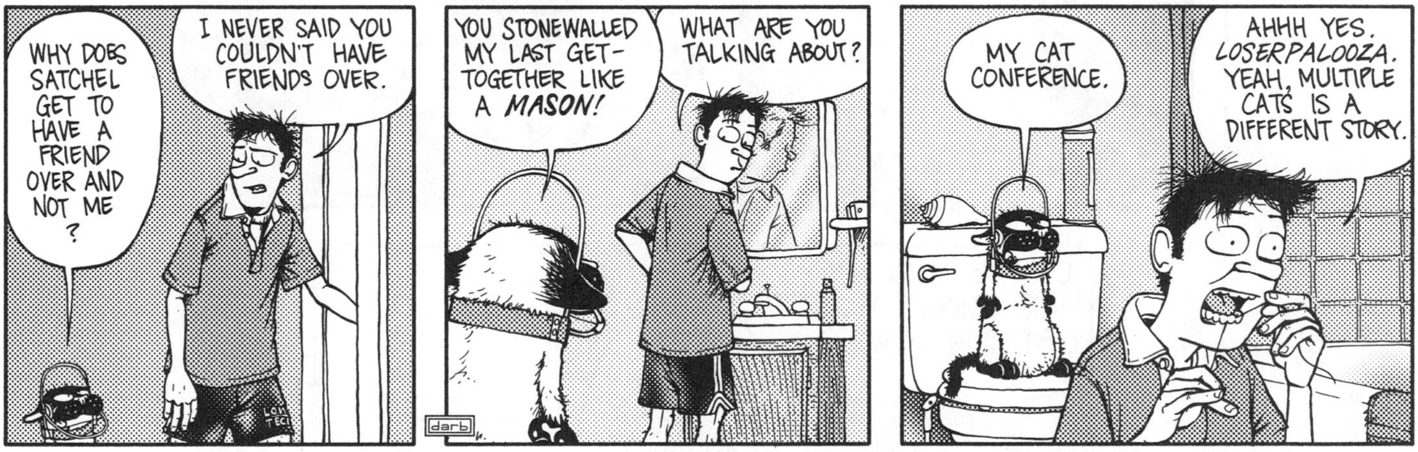
WHY DOES SATCHEL GET TO HAVE A FRIEND OVER AND NOT ME?
I NEVER SAID YOU COULDN'T HAVE FRIENDS OVER.
YOU STONEWALLED MY LAST GET-TOGETHER LIKE A *MASON!*
WHAT ARE YOU TALKING ABOUT?
MY CAT CONFERENCE.
AHHH YES. *LOSERPALOOZA.* YEAH, MULTIPLE CATS IS A DIFFERENT STORY.
darb

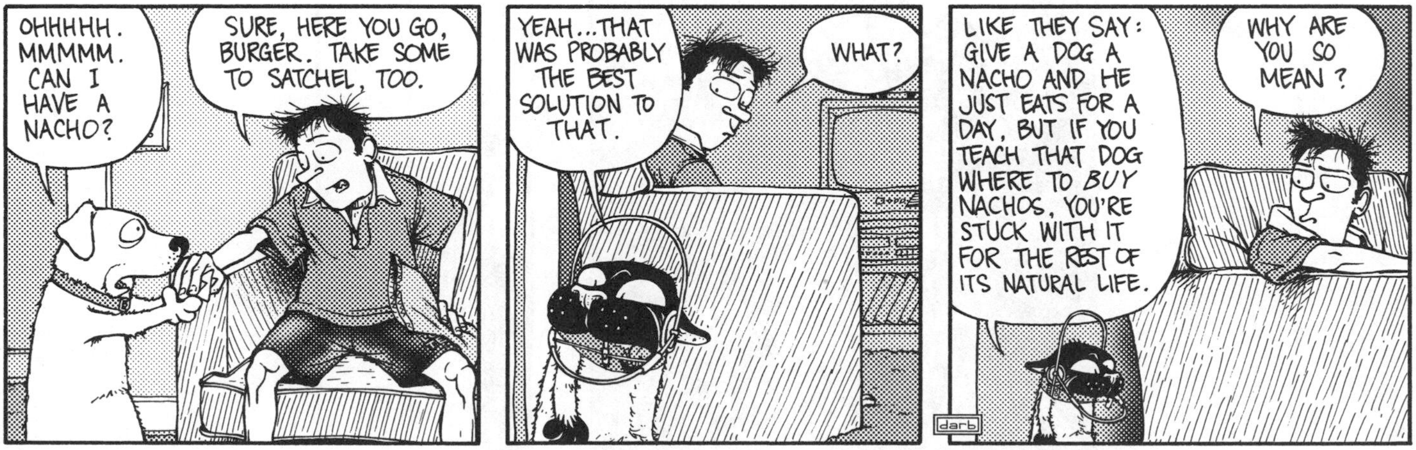
OHHHHH. MMMMM. CAN I HAVE A NACHO?
SURE, HERE YOU GO, BURGER. TAKE SOME TO SATCHEL, TOO.
YEAH...THAT WAS PROBABLY THE BEST SOLUTION TO THAT.
WHAT?
LIKE THEY SAY: GIVE A DOG A NACHO AND HE JUST EATS FOR A DAY, BUT IF YOU TEACH THAT DOG WHERE TO *BUY* NACHOS, YOU'RE STUCK WITH IT FOR THE REST OF ITS NATURAL LIFE.
WHY ARE YOU SO MEAN?
darb

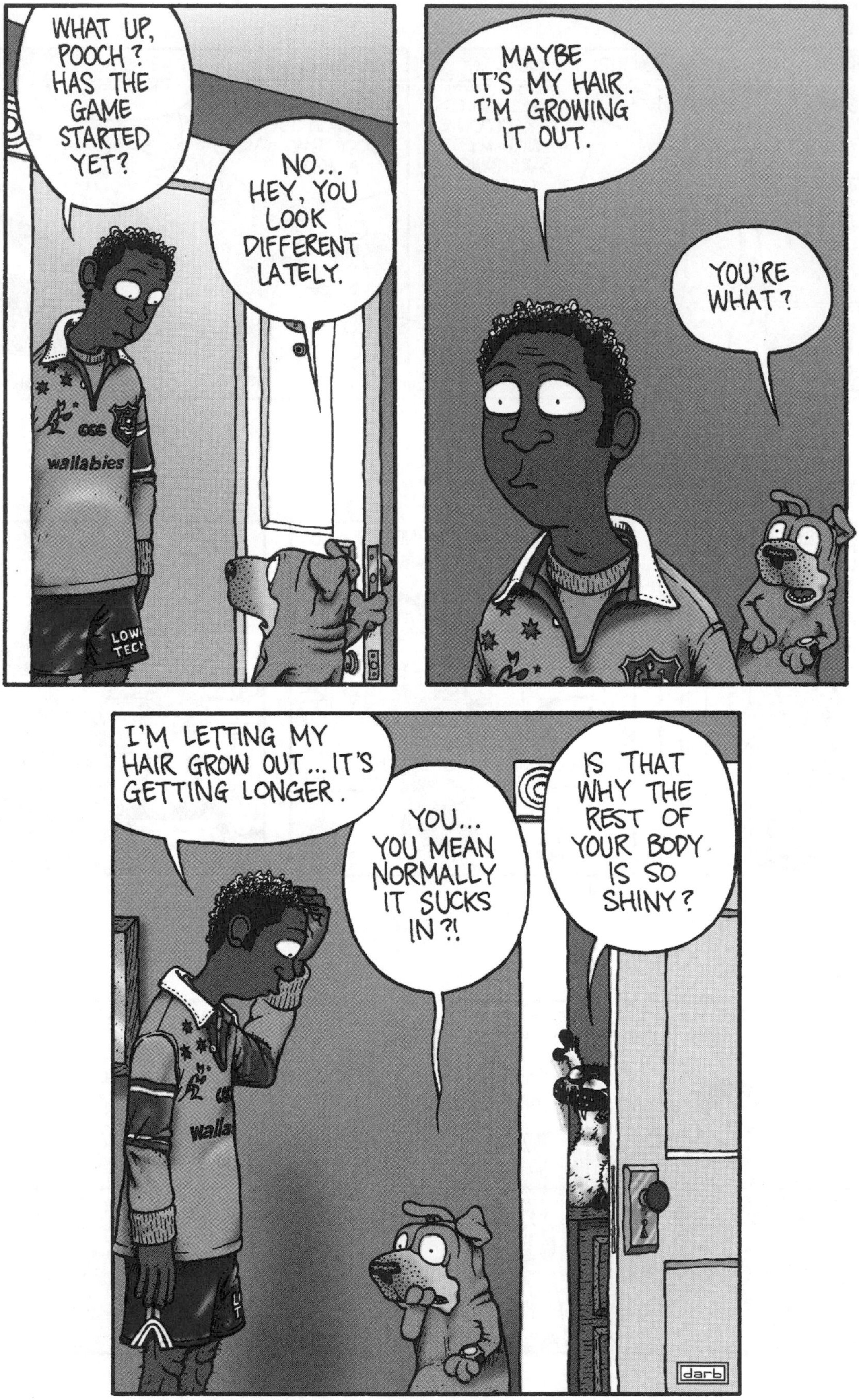
WHAT UP, POOCH? HAS THE GAME STARTED YET?
NO... HEY, YOU LOOK DIFFERENT LATELY.
wallabies
LOW TECH
MAYBE IT'S MY HAIR. I'M GROWING IT OUT.
YOU'RE WHAT?
I'M LETTING MY HAIR GROW OUT... IT'S GETTING LONGER.
YOU... YOU MEAN NORMALLY IT SUCKS IN?!
IS THAT WHY THE REST OF YOUR BODY IS SO SHINY?
darb

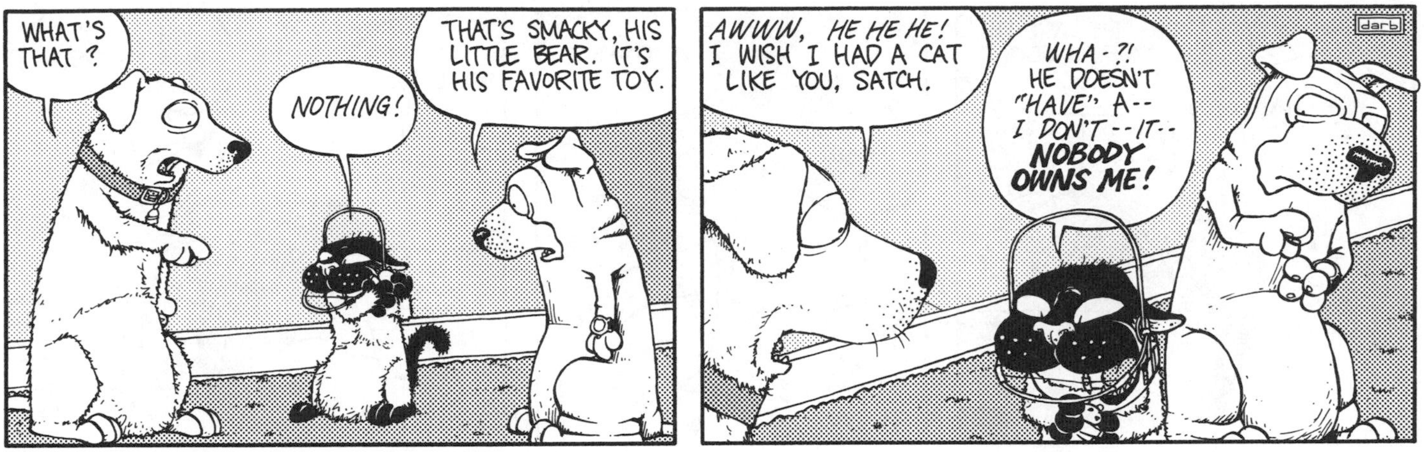
WHAT'S THAT ?
NOTHING!
THAT'S SMACKY, HIS LITTLE BEAR. IT'S HIS FAVORITE TOY.
darb
AWWW, HE HE HE! I WISH I HAD A CAT LIKE YOU, SATCH.
WHA-?! HE DOESN'T "HAVE" A-- I DON'T --IT-- NOBODY OWNS ME!

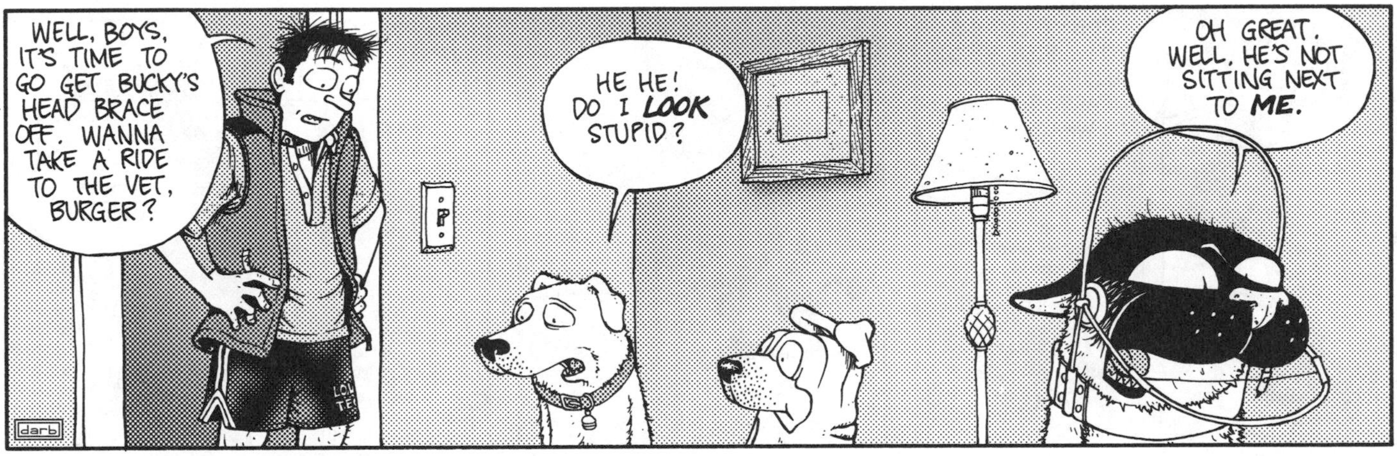
WELL, BOYS, IT'S TIME TO GO GET BUCKY'S HEAD BRACE OFF. WANNA TAKE A RIDE TO THE VET, BURGER?
HE HE! DO I LOOK STUPID?
OH GREAT. WELL, HE'S NOT SITTING NEXT TO ME.
darb

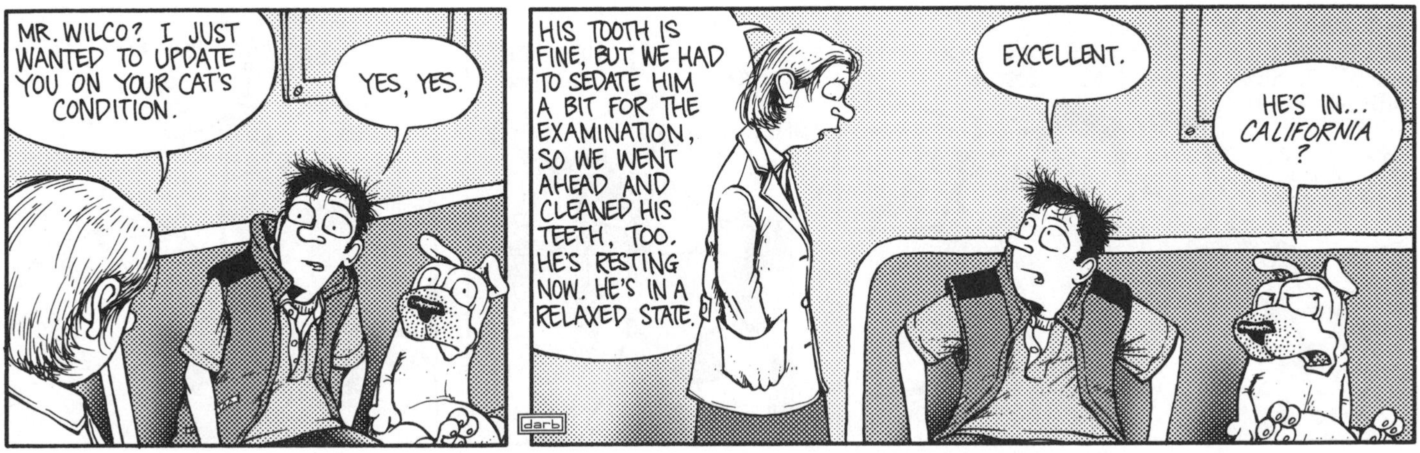
MR. WILCO? I JUST WANTED TO UPDATE YOU ON YOUR CAT'S CONDITION.
YES, YES.
darb
HIS TOOTH IS FINE, BUT WE HAD TO SEDATE HIM A BIT FOR THE EXAMINATION, SO WE WENT AHEAD AND CLEANED HIS TEETH, TOO. HE'S RESTING NOW. HE'S IN A RELAXED STATE.
EXCELLENT.
HE'S IN... CALIFORNIA?

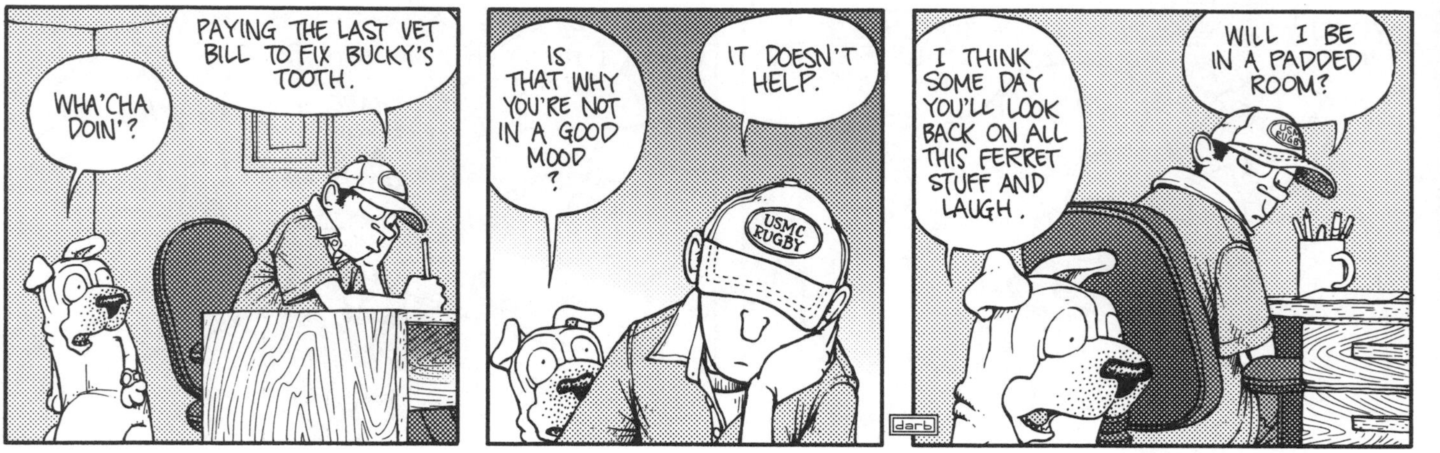
WHA'CHA DOIN'?
PAYING THE LAST VET BILL TO FIX BUCKY'S TOOTH.
IS THAT WHY YOU'RE NOT IN A GOOD MOOD?
IT DOESN'T HELP.
I THINK SOME DAY YOU'LL LOOK BACK ON ALL THIS FERRET STUFF AND LAUGH.
WILL I BE IN A PADDED ROOM?
USMC RUGBY
darb

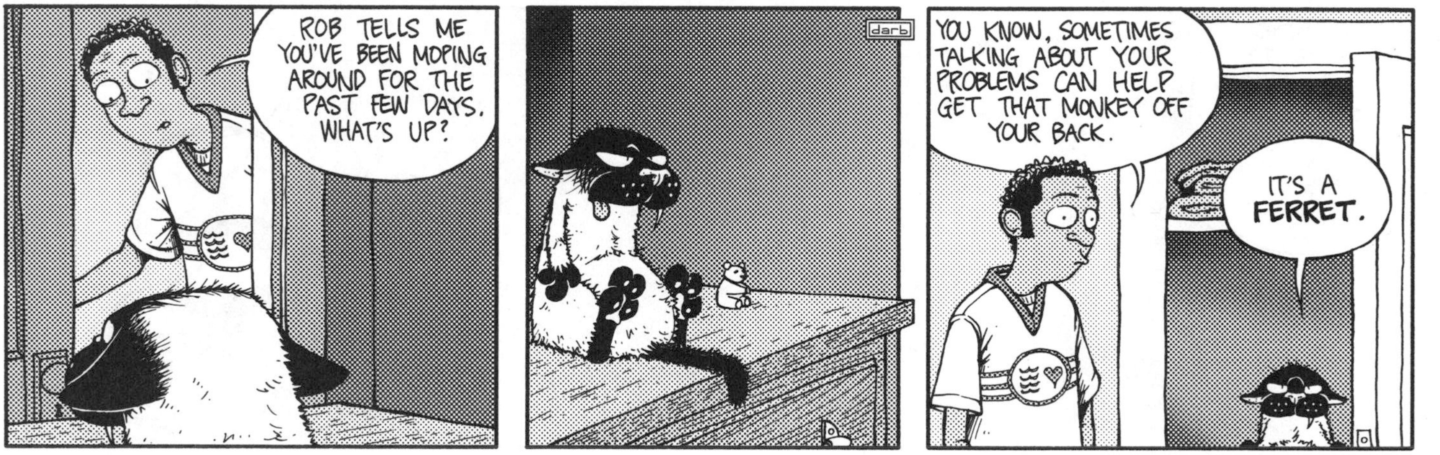
ROB TELLS ME YOU'VE BEEN MOPING AROUND FOR THE PAST FEW DAYS. WHAT'S UP?
darb
YOU KNOW, SOMETIMES TALKING ABOUT YOUR PROBLEMS CAN HELP GET THAT MONKEY OFF YOUR BACK.
IT'S A **FERRET**.

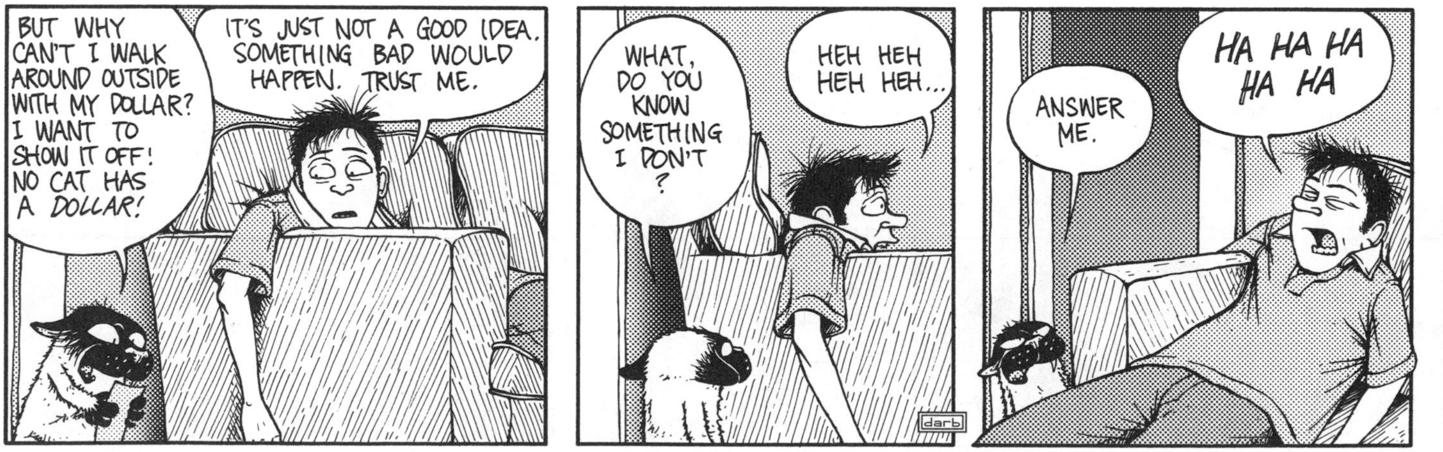
BUT WHY CAN'T I WALK AROUND OUTSIDE WITH MY DOLLAR? I WANT TO SHOW IT OFF! NO CAT HAS A *DOLLAR*!
IT'S JUST NOT A GOOD IDEA. SOMETHING BAD WOULD HAPPEN. TRUST ME.
WHAT, DO YOU KNOW SOMETHING I DON'T?
HEH HEH HEH HEH...
darb
ANSWER ME.
HA HA HA HA HA

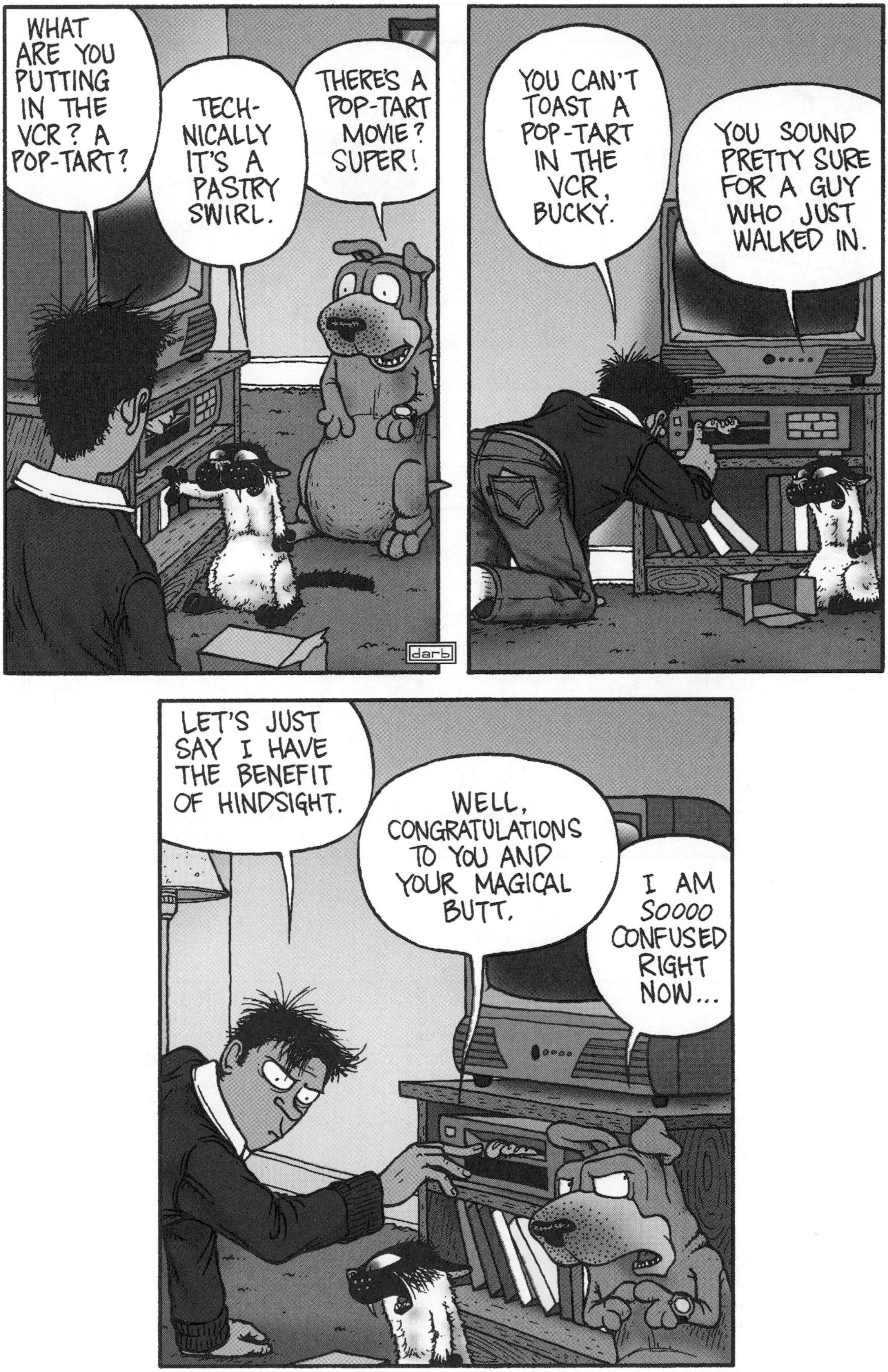
WHAT ARE YOU PUTTING IN THE VCR? A POP-TART?
TECH-NICALLY IT'S A PASTRY SWIRL.
THERE'S A POP-TART MOVIE? SUPER!
darb
YOU CAN'T TOAST A POP-TART IN THE VCR, BUCKY.
YOU SOUND PRETTY SURE FOR A GUY WHO JUST WALKED IN.
LET'S JUST SAY I HAVE THE BENEFIT OF HINDSIGHT.
WELL, CONGRATULATIONS TO YOU AND YOUR MAGICAL BUTT.
I AM *SOOOO* CONFUSED RIGHT NOW...

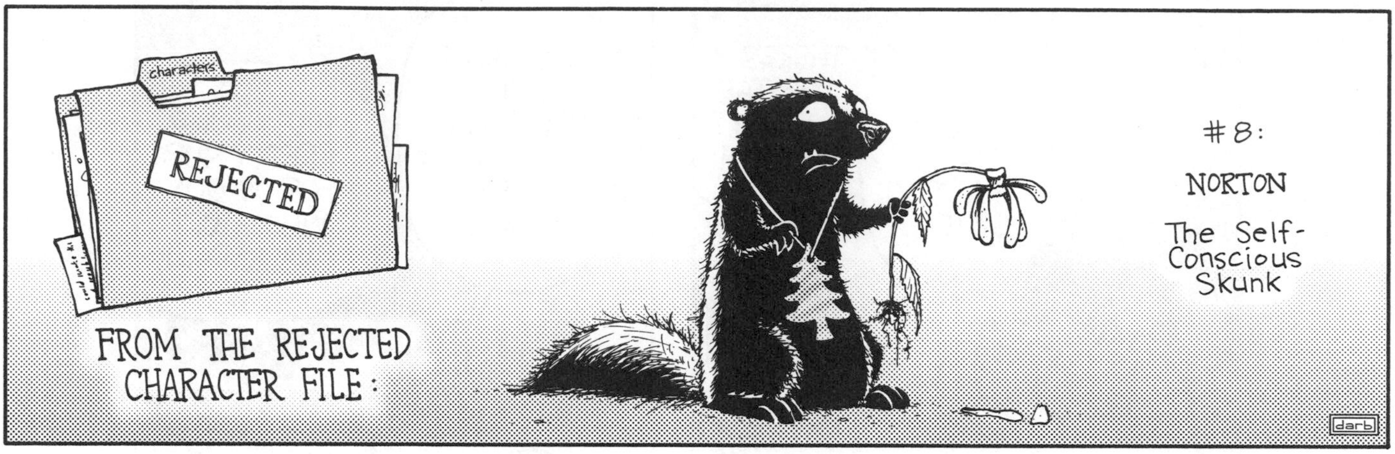
characters
REJECTED
FROM THE REJECTED CHARACTER FILE:
#8:
NORTON
The Self-Conscious Skunk
darb

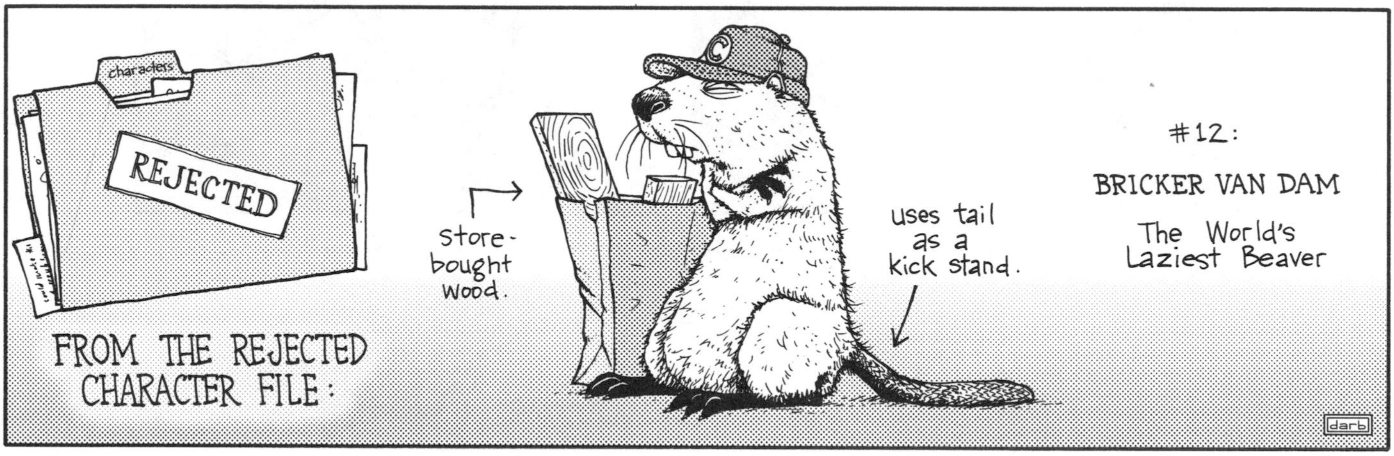
characters
REJECTED
FROM THE REJECTED CHARACTER FILE:
store-bought wood.
uses tail as a kick stand.
#12:
BRICKER VAN DAM
The World's Laziest Beaver
darb

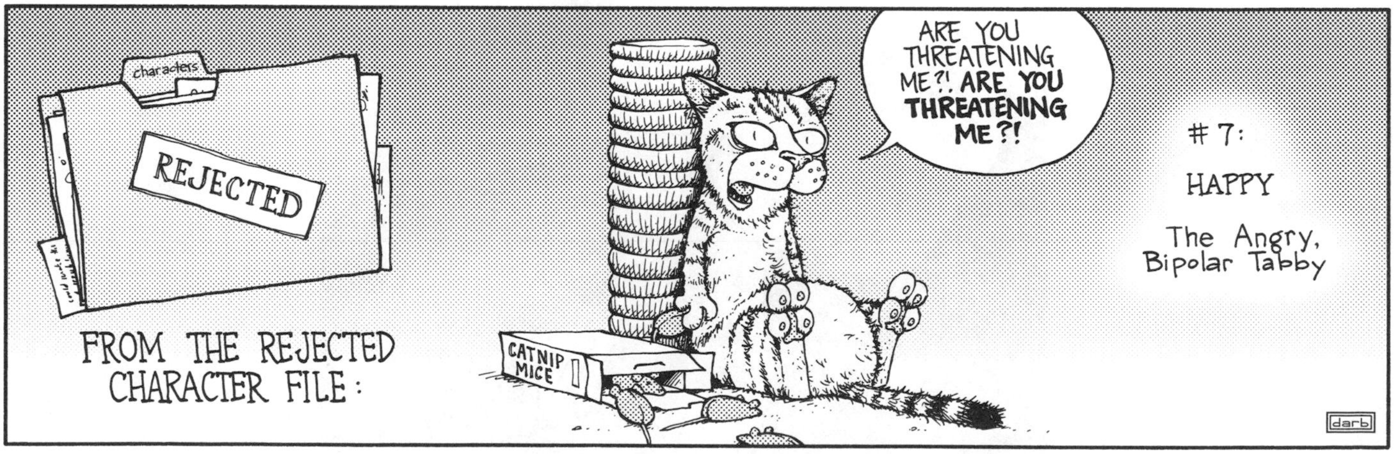
characters
REJECTED
FROM THE REJECTED CHARACTER FILE:
CATNIP MICE
ARE YOU THREATENING ME?! ARE YOU THREATENING ME?!
#7:
HAPPY
The Angry, Bipolar Tabby
darb

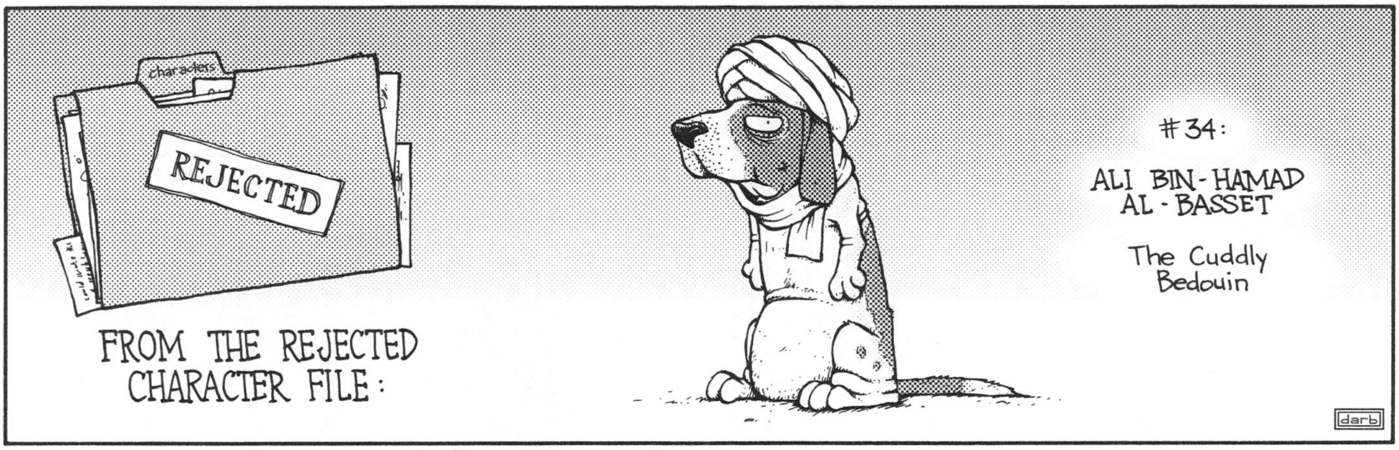
characters
REJECTED
FROM THE REJECTED CHARACTER FILE:
#34:
ALI BIN-HAMAD AL-BASSET
The Cuddly Bedouin
darb

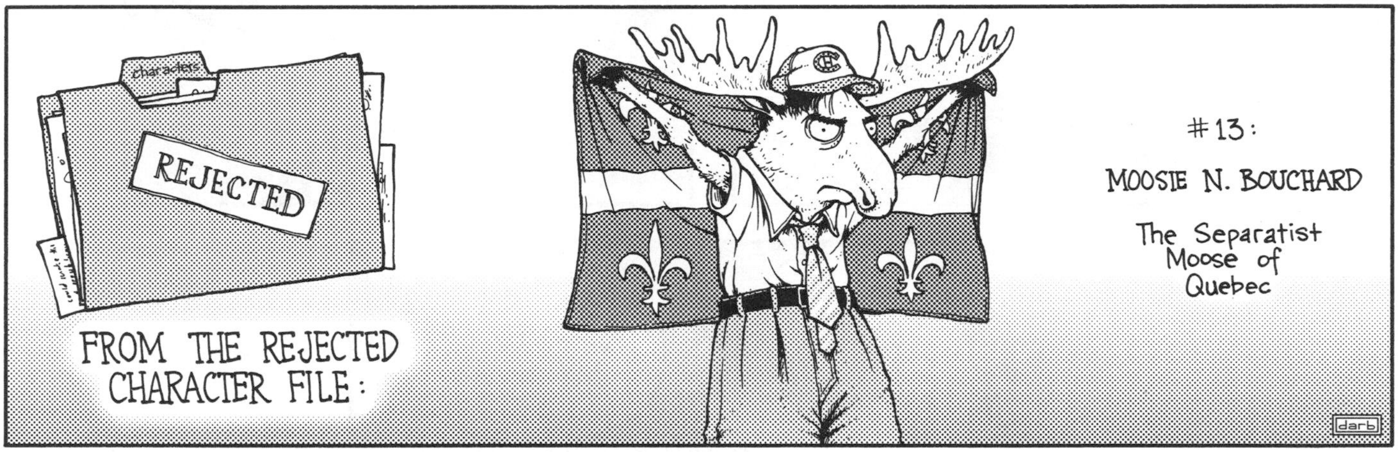
characters
REJECTED
FROM THE REJECTED CHARACTER FILE:
#13:
MOOSIE N. BOUCHARD
The Separatist Moose of Quebec
darb

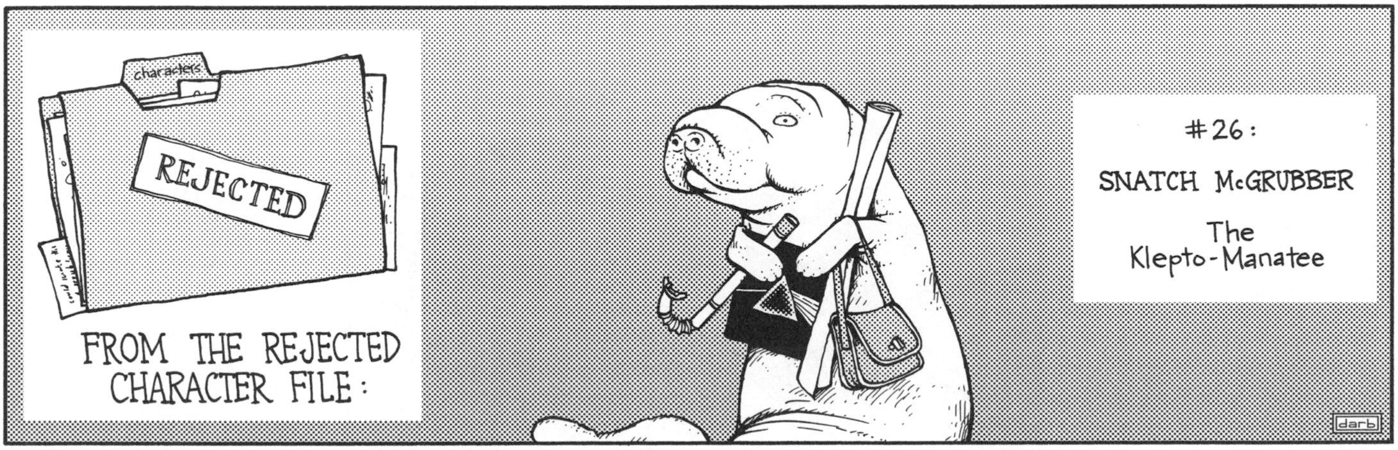
characters
REJECTED
FROM THE REJECTED CHARACTER FILE:
#26:
SNATCH McGRUBBER
The Klepto-Manatee
darb

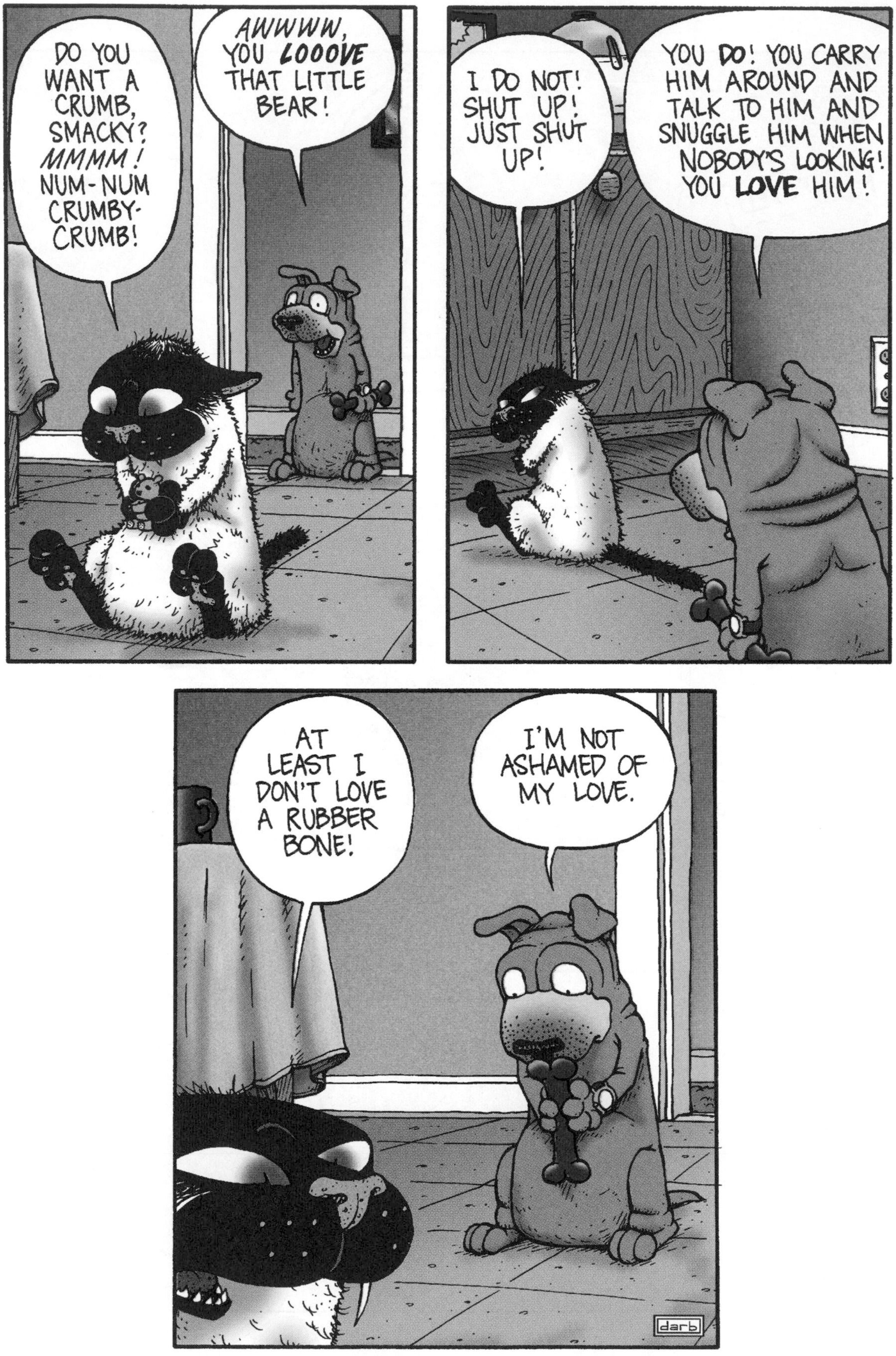
DO YOU WANT A CRUMB, SMACKY? MMMM! NUM-NUM CRUMBY-CRUMB!
AWWWW, YOU LOOOVE THAT LITTLE BEAR!
I DO NOT! SHUT UP! JUST SHUT UP!
YOU DO! YOU CARRY HIM AROUND AND TALK TO HIM AND SNUGGLE HIM WHEN NOBODY'S LOOKING! YOU LOVE HIM!
AT LEAST I DON'T LOVE A RUBBER BONE!
I'M NOT ASHAMED OF MY LOVE.
darb

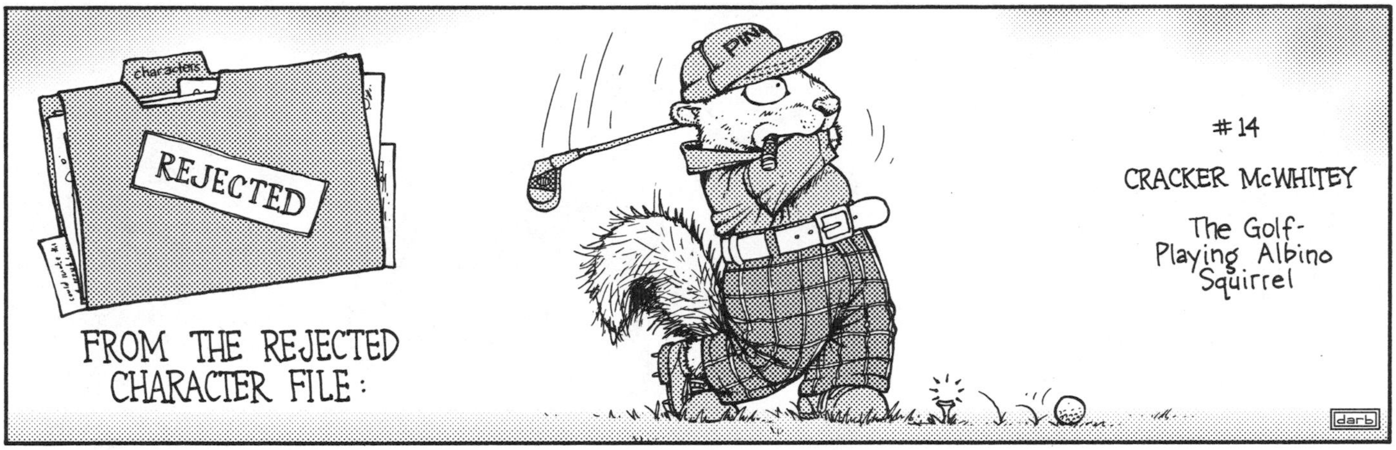
characters
REJECTED
FROM THE REJECTED CHARACTER FILE:
PING
#14
CRACKER McWHITEY
The Golf-Playing Albino Squirrel
darb

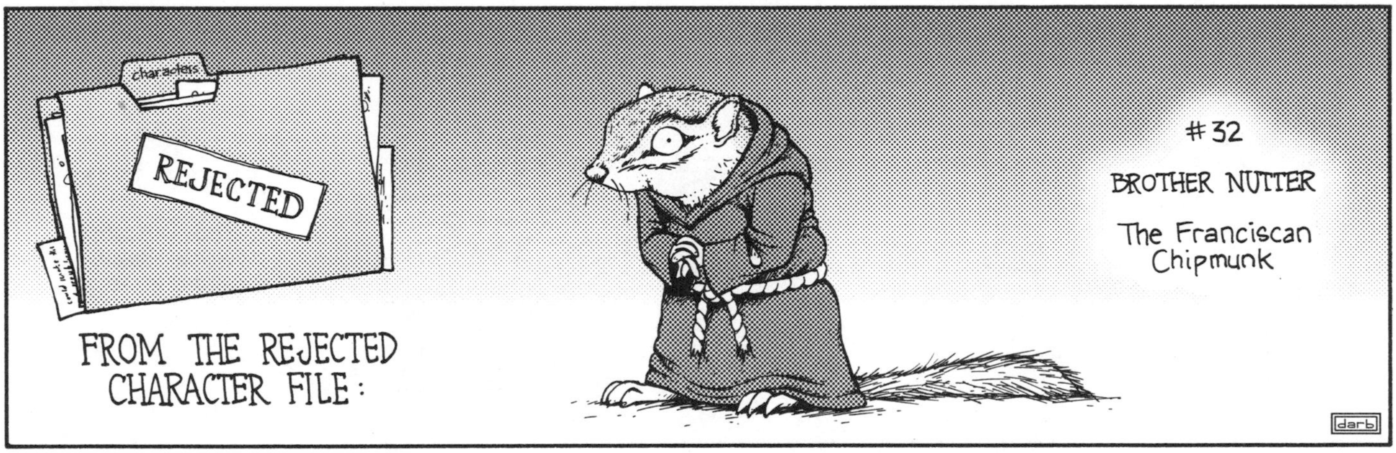
characters
REJECTED
FROM THE REJECTED CHARACTER FILE:
#32
BROTHER NUTTER
The Franciscan Chipmunk
darb

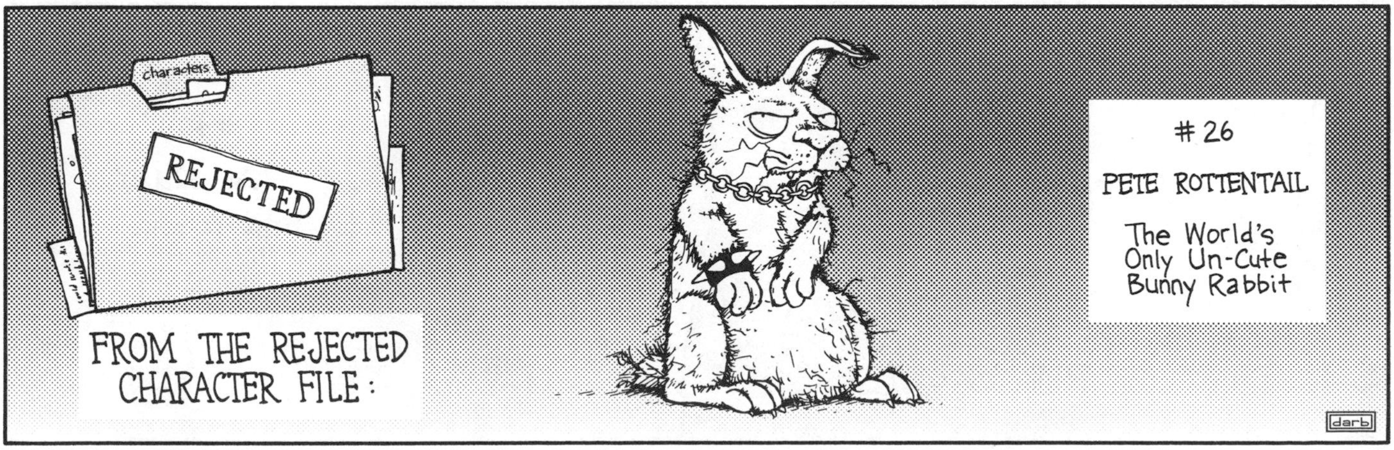
characters
REJECTED
FROM THE REJECTED CHARACTER FILE:
#26
PETE ROTTENTAIL
The World's Only Un-Cute Bunny Rabbit
darb

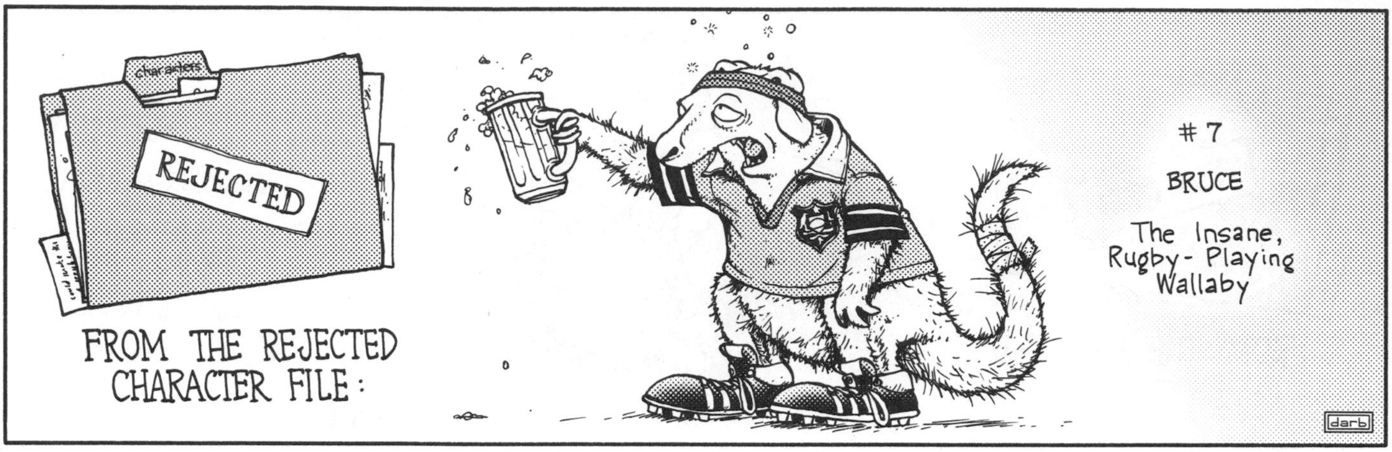
characters
REJECTED
FROM THE REJECTED CHARACTER FILE:
7
BRUCE
The Insane, Rugby-Playing Wallaby
darb

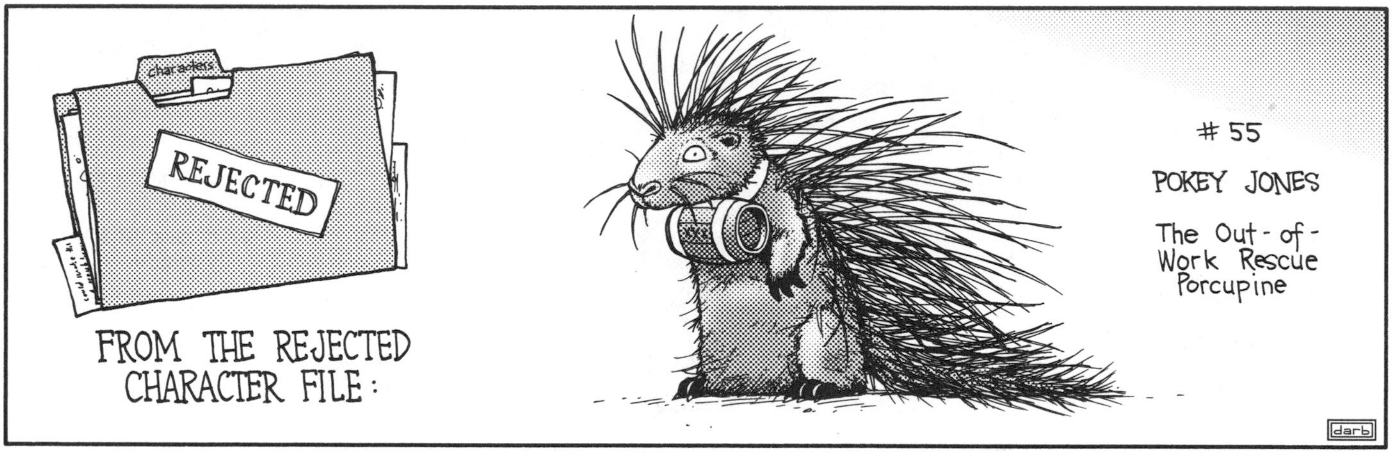
characters
REJECTED
FROM THE REJECTED CHARACTER FILE:
55
POKEY JONES
The Out-of-Work Rescue Porcupine
darb

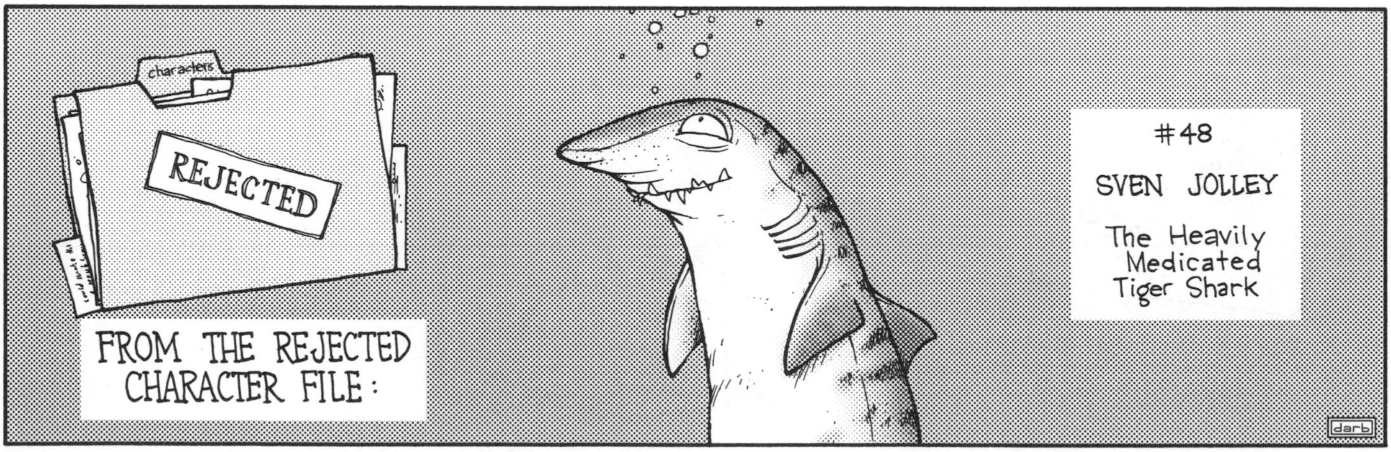
characters
REJECTED
FROM THE REJECTED CHARACTER FILE:
#48
SVEN JOLLEY
The Heavily Medicated Tiger Shark
darb

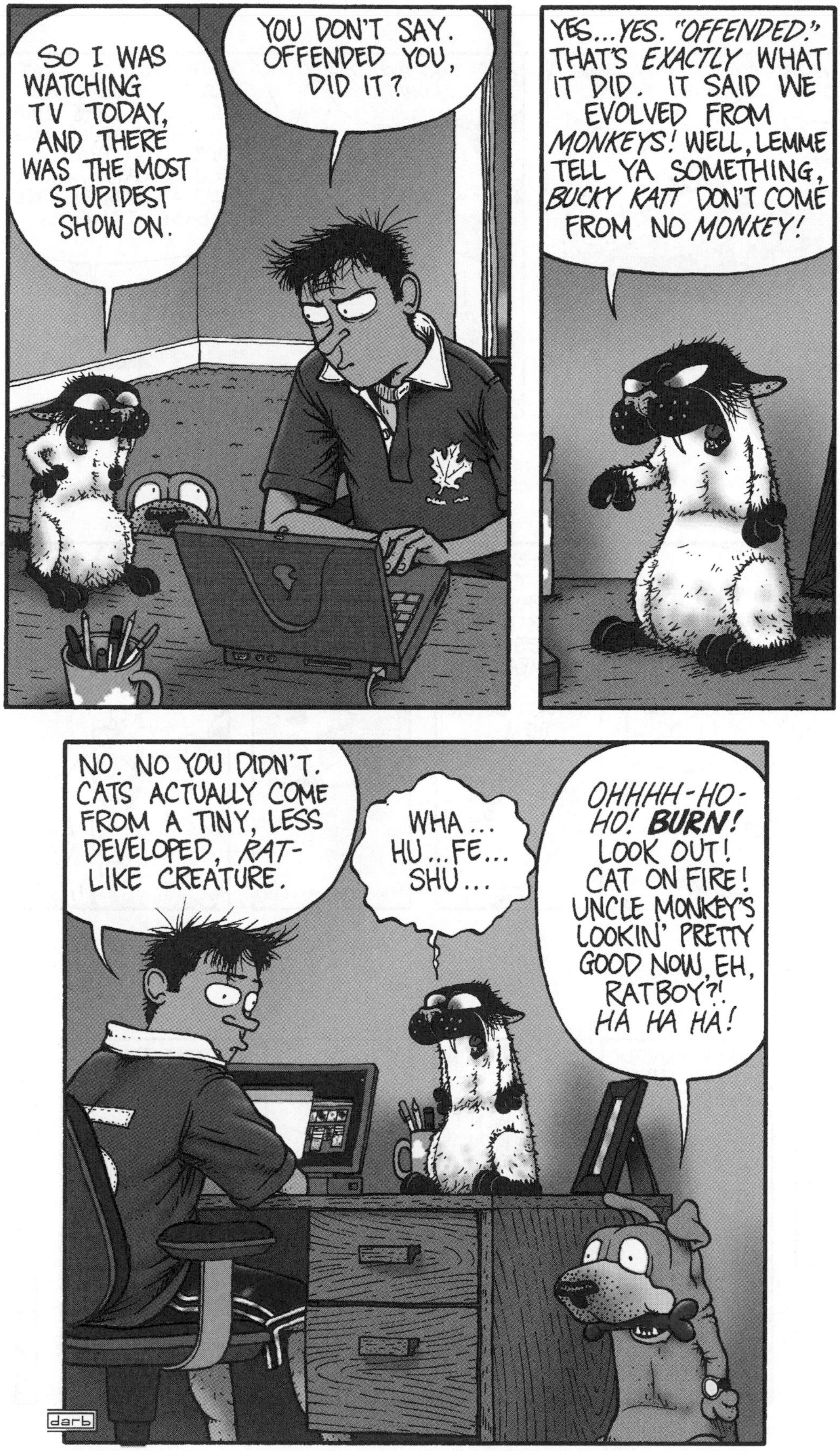
SO I WAS WATCHING TV TODAY, AND THERE WAS THE MOST STUPIDEST SHOW ON.
YOU DON'T SAY. OFFENDED YOU, DID IT?
YES... YES. "OFFENDED." THAT'S EXACTLY WHAT IT DID. IT SAID WE EVOLVED FROM MONKEYS! WELL, LEMME TELL YA SOMETHING, BUCKY KATT DON'T COME FROM NO MONKEY!
NO. NO YOU DIDN'T. CATS ACTUALLY COME FROM A TINY, LESS DEVELOPED, RAT-LIKE CREATURE.
WHA... HU... FE... SHU...
OHHHH-HO-HO! BURN! LOOK OUT! CAT ON FIRE! UNCLE MONKEY'S LOOKIN' PRETTY GOOD NOW, EH, RATBOY?! HA HA HA!
darb

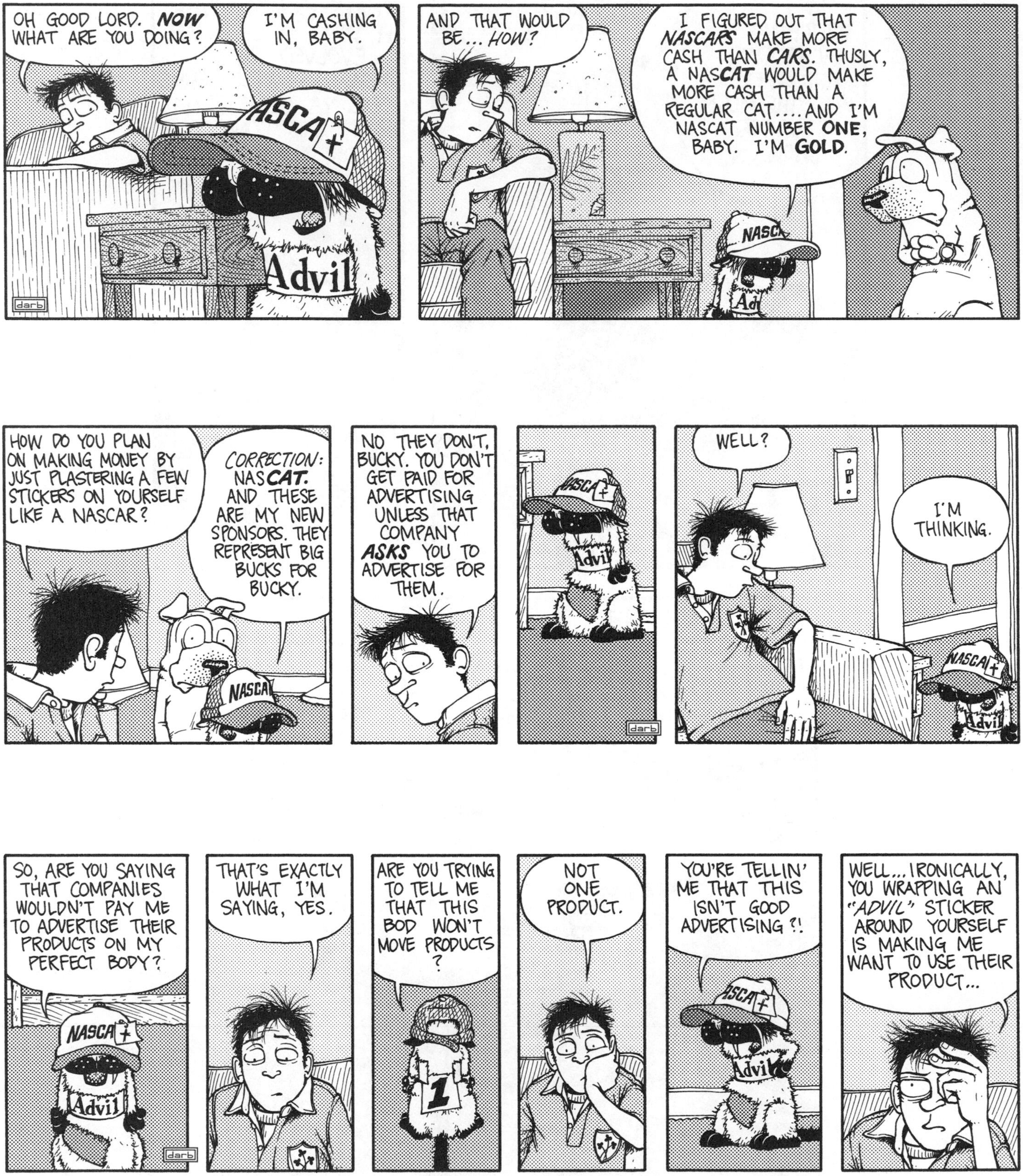
OH GOOD LORD. NOW WHAT ARE YOU DOING?
I'M CASHING IN, BABY.
NASCA
Advil
darb
AND THAT WOULD BE... HOW?
I FIGURED OUT THAT NASCARS MAKE MORE CASH THAN CARS. THUSLY, A NASCAT WOULD MAKE MORE CASH THAN A REGULAR CAT.... AND I'M NASCAT NUMBER ONE, BABY. I'M GOLD.
NASCA
HOW DO YOU PLAN ON MAKING MONEY BY JUST PLASTERING A FEW STICKERS ON YOURSELF LIKE A NASCAR?
CORRECTION: NASCAT. AND THESE ARE MY NEW SPONSORS. THEY REPRESENT BIG BUCKS FOR BUCKY.
NASCA
NO THEY DON'T, BUCKY. YOU DON'T GET PAID FOR ADVERTISING UNLESS THAT COMPANY ASKS YOU TO ADVERTISE FOR THEM.
NASCA
Advil
darb
WELL?
I'M THINKING.
NASCA
Advil
SO, ARE YOU SAYING THAT COMPANIES WOULDN'T PAY ME TO ADVERTISE THEIR PRODUCTS ON MY PERFECT BODY?
NASCA
Advil
darb
THAT'S EXACTLY WHAT I'M SAYING, YES.
ARE YOU TRYING TO TELL ME THAT THIS BOD WON'T MOVE PRODUCTS?
1
NOT ONE PRODUCT.
YOU'RE TELLIN' ME THAT THIS ISN'T GOOD ADVERTISING?!
NASCA
Advil
WELL... IRONICALLY, YOU WRAPPING AN "ADVIL" STICKER AROUND YOURSELF IS MAKING ME WANT TO USE THEIR PRODUCT...

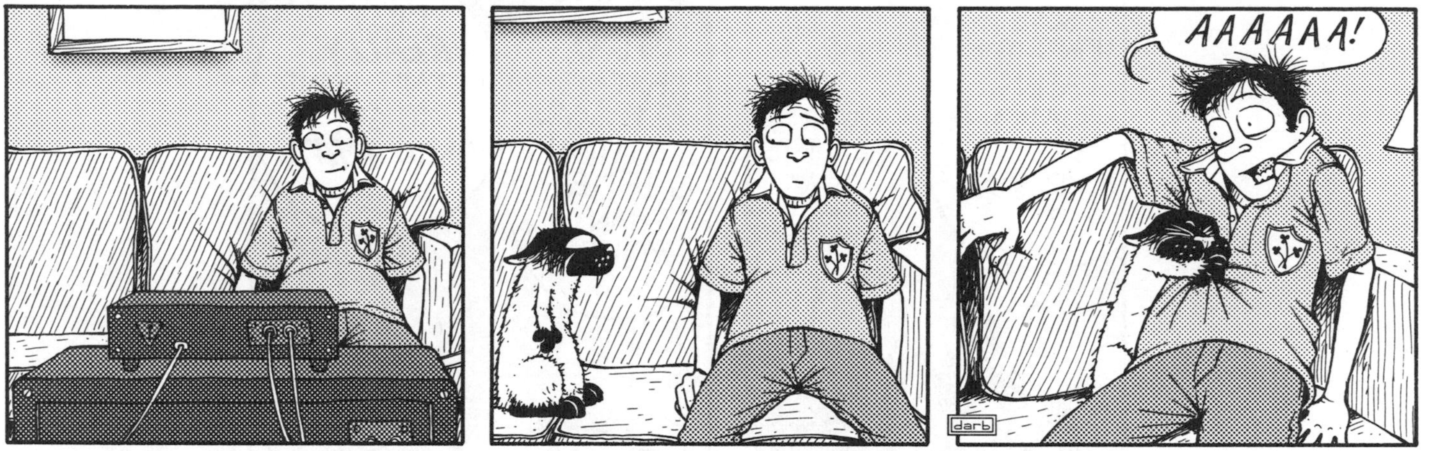
AAAAAA!

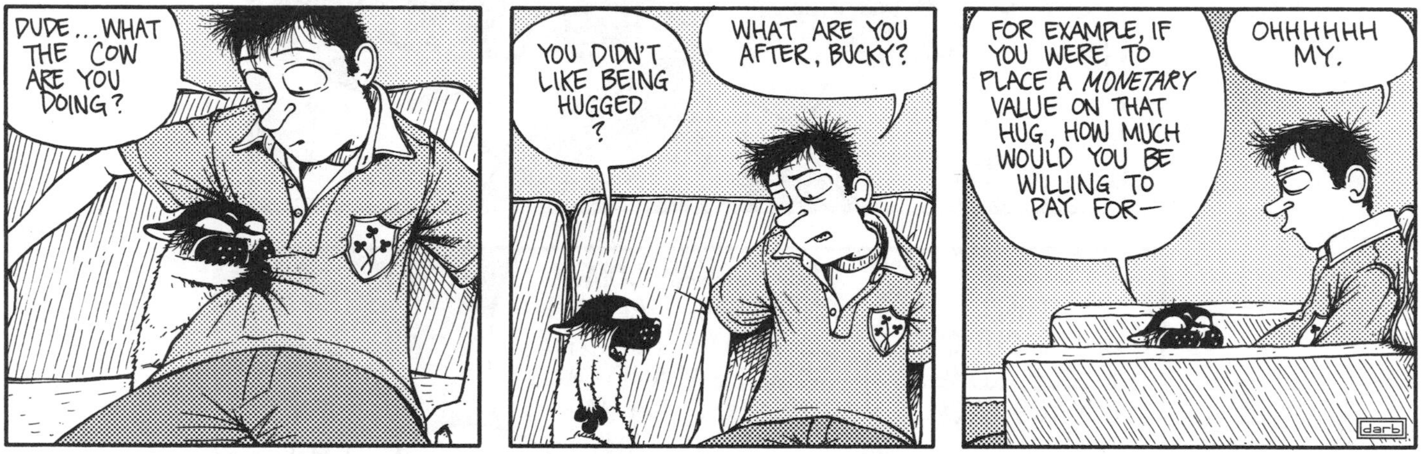
DUDE... WHAT THE COW ARE YOU DOING?
YOU DIDN'T LIKE BEING HUGGED ?
WHAT ARE YOU AFTER, BUCKY?
FOR EXAMPLE, IF YOU WERE TO PLACE A *MONETARY* VALUE ON THAT HUG, HOW MUCH WOULD YOU BE WILLING TO PAY FOR—
OHHHHHH MY.

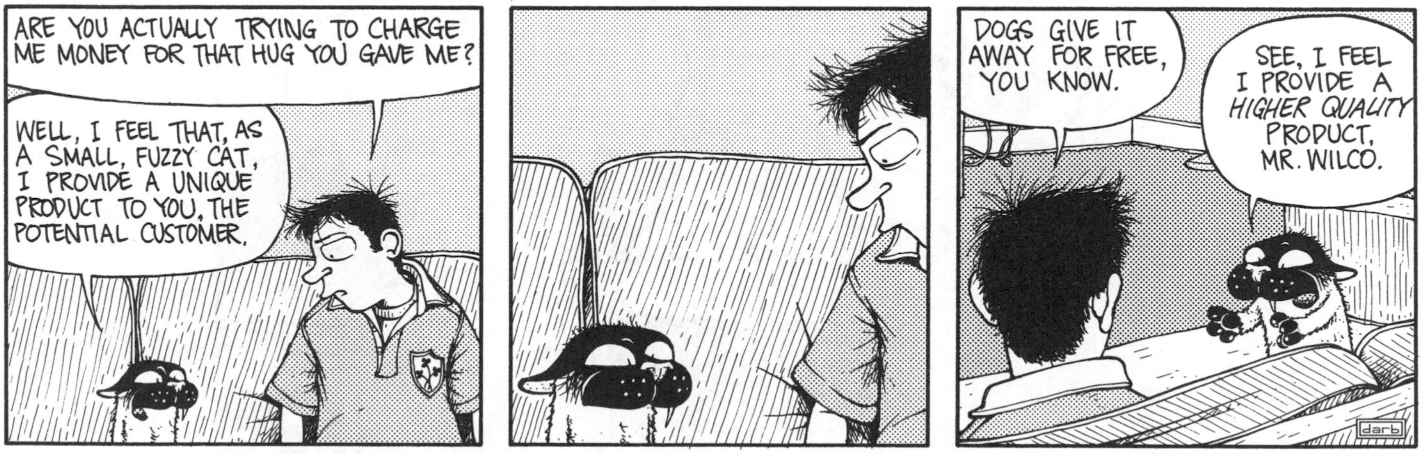
ARE YOU ACTUALLY TRYING TO CHARGE ME MONEY FOR THAT HUG YOU GAVE ME?
WELL, I FEEL THAT, AS A SMALL, FUZZY CAT, I PROVIDE A UNIQUE PRODUCT TO YOU, THE POTENTIAL CUSTOMER.
DOGS GIVE IT AWAY FOR FREE, YOU KNOW.
SEE, I FEEL I PROVIDE A *HIGHER QUALITY* PRODUCT, MR. WILCO.

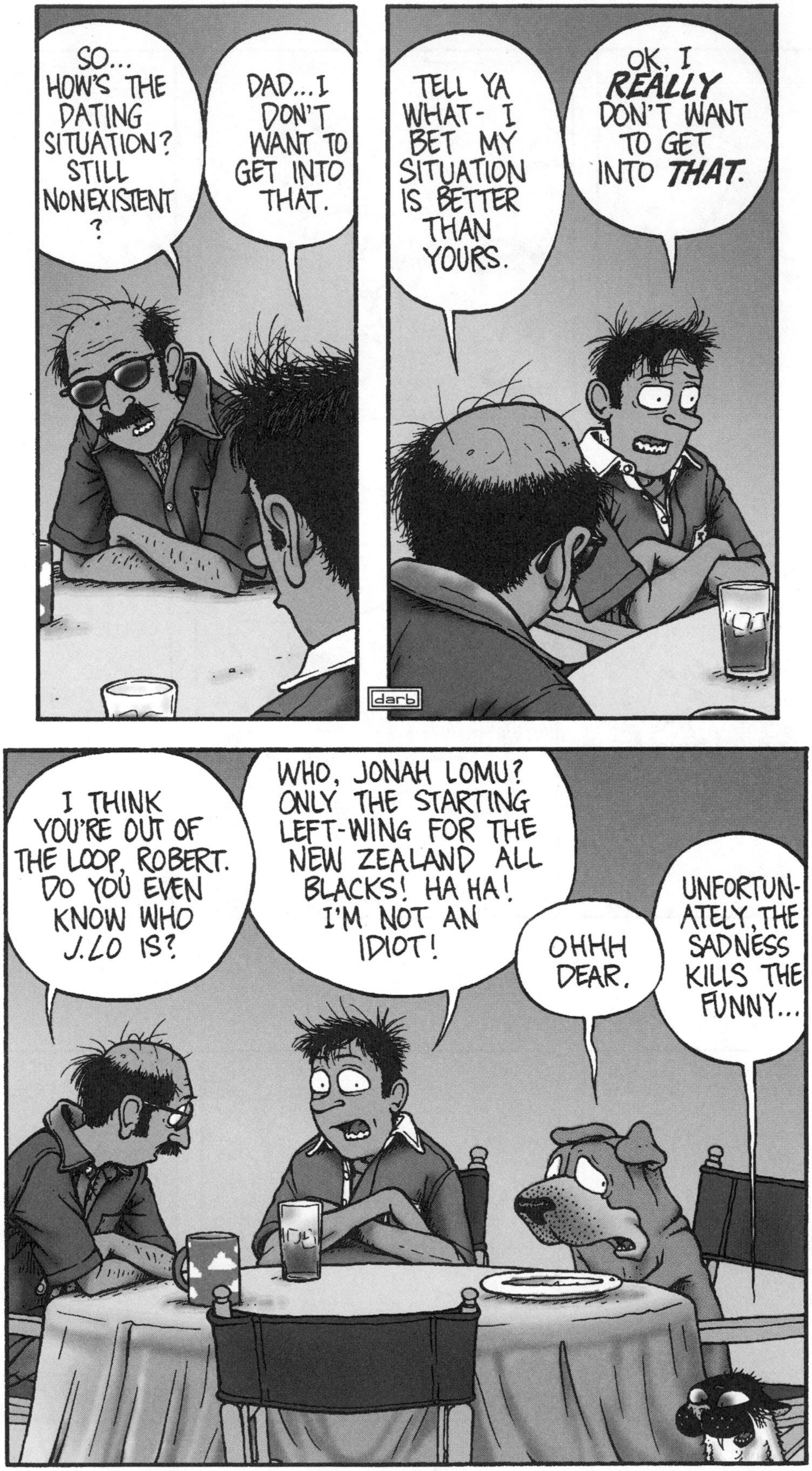
SO... HOW'S THE DATING SITUATION? STILL NONEXISTENT ?
DAD...I DON'T WANT TO GET INTO THAT.
TELL YA WHAT- I BET MY SITUATION IS BETTER THAN YOURS.
OK, I REALLY DON'T WANT TO GET INTO THAT.
darb
I THINK YOU'RE OUT OF THE LOOP, ROBERT. DO YOU EVEN KNOW WHO J.LO IS?
WHO, JONAH LOMU? ONLY THE STARTING LEFT-WING FOR THE NEW ZEALAND ALL BLACKS! HA HA! I'M NOT AN IDIOT!
OHHH DEAR.
UNFORTUN-ATELY, THE SADNESS KILLS THE FUNNY...

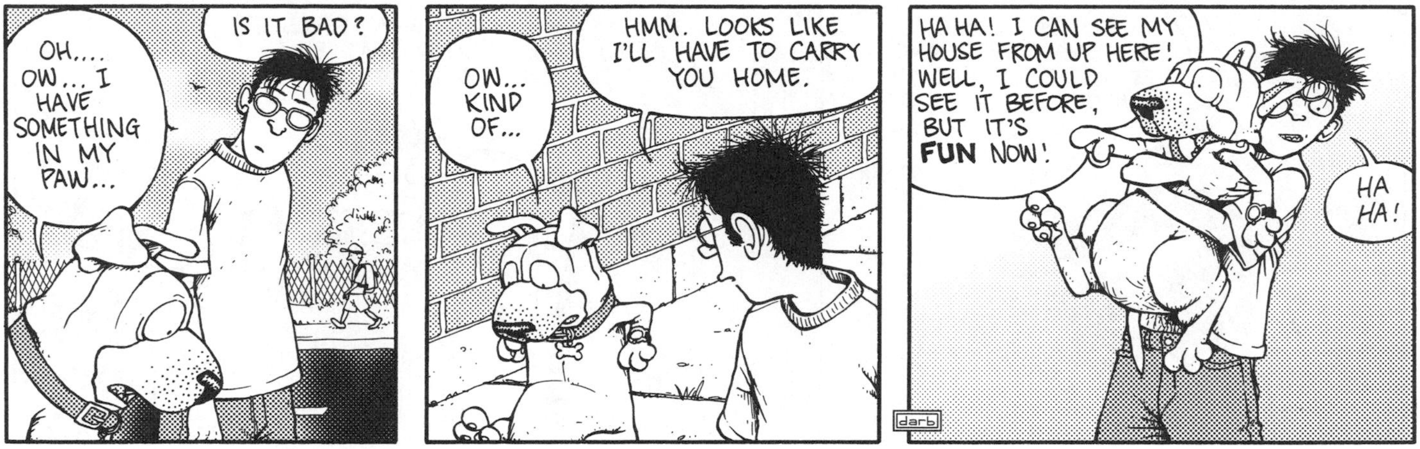
OH.... OW... I HAVE SOMETHING IN MY PAW...
IS IT BAD?
OW... KIND OF...
HMM. LOOKS LIKE I'LL HAVE TO CARRY YOU HOME.
HA HA! I CAN SEE MY HOUSE FROM UP HERE! WELL, I COULD SEE IT BEFORE, BUT IT'S **FUN** NOW!
HA HA!
darb

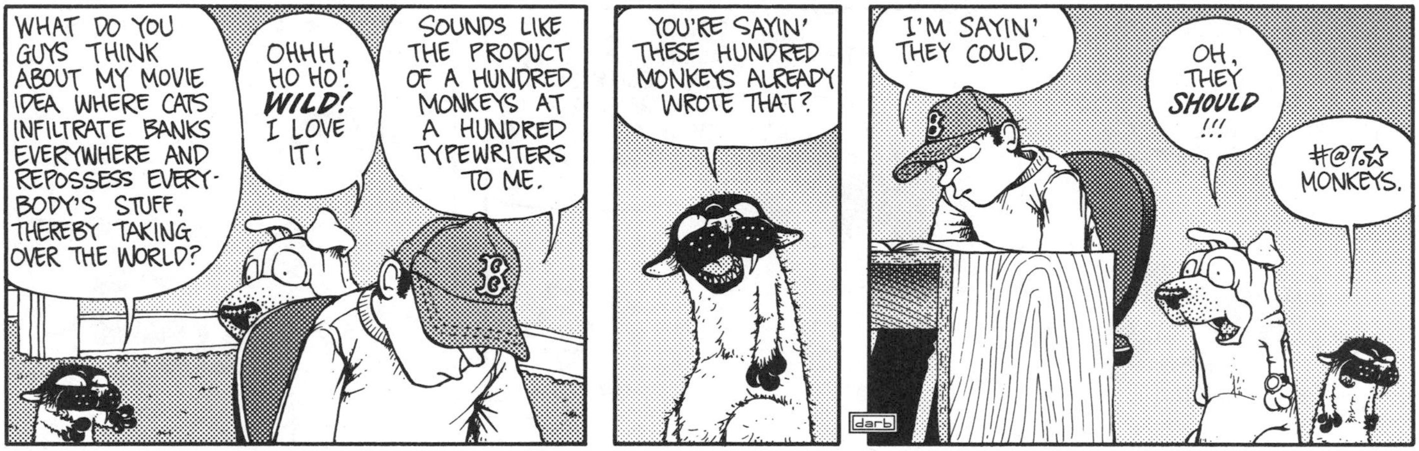
WHAT DO YOU GUYS THINK ABOUT MY MOVIE IDEA WHERE CATS INFILTRATE BANKS EVERYWHERE AND REPOSSESS EVERY-BODY'S STUFF, THEREBY TAKING OVER THE WORLD?
OHHH HO HO! ***WILD!*** I LOVE IT!
SOUNDS LIKE THE PRODUCT OF A HUNDRED MONKEYS AT A HUNDRED TYPEWRITERS TO ME.
YOU'RE SAYIN' THESE HUNDRED MONKEYS ALREADY WROTE THAT?
darb
I'M SAYIN' THEY COULD.
OH, THEY ***SHOULD*** !!!
#@%☆ MONKEYS.

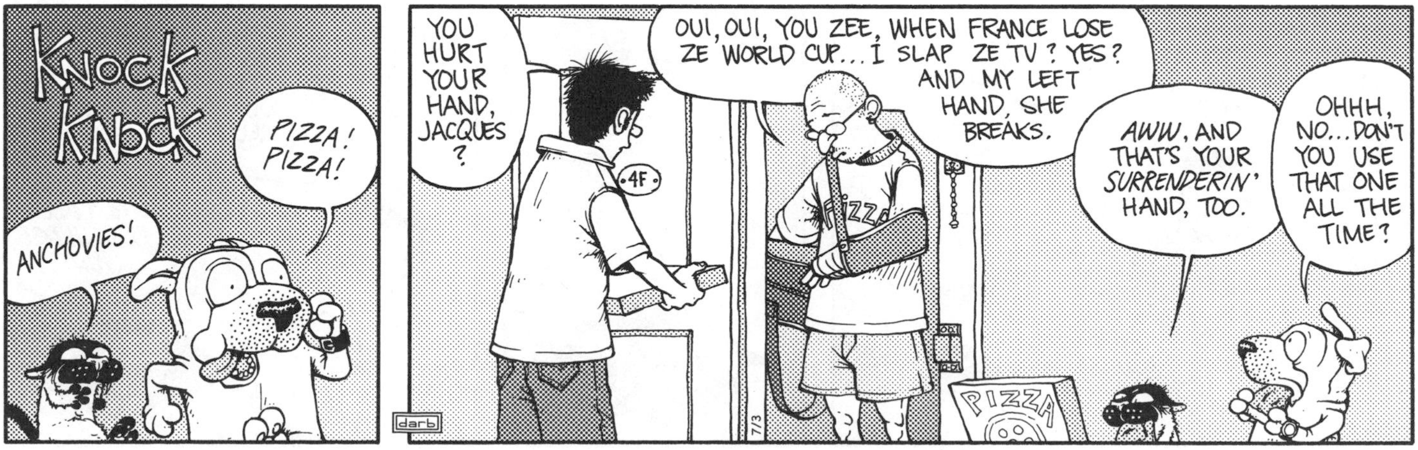
KNOCK KNOCK
PIZZA! PIZZA!
ANCHOVIES!
darb
YOU HURT YOUR HAND, JACQUES?
4F
OUI, OUI, YOU ZEE, WHEN FRANCE LOSE ZE WORLD CUP... I SLAP ZE TV? YES? AND MY LEFT HAND, SHE BREAKS.
PIZZA
7/3
AWW, AND THAT'S YOUR *SURRENDERIN'* HAND, TOO.
OHHH, NO... DON'T YOU USE THAT ONE ALL THE TIME?
PIZZA

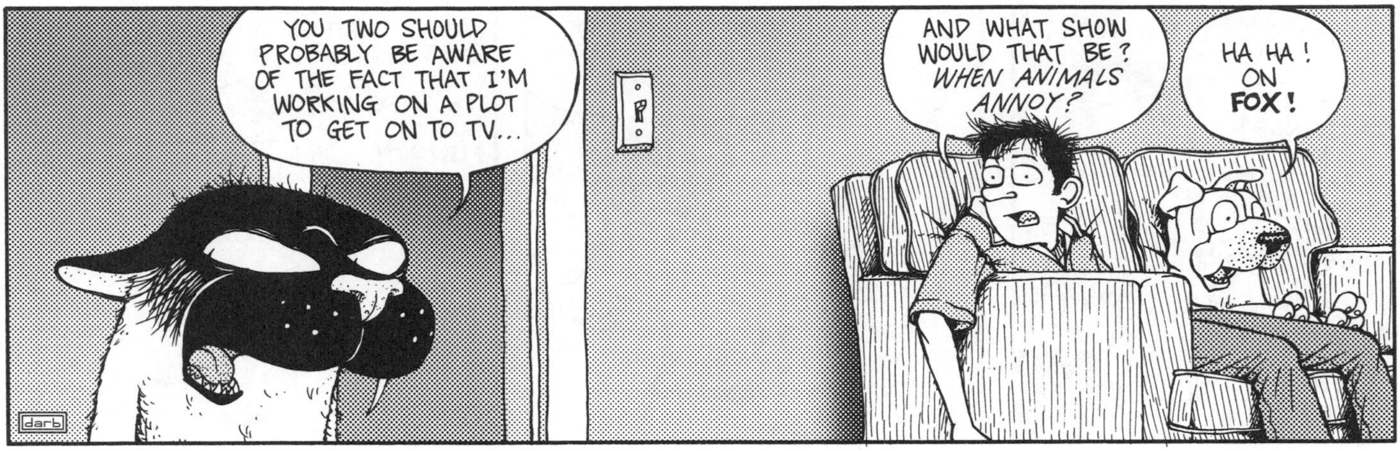
YOU TWO SHOULD PROBABLY BE AWARE OF THE FACT THAT I'M WORKING ON A PLOT TO GET ON TO TV...
AND WHAT SHOW WOULD THAT BE? WHEN ANIMALS ANNOY?
HA HA! ON FOX!
darb

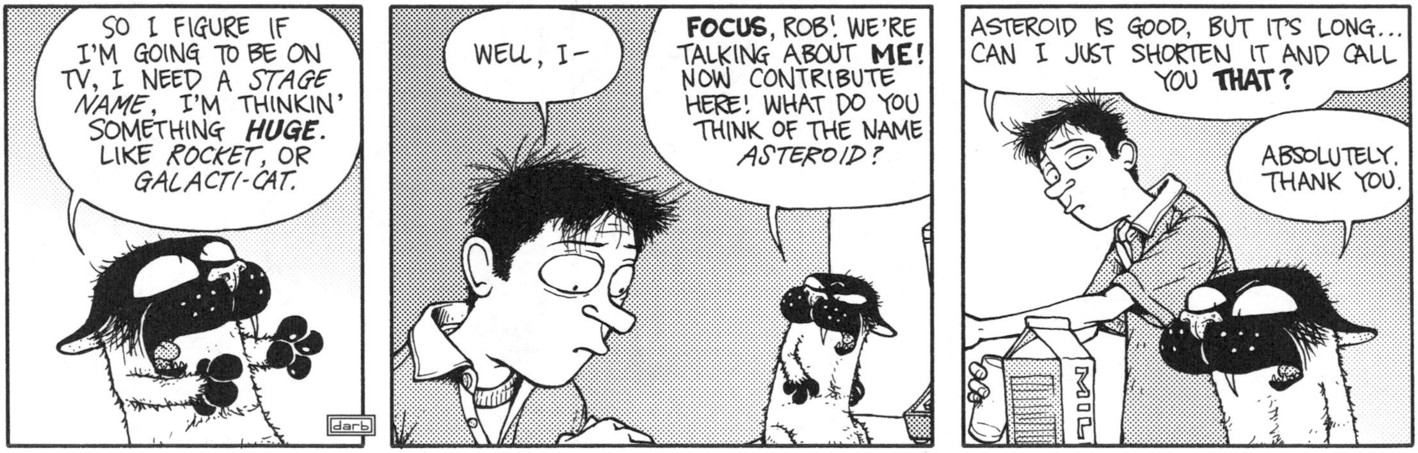
SO I FIGURE IF I'M GOING TO BE ON TV, I NEED A STAGE NAME, I'M THINKIN' SOMETHING HUGE. LIKE ROCKET, OR GALACTI-CAT.
darb
WELL, I-
FOCUS, ROB! WE'RE TALKING ABOUT ME! NOW CONTRIBUTE HERE! WHAT DO YOU THINK OF THE NAME ASTEROID?
ASTEROID IS GOOD, BUT IT'S LONG... CAN I JUST SHORTEN IT AND CALL YOU THAT?
ABSOLUTELY. THANK YOU.

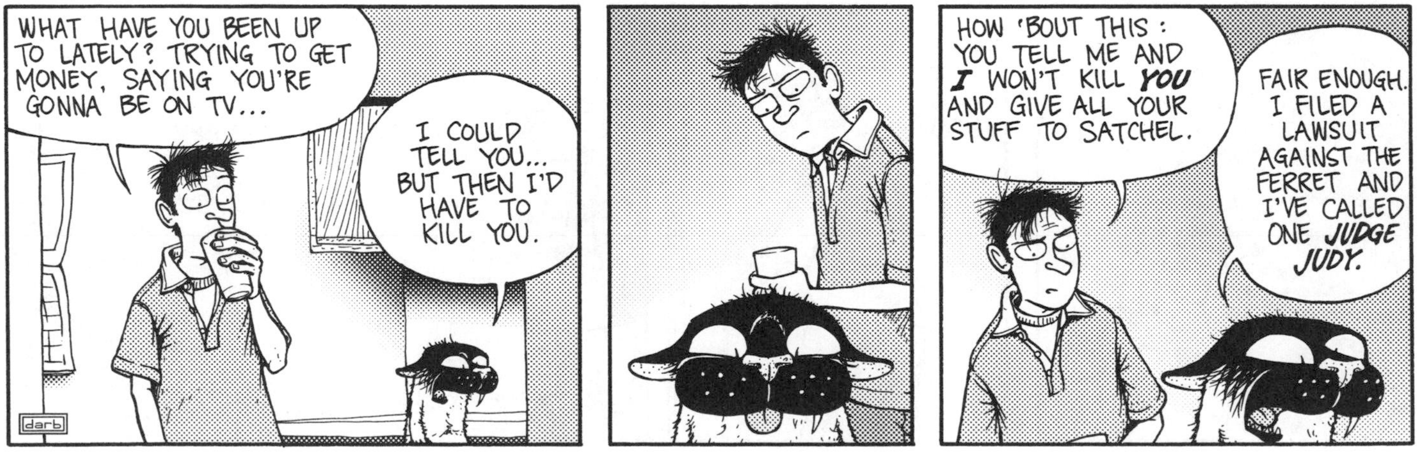
WHAT HAVE YOU BEEN UP TO LATELY? TRYING TO GET MONEY, SAYING YOU'RE GONNA BE ON TV...
I COULD TELL YOU... BUT THEN I'D HAVE TO KILL YOU.
darb
HOW 'BOUT THIS: YOU TELL ME AND I WON'T KILL YOU AND GIVE ALL YOUR STUFF TO SATCHEL.
FAIR ENOUGH. I FILED A LAWSUIT AGAINST THE FERRET AND I'VE CALLED ONE JUDGE JUDY.

WHAT ON EARTH ARE YOU DOING ?
I SAW IT ON TV! SPIRITS CAN TELL YOU THINGS BY MOVING THIS THING AROUND A BOARD!
YOU MEAN *OUIJA?*
YEAH! *WEEE-JEEE!* HA HA HA! ONLY I CAN'T UNDERSTAND WHAT IT'S TRYING TO TELL ME...
LOWE TECH
SEE, THE THING IS, THERE'S A SPECIAL *OUIJA BOARD*... YOU'RE NOT SUPPOSED TO USE A CANDYLAND BOARD.
OHHH, HA HA! I WONDERED WHY A SPIRIT WOULD GO THROUGH MULTIPLE DIMENSIONS TO TELL ME *GUMDROP, GUMDROP, LOLLY!*
I FIGURED YOU CHANNELED AN IDIOT.
darb

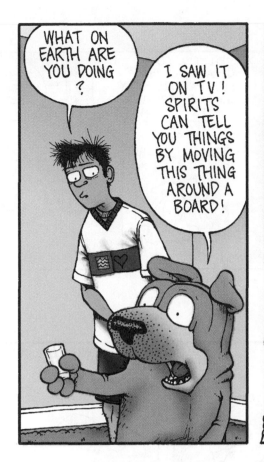

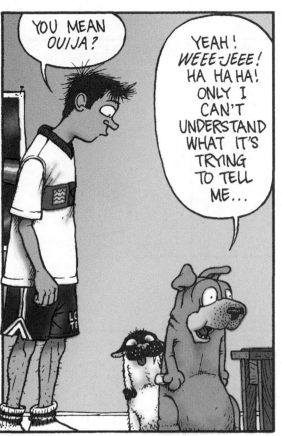

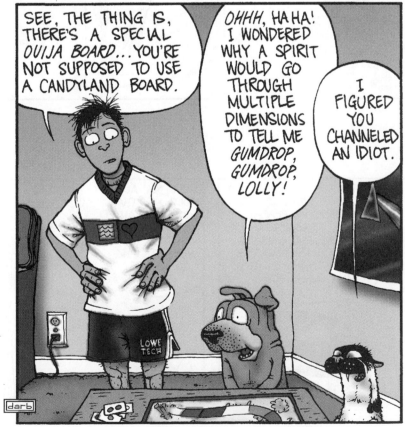

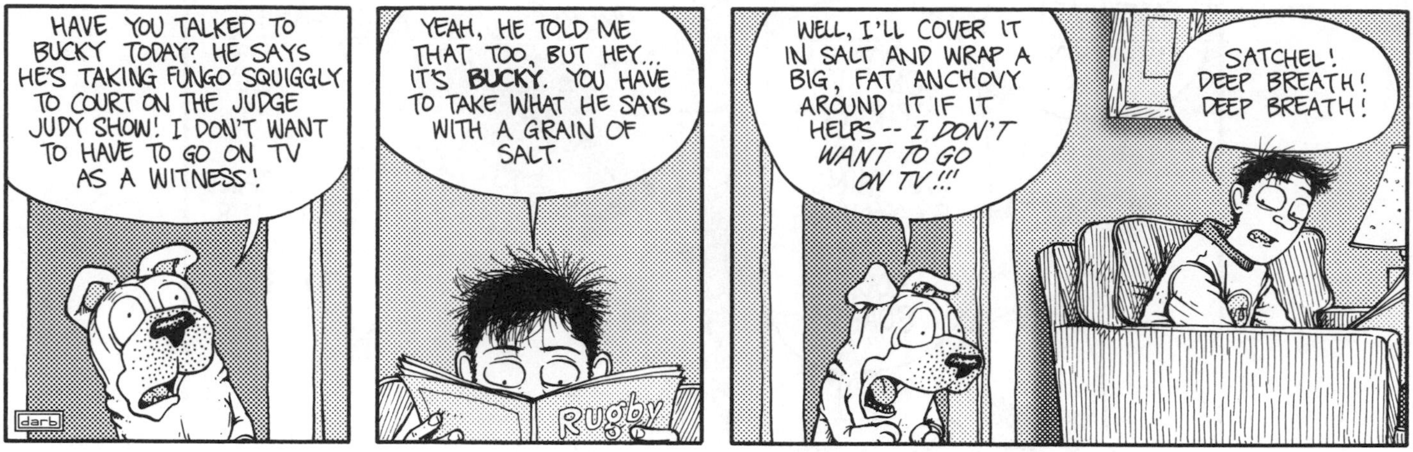
HAVE YOU TALKED TO BUCKY TODAY? HE SAYS HE'S TAKING FUNGO SQUIGGLY TO COURT ON THE JUDGE JUDY SHOW! I DON'T WANT TO HAVE TO GO ON TV AS A WITNESS!
YEAH, HE TOLD ME THAT TOO, BUT HEY... IT'S BUCKY. YOU HAVE TO TAKE WHAT HE SAYS WITH A GRAIN OF SALT.
Rugby
WELL, I'LL COVER IT IN SALT AND WRAP A BIG, FAT ANCHOVY AROUND IT IF IT HELPS -- I DON'T WANT TO GO ON TV!!!
SATCHEL! DEEP BREATH! DEEP BREATH!
darb

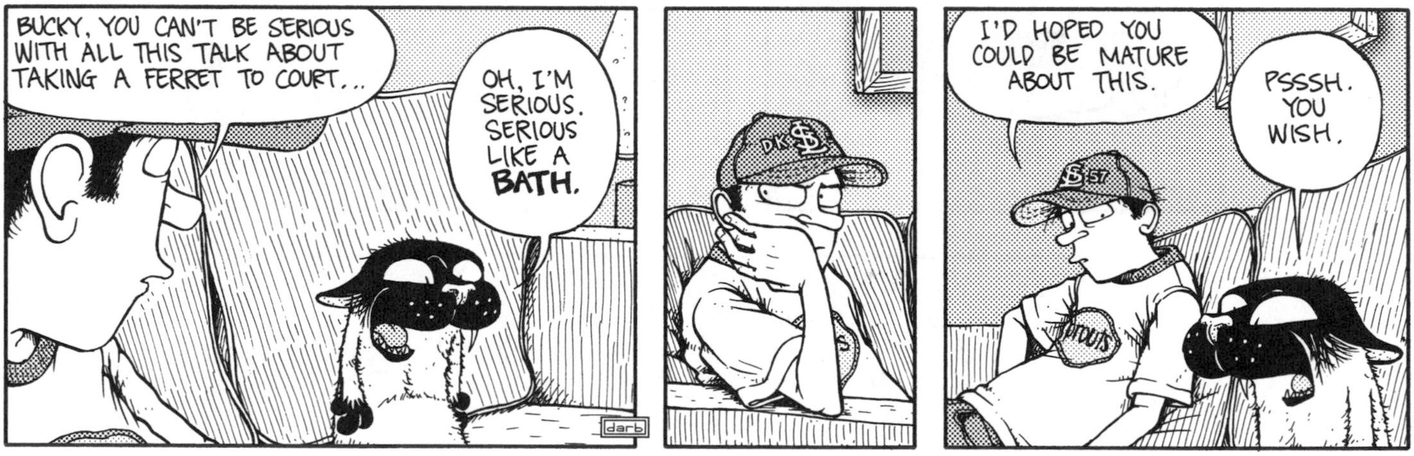
BUCKY, YOU CAN'T BE SERIOUS WITH ALL THIS TALK ABOUT TAKING A FERRET TO COURT...
OH, I'M SERIOUS. SERIOUS LIKE A BATH.
darb
I'D HOPED YOU COULD BE MATURE ABOUT THIS.
PSSSH. YOU WISH.

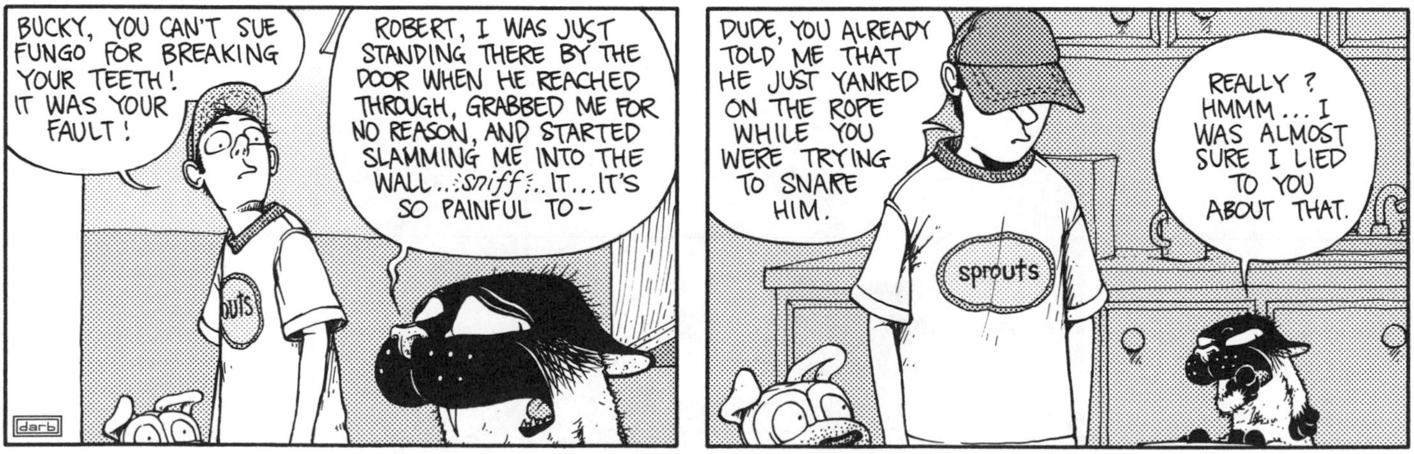
BUCKY, YOU CAN'T SUE FUNGO FOR BREAKING YOUR TEETH! IT WAS YOUR FAULT!
ROBERT, I WAS JUST STANDING THERE BY THE DOOR WHEN HE REACHED THROUGH, GRABBED ME FOR NO REASON, AND STARTED SLAMMING ME INTO THE WALL... sniff... IT... IT'S SO PAINFUL TO-
darb
DUDE, YOU ALREADY TOLD ME THAT HE JUST YANKED ON THE ROPE WHILE YOU WERE TRYING TO SNARE HIM.
REALLY? HMMM... I WAS ALMOST SURE I LIED TO YOU ABOUT THAT.
sprouts

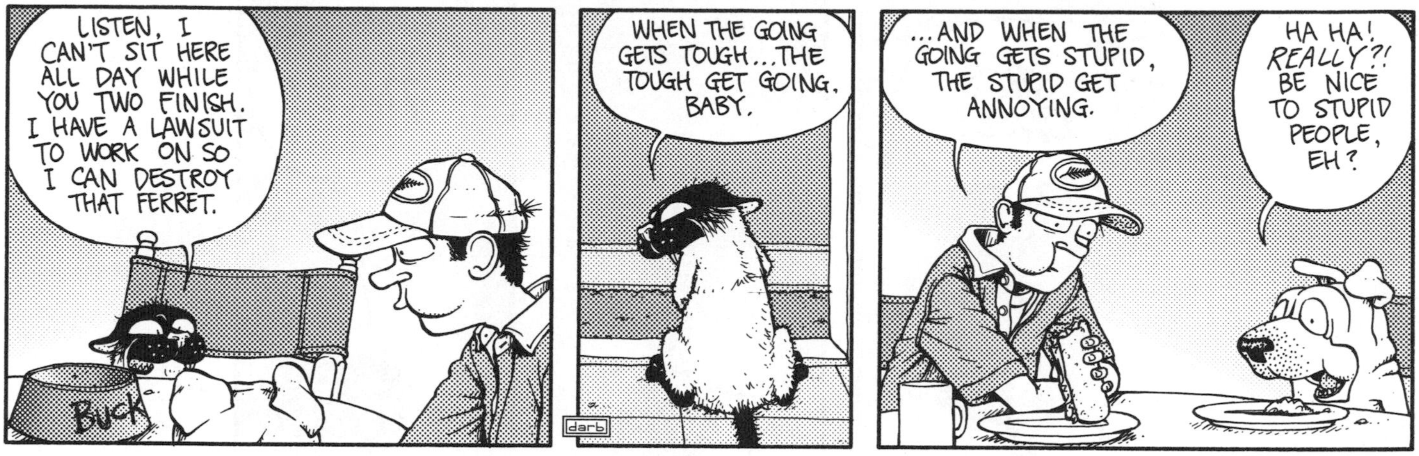
LISTEN, I CAN'T SIT HERE ALL DAY WHILE YOU TWO FINISH. I HAVE A LAWSUIT TO WORK ON SO I CAN DESTROY THAT FERRET.
BUCK
WHEN THE GOING GETS TOUGH...THE TOUGH GET GOING. BABY.
darb
...AND WHEN THE GOING GETS STUPID, THE STUPID GET ANNOYING.
HA HA! *REALLY?!* BE NICE TO STUPID PEOPLE, EH?

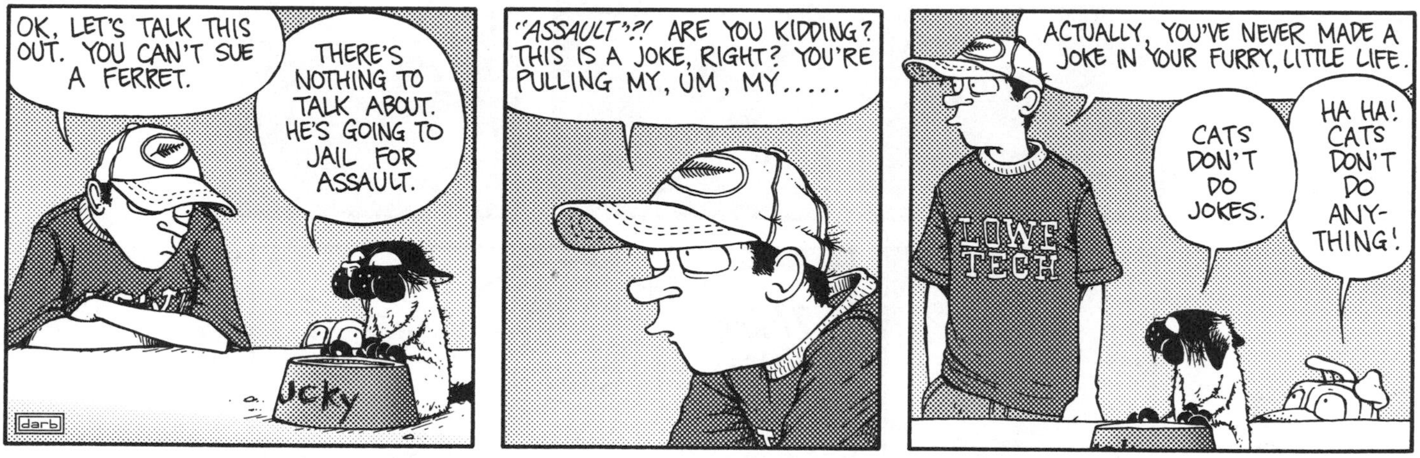
OK, LET'S TALK THIS OUT. YOU CAN'T SUE A FERRET.
THERE'S NOTHING TO TALK ABOUT. HE'S GOING TO JAIL FOR ASSAULT.
darb
"*ASSAULT*"?! ARE YOU KIDDING? THIS IS A JOKE, RIGHT? YOU'RE PULLING MY, UM, MY.....
ACTUALLY, YOU'VE NEVER MADE A JOKE IN YOUR FURRY, LITTLE LIFE.
CATS DON'T DO JOKES.
HA HA! CATS DON'T DO ANYTHING!
LOWE TECH

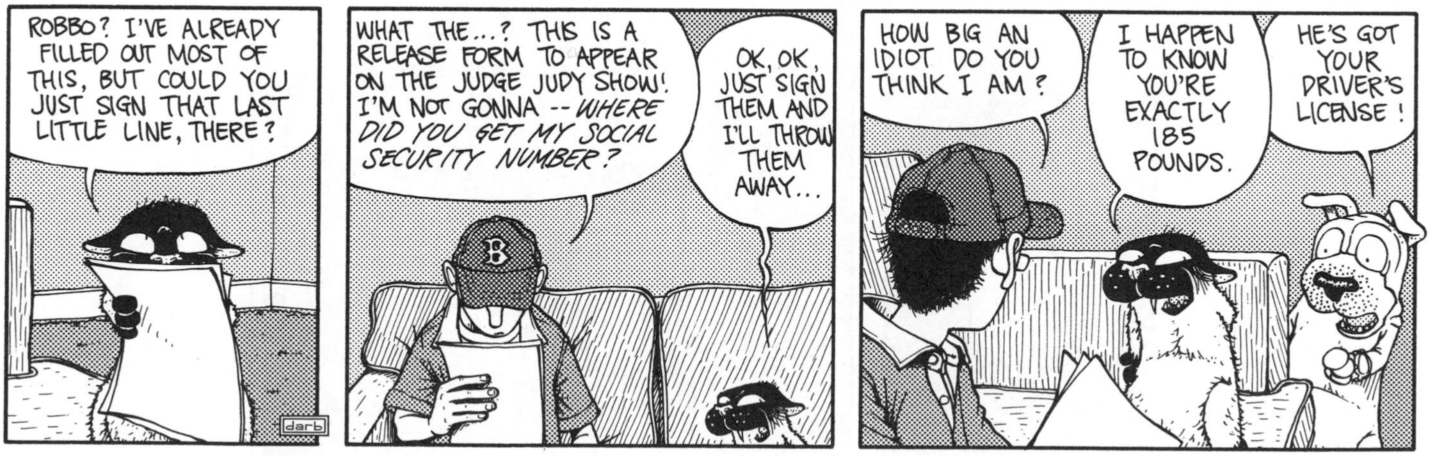
ROBBO? I'VE ALREADY FILLED OUT MOST OF THIS, BUT COULD YOU JUST SIGN THAT LAST LITTLE LINE, THERE?
darb
WHAT THE...? THIS IS A RELEASE FORM TO APPEAR ON THE JUDGE JUDY SHOW! I'M NOT GONNA -- *WHERE DID YOU GET MY SOCIAL SECURITY NUMBER?*
OK, OK, JUST SIGN THEM AND I'LL THROW THEM AWAY...
HOW BIG AN IDIOT DO YOU THINK I AM?
I HAPPEN TO KNOW YOU'RE EXACTLY 185 POUNDS.
HE'S GOT YOUR DRIVER'S LICENSE!

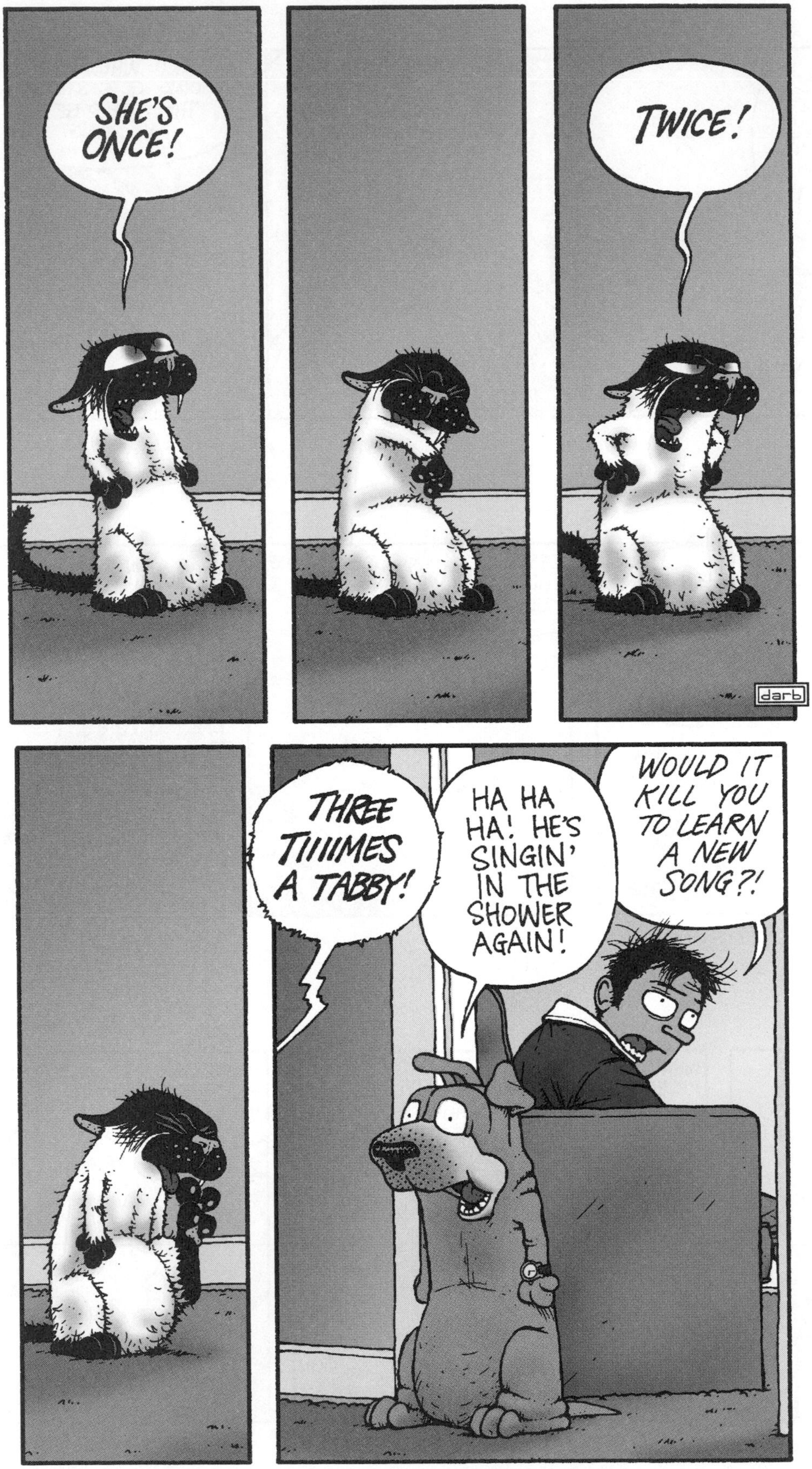
SHE'S ONCE!
TWICE!
darb
THREE TIIIIMES A TABBY!
HA HA HA! HE'S SINGIN' IN THE SHOWER AGAIN!
WOULD IT KILL YOU TO LEARN A NEW SONG?!

Panel 1: I NEED YOU TO TAKE THESE PAPERS OVER TO THE FERRET. / WHY? WHAT ARE THEY?

Panel 2: THEY'RE LAW THINGIES. THEY TELL HIM HE'S BEING SUED. / OHHH NO NO NO, I'M NOT GIVING HIM THOSE. / YOU'RE ALONE ON THIS ONE, BUCK... JUST REMEMBER: *NO MAN IS AN ISLAND.*

Panel 3: YES, BUT I PUT IT TO YOU THAT CATS ARE, LIKE, SMALL BOATS. / CATS ARE DINGHIES!

Panel 4: WHAT TOOK YOU SO LONG? DID YOU SERVE THE WEASEL MY LEGAL PAPERS? / YES, YES, CALM DOWN. WE WERE HANGING OUT IN HIS ROOM.

Panel 5: *ROOM?* I THOUGHT YOU SAID HE LIVED IN A CLOSET... IS IT NICER THAN MY CLOSET? / OH, YEAH, IT'S A *WALK-IN!* IT'S QUITE A DRAMATIC SPACE, ACTUALLY!

Panel 6: SEE, LOOK, HERE'S A PICTURE OF US FROM HIS WEB-CAM WE PRINTED OFF OF HIS WEB SITE. / THE FERRET HAS A WEB SITE? **WOW,** IS THAT A PLASMA TV WITH A SATELLITE RECEIVER BEHIND YOU? / *PFFF...* HE'S PROBABLY JUST GOT THE BASIC PROGRAM PACKAGE.

Panel 7: YOU KNOW WHAT? I *ROCK.* I AM ONE COOL— / DUDE, YOU CAN'T SAY THAT **YOU** ROCK, SOMEONE **ELSE** HAS TO SAY IT! IF YOU HAVE TO SAY IT YOURSELF, IT AIN'T TRUE.

Panel 8: WELL, **ONE** THING IS FOR SURE- **YOU** DON'T ROCK! YOU'RE MOTIONLESS, BABY! / MOTIONLESS LIKE A *ROCK!* I ROCK LIKE A RETIRED "LA-Z-BOY" EMPLOYEE! / GUYS! GUYS! LET'S NOT ARGUE! IN ALL PROBABILITY, EACH ONE OF YOU DOES THIS ROCKING...

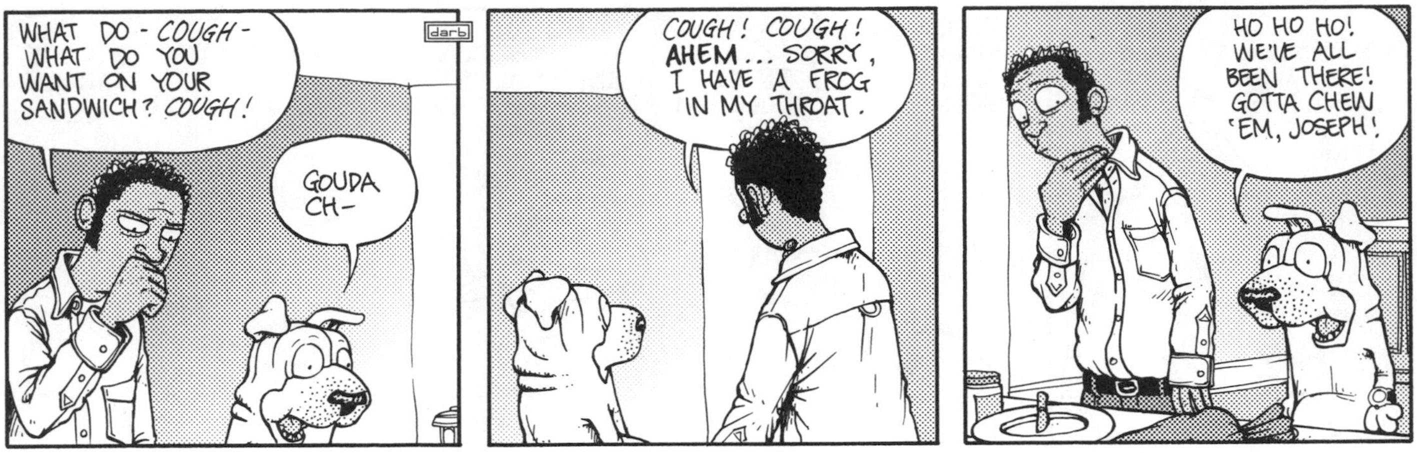
WHAT DO - COUGH - WHAT DO YOU WANT ON YOUR SANDWICH? COUGH!
GOUDA CH-
COUGH! COUGH! AHEM... SORRY, I HAVE A FROG IN MY THROAT.
HO HO HO! WE'VE ALL BEEN THERE! GOTTA CHEW 'EM, JOSEPH!

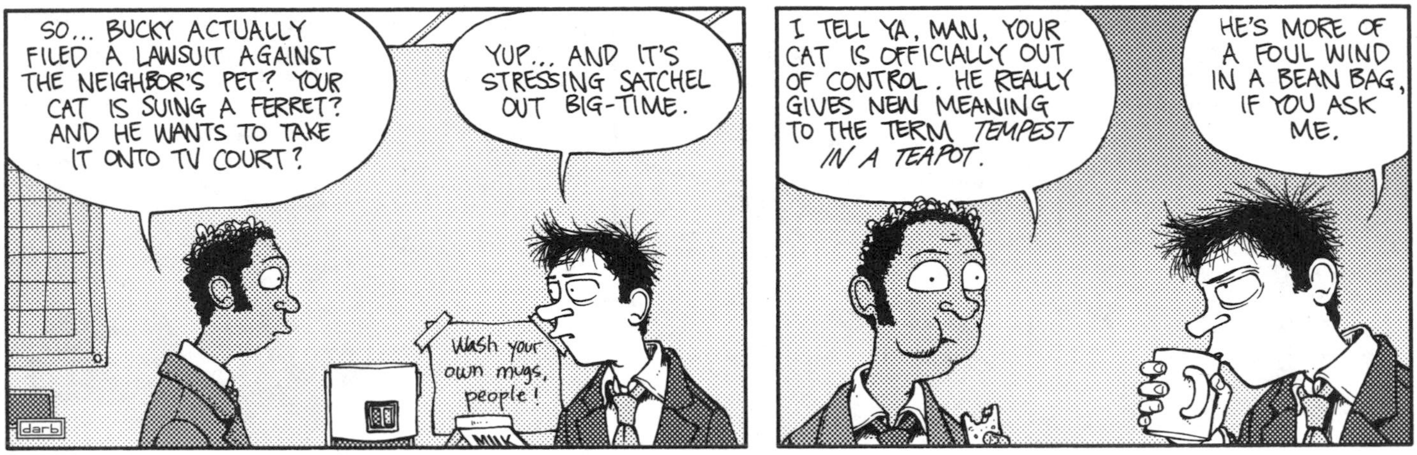
SO... BUCKY ACTUALLY FILED A LAWSUIT AGAINST THE NEIGHBOR'S PET? YOUR CAT IS SUING A FERRET? AND HE WANTS TO TAKE IT ONTO TV COURT?
YUP... AND IT'S STRESSING SATCHEL OUT BIG-TIME.
Wash your own mugs, people!
I TELL YA, MAN, YOUR CAT IS OFFICIALLY OUT OF CONTROL. HE REALLY GIVES NEW MEANING TO THE TERM TEMPEST IN A TEAPOT.
HE'S MORE OF A FOUL WIND IN A BEAN BAG, IF YOU ASK ME.

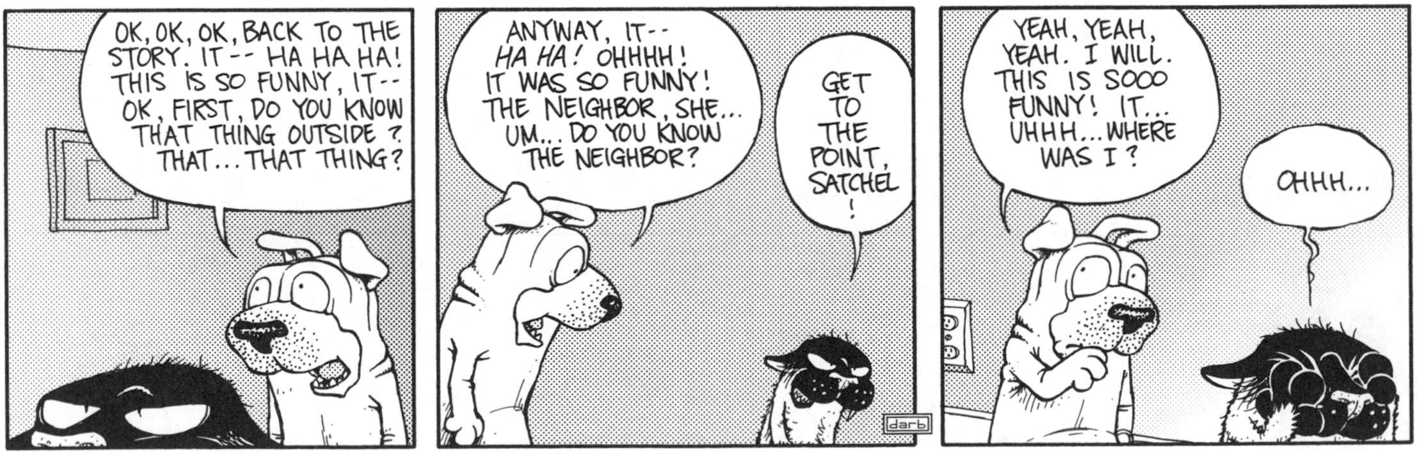
OK, OK, OK, BACK TO THE STORY. IT-- HA HA HA! THIS IS SO FUNNY, IT-- OK, FIRST, DO YOU KNOW THAT THING OUTSIDE? THAT... THAT THING?
ANYWAY, IT-- HA HA! OHHHH! IT WAS SO FUNNY! THE NEIGHBOR, SHE... UM... DO YOU KNOW THE NEIGHBOR?
GET TO THE POINT, SATCHEL!
YEAH, YEAH, YEAH. I WILL. THIS IS SOOO FUNNY! IT... UHHH... WHERE WAS I?
OHHH...

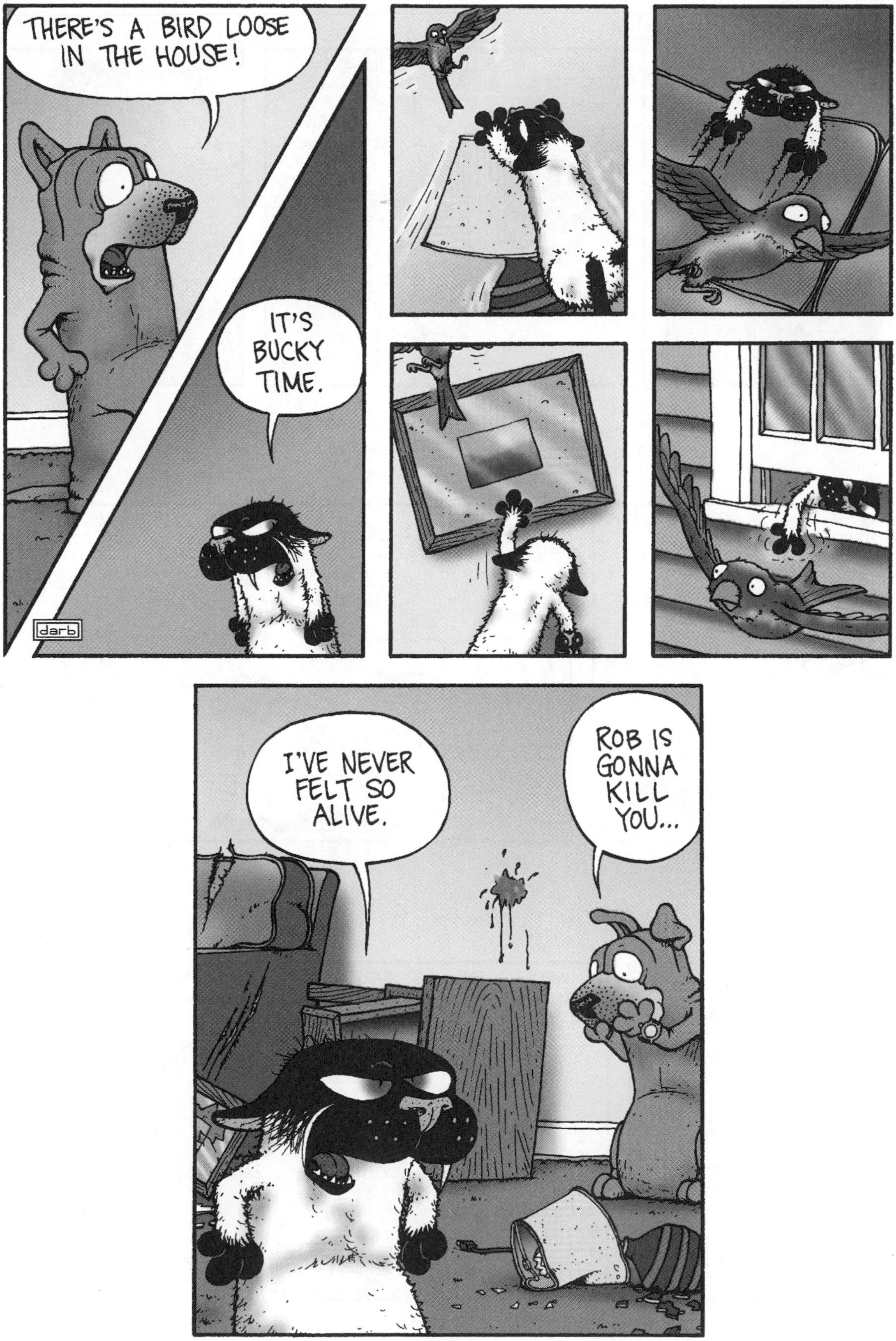
THERE'S A BIRD LOOSE IN THE HOUSE!
IT'S BUCKY TIME.
darb
I'VE NEVER FELT SO ALIVE.
ROB IS GONNA KILL YOU...

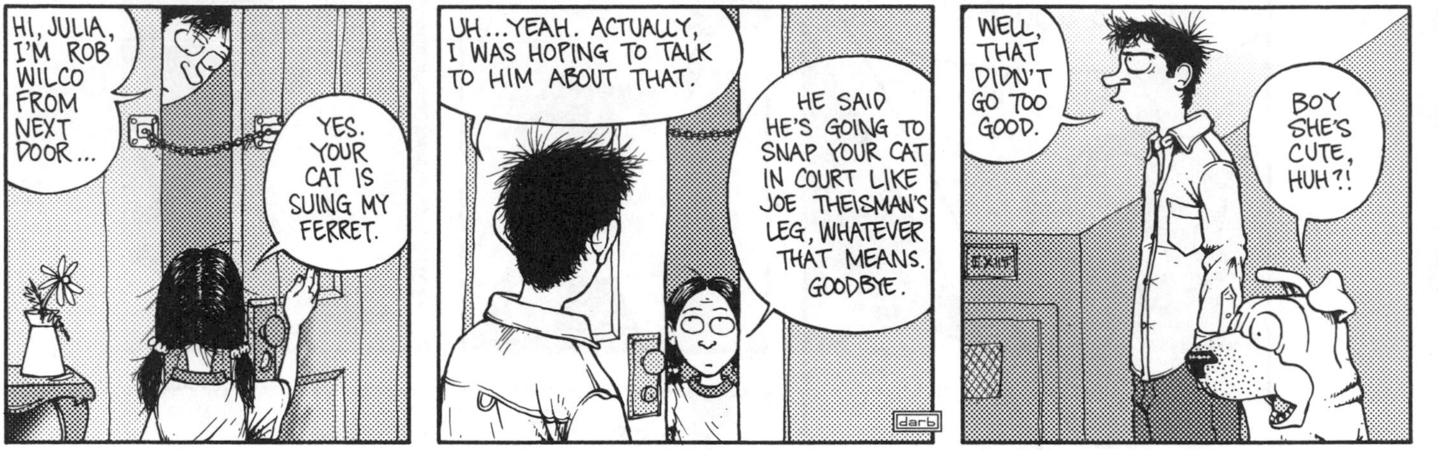
HI, JULIA, I'M ROB WILCO FROM NEXT DOOR...
YES. YOUR CAT IS SUING MY FERRET.
UH...YEAH. ACTUALLY, I WAS HOPING TO TALK TO HIM ABOUT THAT.
HE SAID HE'S GOING TO SNAP YOUR CAT IN COURT LIKE JOE THEISMAN'S LEG, WHATEVER THAT MEANS. GOODBYE.
WELL, THAT DIDN'T GO TOO GOOD.
BOY SHE'S CUTE, HUH?!
darb

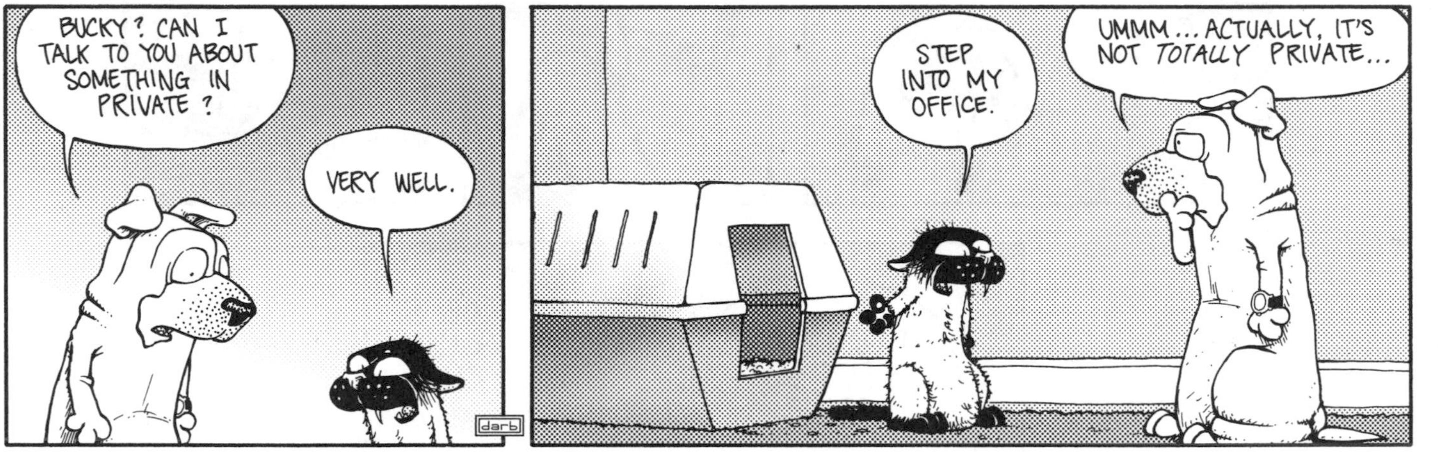
BUCKY? CAN I TALK TO YOU ABOUT SOMETHING IN PRIVATE?
VERY WELL.
STEP INTO MY OFFICE.
UMMM... ACTUALLY, IT'S NOT TOTALLY PRIVATE...
darb

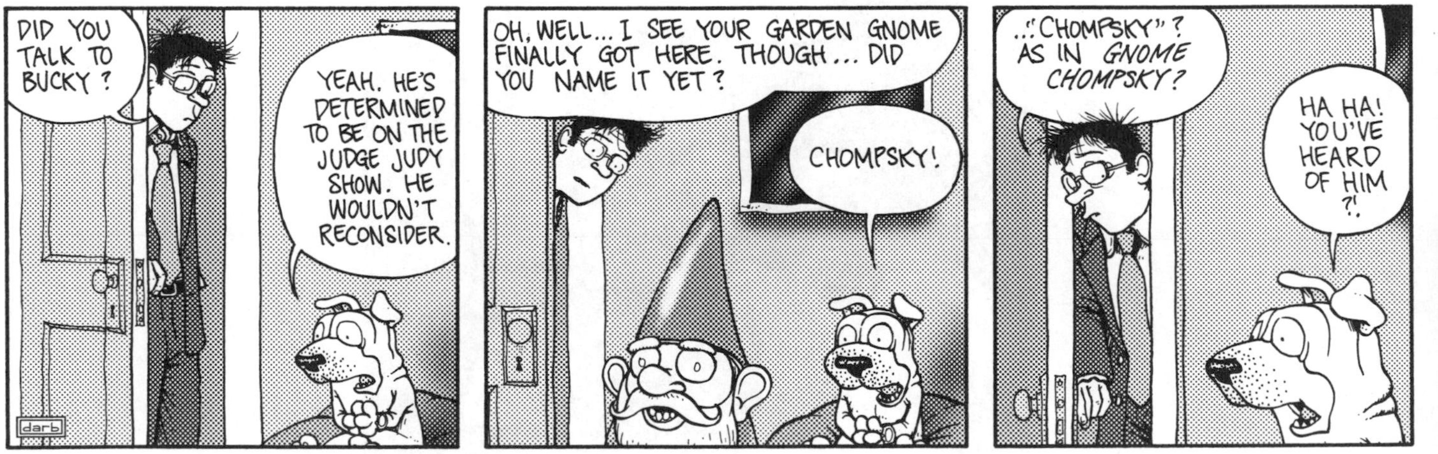
DID YOU TALK TO BUCKY?
YEAH. HE'S DETERMINED TO BE ON THE JUDGE JUDY SHOW. HE WOULDN'T RECONSIDER.
OH, WELL... I SEE YOUR GARDEN GNOME FINALLY GOT HERE. THOUGH... DID YOU NAME IT YET?
CHOMPSKY!
..."CHOMPSKY"? AS IN GNOME CHOMPSKY?
HA HA! YOU'VE HEARD OF HIM?!
darb

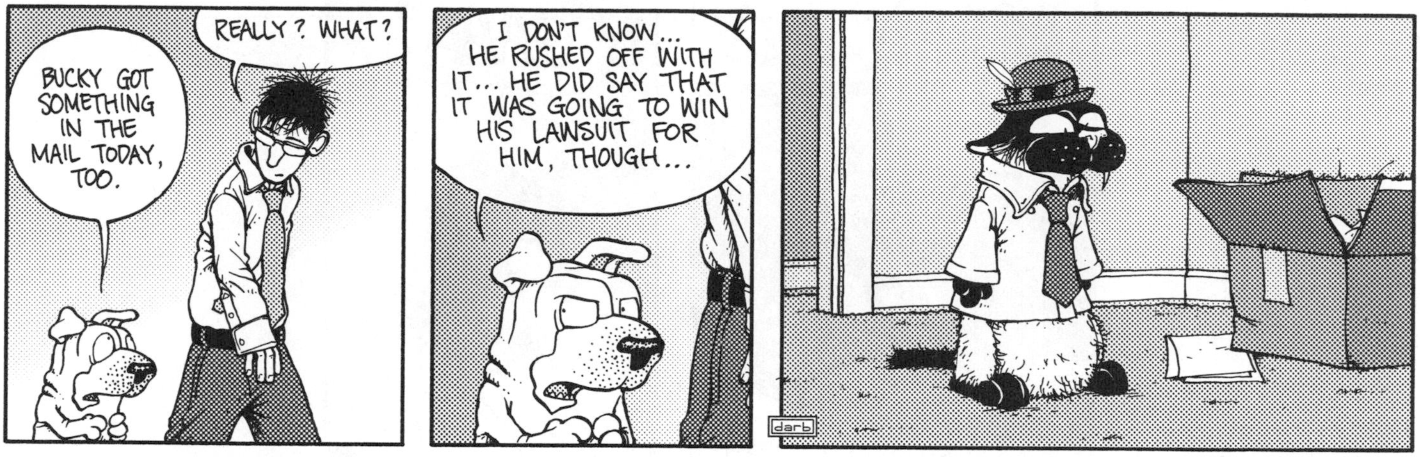
BUCKY GOT SOMETHING IN THE MAIL TODAY, TOO.
REALLY? WHAT?
I DON'T KNOW... HE RUSHED OFF WITH IT... HE DID SAY THAT IT WAS GOING TO WIN HIS LAWSUIT FOR HIM, THOUGH...
darb

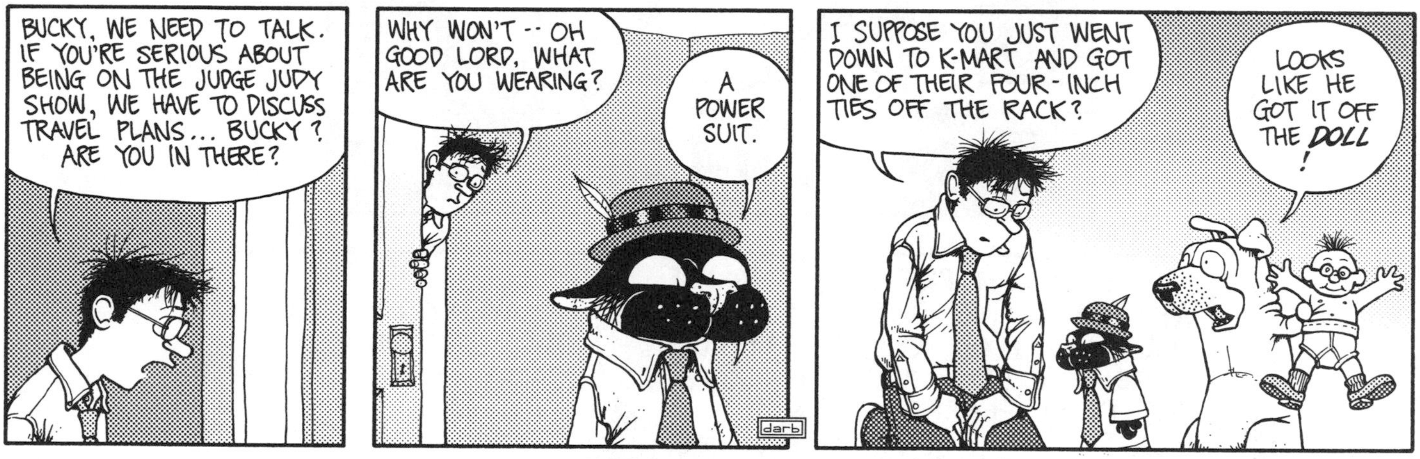
BUCKY, WE NEED TO TALK. IF YOU'RE SERIOUS ABOUT BEING ON THE JUDGE JUDY SHOW, WE HAVE TO DISCUSS TRAVEL PLANS... BUCKY? ARE YOU IN THERE?
WHY WON'T -- OH GOOD LORD, WHAT ARE YOU WEARING?
A POWER SUIT.
darb
I SUPPOSE YOU JUST WENT DOWN TO K-MART AND GOT ONE OF THEIR FOUR-INCH TIES OFF THE RACK?
LOOKS LIKE HE GOT IT OFF THE *DOLL*!

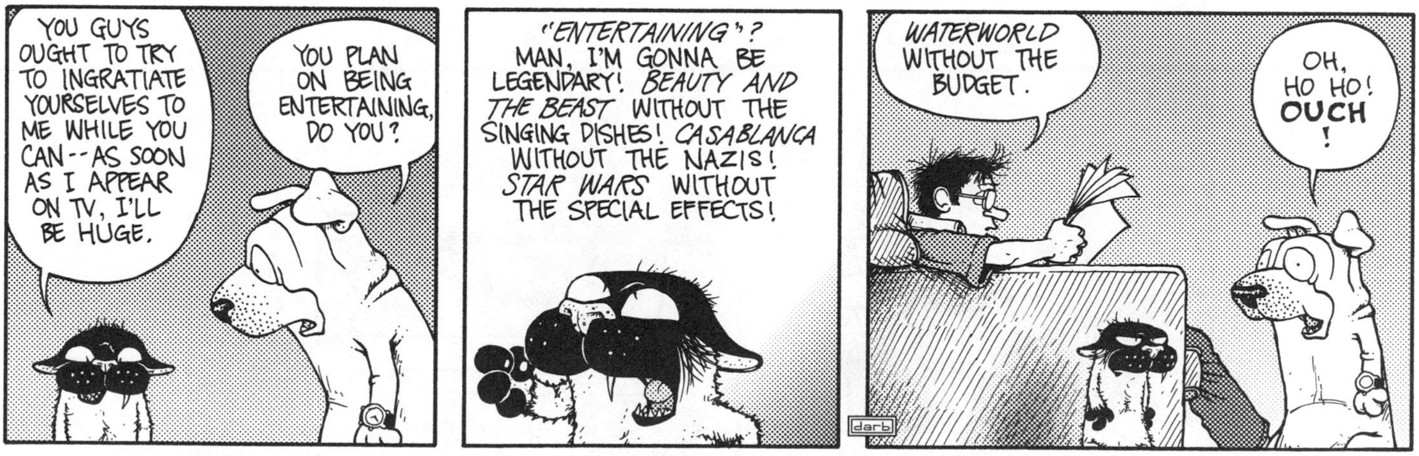
YOU GUYS OUGHT TO TRY TO INGRATIATE YOURSELVES TO ME WHILE YOU CAN -- AS SOON AS I APPEAR ON TV, I'LL BE HUGE.
YOU PLAN ON BEING ENTERTAINING, DO YOU?
"*ENTERTAINING*"? MAN, I'M GONNA BE LEGENDARY! *BEAUTY AND THE BEAST* WITHOUT THE SINGING DISHES! *CASABLANCA* WITHOUT THE NAZIS! *STAR WARS* WITHOUT THE SPECIAL EFFECTS!
WATERWORLD WITHOUT THE BUDGET.
OH, HO HO! **OUCH**!
darb

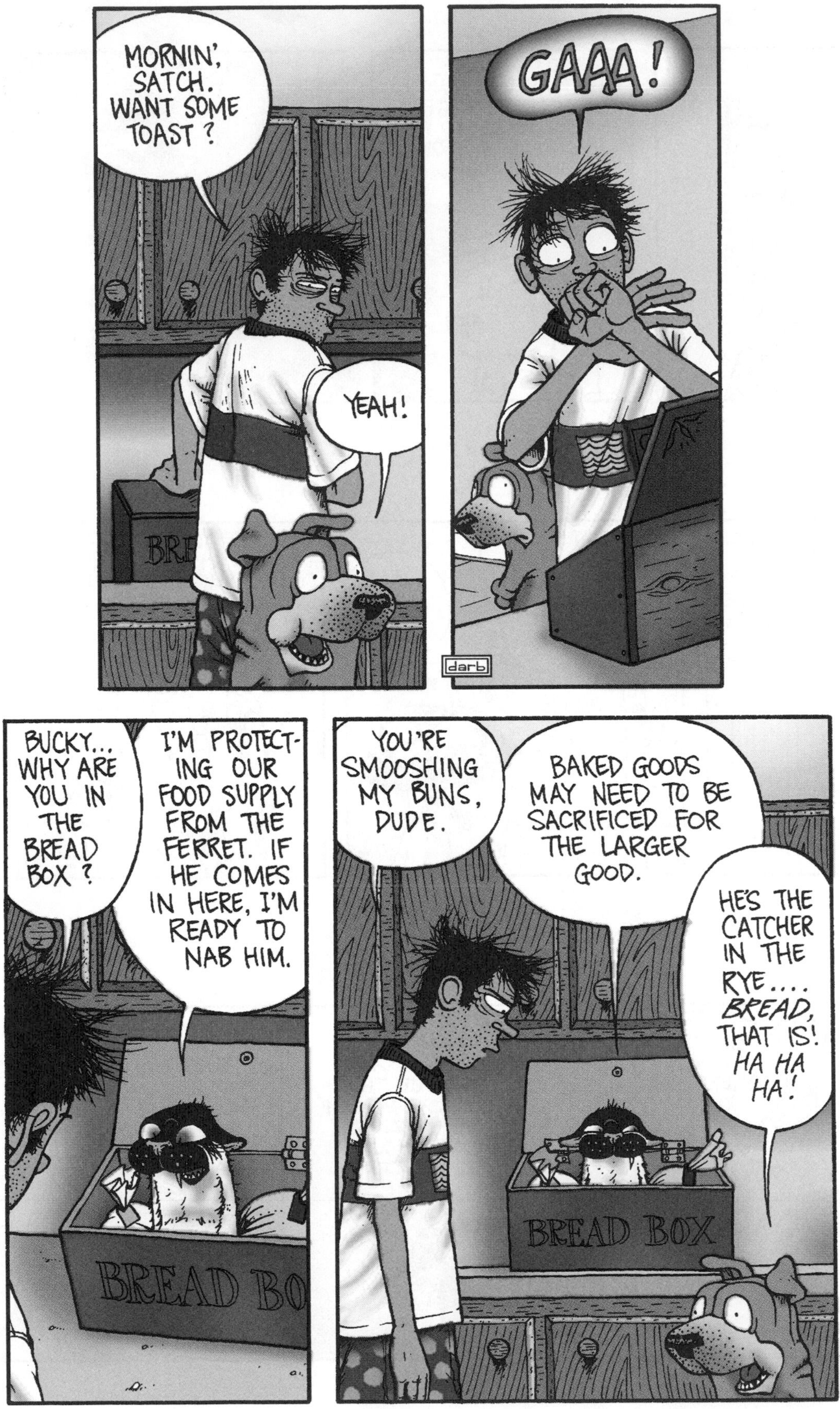
MORNIN', SATCH. WANT SOME TOAST ?
YEAH!
GAAA!
darb
BUCKY... WHY ARE YOU IN THE BREAD BOX ?
I'M PROTECTING OUR FOOD SUPPLY FROM THE FERRET. IF HE COMES IN HERE, I'M READY TO NAB HIM.
BREAD BO
YOU'RE SMOOSHING MY BUNS, DUDE.
BAKED GOODS MAY NEED TO BE SACRIFICED FOR THE LARGER GOOD.
HE'S THE CATCHER IN THE RYE.... *BREAD*, THAT IS! HA HA HA!
BREAD BOX

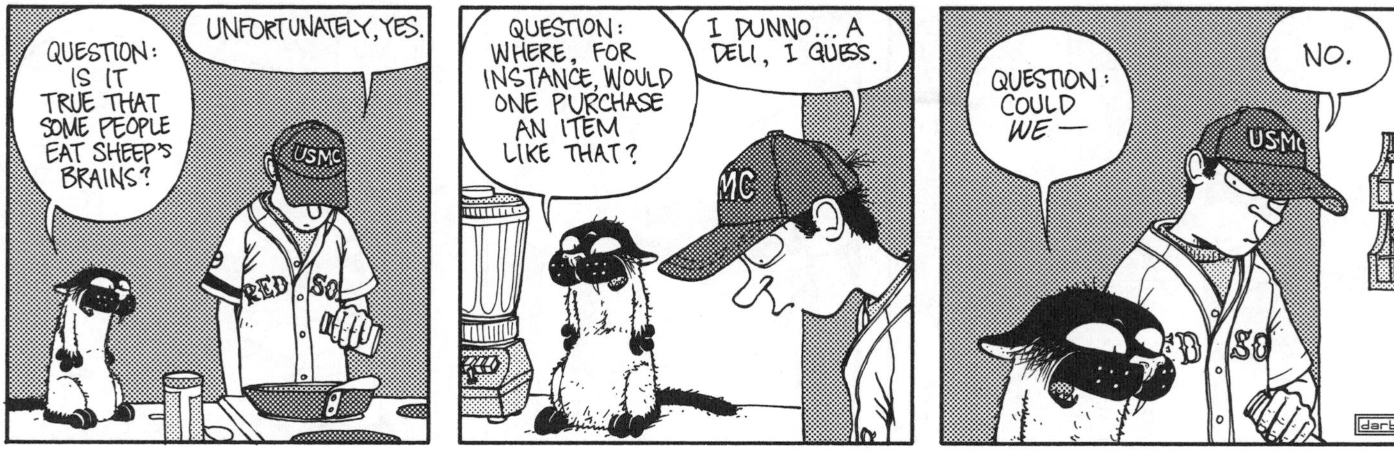
QUESTION: IS IT TRUE THAT SOME PEOPLE EAT SHEEP'S BRAINS?
UNFORTUNATELY, YES.
QUESTION: WHERE, FOR INSTANCE, WOULD ONE PURCHASE AN ITEM LIKE THAT?
I DUNNO... A DELI, I GUESS.
QUESTION: COULD *WE* —
NO.

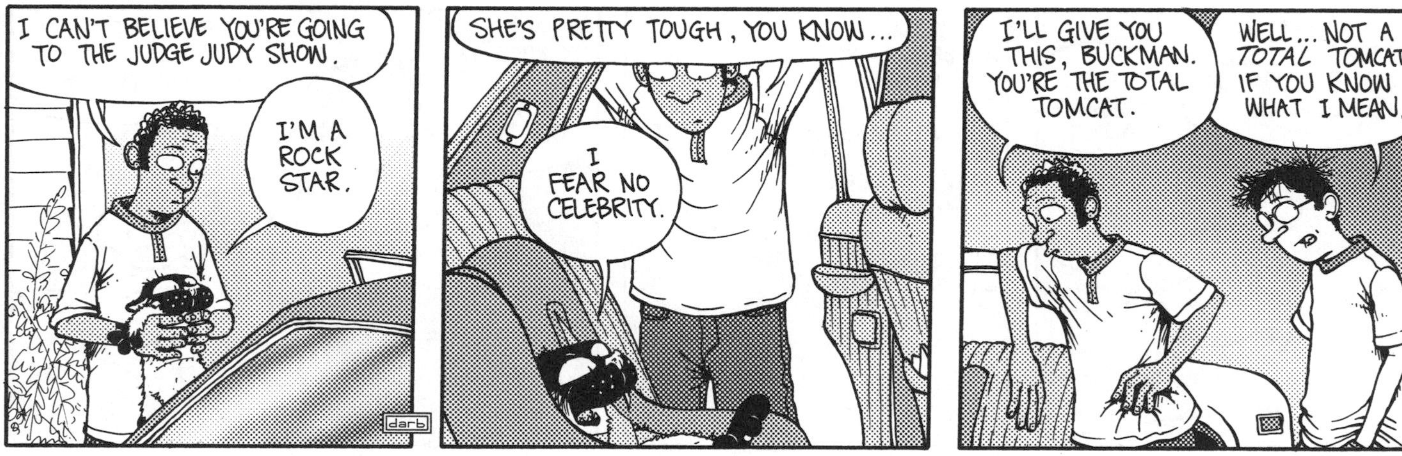
I CAN'T BELIEVE YOU'RE GOING TO THE JUDGE JUDY SHOW.
I'M A ROCK STAR.
SHE'S PRETTY TOUGH, YOU KNOW...
I FEAR NO CELEBRITY.
I'LL GIVE YOU THIS, BUCKMAN. YOU'RE THE TOTAL TOMCAT.
WELL... NOT A *TOTAL* TOMCAT, IF YOU KNOW WHAT I MEAN.

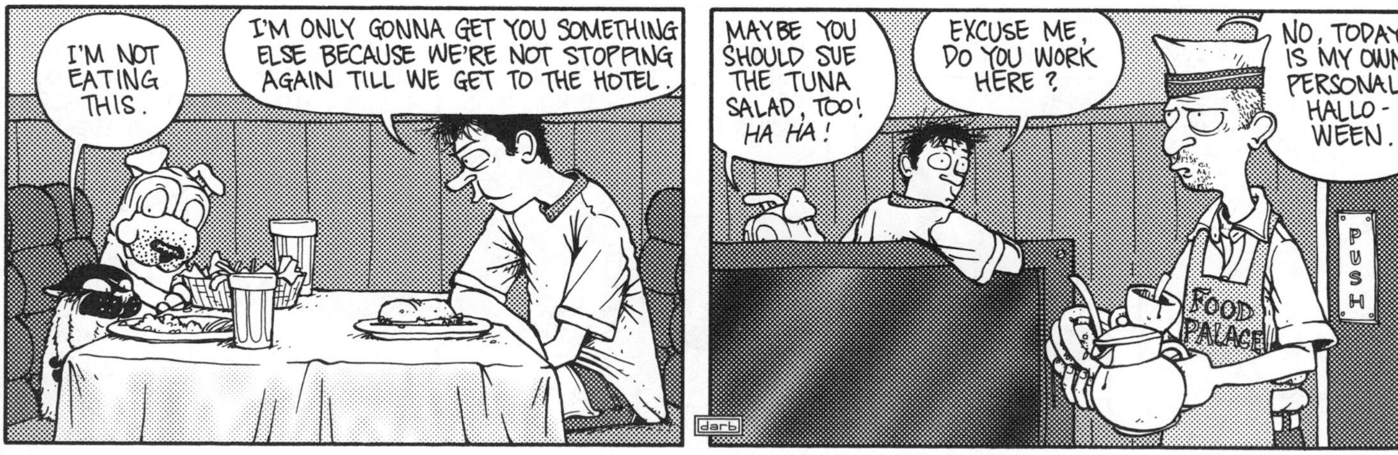
I'M NOT EATING THIS.
I'M ONLY GONNA GET YOU SOMETHING ELSE BECAUSE WE'RE NOT STOPPING AGAIN TILL WE GET TO THE HOTEL.
MAYBE YOU SHOULD SUE THE TUNA SALAD, TOO! *HA HA!*
EXCUSE ME, DO YOU WORK HERE?
NO, TODAY IS MY OWN PERSONAL HALLO-WEEN.
PUSH
FOOD PALACE

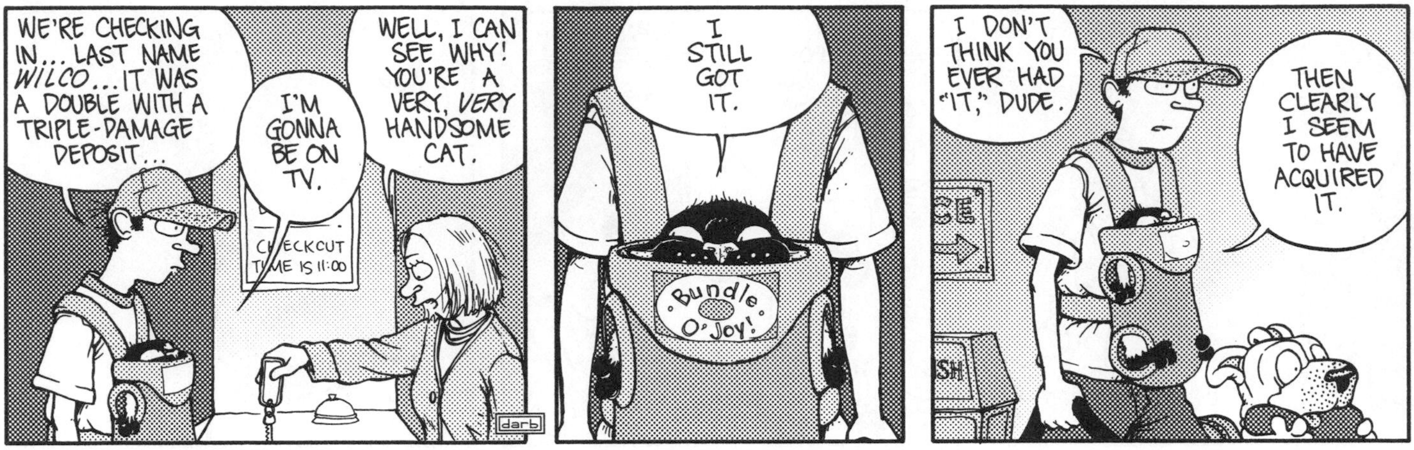
WE'RE CHECKING IN... LAST NAME *WILCO*... IT WAS A DOUBLE WITH A TRIPLE-DAMAGE DEPOSIT...
I'M GONNA BE ON TV.
CHECKOUT TIME IS 11:00
WELL, I CAN SEE WHY! YOU'RE A VERY, *VERY* HANDSOME CAT.
darb
I STILL GOT IT.
Bundle O'Joy!
I DON'T THINK YOU EVER HAD "IT," DUDE.
THEN CLEARLY I SEEM TO HAVE ACQUIRED IT.

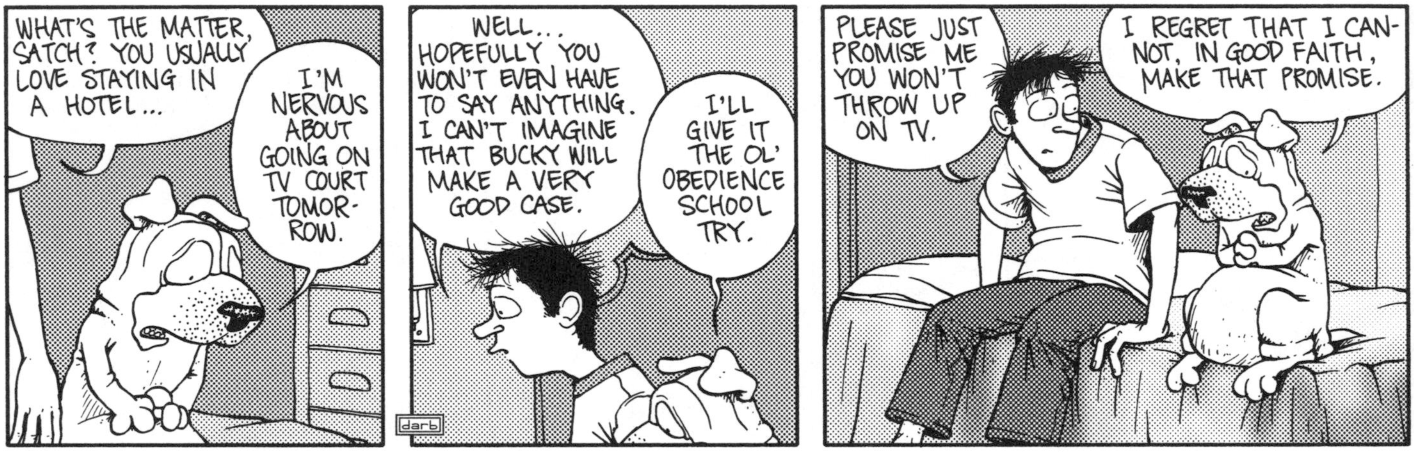
WHAT'S THE MATTER, SATCH? YOU USUALLY LOVE STAYING IN A HOTEL...
I'M NERVOUS ABOUT GOING ON TV COURT TOMORROW.
WELL... HOPEFULLY YOU WON'T EVEN HAVE TO SAY ANYTHING. I CAN'T IMAGINE THAT BUCKY WILL MAKE A VERY GOOD CASE.
I'LL GIVE IT THE OL' OBEDIENCE SCHOOL TRY.
darb
PLEASE JUST PROMISE ME YOU WON'T THROW UP ON TV.
I REGRET THAT I CANNOT, IN GOOD FAITH, MAKE THAT PROMISE.

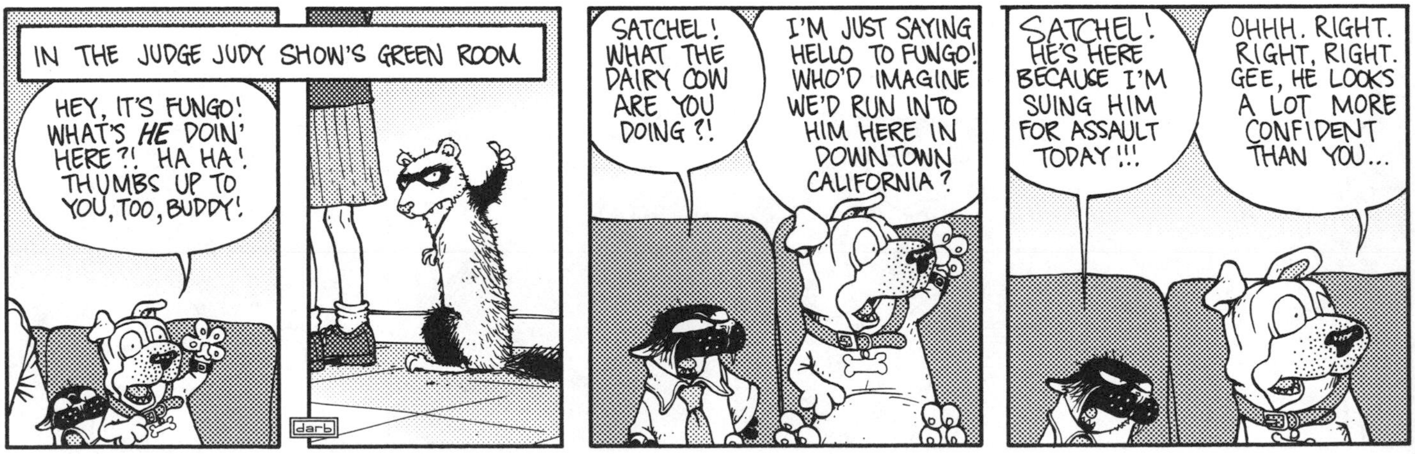
IN THE JUDGE JUDY SHOW'S GREEN ROOM
HEY, IT'S FUNGO! WHAT'S *HE* DOIN' HERE?! HA HA! THUMBS UP TO YOU, TOO, BUDDY!
darb
SATCHEL! WHAT THE DAIRY COW ARE YOU DOING?!
I'M JUST SAYING HELLO TO FUNGO! WHO'D IMAGINE WE'D RUN INTO HIM HERE IN DOWNTOWN CALIFORNIA?
SATCHEL! HE'S HERE BECAUSE I'M SUING HIM FOR ASSAULT TODAY!!!
OHHH. RIGHT. RIGHT, RIGHT. GEE, HE LOOKS A LOT MORE CONFIDENT THAN YOU...

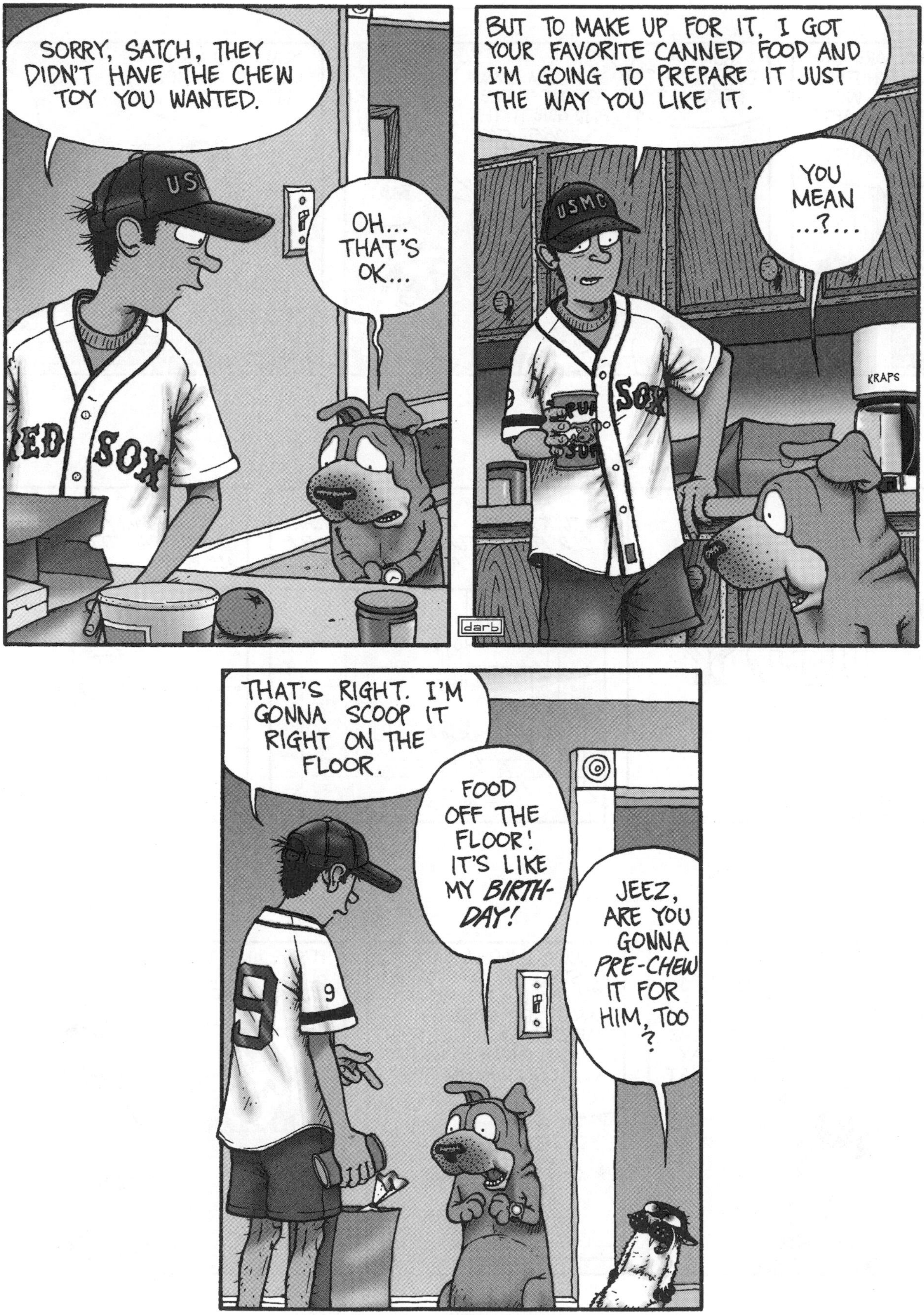
SORRY, SATCH, THEY DIDN'T HAVE THE CHEW TOY YOU WANTED.
OH... THAT'S OK...
BUT TO MAKE UP FOR IT, I GOT YOUR FAVORITE CANNED FOOD AND I'M GOING TO PREPARE IT JUST THE WAY YOU LIKE IT.
YOU MEAN ...?...
KRAPS
THAT'S RIGHT. I'M GONNA SCOOP IT RIGHT ON THE FLOOR.
FOOD OFF THE FLOOR! IT'S LIKE MY *BIRTH-DAY!*
JEEZ, ARE YOU GONNA *PRE-CHEW* IT FOR HIM, TOO?

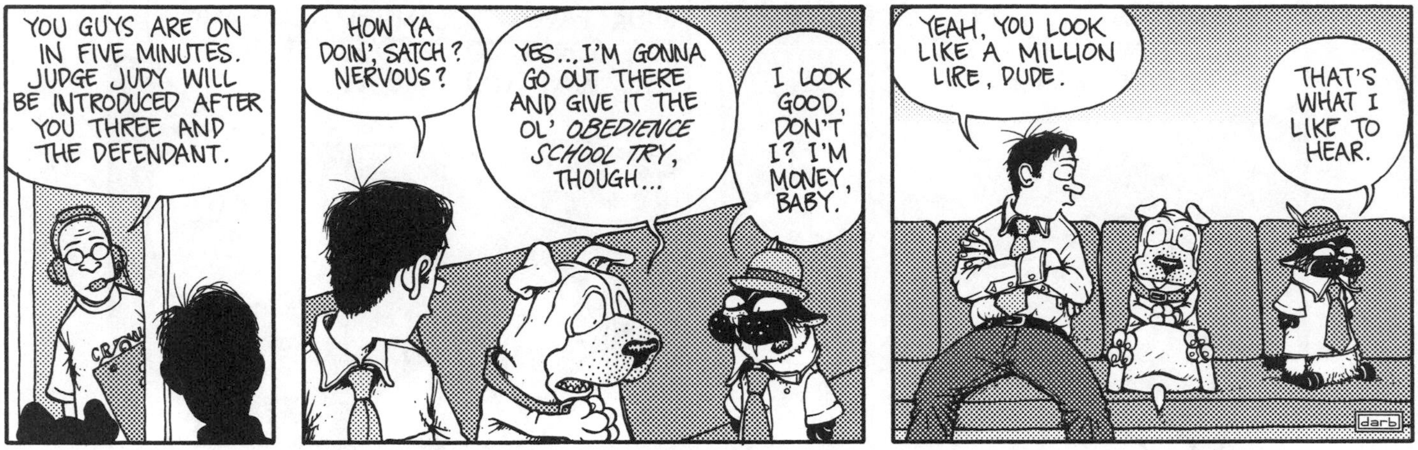
YOU GUYS ARE ON IN FIVE MINUTES. JUDGE JUDY WILL BE INTRODUCED AFTER YOU THREE AND THE DEFENDANT.
CREW
HOW YA DOIN', SATCH? NERVOUS?
YES... I'M GONNA GO OUT THERE AND GIVE IT THE OL' *OBEDIENCE SCHOOL TRY*, THOUGH...
I LOOK GOOD, DON'T I? I'M MONEY, BABY.
YEAH, YOU LOOK LIKE A MILLION
LIKE, DUDE.
THAT'S WHAT I LIKE TO HEAR.
darb

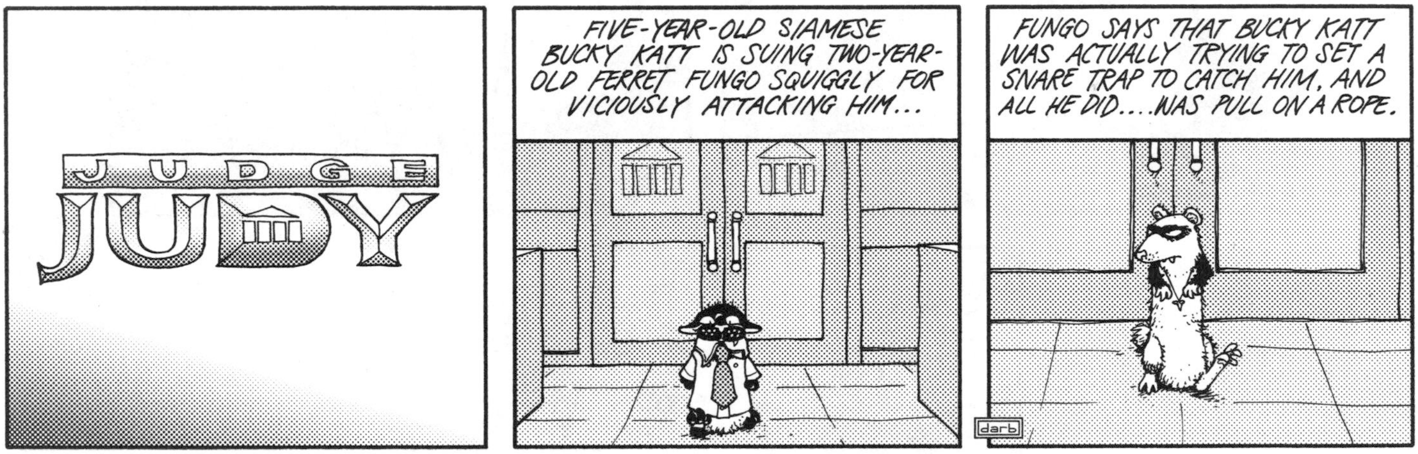
JUDGE
JUDY
FIVE-YEAR-OLD SIAMESE BUCKY KATT IS SUING TWO-YEAR-OLD FERRET FUNGO SQUIGGLY FOR VICIOUSLY ATTACKING HIM...
FUNGO SAYS THAT BUCKY KATT WAS ACTUALLY TRYING TO SET A SNARE TRAP TO CATCH HIM, AND ALL HE DID.... WAS PULL ON A ROPE.
darb

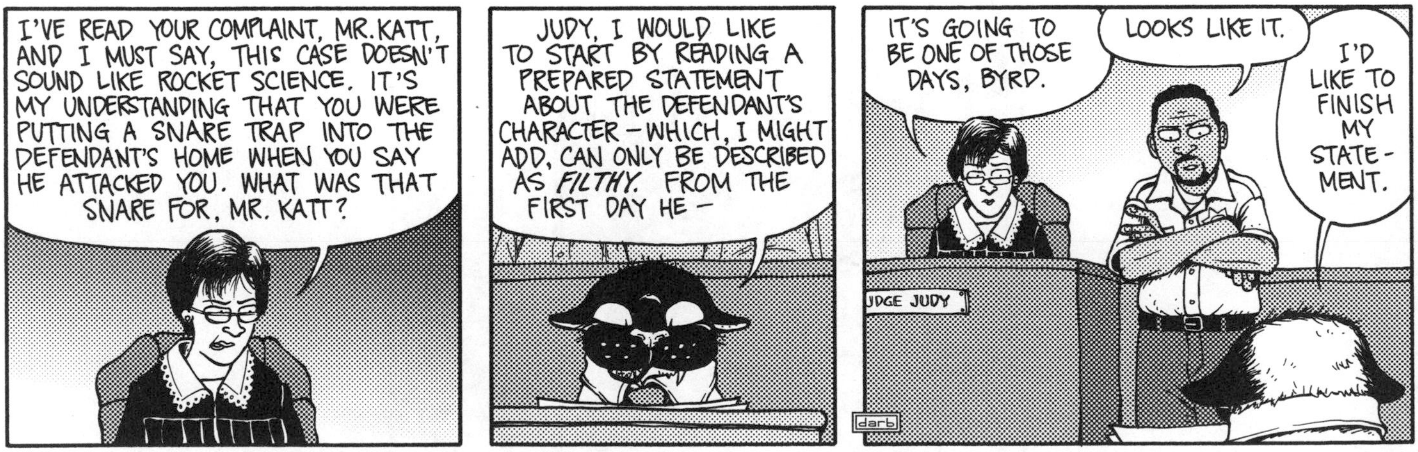
I'VE READ YOUR COMPLAINT, MR. KATT, AND I MUST SAY, THIS CASE DOESN'T SOUND LIKE ROCKET SCIENCE. IT'S MY UNDERSTANDING THAT YOU WERE PUTTING A SNARE TRAP INTO THE DEFENDANT'S HOME WHEN YOU SAY HE ATTACKED YOU. WHAT WAS THAT SNARE FOR, MR. KATT?
JUDY, I WOULD LIKE TO START BY READING A PREPARED STATEMENT ABOUT THE DEFENDANT'S CHARACTER — WHICH, I MIGHT ADD, CAN ONLY BE DESCRIBED AS *FILTHY*. FROM THE FIRST DAY HE —
IT'S GOING TO BE ONE OF THOSE DAYS, BYRD.
LOOKS LIKE IT.
I'D LIKE TO FINISH MY STATE-MENT.
JUDGE JUDY
darb

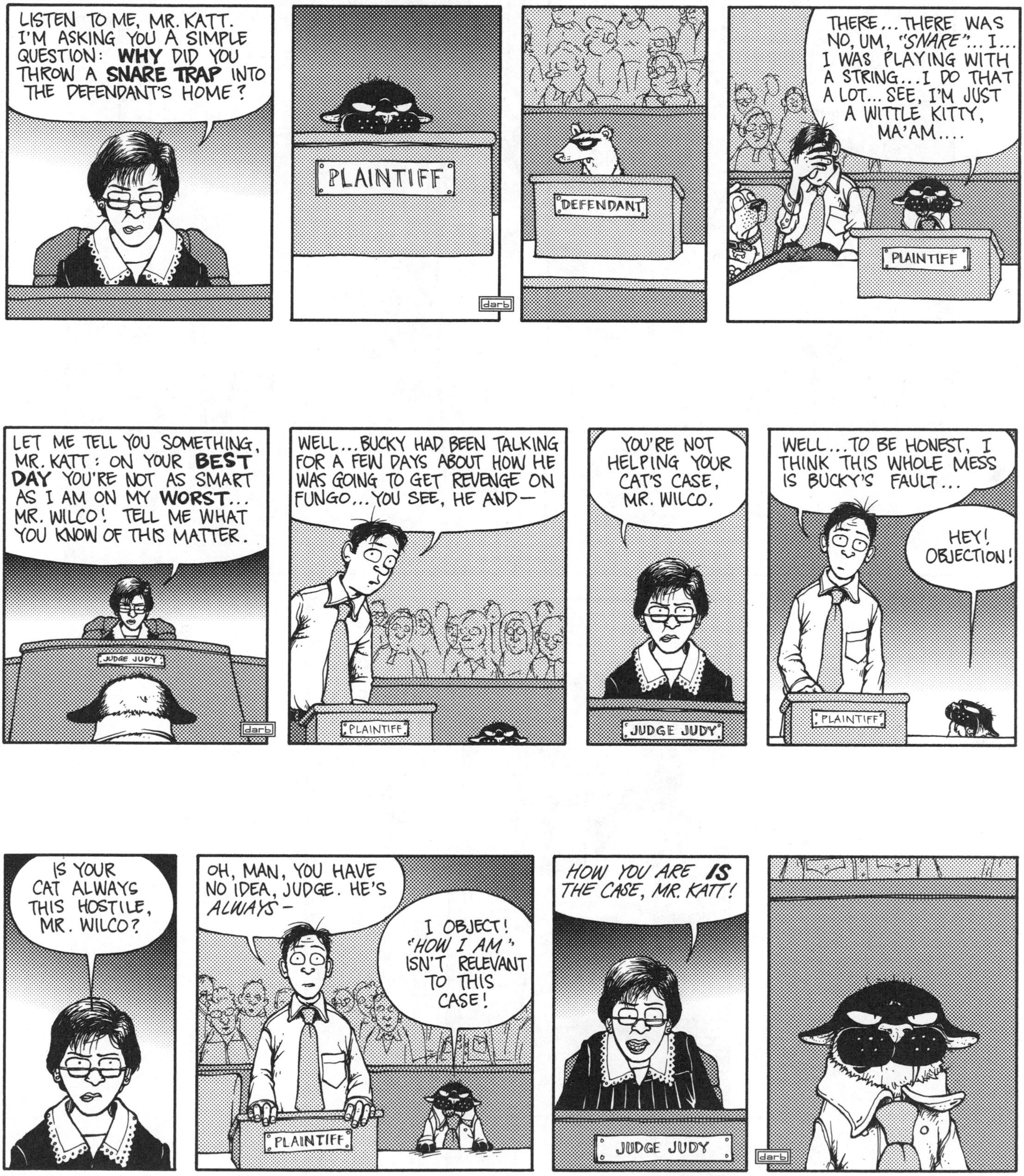
LISTEN TO ME, MR. KATT. I'M ASKING YOU A SIMPLE QUESTION: WHY DID YOU THROW A SNARE TRAP INTO THE DEFENDANT'S HOME?
PLAINTIFF
darb
DEFENDANT
THERE... THERE WAS NO, UM, "SNARE"... I... I WAS PLAYING WITH A STRING... I DO THAT A LOT... SEE, I'M JUST A WITTLE KITTY, MA'AM....
PLAINTIFF
LET ME TELL YOU SOMETHING, MR. KATT: ON YOUR BEST DAY YOU'RE NOT AS SMART AS I AM ON MY WORST... MR. WILCO! TELL ME WHAT YOU KNOW OF THIS MATTER.
JUDGE JUDY
darb
WELL... BUCKY HAD BEEN TALKING FOR A FEW DAYS ABOUT HOW HE WAS GOING TO GET REVENGE ON FUNGO... YOU SEE, HE AND—
PLAINTIFF
YOU'RE NOT HELPING YOUR CAT'S CASE, MR. WILCO.
JUDGE JUDY
WELL... TO BE HONEST, I THINK THIS WHOLE MESS IS BUCKY'S FAULT...
HEY! OBJECTION!
PLAINTIFF
IS YOUR CAT ALWAYS THIS HOSTILE, MR. WILCO?
OH, MAN, YOU HAVE NO IDEA, JUDGE. HE'S ALWAYS –
I OBJECT! "HOW I AM" ISN'T RELEVANT TO THIS CASE!
PLAINTIFF
HOW YOU ARE IS THE CASE, MR. KATT!
JUDGE JUDY
darb

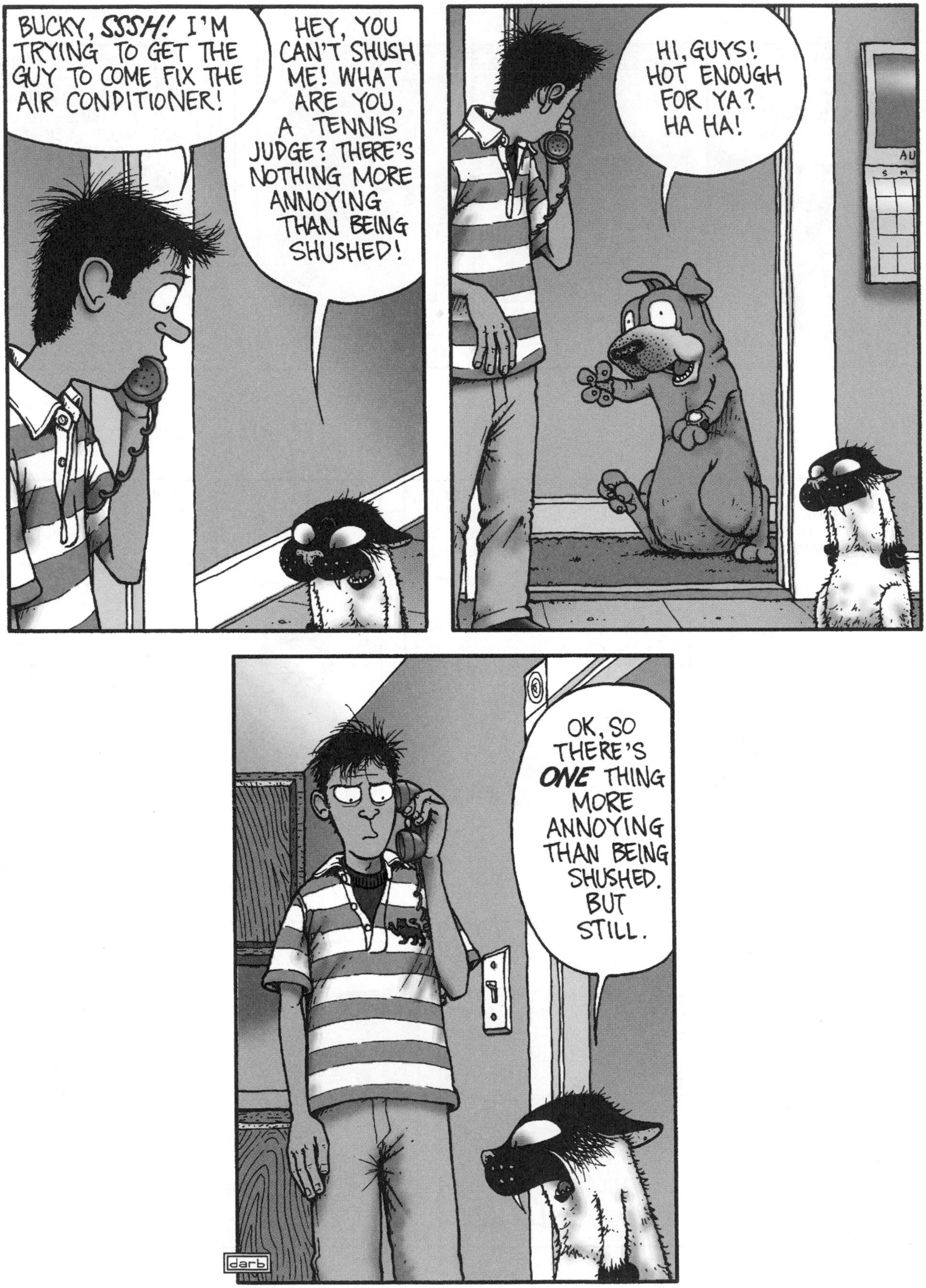
BUCKY, SSSH! I'M TRYING TO GET THE GUY TO COME FIX THE AIR CONDITIONER!
HEY, YOU CAN'T SHUSH ME! WHAT ARE YOU, A TENNIS JUDGE? THERE'S NOTHING MORE ANNOYING THAN BEING SHUSHED!
HI, GUYS! HOT ENOUGH FOR YA? HA HA!
OK, SO THERE'S ONE THING MORE ANNOYING THAN BEING SHUSHED. BUT STILL.
darb

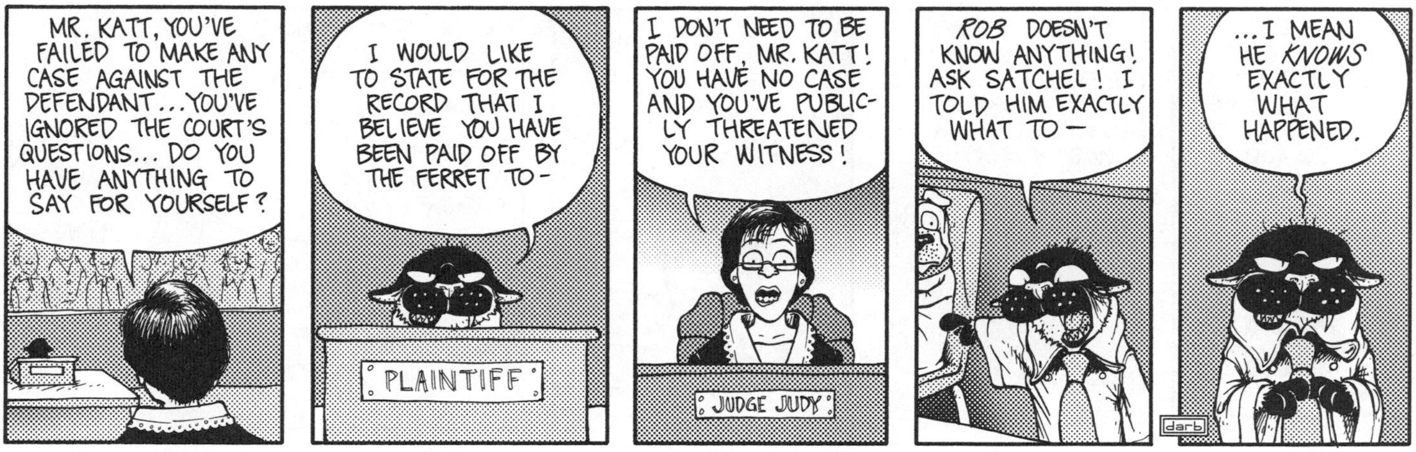
MR. KATT, YOU'VE FAILED TO MAKE ANY CASE AGAINST THE DEFENDANT... YOU'VE IGNORED THE COURT'S QUESTIONS... DO YOU HAVE ANYTHING TO SAY FOR YOURSELF?
I WOULD LIKE TO STATE FOR THE RECORD THAT I BELIEVE YOU HAVE BEEN PAID OFF BY THE FERRET TO-
PLAINTIFF
I DON'T NEED TO BE PAID OFF, MR. KATT! YOU HAVE NO CASE AND YOU'VE PUBLICLY THREATENED YOUR WITNESS!
JUDGE JUDY
ROB DOESN'T KNOW ANYTHING! ASK SATCHEL! I TOLD HIM EXACTLY WHAT TO—
...I MEAN HE KNOWS EXACTLY WHAT HAPPENED.
darb

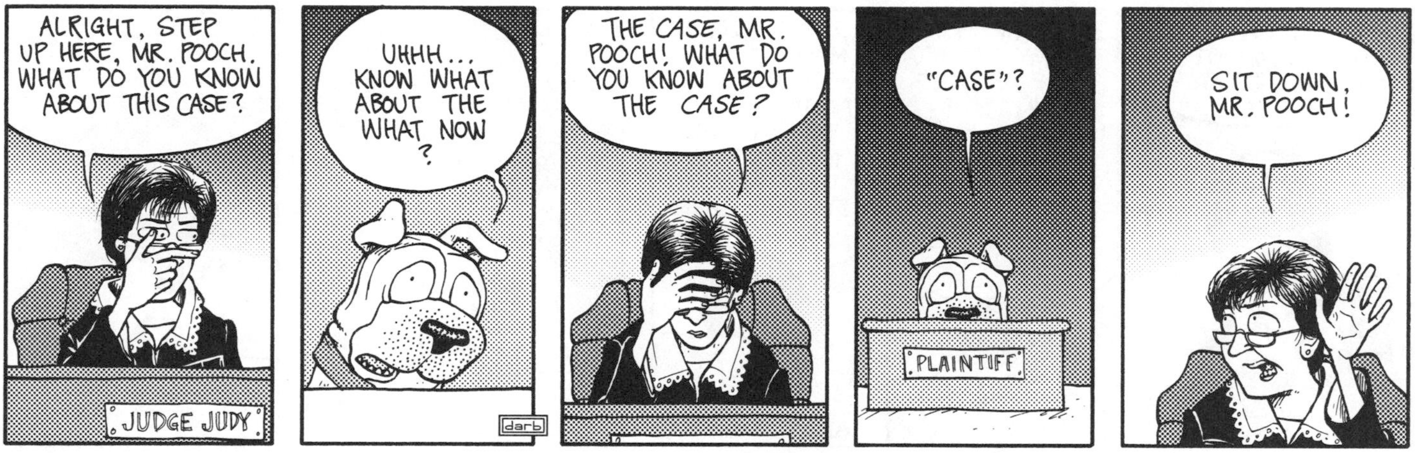
ALRIGHT, STEP UP HERE, MR. POOCH. WHAT DO YOU KNOW ABOUT THIS CASE?
JUDGE JUDY
UHHH... KNOW WHAT ABOUT THE WHAT NOW?
darb
THE CASE, MR. POOCH! WHAT DO YOU KNOW ABOUT THE CASE?
"CASE"?
PLAINTIFF
SIT DOWN, MR. POOCH!

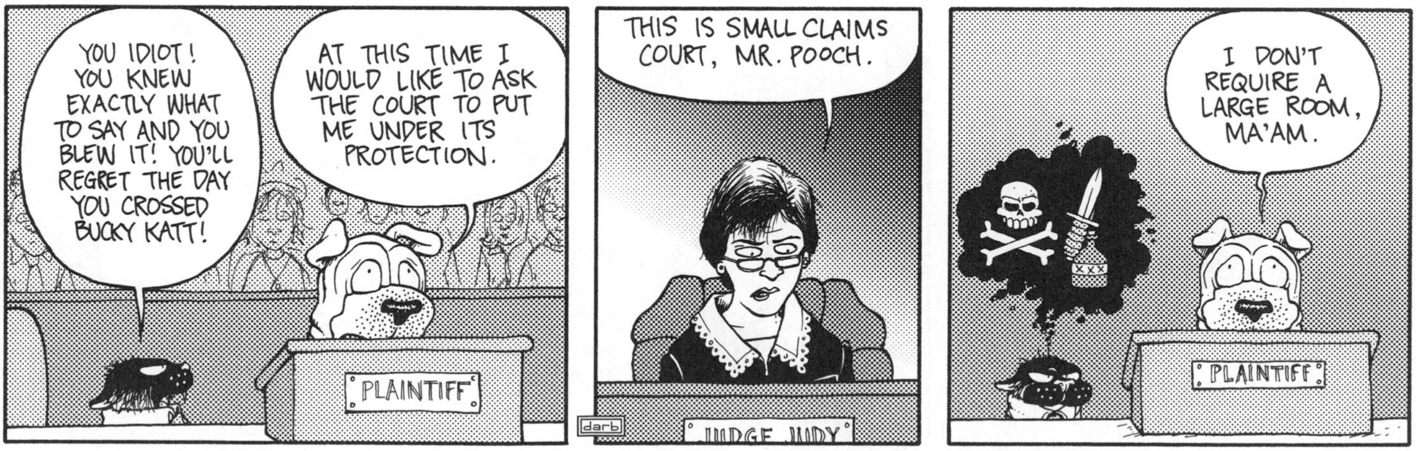
YOU IDIOT! YOU KNEW EXACTLY WHAT TO SAY AND YOU BLEW IT! YOU'LL REGRET THE DAY YOU CROSSED BUCKY KATT!
AT THIS TIME I WOULD LIKE TO ASK THE COURT TO PUT ME UNDER ITS PROTECTION.
PLAINTIFF
THIS IS SMALL CLAIMS COURT, MR. POOCH.
darb
JUDGE JUDY
I DON'T REQUIRE A LARGE ROOM, MA'AM.
PLAINTIFF

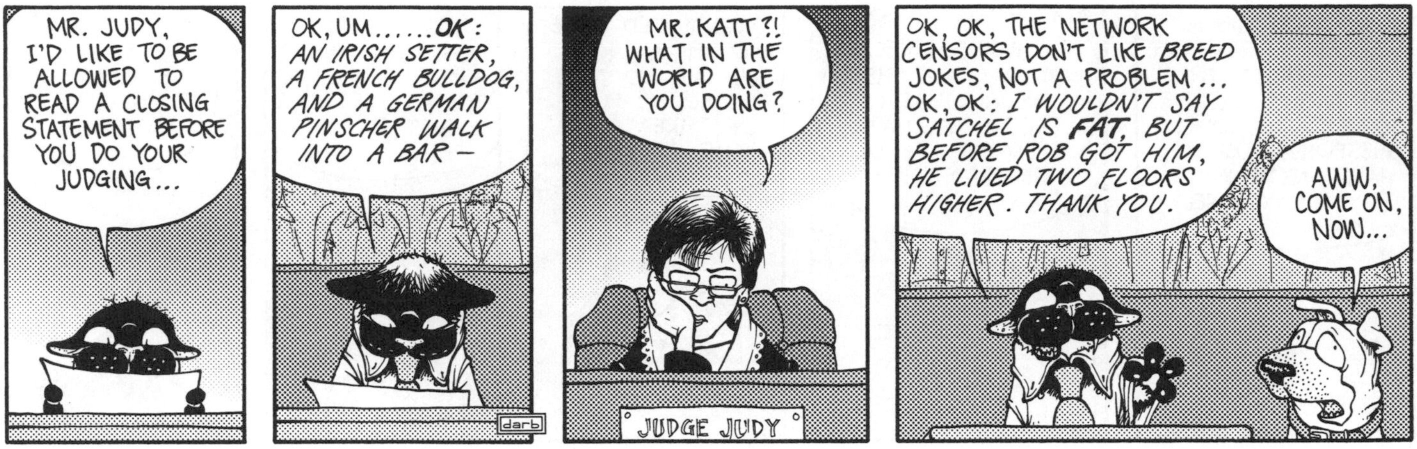
MR. JUDY, I'D LIKE TO BE ALLOWED TO READ A CLOSING STATEMENT BEFORE YOU DO YOUR JUDGING...
OK, UM......OK: AN IRISH SETTER, A FRENCH BULLDOG, AND A GERMAN PINSCHER WALK INTO A BAR —
darb
MR. KATT?! WHAT IN THE WORLD ARE YOU DOING?
JUDGE JUDY
OK, OK, THE NETWORK CENSORS DON'T LIKE BREED JOKES, NOT A PROBLEM... OK, OK: I WOULDN'T SAY SATCHEL IS FAT, BUT BEFORE ROB GOT HIM, HE LIVED TWO FLOORS HIGHER. THANK YOU.
AWW, COME ON, NOW...

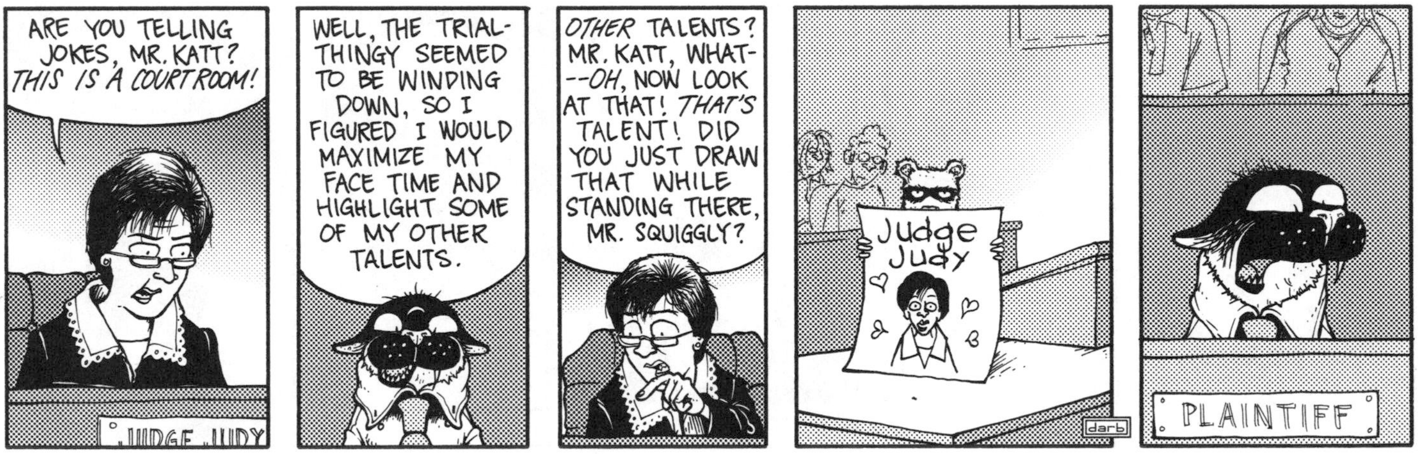
ARE YOU TELLING JOKES, MR. KATT? THIS IS A COURTROOM!
JUDGE JUDY
WELL, THE TRIAL-THINGY SEEMED TO BE WINDING DOWN, SO I FIGURED I WOULD MAXIMIZE MY FACE TIME AND HIGHLIGHT SOME OF MY OTHER TALENTS.
OTHER TALENTS? MR. KATT, WHAT- --OH, NOW LOOK AT THAT! THAT'S TALENT! DID YOU JUST DRAW THAT WHILE STANDING THERE, MR. SQUIGGLY?
Judge Judy
darb
PLAINTIFF

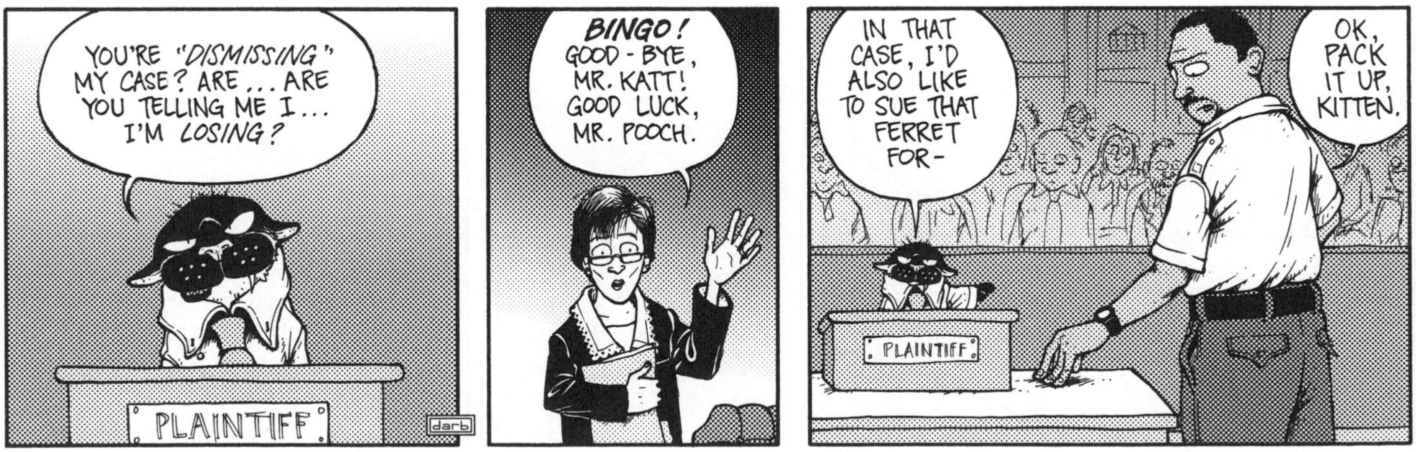
YOU'RE "DISMISSING" MY CASE? ARE... ARE YOU TELLING ME I... I'M LOSING?
PLAINTIFF
darb
BINGO! GOOD-BYE, MR. KATT! GOOD LUCK, MR. POOCH.
IN THAT CASE, I'D ALSO LIKE TO SUE THAT FERRET FOR-
OK, PACK IT UP, KITTEN.
PLAINTIFF

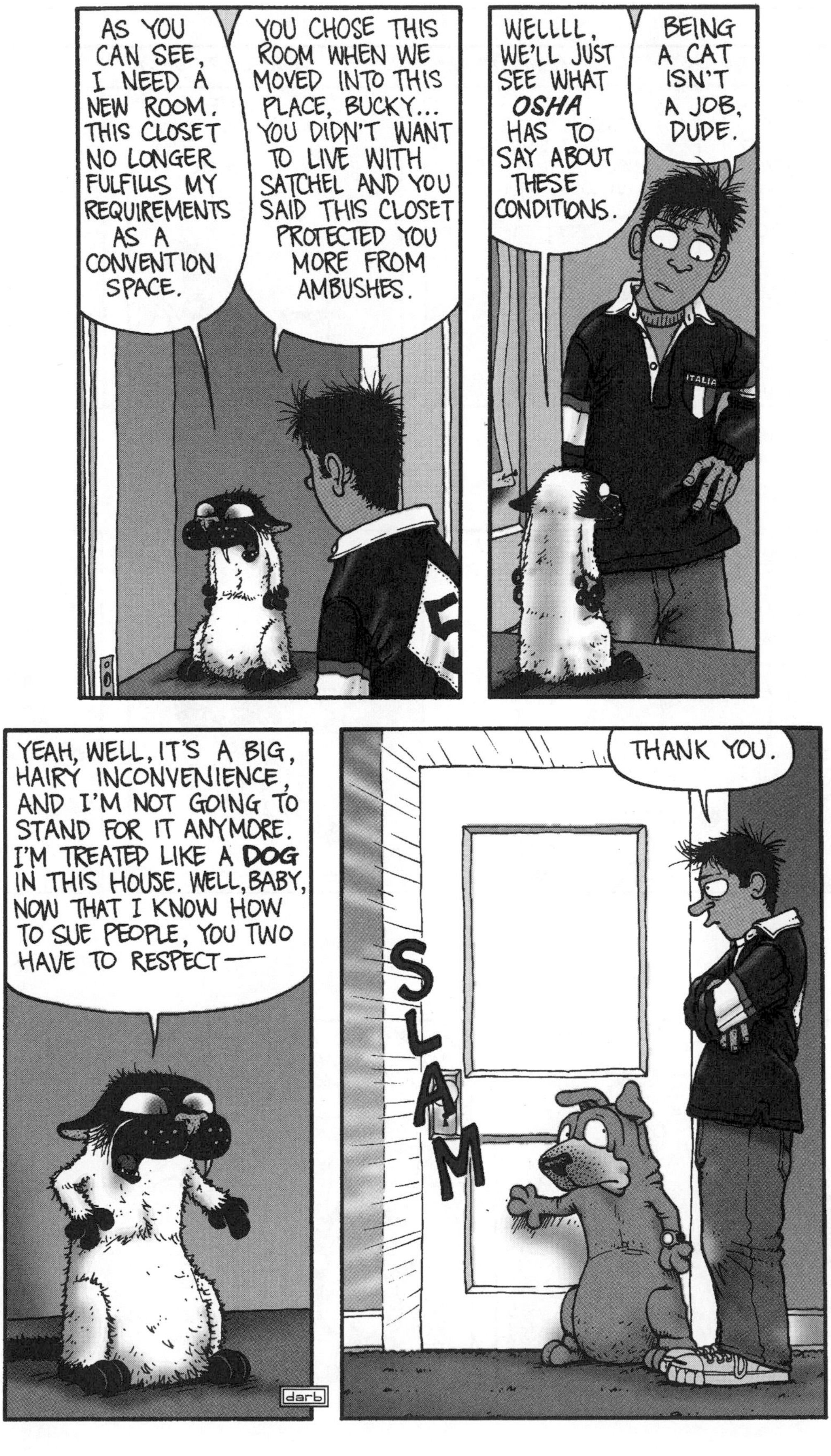
AS YOU CAN SEE, I NEED A NEW ROOM. THIS CLOSET NO LONGER FULFILLS MY REQUIREMENTS AS A CONVENTION SPACE.
YOU CHOSE THIS ROOM WHEN WE MOVED INTO THIS PLACE, BUCKY... YOU DIDN'T WANT TO LIVE WITH SATCHEL AND YOU SAID THIS CLOSET PROTECTED YOU MORE FROM AMBUSHES.
WELLLL, WE'LL JUST SEE WHAT OSHA HAS TO SAY ABOUT THESE CONDITIONS.
BEING A CAT ISN'T A JOB, DUDE.
ITALIA
YEAH, WELL, IT'S A BIG, HAIRY INCONVENIENCE, AND I'M NOT GOING TO STAND FOR IT ANYMORE. I'M TREATED LIKE A DOG IN THIS HOUSE. WELL, BABY, NOW THAT I KNOW HOW TO SUE PEOPLE, YOU TWO HAVE TO RESPECT—
darb
THANK YOU.
SLAM

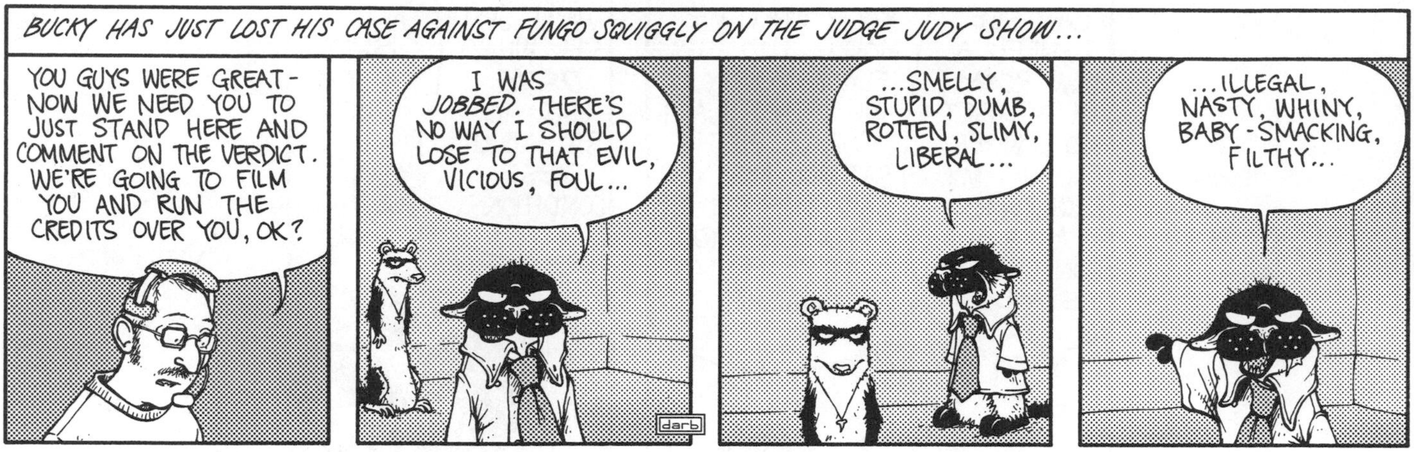
BUCKY HAS JUST LOST HIS CASE AGAINST FUNGO SQUIGGLY ON THE JUDGE JUDY SHOW...
YOU GUYS WERE GREAT - NOW WE NEED YOU TO JUST STAND HERE AND COMMENT ON THE VERDICT. WE'RE GOING TO FILM YOU AND RUN THE CREDITS OVER YOU, OK?
I WAS JOBBED. THERE'S NO WAY I SHOULD LOSE TO THAT EVIL, VICIOUS, FOUL...
...SMELLY, STUPID, DUMB, ROTTEN, SLIMY, LIBERAL...
...ILLEGAL, NASTY, WHINY, BABY-SMACKING, FILTHY...
darb

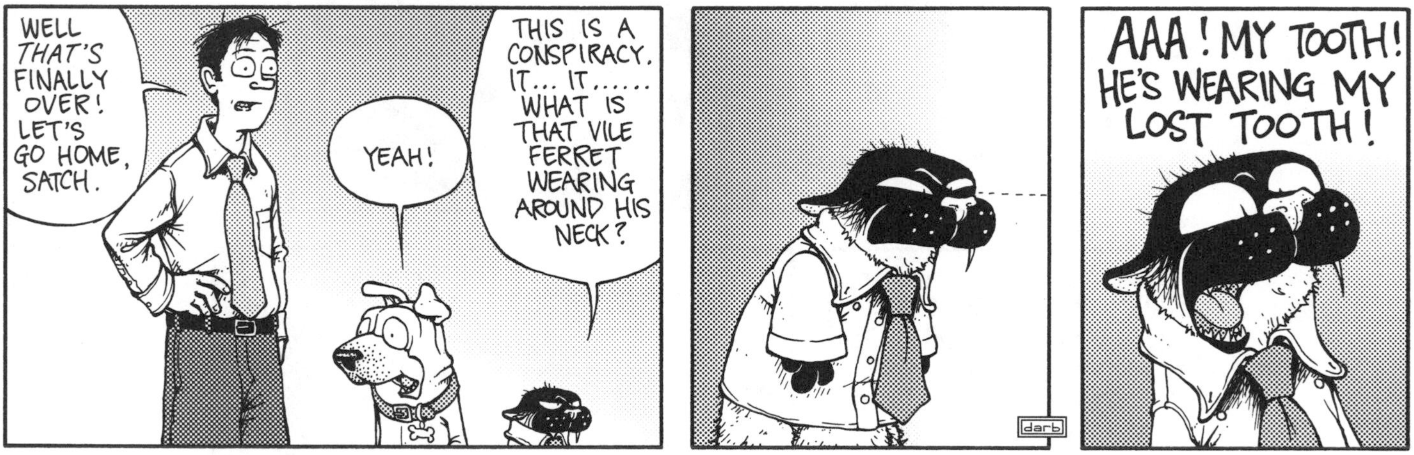
WELL THAT'S FINALLY OVER! LET'S GO HOME, SATCH.
YEAH!
THIS IS A CONSPIRACY. IT... IT...... WHAT IS THAT VILE FERRET WEARING AROUND HIS NECK?
darb
AAA! MY TOOTH! HE'S WEARING MY LOST TOOTH!

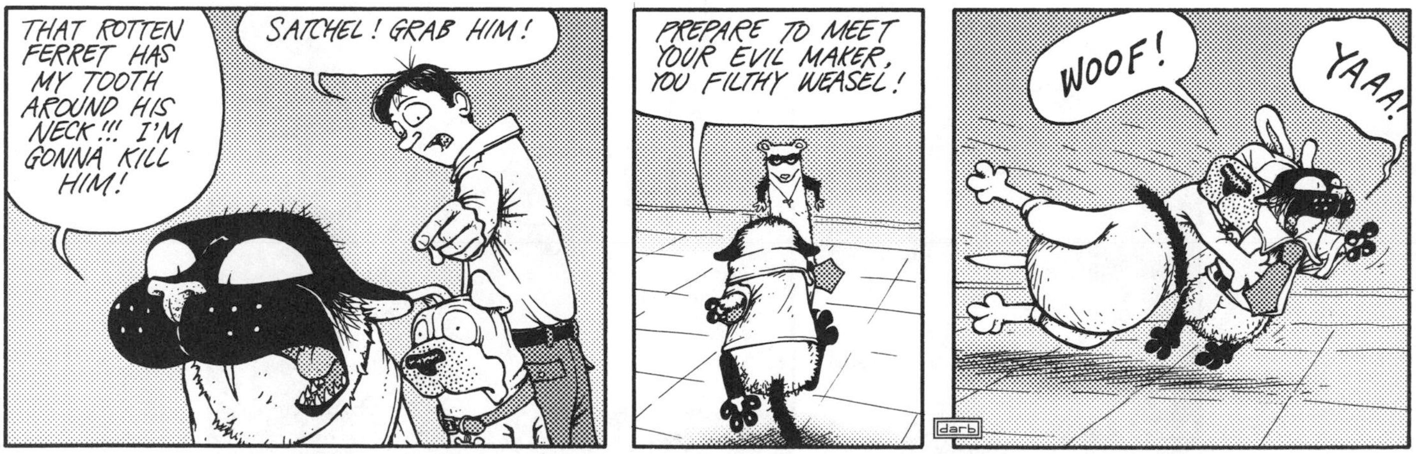
THAT ROTTEN FERRET HAS MY TOOTH AROUND HIS NECK!!! I'M GONNA KILL HIM!
SATCHEL! GRAB HIM!
PREPARE TO MEET YOUR EVIL MAKER, YOU FILTHY WEASEL!
darb
WOOF!
YAAA!

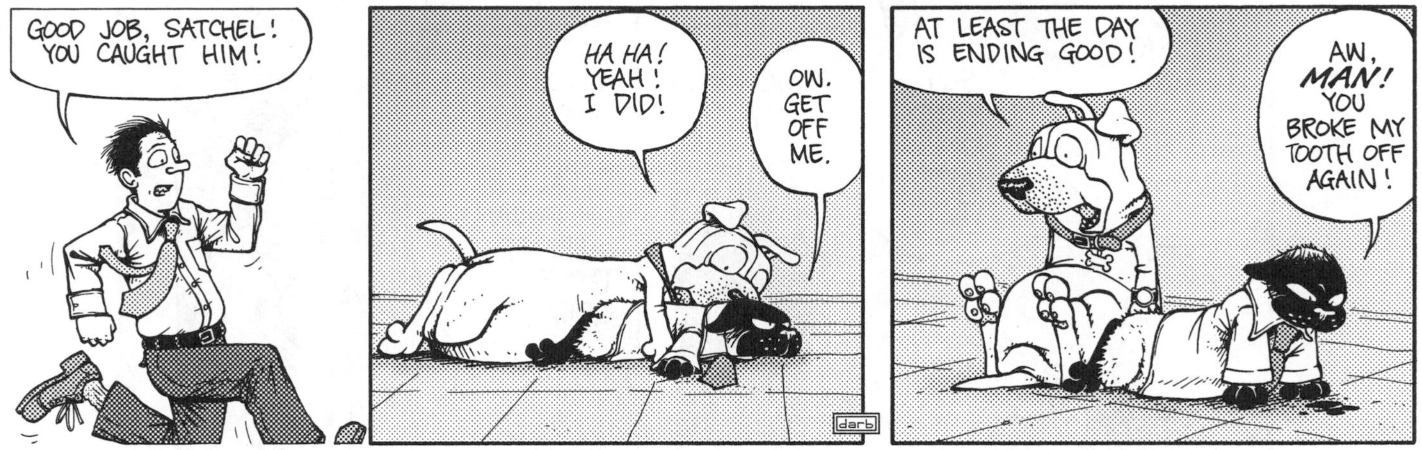
GOOD JOB, SATCHEL! YOU CAUGHT HIM!
HA HA! YEAH! I DID!
OW. GET OFF ME.
AT LEAST THE DAY IS ENDING GOOD!
AW, MAN! YOU BROKE MY TOOTH OFF AGAIN!
darb

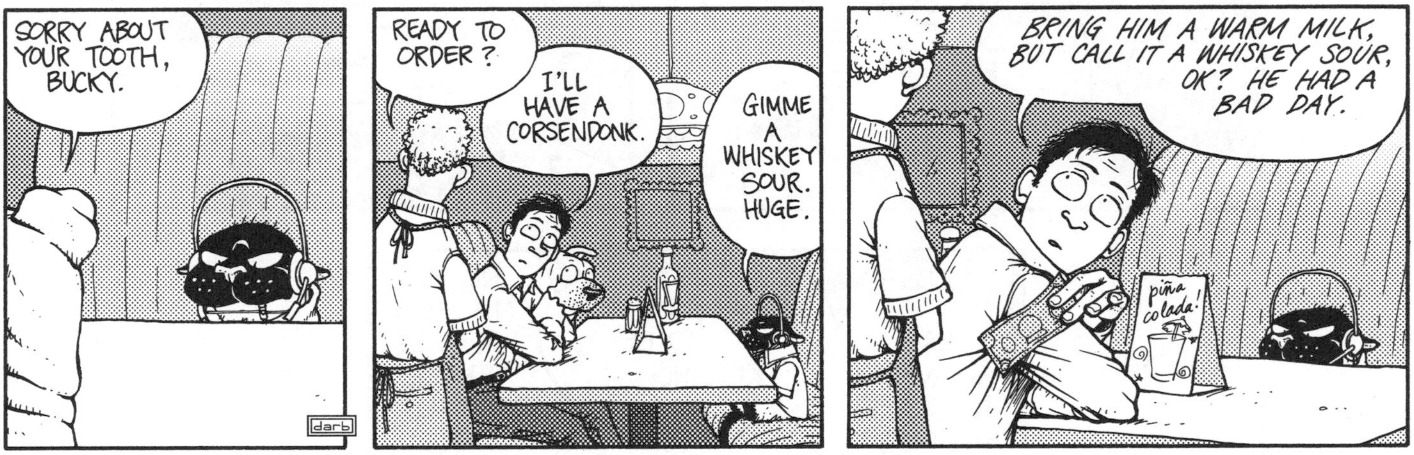
SORRY ABOUT YOUR TOOTH, BUCKY.
darb
READY TO ORDER?
I'LL HAVE A CORSENDONK.
GIMME A WHISKEY SOUR. HUGE.
BRING HIM A WARM MILK, BUT CALL IT A WHISKEY SOUR, OK? HE HAD A BAD DAY.
piña colada!

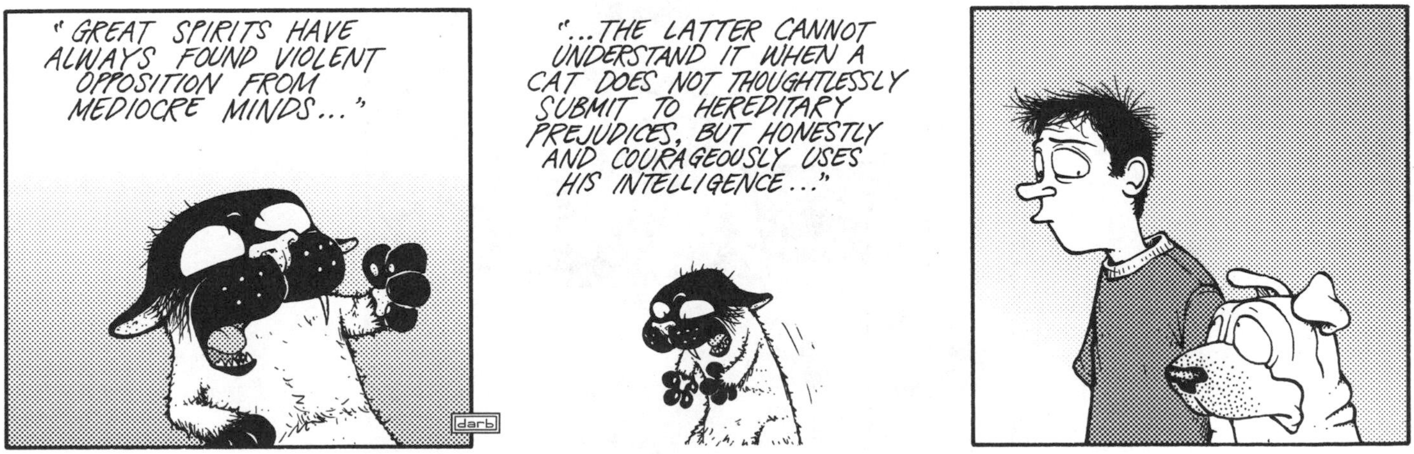
"GREAT SPIRITS HAVE ALWAYS FOUND VIOLENT OPPOSITION FROM MEDIOCRE MINDS..."
darb
"...THE LATTER CANNOT UNDERSTAND IT WHEN A CAT DOES NOT THOUGHTLESSLY SUBMIT TO HEREDITARY PREJUDICES, BUT HONESTLY AND COURAGEOUSLY USES HIS INTELLIGENCE..."

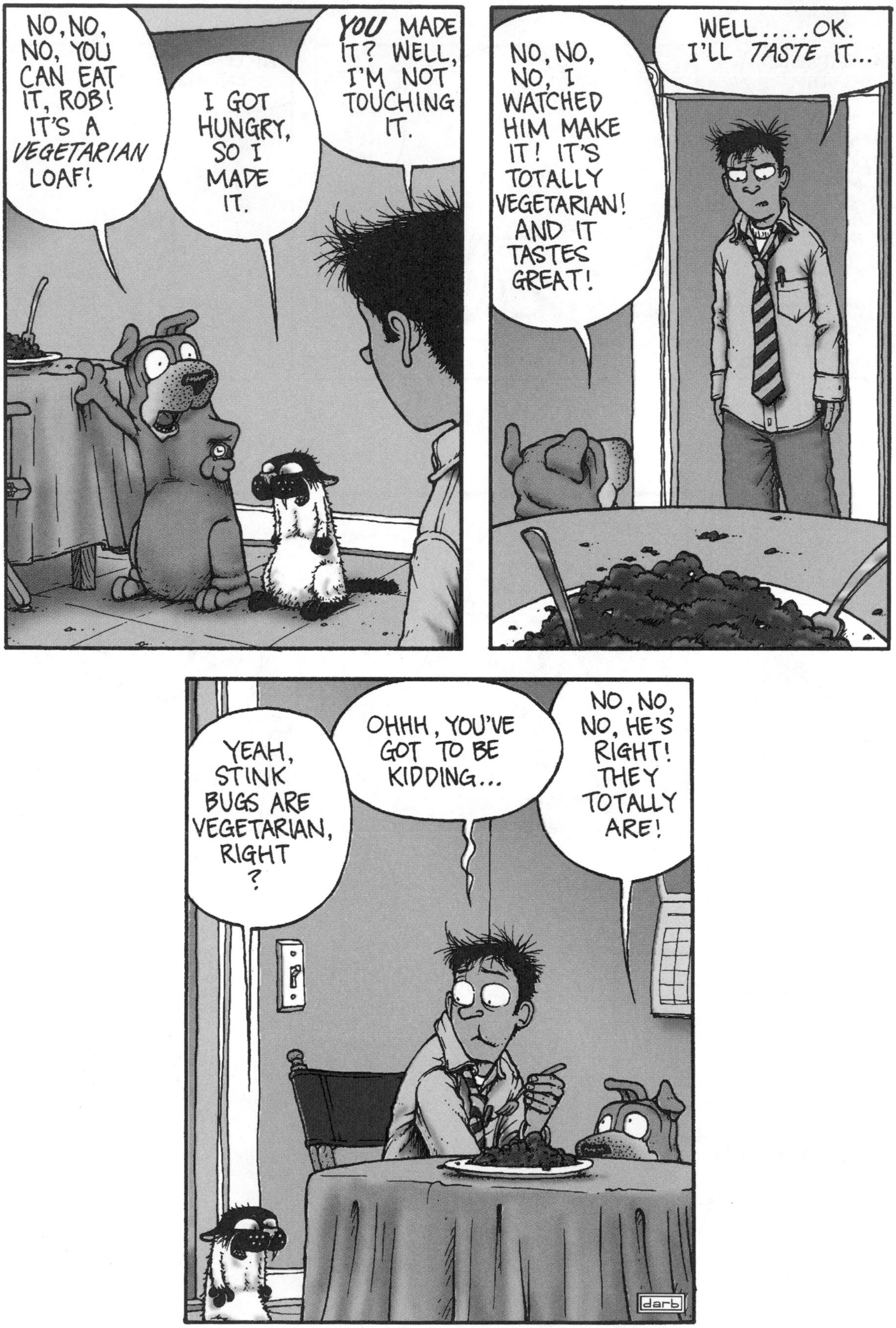
NO, NO, NO, YOU CAN EAT IT, ROB! IT'S A *VEGETARIAN* LOAF!
I GOT HUNGRY, SO I MADE IT.
YOU MADE IT? WELL, I'M NOT TOUCHING IT.
NO, NO, NO, I WATCHED HIM MAKE IT! IT'S TOTALLY VEGETARIAN! AND IT TASTES GREAT!
WELL.....OK. I'LL *TASTE* IT...
YEAH, STINK BUGS ARE VEGETARIAN, RIGHT?
OHHH, YOU'VE GOT TO BE KIDDING...
NO, NO, NO, HE'S RIGHT! THEY TOTALLY ARE!
darb

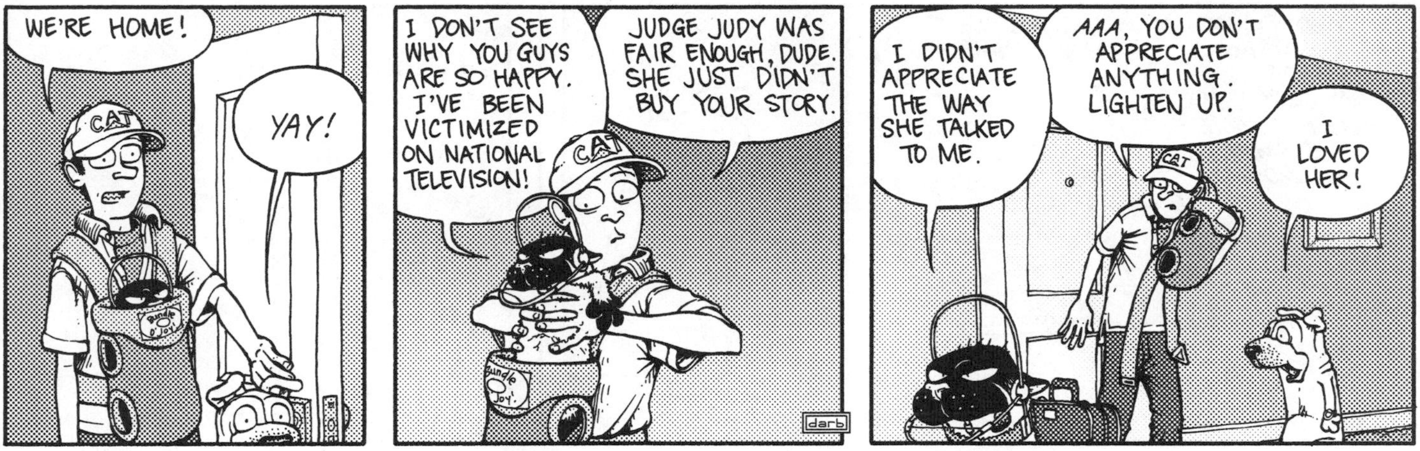
WE'RE HOME!
YAY!
I DON'T SEE WHY YOU GUYS ARE SO HAPPY. I'VE BEEN VICTIMIZED ON NATIONAL TELEVISION!
JUDGE JUDY WAS FAIR ENOUGH, DUDE. SHE JUST DIDN'T BUY YOUR STORY.
I DIDN'T APPRECIATE THE WAY SHE TALKED TO ME.
AAA, YOU DON'T APPRECIATE ANYTHING. LIGHTEN UP.
I LOVED HER!

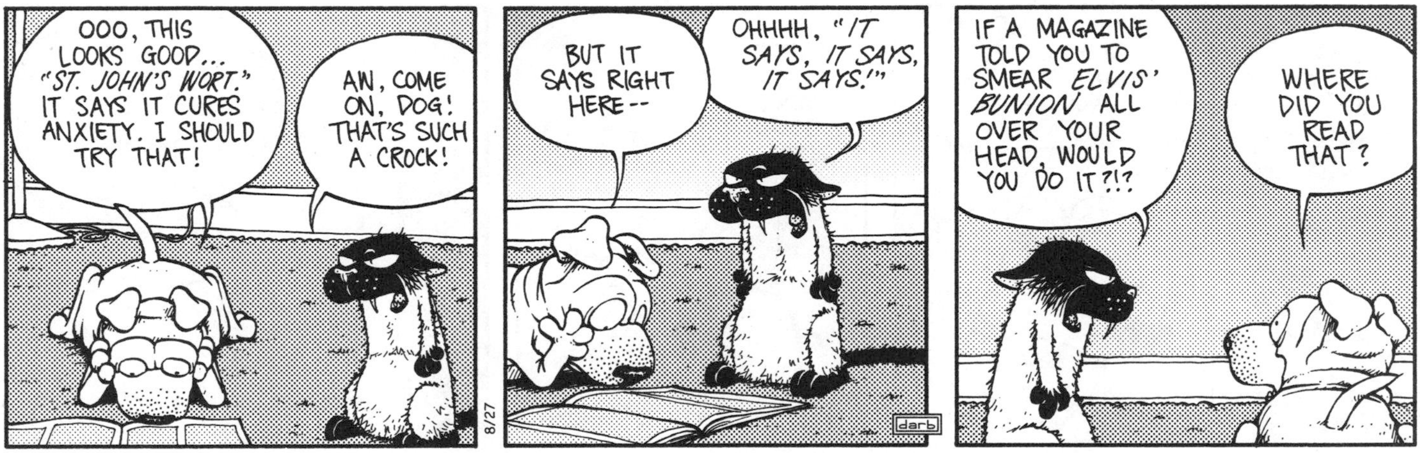
OOO, THIS LOOKS GOOD... *"ST. JOHN'S WORT."* IT SAYS IT CURES ANXIETY. I SHOULD TRY THAT!
AW, COME ON, DOG! THAT'S SUCH A CROCK!
8/27
BUT IT SAYS RIGHT HERE--
OHHHH, *"IT SAYS, IT SAYS, IT SAYS!"*
IF A MAGAZINE TOLD YOU TO SMEAR *ELVIS' BUNION* ALL OVER YOUR HEAD, WOULD YOU DO IT?!?
WHERE DID YOU READ THAT?

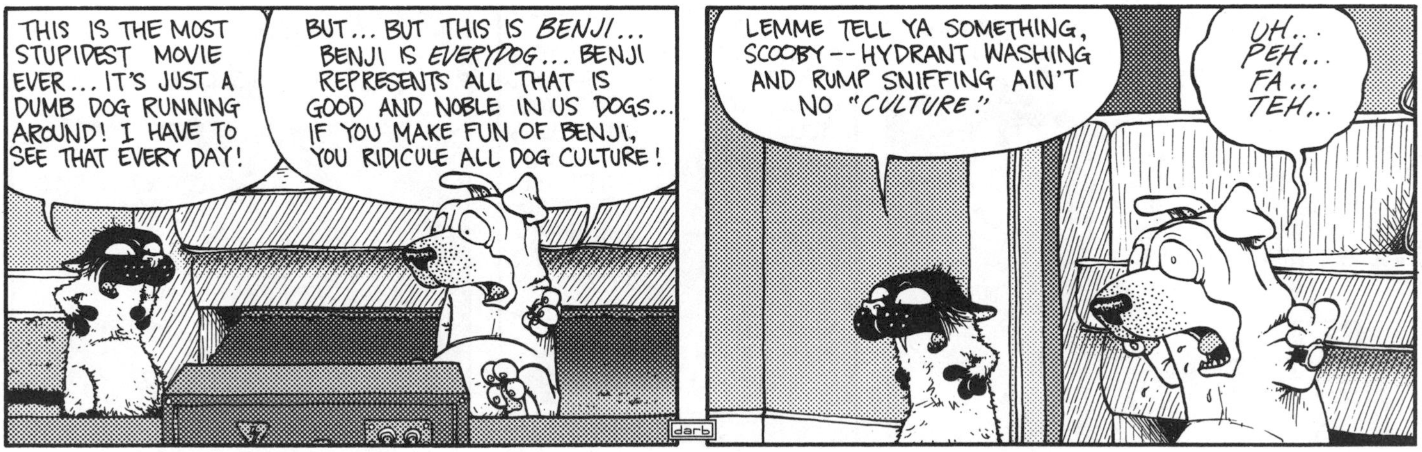
THIS IS THE MOST STUPIDEST MOVIE EVER... IT'S JUST A DUMB DOG RUNNING AROUND! I HAVE TO SEE THAT EVERY DAY!
BUT... BUT THIS IS *BENJI*... BENJI IS *EVERYDOG*... BENJI REPRESENTS ALL THAT IS GOOD AND NOBLE IN US DOGS... IF YOU MAKE FUN OF BENJI, YOU RIDICULE ALL DOG CULTURE!
LEMME TELL YA SOMETHING, SCOOBY--HYDRANT WASHING AND RUMP SNIFFING AIN'T NO *"CULTURE."*
UH... PEH... FA... TEH...

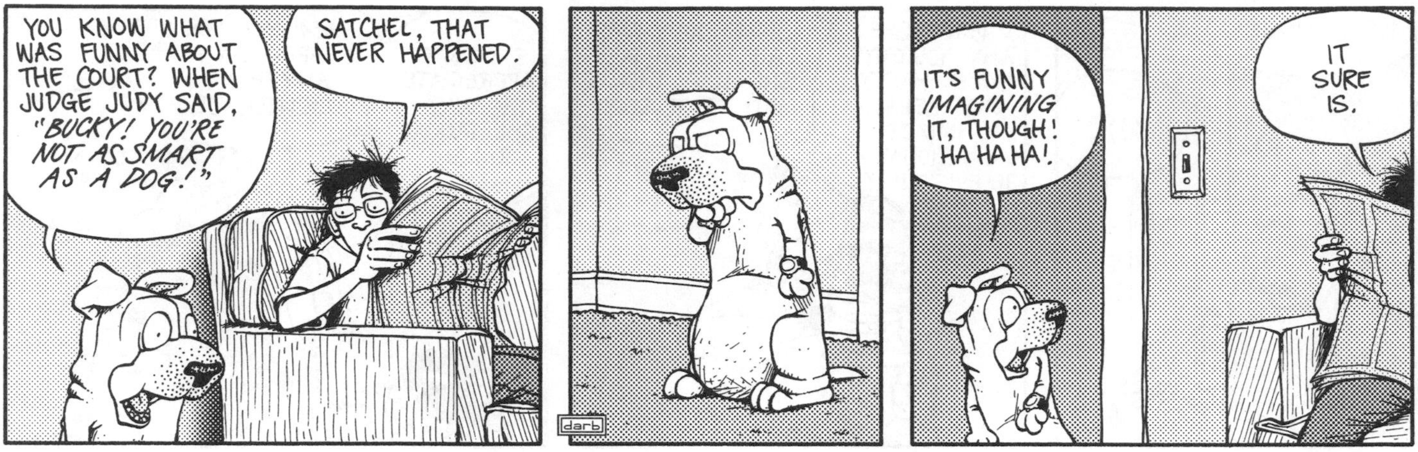
YOU KNOW WHAT WAS FUNNY ABOUT THE COURT? WHEN JUDGE JUDY SAID, "*BUCKY! YOU'RE NOT AS SMART AS A DOG!*"
SATCHEL, THAT NEVER HAPPENED.
darb
IT'S FUNNY *IMAGINING* IT, THOUGH! HA HA HA!
IT SURE IS.

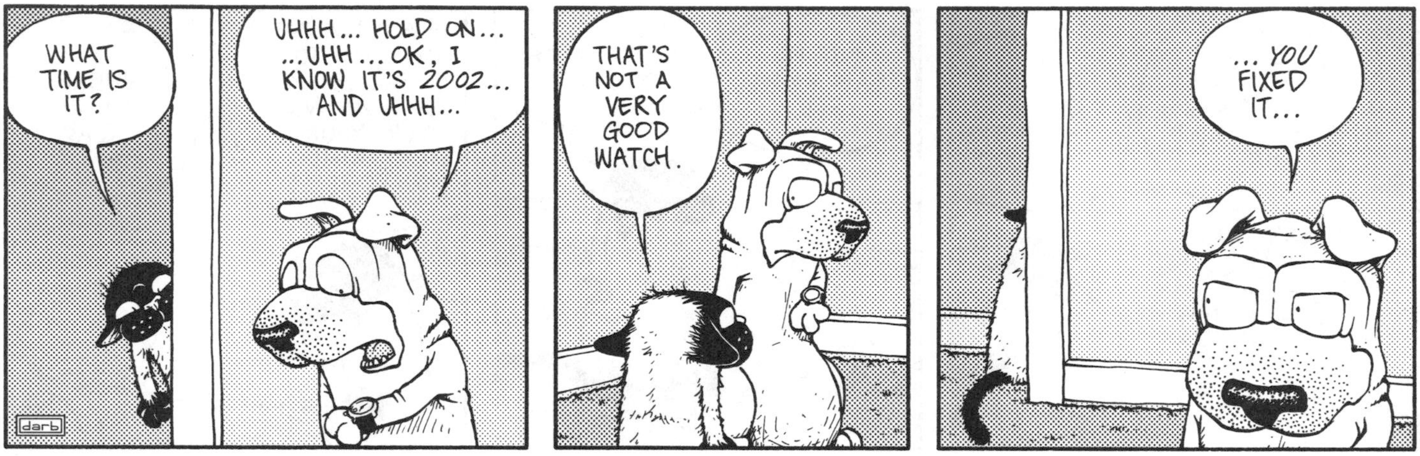
WHAT TIME IS IT?
UHHH... HOLD ON... ...UHH... OK, I KNOW IT'S *2002*... AND UHHH...
darb
THAT'S NOT A VERY GOOD WATCH.
...*YOU* FIXED IT...

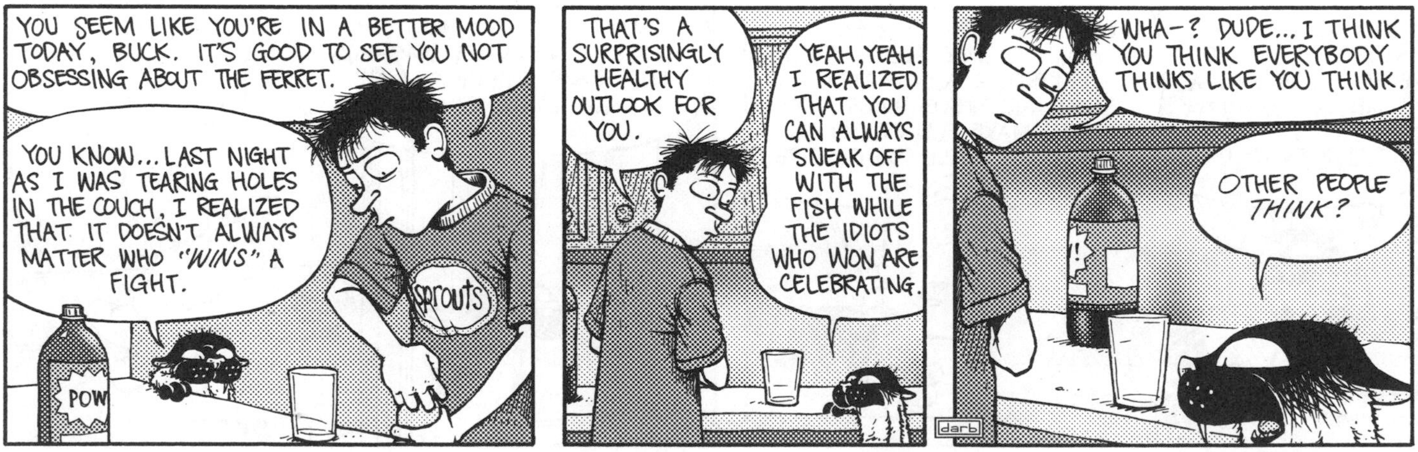
YOU SEEM LIKE YOU'RE IN A BETTER MOOD TODAY, BUCK. IT'S GOOD TO SEE YOU NOT OBSESSING ABOUT THE FERRET.
YOU KNOW... LAST NIGHT AS I WAS TEARING HOLES IN THE COUCH, I REALIZED THAT IT DOESN'T ALWAYS MATTER WHO "*WINS*" A FIGHT.
sprouts
POW
THAT'S A SURPRISINGLY HEALTHY OUTLOOK FOR YOU.
YEAH, YEAH. I REALIZED THAT YOU CAN ALWAYS SNEAK OFF WITH THE FISH WHILE THE IDIOTS WHO WON ARE CELEBRATING.
darb
WHA-? DUDE... I THINK YOU THINK EVERYBODY THINKS LIKE YOU THINK.
OTHER PEOPLE *THINK*?

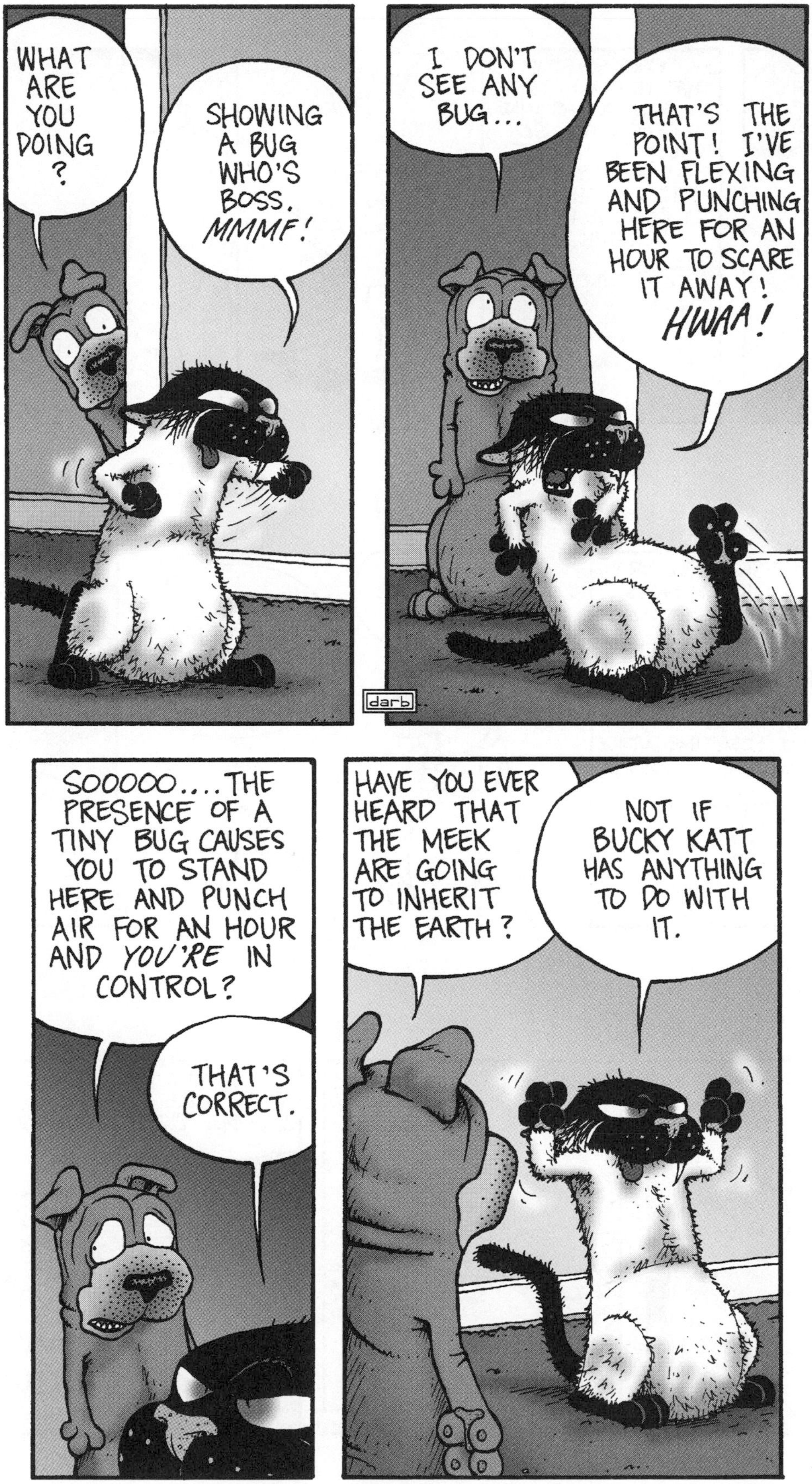
WHAT ARE YOU DOING ?
SHOWING A BUG WHO'S BOSS. MMMF!
I DON'T SEE ANY BUG...
THAT'S THE POINT! I'VE BEEN FLEXING AND PUNCHING HERE FOR AN HOUR TO SCARE IT AWAY! HWAA!
darb
SOOOOO....THE PRESENCE OF A TINY BUG CAUSES YOU TO STAND HERE AND PUNCH AIR FOR AN HOUR AND YOU'RE IN CONTROL?
THAT'S CORRECT.
HAVE YOU EVER HEARD THAT THE MEEK ARE GOING TO INHERIT THE EARTH ?
NOT IF BUCKY KATT HAS ANYTHING TO DO WITH IT.

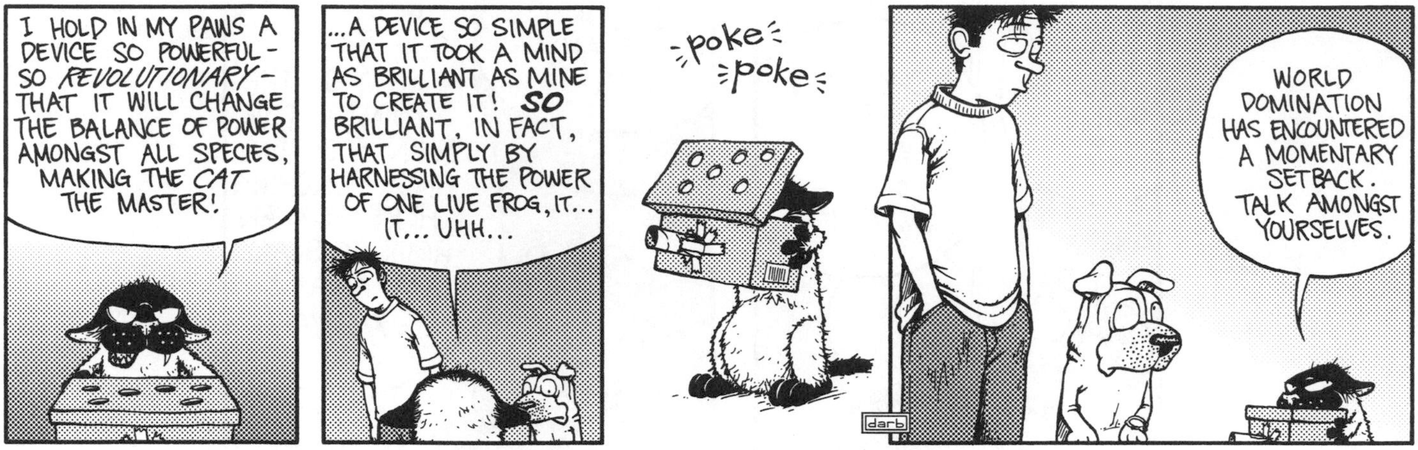
I HOLD IN MY PAWS A DEVICE SO POWERFUL - SO *REVOLUTIONARY* - THAT IT WILL CHANGE THE BALANCE OF POWER AMONGST ALL SPECIES, MAKING THE *CAT* THE MASTER!
...A DEVICE SO SIMPLE THAT IT TOOK A MIND AS BRILLIANT AS MINE TO CREATE IT! ***SO*** BRILLIANT, IN FACT, THAT SIMPLY BY HARNESSING THE POWER OF ONE LIVE FROG, IT... IT... UHH...
poke
poke
WORLD DOMINATION HAS ENCOUNTERED A MOMENTARY SETBACK. TALK AMONGST YOURSELVES.
darb

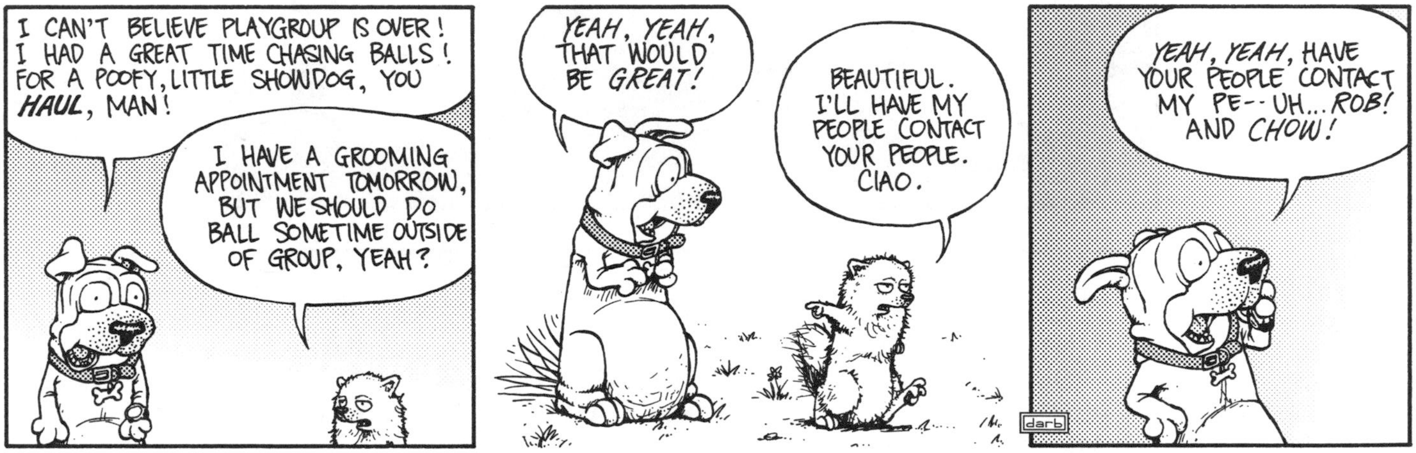
I CAN'T BELIEVE PLAYGROUP IS OVER! I HAD A GREAT TIME CHASING BALLS! FOR A POOFY, LITTLE SHOWDOG, YOU ***HAUL***, MAN!
I HAVE A GROOMING APPOINTMENT TOMORROW, BUT WE SHOULD DO BALL SOMETIME OUTSIDE OF GROUP, YEAH?
YEAH, YEAH, THAT WOULD BE *GREAT*!
BEAUTIFUL. I'LL HAVE MY PEOPLE CONTACT YOUR PEOPLE. CIAO.
YEAH, YEAH, HAVE YOUR PEOPLE CONTACT MY PE-- UH... *ROB*! AND *CHOW*!
darb

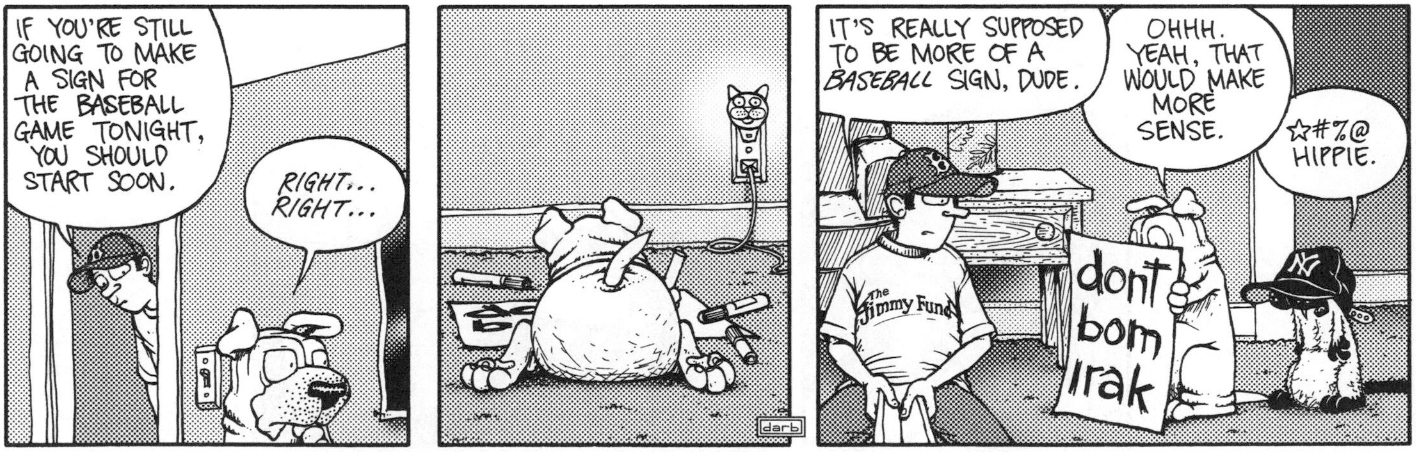
IF YOU'RE STILL GOING TO MAKE A SIGN FOR THE BASEBALL GAME TONIGHT, YOU SHOULD START SOON.
RIGHT... RIGHT...
darb
IT'S REALLY SUPPOSED TO BE MORE OF A *BASEBALL* SIGN, DUDE.
The Jimmy Fund
dont bom irak
OHHH. YEAH, THAT WOULD MAKE MORE SENSE.
☆#%@ HIPPIE.

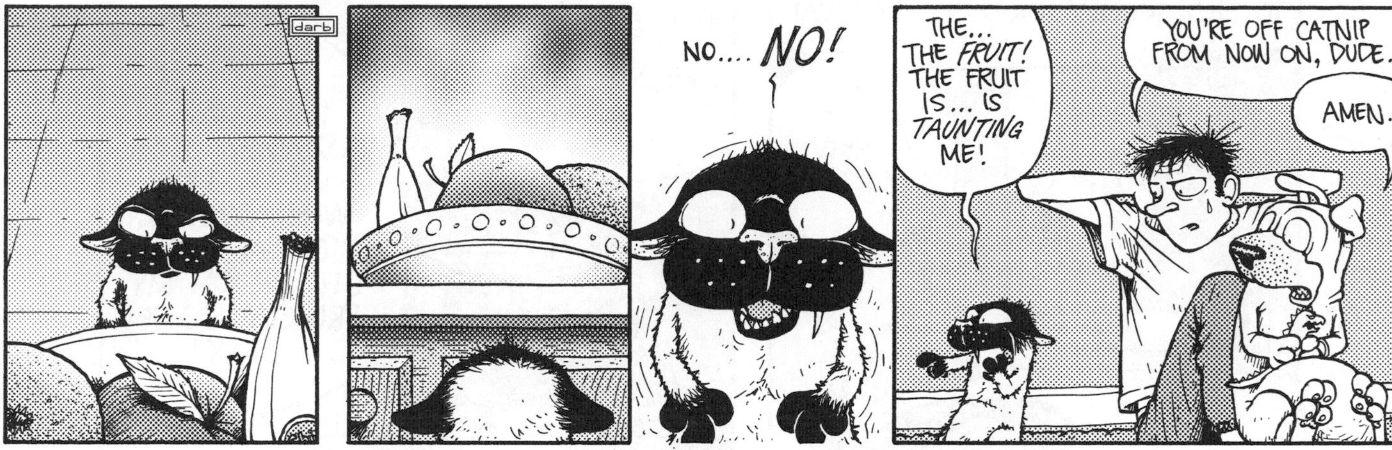
darb
NO.... NO!
THE... THE FRUIT! THE FRUIT IS... IS TAUNTING ME!
YOU'RE OFF CATNIP FROM NOW ON, DUDE.
AMEN.

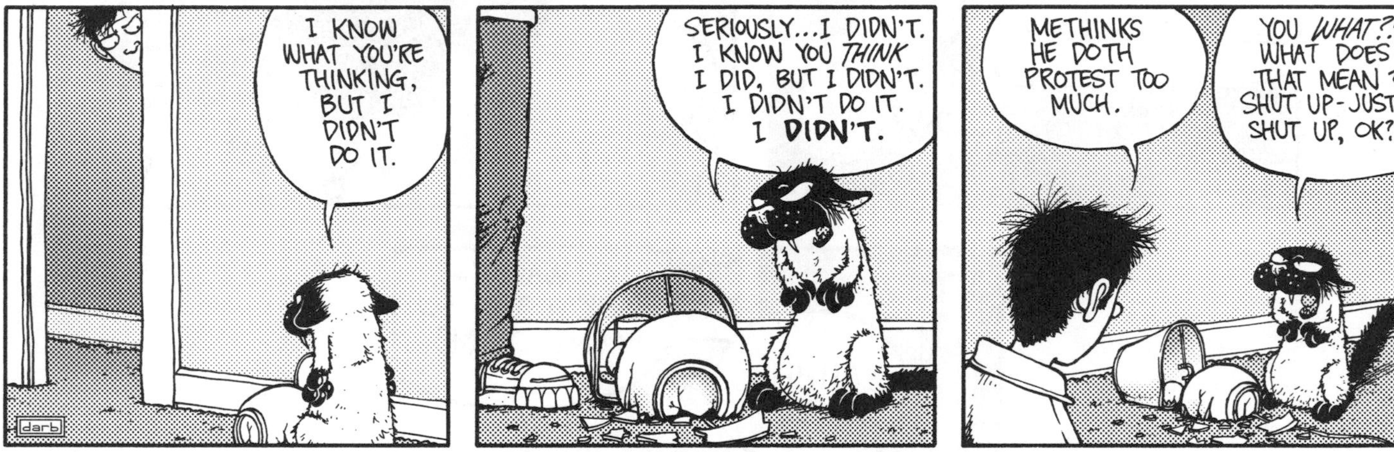
I KNOW WHAT YOU'RE THINKING, BUT I DIDN'T DO IT.
darb
SERIOUSLY...I DIDN'T. I KNOW YOU THINK I DID, BUT I DIDN'T. I DIDN'T DO IT. I DIDN'T.
METHINKS HE DOTH PROTEST TOO MUCH.
YOU WHAT?! WHAT DOES THAT MEAN ? SHUT UP-JUST SHUT UP, OK?!

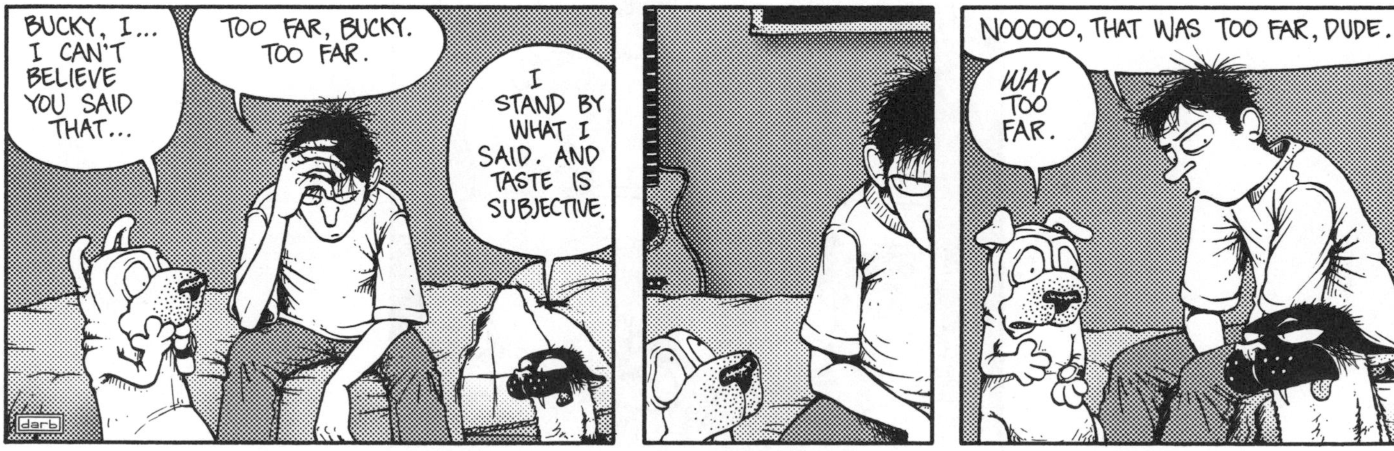
BUCKY, I... I CAN'T BELIEVE YOU SAID THAT...
TOO FAR, BUCKY. TOO FAR.
I STAND BY WHAT I SAID. AND TASTE IS SUBJECTIVE.
darb
NOOOOO, THAT WAS TOO FAR, DUDE.
WAY TOO FAR.

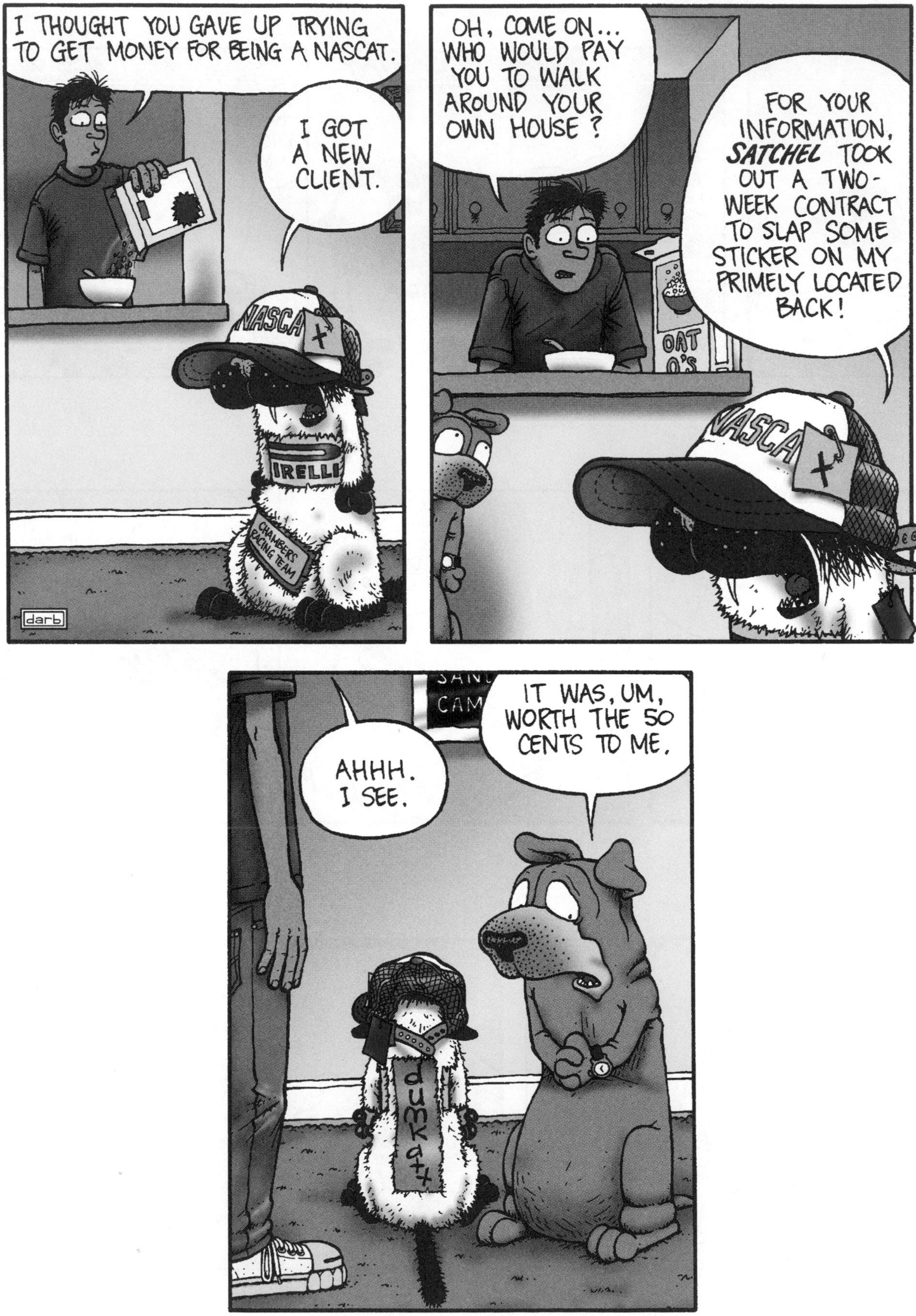
I THOUGHT YOU GAVE UP TRYING TO GET MONEY FOR BEING A NASCAT.
I GOT A NEW CLIENT.
NASCA
IRELLI
CHAMBERS RACING TEAM
darb
OH, COME ON... WHO WOULD PAY YOU TO WALK AROUND YOUR OWN HOUSE?
FOR YOUR INFORMATION, SATCHEL TOOK OUT A TWO-WEEK CONTRACT TO SLAP SOME STICKER ON MY PRIMELY LOCATED BACK!
OAT O'S
AHHH. I SEE.
IT WAS, UM, WORTH THE 50 CENTS TO ME.
dumk a++

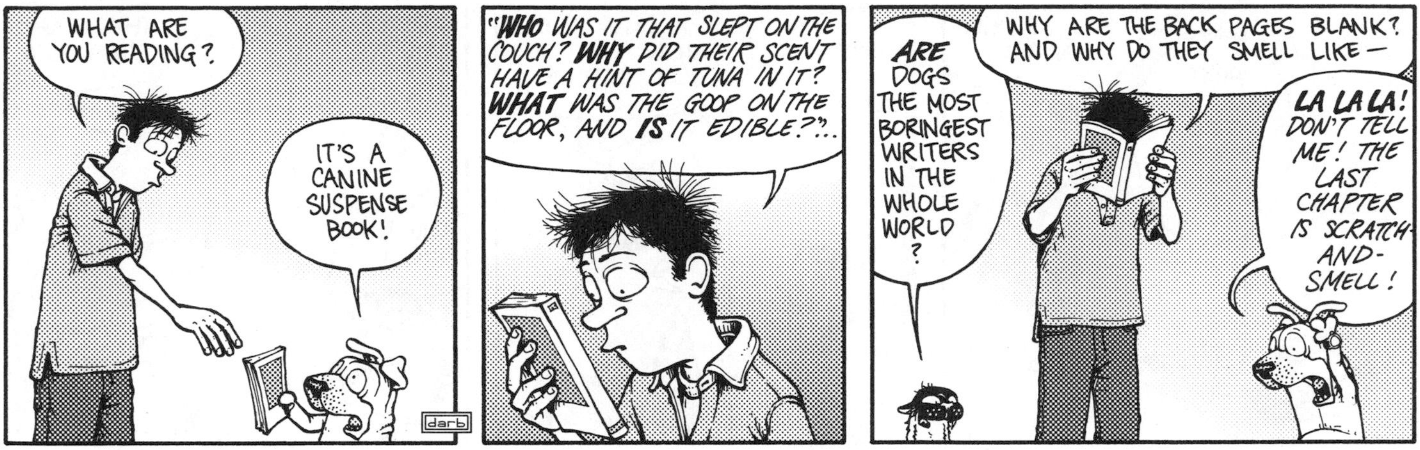
WHAT ARE YOU READING?
IT'S A CANINE SUSPENSE BOOK!
"WHO WAS IT THAT SLEPT ON THE COUCH? WHY DID THEIR SCENT HAVE A HINT OF TUNA IN IT? WHAT WAS THE GOOP ON THE FLOOR, AND IS IT EDIBLE?"...
ARE DOGS THE MOST BORINGEST WRITERS IN THE WHOLE WORLD?
WHY ARE THE BACK PAGES BLANK? AND WHY DO THEY SMELL LIKE—
LA LA LA! DON'T TELL ME! THE LAST CHAPTER IS SCRATCH-AND-SMELL!
darb

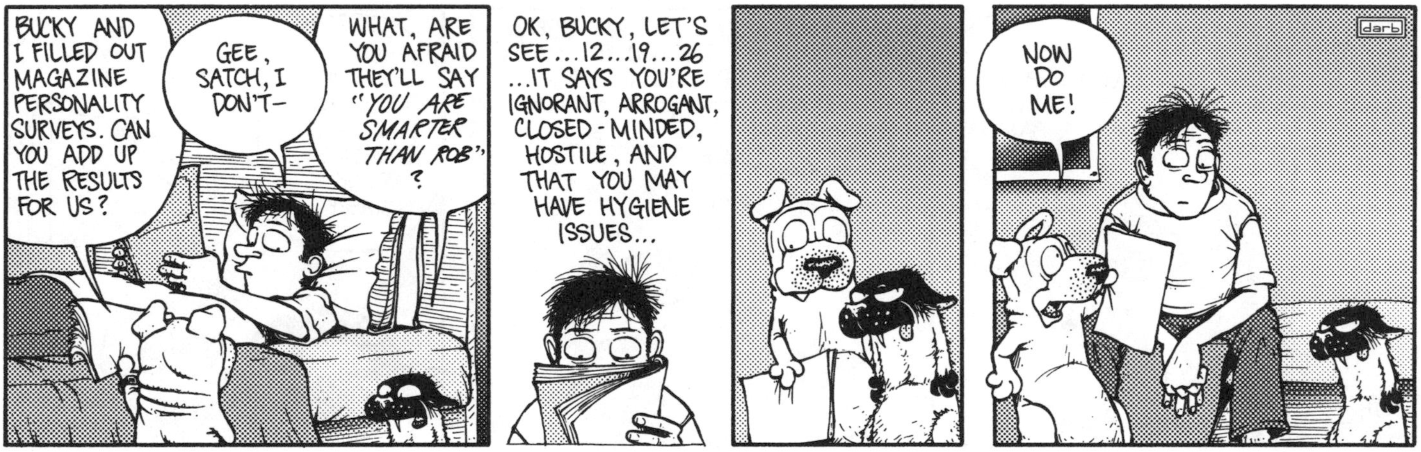
BUCKY AND I FILLED OUT MAGAZINE PERSONALITY SURVEYS. CAN YOU ADD UP THE RESULTS FOR US?
GEE, SATCH, I DON'T-
WHAT, ARE YOU AFRAID THEY'LL SAY "YOU ARE SMARTER THAN ROB"?
OK, BUCKY, LET'S SEE...12...19...26 ...IT SAYS YOU'RE IGNORANT, ARROGANT, CLOSED-MINDED, HOSTILE, AND THAT YOU MAY HAVE HYGIENE ISSUES...
NOW DO ME!
darb

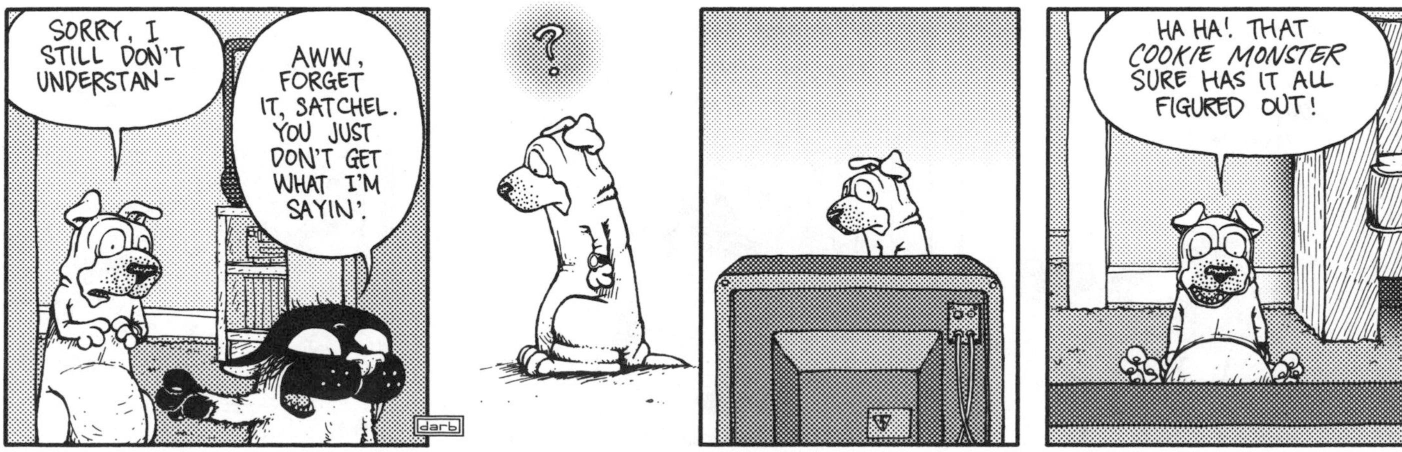
SORRY, I STILL DON'T UNDERSTAN-
AWW, FORGET IT, SATCHEL. YOU JUST DON'T GET WHAT I'M SAYIN'.
darb
?
HA HA! THAT COOKIE MONSTER SURE HAS IT ALL FIGURED OUT!

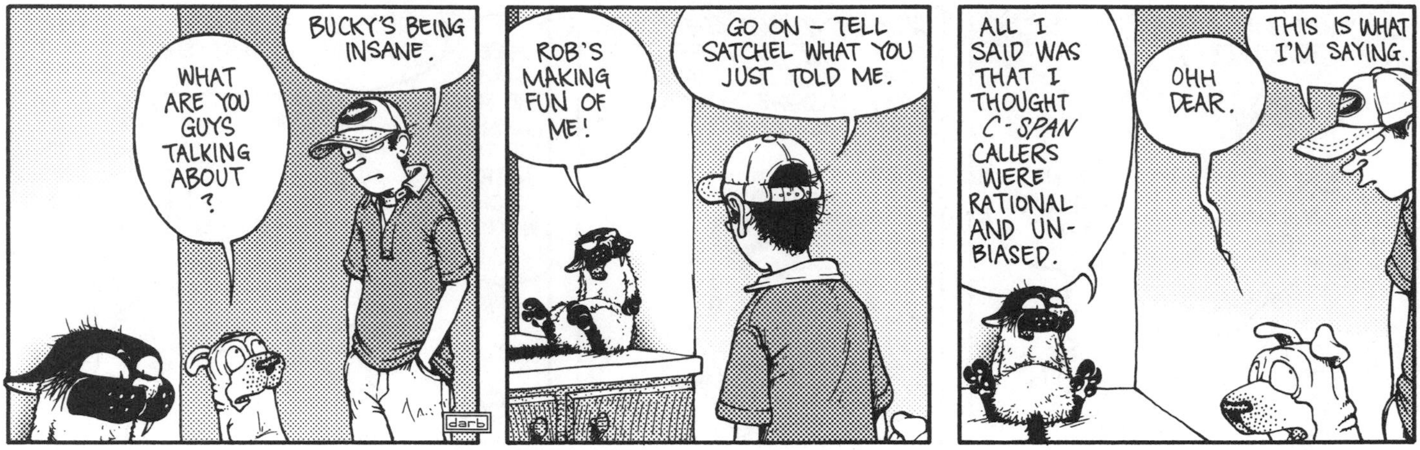

WHAT ARE YOU GUYS TALKING ABOUT?
BUCKY'S BEING INSANE.
ROB'S MAKING FUN OF ME!
GO ON – TELL SATCHEL WHAT YOU JUST TOLD ME.
ALL I SAID WAS THAT I THOUGHT *C-SPAN* CALLERS WERE RATIONAL AND UN-BIASED.
OHH DEAR.
THIS IS WHAT I'M SAYING.

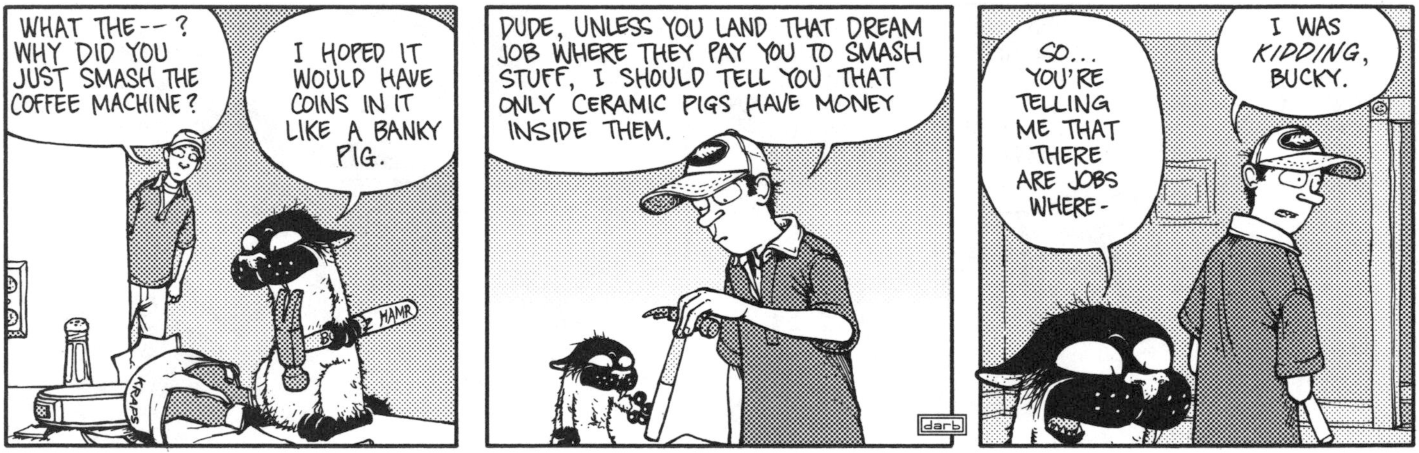

WHAT THE--? WHY DID YOU JUST SMASH THE COFFEE MACHINE?
I HOPED IT WOULD HAVE COINS IN IT LIKE A BANKY PIG.
KRAPS
DUDE, UNLESS YOU LAND THAT DREAM JOB WHERE THEY PAY YOU TO SMASH STUFF, I SHOULD TELL YOU THAT ONLY CERAMIC PIGS HAVE MONEY INSIDE THEM.
SO... YOU'RE TELLING ME THAT THERE ARE JOBS WHERE-
I WAS *KIDDING*, BUCKY.

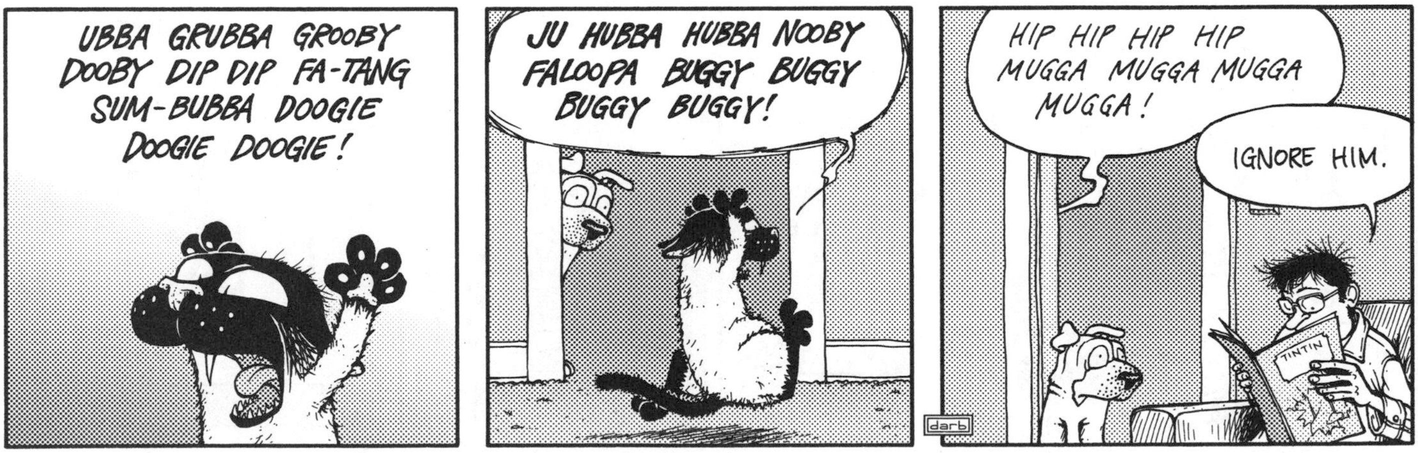

UBBA GRUBBA GROOBY DOOBY DIP DIP FA-TANG SUM-BUBBA DOOGIE DOOGIE DOOGIE!
JU HUBBA HUBBA NOOBY FALOOPA BUGGY BUGGY BUGGY BUGGY!
HIP HIP HIP HIP MUGGA MUGGA MUGGA MUGGA!
IGNORE HIM.
TINTIN

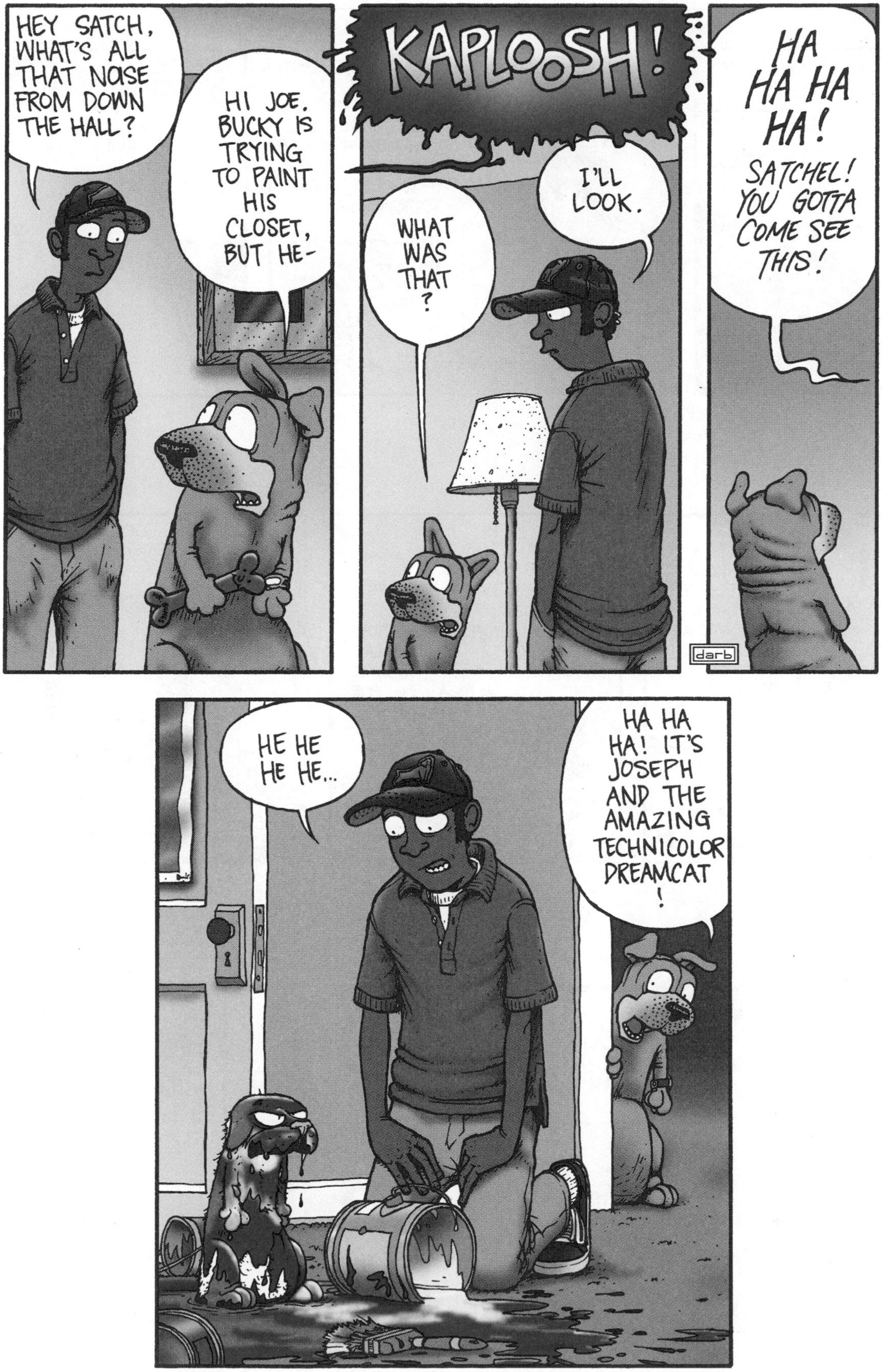
HEY SATCH, WHAT'S ALL THAT NOISE FROM DOWN THE HALL?
HI JOE. BUCKY IS TRYING TO PAINT HIS CLOSET, BUT HE-
KAPLOOSH!
WHAT WAS THAT?
I'LL LOOK.
HA HA HA HA!
SATCHEL! YOU GOTTA COME SEE THIS!
darb
HE HE HE HE...
HA HA HA! IT'S JOSEPH AND THE AMAZING TECHNICOLOR DREAMCAT!

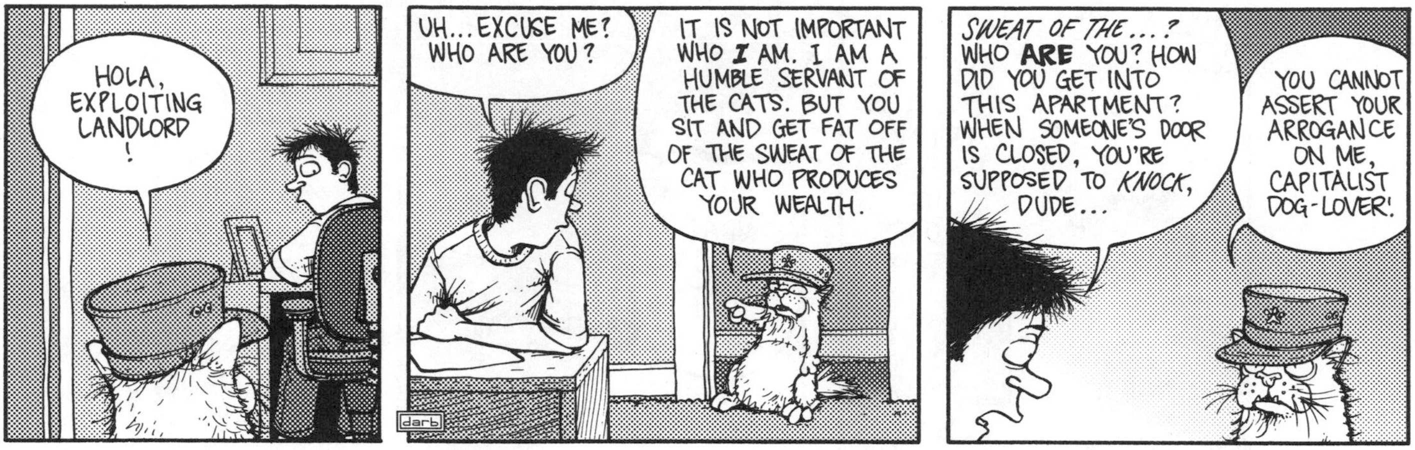
HOLA, EXPLOITING LANDLORD!
UH... EXCUSE ME? WHO ARE YOU?
IT IS NOT IMPORTANT WHO *I* AM. I AM A HUMBLE SERVANT OF THE CATS. BUT YOU SIT AND GET FAT OFF OF THE SWEAT OF THE CAT WHO PRODUCES YOUR WEALTH.
darb
SWEAT OF THE...? WHO **ARE** YOU? HOW DID YOU GET INTO THIS APARTMENT? WHEN SOMEONE'S DOOR IS CLOSED, YOU'RE SUPPOSED TO *KNOCK*, DUDE...
YOU CANNOT ASSERT YOUR ARROGANCE ON ME, CAPITALIST DOG-LOVER!

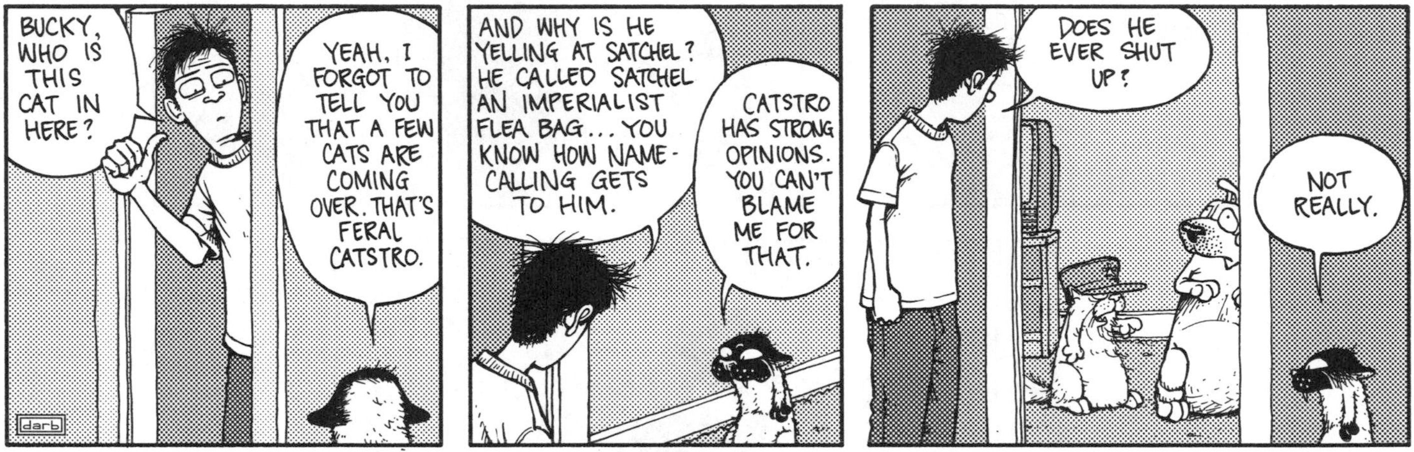
BUCKY, WHO IS THIS CAT IN HERE?
YEAH, I FORGOT TO TELL YOU THAT A FEW CATS ARE COMING OVER. THAT'S FERAL CATSTRO.
darb
AND WHY IS HE YELLING AT SATCHEL? HE CALLED SATCHEL AN IMPERIALIST FLEA BAG... YOU KNOW HOW NAME-CALLING GETS TO HIM.
CATSTRO HAS STRONG OPINIONS. YOU CAN'T BLAME ME FOR THAT.
DOES HE EVER SHUT UP?
NOT REALLY.

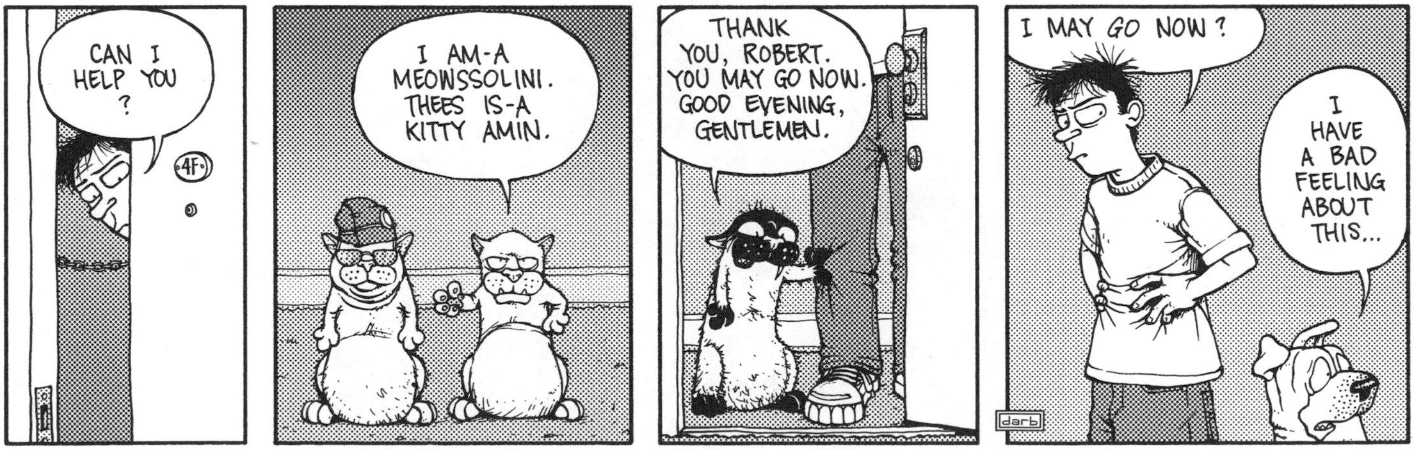
CAN I HELP YOU?
4F
I AM-A MEOWSSOLINI. THEES IS-A KITTY AMIN.
THANK YOU, ROBERT. YOU MAY GO NOW. GOOD EVENING, GENTLEMEN.
I MAY *GO* NOW?
I HAVE A BAD FEELING ABOUT THIS...
darb

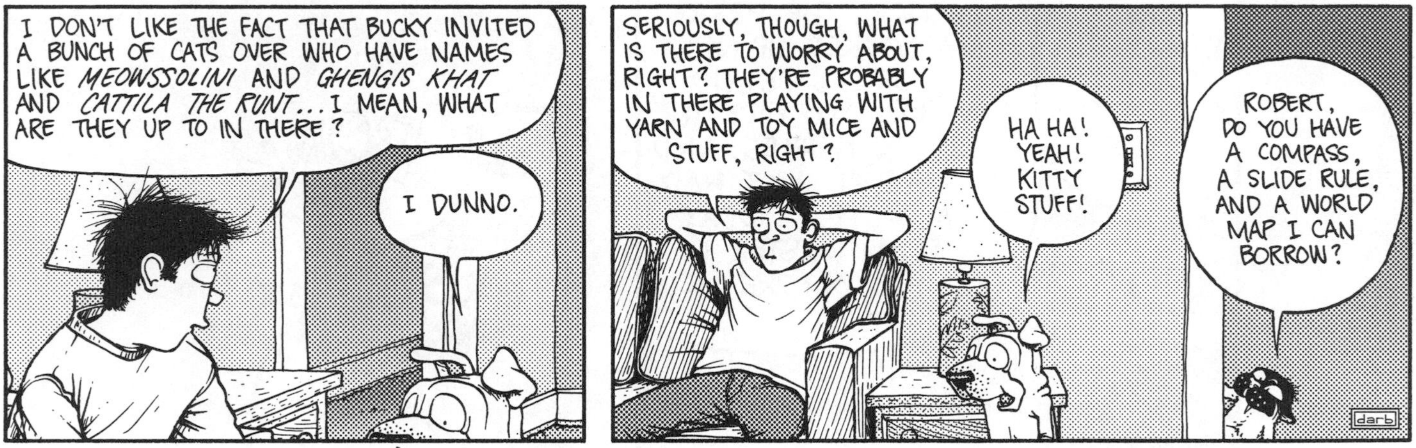
I DON'T LIKE THE FACT THAT BUCKY INVITED A BUNCH OF CATS OVER WHO HAVE NAMES LIKE MEOWSSOLINI AND GHENGIS KHAT AND CATTILA THE RUNT... I MEAN, WHAT ARE THEY UP TO IN THERE?
I DUNNO.
SERIOUSLY, THOUGH, WHAT IS THERE TO WORRY ABOUT, RIGHT? THEY'RE PROBABLY IN THERE PLAYING WITH YARN AND TOY MICE AND STUFF, RIGHT?
HA HA! YEAH! KITTY STUFF!
ROBERT, DO YOU HAVE A COMPASS, A SLIDE RULE, AND A WORLD MAP I CAN BORROW?
darb

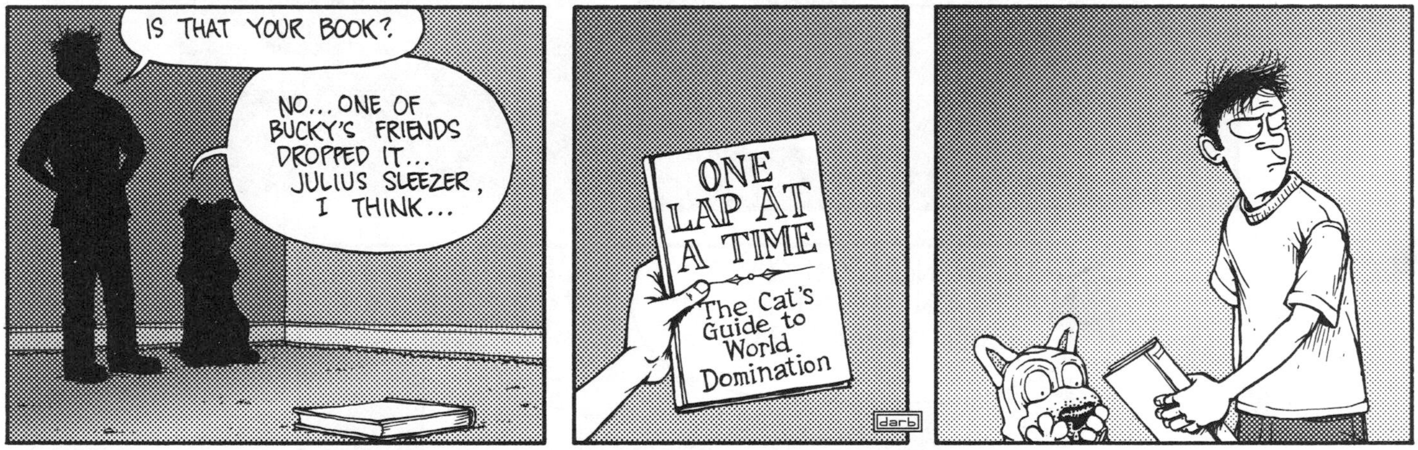
IS THAT YOUR BOOK?
NO... ONE OF BUCKY'S FRIENDS DROPPED IT... JULIUS SLEEZER, I THINK...
ONE LAP AT A TIME
The Cat's Guide to World Domination
darb

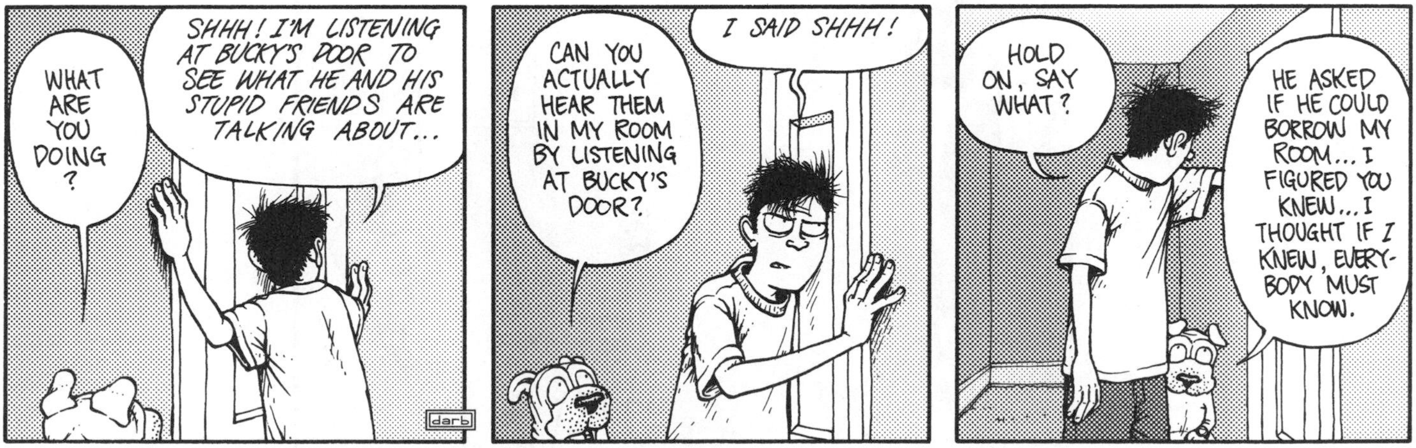
WHAT ARE YOU DOING?
SHHH! I'M LISTENING AT BUCKY'S DOOR TO SEE WHAT HE AND HIS STUPID FRIENDS ARE TALKING ABOUT...
darb
CAN YOU ACTUALLY HEAR THEM IN MY ROOM BY LISTENING AT BUCKY'S DOOR?
I SAID SHHH!
HOLD ON, SAY WHAT?
HE ASKED IF HE COULD BORROW MY ROOM... I FIGURED YOU KNEW... I THOUGHT IF I KNEW, EVERY-BODY MUST KNOW.

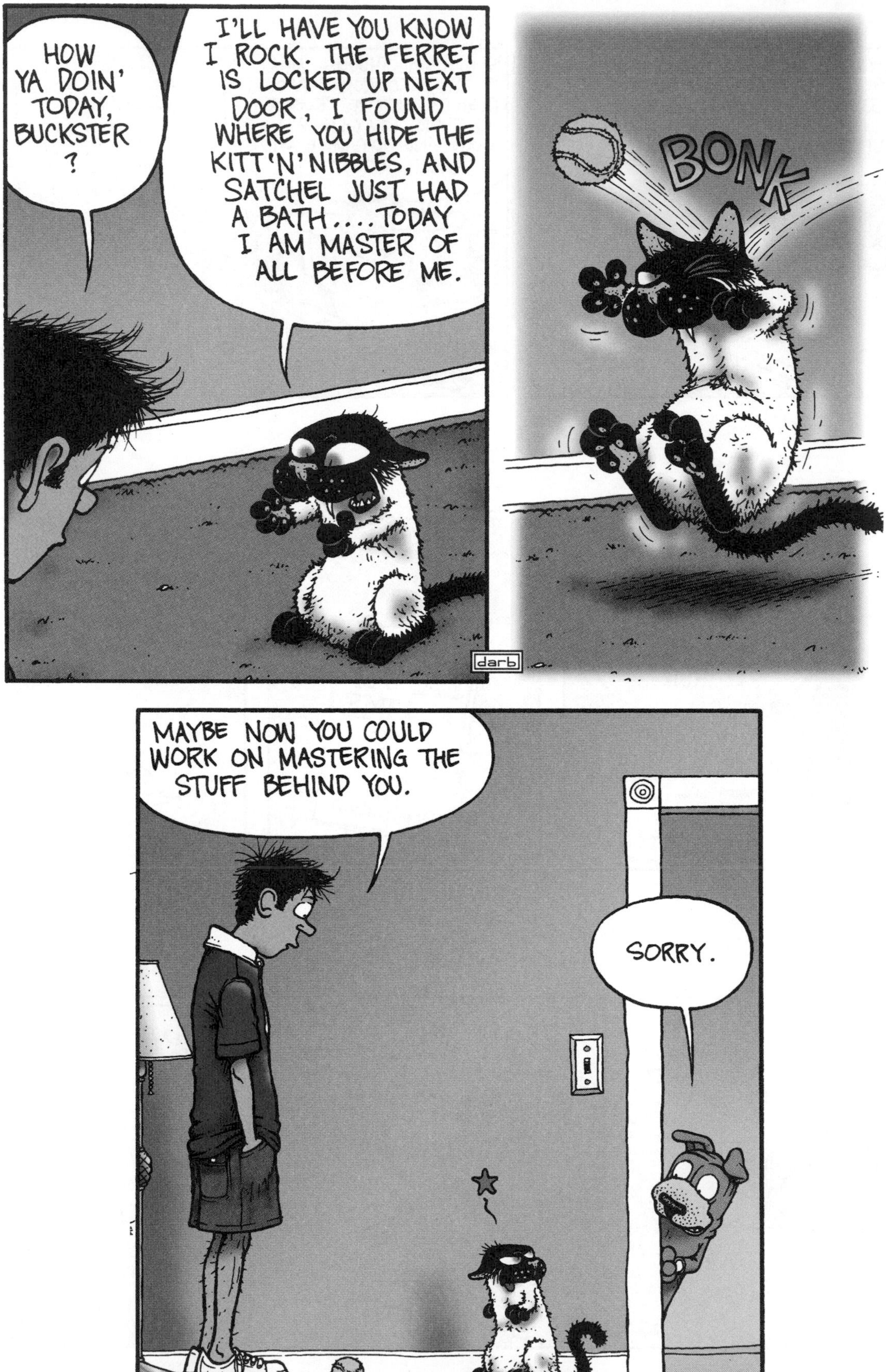
HOW YA DOIN' TODAY, BUCKSTER ?
I'LL HAVE YOU KNOW I ROCK. THE FERRET IS LOCKED UP NEXT DOOR, I FOUND WHERE YOU HIDE THE KITT'N'NIBBLES, AND SATCHEL JUST HAD A BATH....TODAY I AM MASTER OF ALL BEFORE ME.
darb
BONK
MAYBE NOW YOU COULD WORK ON MASTERING THE STUFF BEHIND YOU.
SORRY.

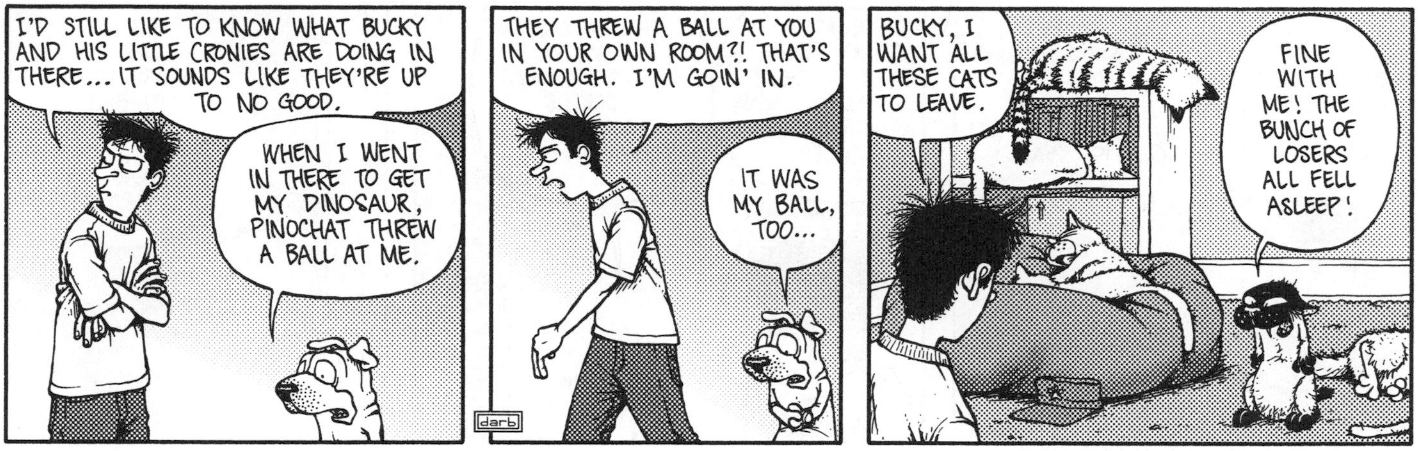
I'D STILL LIKE TO KNOW WHAT BUCKY AND HIS LITTLE CRONIES ARE DOING IN THERE... IT SOUNDS LIKE THEY'RE UP TO NO GOOD.
WHEN I WENT IN THERE TO GET MY DINOSAUR, PINOCHAT THREW A BALL AT ME.
darb
THEY THREW A BALL AT YOU IN YOUR OWN ROOM?! THAT'S ENOUGH. I'M GOIN' IN.
IT WAS MY BALL, TOO...
BUCKY, I WANT ALL THESE CATS TO LEAVE.
FINE WITH ME! THE BUNCH OF LOSERS ALL FELL ASLEEP!

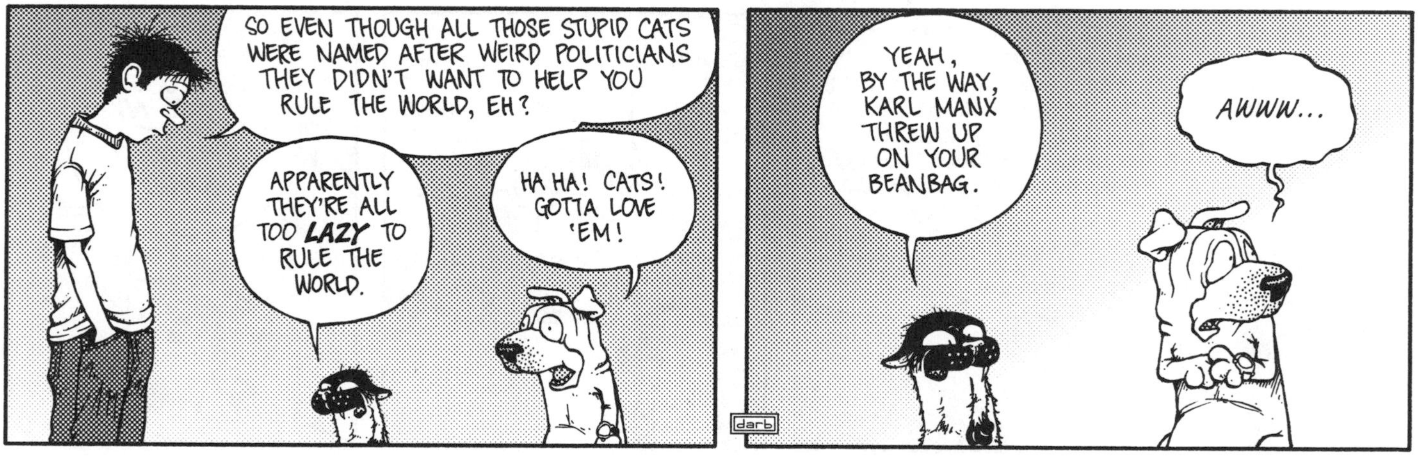
SO EVEN THOUGH ALL THOSE STUPID CATS WERE NAMED AFTER WEIRD POLITICIANS THEY DIDN'T WANT TO HELP YOU RULE THE WORLD, EH?
APPARENTLY THEY'RE ALL TOO LAZY TO RULE THE WORLD.
HA HA! CATS! GOTTA LOVE 'EM!
darb
YEAH, BY THE WAY, KARL MANX THREW UP ON YOUR BEANBAG.
AWWW...

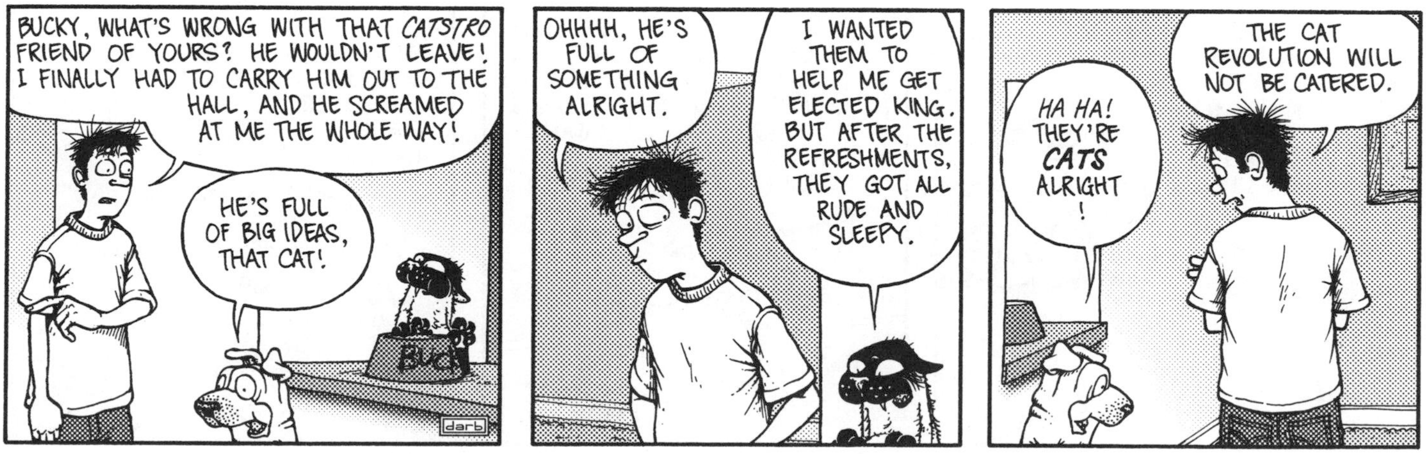
BUCKY, WHAT'S WRONG WITH THAT CATSTRO FRIEND OF YOURS? HE WOULDN'T LEAVE! I FINALLY HAD TO CARRY HIM OUT TO THE HALL, AND HE SCREAMED AT ME THE WHOLE WAY!
HE'S FULL OF BIG IDEAS, THAT CAT!
BUCK
darb
OHHHH, HE'S FULL OF SOMETHING ALRIGHT.
I WANTED THEM TO HELP ME GET ELECTED KING. BUT AFTER THE REFRESHMENTS, THEY GOT ALL RUDE AND SLEEPY.
HA HA! THEY'RE CATS ALRIGHT!
THE CAT REVOLUTION WILL NOT BE CATERED.

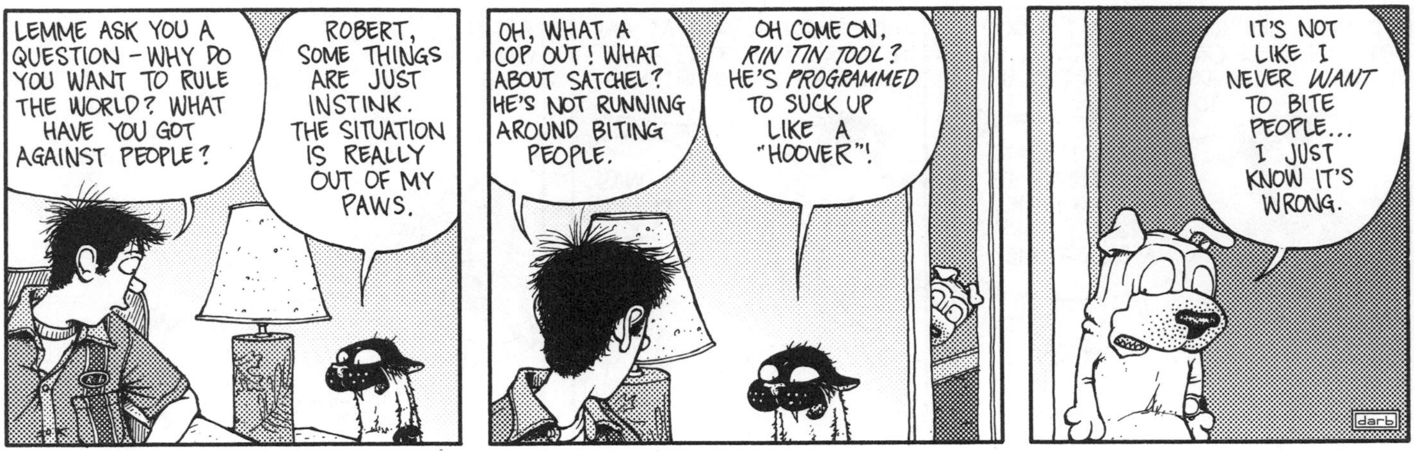
LEMME ASK YOU A QUESTION – WHY DO YOU WANT TO RULE THE WORLD? WHAT HAVE YOU GOT AGAINST PEOPLE?
ROBERT, SOME THINGS ARE JUST INSTINK. THE SITUATION IS REALLY OUT OF MY PAWS.
OH, WHAT A COP OUT! WHAT ABOUT SATCHEL? HE'S NOT RUNNING AROUND BITING PEOPLE.
OH COME ON, *RIN TIN TOOL?* HE'S *PROGRAMMED* TO SUCK UP LIKE A "HOOVER"!
IT'S NOT LIKE I NEVER *WANT* TO BITE PEOPLE... I JUST KNOW IT'S WRONG.
darb

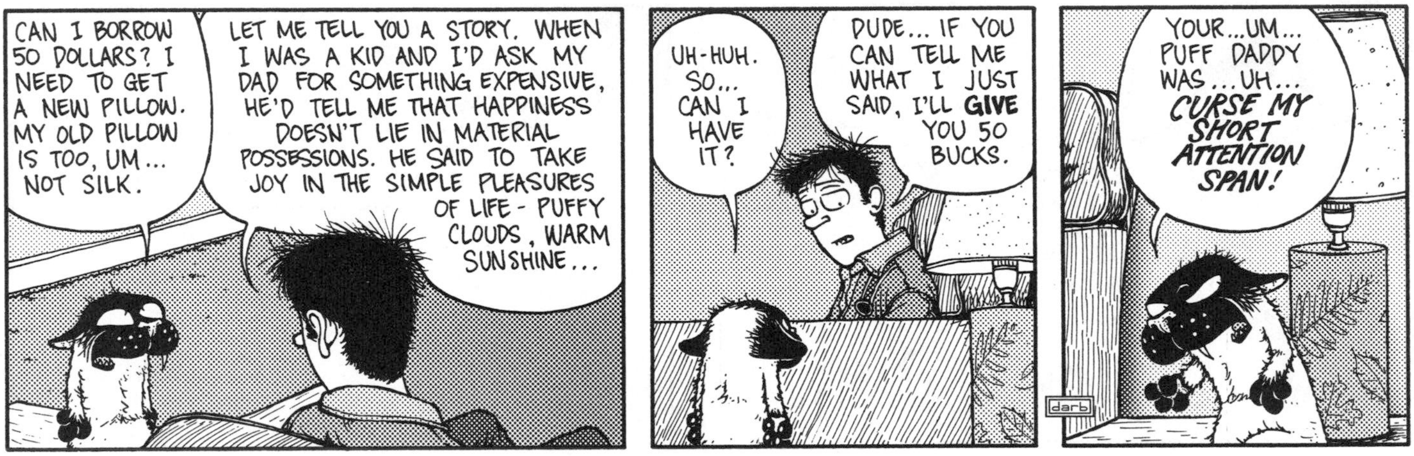
CAN I BORROW 50 DOLLARS? I NEED TO GET A NEW PILLOW. MY OLD PILLOW IS TOO, UM... NOT SILK.
LET ME TELL YOU A STORY. WHEN I WAS A KID AND I'D ASK MY DAD FOR SOMETHING EXPENSIVE, HE'D TELL ME THAT HAPPINESS DOESN'T LIE IN MATERIAL POSSESSIONS. HE SAID TO TAKE JOY IN THE SIMPLE PLEASURES OF LIFE - PUFFY CLOUDS, WARM SUNSHINE...
UH-HUH. SO... CAN I HAVE IT?
DUDE... IF YOU CAN TELL ME WHAT I JUST SAID, I'LL **GIVE** YOU 50 BUCKS.
darb
YOUR...UM... PUFF DADDY WAS...UH... ***CURSE MY SHORT ATTENTION SPAN!***

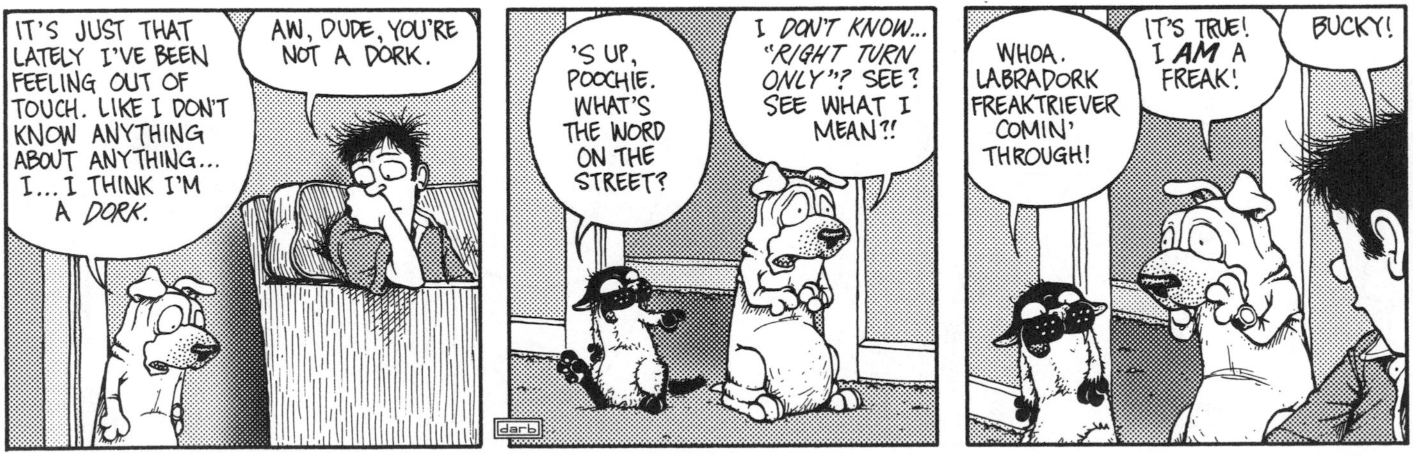
IT'S JUST THAT LATELY I'VE BEEN FEELING OUT OF TOUCH. LIKE I DON'T KNOW ANYTHING ABOUT ANYTHING... I... I THINK I'M A *DORK*.
AW, DUDE, YOU'RE NOT A DORK.
'S UP, POOCHIE. WHAT'S THE WORD ON THE STREET?
I *DON'T KNOW*... "*RIGHT TURN ONLY*"? SEE? SEE WHAT I MEAN?!
darb
WHOA. LABRADORK FREAKTRIEVER COMIN' THROUGH!
IT'S TRUE! I ***AM*** A FREAK!
BUCKY!

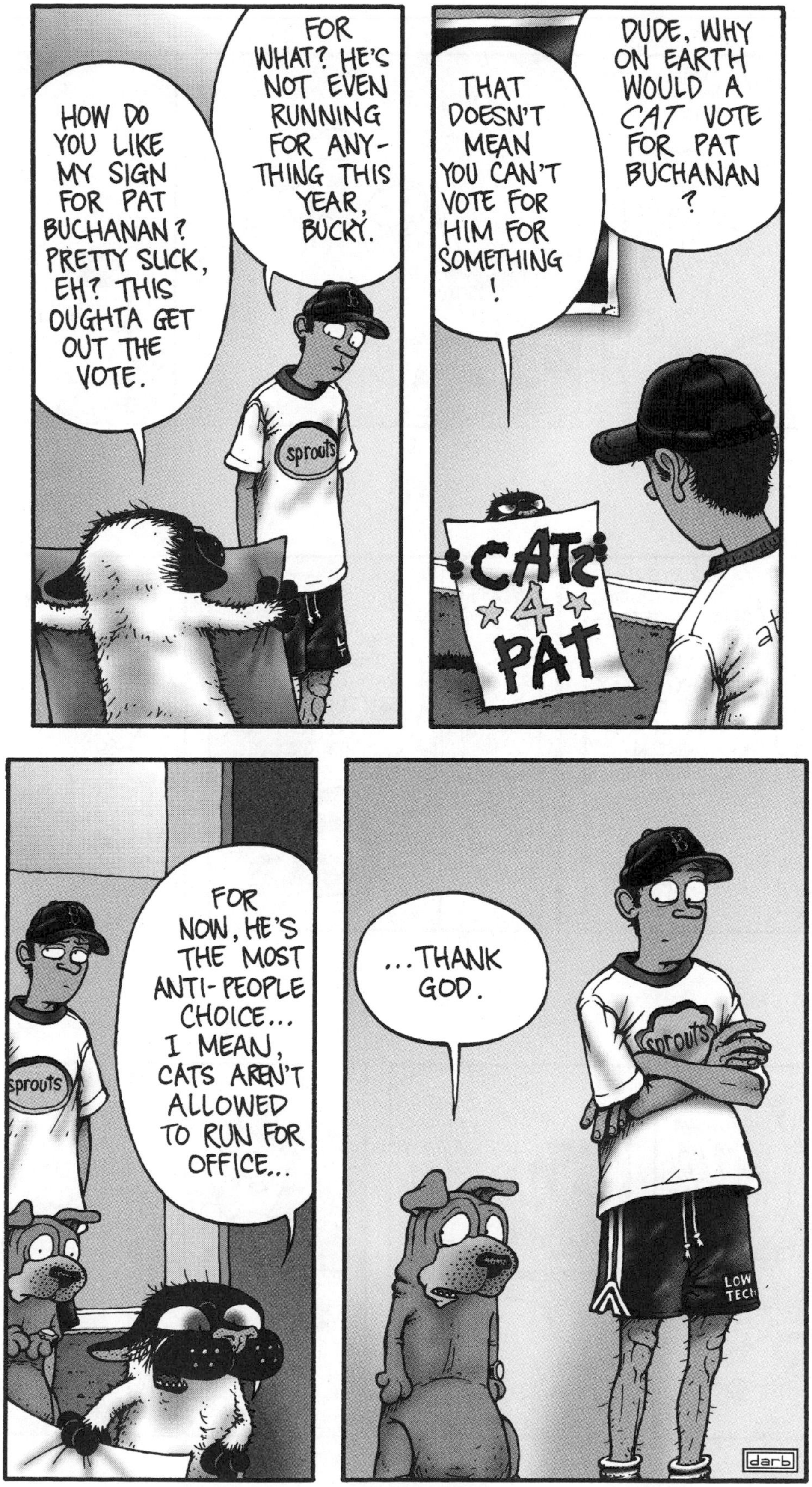
HOW DO YOU LIKE MY SIGN FOR PAT BUCHANAN? PRETTY SLICK, EH? THIS OUGHTA GET OUT THE VOTE.
FOR WHAT? HE'S NOT EVEN RUNNING FOR ANYTHING THIS YEAR, BUCKY.
sprouts
DUDE, WHY ON EARTH WOULD A *CAT* VOTE FOR PAT BUCHANAN?
THAT DOESN'T MEAN YOU CAN'T VOTE FOR HIM FOR SOMETHING!
CATS 4 PAT
FOR NOW, HE'S THE MOST ANTI-PEOPLE CHOICE... I MEAN, CATS AREN'T ALLOWED TO RUN FOR OFFICE...
sprouts
...THANK GOD.
sprouts
LOW TECH
darb

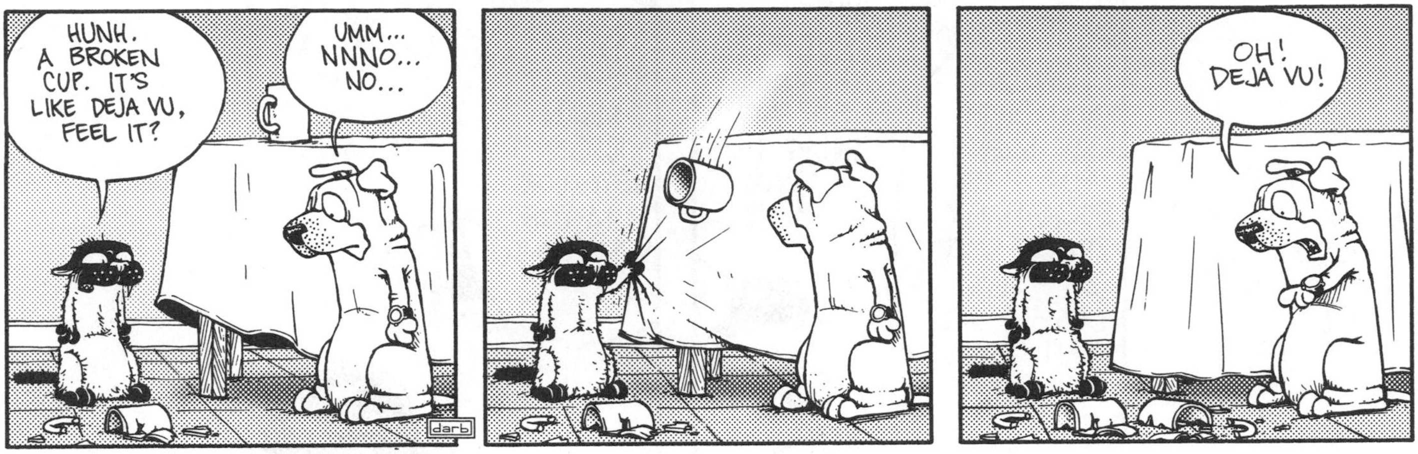
HUNH. A BROKEN CUP. IT'S LIKE DEJA VU, FEEL IT?
UMM... NNNO... NO...
OH! DEJA VU!

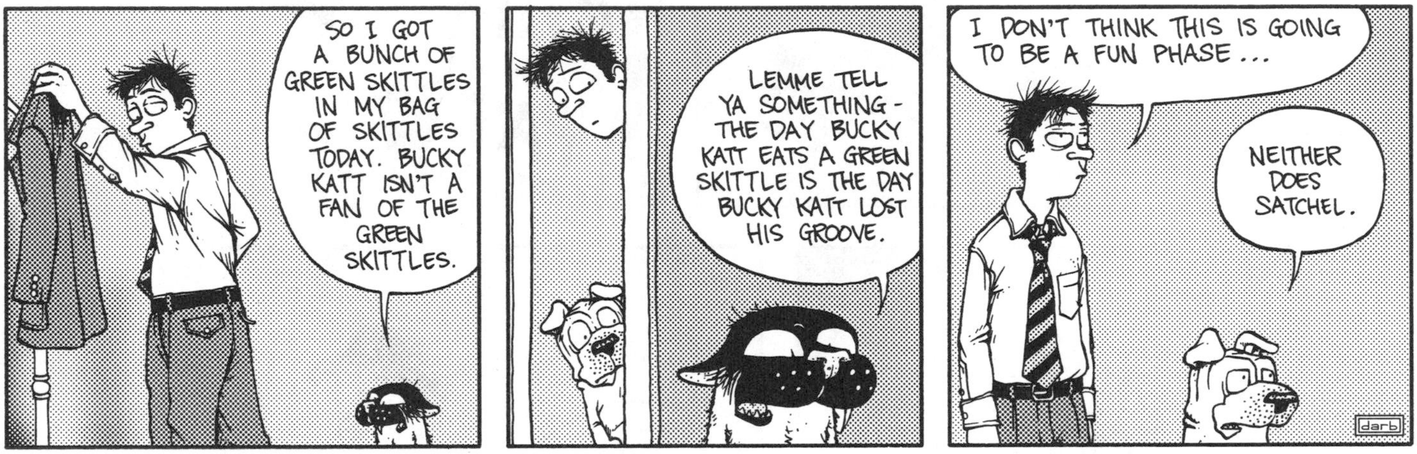
SO I GOT A BUNCH OF GREEN SKITTLES IN MY BAG OF SKITTLES TODAY. BUCKY KATT ISN'T A FAN OF THE GREEN SKITTLES.
LEMME TELL YA SOMETHING - THE DAY BUCKY KATT EATS A GREEN SKITTLE IS THE DAY BUCKY KATT LOST HIS GROOVE.
I DON'T THINK THIS IS GOING TO BE A FUN PHASE...
NEITHER DOES SATCHEL.

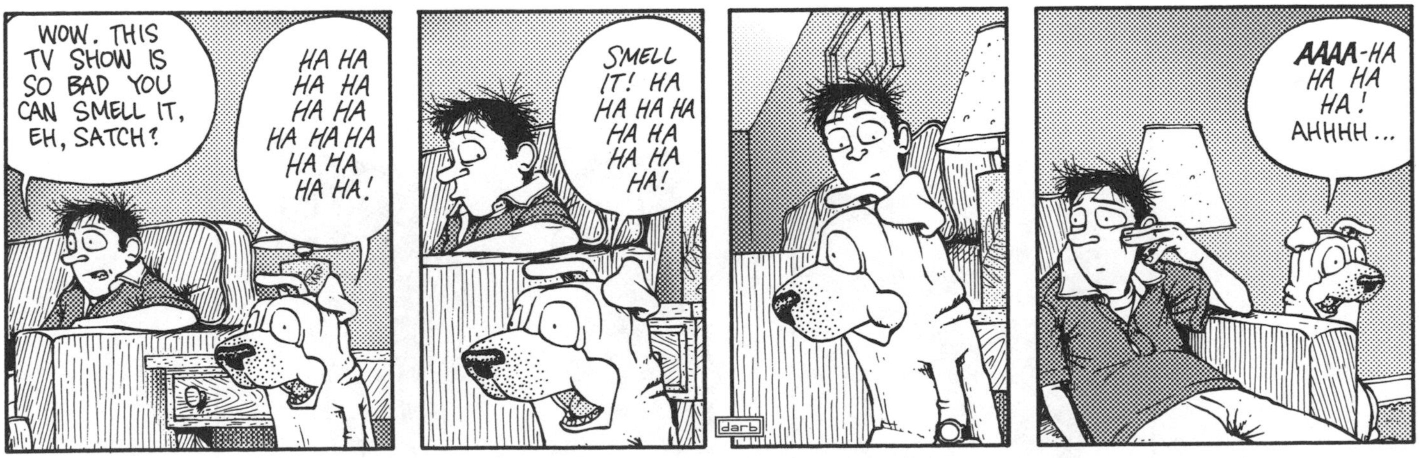
WOW. THIS TV SHOW IS SO BAD YOU CAN SMELL IT, EH, SATCH?
HA HA HA HA HA HA HA HA HA HA HA HA HA!
SMELL IT! HA HA HA HA HA HA HA HA HA!
AAAA-HA HA HA HA! AHHHH...

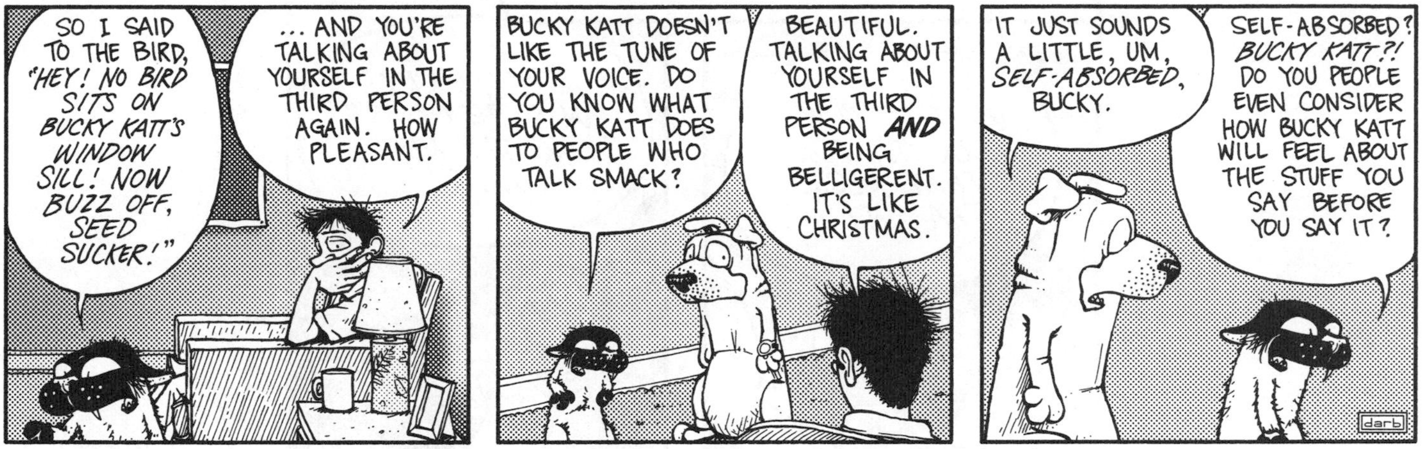
SO I SAID TO THE BIRD, "HEY! NO BIRD SITS ON BUCKY KATT'S WINDOW SILL! NOW BUZZ OFF, SEED SUCKER!"
... AND YOU'RE TALKING ABOUT YOURSELF IN THE THIRD PERSON AGAIN. HOW PLEASANT.
BUCKY KATT DOESN'T LIKE THE TUNE OF YOUR VOICE. DO YOU KNOW WHAT BUCKY KATT DOES TO PEOPLE WHO TALK SMACK?
BEAUTIFUL. TALKING ABOUT YOURSELF IN THE THIRD PERSON AND BEING BELLIGERENT. IT'S LIKE CHRISTMAS.
IT JUST SOUNDS A LITTLE, UM, SELF-ABSORBED, BUCKY.
SELF-ABSORBED? BUCKY KATT?! DO YOU PEOPLE EVEN CONSIDER HOW BUCKY KATT WILL FEEL ABOUT THE STUFF YOU SAY BEFORE YOU SAY IT?
darb

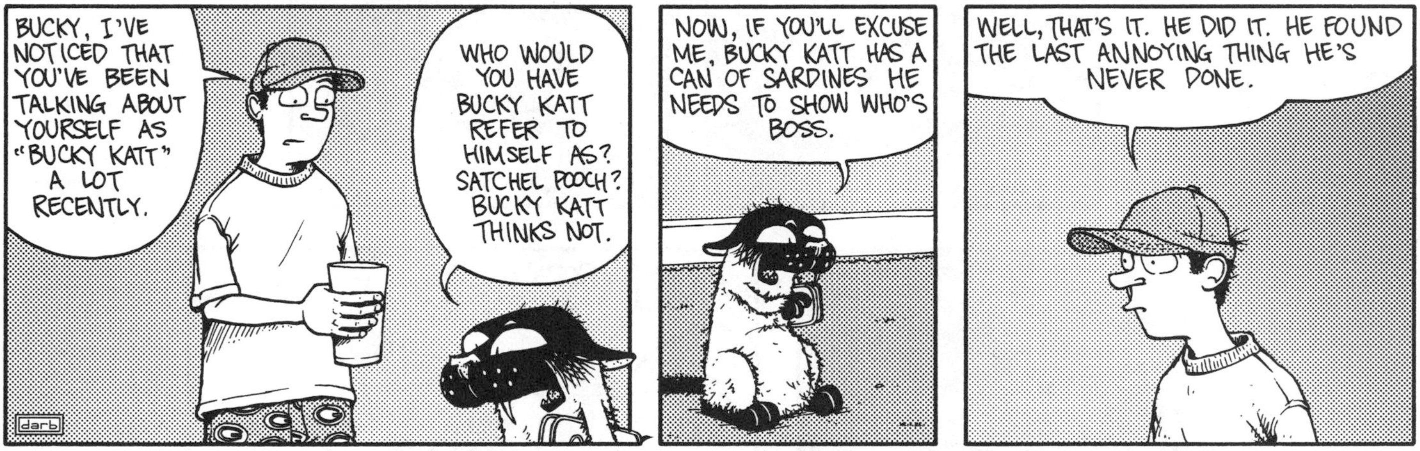
BUCKY, I'VE NOTICED THAT YOU'VE BEEN TALKING ABOUT YOURSELF AS "BUCKY KATT" A LOT RECENTLY.
WHO WOULD YOU HAVE BUCKY KATT REFER TO HIMSELF AS? SATCHEL POOCH? BUCKY KATT THINKS NOT.
NOW, IF YOU'LL EXCUSE ME, BUCKY KATT HAS A CAN OF SARDINES HE NEEDS TO SHOW WHO'S BOSS.
WELL, THAT'S IT. HE DID IT. HE FOUND THE LAST ANNOYING THING HE'S NEVER DONE.
darb

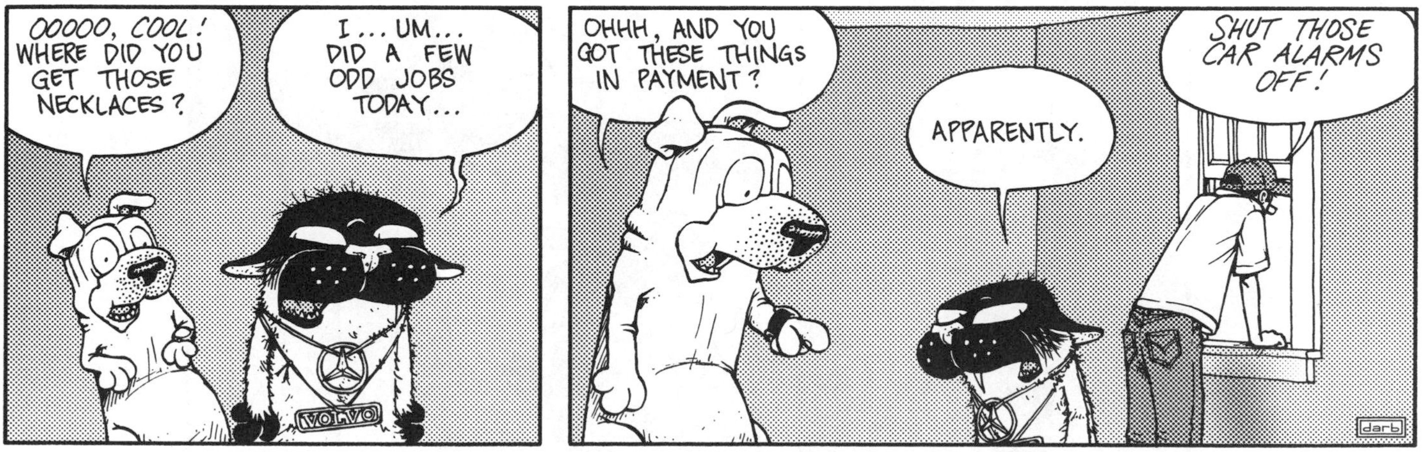
OOOOO, COOL! WHERE DID YOU GET THOSE NECKLACES?
I... UM... DID A FEW ODD JOBS TODAY...
VOLVO
OHHH, AND YOU GOT THESE THINGS IN PAYMENT?
APPARENTLY.
SHUT THOSE CAR ALARMS OFF!
darb

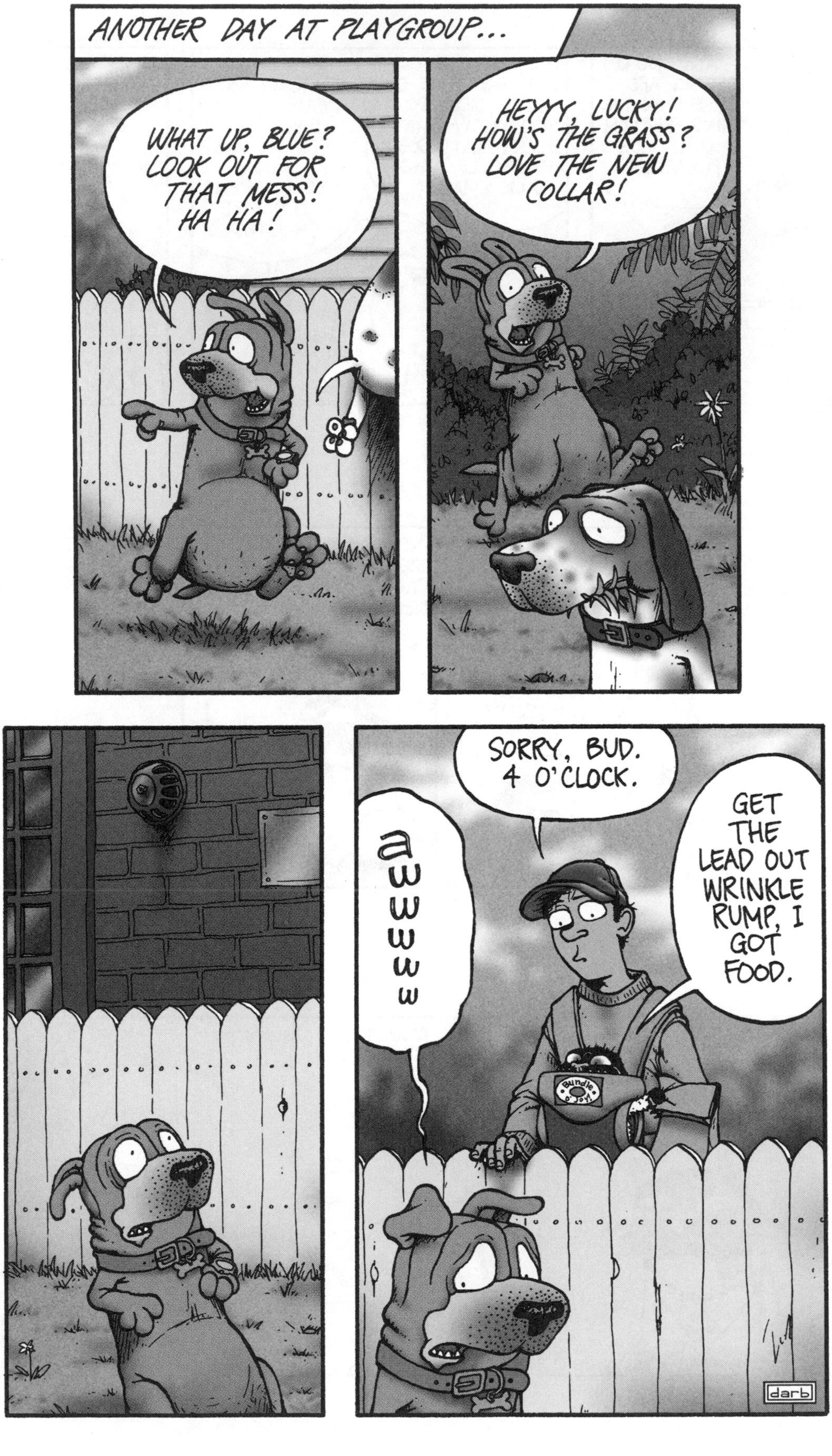
ANOTHER DAY AT PLAYGROUP...
WHAT UP, BLUE? LOOK OUT FOR THAT MESS! HA HA!
HEYYY, LUCKY! HOW'S THE GRASS? LOVE THE NEW COLLAR!
awwwww
SORRY, BUD. 4 O'CLOCK.
GET THE LEAD OUT WRINKLE RUMP, I GOT FOOD.
Bundle o' Joy!
darb

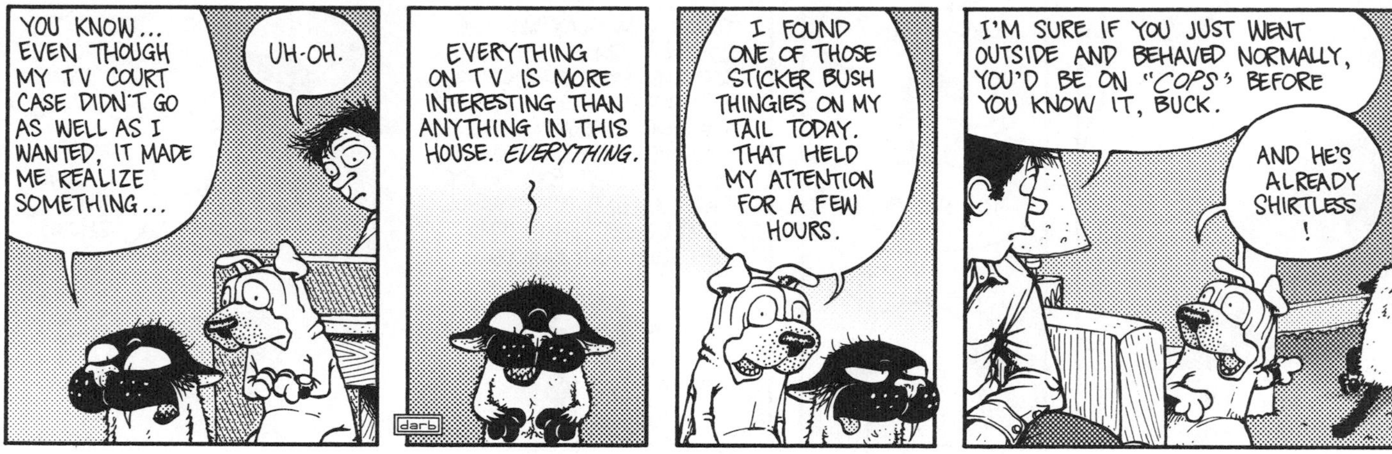
YOU KNOW... EVEN THOUGH MY TV COURT CASE DIDN'T GO AS WELL AS I WANTED, IT MADE ME REALIZE SOMETHING...
UH-OH.
EVERYTHING ON TV IS MORE INTERESTING THAN ANYTHING IN THIS HOUSE. EVERYTHING.
I FOUND ONE OF THOSE STICKER BUSH THINGIES ON MY TAIL TODAY. THAT HELD MY ATTENTION FOR A FEW HOURS.
I'M SURE IF YOU JUST WENT OUTSIDE AND BEHAVED NORMALLY, YOU'D BE ON "COPS" BEFORE YOU KNOW IT, BUCK.
AND HE'S ALREADY SHIRTLESS!
darb

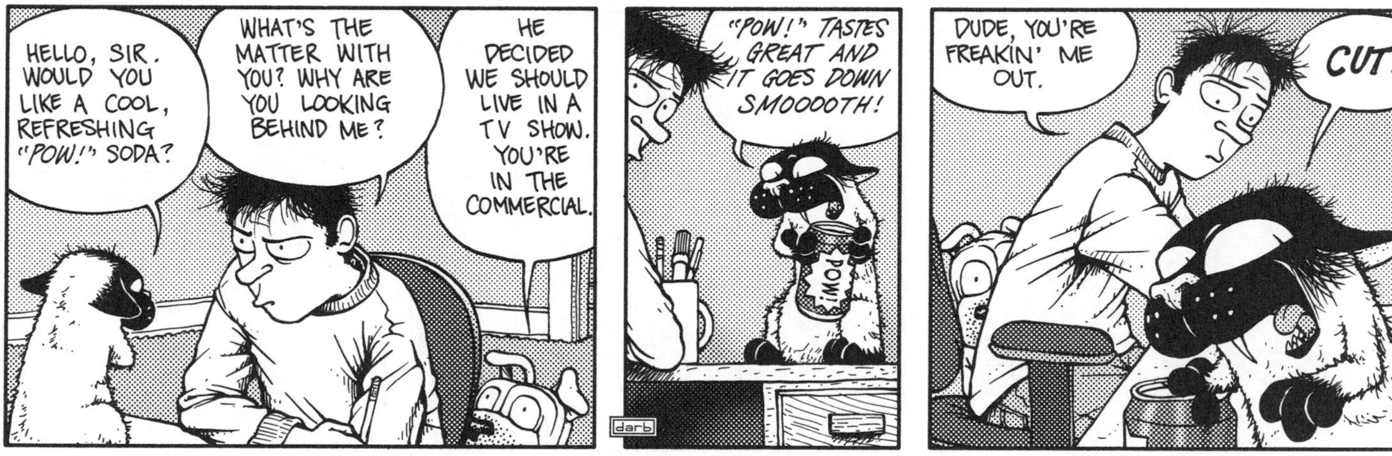
HELLO, SIR. WOULD YOU LIKE A COOL, REFRESHING "POW!" SODA?
WHAT'S THE MATTER WITH YOU? WHY ARE YOU LOOKING BEHIND ME?
HE DECIDED WE SHOULD LIVE IN A TV SHOW. YOU'RE IN THE COMMERCIAL.
"POW!" TASTES GREAT AND IT GOES DOWN SMOOOOTH!
POW!
DUDE, YOU'RE FREAKIN' ME OUT.
CUT!
darb

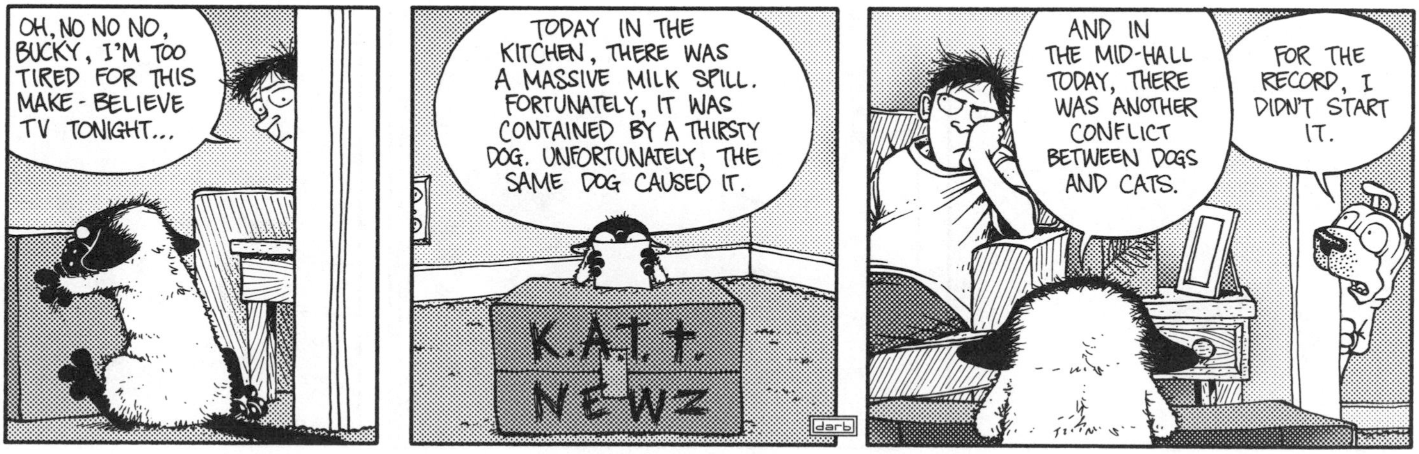
OH, NO NO NO, BUCKY, I'M TOO TIRED FOR THIS MAKE-BELIEVE TV TONIGHT...
TODAY IN THE KITCHEN, THERE WAS A MASSIVE MILK SPILL. FORTUNATELY, IT WAS CONTAINED BY A THIRSTY DOG. UNFORTUNATELY, THE SAME DOG CAUSED IT.
K.A.T. t. NEWZ
AND IN THE MID-HALL TODAY, THERE WAS ANOTHER CONFLICT BETWEEN DOGS AND CATS.
FOR THE RECORD, I DIDN'T START IT.
darb

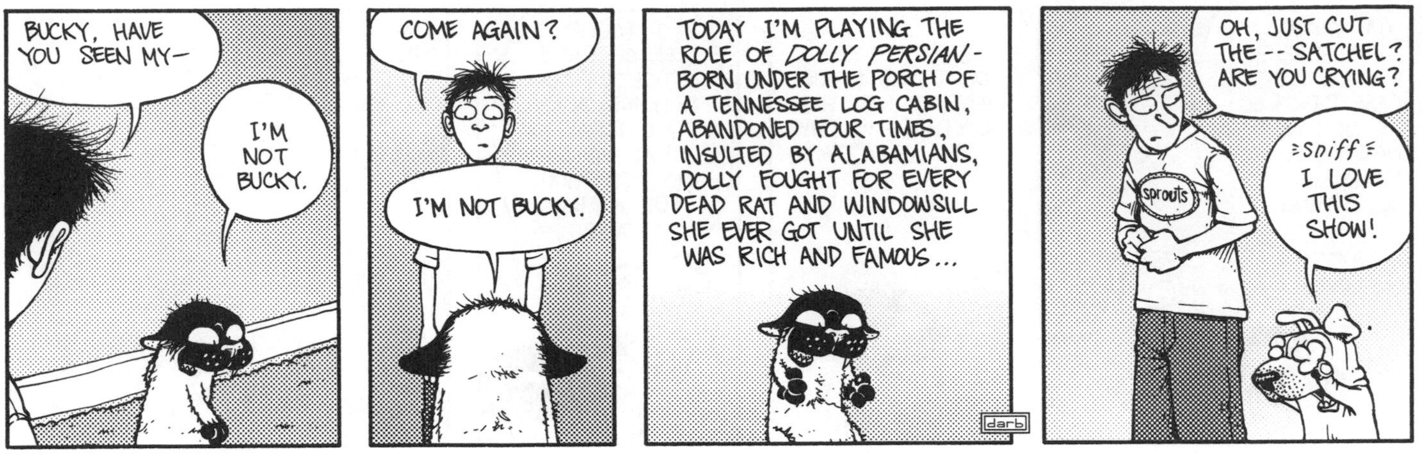

BUCKY, HAVE YOU SEEN MY—
I'M NOT BUCKY.
COME AGAIN?
I'M NOT BUCKY.
TODAY I'M PLAYING THE ROLE OF *DOLLY PERSIAN* - BORN UNDER THE PORCH OF A TENNESSEE LOG CABIN, ABANDONED FOUR TIMES, INSULTED BY ALABAMIANS, DOLLY FOUGHT FOR EVERY DEAD RAT AND WINDOWSILL SHE EVER GOT UNTIL SHE WAS RICH AND FAMOUS...
darb
OH, JUST CUT THE -- SATCHEL? ARE YOU CRYING?
sprouts
sniff
I LOVE THIS SHOW!

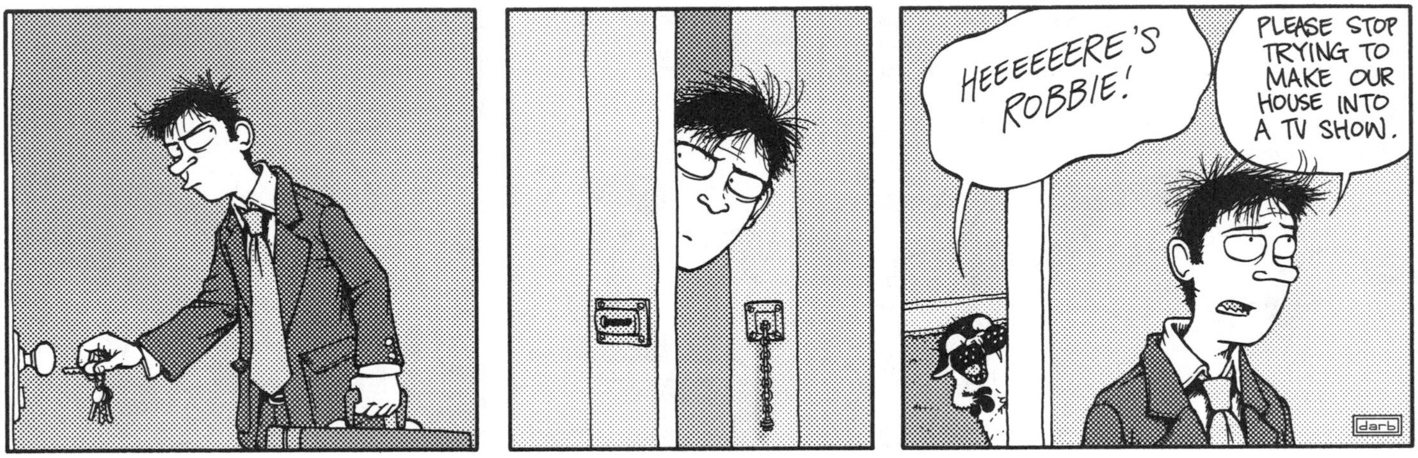

HEEEEEERE'S ROBBIE!
PLEASE STOP TRYING TO MAKE OUR HOUSE INTO A TV SHOW.
darb

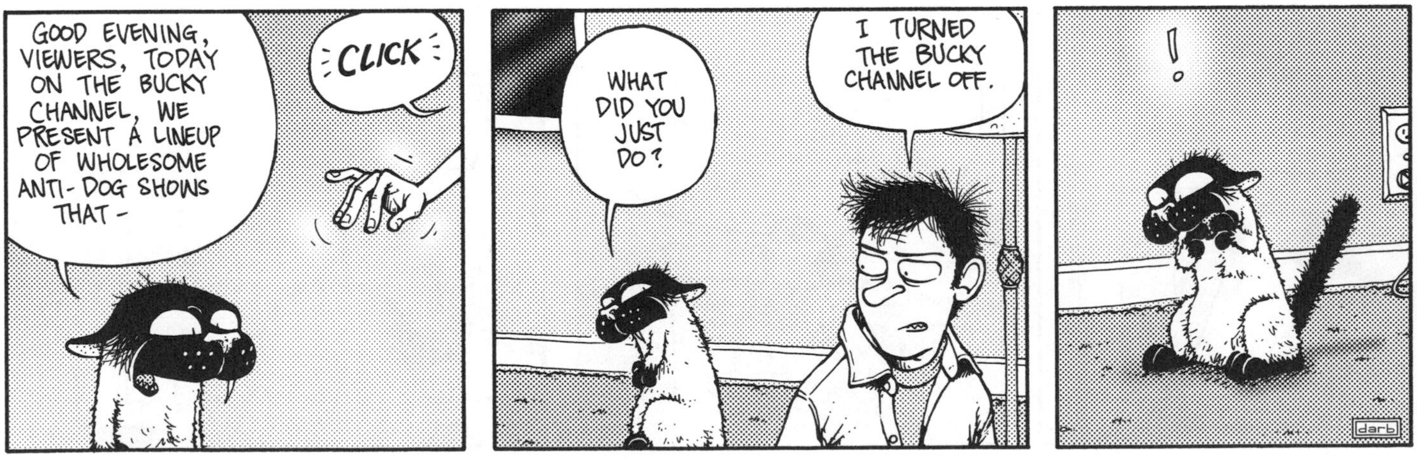

GOOD EVENING, VIEWERS, TODAY ON THE BUCKY CHANNEL, WE PRESENT A LINEUP OF WHOLESOME ANTI-DOG SHOWS THAT -
CLICK
WHAT DID YOU JUST DO?
I TURNED THE BUCKY CHANNEL OFF.
!
darb

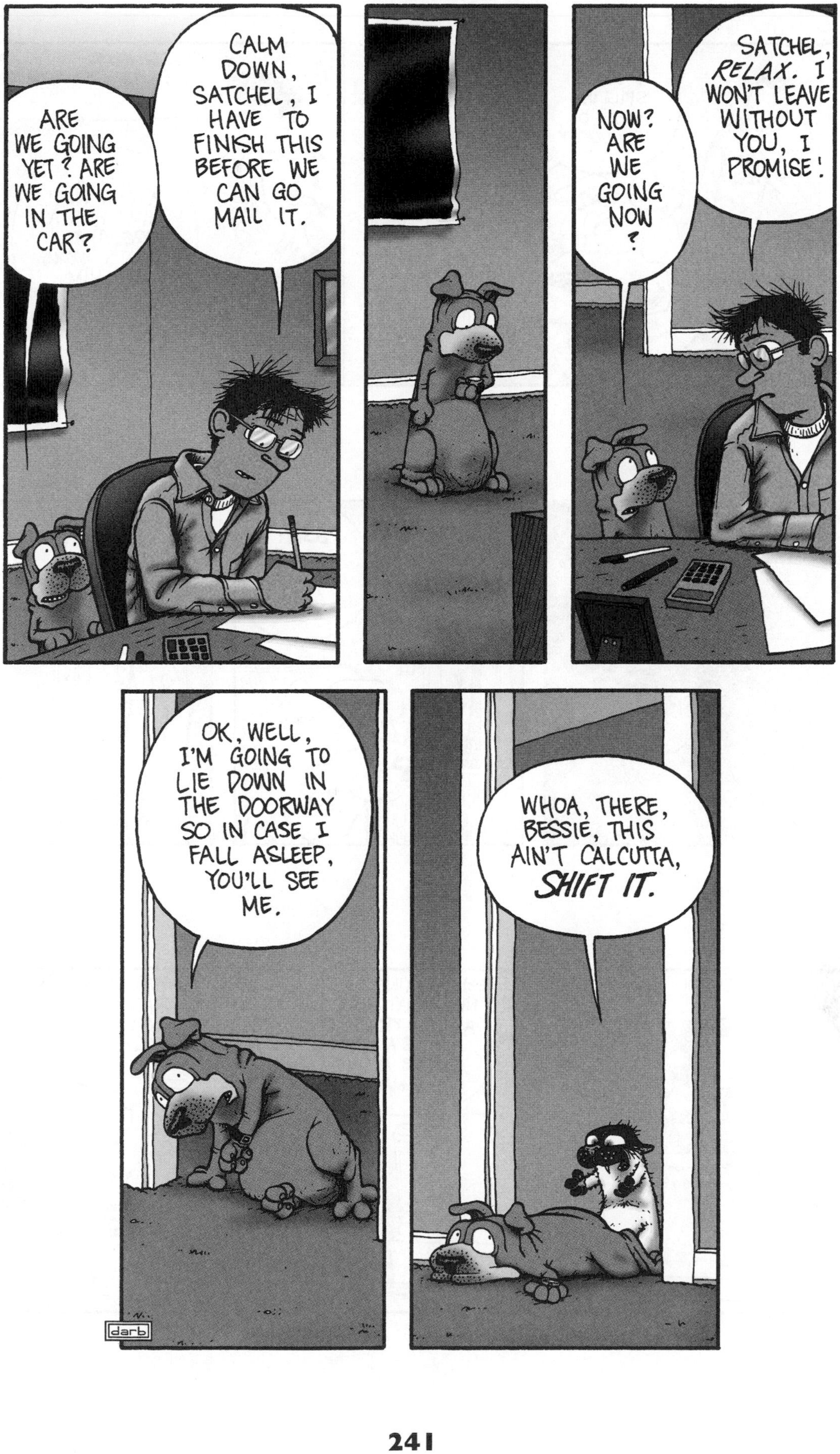
ARE WE GOING YET? ARE WE GOING IN THE CAR?
CALM DOWN, SATCHEL, I HAVE TO FINISH THIS BEFORE WE CAN GO MAIL IT.
NOW? ARE WE GOING NOW?
SATCHEL, RELAX. I WON'T LEAVE WITHOUT YOU, I PROMISE!
OK, WELL, I'M GOING TO LIE DOWN IN THE DOORWAY SO IN CASE I FALL ASLEEP, YOU'LL SEE ME.
WHOA, THERE, BESSIE, THIS AIN'T CALCUTTA, SHIFT IT.
darb

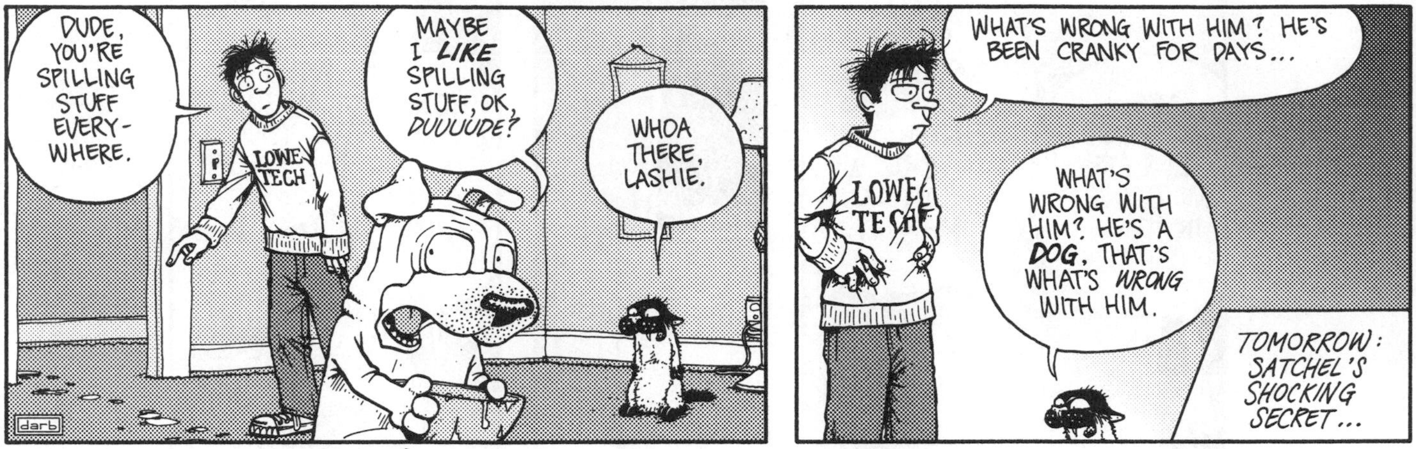
DUDE, YOU'RE SPILLING STUFF EVERY-WHERE.
LOWE TECH
MAYBE I **LIKE** SPILLING STUFF, OK, *DUUUUDE?*
WHOA THERE, LASHIE.
darb
WHAT'S WRONG WITH HIM? HE'S BEEN CRANKY FOR DAYS...
LOWE TECH
WHAT'S WRONG WITH HIM? HE'S A **DOG**, THAT'S WHAT'S *WRONG* WITH HIM.
TOMORROW: SATCHEL'S SHOCKING SECRET...

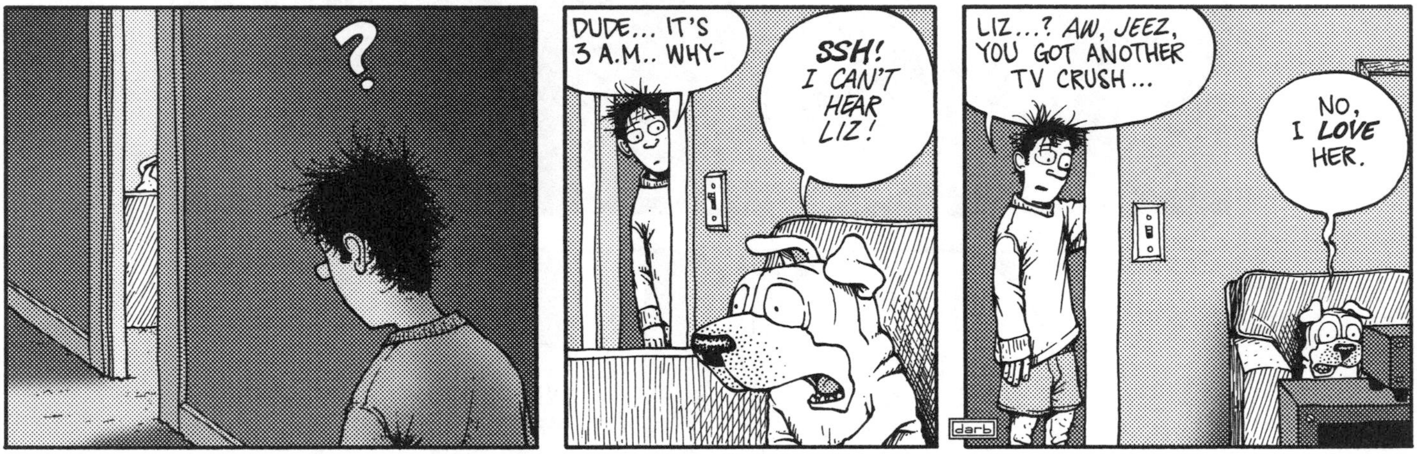
?
DUDE... IT'S 3 A.M.. WHY-
SSH! *I CAN'T HEAR LIZ!*
LIZ...? *AW*, JEEZ, YOU GOT ANOTHER TV CRUSH...
NO, I **LOVE** HER.
darb

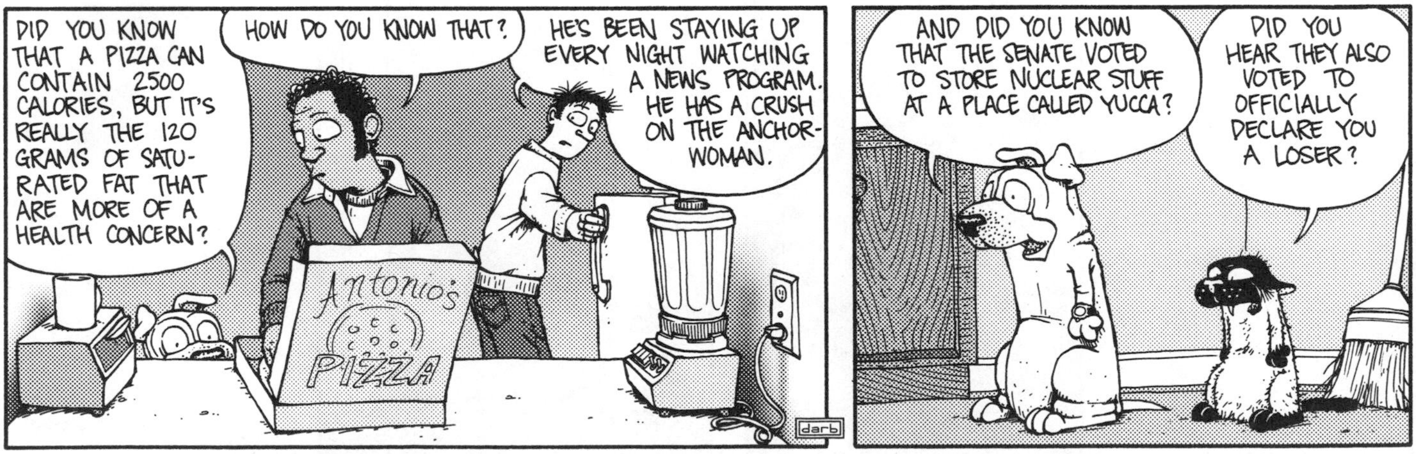
DID YOU KNOW THAT A PIZZA CAN CONTAIN 2500 CALORIES, BUT IT'S REALLY THE 120 GRAMS OF SATU-RATED FAT THAT ARE MORE OF A HEALTH CONCERN?
HOW DO YOU KNOW THAT?
HE'S BEEN STAYING UP EVERY NIGHT WATCHING A NEWS PROGRAM. HE HAS A CRUSH ON THE ANCHOR-WOMAN.
Antonio's PIZZA
darb
AND DID YOU KNOW THAT THE SENATE VOTED TO STORE NUCLEAR STUFF AT A PLACE CALLED YUCCA?
DID YOU HEAR THEY ALSO VOTED TO OFFICIALLY DECLARE YOU A LOSER?

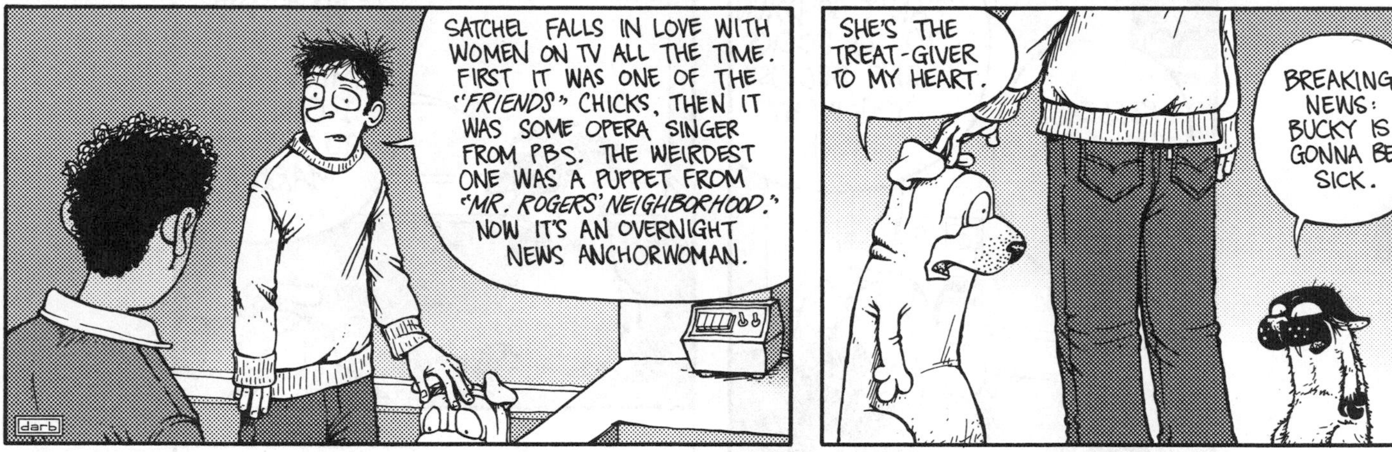
SATCHEL FALLS IN LOVE WITH WOMEN ON TV ALL THE TIME. FIRST IT WAS ONE OF THE "FRIENDS" CHICKS, THEN IT WAS SOME OPERA SINGER FROM PBS. THE WEIRDEST ONE WAS A PUPPET FROM "MR. ROGERS' NEIGHBORHOOD." NOW IT'S AN OVERNIGHT NEWS ANCHORWOMAN.
SHE'S THE TREAT-GIVER TO MY HEART.
BREAKING NEWS: BUCKY IS GONNA BE SICK.

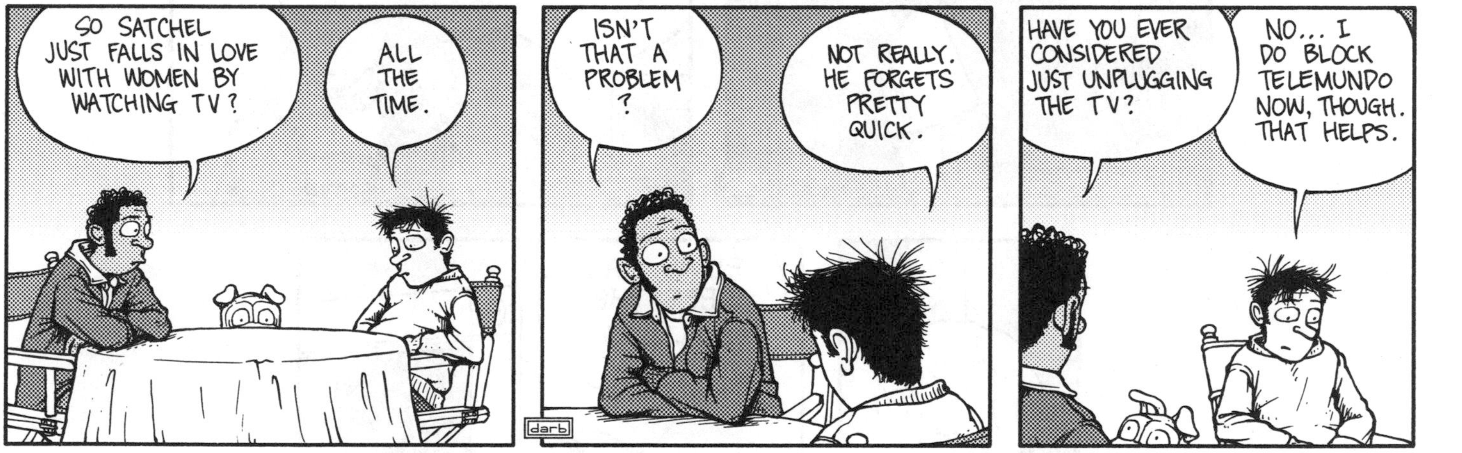
SO SATCHEL JUST FALLS IN LOVE WITH WOMEN BY WATCHING TV?
ALL THE TIME.
ISN'T THAT A PROBLEM?
NOT REALLY. HE FORGETS PRETTY QUICK.
HAVE YOU EVER CONSIDERED JUST UNPLUGGING THE TV?
NO... I DO BLOCK TELEMUNDO NOW, THOUGH. THAT HELPS.

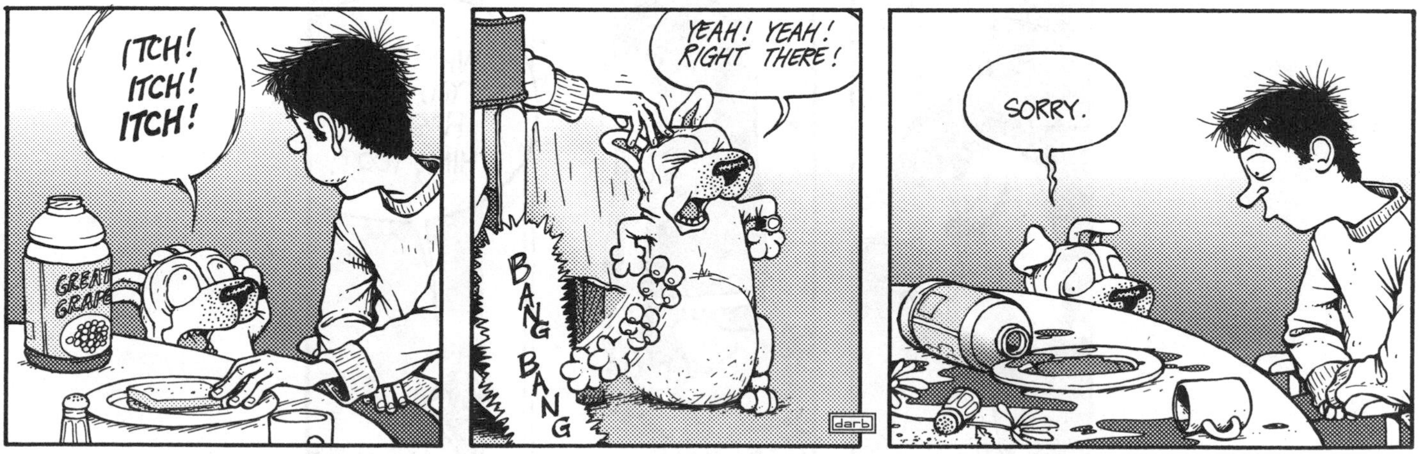
ITCH! ITCH! ITCH!
GREAT GRAPE
YEAH! YEAH! RIGHT THERE!
BANG BANG
SORRY.

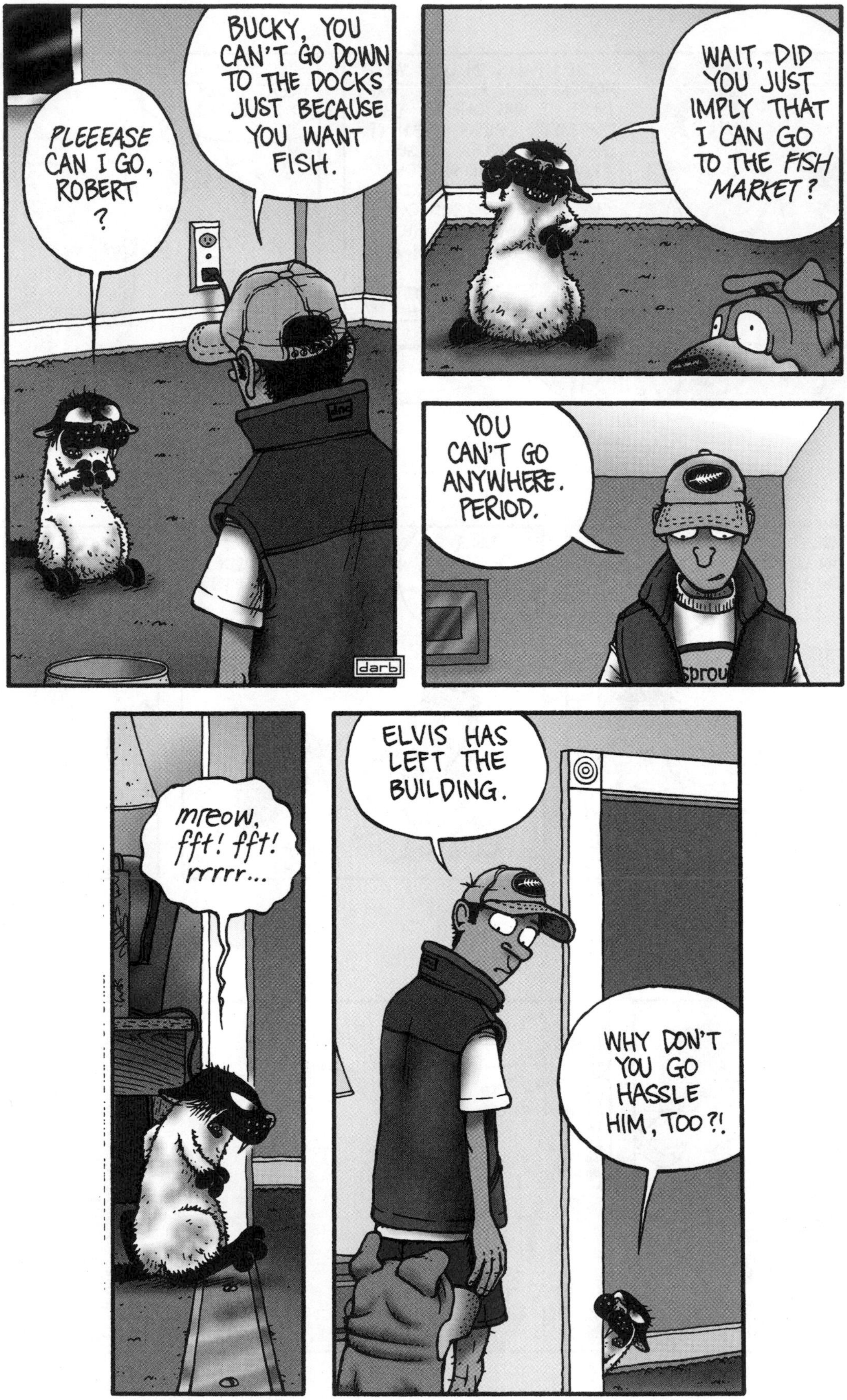
PLEEEASE CAN I GO, ROBERT ?
BUCKY, YOU CAN'T GO DOWN TO THE DOCKS JUST BECAUSE YOU WANT FISH.
darb
WAIT, DID YOU JUST IMPLY THAT I CAN GO TO THE *FISH MARKET* ?
YOU CAN'T GO ANYWHERE. PERIOD.
sprou
mreow, fft! fft! rrrrr...
ELVIS HAS LEFT THE BUILDING.
WHY DON'T YOU GO HASSLE HIM, TOO?!

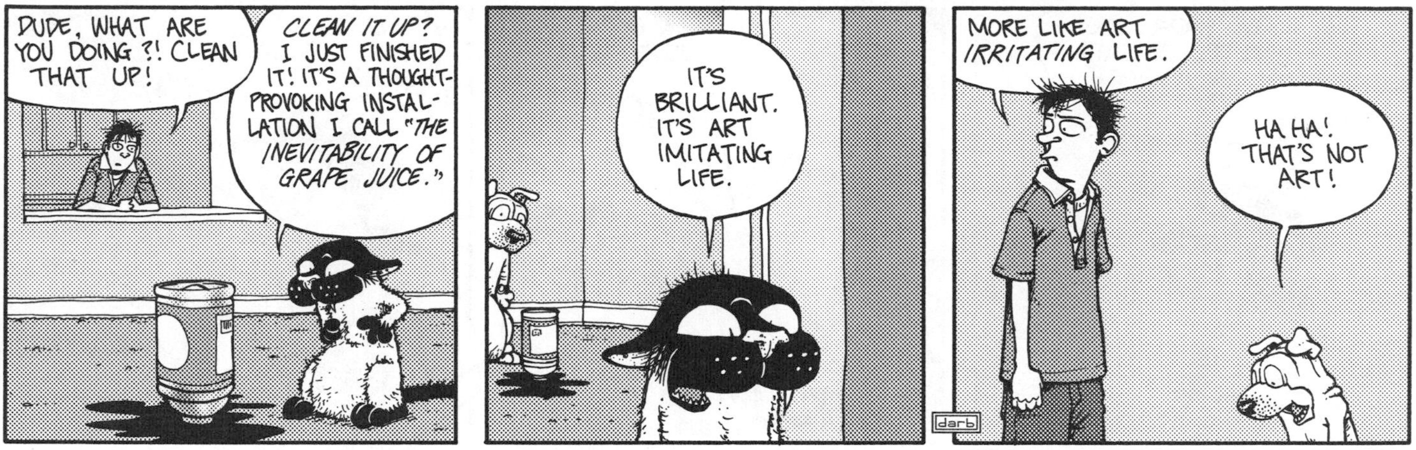
DUDE, WHAT ARE YOU DOING ?! CLEAN THAT UP!
CLEAN IT UP? I JUST FINISHED IT! IT'S A THOUGHT-PROVOKING INSTALLATION I CALL "THE INEVITABILITY OF GRAPE JUICE."
IT'S BRILLIANT. IT'S ART IMITATING LIFE.
MORE LIKE ART IRRITATING LIFE.
HA HA! THAT'S NOT ART!
darb

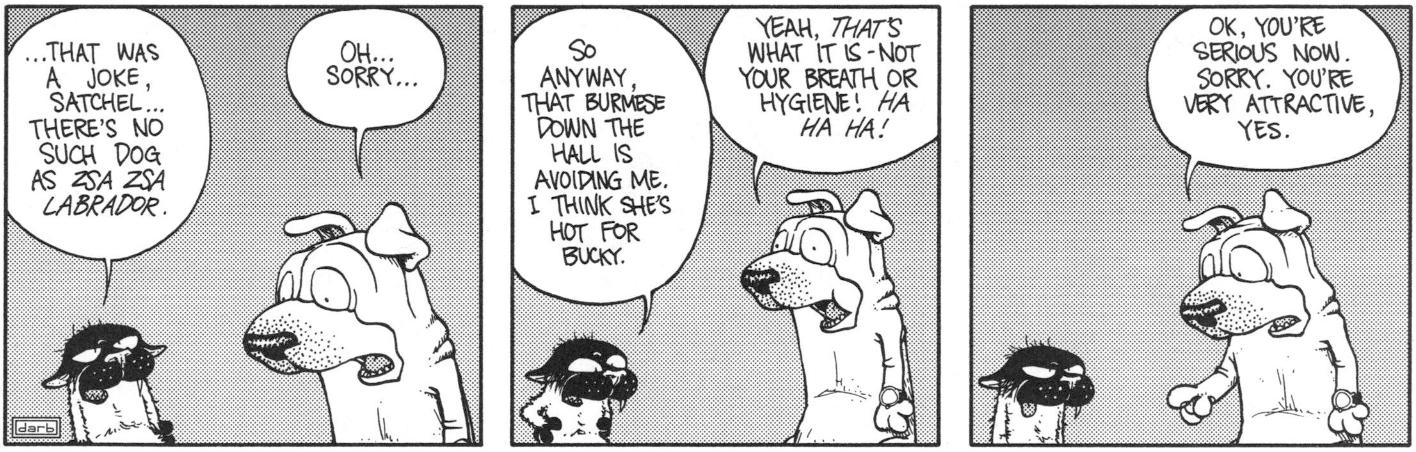
...THAT WAS A JOKE, SATCHEL... THERE'S NO SUCH DOG AS ZSA ZSA LABRADOR.
OH... SORRY...
darb
SO ANYWAY, THAT BURMESE DOWN THE HALL IS AVOIDING ME. I THINK SHE'S HOT FOR BUCKY.
YEAH, THAT'S WHAT IT IS - NOT YOUR BREATH OR HYGIENE! HA HA HA!
OK, YOU'RE SERIOUS NOW. SORRY. YOU'RE VERY ATTRACTIVE, YES.

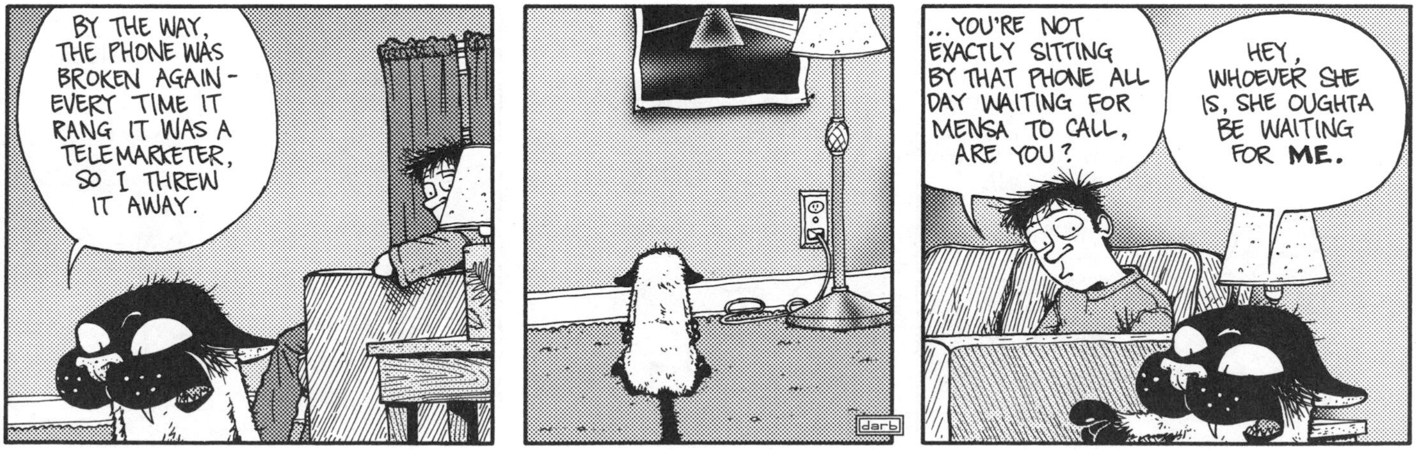
BY THE WAY, THE PHONE WAS BROKEN AGAIN - EVERY TIME IT RANG IT WAS A TELEMARKETER, SO I THREW IT AWAY.
darb
...YOU'RE NOT EXACTLY SITTING BY THAT PHONE ALL DAY WAITING FOR MENSA TO CALL, ARE YOU?
HEY, WHOEVER SHE IS, SHE OUGHTA BE WAITING FOR ME.

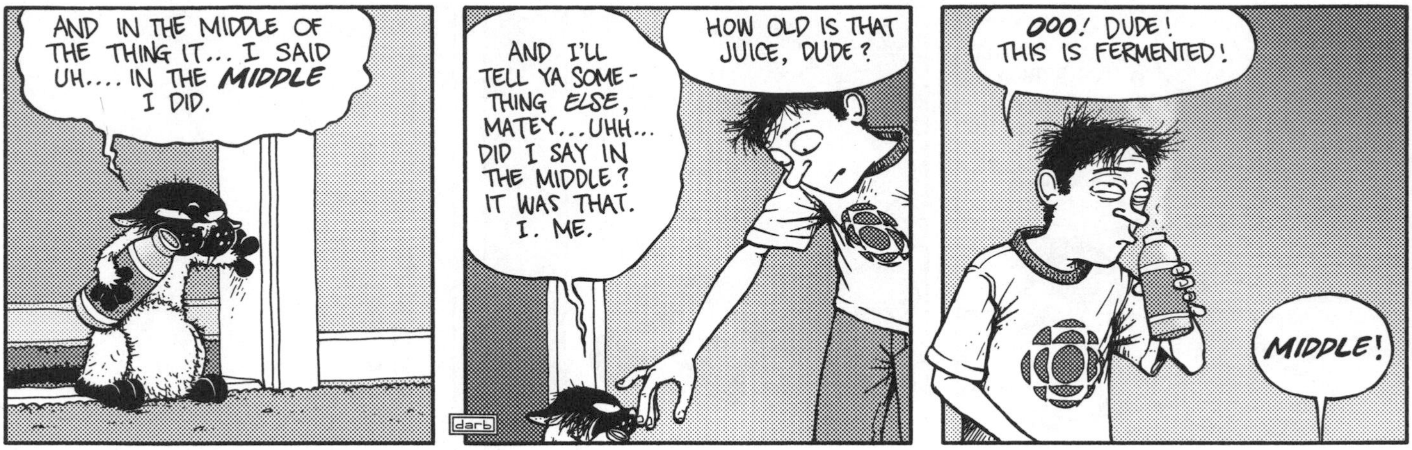
AND IN THE MIDDLE OF THE THING IT... I SAID UH.... IN THE *MIDDLE* I DID.
AND I'LL TELL YA SOME-THING *ELSE*, MATEY...UHH... DID I SAY IN THE MIDDLE? IT WAS THAT. I. ME.
HOW OLD IS THAT JUICE, DUDE?
darb
OOO! DUDE! THIS IS FERMENTED!
MIDDLE!

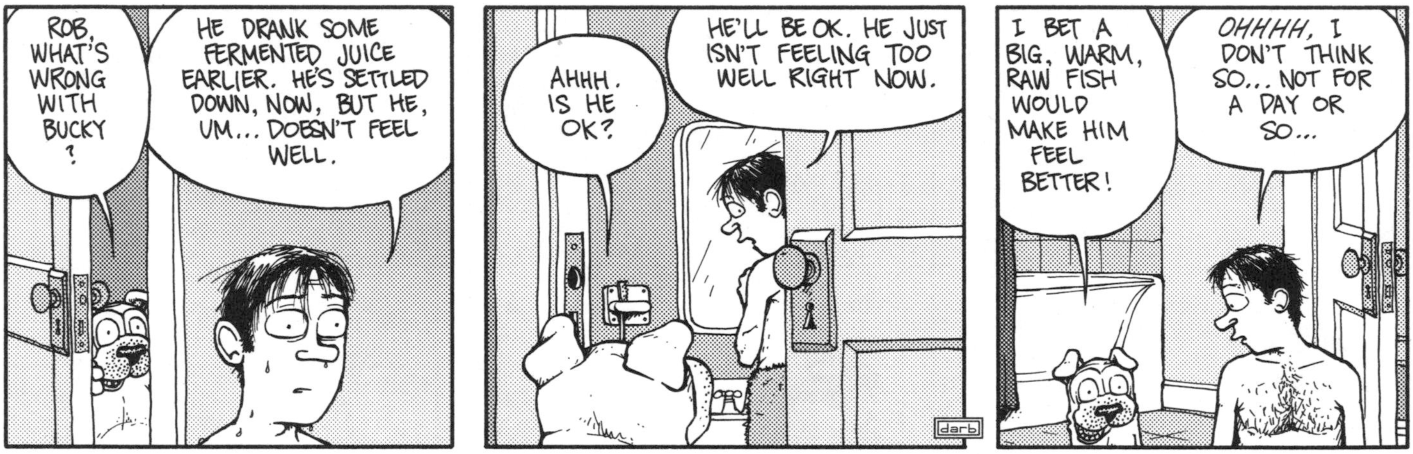
ROB, WHAT'S WRONG WITH BUCKY?
HE DRANK SOME FERMENTED JUICE EARLIER. HE'S SETTLED DOWN, NOW, BUT HE, UM... DOESN'T FEEL WELL.
AHHH. IS HE OK?
HE'LL BE OK. HE JUST ISN'T FEELING TOO WELL RIGHT NOW.
darb
I BET A BIG, WARM, RAW FISH WOULD MAKE HIM FEEL BETTER!
OHHHH, I DON'T THINK SO... NOT FOR A DAY OR SO...

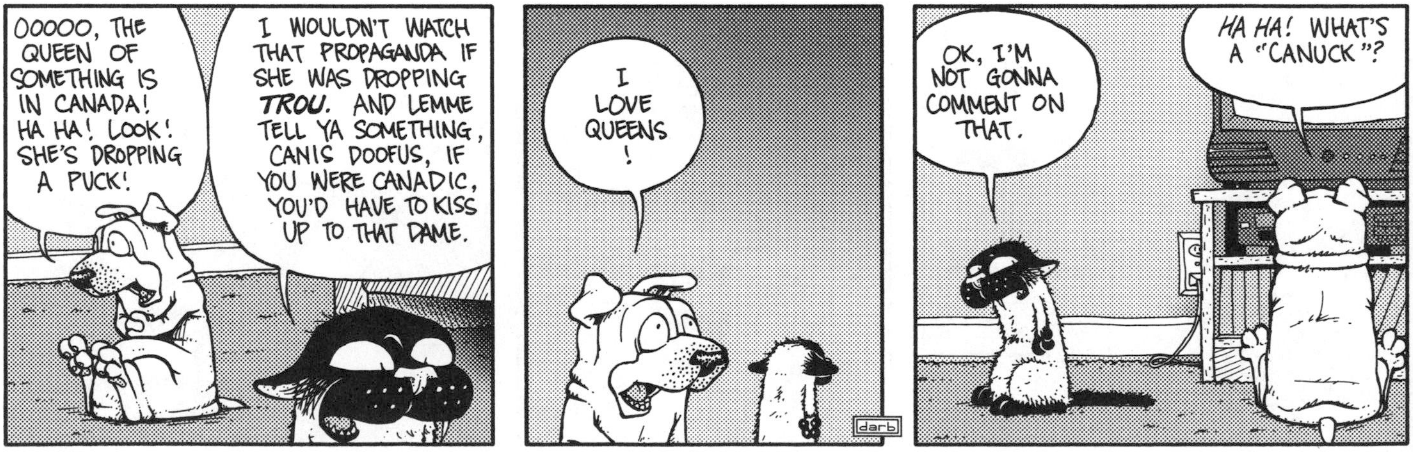
OOOOO, THE QUEEN OF SOMETHING IS IN CANADA! HA HA! LOOK! SHE'S DROPPING A PUCK!
I WOULDN'T WATCH THAT PROPAGANDA IF SHE WAS DROPPING ***TROU.*** AND LEMME TELL YA SOMETHING, CANIS DOOFUS, IF YOU WERE CANADIC, YOU'D HAVE TO KISS UP TO THAT DAME.
I LOVE QUEENS!
darb
OK, I'M NOT GONNA COMMENT ON THAT.
HA HA! WHAT'S A "CANUCK"?

DO THEY HAVE SKUNK PIE OR RAT KEBAB ?
NO.
WELL, DO THEY HAVE RABBIT HASH OR MONKEY NUGGETS ?
NO.
MAN, WHAT'S THE POINT IN EATING OUT IF YOU'RE JUST GETTING THE SAME STUFF YOU GET AT HOME ?
HI, I'M SHELLEY. I'LL BE YOUR WAITRESS THIS EVENING.
HI, SHELLEY! I'M SATCHEL. I'LL BE YOUR DOG THIS EVENING.

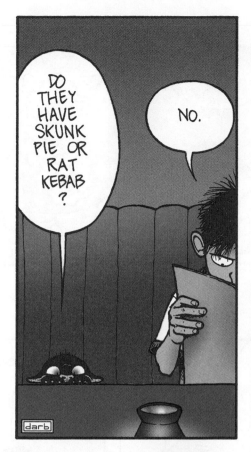

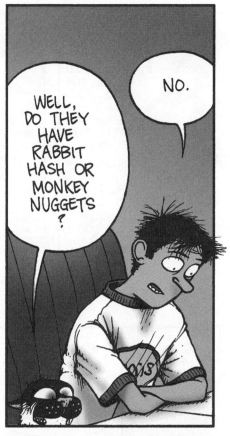

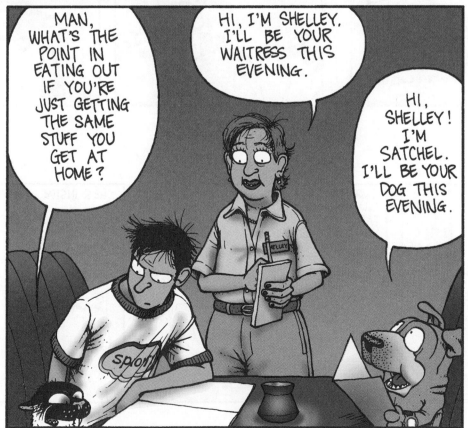

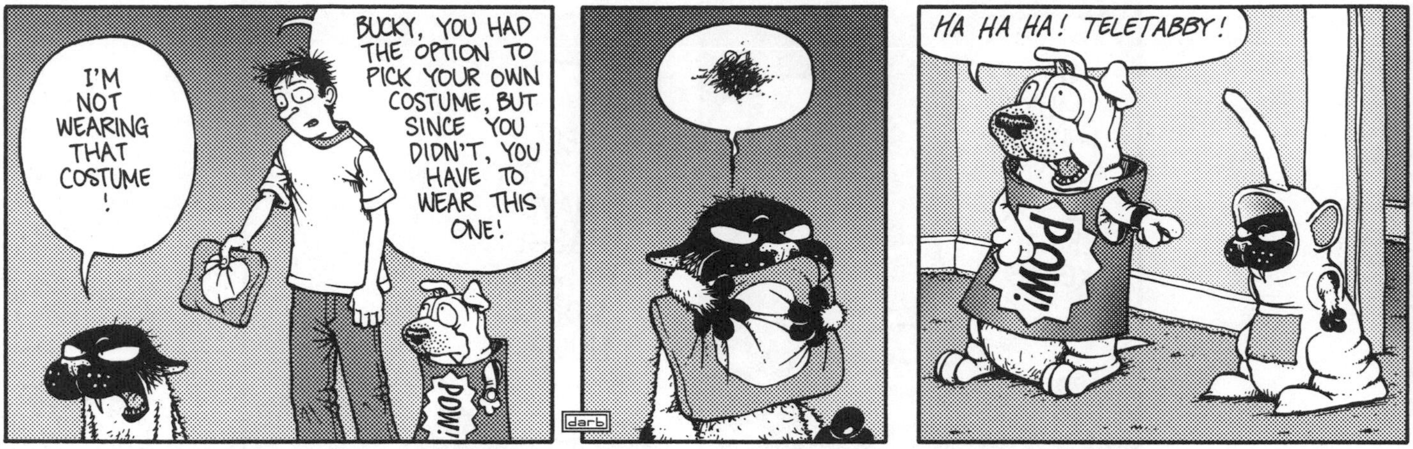
I'M NOT WEARING THAT COSTUME!
BUCKY, YOU HAD THE OPTION TO PICK YOUR OWN COSTUME, BUT SINCE YOU DIDN'T, YOU HAVE TO WEAR THIS ONE!
POW!
darb
HA HA HA! TELETABBY!
POW!

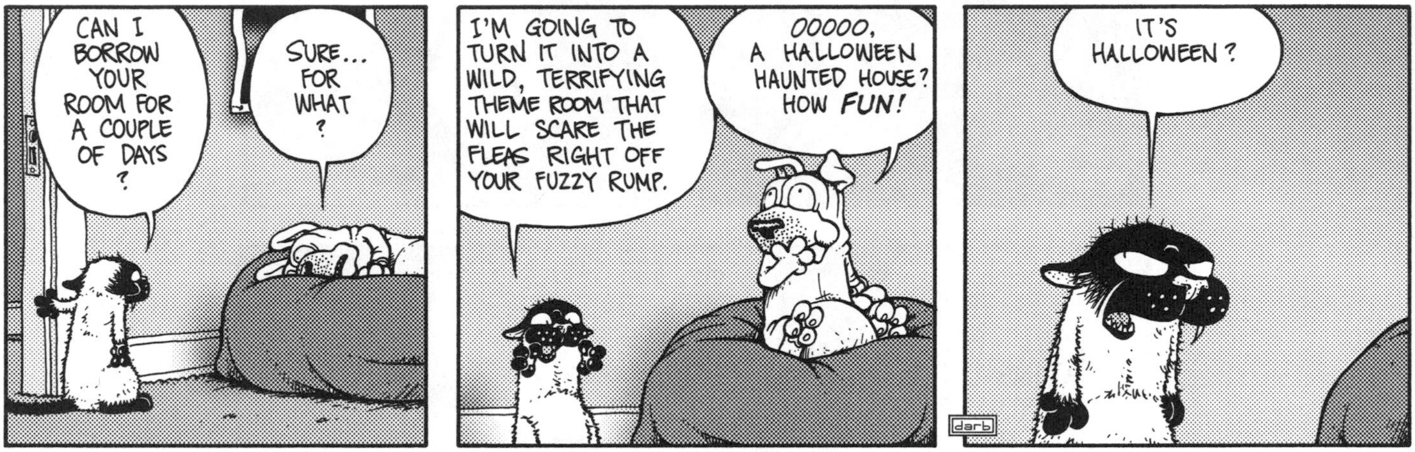
CAN I BORROW YOUR ROOM FOR A COUPLE OF DAYS?
SURE... FOR WHAT?
I'M GOING TO TURN IT INTO A WILD, TERRIFYING THEME ROOM THAT WILL SCARE THE FLEAS RIGHT OFF YOUR FUZZY RUMP.
OOOOO, A HALLOWEEN HAUNTED HOUSE? HOW *FUN*!
darb
IT'S HALLOWEEN?

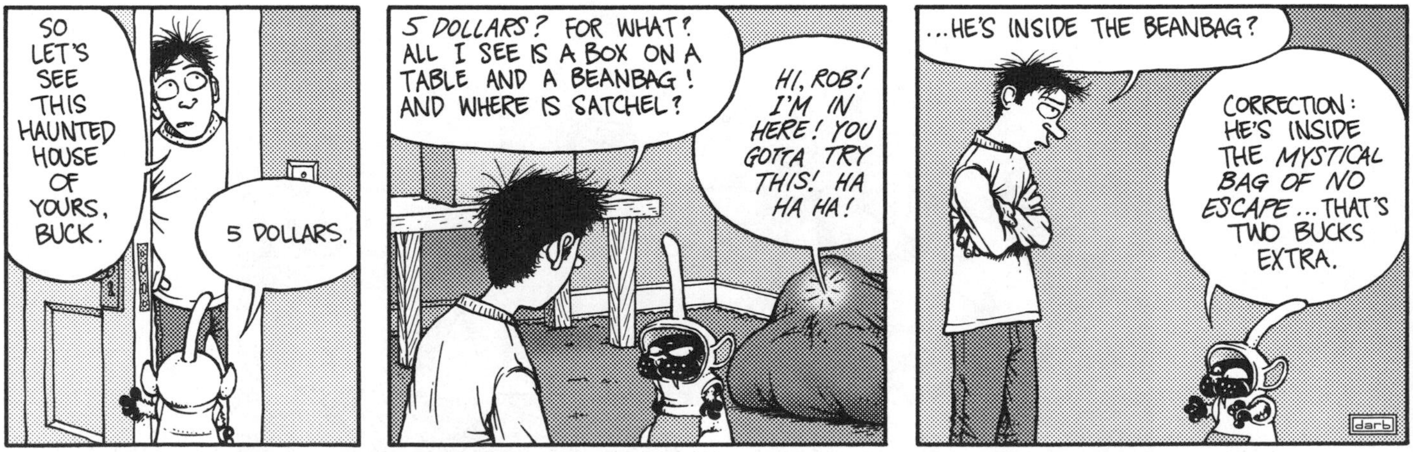
SO LET'S SEE THIS HAUNTED HOUSE OF YOURS, BUCK.
5 DOLLARS.
5 DOLLARS? FOR WHAT? ALL I SEE IS A BOX ON A TABLE AND A BEANBAG! AND WHERE IS SATCHEL?
HI, ROB! I'M IN HERE! YOU GOTTA TRY THIS! HA HA HA!
...HE'S INSIDE THE BEANBAG?
CORRECTION: HE'S INSIDE THE *MYSTICAL BAG OF NO ESCAPE*... THAT'S TWO BUCKS EXTRA.
darb

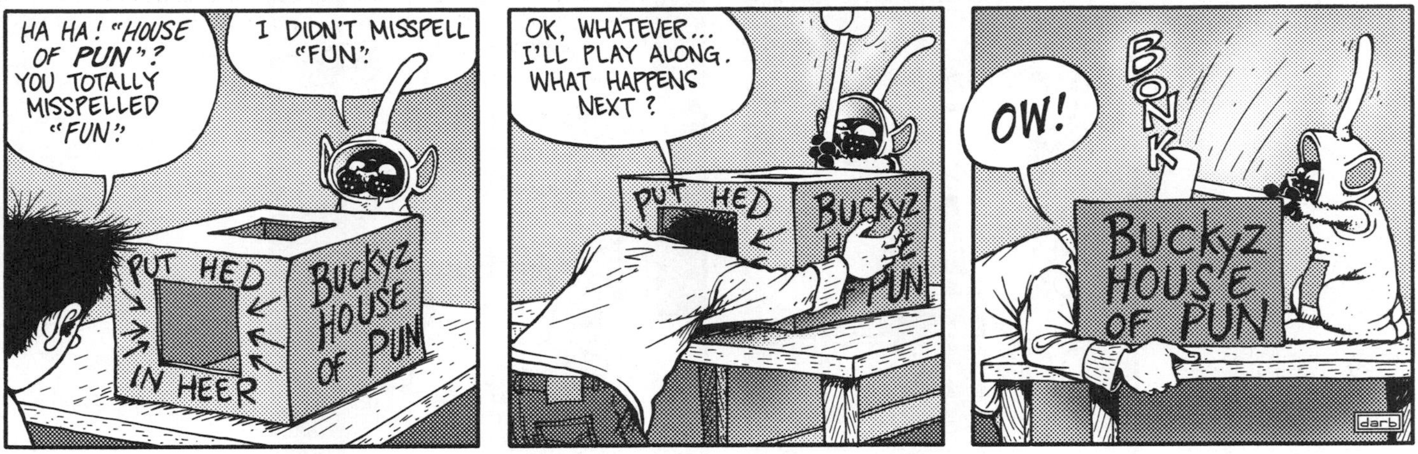
HA HA! "HOUSE OF PUN"? YOU TOTALLY MISSPELLED "FUN".
I DIDN'T MISSPELL "FUN".
PUT HED IN HEER
BUCKYZ HOUSE OF PUN
OK, WHATEVER... I'LL PLAY ALONG. WHAT HAPPENS NEXT?
PUT HED
BUCKYZ HOUSE OF PUN
OW!
BONK
BUCKYZ HOUSE OF PUN
darb

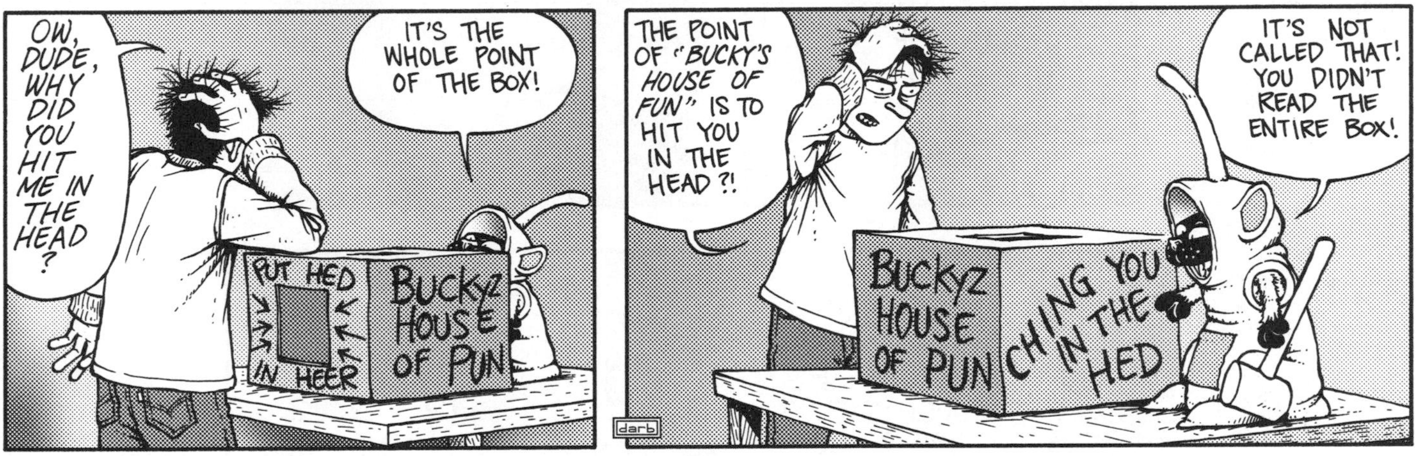
OW, DUDE, WHY DID YOU HIT ME IN THE HEAD?
IT'S THE WHOLE POINT OF THE BOX!
PUT HED IN HEER
BUCKYZ HOUSE OF PUN
darb
THE POINT OF "BUCKY'S HOUSE OF FUN" IS TO HIT YOU IN THE HEAD?!
IT'S NOT CALLED THAT! YOU DIDN'T READ THE ENTIRE BOX!
BUCKYZ HOUSE OF PUNCHING YOU IN THE HED

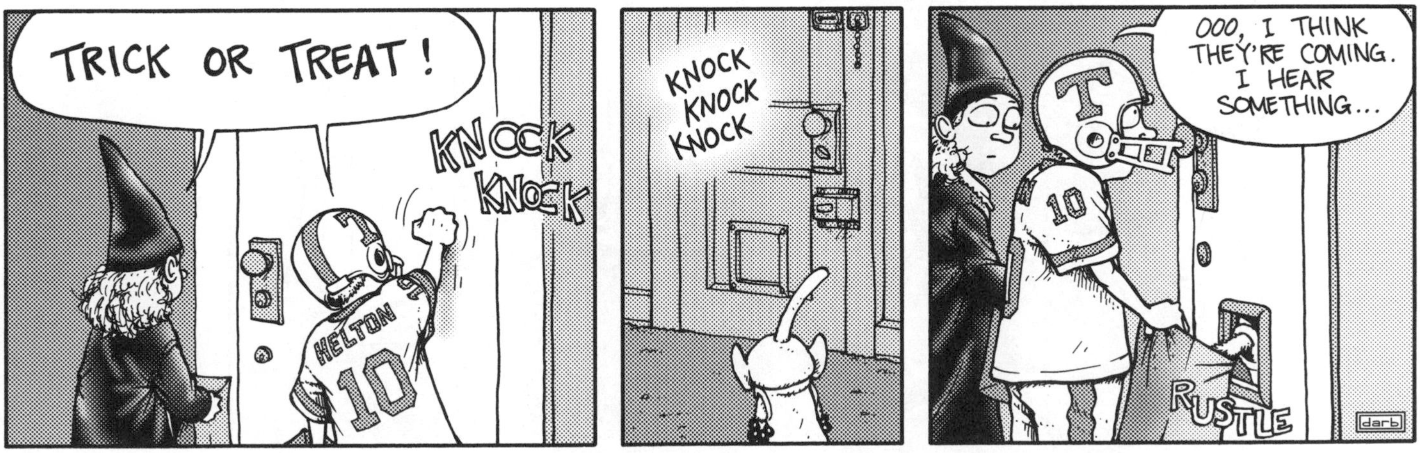
TRICK OR TREAT!
KNOCK KNOCK
HELTON 10
KNOCK KNOCK KNOCK
OOO, I THINK THEY'RE COMING. I HEAR SOMETHING...
10
RUSTLE
darb

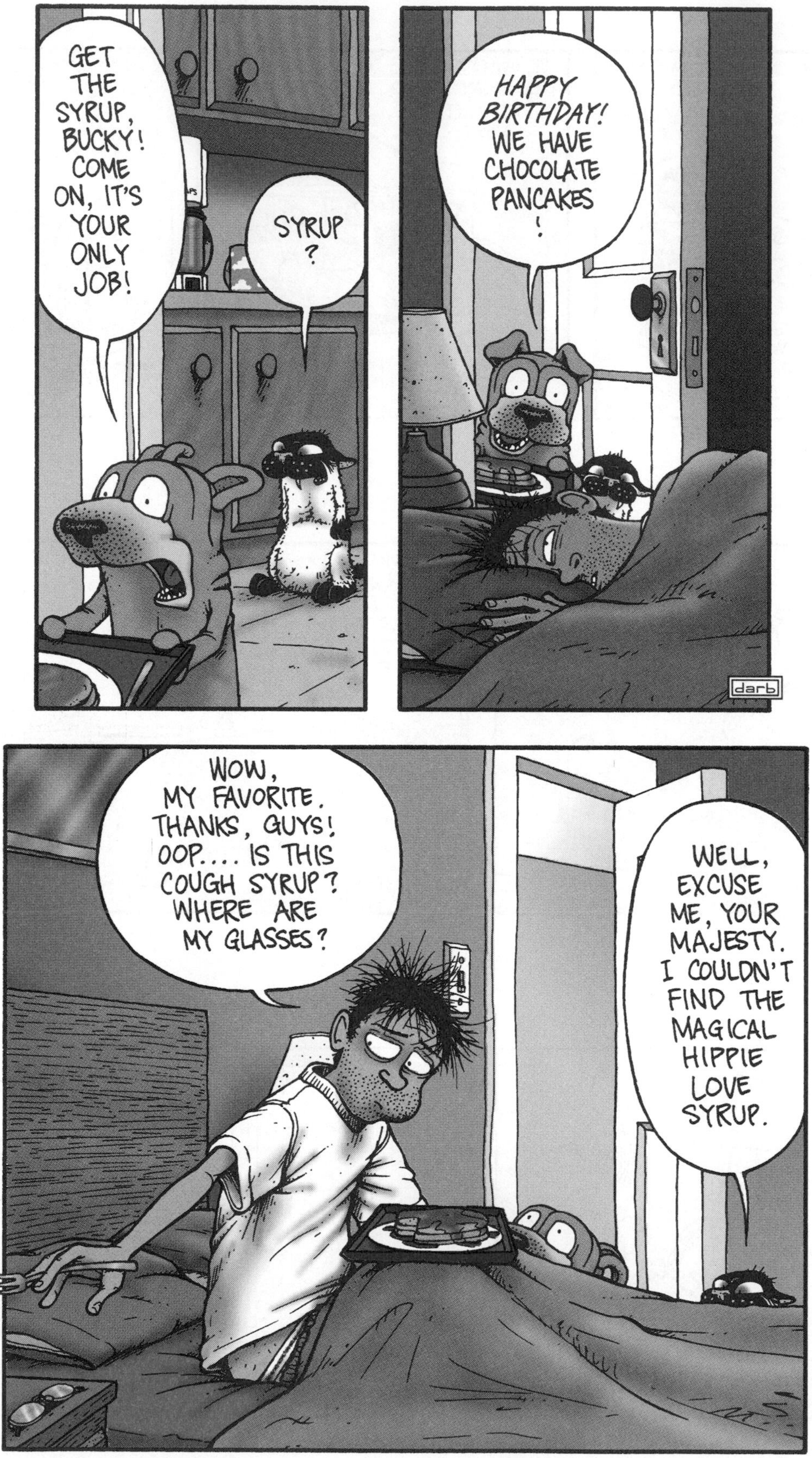
GET THE SYRUP, BUCKY! COME ON, IT'S YOUR ONLY JOB!
SYRUP ?
HAPPY BIRTHDAY! WE HAVE CHOCOLATE PANCAKES !
darb
WOW, MY FAVORITE. THANKS, GUYS! OOP.... IS THIS COUGH SYRUP? WHERE ARE MY GLASSES?
WELL, EXCUSE ME, YOUR MAJESTY. I COULDN'T FIND THE MAGICAL HIPPIE LOVE SYRUP.

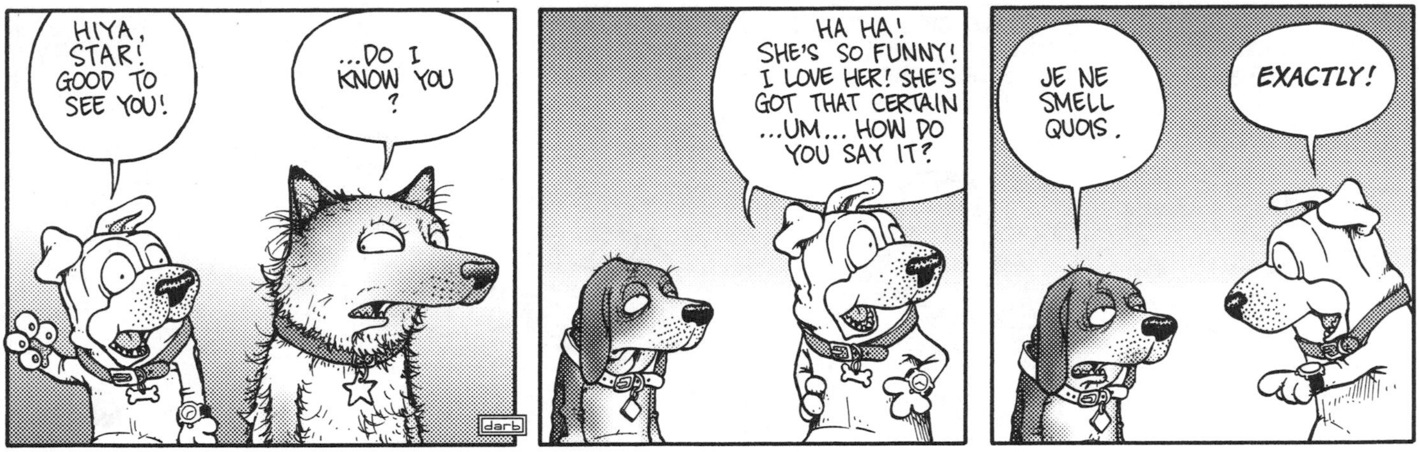
HIYA, STAR! GOOD TO SEE YOU!
...DO I KNOW YOU ?
HA HA! SHE'S SO FUNNY! I LOVE HER! SHE'S GOT THAT CERTAIN ...UM... HOW DO YOU SAY IT?
JE NE SMELL QUOIS.
EXACTLY!

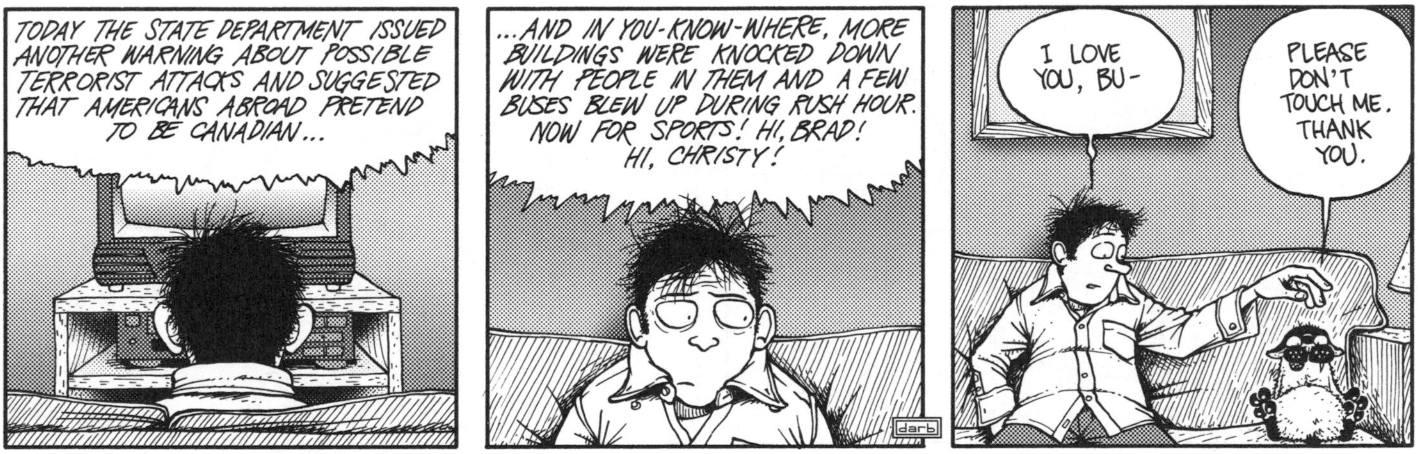
TODAY THE STATE DEPARTMENT ISSUED ANOTHER WARNING ABOUT POSSIBLE TERRORIST ATTACKS AND SUGGESTED THAT AMERICANS ABROAD PRETEND TO BE CANADIAN...
...AND IN YOU-KNOW-WHERE, MORE BUILDINGS WERE KNOCKED DOWN WITH PEOPLE IN THEM AND A FEW BUSES BLEW UP DURING RUSH HOUR. NOW FOR SPORTS! HI, BRAD! HI, CHRISTY!
I LOVE YOU, BU-
PLEASE DON'T TOUCH ME. THANK YOU.

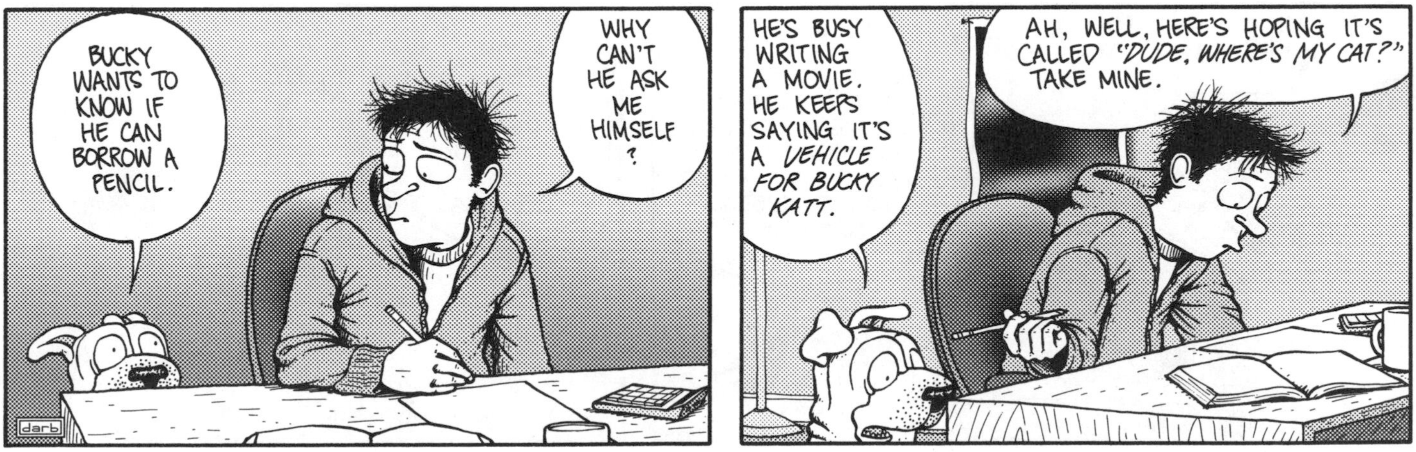
BUCKY WANTS TO KNOW IF HE CAN BORROW A PENCIL.
WHY CAN'T HE ASK ME HIMSELF ?
HE'S BUSY WRITING A MOVIE. HE KEEPS SAYING IT'S A *VEHICLE FOR BUCKY KATT.*
AH, WELL, HERE'S HOPING IT'S CALLED *"DUDE, WHERE'S MY CAT?"* TAKE MINE.

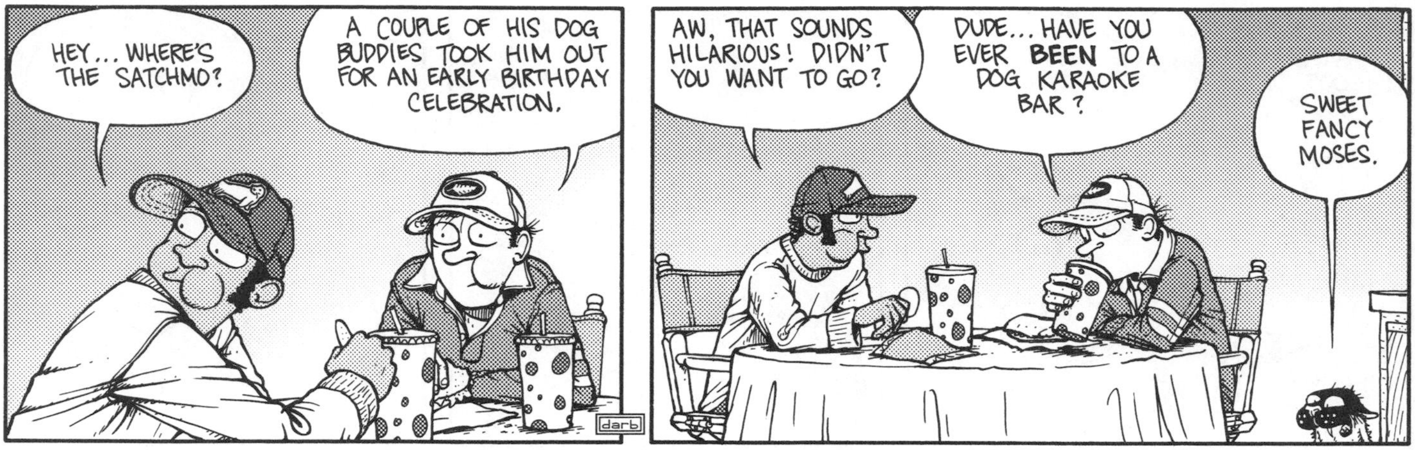
HEY... WHERE'S THE SATCHMO?
A COUPLE OF HIS DOG BUDDIES TOOK HIM OUT FOR AN EARLY BIRTHDAY CELEBRATION.
darb
AW, THAT SOUNDS HILARIOUS! DIDN'T YOU WANT TO GO?
DUDE... HAVE YOU EVER **BEEN** TO A DOG KARAOKE BAR?
SWEET FANCY MOSES.

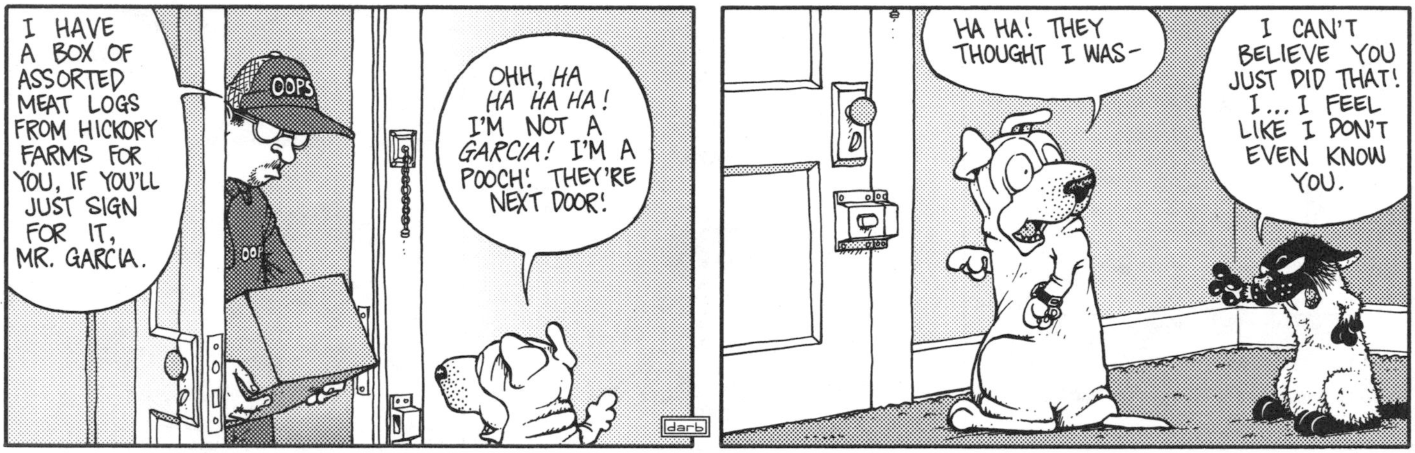
I HAVE A BOX OF ASSORTED MEAT LOGS FROM HICKORY FARMS FOR YOU, IF YOU'LL JUST SIGN FOR IT, MR. GARCIA.
OOPS
OHH, *HA HA HA HA!* I'M NOT A *GARCIA!* I'M A POOCH! THEY'RE NEXT DOOR!
darb
HA HA! THEY THOUGHT I WAS-
I CAN'T BELIEVE YOU JUST DID THAT! I... I FEEL LIKE I DON'T EVEN KNOW YOU.

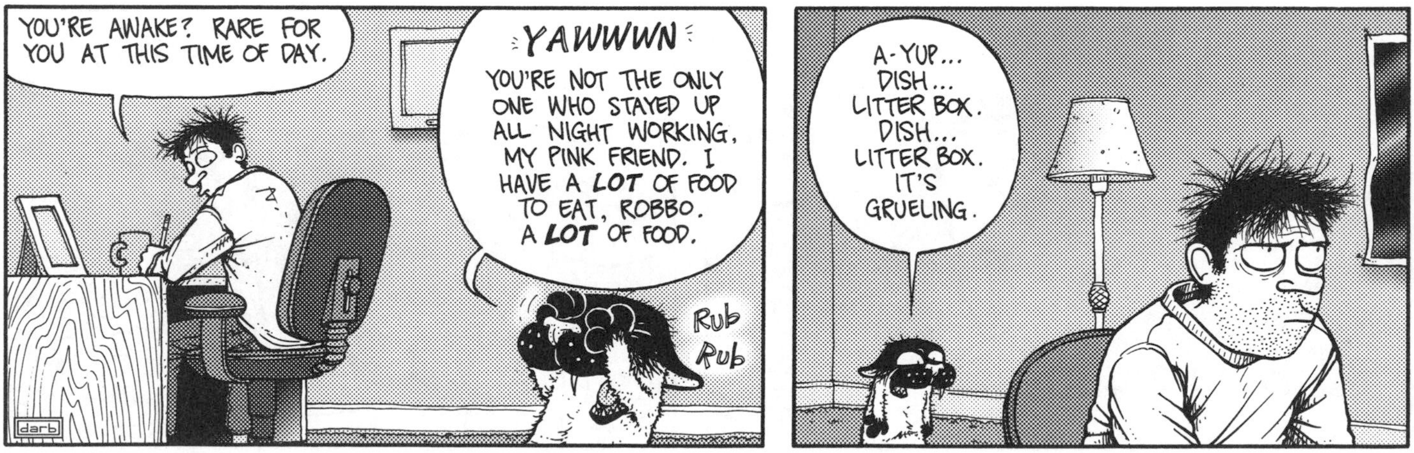
YOU'RE AWAKE? RARE FOR YOU AT THIS TIME OF DAY.
YAWWWN
YOU'RE NOT THE ONLY ONE WHO STAYED UP ALL NIGHT WORKING, MY PINK FRIEND. I HAVE A ***LOT*** OF FOOD TO EAT, ROBBO. A ***LOT*** OF FOOD.
Rub Rub
darb
A-YUP... DISH... LITTER BOX. DISH... LITTER BOX. IT'S GRUELING.

NOTES

NOTES

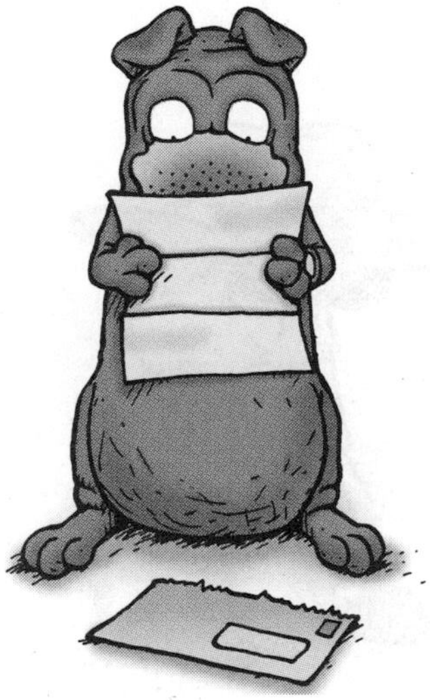

NOTES

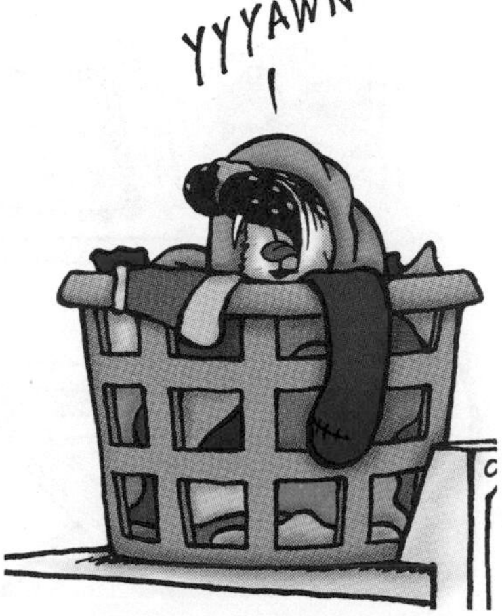
YYYAWN

NOTES